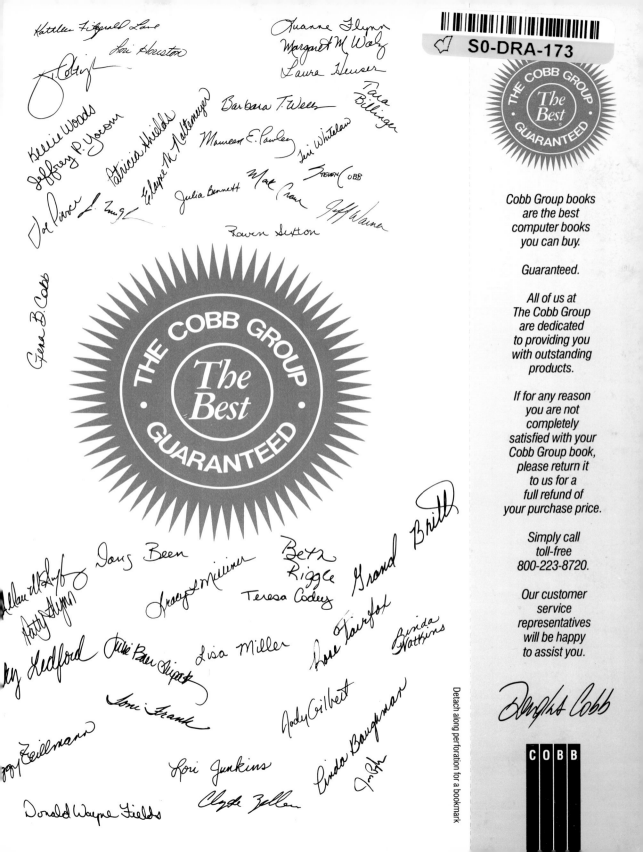

THE COBB GROUP
The Best
GUARANTEED

THE COBB GROUP
The Best
GUARANTEED

Cobb Group books
are the best
computer books
you can buy.

Guaranteed.

All of us at
The Cobb Group
are dedicated
to providing you
with outstanding
products.

If for any reason
you are not
completely
satisfied with your
Cobb Group book,
please return it
to us for a
full refund of
your purchase price.

Simply call
toll-free
800-223-8720.

Our customer
service
representatives
will be happy
to assist you.

Detach along perforation for a bookmark

COBB

WORD 4
COMPANION

The Cobb Group supports many business software programs with books, workbooks, and journals:

IBM PC and Compatibles

BORLAND PARADOX
Douglas Cobb's Paradox 3.0 Handbook
Hands-On Paradox
Paradox User's Journal

BORLAND QUATTRO
Quattro Companion
For Quattro

HEWLETT-PACKARD LASERJET
LaserJet Companion
LaserJet Companion TechNotes

LOTUS SYMPHONY
Mastering Symphony
The Hidden Power of Symphony
The Symphony User's Journal

LOTUS 1-2-3
Douglas Cobb's 1-2-3 Handbook
123 User's Journal

MICROSOFT EXCEL
Running Microsoft Excel
The Expert

MICROSOFT WORKS
Works Companion
The Workshop

MICROSOFT WORD
Word for Word

Apple Macintosh

MICROSOFT EXCEL
Excel in Business
Doug Cobb's Tips for Microsoft Excel
Hands-On Microsoft Excel
Microsoft Excel Functions Library
Excellence

MICROSOFT WORD
Word 4 Companion
Inside Word

PROVUE OVERVUE
Understanding OverVUE

For more information, please call toll-free 1-800-223-8720.

WORD 4
COMPANION

Gena Cobb
Judy Mynhier
Allan McGuffey

With:
Steven Cobb
Mark Crane

Louisville, Kentucky

WORD 4 COMPANION

Published by
The Cobb Group, Inc.
9420 Bunsen Parkway
Louisville, Kentucky 40220

Library of Congress Catalog Number: 88-64170
ISBN 0-936767-14-6

Editing	Production	Design
Toni Frank	Maureen Pawley	Julie Baer Tirpak
Linda Watkins	Beth Riggle	
	Tara Billinger	

Throughout this book, the trade names and trademarks of many companies and products have been used, and no such uses are intended to convey endorsement of or other affiliations with this book.

Printed in the United States of America

RRD-C 0 9 8 7 6 5

Table of Contents

Turn the page for a more
in-depth look at what's inside...

Extended Table of Contents

Dedication

To Bear and David
GBC

To the folks at The Cobb Group
JLM

To Karen Elizabeth, with love;
and Matthew, with hope
AMcG

Acknowledgments

No project of this magnitude can be carried out without the encouragement and help of dozens of people. We'd like to take this opportunity to say thanks to those who made this project possible.

Douglas Cobb, for the opportunity, encouragement, and advice.

Tom Cottingham, marketing guru and music man, for setting up the deal, travelling the country on an expense account, and rediscovering the Filmore.

Toni Frank Bowers, Linda Watkins, Linda Baughman, Jody Gilbert, Clyde Zellers, and Marjorie Maddox, editors extraordinaire, for their eyes and judgment.

Maureen Pawley, Beth Riggle, Tara Billinger, and Elayne Noltemeyer, the tireless group of PageMaker magicians, for putting it all together.

Julie Baer Tirpak, painstaking designer, for the lovely cover.

Paul J. Davis, program manager at Microsoft, for listening and answering with patience and intelligence.

Dave and Jo-Ann Parks at Printer's Type Service, for unstinting labor above and beyond the call of duty.

Theresa Wheatley and Lynda Robertson, for the long hours and loving care.

Finally, to the rest of The Cobb Group—Doug Been, Julia Bennett, Grand Britt, Steve Cobb, Teresa Codey, Mark Crane, Rose Fairfax, Donald Fields, Luanne Flynn, Patty Flynn, Laura Heuser, Lori Houston, Lori Junkins, Tim Landgrave, Kathleen Lane, Becky Ledford, Lisa Miller, Tracy Milliner, Keith Nicholson, Joe Pierce, Jonathan Pyles, Raven Sexton, Patricia Shields, Margaret Walz, Jeff Warner, Barbara Wells, Teri Whitelaw, Kellie Woods, Jeff Yocom, and Peggy Zeillmann—thanks for sharing the experience.

Preface

There's no doubt about it—Microsoft Word is a great piece of software. We've been using Word at The Cobb Group since 1985, when we began doing all our writing and editing with Macintosh computers. As we have worked with and written about Word over the years, we have come to know and appreciate Word for what it is—absolutely the best word processor money can buy.

From the beginning, Word has set the standard of excellence for word processing on personal computers. The original Word was the first powerful word processor to take advantage of the Mac's exciting graphical user interface. Word 3, which was introduced in 1987, substantially increased the basic capabilities of the original version. It offered all the editing features you would expect from a top-flight word processor, plus a built-in outliner, a spelling checker, style sheets, a hyphenation dictionary, sophisticated multicolumn formatting capabilities, automatic creation of tables of contents and indexes, sorting, and much more. These features combined to make Word 3 the most powerful word processor available for any personal computer.

Even with all of its power, however, there were a few weaknesses in Word 3. For one thing, you couldn't always see on the screen how your final document layout would look. And, although Word 3 allowed you to place side-by-side text on a page, the side-by-side paragraph format was not easy to use and results could be unpredictable.

Word 4—the newest version—addresses many of the weaknesses of Word 3, adding even more power and flexibility to what was already an outstanding program. For instance, with Word 4's new page view feature, you can see a full-size representation of each document page on your screen, with columnar formatting, headers, footers, footnotes, and other elements in place. Not only can you see the text, you also can make editing and formatting changes in page view.

Word 4's new table feature allows you to position text in a grid on the screen. You can use tables to create side-by-side text, set up sophisticated tabular formats with text wrapping in each column, design complex forms, and more. Another important new feature in Word 4 is the Position… command, which allows you to place text or graphics at any fixed position on a page, with text flowing around it. And, with the new, easy-to-use Commands… command, you can quickly customize menus and design your own keyboard shortcuts.

In addition to several major new features, Word 4 incorporates dozens of small changes that make it more flexible and easier to use than Word 3. For example, in Word 4, you can apply a style by selecting a style name from a dropdown list on the ruler. The style names in this list change from document to document. When you create a paragraph border in Word 4, you can specify how much space you want to appear between the border and the paragraph text. A new "Smart" Quotes feature allows you to create curved quotation marks and apostrophes (" " ' ') simply by typing the " and ' characters. These are just three examples of the numerous improvements that help make Word 4 the finest word processing program available.

In short, Word 4 has the depth and sophistication that you need to create every kind of document imaginable, from simple memos and reports to professional-looking newsletters and books. All this power is not without a price, however. If you've ever spent two hours trying to develop a multicolumn layout, or cursing because a page of tabular data keeps jumping from place to place, you know that Word is a complex tool. Although Word's powerful word processing, formatting, editing, and design tools are intuitive and easy to use, you may find that it takes months to explore all the nooks and crannies of this powerful program. Even with the user-friendly features of the Macintosh, learning Word 4 is a big job.

ABOUT THIS BOOK

We wrote *Word 4 Companion* to help make Word easier to learn and use. Regardless of your level of expertise, we think you'll find a great deal of useful information on the following pages. If you are new to word processing and desktop publishing, you can use this book as a tutorial to help you get started. If you are an experienced word processor, you can use this book as a reference guide to help you solve specific design and technical problems. If you've used previous versions of Word, you can use this book to come up to speed quickly on the new features of Word 4.

We had three goals in mind as we created this book. First, we wanted to help you learn to use Word 4 efficiently—after all, a productivity tool is supposed to save time. Second, we wanted to provide an in-depth source of reference information that you will return to time and time again, whether you're a Word novice or an expert. Third, we wanted to introduce you to some of the basic concepts of word processing, typography, and design so that you will be able to create professional-looking documents with ease and confidence. We think we've achieved all of these goals.

Word 4 Companion has three sections. Section One offers a basic overview of Microsoft Word and the Macintosh environment. If you are new to the Macintosh or to Word, you will want to read this section carefully before you dive into the more complex aspects of the program. If you've been using Word for awhile, we suggest that you skim this section to familiarize yourself with our terminology and approach before you move on to Sections Two and Three. In Section Two, we cover Word basics—creating documents, editing, formatting, printing, and designing page layouts. Then, in Section Three, we explain the special features that make Word 4 much more than a word processor. Here, you will learn about such features as style sheets, the Outliner, and the merge facility.

About Carts and Horses

Most software manuals provide an abundance of technical information about their products. They present every command, every option, every syntax rule in painstaking detail. Unfortunately, none of this encyclopedic information is geared toward helping you do your job. Until you become familiar with the program, you may not be able to look up the information you need.

On the other hand, many of the books we've seen on word processing packages go to the opposite extreme—they are almost completely tutorial in nature, offering little or no reference information to help you apply technical concepts to your work. Instead, the author walks you through the development of a standard business letter or the design of a prefab two-column newsletter.

We've tried to strike a balance with *Word 4 Companion*—to give you the technical information you need to use Microsoft Word effectively and to teach by example. For that reason, this book is organized functionally, rather than by command name. We try to walk you through the steps you need to develop different types of documents, introducing new commands and new concepts as they logically arise.

Index

At The Cobb Group, we take pride in the comprehensive indexes we create for our books. *Word 4 Companion*'s index contains more than a thousand entries covering all the concepts, topics, and applications we discuss. In addition, many entries are cross-referenced to facilitate your search for a particular subject. If you have a question about any command or feature in Word 4, the index will help you locate the answer in a matter of seconds.

ABOUT THE COBB GROUP

Based in Louisville, Kentucky, The Cobb Group, Inc., was founded in 1984 by Douglas Cobb, co-author of the best-selling computer book of all time: *Using 1-2-3*. Since then, The Cobb Group has become a leading publisher of books and journals for users of personal computer software and related products. Best-selling books written and/or published by The Cobb Group include *LaserJet Companion*, *Quattro Companion*, *Douglas Cobb's 1-2-3 Handbook*, *Running Microsoft Excel*, *Mastering Symphony*, *Write Companion*, *Word Companion* for Microsoft Word 3.0 and 3.01, *Paradox Companion*, and *Works Companion*.

In addition to its best-selling books, The Cobb Group publishes *Inside Word*, a monthly journal for users of Microsoft Word for the Macintosh, and *Excellence*, a monthly journal written for users of Microsoft Excel on the Macintosh. Other Cobb Group journals include *Word for Word*, for users of Microsoft Word on the PC; *The Workshop*, for users of Microsoft Works on the PC; *The Expert,* for users of Microsoft Excel on the PC; *For Quattro*; *1-2-3 User's Journal*; *The Symphony User's Journal*; and *Paradox User's Journal*. For more information on any Cobb Group book or journal, call 800-223-8720 (502-491-1900 in Kentucky).

ABOUT THE AUTHORS

Gena B. Cobb is vice president of The Cobb Group, Inc., where she serves as an author and editor-in-chief. She is the co-author of several books, including *Douglas Cobb's 1-2-3 Handbook*, *Doug Cobb's Tips for Microsoft Excel*, *Mastering Symphony*, *Write Companion*, and *Word Companion* for Microsoft Word 3.0 and 3.01. She currently is the editor-in-chief of *Inside Word*. Gena received a B.S. from the University of Virginia and an M.B.A. from the Harvard Business School.

Judy Mynhier, a free-lance technical writer, is the co-author of *Excel in Business*, the *Hands-On Excel* workbook, *Doug Cobb's Tips for Microsoft Excel*, the *Excel Functions Library*, *Write Companion*, and *Word Companion* for Microsoft Word 3.0 and 3.01. She holds a B.A. from the Indiana University School of Journalism.

Allan McGuffey is an assistant author at The Cobb Group, Inc. Allan co-authored *Write Companion*, which covers the popular word processor Microsoft Write. He is currently a Ph.D. candidate in English at the University of Louisville.

THE COBB GROUP

The Best

GUARANTEED

Section 1:
The Preliminaries

Section 1 lays the groundwork for using Microsoft Word 4. In this brief section, we'll introduce you to Word 4 on the Macintosh, and show you how to get started with the program. You'll find it well worth the time to become familiar with the concepts presented here before you launch into a full-scale assault on Word, particularly if you are new to the program.

We will assume throughout the course of this book that you are familiar with the Macintosh basics that are common to all programs—how to use the mouse, how to select icons and menu commands, and so forth. If you are not comfortable with these basics, we suggest that you review your Macintosh owner's guide before you proceed. You'll find it much easier to come up to speed on Microsoft Word if you have a feel for the general workings of the Macintosh first.

Although we do not presume to give you a full-length course on the Macintosh in this section, we will review a few Mac basics as they relate directly to using Word. In Chapter 1, we'll discuss the hardware you need to use Word, then we'll show you how to create backup copies of your Word disks and customize your startup disk. In Chapter 2, we'll introduce you to the Word environment and show you some of the tools at your disposal. In Chapter 3, we'll discuss file-handling in Word.

BEFORE YOU BEGIN 1

Before you begin working with Word, you must attend to a few housekeeping chores: You should be sure you have the hardware required to use the program, and you should familiarize yourself with the "layout" of your Word disks. Then, you can create backup disks and, if you don't have a hard disk, customize your startup disk to suit your needs. We'll cover those preliminaries in this chapter.

At more than 650K, Word 4 is a large program, requiring at least two 800K disk drives to operate. However, with only two disk drives, you may encounter storage problems later because you will need to use one disk drive for your System folder and the other disk drive for the Word program.

To use Microsoft Word 4 easily, you should have an Apple Macintosh Plus, Macintosh SE, or Mac II with a hard disk and one floppy disk drive, or a Mac Plus or Mac SE with two internal floppy disk drives and an external floppy drive. If you choose hardware that includes a hard drive, Word will run more quickly. However, once you've loaded Word, the hardware differences are indistinguishable. All your Word windows will look the same, and the commands and dialog boxes will not change. (Through the course of this book, we will address the SE with a hard disk as the most common Macintosh configuration. However, if you have a Mac Plus with an external hard drive, you should have no trouble. Word will run on a regular Mac Plus as well, but two disk drives will severely limit the amount of space for saving documents.)

Word 4 is incompatible with the 128K Mac or the unenhanced 512K Mac, but compatible with the Mac 512K Enhanced. However, since the 512K's keyboard is less accommodating for Word 4 than the SE's, you may feel limited by its keyboard.

HARDWARE CONFIGURA-TIONS

The SE keyboard can help speed your work in Word. Its function keys can save time ordinarily spent using the mouse to issue commands from menus.

If you're using a Mac with three floppy disk drives, the Word 4 program requires one disk for itself. You'll need to put the System folder on another disk, then use a third disk for your Word document files. If you try to save your files to one of the other disks, you'll be able to store only a few short documents, such as letters or memos, before your disk is full. If you try to store your Word files on the disk that holds your System folder, you'll find less than one-fourth of the space that a blank disk contains. Therefore, if you don't save your files to a separate disk, you may encounter frustrating disk-full messages.

THE SOFTWARE

You should have received three double-sided disks in your Microsoft Word 4 package: one program disk and two utilities disks. Your program disk contains the Word application, Word 4 ReadMe document, and the Release Notes file.

Your Microsoft Word Utilities 1 disk contains some sample documents, a Hyphenation file, an MS Dictionary file, Glossary files, and Help files. Your Utilities 2 disk contains the SuperPaint program and related files, so you can enhance your Word documents with graphics features; the AutoMac III files, so you can create macros; the Word Finder files, so you can run Word's Thesaurus application; and a folder of conversion utilities.

Your Startup Disk

Of course, to run Word, you'll need a startup disk containing a System folder. If your Mac has a hard disk, you'll probably use that hard disk as your startup disk. If you have only floppy disk drives, you may want to create two or more startup disks with different fonts and desk accessories installed on each. We'll cover this topic a little later in this chapter. For now, let's look at the contents of the System folder. (If you're an experienced Mac user, this information will be review.)

Inside the System folder on your startup disk, you'll find the System and Finder applications; several desk accessory files, such as the Clipboard, the Chooser, and the Control Panel; and—after you load Word for the first time—a file called Word Settings (4). You also may have some printer resource files.

The System application controls the startup procedures and provides operating information for the Mac. (System file information is stored in RAM or random access memory—the part of your computer's memory that can be altered or updated.) The System also keeps track of the desk accessories, fonts, and printer resources you have installed. If your Mac system is neither an SE nor a Mac II, Word 4 is compatible with system Version 3.2 and later. The SE and the Mac II need system Version 4.1 or later.

No matter what programs you use, you've probably seen the terms *Finder level* and *DeskTop* in every book or reference manual written about the Macintosh. When you insert a system disk into your machine and boot up your computer, you are initially at the Finder level. The Finder application is a part of the Mac system that controls disk procedures and manages documents. It keeps track of where documents are stored and controls the display of all icons and windows that appear on your screen.

Another file in your System folder, called DeskTop, handles the display of the menu bar and the background area of your screen. The DeskTop file, which is invisible, works in conjunction with the Finder application.

The Clipboard is a temporary holding area in which Word stores text and graphics when you copy or move a selection in your Word document. We'll discuss how the Clipboard works in Chapter 6.

Word automatically creates the Word Settings (4) file to keep track of certain environmental settings, such as special markup character displays, the ruler display, and your menu configuration. We'll talk more about the Word Settings (4) file when we discuss Word's default settings in Chapter 14.

GETTING STARTED

The first step in getting started with Word on a hard disk machine is to copy onto your hard disk the Word program file from the master Word program disk. If you don't have a hard disk, your first step in getting started with Word is to back up your master disks. We'll show you how to do that in a moment.

If you're using a Mac with a hard disk, begin by starting up your computer, then insert your master Word program disk into the floppy disk drive. Next, double-click the icon for the master Word program disk so you can view its contents. Drag the Word program file icon from the master disk over the icon for your hard disk. (If you've double-clicked the hard disk icon on your DeskTop, drag the Word program icon into the window for your hard disk.)

After copying the Word program file and other files from your master Word program disk, the next step is to copy onto your hard disk the appropriate files from your master Word utilities disks. You should copy the Standard Glossary file from your Utilities 1 disk to your hard disk. The Standard Glossary file does not need to be in your System folder, although this is the recommended setup. The Glossary file can be kept in your Word program folder or not in a folder at all, if you prefer. You also should copy the MS Dictionary and Word Hyphenation files from the Utilities 1 disk to your hard disk. If you want to take advantage of Word's built-in Help facility, copy the Word Help file as well.

Your Utilities 2 disk contains the SuperPaint program and two conversion programs. (The conversion programs allow you to convert files created in WordPerfect or DisplayWrite on the IBM PC into a format that Word 4 can read.) If you think you'll need these items, you should copy them to your hard disk.

To copy the entire contents of your utilities disks onto the hard disk, just insert each disk and drag the icon for that disk over the icon for the hard disk. You will then see a message like the one in Figure 1-1.

FIGURE 1-1

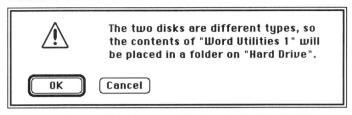

When you drag a disk icon over the icon for the hard disk, you will see a message like this one.

When you click OK, your Mac will automatically create a folder on the hard disk to store the utilities files. This folder will have the same name as the disk from which the files were copied. In a moment, we'll explain some tips on how to arrange the utilities files on your hard disk.

Even though you probably have plenty of storage space on the hard disk—especially if it's relatively new—you may want to conserve space by copying only selected files from the utilities disk instead of copying the entire disk.

Back It Up!

We cannot stress strongly enough the importance of making backup copies of your Word disks before you begin working with the program. Even with Word installed on a hard disk, we recommend that you make an additional backup copy of your master disks. Because Word 4 is not copy-protected, creating and using backup disks is very easy. You should always use these backup disks as your working copies.

Keep in mind that your Word disks are extremely vulnerable. A misguided magnetic force (your telephone, for example), an errant cup of coffee, or even a serious system error could mean that your software investment is gone forever. The process of backing up your Word disks takes only a few minutes and can help you avoid catastrophe.

Before you make your backup copies, place the write-protection tabs at the top-right corner of each Word master disk in the up position. You should be able to see through the small square hole near the corner of each disk. This ensures that you will not inadvertently alter your master disks as you duplicate them.

Backing up your disks on a Mac with a hard drive

If you have a hard drive and one floppy disk drive, you'll need to copy the entire contents of the master Word program disk and the two master utilities disks onto the hard disk, if you have not already done so. (On your Mac DeskTop, just drag each disk icon over the icon for the hard disk.) Word will automatically create a folder to hold the files on each disk, and you can copy these folders onto two blank floppy disks. After copying your master files onto your hard disk and making an additional backup, store the master disks and backups in a safe place. If you have two floppy

disk drives in addition to your hard disk, you can back up your master disks by
following the procedure we'll describe next.

If you have a Macintosh with three 800K disk drives, these are the steps for
backing up your master Word disks:

1. If you have started your Macintosh with another program, select Shut Down
   from the Special menu, then reboot your computer. Place your system disk and
   the master Word program disk in your internal drives. In a few seconds, you'll
   see icons for these disks in the upper-right corner of your screen.
2. Place a blank, 800K disk into your external drive. When you see the message
   This disk is unreadable. Do you want to initialize it?, click on the Two-Sided
   button. Then, click the Erase button that appears next on the screen.
3. When you see the message *Please name this disk*, type a name for your new
   disk, such as *Word4 Copy*. Press OK to lock in your new disk name. Notice
   that the Word4 Copy disk icon appears just below the icon for the master Word
   disk on the Mac DeskTop.
4. Drag the icon for the master Word disk over the icon for the Word4 Copy disk.
   You'll see the message *Completely replace contents of "Word4 Copy" (external drive) with contents of "Word Program" (internal drive)?* Press OK to
   proceed. You'll see a status message at the top of your screen as the master files
   are copied to your new disk.
5. When the status message at the top of your screen disappears, drag the icon for
   the newly created Word program disk over the Trash icon to eject that disk from
   the external drive. Then, drag the icon for the master Word program disk over
   the Trash icon to eject it as well. (You also can click on a disk icon and press
   ⌘-e to eject it.)
6. Insert the master Utilities 1 disk in the internal drive from which you ejected
   the master Word program disk. Then, insert another new blank disk in the
   external drive and initialize it as described in Step 2. Use a name like *Utilities
   1 Copy* to name this new disk.
7. Drag the icon for the master Utilities 1 disk over the icon for the Utilities 1
   Copy disk, and click OK when you see the message *Completely replace
   contents of "Utilities 1 Copy" (external drive) with contents of "Word
   Utilities 1" (internal drive)?*
8. Repeat steps 5 through 7 to create a backup of your Utilities 2 disk.

If your Macintosh has only two floppy disk drives, follow these simple steps
to make backup copies of your Word master disks:

1. If you have started your Macintosh with another program, select Shut Down
   from the Special menu, then reboot your computer. Place your system disk in

*Backing up your
disks on a Mac
with three floppy
drives*

*Backing up your
disks on a Mac
with two floppy
drives*

the Mac's internal drive. In a few seconds, you'll see the disk's icon in the upper-right corner of your screen.

2. Place a blank, 800K disk into your external drive. When you see the message *This disk is unreadable. Do you want to initialize it?*, click on the Two-Sided button. Then, click the Erase button that appears next on the screen.

3. When you see the message *Please name this disk*, type a name, like *Word4 Copy*, for your new disk. Click OK to lock in your new disk name. Notice that the Word4 Copy disk icon appears just below the icon for the system disk on the Mac DeskTop.

4. To make a copy of the master Word program disk, press Shift-⌘-1 or drag the icon for the system disk into the Trash. When the system disk ejects, place the master Word program disk in the empty drive. Drag the icon for the master Word disk over the icon for the Word4 Copy disk. You'll see the message *Completely replace contents of "Word4 Copy" (external drive) with contents of "Word Program" (internal drive)?* Press OK to proceed. You'll see a status message at the top of your screen as the master files are copied to your new disk.

5. When the status message at the top of your screen disappears, press Shift-⌘-2 to eject the newly created Word program disk from the external drive. Insert another new blank disk in the external drive and initialize it as described in Step 2. Use a name like *Utilities 1 Copy* to name this new disk.

6. Now, press Shift-⌘-1 to eject the master Word program disk from your internal drive and insert the master copy of your Utilities 1 disk into the internal drive.

7. Drag the icon for the master Utilities 1 disk over the icon for the Utilities 1 Copy disk, and click OK when you see the message *Completely replace contents of "Utilities 1 Copy" (external drive) with contents of "Word Utilities 1" (internal drive)?*

8. Repeat steps 5 through 7 to back up the Utilities 2 master disk.

Installing a Printer

You'll need to install a printer if you want to view the results of your work in hard-copy form. The most common printers for the Mac are the Apple LaserWriter, the LaserWriter Plus, the LaserWriter II, and the Apple ImageWriter. Although you can use other printers with your Macintosh, you may run into some compatibility problems. For instance, you may find that many of the fonts available for Macintosh programs cannot be reproduced on other printers. In addition, many printers support only fixed-pitch fonts and cannot handle proportionally spaced fonts.

Before you can use any printer, you must copy a resource file for that printer into the System folder of your startup disk. On the Macintosh Printing Tools disk that comes with your Macintosh Utilities and System Tools disks, you'll find the ImageWriter and LaserWriter printer resources. There is also a Print Monitor resource, which you'll need if you plan to do background printing with MultiFinder.

If your printer is not an ImageWriter or LaserWriter, don't panic; you may still be able to use that printer with the Mac. See your printer owner's manual for more information about configuring your printer to communicate with the Macintosh.

You can contact Microsoft to obtain a copy of the appropriate printer resource file. (Before you decide to use a printer other than the LaserWriter or ImageWriter, we suggest you ask your local dealer for more information and a demonstration concerning the printer's compatibility and performance.)

We recommend the LaserWriter printers for any user who requires high-quality print. In this book, we will use a LaserWriter printer to produce our sample output because the ImageWriter's dot matrix output does not lend itself well to reproduction. Next to phototypesetting, the LaserWriter is the best output device available for the Mac.

In Chapter 7, we will show you how to install and choose a printer resource, and we'll offer instructions for using both the ImageWriter and LaserWriter printers.

LOADING WORD

You load the Word program as you load any Macintosh application. If you are using 800K disks, you'll begin by placing your program disk in a disk drive. If you have three floppy drives, you'll want to insert a disk for storing documents in your external drive. If you'll be using one of the files on a utilities disk, you can place that disk in your external drive instead. (To prevent overcrowding, you'll generally want to avoid storing documents on your startup disk—the disk that contains your System files. We suggest that you keep at least 20K free on this disk so that Word can back up your work when you are editing a document.)

After inserting your disks, the next step is to double-click on the icon for the disk that contains your Word program to open that disk and view its contents (if it is not already open). Then, double-click on the Word application icon, or click on the Word application icon and then choose Open from the File menu.

The first time you load Word, you will see a dialog box with edit bars in which you can enter your name and the name of your company or organization. Type the appropriate information in each edit bar, then click OK. When you click OK, Word will "stamp" the disk with your name and your company name. This information will appear on the screen every time you load Word, and it will be transferred to each copy you make of the Word program disk.

After your Word disk has been personalized with your name, you will see a new blank document window called Untitled1. (The next time you load Word, this window will appear immediately.)

Other Loading Techniques

If you want to load the Word program and open an existing Word document simultaneously (more about creating and saving documents in Chapter 3), you can double-click on any Word document icon at the Finder level. If the document you want is located in a folder, double-click on the folder icon to open the folder, then double-click the icon that represents the document you want to work with. The Word program and the selected document will be loaded simultaneously. If the document you select is very long, it may take a few moments for the file to be loaded.

To open the Word program and two or more Word files simultaneously, press the Shift key and click on the icons for the files you want. Then, select the Open command from the File menu or double-click on one of the icons.

If you often need to transfer data from other programs into your Word documents, you'll definitely want to take advantage of MultiFinder when you load Word. MultiFinder lets you open two or more applications and move among them. You also can return to the Finder level without closing your applications. You can even attach documents to MultiFinder so that those documents are opened automatically when you start your computer with MultiFinder. The main disadvantage of MultiFinder is that it requires a lot of RAM. If you want to use Word and another application simultaneously, you'll need at least two megabytes of memory.

To use MultiFinder, choose Set Startup... from the Special menu at the Finder level. In the Set Startup dialog box, select the MultiFinder option. Then, restart your computer. We'll talk more about using MultiFinder (and Word's QuickSwitch application) in Appendix 3.

CUSTOMIZING YOUR STARTUP DISK

If you do not have a hard drive, you'll almost certainly want to create several custom startup disks to meet your special project needs. For example, you may want to customize the desk accessories that are available on the ⚫ menu and add some additional fonts to your current collection. You also may want to delete the tools you don't often use in order to free up some disk space.

There are so many fonts, desk accessories, and other tools available for Word that you'll never fit them all on one startup disk. By making several copies of your startup disk, however, you can customize disks for different purposes.

In the next part of this chapter, we'll look at some of the tools available and offer some suggestions on how you can make your Word system operate as efficiently as possible. Because most of these elements are common to all Macintosh programs, much of this information should be review. If you are unfamiliar with any concepts presented in the next few pages, review your Macintosh owner's manuals.

If you want more information about the Macintosh, we suggest *The Apple Macintosh Book*, an excellent reference guide written by Cary Lu and published by Microsoft Press.

The ⚫ Menu

The ⚫ menu contains a special set of commands that let you access handy desk accessory features and tailor the Macintosh environment to your needs. When you are at the Finder level, the first command on your ⚫ menu is About the Finder.... You can choose this command to find out which version of the Finder you are using. Once you have loaded Word, however, this command changes to About Microsoft Word.... As you'll see a little later, you can use the About Microsoft Word... command to access Word's Help menu.

The next portion of the ⌘ menu is devoted to desk accessories. These handy tools are available at all times—both at the Finder level and from within Word. Let's take a brief look at some of the most common desk accessories that are available for Macintosh users.

The three most important desk accessories are the Control Panel, the Chooser, and the Alarm Clock. We recommend that you keep these desk accessories on all of your startup disks.

Desk accessories

The Control Panel desk accessory contains vital settings information that the Macintosh system uses to format your DeskTop, to program your keyboard, and to control other important "environmental conditions." When you select the Control Panel command from the ⌘ menu, you'll see a dialog box like the one in Figure 1-2. You can use this dialog box to control the key repeat rate for your keyboard, set your double-click speed, and change your DeskTop pattern, among other things.

The Control Panel

FIGURE 1-2

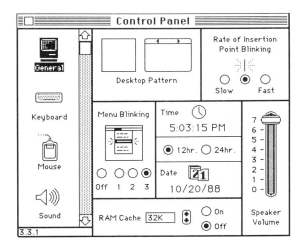

You'll use the Control Panel desk accessory to personalize your Mac environment.

The Chooser lets you select the printer you want to use once you have installed the appropriate printer drivers in the System folder on your startup disk. The contents of this dialog box will change, depending on the type of printer resource files you have installed. In Chapter 7, we'll look at the various Chooser options in more detail.

The Chooser

Although the Alarm Clock desk accessory may seem like a simple convenience item, it is important that you set the Alarm Clock and ensure that the system maintains the correct date and time. The Macintosh is supplied with a battery and keeps track of the current date and time, even when your Mac's power is off.

The Alarm Clock

Whenever you create or save a file, the Mac system records the date and time at which that document was last modified. This information can be critical when you need to locate the most recent version of a file. (By the way, when you are at the Finder level, you can find out when a file was created by choosing Get Info from the File menu, or by choosing the commands by Date, Name, Size, or Kind from the View menu.)

When you select Alarm Clock from the ■ menu, you'll see a small window like the one in Figure 1-3. To provide the Macintosh with the correct time, begin by clicking on the lever icon that appears on the right side of the window. The window will expand to reveal a settings area, as shown in Figure 1-4. When you click on the clock, calendar, or alarm icons to change the Alarm Clock settings, a set of arrows will appear. You can make any needed adjustments by clicking on one of these arrows or simply by typing the correct settings.

FIGURE 1-3

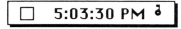

Select Alarm Clock from the ■ menu to see the current time.

FIGURE 1-4

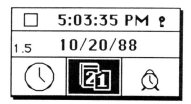

To see the date and time, click on the lever icon on the right side of the alarm window.

Key Caps

The Key Caps desk accessory is another handy tool that lets you see how the character keys on your keyboard are defined. This desk accessory is particularly important when you are using a word processing program. When you choose Key Caps from the ■ menu, you'll see a dialog box like the one in Figure 1-5.

Obviously, this screen doesn't tell you much that you couldn't see by looking at your own keyboard. However, if you press the Shift or Option key (or both) while the Key Caps dialog box is active, you'll see many of the special characters that are available from your keyboard.

When you issue the Key Caps command, you'll also see a special Key Caps menu on your menu bar. This menu lists all the fonts available on your startup disk, which is quite convenient if you are at the Finder level and want to know what fonts you have installed in the Keyboard file in your System folder. In addition, you can select a font name from the Key Caps menu to display the special characters available in each font.

FIGURE 1-5

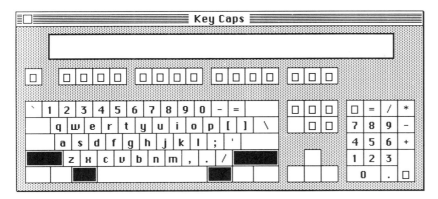

You can use Key Caps to see how your character keys are defined.

The Scrapbook is a storage bin where you can keep text and graphics for later use. As you'll learn in Chapter 5, you can even transfer your Scrapbook desk accessory from one startup disk to another so that you can trade information with other programs.

The Scrapbook

When you choose Calculator from the menu, you'll see a four-function "pocket" calculator like the one in Figure 1-6. Though the Calculator is convenient for performing quick calculations in Word, it will probably be one of the first desk accessories to go if you need to open up more space on your startup disk.

The Calculator

FIGURE 1-6

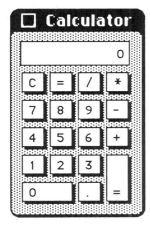

You can use the Calculator desk accessory to perform simple calculations.

Rearranging Your Disks

Obviously, there are as many possible configurations of startup disks as there are Word users. Although we cannot offer you any hard-and-fast rules for customizing your startup disks, we can offer a few recommendations.

Again, if you aren't using a hard drive, and you are beginning to create your own customized system of disks, you need to decide which applications you'll be using most often and how those applications can be grouped to work most efficiently. As we mentioned earlier, you may want to create several sets of startup disks to meet different needs.

One of the first things you can do is use the Font/DA Mover to customize the System folder on your startup disk. Remove any desk accessories and fonts you don't plan to use, and add any others you need. A copy of the Font/DA Mover application is located on the Macintosh Utilities 2 disk that came with your Macintosh, and your *Macintosh Utilities User's Guide* offers step-by-step instructions for using that facility.

In planning a disk configuration, the Font/DA Mover can tell you how much space a font or desk accessory will require. When you click on a font or desk accessory name in the Font/DA Mover dialog box, the size of the selected item appears, as shown in Figure 1-7.

FIGURE 1-7

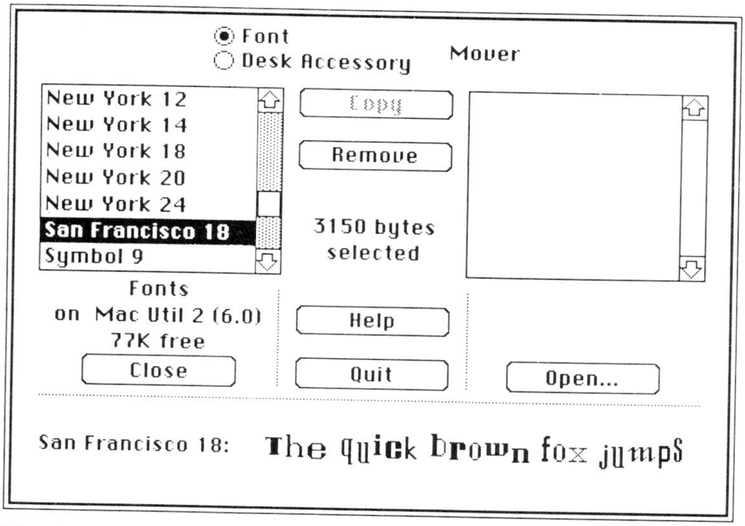

Use the Font/DA Mover to determine how much disk space is required by the fonts and desk accessories you want to use.

If the range of fonts available on the Macintosh doesn't suit your needs, you can purchase special fonts packages with custom display types created especially for the Macintosh. In fact, you can even use applications like Fontastic to create your own custom fonts to use in Word. Your software dealer can give you more information about the variety of fonts, desk accessories, and add-in applications available for Macintosh users.

Besides the common desk accessories that we've mentioned, you may want to place your own desk accessories and add-in applications on your startup disk or on a data disk. Although fonts and the desk accessories on the ⬤ menu must be installed with the Font/DA Mover in your System folder, you can place the Word utilities files and various application programs on the disk that stores your document files.

For example, if you plan to use Word's spelling facility, you may want to place the MS Dictionary file and any of your own custom dictionary files on the same disks on which you'll store your document files. Then, you won't have to pause to insert a utilities disk when you want to check your spelling. Similarly, if you plan to create macros, you'll need to have the AutoMac III application on one of your current disks. To make it easy to transfer graphics from SuperPaint into a Word document, you might copy that program onto the data disk that contains the Word document in which you plan to use graphics.

As you're rearranging various programs, you can use the Get Info command at the Finder level to determine how much disk space is required for each application or folder you want to use. Just click on the appropriate icon and select Get Info from the File menu. You'll see an Info dialog box like the one in Figure 1-8. Note the size of each file or folder you want to use, then calculate how many will fit on each of your disks.

Other Tools and Desk Accessories

FIGURE 1-8

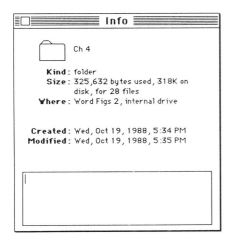

Use the Get Info command to determine how much disk space is required for the files or folders you want to use.

Word Finder

Word Finder is a desk accessory that allows you to access an online thesaurus. Both Word Finder and a file called Large Thesaurus are located on your Word 4 Utilities 2 disk. After you install Word Finder, you'll be able to look up synonyms for a selected word quickly and easily. In Appendix 6, we'll explain how to install and use Word Finder.

GETTING HELP

The Word Help file located on your Word Utilities 1 disk contains quick-reference information about all of Word's commands and options. You can access the Help facility from within Word at any time by choosing Help... from the Window menu or by choosing About Microsoft Word... from the menu and clicking the Help button.

If you try to use the Help facility while the disk that contains your Word Help file is not in one of your disk drives, Word will present a dialog box like the one in Figure 1-9. Just eject the disk currently in one of your drives and insert the Utilities 1 disk (or whichever disk happens to hold your Word Help file). Now, click on the file name Word Help, as shown in Figure 1-10, and click on the Open button or press Return or Enter. In a moment, you'll see a dialog box like the one in Figure 1-11.

FIGURE 1-9

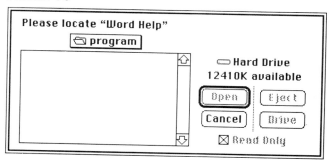

Word will ask you to locate the Help file if it is not currently in one of your disk drives.

FIGURE 1-10

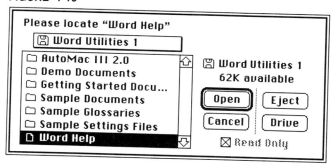

When you locate the Word Help file, use the Open option to access the Help facility.

FIGURE 1-11

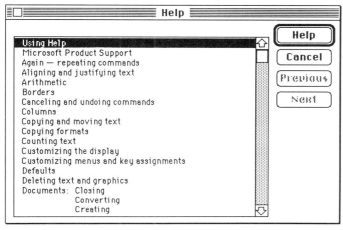

When you select the Word Help file, Word will present you with a list of topics.

FIGURE 1-12

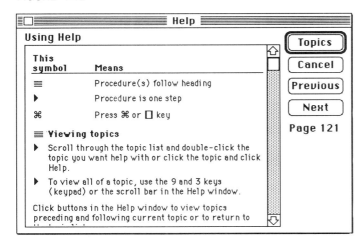

If you select Using Help, you'll see this screen.

Scroll through the list box until the topic you are interested in comes into view. Then, click on the topic name and click the Help button or press Return or Enter. For example, if you select the topic Using Help, you'll see a window like the one in Figure 1-12. To get back to the main list of topics shown in Figure 1-11, click the Topics button. To see the next Help screen in the sequence, click Next. To move to the previous topic in the sequence, click Previous. Finally, to remove the Help window from your screen and return to your document, just click Cancel. If you have inserted the Utilities 1 disk, Word will ask you to reinsert the disk that was originally in the drive.

Context-sensitive Help

Word's Help facility is also context-sensitive, making it easy for you to look up information about a particular command or option. For example, suppose you want to learn more about the Character... command on Word's Format menu. Rather than scrolling through the lists of general topics, just press ⌘-?. When your pointer takes on the question-mark shape, choose the Character... command. Rather than presenting a list of topics from which you can choose, Word will go directly to the Help screen that explains the Character... command, as shown in Figure 1-13. (Again, if your Help files are not currently in one of your disk drives, Word will ask you to locate the Help files before it displays the Help screen.)

FIGURE 1-13

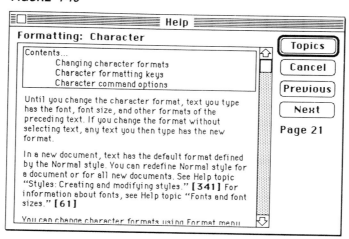

To get context-sensitive help, just press ⌘-? and select a command or option.

You also can receive context-sensitive help after you've opened a dialog box. Just press ⌘-? and Word will immediately display the Help screen for that topic.

A BRIEF TOUR 2

In this chapter, we'll take a tour of the Microsoft Word workspace or DeskTop and introduce some key concepts and terms you'll need throughout the rest of the book. If you are new to Word, please read this chapter carefully. It lays the groundwork for everything to follow. If you've been using Word 4 for a while, we suggest that you skim this chapter just to be sure you're familiar with our terminology. If you've used earlier versions of the program but are not familiar with Word 4, this chapter will highlight many of the program's new features and give you an idea of the variations you should be looking for.

We'll cover a lot of topics at a very general level in this chapter. If you do not understand all the concepts presented here, don't worry about it. We'll return to each concept in much more detail through the course of the book.

THE WORD DESKTOP

Word allows you four views of your document to help you design, create, and print it: the galley view, which we'll discuss in this chapter; the outline view, which we'll discuss in Chapter 9; and the page view and the print preview, which we'll discuss in Chapter 7. The galley view is the standard document view where you create your documents and edit them. The outline view allows you to plan longer documents, then rearrange them by sections. The page view lets you edit your text while Word displays the text as it will appear when printed. Finally, the print preview offers you a view of the page layout in your document.

To open a new or existing document in the galley view, double-click the Word icon on the Macintosh DeskTop. Word will present a screen like the one shown in Figure 2-1. The Word screen is divided into two major areas: the menu bar at the top of the screen and the document window—your workspace—below the menu bar. The document window, which occupies the bulk of the screen, is the blank slate for your creations in Microsoft Word. Through this window, you will create, edit, format, and view your documents.

FIGURE 2-1

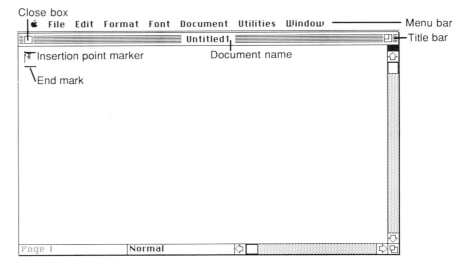

When you load the program, an empty Word document appears.

At this point, your document window will be empty except for a blinking vertical bar called the insertion point marker and a dark horizontal line called the end mark. As you might have guessed, the end mark signals the end of the document. The insertion point marker represents your position in the Word document. As you'll see when we begin working with text, this blinking bar moves one character space to the right each time you type a character in your document. You'll also use the insertion point marker to specify the point at which you want to edit text. If you have worked with PC-based word processors, the insertion point marker is similar to the cursor you have seen in those programs.

At this point, the insertion point marker occupies the first character space in your document window since you have not yet entered any text. Similarly, the end mark appears beneath the first line in the document window since the file Untitled1 is empty.

THE MENU BAR

At the top of the screen is the menu bar, where you will issue instructions to Word. In addition to the menu, which contains your desk accessories, Word offers seven menus to choose from: File, Edit, Format, Font, Document, Utilities, and Window. (In Chapter 14, you will see a custom menu called Work, on which you can place your own Word commands and shortcuts.)

Each menu contains a different set of commands—a different group of tools to work with. The File menu contains document-handling and printing commands. On the Edit menu, you'll find a series of commands that let you copy and move text, specify your type measurement preferences, and control the content of the menus themselves. The Format and Font menus let you control the appearance of the text in your document. From the Document menu, you can take advantage of Word's sophisticated features, such as variable headers and footers, outlining and page view, and other tools for designing and enhancing complex documents. The Utilities menu lets you search for text, change text, go to a specified page in your document, check spelling and hyphenation, create an index, and sort your document. Finally, the Window menu lets you create new windows to view different parts of your document and access the Help facility. You can also move between document windows and see the contents of the Clipboard via the Window menu.

To select a command from a menu, point to that menu name and press the mouse button. When the list of available commands appears below the menu name, hold down the mouse button and drag downward until the command you want is highlighted, then release the mouse button.

Issuing a Command

As you glance through the Word menus, notice the ⌘ characters and letters that appear to the right of many commands. This notation indicates that you can press the ⌘ key and a letter key to issue that command without using the mouse. For example, to save a document, you can press ⌘-s rather than selecting Save from the File menu. Similarly, you can press ⌘-x to issue the Cut command rather than selecting Cut from the Edit menu. You can also use the ⌘ key to perform many actions that are not listed on the Word menus. For example, you can use a ⌘-key combination to split windows into panes and to cancel any command or operation.

⌘-key shortcuts

If you have a numeric keypad, you can browse through the menus without using your mouse. To pull down the desired menu, just press the decimal point key on your numeric keypad and type the first letter of the menu whose contents you want to see. For example, to see the contents of the File menu, begin by pressing the decimal point key. The menu bar will appear in reverse video for about five seconds, then it will return to normal if you don't select a menu. To activate the File menu, type an *f*. Figure 2-2 on the following page shows the results.

Using the keypad

After you have activated a menu, the menu display will remain on your screen until you issue a command or click in another area of the screen. You can also close a menu by pressing the Backspace key, Esc, or the ⌘ and period keys (⌘-.).

FIGURE 2-2

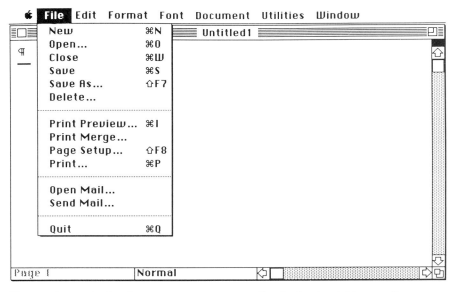

To see the contents of a menu, you can press the decimal point key on the numeric keypad, then type the letter or number that represents the menu you want to see.

Alternatively, you can activate a menu by pressing the decimal point key on the numeric keypad and typing a number from 0 through 8—0 for the menu, 1 for the File menu, 2 for the Edit menu, and so forth. (This technique is particularly handy since three of the menu names begin with an *F* and since there is no letter equivalent for the menu.)

In addition, you can press the decimal point key and then press the ← or → keys to access the first or last item on the menu bar. The first menu, of course, is the menu. The last item on the menu bar may be either the Window menu or the Work menu (if you have created your own custom commands). Once you have activated a menu, you can also press the → and ← keys to move from one menu to the next.

To select a command from a menu you have displayed on the screen, use the ↓ and ↑ keys to move through the list of commands and highlight the one you want. Once the command is highlighted, press Return or Enter to issue the command.

You can also select a command by typing the first letter of the command you want. If more than one command on a menu begins with the same letter, Word moves to those commands in order of their appearance. For example, to select the Save command from the open File menu shown in Figure 2-2, type an *s*. To select the Save As... command, type *s* again. If you type *s* a third time, Word will select Send Mail.... If you type *s* a fourth time, Word will cycle back to the Save command.

Incidentally, the 4, 6, 8, and 2 keys on the numeric keypad serve the same functions as the ←, →, ↑, and ↓ keys, respectively, after you display a menu on the screen. Use the 4 and 6 keys to move from one menu to the next and the 8 and 2 keys to select commands from an open menu.

Short vs. Full Menus

When you first open Word, you will see only some of the commands that are actually available. Word is initially loaded in the Short Menus mode. When the Short Menus setting is in effect, Word displays only the most common commands and options. To see all the commands available in Word, pull down the Edit menu and select the Full Menus command. Now, if you pull down the various menus, you'll see that they are expanded. Throughout this book, we will assume that you are using Full Menus.

By the way, Full Menus is a toggle command. This means the command changes each time you issue it. When you select Full Menus from the Edit menu, that command changes to Short Menus. If you issue the Short Menus command, Word will again display the condensed form of each menu and change the command to read Full Menus again. Figure 2-3 on the following page shows the commands available on the short and full versions of the Word menus.

The Short Menus/Full Menus toggle also affects the appearance of your status box, ruler display, horizontal scroll bar, and many dialog boxes. Let's look at the status box first, then look at dialog boxes and the ruler.

The Status Box

Another change takes place on your screen when you select Full Menus from the Edit menu: The status box at the bottom of your screen is split into two portions. As you can see in Figure 2-4, the word *Normal* appears on the right side of the status box. The *Normal* style notation means that any text you enter into your document at this point will appear in Word's default text format: 12-point New York Plain.

FIGURE 2-4

When you choose Full Menus, a style notation will appear in the status box at the bottom of your screen.

When you begin changing the formats of your document, you'll see the phrase *Normal+...* in this status box. We'll talk about this notation and other style sheet concepts in Chapter 8.

Dialog Boxes

You'll notice that many of the command names on the Word menus are followed by an ellipsis (...). The ellipsis tells you that a second level of options appears "below" that command. These options appear in a special kind of window called a dialog box.

FIGURE 2-3

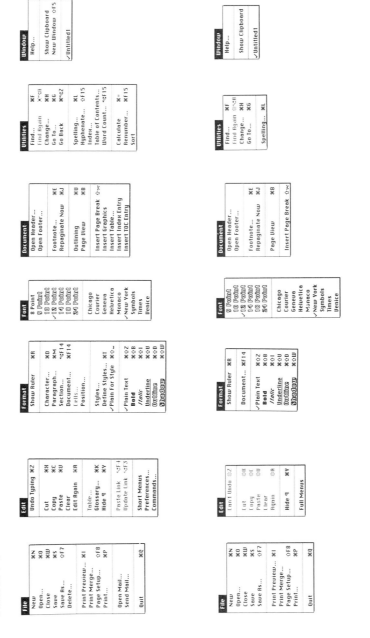

The top row shows commands that are available when you use Full Menus; the bottom row shows the commands available in Short Menus.

For example, if you select the Character... command from the Format menu (this command is available only when the Full Menus setting is in effect), you'll see a dialog box like the one in Figure 2-5.

FIGURE 2-5

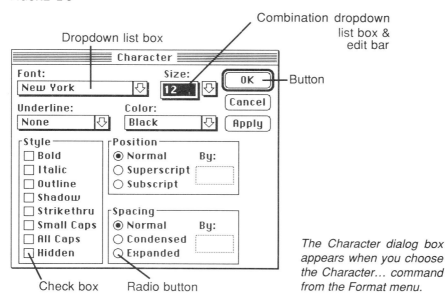

Dropdown list box

Combination dropdown
list box &
edit bar

Button

Check box   Radio button

The Character dialog box appears when you choose the Character... command from the Format menu.

Selecting options

There are several ways to issue instructions from a dialog box. Some dialog boxes contain one or more dropdown list boxes, such as the Font list box in the upper-left corner of the Character dialog box. When you click on the arrow to the right of the list box, a list of options will appear, as shown in Figure 2-6 on the following page. To select an option from the list, just drag the highlighted bar down to the option you want to choose and release the mouse button. (This is similar to selecting an item from a menu.) After you select an option from the list, its name will replace the name of the option that formerly appeared in the box at the top of the list.

You also can click on the name displayed at the top of a dropdown list box to cause the options to appear. Or, you can press the ⌘ key and the first letter of the list box name. For instance, pressing ⌘-f will cause the Font list to drop down.

In some instances, a dropdown list box "drops down" from an edit bar. For instance, in the Character dialog box, the Size list box is actually a combination dropdown list box and edit bar. You can distinguish a combination list box by the space that appears between the arrow and the box that displays the option name. This combination feature gives you two ways to specify a size setting: You can choose an option from the dropdown list, or you can type a new font size in the edit bar at the top of the list. There is one advantage to typing the font size into the edit bar. Word will allow you to use a font size that doesn't appear on the list that drops down from the edit bar. In other words, if you want to type a character in an 8-point font size and that size doesn't appear on the list of font sizes, all you need to do is type that size into the edit bar. When you press OK to close the Character dialog box, the next character you type will appear in 8 point.

FIGURE 2-6

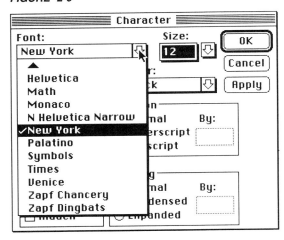

When you click on the arrow to the right of a list box, a list of options will drop down.

The small circles that appear to the left of the Position and Spacing options are called radio buttons. To select an option, just click on the radio button next to the option you want. You can also click on the option name itself to fill in the circle and select that option. For example, to assign the Superscript format to text in your document, you would click on the word Superscript or click on the radio button that appears next to the word.

In most dialog boxes, only one radio button that pertains to a particular group of options can be turned on at a time. That is, radio button options are generally mutually exclusive. For example, when you select the Superscript option, Word will fill in the circle next to the Superscript option and deselect the Normal option. Obviously, your text cannot appear in the Normal and Superscript positions at the same time.

Other options are selected via check boxes, like the ones next to the Style options in Figure 2-5. (Actually, an *x* will appear in one of these boxes when you select it—Microsoft evidently felt that the term *check box* is easier on the tongue than *x box*.) Usually, check boxes represent options that can be activated simultaneously. For example, if you want to display your text in bold, italic type, and you want all the characters to appear in uppercase letters, you can check the Bold, Italic, and All Caps options in the Character dialog box. Word will not usually deselect one check box option when you select another.

This also means that you must manually deselect most check box options when you want to change them; selecting another option won't do it. Thus, if you decide that you want your text to appear in small capital letters with an outline around each character, you must click on the Bold, Italic, and All Caps options to deselect them, then click on the Small Caps and Outline options to assign your new formats.

In the interest of conserving space in dialog boxes, Microsoft has replaced most traditional list boxes with dropdown list boxes like the Font list box we showed earlier. In a few instances, however, Word 4's dialog boxes contain regular list boxes. For example, in the Glossary dialog box, shown in Figure 2-7, the list of glossary terms appears in a list box. To view additional items in the list, you can click on the scroll bar that appears on the right side of the list. You also can drag the scroll box or click on the scroll arrows. To select a glossary term, you simply click on it or use the ↑ or ↓ key to point to it.

FIGURE 2-7

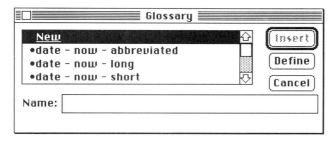

Some of Word's dialog boxes contain list boxes.

The large rectangular objects in the upper-right corner of the Character dialog box are called buttons (not to be confused with radio buttons). Generally, these large buttons are the last options you'll click to lock in your dialog box selections and direct Word to carry out your instructions. For example, if you click the OK button in the Character dialog box, Word will apply the character settings you have chosen and remove the dialog box from your screen. If you click the Cancel button, Word will remove the dialog box from your screen without implementing your changes.

The Apply button allows you to preview the effects of your dialog box selections. If you click the Apply button, Word will implement your character format selections on any selected text, but will not remove the dialog box from your screen. Thus, you can see the effects of an option or setting in your document before you close the dialog box.

Implementing your selections

Navigational buttons

Navigational buttons look like the buttons you use to implement your dialog box selections, except that the name on the button is followed by an ellipsis (…). This tells you that clicking one of these buttons will open another dialog box in which you can specify settings and select options. For example, Figure 2-8 shows Word 4's Paragraph dialog box, which contains three navigational buttons labeled Tabs…, Borders…, and Position.... Clicking these buttons will open the Tabs, Borders, and Position dialog boxes, respectively.

FIGURE 2-8

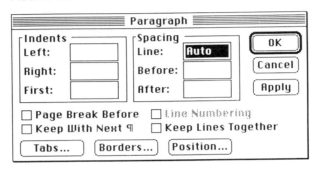

The Paragraph dialog box contains three navigational buttons.

Dialog box shortcuts

Once you become accustomed to using dialog boxes, you'll find that there are several ways to streamline your work. For example, you can use ⌘-key combinations to select many dialog box options and buttons, much as you do when selecting commands from Word menus.

For example, in the Character dialog box shown in Figure 2-5, you can press ⌘-o rather than clicking OK. Similarly, ⌘-c is equivalent to clicking the Cancel button. You can also use the ⌘ and period keys (⌘-.) to cancel any dialog box selections and return to your document. The ⌘-b, ⌘-i, and ⌘-h key combinations let you select the Bold, Italic, and Hidden options, respectively. We'll show you more dialog box shortcuts as we introduce each command in subsequent chapters.

On the expanded Macintosh keyboard, you can move from one group of options to the next by pressing the ← and → keys. When you "activate" a group of options, Word will display a flashing gray bar in that portion of the dialog box. Once you have activated a group of options, you can press the ⌘-Tab or Shift-⌘-Tab key combinations to select individual options from that group.

For example, in the Character dialog box in Figure 2-5, you might press the → key to activate the Position options. Then, you could press ⌘-Tab to move the flashing gray bar under the Subscript option.

If you press ⌘-Tab while the flashing gray bar appears under the last option in a group, Word will move to the first option in the next group. If you have a numeric keypad, you can also press the decimal point key to move from the last option in a group to the next group of options in a dialog box. If you press Shift-⌘-Tab while the flashing gray bar appears under the first option in a group, Word will move to the last option in the previous group. Once the option you want is underlined with the flashing gray bar, you can press ⌘-Spacebar to "click" on that item.

When you see a group of radio buttons or check boxes under one heading—like the Style, Position, and Spacing options shown in Figure 2-5—you can often cancel the selections pertaining to a particular option by clicking on the heading itself. For example, suppose you want to select the Superscript, Expanded, Bold, and Italic options in the Character dialog box.

Now, suppose you decide that you really did not mean to select the Superscript format. You can click on the Position heading above that group of options to cancel your Position selection without altering the remaining selections in the dialog box. When you use this technique, Word will revert to the setting that was selected when you opened the dialog box—not necessarily to the default setting for that group of options.

Selecting dialog box options may seem a bit confusing if you are new to Word. However, once you become proficient with the program, you'll find that these simple shortcuts can speed up your work considerably. We suggest that you experiment with these techniques in a sample document to get a feel for the various keyboard shortcuts.

When the Short Menus setting is in effect, Word changes the format of many of your dialog boxes. For example, when you issue the Document... command on the Format menu while Short Menus is in effect, you'll see a dialog box like the one in Figure 2-9. However, if the Full Menus setting is in effect when you select the Document... command, you will see a dialog box like the one in Figure 2-10 on the following page.

Dialog box options and the Full/Short Menus command

FIGURE 2-9

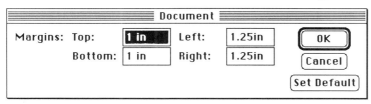

When you use Short Menus, an abbreviated version of the Document dialog box appears.

As you can see, the Document dialog box options grow substantially when the Full Menus setting is in effect. If you are working on a fairly simple document and don't need all these options, you may want to use the Short Menus command to reduce clutter on your screen. If you are working with a complex document with multicolumn formatting, custom menus, or multiple headers and footers, however, you'll want to use the Full Menus setting.

FIGURE 2-10

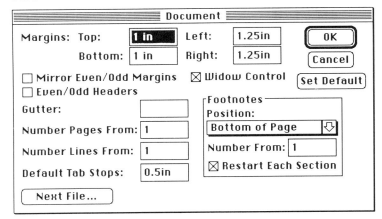

When the Full Menus setting is in effect, the Document dialog box contains more options.

WINDOWS

Since your Macintosh screen measures only nine inches diagonally, it is obvious that you cannot view the contents of an entire file on just one screen—unless you create only very short documents. That is why you need document windows. A window is like a porthole through which you can view a limited portion of your document.

To illustrate, suppose you cut a small square hole in a piece of cardboard and you then place the cardboard over this page. At any given time, you can see only a portion of the page through the square. By moving the cardboard around on the page, however, you can eventually read the entire page through the "window" in your piece of cardboard.

Everything you see on your Macintosh screen is actually viewed through a type of window—dialog boxes, alert boxes, even disk and folder windows at the Finder level. In fact, there are four types of document windows in Word: the standard document workspace, shown in Figure 2-1; a page view window, which we'll talk about in Chapter 7; a print preview window (also in Chapter 7); and an outline window, which we'll introduce in Chapter 9.

At the top of the document window is the title bar. At this point, Word has assigned the generic name *Untitled1* to our document. (We'll show you how to assign names to your documents in Chapter 3.)

However, the title bar does much more than display the name of your document. Notice the two small boxes at either end of the title bar. The one on the left is called the close box. To remove your document from the screen, you can click in this close box. As you'll see in Chapter 3, clicking in the close box is equivalent to selecting the Close command from the File menu.

Resizing Windows

On the right side of the title bar is a zoom box. You can click in this zoom box to change the size of your document window from full-screen to half-screen size. For example, if we click in the zoom box in the document window shown in Figure 2-1, our screen will look like the one in Figure 2-11. If we click the zoom box again, our screen will return to full-screen size. If you prefer, you can press Option-⌘-] to access the zoom feature from the keyboard.

FIGURE 2-11

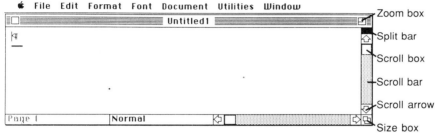

You can click in the zoom box in the title bar to reduce your document window to half-screen size.

You can also use the size box at the lower-right corner of the document window to change the height and width of your window. For example, if you point to the size box on a full-screen window and drag up and to the left, you can create a window like the one in Figure 2-12 on the following page.

Once you have manually resized a window, you can use the zoom box at the upper-right corner of the screen to toggle between the full-screen view and the size that you set manually. Thus, if you click in the zoom box in Figure 2-12, your window will look like the one in Figure 2-1 again. If you click in the zoom box again, your screen will return to the size that you set manually in Figure 2-12. By the way, whenever you open a document, Word will initially display that document in full-screen size—even if you have previously used the zoom box or size box to resize the window.

Resizing windows is not generally necessary unless you have two or more windows open on your DeskTop at the same time. In that case, you may want to create nonoverlapping document windows so that you can see the contents of both windows simultaneously. When you have two or more document windows open at the same time, Word 4 makes it easy to create nonoverlapping windows by automatically repositioning the windows when you click in the zoom box.

For example, suppose you have two document windows open on your screen at the same time: Untitled1 and Untitled2. Currently, Untitled1 is hidden behind

Untitled2, but you want to view the contents of both windows simultaneously. Begin by clicking in the zoom box in the title bar of Untitled2. Your screen will look like the one in Figure 2-13. Notice that Word has not only reduced that window to half-screen size, but has moved the window to the bottom of the screen as well.

FIGURE 2-12

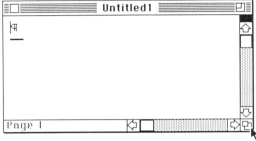

To manually resize a window, drag the size box.

FIGURE 2-13

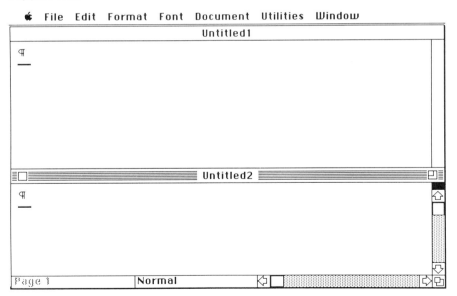

Word has reduced the bottom window to half-screen size.

Next, click on the Untitled1 window to activate it. Untitled1 will now completely cover Untitled2. However, if you click in the zoom box in the Untitled1 window, Word will reduce that window to half-screen size and position it at the top of the screen, as shown in Figure 2-14.

FIGURE 2-14

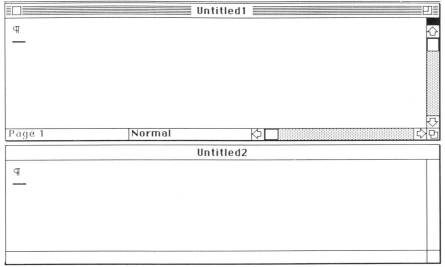

The first window is now stacked above the second.

If you open a third document window and click in its zoom box, Word will automatically reduce that window to quarter-screen size, as shown in Figure 2-15 on the next page. Likewise, if you have four or more windows open at the same time, Word will continue to resize and reposition the windows when you click in the zoom box to make each window as easy as possible to view and access.

If you want to display two windows side by side rather than stacked, you'll need to drag the windows to the desired position on the screen—which brings us to another topic: Whenever you see horizontal stripes at the top of a window (at the Finder level, in a dialog box, or a document window), you can drag that window around on the screen. To move a window, just point anywhere on the title bar (except the close or zoom boxes) and drag.

For example, Figure 2-16 on the next page shows two document windows arranged side by side on the screen. To create these windows, you would begin by dragging the size box for the Untitled1 window to the left until it fills half the screen vertically. Next, click in the Untitled2 window and use the same technique to reduce that window to half-screen size vertically. At this point, the two windows will overlap. Finally, point to the title bar of Untitled2 and drag to the right until the two windows appear side by side.

FIGURE 2-15

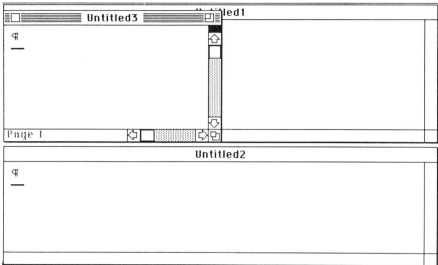

The third window appears in quarter-screen size.

FIGURE 2-16

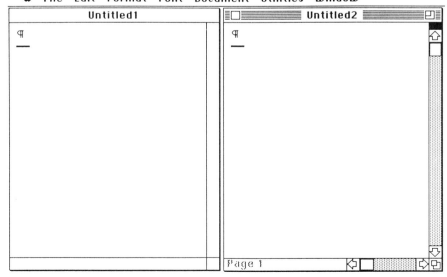

You can create nonoverlapping windows by resizing and dragging the windows manually.

We mentioned that the horizontal lines in your document window indicate that you can drag that window around by its title bar to reposition it. Actually, the horizontal lines mean much more than that. These lines also tell you whether the window is active. The active window on your screen is the one you are currently working in—that is, any commands you issue will apply to the window that is active at the time.

The Active Window

For example, notice that the Untitled1 window in Figure 2-16 does not display horizontal lines (or close and zoom boxes). This window is inactive. In order to edit or make any other changes in this window, you must click on it to reactivate it. (You can also use the Window menu to activate a window, as you'll see in Chapter 2.)

By the way, if you want to move a window around on the screen without deactivating the current window, just press the ⌘ key as you drag the title bar area of the second window. The partially active window will "slide behind" the active window, rather than coming to the top of the stack. If you click anywhere else on the window, however, Word will activate that window and bring it to the top of the stack. To reactivate the window you were working in, you must select it from the Window menu or click on it again.

Moving between windows is much like shuffling a stack of playing cards. To move from one window to another, you can click on the window you want, select the window name from the Window menu, or press Option-⌘-w. When you press Option-⌘-w, the next window in the stack comes into view and the previous window moves to the bottom of the stack.

Moving between Windows

The gray bars at the right and bottom of the screen are called scroll bars. Once you've entered some text into your Word document file, you'll use these scroll bars to move through your document. (More on scrolling and other navigational techniques in Chapter 4.)

Other Window Features

To the left of the horizontal scroll bar at the bottom of your screen is a status box that currently displays a page number. Since we are viewing an empty document window right now, we see the notation *Page 1*. When you begin learning about outlining, formatting, and using the glossary, you'll see other messages in this area as well.

You can also split a window into panes to see two portions of your document at the same time. For example, suppose you are writing a sales report and you have presented a table of statistics at the beginning of the document. If you want to refer to these statistics later in the document, split your document into two panes rather than scroll back and forth to check the contents of your table. This way, you can keep the table in view as you write the body of your report. You can scroll the two panes independently and even copy data from one window pane to the other.

Using the split bar

To split a window into panes, point to the black bar that appears above the vertical scroll bar on the right side of the document window. Drag this split bar downward to the desired position. As you can see in Figure 2-17, Word now gives you two sets of vertical scroll bars so that you can move through the two window panes independently.

FIGURE 2-17

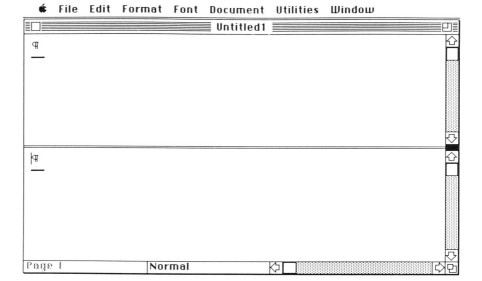

To split a window into panes, you can drag the split bar toward the middle of the screen.

To remove the split pane from your window, just point to the split bar again and drag it past either end of the vertical scroll bar. You can also toggle the split feature on and off by pressing Option-⌘-s.

The New Window command

In addition to the split screen technique, Word offers multiple windowing capabilities for a single document. By creating multiple windows, you can see different parts of the same document at the same time. This is particularly convenient when you are working with very large documents and you want to see several blocks of text simultaneously. When you begin working with outlines in Chapter 9, you may also want to use multiple windows to view your outline and your main document at the same time.

To create a new document window, just select New Window from the Window menu. For example, if we select New Window while the Untitled1 document is active, Word will display a new window called Untitled1:2. It will also rename our original window Untitled1:1. Subsequent windows will be named Untitled1:3, Untitled1:4, and so forth.

Keep in mind that each window is just another porthole through which you view a single document. Any changes you make in one window will affect the entire document—not just the version you see in the active window.

To remove a window from your screen, click the close box or press ⌘-w. Word will automatically renumber the remaining document windows, if necessary. If you click the close box of the only window that is open for a particular document, however, Word will assume that you want to close your document altogether and ask if you want to save any changes before it removes the window from your screen. (You can easily tell if only one window is open for a document since the colon and number that identify multiple windows will not appear.) We'll talk more about closing and saving files in Chapter 3.

THE RULER

You can specify formatting features, such as line lengths, paragraph indentions, paragraph justification, line spacing, and tab settings, by using the ruler. The ruler does not automatically appear on your screen when you open a new document. To access the ruler, select Show Ruler from the Format menu or press ⌘-r.

The appearance of the ruler depends on whether the Short Menus or Full Menus setting is in effect. If you're using Short Menus, your ruler will look like the one in Figure 2-18. As you can see in Figure 2-19, several additional ruler icons are available when the Full Menus setting is activated.

FIGURE 2-18

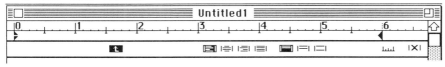

If you're using Short Menus, you'll see this ruler when you select Show Ruler from the Format menu.

FIGURE 2-19

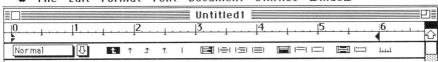

If you're using Full Menus, you'll see this ruler when you select Show Ruler from the Format menu.

If you use Short Menus, Word will display the Normal paragraph icon (|✗|) on the far right side of the ruler, just under the ruler itself. If you click on this icon, Word will change highlighted paragraphs to *Normal* style. If you've inserted any tab stops into your document, they will revert to the default tab stops for the *Normal* style.

If you use Full Menus, you'll see two features on the ruler that are new to Word 4. You now can control your document's style sheet from a dropdown list box on the left side of the ruler, just under the ruler itself. You no longer need to issue the Define Styles... command from the Format menu or use your Work menu to apply styles to your document.

Word 4 also provides you with a scale icon under the 6-inch mark on the ruler. Briefly, Word can format the ruler according to three scales. The normal scale displays the document boundaries, tabs, and indentions. The 0 mark here represents the left column boundary. To change the scales, click on the scale icon.

The page scale displays the position of the document's margins in relation to the paper's edge. Brackets indicate the document's margins, which you can adjust. The 0 mark here represents the left edge of the page.

You can activate the table scale, which shows your columns and column boundaries, only if you have positioned the insertion point marker in a table or if you have highlighted a table. You can reposition the indent and column markers, as well as the brackets, to adjust the size of the columns in your tables.

Show Ruler is another toggle command that changes when issued. When you select Show Ruler from the Format menu, that command changes to Hide Ruler. Once you've specified your ruler settings, you may prefer to suppress the ruler display so that more of your document is visible on the screen. You can select the Hide Ruler command (or press ⌘-r again) to suppress the ruler display. Your ruler specifications will remain in effect even when the ruler is not visible on the screen.

Although you can see only about $6^1/_2$ inches of the ruler on your screen at a time, your ruler (in the normal scale) actually extends from -11 to 22 inches. You can see the remainder of the ruler by clicking on the right and left scroll arrows at the bottom of your screen. To see the negative values on your ruler, you can press the Shift key and then click on the left scroll arrow. We'll talk more about formatting with rulers in Chapter 5.

THE POINTER

As you may have noticed, your mouse pointer takes on a number of shapes as it moves around the screen in Word. Table 2-1 shows the various pointer icons that you'll see as you work in Word.

You'll use the I-beam pointer to select text and to move the blinking insertion point marker around on your screen. The I-beam pointer will probably be the most commonly used pointer shape as you edit and format text.

TABLE 2-1

⃛	I-beam pointer	⌚	Watch
⫰	Italic I-beam pointer	✥	Four-pointed outline pointer
▶	Left arrow pointer	↕	Vertical outline pointer
◢	Right arrow pointer	↔	Horizontal outline pointer
⇕	Split-bar pointer	⌘	Assign to Key pointer
↓	Downward pointing arrow	?	Question mark pointer
→1←	Page number pointer	+	Plus sign pointer
+	Crosshair pointer	−	Minus sign pointer

Word has 16 distinct pointer shapes.

Do not confuse the I-beam pointer with the blinking insertion point marker. You use the I-beam pointer to select an insertion point, but your selection does not go into effect until you actually click the mouse button to place the insertion point marker in your text. (You'll notice the I-beam pointer becomes italic when you move it over italicized text.) In fact, if you use the scroll bars to move through your document, your insertion point marker might be in a part of the document that is not visible on your screen. Make sure the insertion point marker is in the correct spot before you begin typing or editing text. (If you do begin typing while your insertion point marker is positioned beyond the portion of your document visible on the screen, Word will return that portion of the document to the screen.)

The arrow that points to the left appears whenever you point to the menu bar, title bar, or scroll bars. It also appears when you point to options in a Word dialog box. You'll use this arrow to select commands and options and to move through your document via the scroll bars.

The arrow that points to the right appears when you move the pointer to the far-left side of your window. There is an invisible selection bar in this area. When your pointer takes on this shape, you know you are in the selection bar. Then, you can use the right-arrow pointer to select blocks of text quickly.

The split-bar pointer appears when you point to the split bar at the top of the vertical scroll bar. In this shape, the pointer allows you to drag the split bar up or down the scroll bar.

When you're working in a table, the right arrow will appear whenever you move the pointer over the left edge of a column. We'll tell you about Word's table feature in Chapter 10. Also, in the page view, you may see the right arrow in other places on your screen besides the far-left edge. That's because the page view offers selection bars for different elements of text. We'll talk more about the page view in Chapter 7.

The downward pointing arrow appears when you move the pointer over the top of a table column. You can use this pointer to select an entire column of a table.

The page number and crosshair pointers appear when you use the Print Preview... command to see how your document will look when it's printed. The crosshair pointer lets you reposition items on the page, and the page number pointer lets you insert and position a page number on each page of your document. We'll discuss these techniques in Chapter 7.

The watch shape indicates that Word is working to execute your last command. While this watch appears, you cannot use other pointers to issue commands or to select text in Word. However, you can use the keyboard while the watch is visible. You can type text or even get a jump on Word by using ⌘-key combinations to issue commands and select options. Word will catch up with you once it has finished the current task.

The four-pointed outline pointer appears when you point to an outline selection icon to the left of a heading. The vertical outline pointer appears when you drag the heading up or down. The horizontal outline pointer appears when you drag the heading left or right to promote or demote the heading.

When you press ⌘-Option-+(keypad), the Assign to Key pointer appears, allowing you to select menu commands and assign them to any key combination of your choice.

As we told you in Chapter 1, the question-mark pointer appears when you press ⌘-? to access Word's Help facility.

Finally, the plus and minus sign pointers appear when you are creating custom menus in Word. As you'll learn in Chapter 14, you'll use these pointers to select commands and options that you want to add to, or delete from, menus.

THE KEYBOARD   Your Macintosh keyboard is much more than a standard typewriter keyboard. Its extra keys allow you to perform special functions. The Return, Option, and ⌘ keys are the most obvious differences. You'll see a numeric keypad and a set of arrow keys at your disposal as well. Figures 2-20 and 2-21 show diagrams of the Macintosh Plus and Macintosh SE keyboards.

FIGURE 2-20

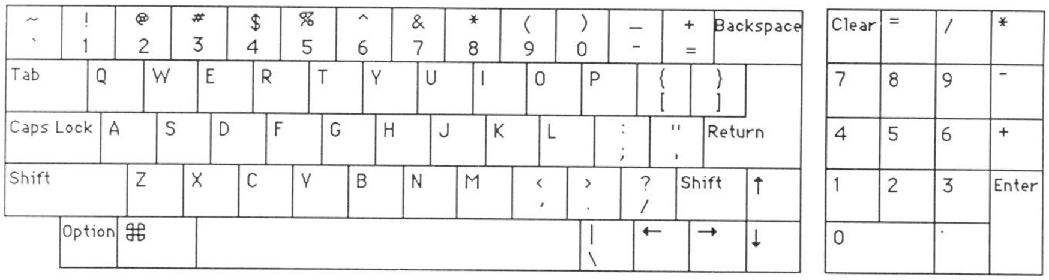

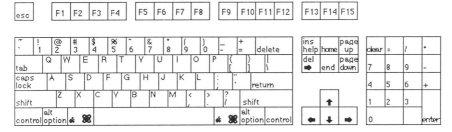

The Macintosh Plus keyboard looks like this.

FIGURE 2-21

The Macintosh SE keyboard has a direction keypad and function keys.

The Option and ⌘ keys are special function keys that let you issue commands and perform tasks quickly—without the aid of your mouse. Generally, these keys are used in conjunction with the alphabetic keys.

The Spacebar works just like the Spacebar on a standard typewriter. Use it to enter blank spaces into your document.

You'll use the Tab key to set up columnar tables of data and to control the positioning of text in your document.

As you might have guessed, the Shift key's primary purpose is to let you type in uppercase characters. The Shift key also serves as a special function key when used in conjunction with the Option and ⌘ keys.

The Caps Lock key on your Mac keyboard is quite similar to the Shift Lock key on a standard typewriter—it allows you to type in all uppercase letters, without pressing the Shift key. Keep in mind that Caps Lock does not apply to the numeric keys along the top of your keyboard. In order to use the top-row characters like !, @, and #, or punctuation marks like :, ", and ?, you must still press the Shift key.

The Backspace (or Delete) key is primarily an editing key that lets you back up over typographical errors or delete blocks of text. As you'll learn in Chapter 13, you also use the Backspace and ⌘ keys to make glossary entries in your document.

On the SE keyboard, the Backspace key is labeled *delete*. We'll use the word "Backspace" when referring to this key, since it functions like the Backspace key on the Mac Plus and other computer keyboards. You'll also notice that the SE keyboard has an extra delete key above the arrow keys. This Del key edits forward in your text. In case you've misplaced your insertion point marker to the left of the character you intended to delete, you can use the Del key to delete forward. You need not reposition your insertion point marker.

Among other things, the Return and Enter keys let you lock in dialog box selections and signal the beginning of a new paragraph in your Word documents. Do not confuse the Return and Enter keys with the carriage return on a standard typewriter. You do not have to press the Return key at the end of each line to move to the beginning of the next line. Word offers a special feature called WordWrap that automatically moves the insertion point marker from one line to the next. Press Return or Enter only when you want to end one paragraph and start a new one.

If you have a Mac Plus or Mac SE keyboard, you can use the numeric keypad and the ←, →, ↑, and ↓ keys as navigational tools to move quickly through your Word documents. You must press the Clear key before you can use the numeric keypad to enter text into your document. Otherwise, you will find yourself moving around the document instead of typing numeric characters. Although the numeric keypad is designed for quick numeric entry for spreadsheet and other business software users, Microsoft has turned it into a navigational tool for Word users. When you press the Clear key, however, Word will allow you to use the keypad for entering numbers. In effect, the Clear key serves as a NumLock key in Word. When you are using the keypad to enter numbers, *Num. Lock* will appear in the status box in the lower-left corner of your screen. To use the keypad for navigation again, just press the Clear key one more time.

Across the top of the SE keyboard, you'll see an Esc key and a row of special function keys labeled [F1], [F2], and so forth. The Esc key allows you to cancel commands and other actions, while the special function keys can be used in conjunction with the ⌘, Shift, and Option keys to issue commands, open dialog boxes, and perform various other operations.

In addition to the special function keys, many of the standard typewriter keys also serve special functions in certain circumstances. As we mentioned earlier, you can use the ⌘ and Option keys in conjunction with certain letter keys to issue Word commands and perform other tasks. We'll introduce these special functions and techniques as we discuss Word's various features throughout the course of the book.

FILE HANDLING 3

In the next section of this book, we'll show you how to create, edit, and format documents. Before you invest your time and energy in building a document, however, you should be familiar with the procedures for opening, closing, deleting, and saving files in Word. In this chapter, we'll show you seven of the commands on Word's File menu: New, Open..., Close, Save, Save As..., Delete..., and Quit. (When we first mention these commands, we'll include in brackets their function key shortcuts for those who use the SE keyboard.) In addition, we'll introduce you to the Word Count... command on the Utilities menu. This feature lets you monitor the size of your document by characters, words, lines, and paragraphs. In Chapter 12 and Appendix 3, we'll show you some additional file-handling techniques for working with the print merge and QuickSwitch facilities.

CREATING AND OPENING FILES

As we explained in Chapter 1, when you double-click the Word icon at the Finder level to load the Word program, Word will automatically create a new blank file. The document name *Untitled1* will appear in the title bar. Similarly, you can simultaneously load Word and open one or more existing files from the Finder level by selecting the icons for the files you want to work with and issuing the Open command. You can also double-click on one of the highlighted file icons to open the files.

If you need to open a new, blank document while you are in Word, you can always select the New command from the File menu, or press [F5]. If you have already opened one untitled document, your new document will be called Untitled2. As you open new files during a session, Word will number those files sequentially—Untitled3, Untitled4, and so forth.

Retrieving Existing Files

If you have already created a file and you want to retrieve it from disk while working in Word, choose the Open... command from the File menu, or press [F6]. Word will present a dialog box like the one in Figure 3-1.

FIGURE 3-1

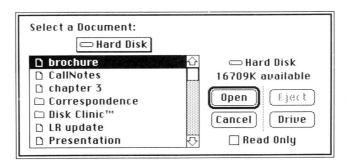

When you issue the Open... command, Word presents a list of files and folders on the active disk.

On the right side of the Open dialog box, Word presents the name of the disk in the active disk drive. The amount of space available on the disk appears below the disk name, just above the Open, Eject, Cancel, and Drive buttons.

On the left side of the dialog box, a disk icon and the disk name also appear. Below that is a list box that contains the names of all the folders and Word files on the active disk. As you can see in Figure 3-1, the small icons on the left side of each item in the list box show whether an item is a folder or a document. Documents created in other applications will not appear in the list box unless they have been stored in a format that Word can read. (In Appendix 3, we'll include more on opening files created in other programs.)

The document and folder names appear in alphabetical order in the Open dialog box list box. If your disk contains more than seven files and folders, you can click on the scroll arrows or in the gray area of the scroll bar to bring additional names into view. You can also use the ↑ and ↓ keys to move through the list of document and folder names. Then, to open a file you've selected, all you need to do is click the Open button or press Return or Enter.

You can move quickly to the file you need by typing the first letter of the file (or folder) name. Word will immediately scroll through the lists of files and folders and highlight the first file name or folder name that begins with the letter you typed. For example, if we type *p* in the Open dialog box shown in Figure 3-1, Word will highlight the document name *Presentation*. If you type quickly, you can narrow your selection even further by typing the first two or three letters of the name.

To open a folder, simply highlight the folder name and click the Open button or press Return or Enter. If you have a Mac Plus or Mac SE keyboard, you can also press ⌘-↓ to open a folder. When you open a folder, your dialog box will look like the one in Figure 3-2. Notice that an open folder icon replaces the disk icon above the list box. Inside the folder, you'll see another list of Word files—and additional folders if you have placed one folder inside another at the Finder level.

FIGURE 3-2

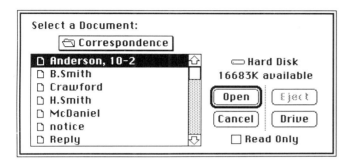

The icon for an open folder differs slightly from the icon for the disk.

To close a folder and move up to the next "level" in the list box, click the pointer on the folder title above the list box and drag down to select the disk icon again. You can also press ⌘-↑ to move up to the next level.

If the file you want to see is on a disk located in another drive, just click the Drive button to see a list of the files and folders on the disk in that drive. You can also press ⌘-d or Tab to activate another disk drive.

If the document you want is not on one of the disks currently in your disk drive(s), click the Eject button or press ⌘-e to eject the disk in the active drive. Then, place in the disk drive the disk that contains the file you want.

Finally, once you have selected the file you want, press either the Return or Enter key, click the Open button, or press ⌘-o to display the document on your Word DeskTop.

The Read Only option is designed primarily for Macintosh networks, where two or more users may have access to the same files. To ensure that no one alters the master version of a file, you can apply the Read Only option. (As you'll see in Chapter 6, Word also applies the Read Only option to your MS Dictionary file to protect it from revisions.)

Even if you are a solo Mac user, if you want only to see the contents of a file without making changes to it, you can click the Read Only option before opening the file. When you use the Read Only option, Word will let you scan the file and even make changes to it, but it will not let you save that file under the name that was originally assigned to it. In other words, if you want to keep any changes you have made to a file that was opened with the Read Only option in effect, you must save that file under a new name. In this way, Word protects your original file while you're in the Read Only mode.

The Read Only option

If you issue the Save command to save a file that you opened with the Read Only option, Word will automatically present the Save As dialog box. If you attempt to assign the original file name to the altered file, Word will present the alert box shown in Figure 3-3.

FIGURE 3-3

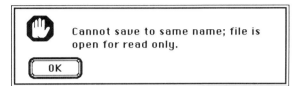

If you use the Read Only option, Word will not let you save an altered file under the same name as the original.

In order to save your changes to the file, you must click OK in this alert box, then assign a new name to the document. (We'll say more about saving files in a moment.) Although the Read Only option is hardly a foolproof security device, you may find it a convenient way to protect your files from inadvertent changes.

SAVING YOUR WORK

Word gives you several ways to save a file. As you might have guessed, to save a document, you need to select the Save or Save As... command from the File menu. The first time you save an untitled document, you'll see the Save As dialog box shown in Figure 3-4. This dialog box appears whether you select Save or Save As... from the File menu. (To select the Save command quickly from the keyboard, press ⌘-s or [F7]. To select the Save As... command, press Shift-[F7].) Once you have assigned a name to a document, however, you can bypass this dialog box by issuing the Save command rather than choosing Save As....

FIGURE 3-4

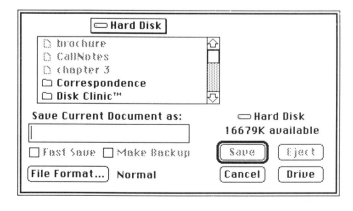

The Save As dialog box appears when you issue the Save As... or Save command to save a file for the first time.

The first thing you need to tell Word is where you want the file to be stored. Use the Drive and Eject buttons, described earlier, to access the disk you want. Notice that the names of the documents already stored on the active disk are dimmed in the list box. You cannot select any of these documents from the list box; they appear only as a reminder of the names you have already used.

You'll also see the folders on the active disk in the Save As dialog box list box. Unlike the file names, folder names are available for selection in the Save As dialog box. If you want to place a document into a folder, just double-click the folder icon or folder name to open it. When you return to the Finder level, you'll see that the document has been stored in the selected folder.

Word also tells you how much room is on the active disk. As you work with documents of various lengths, you'll soon get a feel for the amount of space required to store documents of various lengths and levels of complexity. (For instance, a ten-page document requires about 30K of disk space.)

If there is not enough room on the active disk to save your document, you'll see an alert box like the one in Figure 3-5. At this point, you can either cancel the Save procedure and delete some of the documents on the disk (we'll talk about the Delete... command in a few pages), or you can eject the current disk and save your document on another disk.

FIGURE 3-5

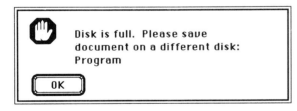

You'll see this alert message if there is not enough room to save your document on the active disk.

Once you decide where you want to store your document, you must provide Word with a name for the file. (The Save button will remain dimmed until you provide a name.) If this is the first time you have saved the document, the Save Current Document As edit bar will be empty. Just type the name you want to use. If you have saved the document before, Word will display the current document name in the Save Current Document As edit bar. You can leave that entry intact, or you can type a new name for your document. After you have entered the name you want to use in the Save As dialog box, click the Save button, press ⌘-s, or press the Return or Enter key.

If you have entered a name in the Save Current Document As edit bar that has already been used on the active disk, you'll see an alert box like the one shown in Figure 3-6. If you want to replace the existing file with the document that is currently open on your screen, click Yes; otherwise, click No. If you click No, Word will redisplay the Save As dialog box and allow you to enter a new document name in the Save Current Document As edit bar.

FIGURE 3-6

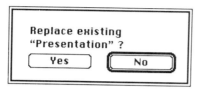

Word asks you to verify your file name when you assign the same name to two documents.

Word will not display the alert message in Figure 3-6 if the existing file on your disk is stored in an unopened folder. That is, Word will allow you to create files with identical names on the same disk, as long as those files are in separate folders. However, we strongly recommend that you avoid duplicate file names.

The Close and Quit Commands

Of course, you can issue the Save or Save As... command at any time during a Word session to save your revisions to a document. If you issue the Save command to save a document that has already been named, Word will assume that you want to save the revised document under the existing name. That is, Word will replace the version of the document that is stored on disk with the revised document.

If you issue the Close command after you have made changes to a document (this includes entering data into a new, blank file), you'll see an alert box like the one in Figure 3-7.

FIGURE 3-7

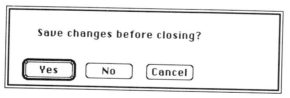

The Close alert box appears when you issue the Close command without saving your changes.

If you click No in the Close alert box, Word will close the current document window without saving your changes. If you click Yes and the current document has previously been saved, Word will automatically save the document under its current name. If the document has not been saved before, Word will present the Save As dialog box shown in Figure 3-4.

Similarly, if you issue the Quit command after you have made changes to a document, you'll see a Save Changes alert box like the one in Figure 3-8. Keep in mind that the Quit command tells Word to close all documents that are open on the

Word DeskTop and return to the Finder level. Therefore, if you choose Quit before you save a document, Word will present the Save Changes alert box for any file that has been changed since your last save (including dictionary and glossary files, which we'll discuss in Chapters 6 and 13). You may elect to save or discard your changes to each file.

FIGURE 3-8

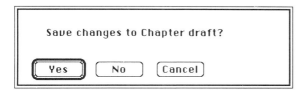

When you issue the Quit command without saving
your changes, Word will display this alert box for
any file that has been changed.

Backing Up
Your Work

If you want to make sure that you have a backup of your document, use the Make Backup option in the Save As dialog box. When you use the Make Backup option, Word does not overwrite the last version of the document that you saved. It renames the last version, "Backup of ...," then saves your changes to the document that is currently open on the DeskTop.

When you use the Make Backup option, Word will add the prefix *Backup of* to the document name that appears in the Save Current Document As edit bar. For example, if your main file is named *Presentation*, your backup file will be named *Backup of Presentation*.

To use the Make Backup option, you must use the Save As... command to save a previously saved file. Word will not make a backup copy of an untitled document or a document whose name you have changed; the document name must already be recorded on disk so that Word can duplicate the original document before it implements your Save As... command to record your changes to the file. Thus, you should leave the existing document name in the Save Current Document As edit bar, click the Make Backup option, then click Save, press ⌘-s, or press Return or Enter to save the document under the same name. Click Yes when Word asks if you want to replace the existing file that is stored under that name.

Keep in mind that Word will never update the backup copy of your document unless you specifically instruct it to do so. If you want to update your backup copy to reflect the status of your document as of the last time you saved, you must reissue the Save As... command and save the document again with the Make Backup option in effect.

Some precautions   We recommend that you save each of the open documents on your DeskTop at least every half hour to ensure that any changes you have made to those files are recorded on disk. As you may have learned the hard way, a momentary power outage or an irreversible editing command can mean the loss of a lot of hard work. By saving your files regularly, you can ensure that you will not lose hours' worth of work.

For important documents, you should also copy the file to a separate backup disk. Although the Make Backup option is a handy way to create backup copies of your files, it will not help you if the disk on which your documents are stored becomes unreadable for some reason. By regularly copying your files to a separate disk, you decrease the chances of losing important work.

By the way, whenever you save a file, Word will replace the page number in the lower-left corner of your window with a character count. This change is temporary; as soon as you click anywhere in your document, type a character, or issue a command, the page number will reappear.

Making a
fast save   To make it easier to save your changes to long documents, Word 4 offers a feature called Fast Save. If you click the Fast Save option in the Save As dialog box, Word will substantially shorten the amount of time it takes to save your documents.

Here's how it works: Word maintains a set of pointer tables to keep track of the changes you make to your document. Normally, when you issue the Save command, Word completely rewrites your document on the disk. When you use Fast Save, Word appends your changes to the last saved version of the document. As a result, when you use Fast Save, your files will get longer each time you issue the Save command to record your changes to a file. To keep your document from getting too long, Word will occasionally perform a full-fledged Save procedure to consolidate your changes. Of course, Word always updates all the pointer tables and rewrites your entire file to disk when you issue the Close or Quit command and save your changes.

You cannot use the Make Backup and Fast Save options simultaneously. However, you can switch options at any time by issuing the Save As… command rather than the Save command. For example, suppose you have been using the Fast Save option to save your revisions to a document as you work, then you decide to make a separate backup file to ensure that the last saved version of your file is kept safe while you make some changes to the current version on your screen. You can issue the Save As… command and select the Make Backup option, as described earlier. Then, the next time you want to save your work, you can issue the Save As… command again and reselect the Fast Save option so that you can make quick saves as you continue your work.

Duplicating a file   Occasionally, you may find it necessary to duplicate a file while you are working in Word. You can accomplish this task by issuing the Save As… command

and typing a new name in the Save Current Document As edit bar. For example, suppose you want to create two very similar versions of a report. After creating and formatting the first report, save it under an appropriate name (let's say Report1). Then, to duplicate the file without returning to the Finder level, issue the Save As… command, and type a new name (like Report2) in the Save Current Document As edit bar. The document on your screen will now carry the name Report2, and the original Report1 will be filed away safely on disk. Now, you can make any necessary changes to the second report, without altering the first.

You can use this technique to save permanent template files so you can create similar sets of documents quickly and easily. When you use the Save As… command to duplicate a file, Word also remembers the print settings, styles, and other formats you have assigned to that file. If you want, you can erase the text of a file once you've duplicated it, then rename the file as a template that contains all the styles, margins, and print settings you can reuse any time.

The Delete... command on Word's File menu was a new addition to Word 3. Word 4 offers it as well. In earlier versions of the program, you could delete files from a disk only by dragging them into the Trash at the Finder level. The Delete… command makes it much easier for you to recover disk space when you need it.

To delete a file from within Word, select the Delete… command from the File menu. Word will display a dialog box like the one in Figure 3-9. As with the Open and Save As dialog boxes, you can use the Drive button to see the contents of any disk drive, and you can use the Eject button to remove your disk.

DELETING A DOCUMENT

FIGURE 3-9

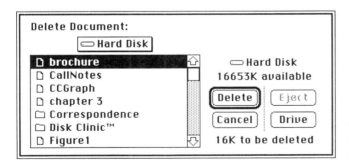

The Delete dialog box is similar to the Open and Save As dialog boxes.

Notice that Word displays in the Delete dialog box the names of all files—not just the Word files—on the current disk. You can delete a file created in any application to make room on the active disk. The only file names that will not appear in the list box are certain protected files, like the System, Finder, and Word applications, and any files that are currently open on the Word DeskTop.

Notice also that Word displays the size of the selected file at the lower-right side of the Delete dialog box. This feature is helpful when you are trying to make enough room on a data disk to save a file. If you can estimate the length of the file you need to save, you may be able to delete one or two unneeded files that consume approximately the same amount of space on the disk. As usual, the amount of available space on the disk appears just below the disk name. Word will update this value after each deletion to let you know how much disk space you have recovered.

To delete a file, simply point to the name of the file you want to delete and click on the Delete button. Word will display an alert box like the one in Figure 3-10. If you're sure you want to delete the file, click Yes. Otherwise, click No or Cancel. If you click No, Word will present the Delete dialog box again. If you click Cancel, Word will return you to the DeskTop.

FIGURE 3-10

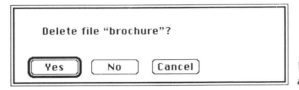

Delete file "brochure"?

Yes   No   Cancel

Word asks you to verify a Delete… command.

Once the file has been deleted, Word will redisplay the Delete dialog box. At this point, you can select another file to delete, or you can click Cancel to remove the dialog box from your screen.

Temporary Files

Word will periodically create special temporary files with names such as *Word Temp 1* and *Word Temp 2* to back up your work. These temporary files often appear in the System folder on your startup disk. For this reason, if you store documents on your startup disk, you'll want to make sure you leave about 20K of space open on that disk so that Word can keep track of your actions. If you fail to leave adequate room on your startup disk for the temporary files, Word may present you with a warning that your disk is running low on space.

We recommend that you never use the Delete… command to delete these temporary files while you are working in Word. You may create a system error and lose a great deal of work. However, if necessary, you can drag these temporary files into the Trash at the Finder level after you have finished a Word session.

A Tip on Naming Files

When you use the Delete… command, keep in mind that Word will display the names of all files located on the selected disk—not just the names of Word documents. It is impossible to tell what type of document you are selecting when you click on a file name in the Delete dialog box. If you commonly store files of different types on the same disk, you may want to store each type of file in a separate folder or identify each file by adding a type code. For example, you might want to use a *W* suffix for Word files, a *C* suffix for Microsoft Chart files, an *E* or *X* suffix for Microsoft Excel files, and so forth. Thus, an Excel budget worksheet might be called *Budget.X*, while your budget proposal text created in Word might be called *Budget.W*.

THE WORD COUNT... COMMAND

Word 4 provides a useful, new feature with the Word Count... command. When you choose this command from the Utilities menu or by pressing Option-[F15], Word presents a dialog box that can specify the number of characters, words, lines, and paragraphs a document contains. The command will examine the main text of a document and its footnotes, but not its headers and footers.

As you can see in Figure 3-11, the Word Count dialog box is simple to operate. The first time you open it, three of the four items will be activated. (Only Lines is deactivated.) Click on the Count button to begin counting. While counting the text, Word presents its count for the Main Text and the Footnotes in the appropriate columns in the dialog box. Until Word finishes its count, you'll see in the lower-right corner of the dialog box the percentage of the document that Word has examined. When the count is complete, Word provides a total for each item in the right-hand column of the dialog box.

FIGURE 3-11

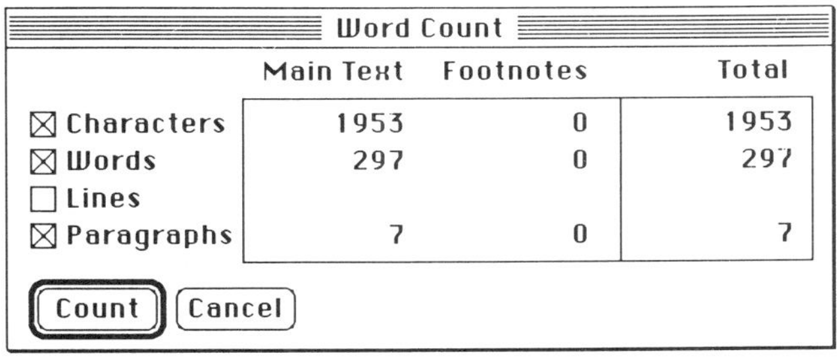

Word Count			
	Main Text	Footnotes	Total
☒ Characters	1953	0	1953
☒ Words	297	0	297
☐ Lines			
☒ Paragraphs	7	0	7
[Count] [Cancel]			

The Word Count procedure allows you to keep track of the units of information in your document.

Word lets you cancel the Word Count procedure at any time by pressing the Stop button. (The Count button becomes the Stop button while Word is counting.) You can press the Cancel button when Word finishes the Word Count procedure.

OTHER TOPICS

In this chapter, we've reviewed the basics of opening, closing, and saving files in Word. However, we've not yet explored the structure or format of those files. If you frequently need to transfer information from one program to another, you need to understand the basic characteristics of the files created in each program so that you can effectively communicate with other applications.

For example, the File Format... option in the Save As dialog box lets you save your documents in different formats so that you can access them from within other programs. Similarly, programs like Microsoft Works and Microsoft Excel let you save files in a text format that is readable by Word. In addition, the QuickSwitch application lets you set up links between files created in different programs. We'll talk more about these topics in Chapter 15, "Sharing Data with Other Programs."

The Best
THE COBB GROUP
GUARANTEED

Working with Word

Section 2:
Working with Word

Now that you've learned the basics, it's time to get some work done! Your first step, of course, will be to enter some text into a Word file. Then, you can use Word's formatting and editing tools to create a finished document.

When you complete this section, you will have mastered the basic tools you need to use Word. In Chapter 4, we'll show you how to enter text into a new document window, then we'll show you how to select and view that text and perform some basic editing tasks. In Chapter 5, we'll explore some formatting techniques and, in Chapter 6, focus on some of Word's more powerful editing facilities. Finally, in Chapter 7, we'll show you how to print your Word documents.

WORD BASICS 4

Presumably, your first task upon opening a new Word document will be to enter some text. Then, you can format and edit the document to suit your needs. In this chapter, we'll show you how to enter text in Word, then we'll show some navigation and selection techniques you'll need in order to view, edit, and format the text. We'll wrap up the chapter with some basic manual editing techniques before we launch into Word's formatting and editing commands in Chapters 5 and 6.

On the following pages, you'll find dozens of keyboard shortcuts and special tools for moving around in your document window, selecting text, and editing your Word files. We urge you to practice these techniques. They will help you work more efficiently in Word. For easy reference, Appendix 2 offers a summary of these keyboard shortcuts.

Entering text in Word is actually easier than typing text on a typewriter. A special facility called WordWrap lets you type a constant stream of characters without the need for carriage returns at the end of each line. If you are new to word processing, you may be tempted to press the Return or Enter key as you approach the end of a line of text in order to move to the next line. Not to worry—if there is not enough room for the word you are typing on the current line, Word will move that word to the beginning of the next line automatically.

In fact, the only time you need to press the Return or Enter key as you enter text in Word is when you want to start a new paragraph. You can significantly hinder your editing and formatting capabilities by placing carriage returns at the end of each line. If you decide later to insert or delete text or change your margins, you'll

ENTERING TEXT

have to edit each line manually in order to reset your line breaks. If you let WordWrap handle this task for you, you can easily change the content, format, and layout of your document and have Word automatically reflow the text for you.

**A Sample
Document**

To illustrate some basic entry, selection, and editing techniques in Word, we'll enter the sample document shown in Figure 4-1 into a new Word file. If you would like to follow along with our example, load Word and open a new document by double-clicking the Word program icon at the Finder level. If you are already in Word and need to open a new blank document, select the New command from Word's File menu. You'll see a blank document window with a name like Untitled1 or Untitled2.

FIGURE 4-1

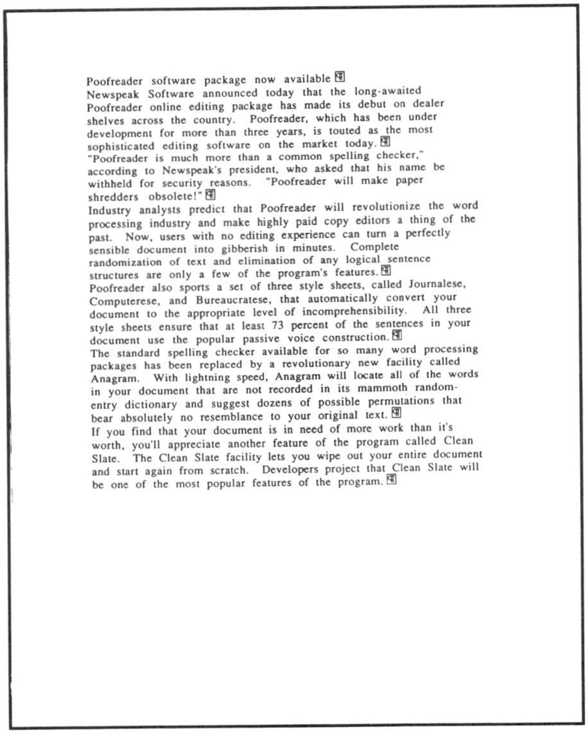

Poofreader software package now available ¶
Newspeak Software announced today that the long-awaited Poofreader online editing package has made its debut on dealer shelves across the country. Poofreader, which has been under development for more than three years, is touted as the most sophisticated editing software on the market today. ¶
"Poofreader is much more than a common spelling checker," according to Newspeak's president, who asked that his name be withheld for security reasons. "Poofreader will make paper shredders obsolete!" ¶
Industry analysts predict that Poofreader will revolutionize the word processing industry and make highly paid copy editors a thing of the past. Now, users with no editing experience can turn a perfectly sensible document into gibberish in minutes. Complete randomization of text and elimination of any logical sentence structures are only a few of the program's features. ¶
Poofreader also sports a set of three style sheets, called Journalese, Computerese, and Bureaucratese, that automatically convert your document to the appropriate level of incomprehensibility. All three style sheets ensure that at least 73 percent of the sentences in your document use the popular passive voice construction. ¶
The standard spelling checker available for so many word processing packages has been replaced by a revolutionary new facility called Anagram. With lightning speed, Anagram will locate all of the words in your document that are not recorded in its mammoth random-entry dictionary and suggest dozens of possible permutations that bear absolutely no resemblance to your original text. ¶
If you find that your document is in need of more work than it's worth, you'll appreciate another feature of the program called Clean Slate. The Clean Slate facility lets you wipe out your entire document and start again from scratch. Developers project that Clean Slate will be one of the most popular features of the program. ¶

We'll use this sample document to illustrate Word's selection, navigation, and editing facilities.

Begin by typing the first line of text shown in Figure 4-1. As you type, keep your eye on the blinking vertical insertion point marker. The marker will move one space to the right as you type each character, indicating your position in the document.

If you make an error as you are typing, just press the Backspace (Delete) key to move the insertion point marker to the left one space at a time and erase the erroneous characters. Then, you can resume typing. If you notice an error after you're several words along, don't worry about it at this point. We'll show you how to correct those mistakes in a few pages.

When you reach the end of the first one-line paragraph shown in Figure 4-1 (this will become a headline when we begin formatting the text in Chapter 5), press the Return or Enter key to begin a new paragraph. Continue typing the sample text, pressing Return or Enter only when you need to begin a new paragraph. We have included ¶ symbols in our sample document to indicate where paragraph breaks are needed. You will not see these symbols in your Word document at first.

Don't worry if some of the text disappears from view as you type. As you will see in a moment, you can use Word's scrolling features to bring that text back into view.

By the way, we used Word's default type formats—12-point New York Plain—to create the sample document in Figure 4-1. If you are using another type style or size, your line breaks may look a bit different from ours. (We'll say more about fonts and formatting in Chapter 5.)

MARKING UP YOUR DOCUMENT

One of Word's strongest selling points is that you can see on the screen exactly what your text will look like when it's printed (with a few exceptions). You don't have to litter the online version of your document with hard-to-read codes every time you want to begin a new paragraph, change margin widths, or assign a special format to some element of your text. This online display is whimsically referred to as the WYSIWYG (What You See Is What You Get) feature.

Without being aware of it, however, you do enter special coding information every time you create a new paragraph or make some formatting change to your document. Word does a lot of work behind the scenes as it implements your editing and formatting instructions. Some of this work is evident in a set of special markup characters that indicate where paragraph breaks, line breaks, blank spaces, optional hyphens, and so forth, occur in your document.

To see these symbols, choose Show ¶ from the Edit menu. Immediately, you'll see a series of ¶ and · markers in your document window, as shown in Figure 4-2 on the next page. These symbols do not appear when you print your document because they appear on the screen only for reference.

When you choose Show ¶ from the Edit menu, Word will change that command to read Hide ¶. As you might have guessed, you can choose the Hide ¶ toggle to suppress the display of all special markup characters again. (Normal hyphens will remain in view at all times.) You can toggle between the Show ¶ and Hide ¶ commands at any time during a Word session by pressing ⌘-y.

FIGURE 4-2

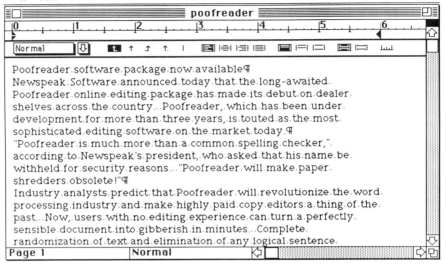

When you use the Show ¶ command, Word displays special markup characters on your screen.

We'll generally display the marker symbols in our sample screen displays throughout this book to help you interpret the content and design of our sample documents. We think that you will find these displays helpful as you begin editing and formatting text in Word and seeing the effects of your changes in the document window.

As you already know, the ¶ symbol represents the end of a paragraph in your Word document. Among other things, it tells Word that you want to begin a new line of text. As you'll learn when we begin formatting text in Chapter 5, the paragraph marker also "stores" the formatting characteristics you have assigned to your text.

The dots (·) that appear between the words and sentences in Figure 4-2 represent blank spaces. It's a little difficult at first to distinguish the space markers from period characters, but if you look closely, you'll see that the space markers sit slightly higher than the periods. Table 4-1 lists some of the other marker symbols that Word displays on your screen when you use the Show ¶ command.

In addition to these marker symbols, the Show ¶ command affects the display of tables, graphics, dates, times, page numbers, and footnote entries in your Word documents. It also affects the display of text boundaries in page view. We'll discuss each of these topics as they arise through the course of this book. For now, let's explore some of the effects of the · and ¶ markers on your Word document.

TABLE 4-1

Symbol	Name	To enter, type
¶	Paragraph marker	Return or Enter
↵	End-of-line marker	Shift-Return
...	Normal blank space	Spacebar
~ ~ ~	Nonbreaking space	⌘-Spacebar
→	Tab marker	Tab
•	End-of-cell marker	Option-8
≃ ≃ ≃	Nonbreaking hyphen	⌘- ~
⊤ ⊤ ⊤	Optional hyphen	⌘-hyphen (-)

When you issue the Show ¶ command, Word displays marker symbols on your screen.

Now that we've entered some text and have seen how Word operates, let's review some basic definitions. As you begin selecting, editing, and formatting text in your document, you'll need to understand how Word defines elements like characters, words, sentences, and paragraphs. While these concepts are not difficult to grasp, they can be quite different from the definitions you may have become accustomed to in writing or typing text. Many new users become extremely frustrated as they begin editing and formatting documents because they've never been exposed to this new mindset.

DEFINING THE BASIC ELEMENTS OF A DOCUMENT

The most basic element of text in your Word document is a character. A character can be any element you enter onto the screen. It can be a blank space, letter, number, punctuation mark, or any other special symbol. Words, sentences, and paragraphs are nothing more than predefined combinations of characters.

Characters

Word does not look at words in your document as nouns, verbs, adjectives, and so forth. A word is any group of alphabetic and/or numeric characters set apart by one or more blank spaces, a period, comma, hyphen, colon, semicolon, question mark, exclamation point, or quotation mark. Other characters that can serve as word separators include parentheses, braces, brackets, greater than or less than signs, the pound sign, the @ symbol, the dollar sign, the ampersand, left and right slash marks, guillemet characters (« and »), and the asterisk.

Words

Oddly enough, characters like <, ?, >, !, @, -, +, and = mark the end of a word only when they are mixed with alphabetic or numeric characters—not when they are grouped together. For example, the character string =-+ would be interpreted as one word, but the character string *abc+=-def* would be considered as three words: *abc*, *+=-*, and *def*.

In short, all the characters below serve as word delimiters, except when they are grouped together:

! @ # $ % & * ( ) - = + [ ] { } ; : " , . < > \ | / ?«»

Keep in mind that a blank space always marks the end of a word, even when it is used in conjunction with the characters above.

Unlike most punctuation marks, an apostrophe doesn't end a word since that character is commonly used in contractions and in creating the possessive form of a noun. Likewise, the ^, `, _, and ~ characters don't mark the ends of words. Word treats these characters exactly as it does alphabetic characters and numbers.

With all these definitions in mind, how many words would you say make up the quote *"Poofreader will make paper shredders obsolete!"* at the end of the third paragraph in Figure 4-2? You might be tempted to answer six, but by Word's definition, there are actually eight distinct words in this sentence, as shown by the vertical lines below

|"|Poofreader·|will·|make·|paper·|shredders·|obsolete|!"|

The ¶ symbol at the end of the sentence also counts as a word, but Word does not consider the paragraph marker as part of the sentence. As you know by now, Word always tries to keep the characters in a word together in your document. That is, if a word is too long to fit at the end of a line, the WordWrap feature will push that word forward to the beginning of the next line. There are two exceptions to this. In keeping with our definitions above, if a word contains a hyphen, Word will treat it as two words. Thus, if a hyphenated word will not fit on one line, all the characters up to and including the hyphen will appear at the end of the first line, while the remaining characters wrap to the beginning of the next line. You can control these breaks to some extent with Word's special hyphenation features, which we'll cover in Chapters 5 and 6.

The only other time that WordWrap will not keep all the characters in a word together is when the word is simply too long to fit on a single line. This most likely will be a problem when you are working with very narrow columns. For example, in Figure 4-3, we typed the word *supercalifragilisticexpialidocious* into an empty Word document with a 1-inch column width (more on column widths in Chapter 10). As you can see, Word included as many characters in the first line as possible, allowing the remaining characters to flow to the next two lines.

By the way, when you use the Word Count… command, Word will not include punctuation marks (such as the quotation marks in the sentence above) in its word total. The sentence that we have delimited above simply shows how words are defined for selection purposes. We will talk more about selection techniques in a few pages.

FIGURE 4-3

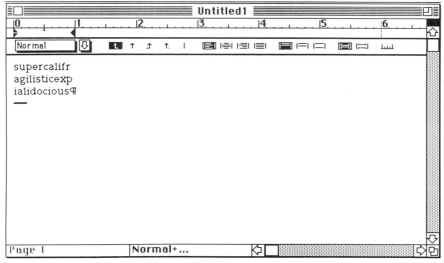

If all the characters in a word will not fit on one line, Word will allow the characters to flow to the next lines.

Sentences

A sentence is a group of characters and words set apart by a period, exclamation point, or question mark. A forced line break (which is represented by the ↵ symbol and entered into the document by pressing the Shift and Return keys) or a ¶ marker may also mark the end of a sentence. Of course, as you may have guessed from our discussion of words, any character that marks the end of a sentence also marks the end of the last word in that sentence.

For example, consider the sentence *Poofreader... is touted as the most sophisticated editing software on the market today.* in the second paragraph of our sample document. The period at the end of this series of characters marks the end of the sentence, as well as the end of the word *today*.

Paragraphs

A paragraph can be any combination of characters, words, and symbols, set apart by a ¶ symbol. Keep in mind that the ¶ symbol at the end of a paragraph is considered part of that paragraph. In fact, the ¶ symbol is treated as an individual word, which marks the end of the last word and the last sentence in a paragraph. And, as you might have guessed, the first sentence at the beginning of a paragraph is delimited by the ¶ symbol at the end of the previous paragraph. Similarly, the first word in a paragraph is delimited by the ¶ symbol from above.

For example, in the sample document shown in Figure 4-2, the first line of the document ends with a ¶ symbol, which marks the end of the first sentence, as well as the first paragraph. It also marks the end of the word *available* and the beginning of the first word and sentence in the next paragraph, *Newspeak*.

These definitions may seem difficult to grasp at this point, but they will become apparent to you when you begin selecting text blocks and editing your document. As you will learn in Chapter 6, a thorough understanding of these definitions is also critical to using Word's Find... and Change... commands effectively.

SELECTING TEXT

Now that you know how Word defines the basic elements of your document, you can learn how to work with these elements so that you can edit and format them. Before you can edit or format any text you have created in Word, however, you must select the text you want to work with.

When you select text in Word, that block of characters will appear in reverse video—that is, you'll see white type on a black background rather than the normal black type on white background. Throughout this book, you'll see this reverse-video text referred to as highlighted or selected text.

Selecting Text with the Mouse

If you've used previous versions of Word, or if you've used other word processing software on the Macintosh, you know that most of your text selection and navigation is done with the mouse. However, Microsoft has also added several keyboard shortcuts to help you select text and move around your document quickly. Let's begin with the standard mouse selection techniques, then we'll explore Word's many keyboard shortcuts.

Click and drag

The most basic mouse selection technique is the click and drag method. For example, suppose you want to select the words *common spelling checker* in the third paragraph of our sample document. Begin by clicking just to the left of the letter *c* in the word *common*. Now, without releasing the mouse button, drag to the right until the desired characters are highlighted, as shown in Figure 4-4. You can use this dragging technique to select any size block of text, from a single character to an entire document.

The click/Shift-click method

Of course, if you need to select a large block of text, you might find it tiresome to drag through line after line of text. Another technique for selecting text is the click/Shift-click method. For example, suppose you want to highlight all the text beginning with the words *Industry analysts* and ending with *gibberish in minutes*. Begin by clicking just to the left of the word *Industry*, then hold the Shift key as you click just to the right of the period that follows the word *minutes*. Figure 4-5 shows the results.

FIGURE 4-4

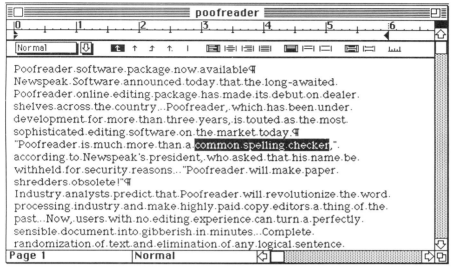

Use the click and drag method to select a block of text.

FIGURE 4-5

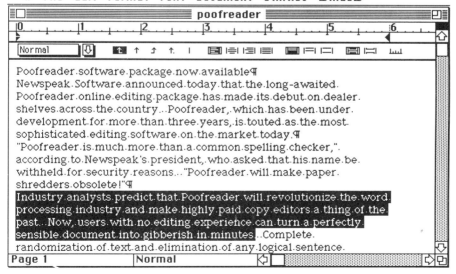

You can select any size block of text by clicking at the beginning of the block, then holding the Shift key as you click at the end of the block.

Selecting a word

You can select an entire word by double-clicking anywhere on that word. For example, to select the word *software* in the first line of our sample document, just place the mouse pointer over that word and double-click. As you can see in Figure 4-6, Word will highlight the entire word, as well as any blank spaces that appear to the right of the word.

FIGURE 4-6

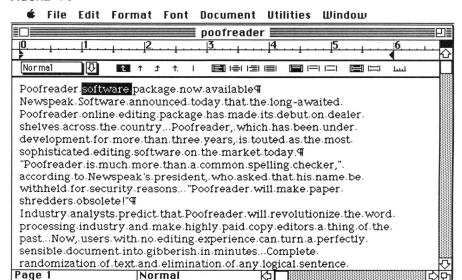

To select an entire word, double-click anywhere on that word.

If you double-click on a word that is followed by a period, comma, or some other demarcation character, Word will not highlight the demarcation character or blank spaces after that word. For example, if you double-click on the word *country* in the fourth line of our sample document, Word will highlight only the characters *country*, not the period or two blank spaces that appear after that word. Instead, those trailing characters will be treated as a separate word. In fact, if you double-click just to the right of the word *country*, Word will highlight the period and blank spaces that mark the end of that word and sentence.

Selecting a sentence

There's also a special technique for selecting an entire sentence in Word. Just press the ⌘ key and click anywhere on the sentence you want to select. Word will highlight the entire sentence, as well as any trailing blank spaces. If a sentence falls at the end of a paragraph, Word will not highlight the ¶ character. Like the period and blank spaces in word selection, the ¶ symbol is treated separately when you are selecting sentences.

To select an entire line or paragraph in Word, use the invisible selection bar on the left side of your document window. Although you cannot see this selection bar, you'll know you are there when your mouse pointer takes on the right arrow shape.

To select an entire line of text, just move the pointer to the left of the screen until it takes on the right arrow shape, then point to the line of text you want to select, and click. For example, if we click in the selection bar to the left of the line that begins *Poofreader online editing package* in the second paragraph in our sample document, our screen will look like the one in Figure 4-7.

Selecting lines and paragraphs

FIGURE 4-7

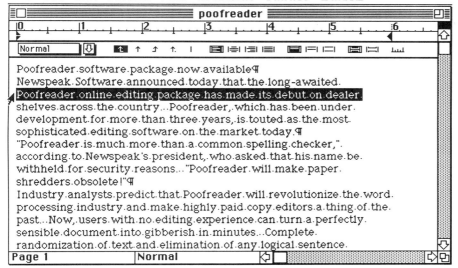

To select an entire line, click next to that line in the selection bar.

To select an entire paragraph, move your pointer to the selection bar and double-click anywhere to the left of the paragraph. Figure 4-8 on the following page shows the screen after we selected the entire second paragraph of the document. As you can see, the ¶ marker at the end of the paragraph is also highlighted. Notice the right arrow shape of the mouse pointer as it lies in the selection bar in Figures 4-7 and 4-8.

Finally, to select the entire Word document, move the pointer to the selection bar and press the ⌘ key as you click. All of your text will appear highlighted in reverse video to indicate your selection. As you will learn in Chapter 6, this technique is particularly helpful when you need to make a global change to your document—for instance, changing the font or indentions for all your text.

Selecting an entire document

FIGURE 4-8

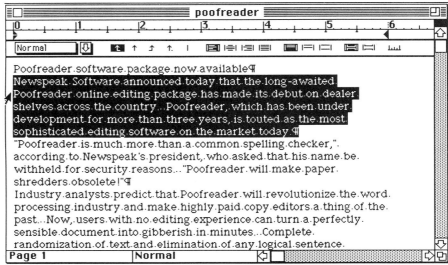

Double-click in the invisible selection bar to select a paragraph of text.

Making block selections

Another selection technique you'll find particularly convenient when working with tabular data is the block selection. To make a block selection, press the Option key, then drag through the desired characters.

For example, in our sample document, if we press the Option key, click to the left of the word *package* in the first line of the document, then drag down and to the right, our selection will look like the one in Figure 4-9.

As you can see, we have selected a strip of text from the middle of the document, disregarding word, sentence, or paragraph breaks. In fact, some of the characters in our selection are only partially highlighted. When you use the Option key to make a block selection, Word considers any character that is more than half highlighted to be part of the selection.

We'll look at this technique in more detail in Chapters 5 and 6 when we talk about formatting and editing tables.

FIGURE 4-9

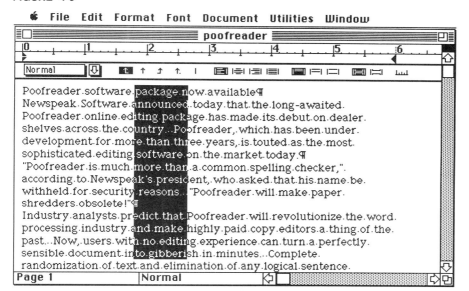

To make a block selection, press the Option key, then drag through the desired text.

Anchoring Your Selection

When you select text in Word, your insertion point marker serves as the pivot or anchor point for one end of the selection. Whether you drag or click above, below, to the left, or to the right of the insertion point marker, it always represents one edge of your selection. For example, if you click to the left of the word *much* in line 7 of our sample document, then drag down and to the left of the comma after the word *president*, your screen will look like the one in Figure 4-10 on the following page. However, if you now drag up and to the left of the word *is* in the previous line without releasing the mouse button, your screen will look like the one in Figure 4-11 on the next page. As you can see, our initial anchor point becomes the pivot for our selection. You can continue to change the size and shape of your selection by dragging around this anchor point, as long as you don't release the mouse button.

The easiest way to see the effect of the pivot point is to click in the middle of a line of text in your document and move your mouse in a broad circular motion. As you drag up, right, down, and left, the size and shape of your highlighted selection will change, but the insertion point will always mark one end of your selection.

FIGURE 4-10

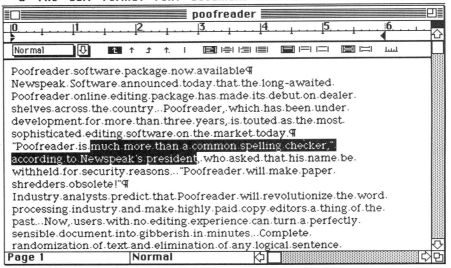

When you drag down or to the right, your insertion point marks the start of your selection.

FIGURE 4-11

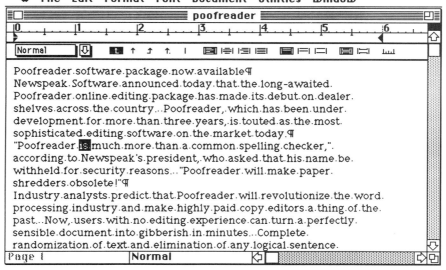

When you drag up or to the left, your insertion point marks the end of your selection.

Interestingly, when you use one of the mouse selection techniques described above, Word will "remember" that technique as you drag through additional text. For example, suppose you have double-clicked on a word to select it. In effect, you have entered the "word selection mode." If you drag to the right or left, Word will highlight the next word that your pointer touches. Even if you drag up or down through several lines, Word will continue to highlight entire words.

Similarly, if you press the ⌘ key and click on a sentence to select it, you can select adjacent sentences by dragging up, down, left, or right. The selection mode that you started with will remain in effect until you release the mouse button.

Selection Modes

As we mentioned earlier, you can select an entire Word document by pressing the ⌘ key and clicking the mouse pointer in the selection bar. You can achieve the same effect without using your mouse by pressing Option-⌘-m.

Mouseless Selection Techniques

If your Macintosh has a numeric keypad, another special selection feature lets you extend your selection from the current insertion point to a specified character in your document. For example, suppose you want to select all the text beginning with the phrase *Poofreader, which has been under development* through the period that ends the sentence. Just click to the left of the character *P* in *Poofreader*, then press the minus key (-) on the numeric keypad. You'll see the prompt *Extend to* in the status box at the lower-left corner of your screen. Just type the character to which you want to extend your selection—in this case, you'll press the period key on your standard keyboard (not the decimal point on the numeric keypad). Word will highlight everything from the insertion point marker to the right of the next occurrence of the period, as shown in Figure 4-12 on the following page.

When you are using the minus key to extend your selection from the insertion point to a specified character, Word will continue to display the *Extend to* prompt in the status box until you issue a command or click anywhere on your screen. Thus, after typing the first character to which you want to extend your selection, you can type another character if you want to extend your selection beyond the current highlighted text to the next occurrence of a given character. For example, in the sample screen shown in Figure 4-12, if we type the character *g*, Word will extend our selection from the original insertion point—to the left of the word *Poofreader*—through the end of the word *spelling* in the seventh line.

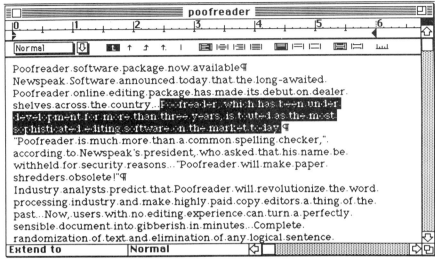

FIGURE 4-12

You can also select a block of text by clicking at the beginning of the block, pressing the minus key on the numeric keypad, and typing the character through which you want to extend your selection.

NAVIGATION

As we mentioned earlier, the text at the beginning of your document becomes lost from view after you fill up the screen. If you have created a document that is more than 18 or 20 lines long, you won't be able to see all of that document on the small Macintosh screen. The amount you can view at one time depends, of course, on the size of the window and the size of the type you are using.

Word offers several techniques for navigating through your document, some of which require the use of your mouse and some of which can be performed directly from the keyboard. We'll start with the standard mouse techniques, then we'll show you some keyboard navigational devices.

Navigating with the Mouse

The primary means of viewing all the text in your document is a technique called scrolling. As you learned in Chapter 2, the gray bars to the right and at the bottom of your document windows are called scroll bars. The white boxes within the scroll bars are called scroll boxes, and the white arrows at either end of each scroll bar are called scroll arrows.

To move through your document one line at a time (without necessarily selecting any text), you can click on the scroll arrows that appear above and below the vertical scroll bar.

Since the ruler is displayed in our previous screen samples, only the first 15 lines of our document are in view. If we click on the scroll arrow below the vertical scroll bar, we'll see lines 2 through 16. Line 1 will move out of view, as shown in Figure 4-13.

FIGURE 4-13

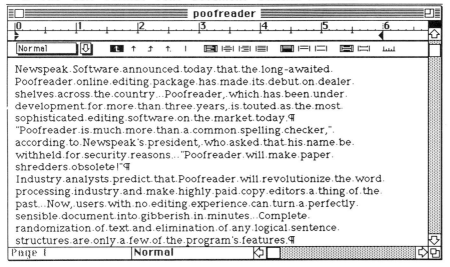

Use the scroll arrows at either end of the vertical scroll bar to move through your document one line at a time.

Moving through your document one line at a time is satisfactory for fine-tuning your view through the document window, but you'd soon find this method tedious in a long document. To move through your document a full screen at a time, click in the gray area of the scroll bar, above or below the scroll box. Word will scroll the next screenful into view.

For example, if we click below the scroll box in the vertical scroll bar while lines 1 through 15 of our sample document are in view, our screen will look like the one in Figure 4-14 on the next page. As you can see, lines 15 through 29 are now in view. Notice that two lines from the bottom of the previous screen remain in view at the top of the second screen to help you get your bearings.

Of course, the distance that you scroll depends on the size of the document window. For example, if we reduce our window to half-screen size, as shown in Figure 4-15, only the first five lines of our document will be in view. If we now click in the gray area of the scroll bar, Word will bring lines 4 through 8 into view. In Figure 4-16 on page 77, the last two lines from the bottom of the previous screen now appear at the top of the document window.

FIGURE 4-14

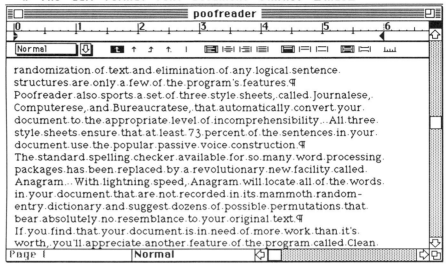

To move a new screenful of data into view, click in the gray area of the scroll bar.

FIGURE 4-15

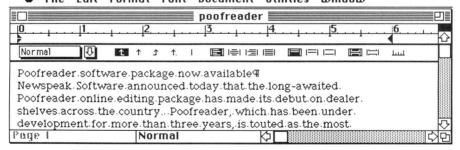

We reduced our document window to half-screen size to show how window size affects scrolling.

FIGURE 4-16

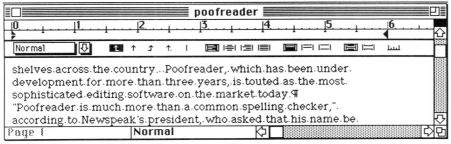

Word brings lines 4 through 8 into view when you click in the gray area of the scroll bar.

You can also drag the white scroll box to the desired position in the scroll bar to travel quickly through long passages in your document. The distance you travel by dragging the white scroll box depends on the length of your document. The scroll bar is relative to the length of your document. Thus, in a very short document like the one that holds our sample Poofreader text, dragging the scroll box to the middle of the scroll bar will advance you to the third or fourth paragraph of the document. However, if you drag to the middle of the vertical scroll bar in a 50-page document, you'd be scrolling through 25 pages of text. As you might have guessed, if you drag the scroll box to the top of the scroll bar, you'll see the first screen of your document; if you drag the scroll box to the bottom of the scroll bar, you'll see the last screenful of information.

Although it's difficult to fine-tune your navigation by dragging the scroll box, you'll soon get a feel for the relative distances you are traveling. You can watch the page number in the status bar of your window change as you drag the scroll box. This helps you zero in on the page you want to view. Generally, in a long document, you'll want to drag the scroll box to the approximate location you want to view, then click in the scroll bar or on the scroll arrows to fine-tune your position.

Using the horizontal scroll bar

If you are working with a document that is too wide to be displayed on one screen—for example, if you are printing a document with wide margins or if you are viewing your text through a partial-screen window—you can use the scroll arrows at either end of the horizontal scroll bar to move right and left through your document. As you might guess, horizontal scrolling is much like vertical scrolling. You use the scroll arrows to move short distances through your document; you click in the scroll bar to move a new screenful of information into view; and you drag the scroll box to reposition the window manually.

Starting with the scroll arrows, let's look at a few examples. We have narrowed our sample document window in Figure 4-17 so that only the first four inches of the document are visible. To see the remaining text on the right side of the document, we can click on the right scroll arrow. As you can see in Figure 4-18, Word scrolls the document window about $^1/_2$ inch to the right. If we now click on the left scroll arrow, our screen will look like the one in Figure 4-17 again.

FIGURE 4-17

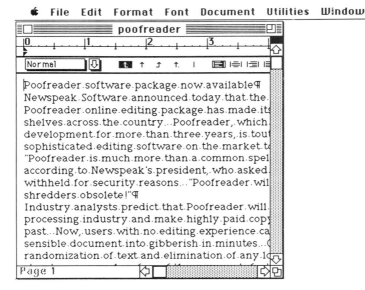

We have narrowed our document window to illustrate Word's horizontal scrolling features.

When you click in the gray area of the scroll bar, to the left or right of the scroll box, Word will scroll the document $3^1/_4$ inches to the left or right. Again, the distance that you travel depends on the size of the document window. For example, in Figure 4-18, if you click to the right of the scroll box, Word will bring the next $1^1/_2$ inches of the document into view, as shown in Figure 4-19. If you now click to the left of the scroll box, your screen will again look like the one in Figure 4-18.

FIGURE 4-18

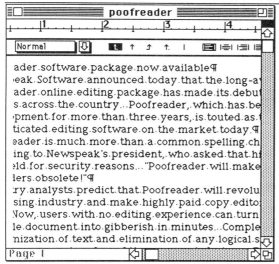

When you click on a scroll arrow, the next $^1/_2$ inch of the document scrolls into view.

FIGURE 4-19

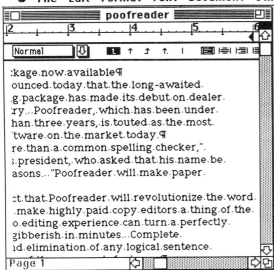

Click in the gray area of the scroll bar to bring a new screenful of information into view.

Unlike the vertical scroll bar, the distance you travel when you drag the scroll box in the horizontal scroll bar is constant. Although only about $6^3/_4$ inches of your document are visible in a full-screen window, Word actually allows you to create columns as wide as $21^3/_4$ inches. Thus, if you drag the scroll box to the extreme right side of the scroll bar, you'll travel $21^3/_4$ inches; if you drag the scroll box to the middle of the horizontal scoll bar, you'll travel a little over ten inches. If you want to scroll to the far left (past the zero point on the ruler), press the Shift key as you click the left scroll arrow.

Scrolling as you select text

Often, you'll want to select a block of text that is too large to display on one screen. In this event, you'll need to combine the selection technique described earlier in this chapter with the navigational techniques we've just discussed.

For example, suppose lines 15 through 29 of your document are in view and you want to select the block of text that begins with *worth, you'll appreciate* and ends with *most popular features of the program*. Since the last part of this text block is not currently visible on the screen when you begin your selection, clicking to the left of the word *worth* in line 25 and dragging downward selects the final line in Figure 4-20. As you drag the pointer past the horizontal scroll bar at the bottom of the screen, the rest of your text will scroll into view one line at a time, and the text at the top of the window will scroll out of view, as shown in Figure 4-20.

FIGURE 4-20

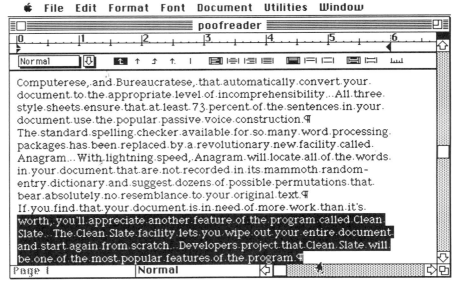

If you drag past the bottom of the document window, Word will scroll succeeding lines of text into view.

Similarly, if you drag toward the top of the screen, Word will scroll the document window upward as your mouse pointer comes in contact with the title bar at the top of the document window. Word will highlight the text automatically as you drag.

You also can drag to the left or right edge of the document window to scroll horizontally as you select text. Word will select the text and scroll the document window so you can see your selection.

You also can use the scroll bars in conjunction with the click/Shift-click technique described on page 66 to select large areas of text. Just click at the beginning of your selection, scroll to the end of the block you want to highlight, then hold down the Shift key as you click at the end of the block.

Mouseless Navigational Techniques

In addition to the horizontal and vertical scroll bars, you can use the keyboard to move through your Word text. Keep in mind that when you use the scroll bars to move through your document, your insertion point does not move with you. You must still click in the text area of your screen to move your insertion point marker.

When you use most of the keyboard techniques described below, however, your insertion point marker will travel with you as you navigate through your document window.

The Go To... command

In addition to the scroll bars, you can use the Go To... command on Word's Utilities menu to go to the top of a specific page in your document. To access the Go To dialog box quickly, just press ⌘-g. You'll see a dialog box like the one in Figure 4-21. Notice that the value in the Page Number edit bar is already highlighted. All you need to do is type the number of the page you want to view in the Page Number edit bar and click OK or press Return or Enter. Word will display the specified page on your screen and place the insertion point marker at the beginning of the first line.

The page numbers, which appear in the status box, relate to the way the document will appear when it is printed. (More on page breaks and page numbering in Chapters 5 and 7.)

FIGURE 4-21

Use the Go To... command to move quickly to a specified page in your document.

Moving the insertion point to its previous location

When you are editing a document, you'll often find yourself skipping from one spot to another to move text or to make minor changes. Word 4 offers a navigational feature to help streamline this process: you can quickly return to your last insertion point by choosing the Go Back command on Word's Utilities menu or by pressing Option-⌘-z. If you have a numeric keypad, you can press the 0 key to move back to your previous insertion point location.

This technique is also convenient for toggling between two remote areas of your document when you need to compare two sets of text. For example, suppose you have just finished editing a table that appears on the first page of your document, then you move to the end of your document to transfer some of the data from that table into your text. You need to move back to the table and pick up some more information. Just press Option-⌘-z or 0 on the numeric keypad or issue the Go Back command to move between the two areas quickly.

Word can remember as many as three insertion point locations as well as your current location. For example, suppose you've made editing changes in the four locations marked in the sample screen in Figure 4-22. If you press Option-⌘-z or 0 on the numeric keypad after making your change at point 4, Word will move you back to point 3. Pressing Option-⌘-z or 0 again will take you to point 2, then to point 1. If you press Option-⌘-z or 0 a fourth time, Word will cycle back to point 4.

FIGURE 4-22

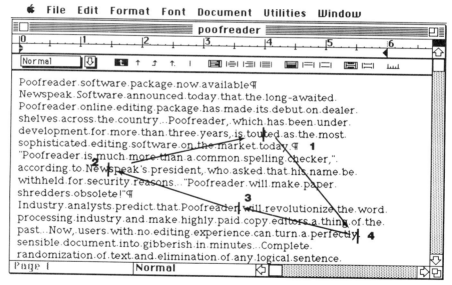

Word will remember your last three insertion point locations.

Using the arrow keys

If you have an expanded keyboard, you'll find that the ↑, ↓, ←, and → arrow keys are tremendously convenient for moving short distances in your document. As you might expect, the ↑ and ↓ keys let you move the insertion point marker up or down one line at a time. Generally, when you use the ↑ and ↓ keys, your insertion point marker will move in a straight line. However, because line lengths vary and characters occupy different amounts of space, you may notice that your insertion point marker jumps around a bit as you press the ↑ and ↓ keys.

For example, Figure 4-23 shows the path of the insertion point marker as we press the ↓ key to move through our sample document. As you can see, the marker moves slightly to the right and left as we travel downward through the document, staying in line as much as possible with our original insertion point between the characters *a* and *v* in line 1. Also, notice that the insertion point jumps to the left when we reach line 10 since that line does not extend as far as our insertion point. When we reach line 11, the marker moves back toward the middle of the screen.

FIGURE 4-23

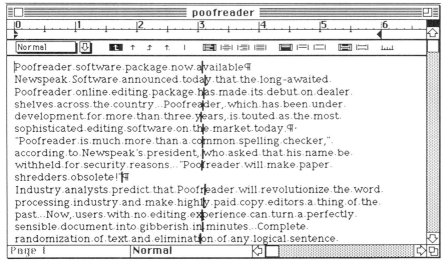

When you press the ↑ and ↓ keys, the insertion point marker will follow a fairly straight path through your document.

If you press the ↑ or ↓ key while the insertion point marker is at the top or bottom of the document window, Word will scroll additional text into view automatically.

When you press the ← and → arrow keys, the insertion point marker moves one space to the left or right. When you press ← at the beginning of a line, the insertion point marker will move to the end of the previous line. Similarly, when you press → at the end of a line, the marker jumps to the beginning of the next line.

For example, suppose your insertion point marker is between the characters *e* and *v* of the word *development* in the fifth line of our sample document. If you press the ← key twice, the insertion point marker will appear at the beginning of the line, just to the left of the character *d*. If you press ← again, the insertion point marker will jump to the end of the previous line, just to the right of the word *under*.

Particularly when you are working with very small font sizes or italicized text, it can be difficult to click in the exact location you need. The ← and → keys are very convenient for fine-tuning your selection once you've clicked in the general area in which you want to work.

To move through your document a little more quickly, you can press the ⌘ key as you press the ↑, ↓, ←, and → keys. If your insertion point marker is currently in the middle of a paragraph, the ⌘-↑ combination lets you jump to the beginning of that paragraph. If your insertion point marker is already at the beginning of a paragraph, ⌘-↑ takes you to the beginning of the previous paragraph. Similarly, the ⌘-↓ combination takes you to the beginning of the next paragraph.

For example, suppose your insertion point marker is currently in the middle of the word *common* in the third paragraph of our sample document. If you press ⌘-↑, the insertion point marker will move to the left of the " character at the beginning of the paragraph. Pressing ⌘-↑ again will land you just to the left of the character *N* at the beginning of the second paragraph. If you press ⌘-↓ while the insertion point marker is in the middle of the word *common* in the third paragraph, you'll land just to the left of the character *I* at the beginning of the fourth paragraph.

You can also jump from one word to the next by pressing ⌘ as you press the ← and → keys. The ⌘-← key combination lets you move one word to the left while the ⌘-→ key combination lets you move one word to the right. In either case, the insertion point marker will land just to the left of the next word, between the first character in that word and any preceding blank spaces or demarcation characters.

For example, suppose your insertion point marker is currently just to the left of the word *today* in the second line of our sample document. If you press ⌘-←, your insertion point marker will appear just to the left of the word *announced*. Similarly, if you press ⌘-→ while the insertion point marker is just to the left of the word *today* in the second line, your insertion point marker will move just to the left of the word *that*. If your insertion point marker is in the middle of a word when you press ⌘-←, Word will jump to the beginning of that word. If you press ⌘-→ while the insertion point marker is in the middle of a word, Word will move to the beginning of the next word.

Navigating with the numeric keypad

You can simulate the action of the ↑, ↓, ←, and → arrow keys with the 8, 2, 4, and 6 keys. You'll find these navigational keys easier to remember if you visualize the 8, 2, 4, and 6 keys as a diamond shape, radiating from the 5 key at the center of the keypad.

You can also use the ⌘ key in conjunction with the 8, 2, 4, and 6 keys on your keypad to move up and down one paragraph at a time and left and right one word at a time. The highlighted keys in Figure 4-24 work exactly like the arrow keys described above.

FIGURE 4-24

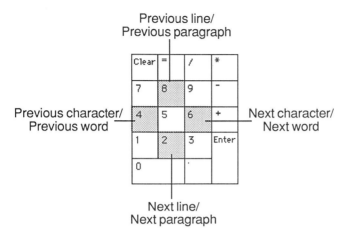

The 8, 2, 4, and 6 keys let you move the insertion point marker
up, down, left, and right.

In addition to the 8, 2, 4, and 6 keys, you can use the 7, 9, 1, 3, and 5 keys on
your numeric keypad to move through your Word document. Press the 7 key on your
numeric keypad to move to the beginning of the current line, and the 1 key to move
to the end of the current line. To continue with our sample document, if the insertion
point marker is currently in the middle of the word *package* in line 3 when you press
the 7 key, Word will move just to the left of the letter *P* at the beginning of that line.
If you press 1 on the numeric keypad, Word will move to the right of the letter *r* at
the end of that line. (Oddly, Word does not move to the right of the blank space at
the end of the line as you might expect. Thus, if you want to insert a new word at
this point, you'll need to press the Spacebar before you begin typing new text.)

If your insertion point marker is already at the beginning of a line when you
press the 7 key, Word will move to the beginning of the previous line. As you might
have guessed, if the insertion point marker is already at the end of a line when you
press 1, Word will move to the end of the next line.

You can also use the ⌘ key in conjunction with the 1 and 7 keys to move through
your document one sentence at a time. Press ⌘-1 to move to the beginning of the
next sentence and ⌘-7 to move to the beginning of the previous sentence. If you
press ⌘-1 while your insertion point marker is in the final sentence of a paragraph,
Word will move to the left of the ¶ marker. If your insertion point marker is in the
middle of a sentence when you press ⌘-7, Word will move to the beginning of that
sentence. However, if your insertion point marker is already at the beginning when
you press ⌘-7, Word will move to the beginning of the previous sentence.

For example, if your insertion point marker is in the middle of the word *touted* in line 5 of our sample document and you press the ⌘-7 key combination, the insertion point marker will appear just in front of the letter *P* at the beginning of that sentence. If you press ⌘-7 again at this point, your insertion point marker will appear just to the left of the letter *N* in the sentence that begins *Newspeak Software announced*.

Similarly, if your insertion point marker is in the middle of the word *online* in line 3 of our sample document and you press ⌘-1, the insertion point marker will appear just in front of the letter *P* at the beginning of the next sentence, which begins with the word *Poofreader*. If you press ⌘-1 again at this point, your insertion point marker will appear just to the left of the ¶ character at the end of the paragraph. If you press ⌘-1 a third time, you'll land to the left of the ″ character at the beginning of the next paragraph.

The 9 and 3 keys let you move through your document one screen at a time, just as if you had clicked in the vertical scroll bar on the right side of your screen. To move up one screen, press 9 on the keypad; to move down one screen, press 3. One difference between using the numeric keypad rather than the vertical scroll bar is that your insertion point marker moves when you use the keypad to travel through your document. When you press the 9 or 3 keys, Word places your insertion point marker at relatively the same position in the screenful of text. For example, if your insertion point marker is on the last line of text on your screen when you press 9, the marker will appear on the last line of text in the new screenful of information.

You can also use the ⌘ key in conjunction with the 9 and 3 keys to move the insertion point marker to the beginning or end of your document. Regardless of your current location, ⌘-9 will place the insertion point marker at the very first character space in your document, and ⌘-3 will place the insertion point marker at the very last character space in your document.

Finally, to move the insertion point marker to the top-left corner of your Word screen, press ⌘-5. Figure 4-25 summarizes the functions of the 7, 9, 1, 3, and 5 keys.

FIGURE 4-25

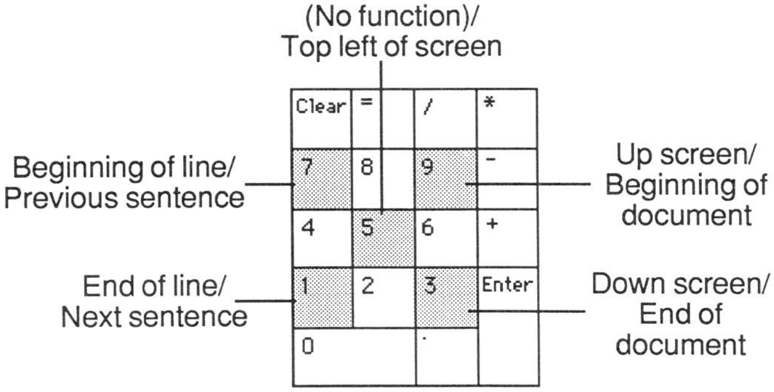

You can also use the 7, 9, 1, 3, and 5 keys for navigation in Word.

By the way, you can also use your numeric keypad to enter numbers into your document; however, the default "mode" for the keypad is navigational. In order to enter numbers, you must press the Clear key before you begin typing. The legend *Num. Lock* will appear in the status box to indicate that you are in the "numbers" mode. Before you can use the numeric keypad for navigation again, you must press the Clear key again to remove the *Num. Lock* legend from your screen.

Selecting Text with the Shift Key

If we haven't overwhelmed you yet with all the selection and navigation shortcuts that we've explored so far, here's one more technique to try: press the Shift key as you use the various navigational devices described above to select text as you move around in your Word document.

For example, you already know that you can press ⌘-7 to move to the beginning of the sentence you are currently in. If you press Shift-⌘-7, Word will highlight everything from the current insertion point marker to the beginning of the current sentence. If you press Shift-⌘-7 again while this partial sentence is highlighted, Word will extend your selection through the beginning of the previous sentence.

Similarly, you can press Shift-⌘-→ to select words as you scroll through your document or Shift-⌘-↓ to select entire paragraphs. In short, all the navigational shortcuts we have discussed in this section double as selection shortcuts when you add the Shift key to the original key combination.

BASIC EDITING TECHNIQUES

The simplest way to edit text in your Word document is to insert new characters, delete existing characters, or overwrite the characters you want to change. These three techniques are among Word's most basic—and most important—editing features. Although we'll elaborate on editing in Chapter 6, we'll introduce these basic editing techniques now because they relate closely to the selection and navigation techniques we've explored over the last several pages.

As we mentioned earlier, the WordWrap feature lets Word reflow your text whenever you make editing or formatting changes—that is why we cautioned you against entering carriage returns at the ends of lines of text. As we walk through the insertion, deletion, and overwriting techniques in the next few pages, notice the way that Word reflows your text to adjust for your changes. As you'll see, WordWrap is one of the features that make electronic word processing so popular. This vital feature makes editing text virtually effortless.

Inserting New Text

Inserting text in your Word document is as easy as typing. To insert a block of text into an existing document, simply move the insertion point marker to the spot where you want to insert the text, and click. When your blinking insertion bar appears to mark the insertion spot, just begin typing. Make sure that you have not highlighted any characters before you begin typing, or Word will overwrite those characters.

For example, suppose you want to change the phrase *users with no editing experience,* in line 13 of our sample document, to read *users with no proofreading or editing experience.* Begin by clicking just to the right of the space after the word *no,* and type the rest of the new phrase.

As you can see in Figure 4-26, when you type the new characters, Word pushes the remaining characters on the line to the right to make room for your insertion. Thanks to the WordWrap feature, Word will push the words at the end of the line to the beginning of the next line as you go, reflowing your existing text all the way through to the end of the document, if necessary, to make room for your insertion.

FIGURE 4-26

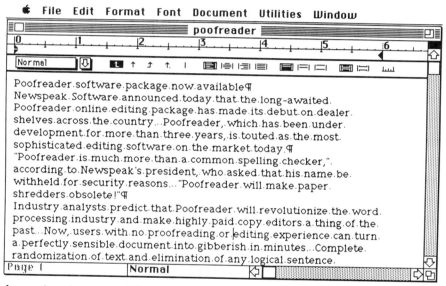

As you insert new text, Word will reflow your text to make room for your changes.

Inserting a ¶ marker

If you find it distracting to watch Word reflow the remaining text in a paragraph as you insert text, try pressing Option-⌘-Return to begin a new paragraph before you begin typing. Word will insert a new ¶ marker (which will be visible only if the Show ¶ command is in effect) and move the text to the right of the insertion point marker into a new paragraph.

Of course, you can press the Return key at any time to insert a new ¶ marker and break the current paragraph into two smaller paragraphs. When you simply press Return, however, your insertion point marker moves down to the beginning of the next paragraph. When you use the Option-⌘-Return technique, your insertion point marker will remain in place so that you can continue to insert text in the current paragraph.

If you want to recombine the two paragraphs after inserting your text, just press Option-⌘-f to delete the ¶ marker. Option-⌘-f lets you delete the character immediately to the right of the insertion point. (Of course, the expanded SE and Mac II keyboards have a Del key that deletes the character to the right of the insertion point marker.) This brings us to our next topic: deleting text in Word.

As we mentioned at the beginning of this chapter, the easiest way to delete individual characters in your text is to click to the right of the character(s) that you want to delete and press the Backspace key. Word will delete the characters immediately to the left of the insertion point marker one at a time. This action pulls the line of text to the right of the insertion point marker one character space leftward each time you press the Backspace key. To delete several characters at once, you can highlight the unwanted block and then press the Backspace key to delete the entire selection.

Deleting Text

Suppose you want to delete the words *proofreading or* in line 13 of our sample document in Figure 4-26. Begin by highlighting the words *proofreading or*, then press the Backspace key to erase them. As you can see in Figure 4-27, Word will delete the selected words and automatically pull the remaining characters in your document up and to the left to fill the gap.

FIGURE 4-27

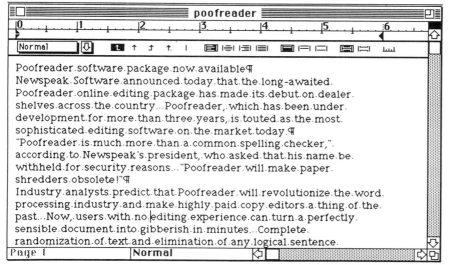

When you delete a highlighted block of text, Word will reflow your document to fill the gap.

If you press the Backspace key while your insertion point marker is at the beginning of a line, Word will move the insertion point to the end of the previous line and delete the last character in that line. Similarly, if you press Backspace while the insertion point marker is at the beginning of a paragraph, Word will delete the ¶ marker at the end of the previous paragraph and reflow your text to combine the two paragraphs—as long as your paragraphs are formatted in the same style.

If you try to combine two paragraphs that carry different formatting styles, Word will beep. If you're determined to combine the two paragraphs anyway, you'll need to highlight the ¶ marker at the end of the first one, then press the Backspace key. If you have an SE or Mac II keyboard, place the insertion point marker to the left of the ¶ marker, then press the Del key. The combined paragraph will take on the style characteristics of the second paragraph. We'll elaborate on this topic in the next chapter.

Deletion shortcuts

Word also offers some special keyboard shortcuts for deleting text. For example, rather than using the Backspace key to delete the characters to the left of the insertion point marker one at a time, you can press ⌘-Option-Backspace to delete the entire word to the left of the insertion point marker. If you want to delete the space to the right of the word as well, click to the right of that space before you press ⌘-Option-Backspace. If you want to leave that space intact (for instance, so that you can insert another word or phrase in that spot), click to the left of the blank space, just after the word to be deleted.

For example, to change the phrase *users with no proofreading or editing experience can* to *users with no editing experience can*, you could click to the right of the blank space after the word *or* and press ⌘-Option-Backspace. Word will delete the word *or* and the blank space after it. Repeat this process to delete the word *proofreading* and the blank space after it.

If you click in the middle of a word and press ⌘-Option-Backspace, Word will delete all the characters to the left of the insertion point marker up to, but not including, the blank space that divides the current word from the previous word.

For example, suppose you want to change the phrase *level of incomprehensibility* to *level of comprehensibility* in the fifth paragraph of our sample document. You can click between the letters *n* and *c* in the word *incomprehensibility* and press ⌘-Option-Backspace to delete the characters *in*. The blank space to the right of the word *of* will remain intact.

Overwriting Text

When you delete a block of text in Word, you'll often need to insert some new text to replace the text you deleted. Rather than erasing a block of text before you insert new characters, you can overwrite existing characters by highlighting the characters you want to replace, then—rather than pressing the Backspace key—typing your new text. Word will automatically delete the highlighted characters and replace them with the new characters you type. This overwriting technique merely combines the deletion/insertion process.

For example, suppose you want to replace the phrase *has made its debut on dealer shelves* in lines 3 and 4 with the new phrase *is being shipped to dealers*. Just drag through the characters *has made its debut on dealer shelves,* then type the replacement text. As you can see in Figure 4-28, Word replaces the old characters with the new ones and reflows the remaining text in our document.

FIGURE 4-28

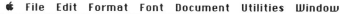

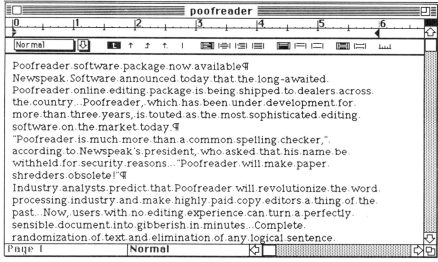

To overwrite text, just select the characters you want to delete and type your replacement text.

Interestingly, Word will not allow you to overwrite a ¶ marker by selecting it and typing. Instead, you must select the ¶ marker, press the Delete key, then type your new text. When you press Delete, Word will combine the current paragraph with the paragraph below, as we described in our discussion of deleting text. As you might have guessed, this idiosyncrasy occurs because Word tries to prevent you from inadvertently changing the style of the current paragraph by picking up the format styles assigned to the next paragraph. Again, we'll talk more about the ¶ marker and its function in Chapter 5.

Selection Modes and Editing

As you know, when you double-click on a word to select it, Word automatically highlights any trailing blank spaces that fall after that word. Naturally, if you press the Delete key to delete that word, those trailing blank spaces will be deleted as well. However, if you double-click on a word, then overwrite it by typing new characters,

Word will leave any trailing blank spaces intact. Basically, the program assumes you are replacing one (or more) words with another word and saves you a few keystrokes by leaving the blank spaces in place for you.

This technique works even if you have selected several words. As long as you entered the word selection mode by double-clicking on a word and then dragging through additional words, Word will apply this treatment. The last set of blank spaces will be deleted if you press Backspace , but will be left intact if you overwrite the selected text.

If you double-click in the selection bar to highlight an entire paragraph, Word will use a similar technique to decide whether the ¶ marker at the end of the paragraph should stay or go. As you might have guessed, if you press Backspace to delete the paragraph, the ¶ marker will disappear as well. However, if you overwrite the paragraph, the ¶ marker will remain in place. Again, as long as you entered the paragraph selection mode by double-clicking in the selection bar to select the paragraph, Word will apply this technique, no matter how many paragraphs you have selected.

If you plan to insert new text, but want to delete the ¶ marker or blank spaces that appear after your selection, you can drag through the block you want to overwrite rather than double-clicking. Alternatively, you can double-click on the word or paragraph, press Backspace, then type your new text.

Interestingly, Word does not apply this technique when you select entire sentences. Although the program will highlight the punctuation mark and trailing spaces that appear after a sentence when you use the ⌘-click technique to select it, Word will always delete those characters when you delete or overwrite the selection.

CANCELLING AND REPEATING ACTIONS

When you insert, delete, or overwrite text in your document, Word remembers the last set of keystrokes you performed. Consequently, you can elect to do two things: undo an editing change by selecting the Undo command from the Edit menu, or repeat a command or a series of keystrokes automatically. First, let's explore the workings of the Undo command, then we'll show you how to repeat a command or a series of keystrokes in Word.

The Undo Command

The Undo command is one of the most important commands on the Edit menu because it gives you a second chance when you make a mistake. As you'll undoubtedly learn at some time in your work with Word, Undo can be a real lifesaver when you find that you have inadvertently altered a critical passage in your document.

Undo is a context-sensitive command; that is, it changes to reflect your last action. If you've inserted new text or overwritten some existing text, you'll see the command Undo Typing at the top of the Edit menu. If you have applied some formatting, such as boldface, to some characters, you'll see the command Undo Formatting. There are two keyboard shortcuts for the Undo command: ⌘-z and, if you have an SE or Mac II keyboard, [F1].

You can even undo an Undo command. When you issue the Undo command or press ⌘-z or [F1], Word changes that command to Redo. Thus, if you cut a block of text, then select Undo Cut, you can select Redo Cut to delete the text again. You should keep in mind, however, that the Undo command remains in effect only until you issue another command or begin typing new text. As soon as you perform another action, Word will change the Undo command to reflect your new activity.

In addition to undoing the manual editing procedures we have discussed in this chapter, you can also undo many of Word's other commands. If a command or action cannot be undone, you'll see the notation *Can't Undo* in dimmed characters at the top of the Edit menu.

None of the commands on the menu, File menu, or Window menu can be reversed with the Undo command. Table 4-2 summarizes the actions on the other Word menus that can and cannot be undone.

TABLE 4-2

Menu	Command	Can Undo
Edit	Undo/Redo	•
	Cut	•
	Copy	•
	Paste	•
	Clear	•
	Again	
	Table...	•
	Glossary...	•Insert option only
	Hide ¶/Show ¶	
	Paste Link	•
	Update Link	•
	Short Menus/Full Menus	
	Preferences...	
	Commands...	
Format	Show Ruler/Hide Ruler	
	Character...	•
	Paragraph...	•
	Section...	•
	Document...	
	Cells...	•
	Position...	
	Styles...	•Apply option only
	Define Styles...	•Apply option only
	Plain For Style	•for Plain For Style
	(Character Format Options)	•

Menu	Command	Can Undo
Font	(Font Names)	•
	(Font Sizes)	•
Document	Open Header...	
	Open Footer...	
	Footnote...	•
	Repaginate Now	
	Outlining	
	Page View	
	Insert Page Break	•
	Insert Graphics	•
	Insert Table...	•
	Insert Index Entry	•
	Insert TOC Entry	•
Utilities	Find...	
	Find Again	
	Change...	•
	Go To...	
	Go Back	
	Spelling...	
	Hyphenate...	•
	Index...	•
	Table of Contents...	•
	Word Count...	
	Calculate	
	Renumber...	•
	Sort	•
Work	(Glossary entries)	•
	(Style names)	•

You can use the Undo/Redo command to reverse those actions marked by a • character in this table.

We'll talk more about these commands later. For now, just make a mental note about which actions in Word are easily remedied and which are not. Some commands—like Page Setup..., which we'll discuss in Chapter 7—can easily be "undone" by reissuing the command and selecting the correct options. However, if you use the Delete... command to erase a file or accidentally overwrite a file with the Save As... command, you won't be able to reverse that action. Consequently, you should use extreme caution when handling files.

As we mentioned in our discussion of the Undo command, Word remembers the last action you performed so that it can undo that action for you. Word also remembers your last action so that it can repeat a command or a series of keystrokes for you automatically. To repeat an action, choose the Again command from the Edit menu or press ⌘-a.

For example, if you insert a series of characters at one spot in your document, then decide that you need to insert the same series of characters in another location, you can click in the second location and press ⌘-a to "replay" your keystrokes. Similarly, if you select a block of text and overwrite it, you can select another block and press ⌘-a to repeat the same action.

Although you can use the Again command or ⌘-a to repeat just about any command or series of keystrokes, one of the most common uses for this shortcut is to "replay" complex formatting instructions that you want to apply in more than one area of your document.

Repeating an Action

FORMATTING 5

Word's formatting capabilities are among the most sophisticated and easy to use that we've seen in any word processing program. As we mentioned earlier, one reason that formatting in Word is so easy is that you see on screen exactly how your printed document will look. You can also see special formatting effects, including fonts and borders, and character styles, such as boldfacing.

On Word's Format and Font menus, you'll find lots of options to help you lay out and design your document. Another important formatting feature is the ruler, which you'll use to control tabs, line and paragraph spacing, and margin settings in your Word documents.

Because Word offers so many options for controlling the appearance of your documents—and because these options often interact—formatting is a vast and complex topic. But don't be intimidated. Once you've learned a few basic techniques, you should be able to handle the majority of your formatting needs. In this chapter, we'll introduce you to those basic formatting techniques: setting margins, applying paragraph formats, and formatting individual characters and words. We'll also talk about some related topics, including page breaks and special characters. In Chapter 8, we'll explain style sheets, one of the most powerful formatting tools available in Word. In Chapter 10, we'll address a variety of advanced formatting topics, including multicolumn formatting, the Position... command, and tables.

TOP-DOWN DOCUMENT DESIGN

Formatting a document in Word occurs on four levels: the overall document level, the section level, the paragraph level, and finally, the character level. Any changes you make at one level can affect the formatting characteristics of subsequent levels. For example, if you change your document's margins (a document-level formatting change), you'll affect every paragraph in the document. Because the different formatting levels are interrelated, it makes sense to design your documents "from the top down."

By top-down document design, we mean that you should move from the general to the specific. Decide first on the most general aspects of your document layout (your paper size and margins, for example); then, you can fine-tune factors like paragraph and character formats. We think you'll find that this approach simplifies the document design process and eliminates a lot of backtracking. Figure 5-1 illustrates the concept of top-down document design.

In this chapter, we'll look at three of Word's four formatting levels: document, paragraph, and character formatting. We'll save our discussion of section-level formatting for Chapter 10 since it applies only to documents with multiple sections. Generally, you'll use multiple sections when you need to change certain characteristics—such as the number of columns on a page or the header or footer text—from one part of a document to another.

BASIC PAGE LAYOUT

In keeping with the principle of top-down document design, the first step in formatting a document is to establish your overall page layout. In a simple document, there are three factors that affect your page layout: paper size, print orientation, and margin settings. In a more complex document, you may also have to consider such factors as multiple columns, mirror margins (different margins on the right and left pages, as you often see in bound documents), headers, and footers. We'll discuss these topics in detail in Chapter 10. For now, however, let's consider how paper size, orientation, and margin settings work together to determine your page layout.

Figure 5-2 on page 100 shows a sketch of Word's default page layout characteristics. Notice that the paper size is assumed to be $8^1/_2$ inches wide by 11 inches tall (US Letter size). In addition, Word assumes you're using what is sometimes referred to as "portrait" or "tall" orientation—that is, printing your document with the lines of text running across the short side of the paper. The default width for both the left and right margins is $1^1/_4$ inches, and the default top and bottom margins are each 1 inch. Each of these margin settings indicates the amount of white space between the edge of your paper and the edge of your text area.

Determining the Size of the Text Area

As Figure 5-2 illustrates, your paper size, orientation, and margins work together to determine the width and height of your document's text area. The width of the text area is determined by subtracting the left and right margins from the width of the paper, like this:

Width of text area = paper width - left margin - right margin

FIGURE 5-1

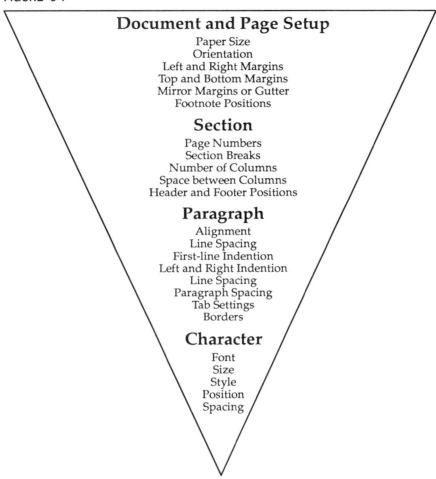

You can simplify the document design process by moving from the general to the specific.

Similarly, the height of your text area is determined by subtracting the top and bottom margins from the height of the paper:

Height of text area = paper height - top margin - bottom margin

When you're using Word's default settings, your text area on each page will be 6 inches wide ($8^1/_2$ - $1^1/_4$ - $1^1/_4$) and 9 inches long (11 - 1 - 1).

FIGURE 5-2

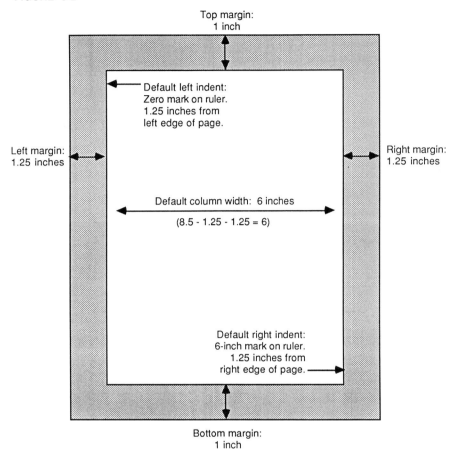

Top margin:
1 inch

Default left indent:
Zero mark on ruler.
1.25 inches from
left edge of page.

Left margin:
1.25 inches

Right margin:
1.25 inches

Default column width: 6 inches

(8.5 - 1.25 - 1.25 = 6)

Default right indent:
6-inch mark on ruler.
1.25 inches from
right edge of page.

Bottom margin:
1 inch

This layout sketch reflects Word's default page layout settings.

In a multicolumn document or a table, the text area is divided into two or more text columns. In the documents we'll look at in this chapter, only one column of text will appear in the text area. Unless you change the indents on your paragraphs, the width of the text column will be the same as the width of the text area.

Since the size of your document's text area will affect the appearance of each paragraph within the document, you should establish your page size, margin settings, and print orientation before you do any other formatting. If you change the size of your text area after you've made other formatting changes, you may find that you need to redo some of your section or paragraph formatting in various places throughout the document.

To establish your margin and page size settings, you use the Document dialog box, shown in Figure 5-3, and the Page Setup dialog box, shown in Figure 5-4 below and in Figure 5-5 on the following page. (The appearance of the Page Setup dialog box depends on what type of printer you are using. As you can see, we've shown a LaserWriter and an ImageWriter version of this dialog box.)

To open the Document dialog box, just select the Document... command on the Format menu or press ⌘-[F14]. You can open the Page Setup dialog box by choosing Page Setup... from the File menu or by pressing Shift-[F8]. (By the way, if you click on the button labeled *Document...* in the Page Setup dialog box, you will open the Document dialog box.)

FIGURE 5-3

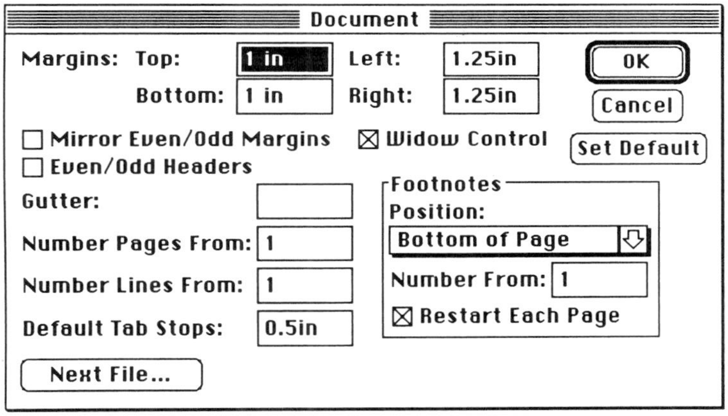

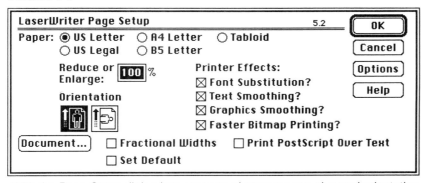

You can use the Document dialog box to change your margin settings.

FIGURE 5-4

With the Page Setup dialog box, you can alter your page size and orientation.

FIGURE 5-5

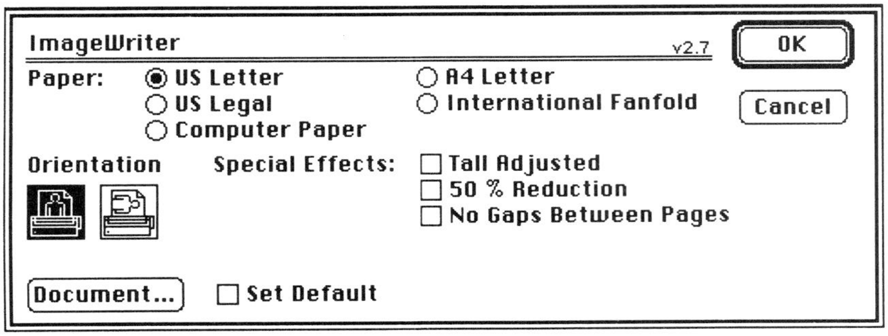

This is the Page Setup dialog box for an ImageWriter printer.

As you can see, the Document dialog box contains edit bars for entering the Top, Bottom, Left, and Right margin settings. In Figure 5-3, these edit bars all contain Word's default settings. The Page Setup dialog box includes several Paper size options and two Orientation options. These options are set to Word's defaults in Figures 5-4 and 5-5. Of course, there are a number of other elements in the Document and Page Setup dialog boxes as well. We'll discuss these later in this chapter and in other sections of this book.

Before we change any of the Document or Page Setup settings, let's look at how margins, page size, and orientation affect the appearance of the ruler.

The Ruler

As you might guess, the ruler gives some helpful clues about the page layout of a document. When we introduced the ruler in Chapter 2, we explained that it can have three possible scales: the normal scale (this is the default), the page scale, and the table scale. When you're using the normal scale, the ruler shows you the width of your document's text column. The ruler in the page scale shows your Left and Right margin settings relative to the width of the paper, and the table scale shows the boundaries of your text when you're working in a table. We'll discuss the table scale in Chapter 10, when we cover tabular text. For now, let's see how your margin and page settings affect the appearance of the ruler in the first two scales.

When you're using Word's default settings, the ruler in the normal scale will look like the one in Figure 5-6. In the normal scale, the zero point on the ruler always indicates the left edge of your text column—regardless of what you've specified as your Left margin setting or what size paper and orientation you're using. For example, with Word's default Left margin setting of 1.25, the zero point on the ruler represents a position that is $1^1/_4$ inches from the left edge of the paper. If you change your left margin to 3, the zero point on the ruler will represent a position that is three inches from the left edge of the paper.

FIGURE 5-6

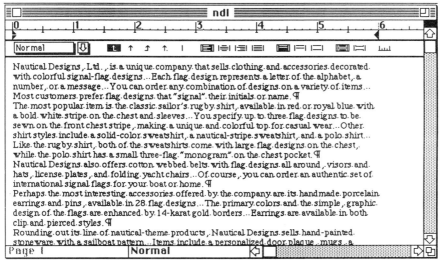

This is how the ruler will look in the normal scale when you're using Word's default page and margin settings.

The right edge of your text—or the width of your text column—is marked by a dotted vertical line. As we've mentioned, when you're using Word's default page and margin settings, the width of your text area (and your text column) will be six inches. Thus, the dotted vertical line appears at the 6-inch position on the ruler in Figure 5-6.

Initially, Word will always align the right indent marker (◀) with the dotted vertical line marking the right edge of your text. Similarly, Word will always align the first-line and left indent markers with the zero point on the ruler. You should not confuse these indent markers with your left and right margins. Although the indent markers will initially be aligned at the left and right edges of your text column, you can drag them along the ruler to change the left or right boundary of the text column in one or more paragraphs. (We'll talk more about this when we discuss paragraph formatting later in this chapter.) When you move an indent marker, however, you do *not* change your overall document margins—you merely change the position of text relative to these margins. To change your document margins, you must enter new settings in the Document dialog box or drag the margin markers that appear when the ruler is in the page scale. When you do this, Word will automatically adjust the width of your text area and move the dotted line that appears on the ruler in the normal scale. Before we demonstrate changing margins, however, let's look at Word's ruler in the page scale.

To change from the normal scale to the page scale on the ruler, just click on the scale icon () that appears in the far-right portion of the ruler. Word will then toggle into the page scale, as shown in Figure 5-7.

FIGURE 5-7

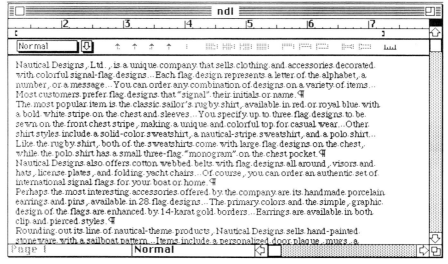

The ruler's page scale shows your left and right document margins relative to the edges of the page.

The main difference between the normal scale and the page scale of the ruler is the orientation of the numbers on the ruler. As we mentioned, in the normal scale, the zero point on the ruler represents the left edge of your text column. In the page scale, however, the ruler's zero point represents the left edge of the paper. The length of the ruler is determined by the Paper option you select in the Page Setup dialog box. For example, if you choose the US Letter option, the ruler in the page scale will be $8^1/_2$ inches long.

Instead of indent markers and a dotted vertical line marking the boundaries of the text, the ruler in the page scale shows two margin markers (**[** and **]**). The positions of these markers correspond to your Left and Right margin settings in the Document dialog box. When you're using Word's default settings, the left margin marker will appear at the $1^1/_4$-inch mark on the ruler and the right margin marker will appear at the $7^1/_4$-inch mark.

Let's look at how you can change your document's margins using either the ruler or the Document dialog box.

The easiest way to change the left and right margins of a document is to switch to the page scale on the ruler and then drag the margin markers to the appropriate positions. Alternatively, you can open the Document dialog box and enter new margin settings in the Left and Right edit bars. (You also can change your margins in the Print Preview window. We'll show you how to do this in Chapter 7.)

Changing Margins

When you enter margin settings in the Document dialog box, you can specify your measurements in inches, centimeters, points, or picas. Use the abbreviations *in*, *cm*, *pt*, or *pi* to indicate the unit you're using. If you're using the default unit (inches, unless you've specified a different default), you don't need to type a unit abbreviation.

Suppose you want to create a document in which your text lines are $4^1/_2$ inches wide and your left and right margins are of equal width. To figure out how to change your margin settings to fit these specifications, you would begin by subtracting your desired text width from the width of your paper. Assuming you're using paper that is $8^1/_2$ inches wide, you would use the formula:

$$8^1/_2 - 4^1/_2 = 4$$

The result, 4, is your total margin area. Since you want your left and right margins to be equal , you would divide the total margin area by 2 to determine your Left and Right margin settings. Thus, the left and right margins would each be 2 inches.

Now, to change your margins on the ruler, you would first click on the scale icon to switch to the page scale. Then, drag the left margin marker to the 2-inch point on the ruler and drag the right margin marker to the $6^1/_2$-inch point (two inches from the right edge of the ruler). As you drag, Word will display the width of the margin in the status box at the lower-left corner of your window.

Alternatively, you can change your margins using the Document dialog box. Just choose Document... from the Format menu and enter 2 in both the Left and Right edit bars.

Figure 5-8 on the next page shows the sample document from Figure 5-7 with new margin settings. Figure 5-9, also on the next page, shows this same document after switching to the normal scale on the ruler. As you can see, Word not only changed the appearance of the ruler, but also reformatted the text of the original document to reflect the new margin settings.

When you switch to the normal scale on the ruler, as shown in Figure 5-9, Word automatically moves both the right indent marker and the dotted vertical line marking the right edge of the text to the $4^1/_2$-inch position on the ruler.

Now, suppose you want your left margin to be $1^1/_2$ inches, but want to leave your overall text width at $4^1/_2$ inches. To determine what your Right margin setting should be, just subtract the left margin and the text width from the width of your paper, like this:

$$8^1/_2 - 1^1/_2 - 4^1/_2 = 2^1/_2$$

FIGURE 5-8

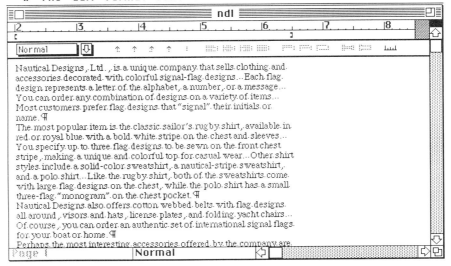

The margin markers on the ruler define the new margins in this document.

FIGURE 5-9

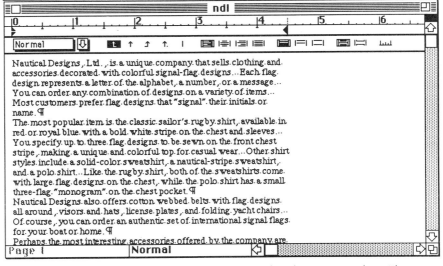

Using the normal scale on the ruler, you can see that the new margin settings reduce the width of the text area to 4¹/₂ inches.

Thus, your Left margin setting would be 1.5 and your Right margin setting would be 2.5. After you change your margin settings in the Document dialog box or on the ruler (in the page scale), you won't see any change on the normal scale of the ruler or in the text on your screen. The left edge of your text will still begin at the zero point, and the dotted vertical line marking the right edge will still appear at the $4^1/_2$-inch mark. However, if you switch to the page scale on the ruler, you'll see that the left margin is now narrower than the right margin, indicating that the text has been shifted left on the page. In other words, the width of your text area hasn't changed—only its position on the page.

In order to change the top or bottom margin in a document, you must open the Document dialog box—you cannot change these margins using the ruler. When you increase the size of the top and/or bottom margin, you decrease the size of your text area, and consequently, the number of lines that can fit on each page. On the other hand, when you decrease the top and/or bottom margin, you increase the size of your text area.

Changing top and bottom margins

Suppose you want to increase the top margin of a document to $1^1/_2$ inches and increase the bottom margin to 2 inches. Just choose Document... from the Format menu, select the default *1 in* that appears in the Top edit bar and replace it by typing *1.5*. (There's no need to enter the *in* abbreviation, unless you want.) Similarly, select the *1 in* that appears in the Bottom edit bar and replace it with *2*. After changing your margins, the height of your text area will be reduced to $7^1/_2$ inches ($11 - 2 - 1^1/_2$).

In our discussion of margins and ruler settings, we have assumed that your document will be printed on $8^1/_2$- by 11-inch paper. If you choose a Paper option other than US Letter in the Page Setup dialog box, however, that change will affect your margins. Table 5-1 on the following page lists the dimensions of some of the common Paper options that appear in the Page Setup dialog box.

Specifying Paper Size

The Paper options you see in your Page Setup dialog box are determined by the printer you have installed and chosen. (For more on installing and selecting a printer, see Chapter 7.) If you're using a printer that can accept custom paper sizes (such as an ImageWriter), you can specify the dimensions of your custom paper in the Preferences dialog box. That custom paper size will then appear as an option in the Page Setup dialog box.

If you choose a Paper option that has a width different than that of the default US Letter paper (which is $8^1/_2$ inches wide), the change will be reflected on the ruler and in any text you have entered. For example, Figures 5-6 and 5-7 show some text that was entered using Word's default US Letter option. Now, let's see what happens when you change to the A4 Letter option ($8^1/_4$ inches wide). When you click OK to close the dialog box and lock in the new setting, your screen will look like Figure 5-10.

TABLE 5-1

Paper option	Dimensions
US Letter	8.5 by 11 inches 216 by 279 millimeters
US Legal	8.5 by 14 inches 216 by 356 millimeters
A4 Letter	8.25 by 11.667 inches 210 by 297 millimeters
B5 Letter	6.9 by 10.8 inches 176 by 250 millimeters
Tabloid	11 by 17 inches 279 by 432 millimeters
Computer Paper	14 by 11 inches 355 by 279 millimeters
International Fanfold	8.25 by 12 inches 210 by 305 millimeters

These are the dimensions of the types of paper you may choose in the Page Setup dialog box.

FIGURE 5-10

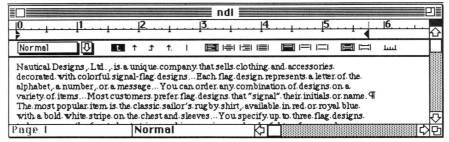

Word has adjusted our text to fit the new paper size we indicated in the Page Setup dialog box.

Notice that the width of the text area has decreased from 6 inches to $5^3/_4$ inches. Word is still using the default Left and Right margin settings of 1.25 inches. However, these margins are now being subtracted from a narrower page width, which results in a narrower text area. If you were to switch to the page scale on the ruler, you would see that the right margin marker now appears at the 7-inch mark, as shown in Figure 5-11. If you were to scroll to the right, you would notice that the ruler is only $8^1/_4$ inches long, reflecting the new paper width.

FIGURE 5-11

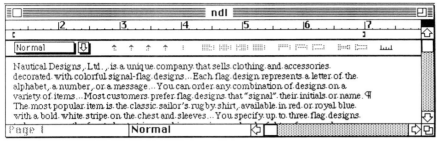

Word will adjust the margin markers in the ruler's page scale to reflect a new paper width.

Again, the Right margin setting has not changed from the default 1.25 inches. However, since the right edge of the paper is assumed to be at the $8^1/_4$-inch mark, Word has shifted the right margin marker accordingly.

As you might guess, if you were to specify a wider paper type, Word would widen the text area. For example, if you were to select the Computer Paper option that is available in the ImageWriter's Page Setup dialog box, Word would shift the right edge of your text $5^1/_2$ inches. That's because computer paper is assumed to be 14 inches wide, which is $5^1/_2$ inches wider than US Letter paper. When you use the normal scale on the ruler, the edge of your text will appear at the $11^1/_2$-inch mark, and in the page scale, the right margin marker would be shifted to the $12^3/_4$ point on the ruler. For more on choosing a paper size, see Chapter 7.

Changing Print Orientation

In most cases, when you change the Orientation setting from "tall" ( ) to "wide" ( ), the effect is similar to choosing a wider type of paper. When tall orientation is in effect (Word's default), Word assumes that you want to print your document across the width of the page. Thus, an $8^1/_2$- by 11-inch page would be taller than it is wide.

Wide orientation, on the other hand, will cause your document to be printed across the length of a page—as though the paper were rotated 90 degrees. A document printed on $8^1/_2$- by 11-inch paper would be wider than it is tall. Figure 5-12 on the following page shows a layout sketch of a page that uses Word's default margin and Paper settings, with wide orientation. Notice that Word rotates the margins as well as the text. Thus, the top and bottom margins now appear on the long sides of the paper, while the left and right margins are on the short sides. Figure 5-13 shows the document from Figure 5-6 after we changed the orientation from tall to wide.

FIGURE 5-12

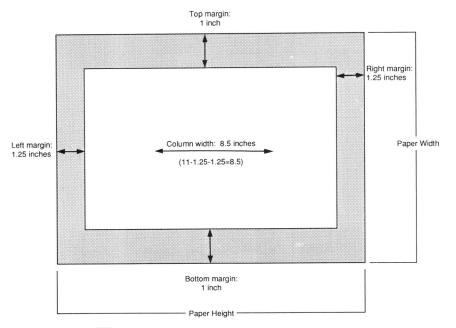

When you use 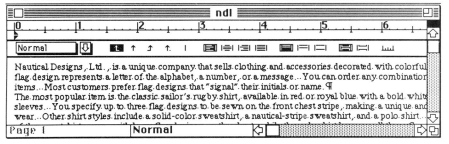 orientation, Word rotates your page 90 degrees.

FIGURE 5-13

After we change our Orientation setting to ⬛, we cannot see both edges of the document without scrolling.

Your text area is now so wide that you cannot see the end of each line on the screen without scrolling horizontally. In fact, if you're using the normal scale on the ruler and you click on the horizontal scroll bar, you will see that the dotted vertical line marking the right edge of your text area now appears at the $8^1/_2$-inch position on the ruler. Word arrived at this new text width by subtracting the Left and Right margin settings from the width of the paper, like this:

$$11 - 1^1/_4 - 1^1/_4 = 8^1/_2$$

If you're changing only your margin settings, paper size, or orientation, it's fairly easy to predict the result. When you need to change two or more of these settings, however, it's quite possible to get lost. If you're new to this process, we recommend that you make one change at a time and view your document after each change. You may even want to use the Print Preview window to get a better idea of how each change affects your document layout.

CONTROLLING LINE AND PAGE BREAKS

As we've illustrated, the size of the text area on each page of your document determines how long individual lines of text can be and how many lines can fit on a page. Word offers a number of options that let you control more precisely where your line and page breaks occur. We'll look at those in this section.

Line Breaks

As you know by now, the WordWrap feature automatically breaks lines of text at the right margin of your document. You can, however, create your own line breaks. One way to create a line break is to press the Return key, which also starts a new paragraph. (If you're displaying paragraph markers on your screen, you'll see the ¶ symbol at the point where you press Return.) If you want to start a new line without beginning a new paragraph, just press Shift-Return. Word will mark the line break on your screen with a ↵ symbol. The new line will be considered part of the same paragraph as the line just above it.

When we discuss paragraph formatting in the next section of this chapter, we'll show you how to move the indent markers on the ruler, creating shorter or longer lines in one or more paragraphs.

Page Breaks

When you create a document that is more than one page long, Word marks the page breaks on your screen with a dotted horizontal line. These are called soft page breaks or automatic page breaks. Word will not display these automatic page breaks on your screen until it has calculated at least once where they should occur. When you first begin to create a document, Word will not automatically calculate page breaks unless you have turned on the Background Repagination feature. If Background Repagination is not active, Word can still determine your page breaks when you want it to. Just choose the Repaginate Now command on the Document menu (or press ⌘-j) when you want Word to repaginate your document. If you choose the Repaginate Now command before you have made any changes to your document that would affect page breaks, Word will not repaginate. You can still force repagination, however, by pressing the Shift key and choosing Full Repaginate Now, which temporarily replaces the Repaginate Now command on the Document menu.

Word will also repaginate your document when you preview it with the Print Preview... command, when you print it, or when you issue the Page View command. After you choose the Page View command from the Document menu, Word will repaginate from the beginning of the document through the current page. If you move the insertion point forward in the document, Word will repaginate through that page.

As we pointed out in Chapter 2, the left edge of Word's status box displays a page number. Often, this page number will appear in dim video, indicating that it is not current. Stated another way, Word has not had a chance to calculate any changes in your document's page breaks that may have resulted from your entering and editing text. After you choose the Repaginate Now command, however, the page number will appear black, indicating that it is current. When the page number is current, it tells you on which page the line at the top of your document window would appear if you were to print the document.

If you want Word to calculate page breaks automatically as you enter and edit text, choose the Preferences... command on the Edit menu. In the Preferences dialog box, select the check box for Background Repagination. When this option is activated, you may notice some slowdown in processing, depending on how long your document is and how much memory your computer has. The page number in the status box will flash between dim video and black as Word recomputes your document's page breaks. That's because Word can repaginate your document only when you're not entering, editing, or formatting text. While you're actually working on the document, Word cannot repaginate it.

Manual page breaks

There may be times when you need to force a page break at a particular location in your document. To do this, just click at the spot where you want the new page to begin, and press the Shift and Enter keys or choose Insert Page Break from the Document menu. Word will insert a manual page-break marker after the current insertion point.

Like the automatic page breaks that appear when you repaginate your document, your manual page breaks will be represented by a single dotted line. You can distinguish between the two types of page-break markers, however, because manual page-break markers are slightly heavier. Figure 5-14 shows an example of an automatic and a manual page-break marker.

Keep in mind that Word's automatic page-break markers will change position each time you repaginate your document. Any manual page breaks you have inserted, however, will always occur at the location you inserted them. For this reason, we suggest you use manual page breaks sparingly. Otherwise, if you reformat or edit your document, these page breaks could cause unwanted gaps and awkward breaks in your printed document. To delete a manual page break, just select it or click in front of it and press the Backspace key.

FIGURE 5-14

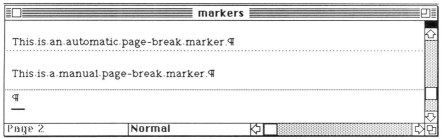

Manual page-break markers are slightly heavier than Word's automatic page-break markers.

If there is a paragraph that you always want to appear at the top of a page, you may want to assign the Page Break Before option to that paragraph. We'll consider this option in more detail later in this chapter when we discuss the Paragraph dialog box.

Widow control

Although the jargon is none too complimentary, the term *widow* refers to those straggling single lines of text that appear at the top or bottom of a printed page. (Sometimes, *widow* refers only to the last line of a paragraph that appears at the top of a printed page, while *orphan* refers to the first line of a paragraph that appears at the bottom of a page. In Word, both of these situations are considered widows.) Generally, it is considered good style to allow at least two lines of a paragraph to appear on a page. That is, the first or last line of a paragraph should never stand alone. If there is not room for at least two lines of a paragraph at the bottom of a page, then you should push the entire paragraph to the beginning of the next page. By the same token, if there is room at the bottom of a page for all but the last line of a paragraph—meaning that the last line of the paragraph would stand alone at the top of the next page—then you should pull a line from the bottom of the first page to the top of the second page.

The Widow Control option in the Document dialog box ensures that no single line of text from a paragraph (unless, of course, it is a single-line paragraph) appears alone on a page. If you use this option, Word will automatically adjust your page breaks as needed to ensure that at least two lines of a paragraph appear on a page. In some cases, this will mean that Word will not print the maximum number of lines on a page, making your bottom margin slightly larger.

When we discuss paragraph formatting later in this chapter, we'll look at the Keep Lines Together option, which goes a step further than Widow Control. When you apply this option to a paragraph, Word will print that paragraph in its entirety on a single page. If an entire paragraph cannot fit at the bottom of one page, Word will push it to the top of the next page.

Other factors that affect page breaks

So far, we've considered the basics of page layout in Word and looked at the primary factors that affect the positioning of page breaks in a document. In later chapters of this book, we'll look at other document elements that can affect page breaks. In Chapter 7, we'll consider headers and footers—text that appears at the top or bottom of each printed page. As you'll see, Word may automatically adjust your top and/or bottom margin to make room for multiline headers and footers. In Chapter 10, we'll look at multisection documents. When you create a document with two or more sections, you can specify that each new section should begin on a new page. Naturally, this will affect the location of page breaks that occur after the start of the new section. Chapter 10 will also cover the Position... command and tables—both of which can affect a document's page breaks. Finally, in Chapter 11, we'll explain footnotes, which you can place at the bottom of a page, at the end of each section, or at the end of a document. Footnotes that are printed at the bottom of a page will likely change the location of page breaks.

PARAGRAPH FORMATTING

Once you've established the page layout of a document, you're ready to move on to formatting individual paragraphs. Word's paragraph formatting options cover a lot of territory, including line spacing, alignment, indentions, and before and after spacing. In many simple documents, your paragraphs may all conform to one or two formats, so you won't need to do much in the way of individual paragraph formatting. In some documents, however, you may need to create a variety of paragraph formats. For example, if you have several levels of subheadings in a document, you may use different formatting for each.

Word's paragraph formatting commands always apply to whole paragraphs. Therefore, to format a paragraph, place the insertion point marker anywhere in that paragraph, then issue the appropriate commands. You also could select some or all of the text in the paragraph before issuing commands. If you want to format two or more paragraphs at once, just select any portion of the text in those paragraphs.

In this section, we'll show you how to apply Word's paragraph formatting features using both the ruler and the Paragraph dialog box. Although we'll cover nearly every paragraph formatting option, there are a couple of topics that we'll save for later in the book. In Chapter 8, we'll show you how to use a style sheet to name and save various combinations of paragraph formatting. As you'll see, using a style sheet can greatly speed up and simplify the process of formatting paragraphs. For now, however, let's begin by reviewing Word's default paragraph formats.

The Defaults

Word's default paragraph settings are flush left, single-spaced, with no first-line, left, or right indents. The term *flush left* refers to how the text is aligned—with an even left and "ragged" right margin. As you'll see in a moment, you can also format paragraphs to appear with centered, flush-right, or justified alignment.

Single-spacing refers to the amount of leading or space between lines of text. Word automatically adds a small amount of space between lines of text to create buffers between the ascenders and descenders of characters on adjacent lines. The amount of space will vary, depending on the font and size you've selected. You can increase or decrease this line spacing to suit your needs.

When we say that Word's default paragraph formatting calls for no indents, we mean that all the text is aligned within the text column established by your document's margins. By dragging the ruler indent markers, you can increase or decrease the width of one or more paragraphs. For example, if you need to set a quotation off from the rest of your document, you might shift the left and right indent markers to narrow that paragraph. You can also indent the first line of text in a paragraph.

(A note of warning: You may be tempted to change your overall margin settings by moving the indent markers on your ruler. We strongly urge you to resist this temptation. As we explained earlier, if you later make any changes to your margin, paper size, or orientation settings, Word will automatically move the indent markers on the ruler to reflect the new settings—and thoroughly scramble the "margins" you established with the indent markers.)

Ruler Icons

Earlier in this chapter, we explained how the ruler can show you the width of your text column and page margins. The ruler also can be used to apply most paragraph formatting features and show you which features are in effect for any individual paragraph in a document. To display the ruler at the top of a document window, just choose Show Ruler from the Format menu or press ⌘-r. (The ruler display is window-specific. If you have more than one document window open, you can choose to view the ruler in some windows and not in others.)

As you can see from the tick marks that appear along the ruler line, Word divides the ruler into $1/_8$-inch increments. However, as we'll demonstrate in this chapter, you can position the indent markers and tabs along the ruler at much more precise intervals.

When the ruler appears in the normal scale, you'll see indent markers at both ends. You'll also see icons below the ruler line that allow you to control paragraph alignment, line spacing, paragraph spacing, and tabs. The vertical line icon (l) allows you to position vertical lines in one or more paragraphs. The ruler also contains a dropdown list box that can be used to apply a style to a paragraph. We'll show you how to use this list box in our discussion of style sheets in Chapter 8.

If you're using Short Menus, Word will hide some of these ruler icons and the dropdown list box of style names. Word will also add an |✖| icon at the far right of the ruler. You can click on this icon to format the current paragraph in the *Normal* style. When you switch to the page scale or table scale on the ruler, Word disables all the ruler icons.

The ruler offers an excellent visual summary of the formatting features that have been applied to any paragraph in your document. If you place the insertion point marker on a paragraph while the ruler is displayed at the top of the document window, the ruler icons, indent markers, and tab markers will show you how that paragraph is formatted. Word will highlight the appropriate icons and display the tabs and indent markers at the correct positions. For example, the ruler in Figure 5-15 shows that the current paragraph contains all of Word's default formatting features. The icons for left alignment, single spacing, and closed spacing are all highlighted; the left and first-line indent markers appear at the zero position; and the right indent marker appears at the 6-inch position.

FIGURE 5-15

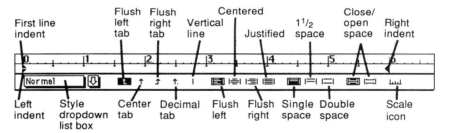

You can use the ruler icons to control paragraph formatting.

If you select two or more paragraphs that have different formatting, Word will dim the icons and shade the area below the ruler line where the tab and indent markers appear. In the shaded area, Word will show only the tab and indent markers for the first paragraph in the selection. For example, suppose a document contains two adjacent paragraphs whose formatting is identical except that the first paragraph has left alignment and the second paragraph has centered alignment. If you were to select both paragraphs (or some text in both of the paragraphs), Word would dim not only the alignment icons on the ruler, but also the tab icons and the line and paragraph spacing icons.

Now that we've seen how the ruler can display a paragraph's format, let's look at how the ruler icons and indent markers can change a paragraph's format. We'll then show you how to use the Paragraph dialog box to format paragraphs. Afterward, we'll demonstrate how to create tab stops and insert vertical lines in your text.

Your overall document margins are controlled by the margin settings in the Document dialog box or by the margin markers that appear on the ruler when it is shown in the page scale. Initially, Word will align the left and first-line indent markers with the left edge of your text column. Similarly, Word will align the right indent marker with the right edge of your text column. However, you can move these markers when you need to change the width of the text in one or more paragraphs. In fact, you might think of the indent markers as tools for making a temporary margin change in a document. While the Left and Right margin settings control the margins throughout an entire document, the indent markers can be used to control the margins or text width of an individual paragraph.

To change the width of a paragraph, first be sure that your ruler appears in the normal scale. (You can click on the scale icon to switch to the normal scale.) Then, place the insertion point marker anywhere on that paragraph and drag the left and right indent markers on the ruler. For example, the second paragraph in the sample document in Figure 5-16 is a quotation from James Joyce's *Dubliners*. To set this quotation apart from the rest of the text, begin by clicking on or selecting some portion of the paragraph, then point to the left indent marker (the bottom of the two indent markers on the left side of the ruler) and drag it to the $^1/_2$-inch mark. The first-line indent marker will move with the left indent marker. Next, to indent the right edge of the paragraph, point to the right indent marker and drag it to the $5^1/_2$-inch mark. Figure 5-17 on the next page shows the results.

Indents

FIGURE 5-16

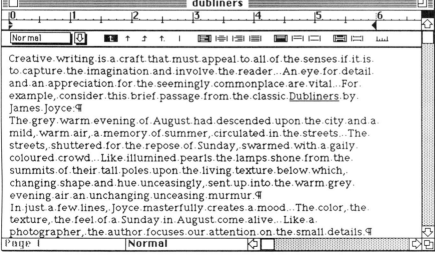

The second paragraph in this sample document is a quotation.

FIGURE 5-17

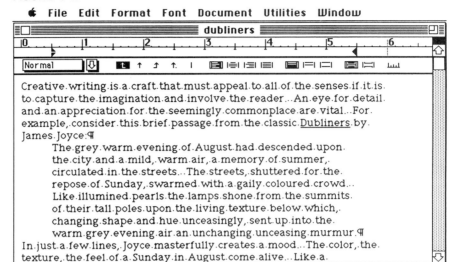

To indent the left and right edges of a paragraph, just move the indent markers on the ruler.

As you move your indent markers, keep in mind that your paragraph indentions are relative to the margin settings you've specified in the Document dialog box or in the page scale of the ruler. In our sample document, the quotation will appear $1^3/_4$ inches from the left and right edges of the page ($1^1/_4$ inch for the margin plus $^1/_2$ inch for the indent).

Paragraph nesting

Word offers a keyboard shortcut that allows you to move the left indent of a paragraph by an amount equal to the width of a default tab stop. (Unless you change them, Word's default tab stops occur every $^1/_2$ inch along the ruler.) When you press ⌘-Shift-n, Word will "nest" the current paragraph(s). That is, Word will move its left indent to the right by $^1/_2$ inch. Each time you press ⌘-Shift-n, Word will nest the paragraph another $^1/_2$ inch (or the width of a default tab stop). To "unnest" a paragraph—that is, to move its left indent to the left by $^1/_2$ inch—press ⌘-Shift-m. Normally, when you press ⌘-Shift-m, Word will not allow the current paragraph to move into the left margin. However, if you have manually changed the position of a paragraph's left indent marker, then you can move the left edge of that paragraph beyond the zero position on the ruler by pressing ⌘-Shift-m

Indenting the first line in a paragraph

Often, you'll want to indent only the first line of each paragraph in your documents to make it easier to distinguish paragraph breaks. That's why the indent marker on the left edge of the ruler is split into two parts. The top half of the icon, called the first-line indent marker, lets you format the first line of a paragraph independently of the rest. To change your first-line indention setting, just drag the top marker. (Instead of dragging the marker, you can press Shift-⌘-f. Word will move the first-line indent marker to the first default tab stop on the ruler.)

For example, Figure 5-18 shows our sample document with a $1/2$-inch first-line indention added to each paragraph. As you can see on the ruler, the first-line indent marker for the first and third paragraphs now appears at the $1/2$-inch mark, while the left indent marker remains at zero. In the quotation paragraph, the left indent marker is at the $1/2$-inch point and the first-line indent marker is at the 1-inch point.

FIGURE 5-18

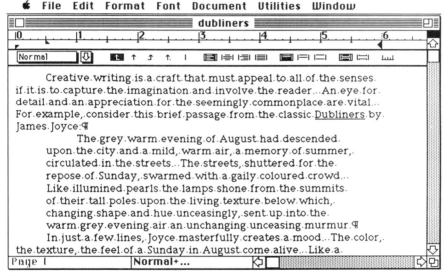

You can move the first-line indent marker to indent the first lines of paragraphs.

Once you split the first-line indent and left indent markers, you can still move both markers simultaneously by dragging the left indent marker. The distance between the two markers will remain unchanged. For example, suppose we want to shift the quotation in our sample document an additional $1/2$ inch to the right. We can point to the left indent marker and drag it to the 1-inch mark on the ruler. When we move the left indent marker, Word will move the first-line indent marker as well, so that it will be set at $1\frac{1}{2}$ inches.

If you want to move the left indent marker without changing the first-line indent, just press the Shift key as you drag the marker. Word will "release" the left indent marker so that you can move it independently.

Hanging indentions

Sometimes, you'll want to format a paragraph so that the first line starts to the left of the left indention. This effect is called a hanging indention or outjustified text, since the first line of the paragraph "hangs" outside the left margin of the paragraph.

For example, to create the paragraph formatting shown in Figure 5-19, we moved the left indent marker to the $^1/_2$-inch position, and kept the first-line indent at the zero position. To create a hanging indention quickly, press Shift-⌘-t. Word will move the left indent marker to the first default tab stop on the ruler.

FIGURE 5-19

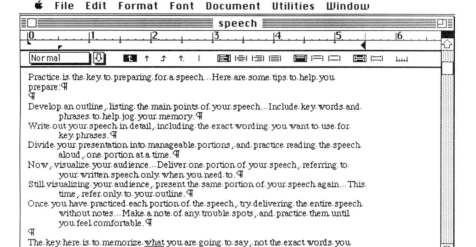

To create a hanging indention, drag the left indent marker to the right of the first-line indent marker.

Hanging indentions are particularly useful when you want to create a numbered or bulleted list of items, with your numbers or bullets hanging outside the main list. We'll show you how to create this kind of list when we discuss paragraph numbering in Chapter 13.

Placing text in the margins

Generally, you'll use the left, right, and first-line indent markers to decrease the width of a selected paragraph, as illustrated in Figure 5-17. However, Word also lets you increase the width of a selected paragraph, placing text in the margin areas of your printed page. To do this, move the left and first-line indent markers to the left of the zero point on the ruler and move the right indent marker to the right of the dotted vertical line that marks the edge of your text area. The ruler (in the normal scale) extends far beyond the $6^1/_2$ inches or so that are visible in a standard document window. In fact, the ruler extends from -11 inches to 22 inches. Figure 5-20 shows a document in which the title extends beyond the left and right margins of the main text area.

FIGURE 5-20

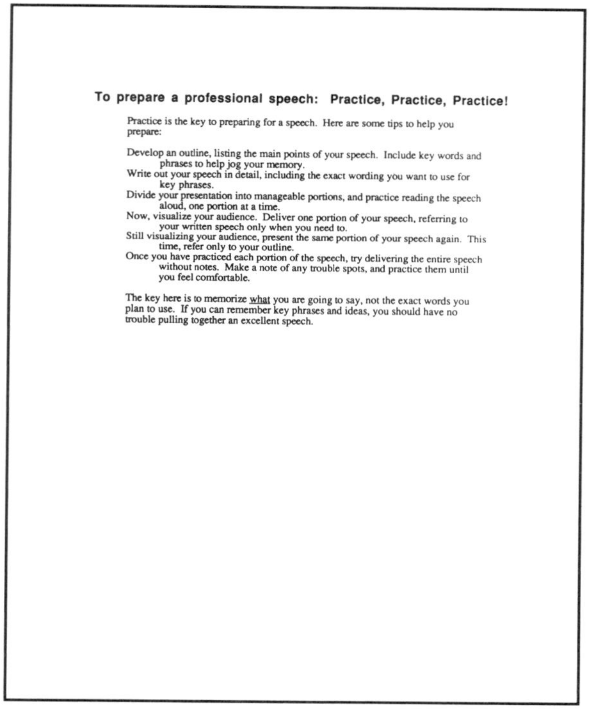

To prepare a professional speech: Practice, Practice, Practice!

Practice is the key to preparing for a speech. Here are some tips to help you prepare:

Develop an outline, listing the main points of your speech. Include key words and phrases to help jog your memory.
Write out your speech in detail, including the exact wording you want to use for key phrases.
Divide your presentation into manageable portions, and practice reading the speech aloud, one portion at a time.
Now, visualize your audience. Deliver one portion of your speech, referring to your written speech only when you need to.
Still visualizing your audience, present the same portion of your speech again. This time, refer only to your outline.
Once you have practiced each portion of the speech, try delivering the entire speech without notes. Make a note of any trouble spots, and practice them until you feel comfortable.

The key here is to memorize what you are going to say, not the exact words you plan to use. If you can remember key phrases and ideas, you should have no trouble pulling together an excellent speech.

By moving the indent markers outside the text area, you can cause text to be printed in the margins of your document.

To create this effect, first place the insertion point on the title paragraph. Then, drag the right indent marker past the right margin (the 6-inch mark, in this case), and move the left and first-line indent markers to the left of the zero point on the ruler. Word will scroll the document window as the negative ruler values come into view, as shown in Figure 5-21 on the following page.

Another common use for negative indents is to place text or special symbols in the margin of a page to draw attention to certain paragraphs. For example, in Figure 5-22, we used a $-1^1/_8$-inch first-line indent to display the words *Save 33%* to the left of the first paragraph. Notice that the left indent marker remains at the zero point so that the remainder of the paragraph is aligned with the rest of the text in the document.

FIGURE *5-21*

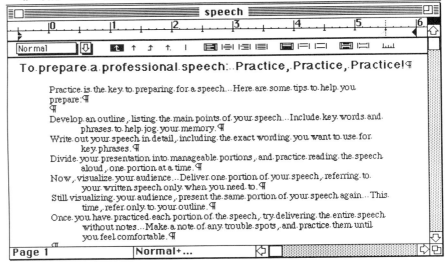

To place text in the left margin, move the left and first-line indent markers to the left of the zero point on the ruler.

FIGURE *5-22*

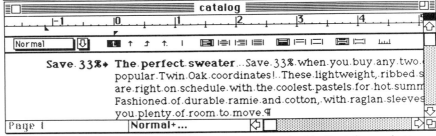

By moving the first-line indent marker, you can place text in the left margin to draw attention to certain paragraphs.

When you enter text in the left margin like this, you may not be able to see that text after you scroll the document window to the right. (In addition, when you close a file and then reopen it, Word will automatically position the window so that the zero point appears at the left edge of the window, with the margin text out of view.) To scroll to the left of the zero point, you need to press the Shift key as you click on the left scroll arrow in the horizontal scroll bar.

As you know, Word's default paragraph formatting aligns all the text in a document evenly with the left indent marker. The length of each line of text varies, creating a ragged right margin. To change this default alignment, place the insertion point marker on the paragraph you want to format (or select some text in all the paragraphs you want to format) and click on one of the alignment icons on the ruler.

Alignment

The effects of the various alignment icons are fairly self-evident: The Centered alignment icon instructs Word to center the selected text between the left and right indent markers. The Left alignment icon aligns the text with the left indent marker, creating a ragged right margin. The Right alignment icon aligns the text with the right indent marker, creating a ragged left margin. The Justified alignment icon aligns both edges of the text evenly with the left and right indent markers. When you choose justified alignment, Word may increase the width of the blank spaces in your text to keep the left and right edges of your text even.

Instead of clicking on a ruler icon, you can use a keyboard shortcut to change a paragraph's alignment. Press Shift-⌘-c to center a paragraph, Shift-⌘-j to create justified alignment, Shift-⌘-l to create left alignment, and Shift-⌘-r to create right alignment.

By the way, it's important to note that Word always aligns text relative to the indent markers on the ruler, not to the page margins you've set up. This can have important implications for how your text is positioned on the page. For example, if you want to center text on the page, you must first be sure that your left and right margins are of equal width. Then, leaving the indent markers at their default positions, select the Centered alignment icon.

Let's use the title page in Figure 5-23 on the following page to illustrate Word's alignment features. With all the text left aligned, this is not a very interesting page. Now, notice the difference when we change the alignment of the various blocks of text, as shown in Figure 5-24 on page 125.

To format the first two lines of the sample page, we simply selected the title lines and clicked the Centered alignment icon on the ruler. Next, to format the summary paragraph in the center of the page, we clicked on that text, then placed the left and right indent markers at the 1-inch and 5-inch marks, respectively. Then, we selected the Justified alignment icon. To format the last few lines of text, we clicked on those lines and selected the Right alignment icon. We also moved the left and first-line indent markers to the 4-inch position on the ruler.

By the way, when you use centered alignment, you'll generally want to keep the left indent and first-line indent settings equal. A first-line indention may throw the first line of the paragraph out of balance with the remaining text.

FIGURE 5-23

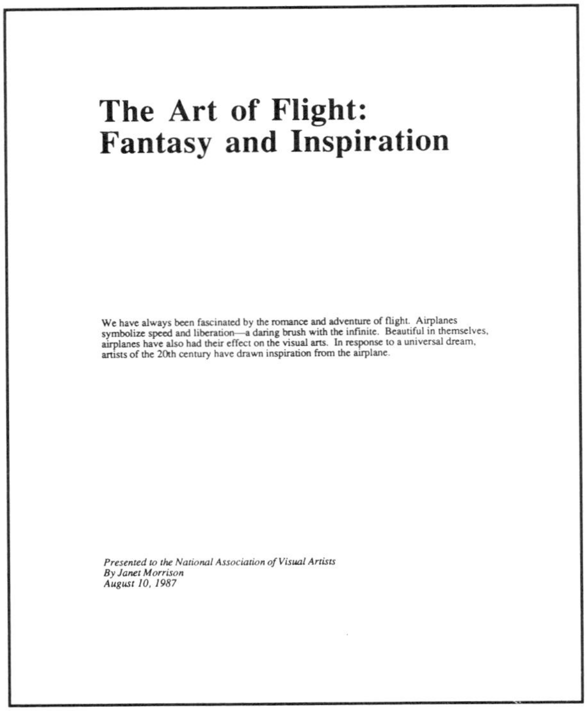

The Art of Flight:
Fantasy and Inspiration

We have always been fascinated by the romance and adventure of flight. Airplanes symbolize speed and liberation—a daring brush with the infinite. Beautiful in themselves, airplanes have also had their effect on the visual arts. In response to a universal dream, artists of the 20th century have drawn inspiration from the airplane.

Presented to the National Association of Visual Artists
By Janet Morrison
August 10, 1987

Currently, all the text in this sample page is left aligned.

Line spacing

As we mentioned earlier, Word automatically adds a small amount of leading, or spacing, between lines of text. The amount of spacing varies, depending on the font and point size you've chosen. In the point sizes that typically are used for the body text of a document (10 and 12), Word will generally allow one or two points of space between the tallest ascenders on one line and the lowest descenders on the line immediately above. For example, if you're using 12-point Helvetica type, Word allows 13 points from the bottom of one line to the bottom of the next line, creating one point of separator space between lines.

When you increase your font size, Word increases the leading as well. For example, if you use 36-point Times type, Word allows four points of space between the characters on two adjacent lines.

Word's default line spacing is called single spacing. Figure 5-25 illustrates single spacing for several point sizes in the Times font.

FIGURE 5-24

The Art of Flight:
Fantasy and Inspiration

We have always been fascinated by the romance and adventure of flight. Airplanes symbolize speed and liberation—a daring brush with the infinite. Beautiful in themselves, airplanes have also had their effect on the visual arts. In response to a universal dream, artists of the 20th century have drawn inspiration from the airplane.

Presented to the National
Association of Visual Artists
By Janet Morrison
August 10, 1987

You can dress up a page design by varying the alignment of paragraphs.

FIGURE 5-25

This is 10-point Times Plain text with default line spacing in effect.
This is 10-point Times Plain text with default line spacing in effect.

This is 12-point Times Plain text with default line spacing in effect. This is 12-point Times Plain text with default line

This is 18-point Times Plain text with default line spacing in effect.This is

This is 36-point Times Plain text

With single spacing, Word adds a small amount of space between lines of text.

The line spacing icons on your ruler let you change the amount of space between lines of text in a paragraph. In addition to single-spaced lines, you can create $1^1/_2$-spaced and double-spaced lines of text. These two formats are convenient for creating manuscript pages because they give you some extra room on the printed page for writing notes and corrections.

To apply the single-space, $1^1/_2$-space and double-space line settings, just place the insertion point marker on (or select) the text you want to format, then click on the appropriate ruler icon.

When you use $1^1/_2$ line spacing, Word increases the amount of space between lines by about six points. (Again, the amount of space between lines will vary, depending on the font and size you've chosen.) Word adds the extra space to its normal leading of one or two points.

When you use double spacing, Word inserts an additional 12 points of white space above each line of text. Figure 5-26 shows examples of single spacing, $1^1/_2$ spacing, and double spacing.

FIGURE 5-26

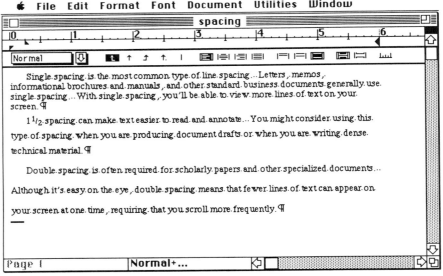

Using the ruler icons, you can create single spacing, $1^1/_2$ spacing, and double spacing.

Using the Paragraph dialog box, you can create more precise line spacing than that allowed by the ruler icons. You also can create line spacing that is larger than double spacing or smaller than single spacing. We'll talk about the Line Spacing setting in the Paragraph dialog box in a few pages.

Unfortunately, when you use larger type sizes, you may find that Word is unable to create $1^1/_2$ or double spacing. For example, Figure 5-27 shows some 24-point Times type in which the first paragraph has single spacing, the second paragraph has $1^1/_2$ spacing, and the third paragraph has double spacing. As you can see, there is no difference in the leading of these three paragraphs. We'll show you how to overcome this problem when we discuss the Line Spacing setting in the Paragraph dialog box.

FIGURE 5-27

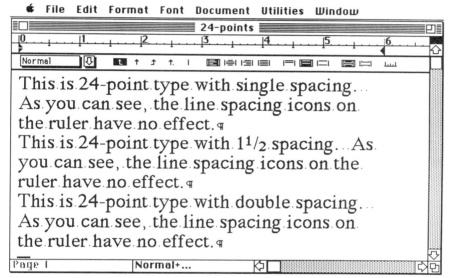

If you use $1^1/_2$ spacing or double spacing with large type, Word will ignore your line spacing setting.

Paragraph spacing

Paragraph spacing is similar to line spacing except that the spacing you choose applies only to the first line of the selected paragraph. Word offers two standard paragraph spacing options: open and closed. When you use closed paragraph spacing, Word does not insert any extra spacing between paragraphs of text, other than the appropriate line spacing. Closed spacing is Word's default. When you use the open setting, Word inserts 12 points of white space before the first line of text in the selected paragraph(s). This space is in addition to any space created by the paragraph's Line Spacing setting or the line spacing icons on the ruler.

To apply the open and closed paragraph settings, just place the insertion point marker on the paragraph you want to format (or select the paragraphs you want to format), then click on the appropriate ruler icon. Instead of clicking on the Open space icon, you can press Shift-⌘-o to insert 12 points of space above a paragraph. Figure 5-28 shows an example of a document in which the paragraphs have been assigned open spacing, creating the extra space between paragraphs.

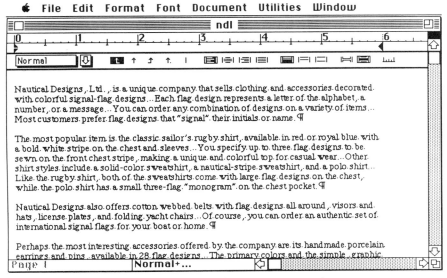

Use open spacing to create extra space between paragraphs.

You can also insert space before and after a paragraph by using the Before and After settings in the Paragraph dialog box. These settings have the advantage of allowing you to specify precisely how much space you want to insert rather than using Word's default spacing of 12 points. We'll talk more about the Before and After settings when we discuss the Paragraph dialog box.

A paragraph spacing tip

Many people create blank spaces between paragraphs by pressing the Return key. When they reach the end of a paragraph, they simply press the Return key twice to insert an extra blank line and begin a new paragraph of text. This technique is inferior to using the Open space icon or the Before and After settings in the Paragraph dialog box.

If you want to remove some of the extra space that you've created with the Return key, you'll need to select each paragraph marker (¶) you've inserted and delete it or reformat it to a smaller size. Moreover, when you press Return to create a blank paragraph, that paragraph will most likely carry the same formats as the paragraph immediately above. Thus, the size of your blank lines may not be consistent throughout a document.

When you use the Open space icon or the Before and After settings to create white space, you can make your blank lines the same size and easily change or remove the spacing around multiple paragraphs. To change or delete the spacing, just select those paragraphs, then choose the Close space icon on the ruler or change the Before and/or After settings in the Paragraph dialog box. This will reformat all the selected paragraphs. (You also can use the style sheet to make this type of formatting change, as you'll learn in Chapter 8.)

Although, in many cases, the ruler offers the quickest and easiest way to format paragraphs, there may be times when the ruler icons do not allow you to create the various kinds of formatting you need. The Paragraph dialog box gives you some options that are not available on the ruler, and it allows you to specify some of the format settings—such as the position of indents and the amount of space between paragraphs—with more precision. The Paragraph dialog box is available only when the Full Menus setting is in effect.

To open the Paragraph dialog box, just choose Paragraph... from the Format menu. You can access the Paragraph dialog box quickly by pressing ⌘-m or Shift-[F14]. You also can open it by double-clicking above the horizontal line on the ruler, double-clicking the right indent marker on the ruler, or double-clicking the paragraph properties mark (■) that appears to the left of some paragraphs. (We'll talk more about the paragraph properties mark later in this chapter.) As it opens the Paragraph dialog box, Word will also display the ruler if it is not already in view. Any settings that have been applied to the current paragraph will appear selected in the dialog box and on the ruler. For example, if you placed the insertion point marker on the second paragraph in Figure 5-18 on page 119 and then choose Paragraph... from the Format menu, Word would display the dialog box shown in Figure 5-29.

The Paragraph Dialog Box

FIGURE 5-29

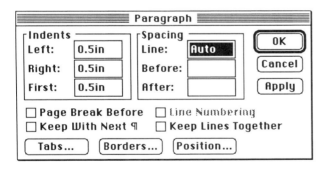

The Paragraph dialog box will display the format settings for the current paragraph.

After you have changed some settings in the Paragraph dialog box, you can apply those settings and close the dialog box by choosing OK. If you want to apply the settings to the current paragraph(s) without closing the dialog box, choose the Apply button. Finally, to close the dialog box without implementing any changes, click on the Cancel button.

Having examined the various formatting options available on the ruler, the Indents and Spacing settings in the Paragraph dialog box should look familiar. Indents can be specified in the three Indents edit bars: Left, Right, and First. As you would expect, entering a value in one of these edit bars has the same effect as moving an indent marker on the ruler. However, when you drag an indent marker on the ruler, you can place that marker with only $\frac{1}{16}$-inch precision. In the Indents edit bars,

Indents and Spacing settings

on the other hand, you can specify the position of an indent to three decimal places of precision. If you don't want to use inches, you can specify your indent positions in points, picas, or centimeters by typing *pt*, *pi*, or *cm* after the number in the edit bar. If you don't specify a unit, Word will assume inches (or whatever unit you're using on the ruler).

After you make an entry in one of the Indents edit bars and close the dialog box, Word will automatically move the appropriate indent marker to reflect the setting you specified. When you specify the first-line indent, keep in mind that Word assumes the measurement in the First edit bar is relative to the Left indent setting. Thus, if you enter .5 in the Left edit bar and .5 in the First edit bar, Word will position the first-line indent marker at the 1-inch position on the ruler—$^1/_2$ inch beyond the left indent.

The Spacing settings in the Paragraph dialog box allow you to specify the amount of space you want to appear before and after a paragraph, as well as the line spacing within the paragraph. The Before setting is similar to the Open space icon on the ruler. It allows you to specify the amount of space you want to insert before the first line of a paragraph. The After setting allows you to insert space after the last line in a paragraph, and the Line setting allows you to specify the total amount of space Word should allow for each line in the paragraph. (We'll talk more about line spacing in a moment.)

When you enter a Spacing setting, you can use points, inches, picas, centimeters, or lines as your unit of measure. Type a number followed by *pt*, *in* (or *"*), *pi*, *cm*, or *li*. Do not include a period after the unit's abbreviation—like *.25 in.*. If you do this, Word will not be able to interpret your entry and will give you an error message. It's not necessary to include a space between the number you type and the unit of measure.

If you do not specify a unit of measure, Word will assume that you intend to use points. If you specify lines, inches, picas, or centimeters as your unit of measure, Word will convert the unit into points. For example, if you enter a Before setting of *.25 in*, then close the Paragraph dialog box and reopen it, you'll see *18 pt* in the Before edit bar.

More on line spacing

When we explained the line spacing icons earlier in this chapter, we mentioned that the Paragraph dialog box allows you to create more precise line spacing than the ruler icons. The entry that you make in the Line edit bar specifies the amount of space that Word should allow from the bottom of one line to the bottom of the next line. For example, if you enter 18 in the Line edit bar, Word will allow 18 points of space from the bottom of one line to the bottom of the next line. (With 12-point type, this is the same as $1^1/_2$ spacing.)

Normally, Word interprets the value you enter in the Line edit bar as a minimum line spacing value. If you have an unusually large character on a line, Word will increase the spacing between lines to accommodate that character. However, Word will never use less line spacing than what you have specified. For example, Figure 5-30 shows some text in which we've specified a Line Spacing setting of 14 points. Notice that all the lines are spaced evenly except the fourth line, which contains some text formatted in a larger type style. Word increased the spacing for this line to prevent the text from overlapping the line above.

FIGURE 5-30

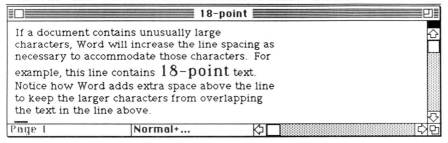

Word may increase line spacing on one line of text to accommodate unusually large characters.

If you don't want Word to increase your line spacing automatically—for example, if you want to overlap two or more lines of text—you can enter a negative number in the Line edit bar. The minus sign in front of the number does not indicate that you want to use negative spacing—if such spacing were possible. Instead, the minus sign indicates that you want the spacing setting to be absolute. Thus, a *-14 pt* Line setting tells Word that you want your line spacing to be 14 points, even if that means some characters will overlap. Figure 5-31 shows some overlapping printed text (24-point Times) that we created by using a Line setting of -11 pt. When you use negative line spacing, some characters may appear truncated on the screen. However, the characters will appear in their entirety when you print them.

FIGURE 5-31

You can create overlapping lines of text by entering a negative value as your Line setting.

Options that affect page breaks

The Paragraph dialog box includes three check box options that allow you to control where page breaks occur. These options are Page Break Before, Keep With Next ¶, and Keep Lines Together.

The Page Break Before option, as its name implies, allows you to force a page break before a paragraph. This option is useful when you want a particular paragraph—such as a subheading—always to appear at the top of a page. Assigning the Page Break Before option to a paragraph is similar to pressing Shift-Enter to insert a manual page break before that paragraph. However, you won't see a line marking the page break on your screen until your document is repaginated. (If Background Repagination is turned on, the line may appear a few seconds after you assign the Page Break Before option.) In addition, with the Page Break Before option, the manual page break is permanently "attached" to the selected paragraph, just like any other paragraph format. If you use the Copy or Cut and Paste commands to copy or move the paragraph to another location in your document, the Page Break Before format will automatically move with the paragraph.

You can use the Keep Lines Together option when you don't want Word to split a paragraph between pages. If you want to ensure that all the lines in a paragraph appear on the same printed page, activate the Keep Lines Together option. Then, if the paragraph falls at the bottom of a page and Word does not have room to print it in its entirety, the whole paragraph will be pushed to the beginning of the next page.

The Keep With Next ¶ option tells Word to print a paragraph on the same page as the following paragraph. If there is not room for both paragraphs on the same page, Word will push them both to the top of the next page. You'll find that the Keep With Next ¶ option comes in handy in many circumstances. For example, if your document contains subheadings, you might want to assign the Keep With Next ¶ option to each subheading to prevent Word from printing a subheading at the bottom of a page and the following text at the top of the next page. When you create a list, you might assign the Keep With Next ¶ option to related items. For example, if you're listing names and addresses, you could assign this option to each name to ensure that it appears on the same page as the address that follows. If you want to keep more than two paragraphs on the same page, assign the Keep With Next ¶ option to all but the last paragraph.

Keep in mind that the Keep With Next ¶ setting does not guarantee that all the lines in each paragraph will remain on the same page. If you have selected the Widow Control option in the Document dialog box, Word will make certain that at least two lines from each paragraph appear together on a page. If you have deselected the Widow Control option, Word will ensure that at least one line from each paragraph appears on the same page as the adjacent paragraph. If you want two paragraphs to appear together on the same page in their entirety, you must assign the Keep Lines Together option to both paragraphs as well as assigning the Keep With Next ¶ setting to the first paragraph.

The paragraph properties mark

When you apply the Page Break Before, Keep Lines Together, or Keep With Next ¶ setting to a paragraph, Word will display a small black box in the left margin next to the first line of that paragraph on your screen. This box, called a paragraph properties mark, is used to designate paragraphs that have been assigned some sort of "invisible" property. That is, if a paragraph has been formatted with a characteristic that doesn't change the appearance of the text on your screen or change the markers and icons on the ruler, it will be displayed with a paragraph properties mark. This mark does not appear in your printed document.

Word also will display a paragraph properties mark next to paragraphs that have been assigned a special position using the Position dialog box. In addition, if you have numbered the paragraphs in a document and turned off line numbering for one paragraph, that paragraph will display a properties mark. (For more on the Position... command, see Chapter 10. Line numbering is discussed in Chapter 13.)

Using borders

With Word 4, you can format a paragraph with one of several standard border options, or you can create your own custom paragraph border. You also can use borders to format the cells of a table. We'll show you how to do that in Chapter 10.

To create a paragraph border, first place the insertion point marker on the paragraph (or paragraphs) where you want the border to appear. Then, open the Paragraph dialog box and click the Borders... button. When you do this, the dialog box shown in Figure 5-32 will appear.

FIGURE 5-32

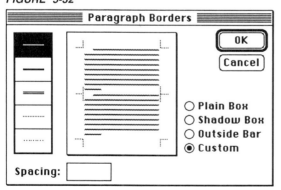

You can use the Paragraph Borders dialog box to assign a standard or custom border to a paragraph.

In the lower-right corner of the Paragraph Borders dialog box, you'll see four option buttons: Plain Box, Shadow Box, Outside Bar, and Custom. The first three options are the standard border types. The Custom option is for anything other than one of Word's standard borders. For example, a border that appears on just two sides of a paragraph would be a custom border. We'll consider some examples of custom borders in a few moments.

Just click on the border type you want to use to select it. (If you want to create a Plain Box border, you also can double-click on the edge of the border diagram that appears in the middle of the dialog box.)

On the left side of the Paragraph Borders dialog box, you'll see five border styles: single line, thick line, double line, dotted line, and hairline. Select the style you want to use by clicking on it. (If you choose the hairline style, the border will appear on your screen as a single line. You must have a PostScript printer, such as an Apple LaserWriter, to print a hairline border.)

Once you have chosen a border type and style, Word will display a diagram of the border in the middle of the dialog box. For example, suppose you have chosen the Plain Box option with a thick line. Word will display that border in the border box, as shown in Figure 5-33.

FIGURE 5-33

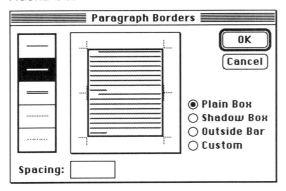

Word will display a diagram of the specified border in the border box.

To apply your border selection in your document, choose OK in the Paragraph Borders dialog box, then choose OK or Apply in the Paragraph dialog box. If you choose Cancel in the Paragraph dialog box, Word will not apply the border you specified. Figure 5-34 shows some printed examples of standard borders.

By the way, the Outside Bar border type normally appears on the left side of a paragraph. When you've set up different right and left page layouts, however, Word will move the bar border so that it always appears on the side of the paragraph opposite the binding edge of the page. For more on this topic, see Chapter 10.

Placing borders around two or more paragraphs

You can place borders around two or more paragraphs simultaneously by selecting some text in those paragraphs before you open the Paragraph Borders dialog box. If you then choose the Plain Box or Shadow Box border type, Word will place the appropriate border box around all the selected paragraphs, as shown in Figure 5-35 on page 136. Word will not place border lines between the paragraphs in the selection. Similarly, if you have placed a box border around a paragraph, and you press Return to start a new paragraph, Word will keep that new paragraph within the border box. (This differs from Word 3, where pressing Return would cause a new border box to be drawn around the new paragraph.)

FIGURE 5-34

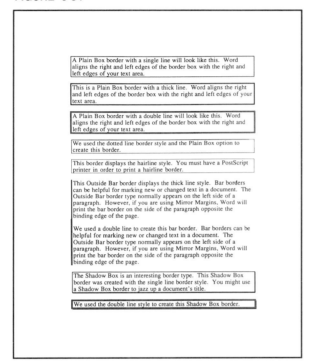

These are some of Word's standard border types.

To insert a horizontal border line between adjacent paragraphs, just select those paragraphs, open the Paragraph Borders dialog box, and click between the center border guides on the border diagram. (We'll talk more about these border guides when we explain custom borders.) For example, Figure 5-36 on the next page shows the document from Figure 5-35 with a border line between paragraphs.

To separate the border boxes of adjacent paragraphs with some white space, press Return to insert a blank paragraph between the two adjacent paragraphs and then remove the border from this blank paragraph. Figure 5-37 on page 137 shows an example of this. You must also use this technique if you want to insert some white space between two Outside Bar borders.

FIGURE *5-35*

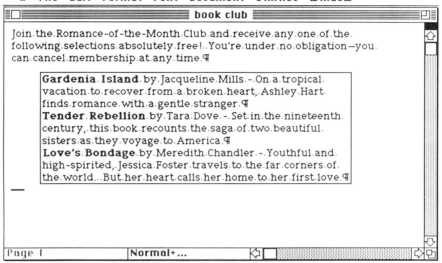

If you select text in two or more paragraphs before you create a border, Word will draw the border around all the paragraphs.

FIGURE *5-36*

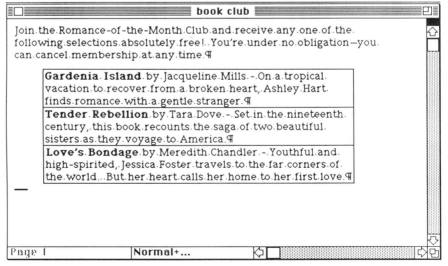

By clicking between the center border guides on the border diagram, you can place a horizontal border line between paragraphs.

FIGURE 5-37

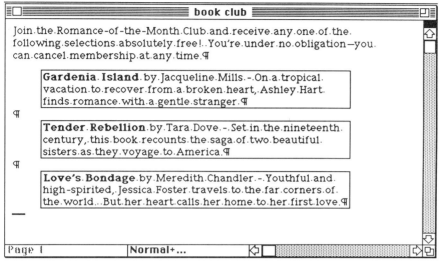

To separate the border boxes of adjacent paragraphs, you must insert a blank paragraph with no border.

Word uses the indent markers on the ruler to determine where a border should be positioned. Normally, Word will allow two points of white space between a border line and the paragraph text. If you have used the Open space icon or the Before and After settings in the Paragraph dialog box to insert some space before or after a paragraph, only two points of that space will be included within the border. An exception to this occurs when you have enclosed two or more paragraphs within a single border. The space before all paragraphs except the first one will be enclosed within the border along with the paragraph text. Similarly, the space after all paragraphs except the last one will be enclosed within the border. This concept is illustrated in Figure 5-38 on the following page. We added 12 points of space before and after the paragraphs in Figure 5-35 and then selected those paragraphs. As you can see, the additional space before the first paragraph and after the third paragraph is not included in the border.

To increase the amount of space between the border and a paragraph's text, use the Spacing edit bar in the Paragraph Borders dialog box. You can enter into this edit bar the amount of space (in points) you want to add between the border and the paragraph text. The space you specify will be added to the default two points. For example, if you enter 4 in the Spacing edit bar, Word will insert a total of 6 points of space between each border line and the paragraph text. (Word will not allow you to enter a negative number in this edit bar to decrease the amount of space between the border and the paragraph text.)

Adding space between a border and text

FIGURE 5-38

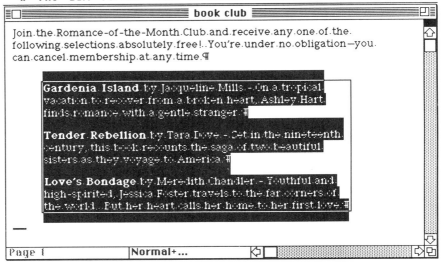

Word does not include within a border the space before the first, or after the last, paragraph in a selection.

When you use the Spacing edit bar, the left and right edges of the border may appear in the margins of your document. To align the border with your document margins, you can use the indent markers to decrease the width of the bordered paragraph somewhat. Then, use the Spacing setting in the Paragraph Borders dialog box to align the right and left sides of the border with your margins.

Adding space to a border can make it much more attractive. Figure 5-39 shows two examples of the same text with borders. In the second example, we used a Spacing setting of 5 to add some "air" between the text and the border.

Custom borders

Creating a custom border is very easy. First, you select a border style (single line, thick line, double line, dotted line, or hairline). Then, you simply click between the border guides on the border diagram that appears in the Paragraph Borders dialog box. The border guides mark five border positions: above, below, left, right, and between. Each time you click between two guides, a border line will appear on the border diagram in the currently selected style.

For example, suppose you want to place a double line both before and after a paragraph. After you have placed the insertion point marker on that paragraph, choose Paragraph... from the Format menu and, in the Paragraph dialog box, click on the Borders... button. When the Paragraph Borders dialog box appears, click on the double-line border style to select it. Then, in the border box, click between the top guides on the border diagram to create the border above the paragraph, and click between the bottom guides to create the border below the paragraph. At this point, the Paragraph Borders dialog box will look like Figure 5-40.

FIGURE 5-39

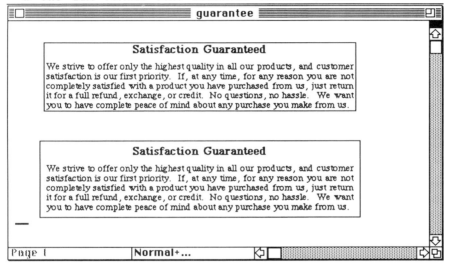

Adding space between a border and the paragraph text can make the border much more attractive.

FIGURE 5-40

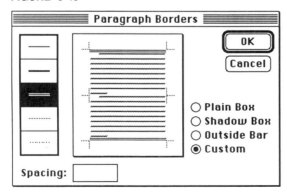

Click between the border guides to create a custom border.

If you select two or more paragraphs before you open the Paragraph Borders dialog box, clicking between the top border guides will place a border line above the first paragraph in the selection only. Similarly, clicking between the bottom border guides will place a border line below the last paragraph only. If you want a border line to appear between paragraphs in the selection as well, you must click between the center border guides.

In creating a custom border, you can use different border styles for different parts of the border. Just select a border style, then click between the border guides to indicate where you want to use that style. You can then select a different style and click between another set of border guides. For example, suppose you want to use a thick line on the left side of your border and a single line for the other three sides of the border. After opening the Paragraph Borders dialog box, click on the thick line style to select it, then click between the left border guides. Next, click on the single-line style and click between the top, right, and bottom border guides to create the other three sides of the border.

If you press the Option key as you click on a border section, Word will highlight the border style for that section. This technique is useful mainly for distinguishing between a single-line border section and a hairline border section. As we've mentioned, Word displays hairline borders as single lines on your screen.

As you are creating a custom border, you can remove a border section by clicking on it. For example, suppose you have clicked between the top border guides and the left border guides. You then decide that you want a top border line only. If you click on the left border line in the border diagram, Word will remove it. In order to remove a border section, be sure that the border style that's selected is the same as the style on the section you want to delete. Otherwise, Word will simply convert the section of the border that you click on to the currently selected border style.

By deleting sections of a border, you can convert a standard box border into a custom border. For example, suppose you want to create a three-sided border. You could begin by choosing the Plain Box border type, which will draw a border around the four sides of the border diagram. You can then click on one side of the border to remove it. When you do this, Word will also change your border type selection from Plain Box to Custom.

Deleting a border

As we just mentioned, you can remove individual border sections by clicking on them in the border diagram that appears in the Paragraph Borders dialog box. Thus, one way to delete a border is to open the Paragraph Borders dialog box and click on each border section in turn until no border sections remain in the border box.

Another way to delete a border is to open the Paragraph Borders dialog box and double-click in the border box outside the border guides. If you have a Plain Box or Outside Bar border, double-clicking once will remove the entire border. If you have a Shadow Box or Custom border, double-clicking once will convert the border to a Plain Box. Double-clicking in the border box again will remove the border.

There are two more options in the Paragraph dialog box that we'll discuss in other parts of the book. As you can see in Figure 5-29, the Paragraph dialog box includes a navigational button labeled *Position....* This allows you to open the Position dialog box, where you can specify precisely where you want to place a paragraph on a page. We'll examine this feature in Chapter 10.

The Paragraph dialog box also contains a check box for Line Numbering. We'll cover this option when we discuss the line numbering feature in Chapter 13.

Other Paragraph options

If you've used a typewriter or another word processor, you're probably familiar with tab stops. Tab stops are simply positions you set within the margins of a document for aligning text. Generally, tabs are used to create columnar text, such as tables and charts. On typewriters and in some word processors, you must also use tabs to create first-line or left indents. As you've already seen, however, Word handles indents with the indent markers on your ruler.

In Word, you'll use tabs to create simple tables, such as a table of contents, or to format documents that contain lists. When you need to create more complex tabular documents, you should use Word's new table feature. This feature allows you to do such things as wrapping text within individual columns of a table. We'll look at the table feature in detail in Chapter 10.

Working with tabs in Word is a two-step process. First, you specify your tab settings on the ruler, then you use the Tab key to position text according to these settings. Each time you press the Tab key, Word will move the insertion point to the next tab stop, creating a tab space. A tab space is marked on your screen by a right-pointing arrow (➡).

WORKING WITH TABS

If you press the Tab key without specifying any tab stops on the ruler, Word will use its default tab settings: left-aligned tab stops at every $1/2$ inch along the ruler. These default tabs are shown as inverted T marks that hang below the ruler line (⊥). To change Word's default tab stops, just choose Document... from the Format menu. In the Document dialog box, you'll see an edit bar labeled *Default Tab Stops*, with the setting *0.5in.* Enter a new tab interval that is less than the right edge of your text and choose OK. For example, if you want default tab stops at every inch along the ruler, enter *1* in the Default Tab Stops edit bar.

Default Tab Stops

When you need to use tabs, you probably won't want them to be spaced uniformly along the ruler line, as are Word's default tab stops. To set tabs at uneven intervals, you must create your own tab stops on the ruler. Word allows you to create up to 50 tab stops for a single paragraph. When you create a tab stop, you can choose from four tab alignments: left, centered, right, and decimal. Table 5-2 shows the four tab alignment icons that appear on your ruler.

Creating, Moving, and Deleting Tab Stops

TABLE 5-2

Icon	Name
ᴸ	Left-aligned tab icon
↑	Centered tab icon
⅃	Right-aligned tab icon
↑.	Decimal tab icon
I	Vertical line icon

The four tab icons on the ruler allow you to select different tab alignments. You use the vertical line icon to create vertical lines in a document.

Word also allows you to create tab leaders. A tab leader is simply a series of characters used to fill the tab space, such as a string of periods. As we'll show in a few pages, you use the Tabs dialog box to specify a tab leader.

Before you create a tab stop, place the insertion point marker on the paragraph that you want to format with tabs. If you want to format a new table or list, just press Return to start a new paragraph. Then, on the ruler, click on the tab alignment icon you want to use. When the appropriate icon is highlighted, click on the ruler where you want the tab to appear. For example, suppose you want to place a left-aligned tab at the 2-inch mark on your ruler. First, click on the left tab icon (ᴸ) if it is not already selected, then click on the 2-inch mark.

When you insert a tab on the ruler, Word will clear all default tabs that appear to the left of the new tab. Continuing with our example, if you insert a tab at the 2-inch mark, Word will delete the default tab stops at the $1/_2$-inch, 1- inch and $1 1/_2$-inch positions on the ruler. Word allows you to place tab stops beyond the right indent marker and the dotted line that marks the right edge of the text on your page. You also can place tabs to the left of the zero point on the ruler (in the normal scale).

If you've already formatted the current paragraph by inserting tab spaces, Word will adjust those spaces according to the new tab stop(s) you've created. Continuing with our example, suppose that before you created the custom tab stop at the 2-inch position, you pressed the Tab key to move the text at the beginning of the current line to the first default tab stop at the $1/_2$-inch position. After you create the custom tab, Word will increase the tab space, moving the beginning of the line to the 2-inch position.

If you need to reposition a tab, point to the tab marker on the ruler and drag. If you press the Shift key as you drag the tab stop, Word will move not only that tab marker, but all tab markers that appear to the right as well.

To clear a tab stop, just point to the tab symbol and drag it up or down off the ruler. When you move or delete tab stops, Word will reformat the text of the current paragraph automatically.

You also can create, move, and delete tabs by using the Tabs dialog box. We'll show you how to do this in a moment. First, however, let's look at an example that illustrates how you might use tabs to create a simple table.

An Example

Perhaps the easiest way to illustrate tabs is to work with a sample document like the one shown in Figure 5-41. Although tables like this require a little planning, they are not difficult to create. Let's walk through the process of building this table.

FIGURE 5-41

Centered Right Decimal Left

Name	Sun	Height	Price	Description
Ageratum	•••	6"	$1.25	Long-lasting blue or white blooms
Alyssum	•••	3"	.75	Great for rock gardens or borders
Aster	•••	6" to 18"	$1.25	Blue, pink, or crimson blooms
Begonia	••	10" to 15"	$1.75	Easy to grow; blooms all summer
Caladium	•	8" to 20"	$1.99	Prefers humid climate and indirect sun
Calendula	••	12" to 15"	$1.99	Bright orange or yellow blooms
Candytuft	••	8"	.75	Hardy pink, white, or lavender blooms
Celosia	•••	7" to 18"	$1.00	Feathery bright plumes
Cineraria	••	8" to 12"	$1.99	Blooms form colorful nosegays
Coleus	•	6" to 15"	$1.00	Beautiful multicolored leaves
Dahlia	••	12" to 20"	$2.25	Compact hardy growth; bright blooms
Fuchsia	•	12" to 20"	$2.75	Needs pampering, but well worth it!
Geranium	••	10" to 12"	$1.25	Long-time favorite for window boxes
Impatiens	••	12" to 20"	$1.00	Easy-care; blooms all summer
Marigold	•••	18" to 20"	$1.25	Sturdy, bright blooms in lots of colors
Nasturtium	•••	12" to 18"	$1.25	Cascades of sky-blue blooms
Pansy	••	7"	$1.75	Charming, delicate blooms; easy-care
Petunia	•••	8" to 14"	$1.00	A window-box champion!
Phlox	••	7"	.75	Compact blooms; great ground cover
Portulaca	•••	6"	$1.75	Roselike blooms; thrives in heat and sun
Snapdragon	•••	12" to 20"	$1.75	Adds color and texture to any garden
Verbena	••	10"	$1.50	Brilliant colors; needs good drainage
Vinca	••	3" to 10"	.75	Fast-spreading hardy ground cover
Zinnia	•••	10" to 18"	$1.75	A hardy sun-loving favorite

This table illustrates Word's four tab alignment options.

Your first step is to decide how many columns you need and how much space you should allow for each column. The space required by each column depends on the size of the type you are using and the length of the entries in each column. You may find it helpful to type the header line for the table and one or two sample lines to get your bearings. Don't worry about the proper ruler settings for now; just enter some sample text, pressing the Tab key at the end of each column to move to the next column. When you press the Tab key, your insertion point marker will automatically jump to the next default tab stop.

Next, assign any desired character and paragraph formats to your sample text so you can get a feel for the space required for each column. Figure 5-42 shows the first two lines of our table at this point. As you can see, our columns are not yet properly aligned because the entries in each line vary in length. When we pressed the Tab key, Word simply pushed each entry to the next $^{1}/_{2}$-inch tab stop.

FIGURE 5-42

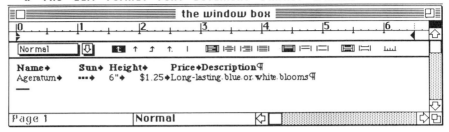

Entering and formatting a couple of lines of sample text can help you determine the appropriate tab stops for a table.

After entering some sample text, you need to decide how you want to align and position the text in each column. Left-aligned tabs generally work best for text entries, like those in the first and fifth columns of our table. A centered tab can be used to align text or symbols, like those in the second column. To align a column of numbers, such as the third column of the table, use a right-aligned tab. When you're working with currency values, you'll probably want to use decimal tabs to align the decimal points in each entry, as we've done in the fourth column.

In deciding where to position your tabs, try to allow enough room between each column to accommodate the longest entry in that column. For example, in the first column of our sample table, the word *Snapdragon* is our longest entry, extending almost to the 1-inch mark. So, we decided to center our second column at the $1\frac{1}{4}$-inch mark. Then, to position columns three, four, and five, we used a right-aligned tab at the $2\frac{1}{2}$-inch mark, a decimal tab at the $3\frac{1}{8}$-inch mark, and a left-aligned tab at the $3\frac{3}{4}$-inch mark. Figure 5-43 shows the results.

FIGURE 5-43

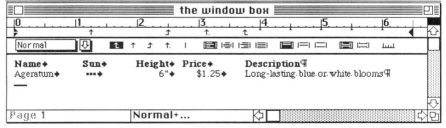

Position tab stops along the ruler according to the length and types of entries in each column.

If you use decimal tabs, you may have to make some adjustments to the header line of your table. As you can see in the Price column of Figure 5-43, our heading is not properly aligned with the subsequent currency values. When Word cannot locate a decimal point in a string of characters, it aligns the last character in that string flush right with the decimal tab stop.

To overcome this problem, we selected just the header line of the table and deleted the decimal tab at the $3^1/_8$-inch mark. Then, we added a right-aligned tab at the $3^3/_8$-inch mark to reposition the fourth column of heading text. Figure 5-44 shows the result.

FIGURE 5-44

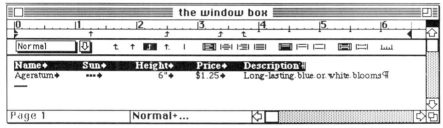

When you use a decimal tab, you may need to realign a line of text that does not have a decimal point, as we have done with the header line of this table.

Once you have defined the width and alignment for each column in your table, you're ready to enter the remainder of your text. Keep in mind that your ruler settings will carry over from one line to the next as you press the Return key. So, once you have set up your tab formats, move the insertion point marker just to the left of the ¶ marker at the end of the last line in your table, then press the Return key to begin a new line.

If you need to adjust your tab settings later, just highlight all the paragraphs in the table and move the tab markers to new positions on the ruler. If you need to change a tab format, just drag the old tab marker off the ruler, select the appropriate tab icon, then click on the ruler to specify the tab position.

Adding Vertical Lines

Next to the tab icons on your ruler, you'll see a vertical line icon. You can use this icon to insert a vertical line in a paragraph. Inserting a vertical line is similar to creating a tab stop. You simply click on the icon to select it, then click on the ruler to specify the position of the line. For example, if you want to add vertical lines between the columns of the sample table, you would first select all the text in the table. Then, you would click on the vertical line icon and click the 1-inch, $1^5/_8$-inch, $2^3/_4$-inch, and $3^5/_8$-inch positions on the ruler. Figure 5-45 shows how your screen would look at this point.

FIGURE 5-45

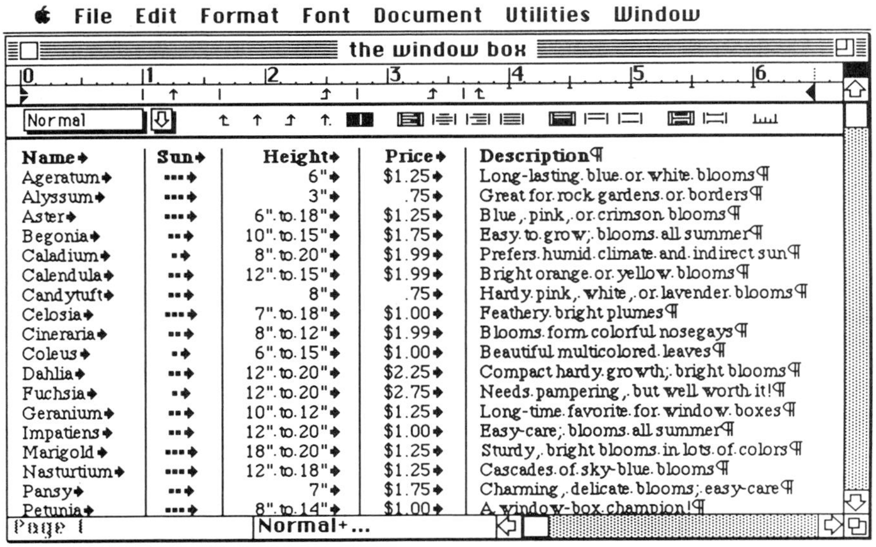

You can use the vertical line icon to insert vertical lines between the columns of the table.

By combining paragraph borders with these vertical lines, you can create a grid effect on the table. Again, select all the text in the table, then open the Paragraph dialog box and choose the Borders... button. In the Paragraph Borders dialog box, make sure that the single line option is selected and select the Plain Box border type. This will draw a box border around the table. To add gridlines between each line of the table, click between the center border guides in the border diagram. When you choose OK in the Paragraph Borders dialog box and in the Paragraph dialog box, your screen will look like Figure 5-46.

As you'll see in Chapter 10, another way to create a table with a grid is to use Word's Insert Table... command to create the table, then use the Cell Borders dialog box to draw a border around the individual cells of the table.

The Tabs Dialog Box

So far, we've shown you how to use the ruler to add, move, and delete tab stops. The Tabs dialog box, which is shown in Figure 5-47, offers another way to manipulate tabs in your document. To access this dialog box, first open the Paragraph dialog box, then click on the Tabs... button. Or, double-click one of the tab icons on your ruler. (If you double-click a tab icon, Word will open only the Tabs dialog box and not the Paragraph dialog box as well.)

FIGURE 5-46

Name◆	Sun◆	Height◆	Price◆	Description¶
Ageratum◆	···◆	6"◆	$1.25◆	Long-lasting.blue.or.white.blooms¶
Alyssum◆	···◆	3"◆	.75◆	Great.for.rock.gardens.or.borders¶
Aster◆	···◆	6".to.18"◆	$1.25◆	Blue,.pink,.or.crimson.blooms¶
Begonia◆	··◆	10".to.15"◆	$1.75◆	Easy.to.grow;.blooms.all.summer¶
Caladium◆	·◆	8".to.20"◆	$1.99◆	Prefers.humid.climate.and.indirect.sun¶
Calendula◆	··◆	12".to.15"◆	$1.99◆	Bright.orange.or.yellow.blooms¶
Candytuft◆	··◆	8"◆	.75◆	Hardy.pink,.white,.or.lavender.blooms¶
Celosia◆	···◆	7".to.18"◆	$1.00◆	Feathery.bright.plumes¶
Cineraria◆	··◆	8".to.12"◆	$1.99◆	Blooms.form.colorful.nosegays¶
Coleus◆	·◆	6".to.15"◆	$1.00◆	Beautiful.multicolored.leaves¶
Dahlia◆	··◆	12".to.20"◆	$2.25◆	Compact.hardy.growth;.bright.blooms¶
Fuchsia◆	·◆	12".to.20"◆	$2.75◆	Needs.pampering,.but.well.worth.it!¶
Geranium◆	··◆	10".to.12"◆	$1.25◆	Long-time.favorite.for.window.boxes¶
Impatiens◆	··◆	12".to.20"◆	$1.00◆	Easy-care;.blooms.all.summer¶
Marigold◆	···◆	18".to.20"◆	$1.25◆	Sturdy,.bright.blooms.in.lots.of.colors¶
Nasturtium◆	···◆	12".to.18"◆	$1.25◆	Cascades.of.sky-blue.blooms¶

Using paragraph borders, you can create a grid effect on a table.

FIGURE 5-47

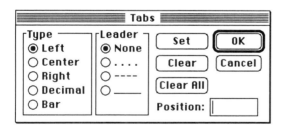

You can set, move, and clear tabs with the Tabs dialog box.

In most cases, you'll probably find that it's more convenient to create, move, and delete tabs directly on the ruler. In fact, the ruler will always be visible and accessible while the Tabs dialog box is open. However, the Tabs dialog box offers some features that are not available on the ruler. First, you can position tab stops more precisely using the dialog box. You also can create tab leader characters. Finally, the Tabs dialog box offers a quick way to clear all tabs (except default tab stops) from the ruler.

To use the Tabs dialog box to change a tab position, first click on that tab's marker on the ruler to select it. Word will enter the current position of the tab in the Position edit bar. You can then type a new position and choose the Set button. Like the Indents settings in the Paragraph dialog box, the tab position you enter can be expressed in inches (*in*), centimeters (*cm*), points (*pt*), or picas (*pi*). If you do not specify a unit of measure, Word will assume inches (or whatever unit of measure you're using on the ruler).

Like tabs, vertical lines can be repositioned using the Position edit bar. First, click on a vertical line marker on the ruler to select it. Word will display the current position of that marker in the Position edit bar. Just type a new position and then click the Set button.

To create a tab stop using the Tabs dialog box, type the tab position in the Position edit bar, specify the tab's alignment by choosing one of the Type options, and choose the Set button. Word will add the type of tab you specified to the ruler. You can add only one tab in this manner. If you enter a new position in the Position edit bar, Word will simply move the currently active tab.

As you might guess, you also can use the Tabs dialog box to change a tab's alignment. First, select the tab marker on the ruler by clicking on it. The position of the tab will appear in the Position edit bar and Word will automatically select the Type option that reflects that tab's alignment. You can select a different alignment by clicking on another Type option.

To clear a tab using the Tabs dialog box, select the tab marker on the ruler (or type its position in the Position edit bar), then choose the Clear button. You can remove all tab stops in the currently selected paragraph(s)—except the defaults— by choosing the Clear All button. The tabs won't actually be cleared until you select OK in the Tabs dialog box and in the Paragraph dialog box (if the Paragraph dialog box is open). If you choose the Cancel button in either dialog box, Word will restore the deleted tabs.

Tab leader characters

As we've mentioned, the Tabs dialog box offers a way to create tab leader characters quickly and easily. A tab leader is simply a character that's repeated on a line to fill in the space between columns of text. Tab leaders are often used to connect items in a table, guiding the reader's eye from one column to the next. Word offers three kinds of tab leaders: periods, hyphens, and underline characters.

Figure 5-48 on the next page shows an example of a document that uses tab leaders. The period characters help guide the reader's eye from the chapter names in the second column to the page numbers in the third column. We also used underline characters to help separate the sections of the table.

To add a tab leader, open the Tabs dialog box, then click on the tab marker on the ruler for which you want to create a leader. After you've selected the tab marker, choose one of the Leader options and choose Set. To delete a tab leader, select the tab marker that has a leader, then choose the None Leader option.

FIGURE 5-48

Contents

The period characters help guide the reader from the chapter title column to the correct page number.

If you want to add leaders to text that you've already formatted with tabs, you must select the text where you want the tab leaders to appear before you open the Tabs dialog box. For example, Figure 5-49 shows the table of contents from Figure 5-48 before we inserted any tab leaders. Each of the lines where a chapter name appears has a left-aligned tab at the $1^1/_2$-inch position and a right-aligned tab at the 6-inch position. To add the tab leaders between the chapter names and page numbers, you would select all the chapter names and page numbers in a section (for example, Chapters 1, 2, 3, and 4), then double-click one of the tab icons on the ruler to open the Tabs dialog box. When the Tabs dialog box appears, click on the tab marker at the 6-inch position on the ruler. Then, select the second leader option (...) and choose Set. When you choose OK to close the dialog box, Word will insert the leader characters between the tab at the $1^1/_2$-inch position and the tab at the 6-inch position. You would follow a similar procedure to create the remaining tab leaders for the chapter names in each section of the table.

FIGURE 5-49

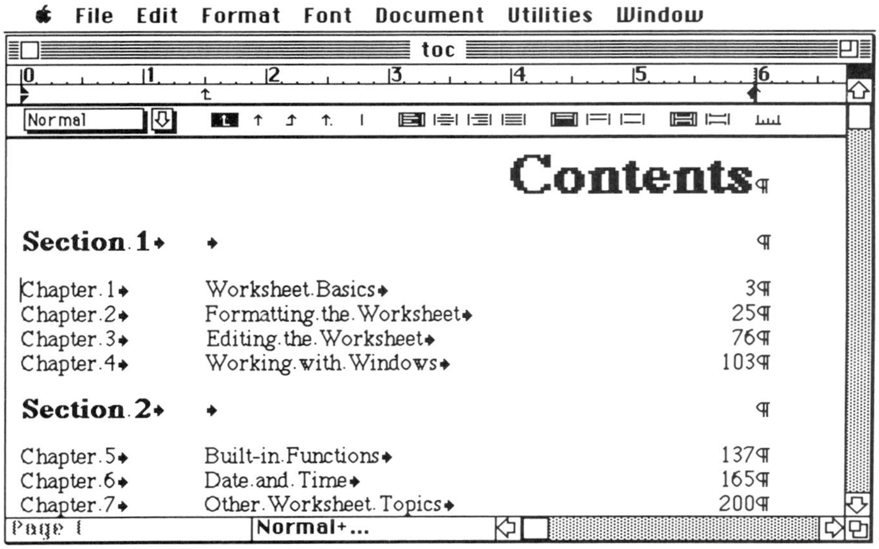

 File Edit Format Font Document Utilities Window

toc

Contents

Section 1

Chapter 1   Worksheet Basics   3
Chapter 2   Formatting the Worksheet   25
Chapter 3   Editing the Worksheet   76
Chapter 4   Working with Windows   103

Section 2

Chapter 5   Built-in Functions   137
Chapter 6   Date and Time   165
Chapter 7   Other Worksheet Topics   200

Page 1   Normal+...

This is how the document in Figure 5-48 looks on the screen before tab leaders are inserted.

Using a tab leader to create a line

As Figure 5-48 illustrates, you also can use a tab leader to create a horizontal line in your document. For example to create the line that appears next to each section name, place the insertion point marker on one of the section names and insert a left-aligned tab at the $1^1/_2$-inch position on the ruler. Then, insert a right-aligned tab at the 6-inch position. The first tab marks the start of the line where the leader characters will begin, and the second tab marks the end of the line. Now, while the insertion point marker is still on the section-name paragraph, open the Tabs dialog box and click on the tab marker at the 6-inch position on the ruler. Then, choose the fourth Leader option (___) and choose Set.

After you close the Tabs dialog box, the horizontal line won't appear in your document until you press the Tab key. With the insertion point marker positioned just after the section name, press the Tab key twice. The first time you press Tab, Word will move the insertion point marker to the first tab stop, which has no leader. When you press Tab again, Word will move the insertion point marker to the second tab stop at the 6-inch position and, at the same time, use the underline characters to fill in the space between the first and second tabs. Depending on the printer you use, this line may print as a solid line or as a dashed line.

CHARACTER FORMATTING

We've now examined two formatting levels in Word: document-level formatting, which includes page layout, and paragraph-level formatting. Let's now look at character formatting, the last formatting level in our top-down scheme of document design.

When you format characters in your Word document, you need to make a number of decisions about how those characters will look: the font you want to use; the size of the characters; special emphasis like boldfacing, italics, and underlining; the amount of space between characters; and the position of those characters in relation to each other. In this section, we'll show you how to control these factors.

In most cases, you will select the text you want to work with before you apply your character formats. All character formatting options—as the name implies—are applied on a character-by-character basis. Thus, the text you format can be as small as a single character or as large as your entire document. Word will apply your formatting commands only to the text that is highlighted.

As you enter text in a Word document, the new text you type will take on the formatting characteristics of the text immediately preceding it. For example, if you move the insertion point to the middle of a line of text that is formatted in 18-point bold type, any new characters you type at that point will appear in 18-point bold as well. If you want to change formats in midstream, you can choose your new formatting options without selecting any text. Word will simply apply those formats to the insertion point. Then, as you begin typing, the text will appear with the formatting characteristics you have chosen. Those characteristics won't change unless you apply new formats or move the insertion point marker to another part of your document.

Before we launch into a discussion of the many character formatting options available in Word, let's consider a few typographical terms and concepts. These will help you understand and apply Word's character formats.

The Language of Type

As you've seen, Word's default character format is 12-point New York Plain text. However, we've never really explained in any detail what this designation means. In this section, we'll explore briefly the concepts of fonts, point size, serifs, letter spacing, and line spacing.

Fonts

Let's start with the concept of fonts. In typographer's terms, a font is defined as a collection of type of one size and "face." The term "face" refers to style elements like bold, italic, and so forth. Thus, 18-point Helvetica type and 12-point Helvetica type are considered different fonts. Similarly, 18-point Helvetica bold type is considered a different font than 18-point Helvetica italic type. Though all of these faces are part of the same type family, each is defined as a very distinct font.

In Word terminology, however, different type sizes and styles do not constitute different fonts. Instead, each family of type, with all its associated formatting options, is considered part of the same font. For instance, 18-point Helvetica, 10-point Helvetica, 12-point Helvetica bold, and 12-point Helvetica italic are looked upon simply as formatting variations of the same font—Helvetica. Therefore, choosing a font is a separate formatting decision from choosing a size and style.

Type sizes

You may also have wondered what the numeric point size specifications actually represent. It's not too hard to figure out that 18-point type is larger than 10-point, but what do these point sizes really mean?

In typography, a point is a printer's unit of measurement of the height of a letter. A point is $\frac{1}{12}$ of a pica. If that doesn't help much, then you should also know that a pica is $\frac{1}{6}$ of an inch. Thus, there are 72 points to an inch. (One point equals $\frac{1}{12}$ x $\frac{1}{6}$, or $\frac{1}{72}$ of an inch.) In other words, if you select a block of text and tell Word to display it in 72-point type, the characters you select will be 1 inch high. Similarly, if you specify 36 points, your type will be $\frac{1}{2}$ inch high; if you specify 18 points, your type will be $\frac{1}{4}$ inch high, and so forth.

Of course, not every letter in the alphabet is the same height. The letter *h* is almost twice as high as the letter *e*. So how do point sizes relate to the height of any given character in your text? Let's back up a step and consider three terms: ascender, descender, and x-height. As Figure 5-50 illustrates, the x-height represents the height of the "body" of the letter. Ascenders and descenders extend above and below the x-height of the letter.

FIGURE 5-50

48 points — abcdefgh — Ascender / X-Height / Descender

Type size is measured from the top of the ascender to the bottom of the descender.

In typography, the height of a character is determined by the distance from the bottom of the lowest descender to the top of the highest ascender. Therefore, the height of any individual letter in your document will depend on whether that character has an ascender or descender. Even when you specify 36 points for your type, the face of any given letter might be only 30 points high. The remaining height is dedicated to the ascending and descending strokes, like the ascending vertical bars in the letters *h* and *k* and the descending strokes in the letters *g* and *q*.

The x-height of corresponding letters of the same type size and different fonts may also vary significantly. (The x-height is equal to the distance between the mean line and the base line, the two gray lines that appear above and below the bodies of the characters in Figure 5-50.) For example, Table 5-3 shows the letters *h* and *g* in several type styles. All the characters in this table appear in 18-point Plain style. As you can see, however, even though the overall height of the letters is the same, the x-height varies significantly, depending on the emphasis given to ascenders and descenders.

TABLE 5-3

Times	Helvetica	Chicago	Venice	Geneva
hg	hg	**hg**	**hg**	hg
New York	**Avant Garde**	**Courier**	**Dover**	**Palatino**
hg	hg	hg	**h g**	hg

The x-height of fonts of the same type size may vary.

Serifs

An important design decision in formatting any document is whether to use serif or sans serif type. Serifs are the short crosslines that appear at the ends of the main strokes of a letter. As you might have guessed, typefaces that use these crosslines are called serif fonts; those that do not are called sans serif fonts.

In Table 5-3, the serif types are Times, New York, Venice, Courier, Dover, and Palatino. Avant Garde, Helvetica, Chicago, and Geneva are sans serif. Figure 5-51 shows a close-up of the letter *k* in Times font with the serifs circled.

FIGURE 5-51

Serifs are the short crosslines at the ends of the main strokes of a letter.

Letter spacing

Before you select a typeface, you should also know whether that font is proportional or nonproportional—that is, whether the width of the character spaces varies. In proportional fonts (also called variable-pitch fonts), the amount of horizontal space assigned to a letter varies according to the width of that letter. In nonproportional fonts (also called fixed-pitch fonts), every letter is assigned the same amount of space. Typewriters and daisy-wheel printers generally use nonproportional spacing.

Table 5-4 shows some examples of proportional and nonproportional fonts. Generally, we think you'll find that a proportional font lends a more finished appearance to a document.

TABLE 5-4

Proportional			
Times	**Helvetica**	**Chicago**	**Venice**
iwiw	iwiw	**iwiw**	*iwiw*
wiwi	wiwi	**wiwi**	*wiwi*
New York	**Avant Garde**	**Palatino**	**Geneva**
iwiw	iwiw	iwiw	iwiw
wiwi	wiwi	wiwi	wiwi

Nonproportional	
Courier	**Dover**
iwiw	iwiw
wiwi	wiwi

The Macintosh offers both proportional and nonproportional font options.

Line spacing

We introduced the concept of line spacing earlier in this chapter. Line spacing, also referred to as leading, is similar to letter spacing except that it applies to the vertical spacing between lines of type rather than the horizontal spacing between individual letters within a line.

Generally, Word considers line spacing to be a paragraph formatting feature. That is, the line spacing you select applies to an entire paragraph. You can, however, change the vertical position of one or more characters in a paragraph by applying the Superscript and Subscript options. We'll look at superscripting and subscripting later in this section.

Using the Format and Font Menus

Now that we've defined some of the basic elements of typography, let's apply these concepts to a Word document. The simplest way to format characters in your Word document is to select a font, size, or style from the Font or Format menu. As you'll see a little later in this chapter, you also can use the Character dialog box to select all the character formatting options on these menus, as well as additional options.

FIGURE 5-52

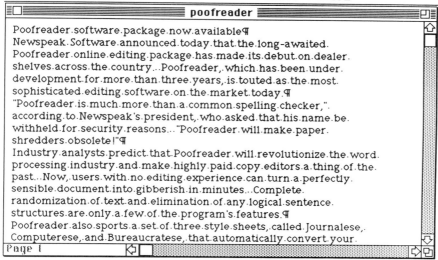

This sample document currently appears in 12-point New York Plain type.

We'll use the sample document that we created in Chapter 4 to illustrate how to apply character formats from the Font and Format menus. Figure 5-52 shows part of that document, which currently appears in 12-point New York Plain type.

Now, suppose we decide to display the first line of our sample document (the title) in 18-point Geneva bold type. We'll begin by selecting the title text, then we'll select the font name Geneva from the Font menu. Next, we'll pull down the Font menu again and choose 18. Finally, we'll choose Bold from the Format menu. Figure 5-53 on the next page shows the results. (We have deselected the text to show the results of our formatting.)

Now, let's format the body of our document to appear in 12-point Times type. After selecting all the text below the title line, we'll pull down the Font menu and choose Times. Since the text is already in 12-point size, there's no need to choose a size from the Font menu. Figure 5-54 on the next page shows the results of choosing a new font.

Notice that all our line breaks have changed because we have selected a different font. Since our characters are now a different size, Word automatically "reflowed" the text within our document margins.

FIGURE 5-53

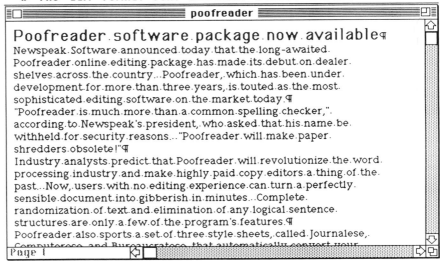

The document heading now appears in 18-point Geneva bold type.

FIGURE 5-54

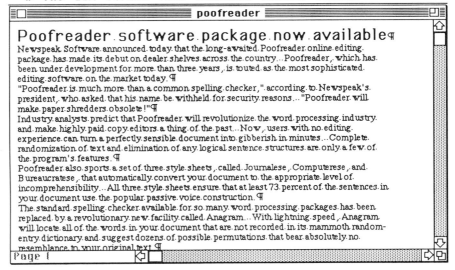

The body of our document now appears in 12-point Times type.

Click on the title of the sample document, then pull down the Font menu, which should look like Figure 5-55. (Your menu may look a bit different, depending on the fonts you have installed on your System file.) As you can see, check marks appear to the left of the Geneva and 18 Point options, indicating the formats that have been applied to the current text. Now, look at the available sizes that appear at the top of the menu.

As you can see in Figure 5-55, all the size options on the Font menu except 24 Point are outlined. The outlined options represent Word's suggested sizes for that font. That is not to say you cannot use another size—only that these are the sizes that have been installed in your System file.

The outlined size options on the Font menu will vary according to the font you have selected. That's because a different range of sizes has been installed for each font on your System file. For example, if you select Chicago from the Font menu, you may see the size options shown in Figure 5-56.

Word's suggested type sizes

FIGURE 5-55

Font
9 Point
10 Point
12 Point
14 Point
✓18 Point
24 Point
Chicago
Courier
✓Geneva
Helvetica
Monaco
Symbol
Symbols
Times

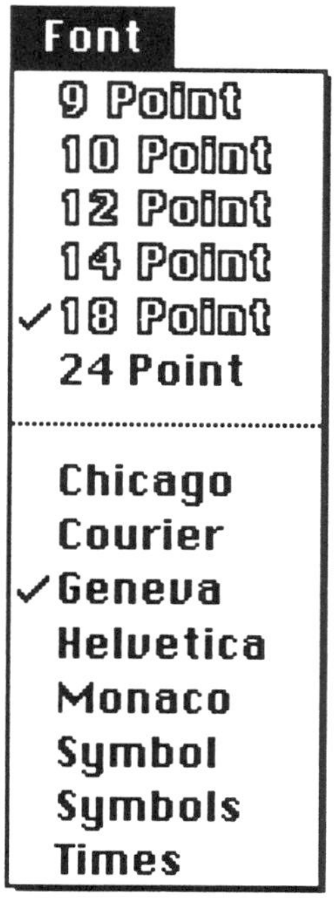

Word displays suggested font sizes in outlined type.

FIGURE 5-56

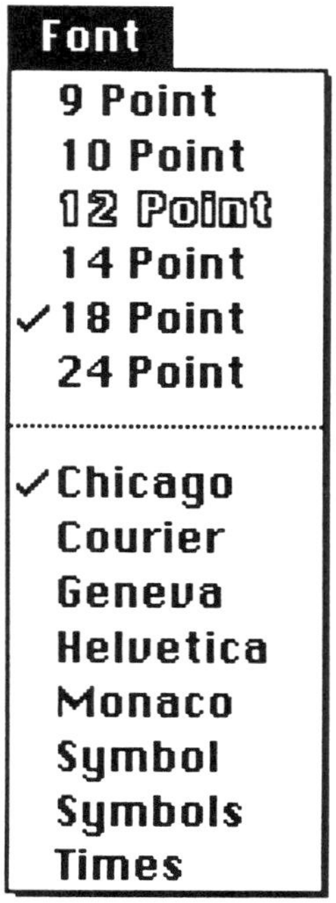

Font
9 Point
10 Point
12 Point
14 Point
✓18 Point
24 Point
✓Chicago
Courier
Geneva
Helvetica
Monaco
Symbol
Symbols
Times

Word's suggested type sizes will vary according to the font you have selected.

When you choose a point size that is not outlined on the Font menu (or if you specify a custom size, which we'll discuss in a moment), Word will extrapolate the size you need from information it has about existing sizes in the System file. Though these scaled fonts may not look too great on your screen, they generally look fine when printed. If you use an ImageWriter printer, you may notice a few jagged edges or some "muddy" characters here and there when the document is printed. If you use a LaserWriter, you'll find that almost any type size between 4 and 127 points looks fine.

Revising a format

You can change the font or size of a block of text simply by selecting that text and choosing a new font or size from the Font menu. Word will move the check mark that appeared to the left of the original option next to the newly selected option.

However, the options on the Format menu work a bit differently. Since you can assign more than one format to the same selection (bold and italic, for example), you must toggle most of the Format menu options on and off by selecting them again. For example, if you select a block of text and then select Bold from the Format menu, Word will display a check mark next to the Bold option. If you choose Bold again with the same text selected, the check mark will disappear, and the text will no longer appear in bold format.

The Plain Text and Plain For Style options

The Plain Text and Plain For Style options are the only Format options that will automatically be deselected when you choose another format. You use these options to remove special formatting you have added to some text. If you used Word 3, you may have found the Plain Text option to be somewhat confusing. Choosing Plain Text from the Format menu in Word 3 did not always result in plain, unformatted text. Rather, this command would apply to your selected text all the character formats defined for the current style. Any additional formats would be stripped from the selected text. For instance, if the style for a paragraph includes boldfacing, then applying Plain Text to some characters in that paragraph would not remove the boldfacing (and might, in fact, add boldfacing if it previously had been removed by manual formatting).

In Word 4, the Plain Text command works more intuitively. When you select some text and then choose the Plain Text command, Word will remove all character formatting from that text except for the font, size, position (superscripting or subscripting), and spacing (condensed or expanded) attributes. Features such as italics, underlining, and color will be stripped away.

The new Plain For Style command in Word 4 has the same effect as the Plain Text command in Word 3. Choosing Plain For Style strips away any manual character formatting, but does not affect the formatting that has been applied as a result of a style. For example, suppose the style for a paragraph specifies 9-point Helvetica italic type. You then select a word in this paragraph, change the font to Times, and add boldfacing. If you later select the word again and choose the Plain

For Style command, Word will return the font to Helvetica and remove the boldfacing. However, the word will remain in italics since that is part of the style definition for the current paragraph. (We'll talk more about using styles in Chapter 8.)

Although the Font and Format menus offer the fastest and easiest way to apply many character formats, you may sometimes need to access some formatting options that are not available on these menus. That's when you'll use the Character... command on the Format menu to open the Character dialog box, shown in Figure 5-57. (You also can open this dialog box by pressing ⌘-d or [F14].) In order to open the Character dialog box, Full Menus must be in effect.

Like the Paragraph dialog box, the Character dialog box reflects the formatting that you have applied to the currently selected text. In Figure 5-57, the dialog box shows the format settings for the title of our sample document in Figure 5-54. If your selection includes characters whose formats vary, the check boxes in the dialog box will appear grayed and the other options will be blank.

**The Character
Dialog Box**

FIGURE 5-57

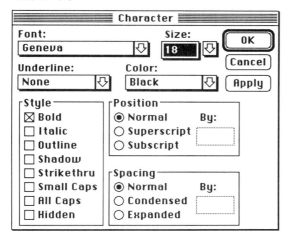

*The Character dialog box
also can be used to apply
character formatting.*

As you can see, the Character dialog box offers more options than the Font and Format menus. In addition to the Bold, Italic, Underline, Outline, and Shadow options that appear on the Format menu, the Character dialog box offers Strikethru, Small Caps, All Caps, and Hidden. A dropdown list box gives you several underline options: None, Single, Word, Double, and Dotted. (Notice that there is no Plain Text option in the Character dialog box. To revert to "plain" text, you'll need to deselect all the character format options and choose the None Underline option.)

The Character dialog box also includes dropdown list boxes for fonts, type sizes, and colors. The Position options allow you to assign superscripting and subscripting to characters. The Spacing options in the lower-right corner of the dialog box allow you to adjust the spacing between characters, creating condensed and expanded text. We'll look at all the Character dialog box options in detail, beginning with the character styles—Bold, Italic, Outline, and so forth.

Character styles

You can select almost any combination of character styles to format text in your document. Just click in the check boxes to select the character formats you want or choose one of the Underline options from the dropdown list. By the way, the Underline options are organized in a list because these options are mutually exclusive. Although you can combine underlining with any of the check box options, you can use only one type of underlining at a time on a given text selection. Also, among the check box options, the All Caps and Small Caps options are mutually exclusive.

Figure 5-58 illustrates several combinations of character format options. All the characters in this document appear in 18-point Times type.

The All Caps and Small Caps options

The All Caps and Small Caps options are interesting in that they appear to change the case of the characters you have entered into your document. When you use All Caps, Word will display the selected text in uppercase letters. However, the underlying characters will still be in the case that you originally typed. For example, if you type the word *microsoft* in all lowercase letters, Word will display that word as *MICROSOFT* after you apply the All Caps format.

Even more interesting is that when you use the Small Caps option, Word displays your text in capital letters, but it also reduces the size of any characters that were originally entered in lowercase. For example, if you format the word *WordWrap* in small caps, Word will display that word as WORDWRAP. As you can see, the appearance of the two *W* characters has not changed. However, the letters O, R, D, R, A, and P now appear in the next smaller type size in capital letters. Again, the underlying characters have not changed. If you remove the Small Caps format, your text will revert to its original form.

The All Caps and Small Caps options are convenient for quickly changing the case of letters without retyping. However, Word will still consider these characters to be lowercase. (As you'll see in the next chapter, the distinction between uppercase and lowercase letters becomes significant when you use Word's Find..., Change..., Spelling..., and Hyphenate... commands.)

We mentioned a moment ago that Word will use the next smallest point size to display lowercase letters when you use the Small Caps option. However, this does not necessarily mean that Word uses the next standard option in the Size list in the Character dialog box for that font. When you use Small Caps, Word will use the sequence of point sizes shown in Figure 5-59 on page 162 to format your lowercase letters.

FIGURE 5-58

Plain
Bold
Italic
Bold Italic
<u>Plain Underline</u>
<u>Word</u> <u>Underline</u>
<u>Double Underline</u>
<u>Dotted Underline</u>
~~Strikethru~~
Outline
Bold Outline
Shadow
Bold Shadow
Outline Shadow
Bold Outline Shadow
Bold Outline Shadow Italic
<u>**Bold Outline Shadow Underline**</u>
SMALL CAPS
BOLD SMALL CAPS
ALL CAPS
BOLD ALL CAPS
BOLD OUTLINE SHADOW SMALL CAPS
BOLD OUTLINE SHADOW ALL CAPS

You can combine style options to create different typographical effects in Word.

FIGURE 5-59

Word uses this sequence of point sizes to scale your letters when you use the Small Caps option.

For example, if you use Small Caps to format 18-point characters, Word will display the lowercase letters in 14 point. If you use Small Caps to format 24-point characters, Word will display the lowercase letters in 18 point. If you use Small Caps to format some text whose size is between the sizes shown in Figure 5-59, Word will use the next smallest size for the lowercase letters. For example, if you format some 20-point text with Small Caps, Word will display the lowercase letters in 18 point.

Hidden text

Although the Hidden option is grouped with the other character styles such as Bold, Italic, and Small Caps, this feature is really in a category by itself. When you apply the Hidden format to text, you can suppress the display of that text on your screen and/or in your printed documents. (We'll show you how to hide text in your printed documents when we talk about printing in Chapter 7.) Though it is used primarily for flagging special items, like PostScript commands and index notations, hidden text is great for entering notes and questions that can be hidden from view when not needed.

You can also use the Hidden format when you need to vary the content of a document. For example, in Figure 5-60, we added a new paragraph to our sample news release that refers to a complimentary review copy of the Poofreader software. We plan to send these complimentary copies only to selected persons on our mailing list.

One way to vary the content of the document for different readers is to hide the optional paragraph when we don't need it. As you can see in Figure 5-60, when we assign the Hidden format to the last paragraph in our sample document, Word displays a gray underline to indicate that the text is hidden. (Unfortunately, this underline is identical to the underline that Word displays when you assign the Dotted Underline format to your text. If you're using both formats, be careful not to confuse the two.)

To suppress the display of Hidden text in your document window, we would select Preferences... from the Edit menu. (Full Menus must be in effect before you can select the Preferences... command.) In the Preferences dialog box, we could click on the Show Hidden Text option to deselect it, as shown in Figure 5-61.

When you turn off the Show Hidden Text setting, any text that has been assigned the Hidden format will disappear from your screen, but will remain in your document "behind the scenes." You can display the hidden text again at any time by reissuing the Preferences… command and reselecting the Show Hidden Text setting.

FIGURE 5-60

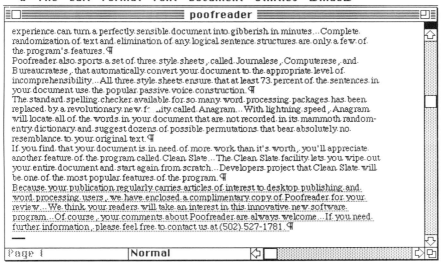

Since the last paragraph in this document is optional, we assigned it the Hidden format.

FIGURE 5-61

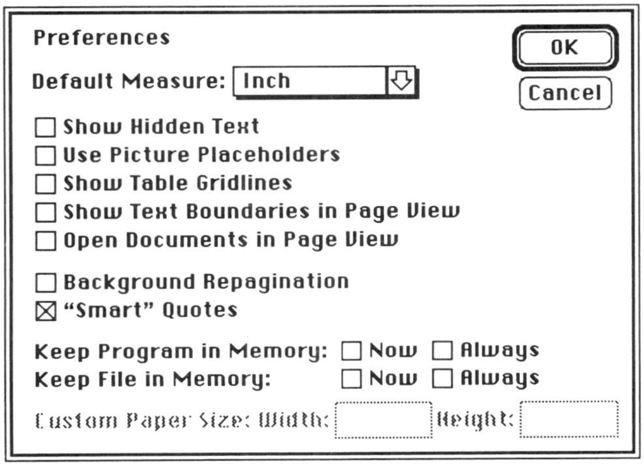

To suppress the display of hidden text, deselect the Show Hidden Text option in the Preferences dialog box.

*Specifying a
font and size*

When you open the Character dialog box, the font that has been applied to the current text selection will appear at the top of the dropdown Font list box. (If your selection includes a variety of formatting, no font name will be displayed. This is true even if all the text is the same font but, for example, includes a couple of different type sizes.) By displaying the dropdown Font list, you can see all the fonts that have been installed on your System file. In many cases, this list will include fonts that do not appear on your Font menu. (In Chapter 14, we'll show you how to customize the Font menu to include any combination of font names.) To apply a font to the current selection, just select its name from the list.

The dropdown Size list box displays the standard type sizes for the currently selected font. As you might have guessed, this list box contains the point size options that appear outlined on the Font menu for the selected font. Because Word displays the sizes in a combination list box and edit bar, you can either select one of the standard options from the dropdown list or enter your own custom size. For example, if you choose the Chicago font from the Font list box, Word may display only one size option, 12. Although this is the only standard size installed on the System file for this font, you can type your own custom size in the edit bar at the top of the Size list box. This value can be any whole number from 4 through 127. Word will not accept decimal values like 10.5 in the Size edit bar.

*The Position
options*

You can also format your text to appear in Superscript or Subscript style by selecting one of the Position options on the right side of the Character dialog box. Of course, the Normal option is the default. The Superscript and Subscript options are used most commonly for mathematical notations like exponents and fractions. However, you may also be able to find some more creative applications for subscripting and superscripting.

To understand the function of the Superscript and Subscript options, you need to visualize all the text in your document as sitting on a base line. This base line appears in the graphic that we used to illustrate type size in Figure 5-50. The Superscript and Subscript options tell Word to shift the selected characters above or below this base line.

When you click the Superscript option in the Character dialog box, Word will automatically display the default value *3 pt* in the By edit bar. Similarly, the default Subscript setting is *2 pt.* You can change this By value to control the distance between the base line of the superscript or subscript character and the base line of the rest of the text on the line. Word will accept any value between 0 and 63.5; however, it will generally round your By setting to the nearest half-point.

To see how superscripting and subscripting can be used, consider the sample text in Figure 5-62. This text contains two mathematical expressions that are very difficult to read because there is no way to distinguish the base and exponent values from the rest of the text.

FIGURE 5-62

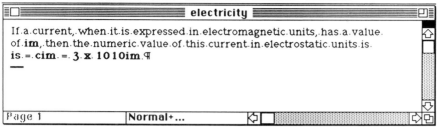

The mathematical expressions in bold type are difficult to read because there is no way to distinguish a base or an exponent.

To correct this problem, we could select the desired characters one at a time, issue the Character... command, and click on the Superscript or Subscript options. Figure 5-63 shows our sample line of text, formatted in Word's default 3-point Superscript and 2-point Subscript.

FIGURE 5-63

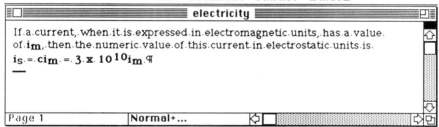

Superscripting and subscripting make the mathematical expressions much easier to read.

Keep in mind that Word may have to adjust your line spacing to prevent the superscript and subscript characters from overlapping succeeding or preceding lines of text. Adding a 3-point superscript to a line of text can have the same effect as using a type size three points larger than the rest of the text on the line. If you find the change in line spacing unattractive, you may be able to avoid this problem by reducing the size of the superscript or subscript characters. For example, notice the gap between the second and third lines of sample text in Figure 5-63. If we change the size of the superscript and subscript characters from 12 points to 9 points, we can close up the line spacing again, as shown in Figure 5-64.

FIGURE 5-64

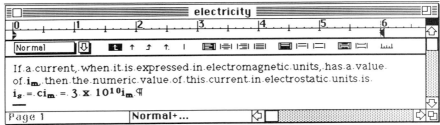

To eliminate the extra line spacing, you can reduce the size of the superscript or subscript characters.

Though the Superscript and Subscript options are used most often for mathematical and scientific expressions, a little imagination can lead to interesting effects. For example, Figure 5-65 shows a logo designed with the Superscript and Subscript options. We created the "rollercoaster" effect by formatting the text in 18-point Times Outline type, then selecting each character in turn and assigning a different Superscript or Subscript setting.

FIGURE 5-65

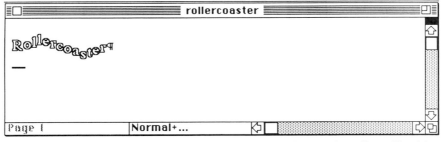

You can use superscripting and subscripting to create interesting effects like this.

Controlling character spacing

Word also lets you control the spacing between characters in your document with three Spacing options in the Character dialog box: Normal, Condensed, and Expanded. The Normal Spacing option is the default.

When you select the Expanded or Condensed options, Word will activate the By edit bar. The default setting for the Expanded format is 3 points, and the default setting for the Condensed format is 1.5 points. However, you can type your own spacing setting in the By edit bar. When you are using the Condensed option, Word will accept any value from 0 to 1.75 points. When you are using the Expanded option, you can use a By setting from 0 to 14 points. Although you can specify decimal values, Word will round the decimal portion of your By setting down to the nearest .25 increment. And, for printing, Word truncates all decimal values to 0. Thus, if you enter a By setting of 1.65, Word will round it to 1.5 the next time you open the Character dialog box, and will use a setting of 1 for printing.

Figure 5-66 illustrates the relationship between the Normal, Condensed, and Expanded formats, respectively. All three lines of text are set in 18-point Times Plain type.

FIGURE 5-66

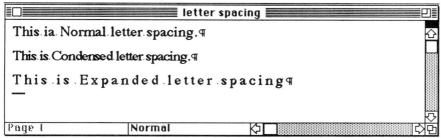

The Normal, Condensed, and Expanded Spacing options control the spacing between characters in your text.

Letter spacing can often be used creatively for special display type. For example, to create the logo shown in Figure 5-67, we formatted both lines of text to appear in 14-point Times type. We used the All Caps option to format the first line, then we used the 13-point Expanded Spacing setting to widen the character spaces in the first line.

FIGURE 5-67

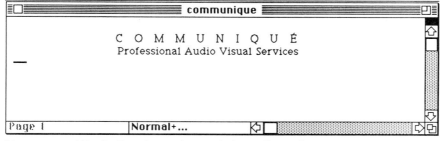

You can use Word's Spacing options to balance lines of text.

Color

Word allows you to apply one of eight colors to a text selection. The default Color choice is Black. Using different colors throughout a document allows you to do such things as flagging certain kinds of text or emphasizing words or phrases. Of course, you must have a color monitor in order to see different colors of text on your screen. If you don't have a color monitor, you can still assign different colors in the Character dialog box. Those colors won't show up until you view your document on a color monitor or print it with a color printer.

To change the color of some text, just select it and choose Character... from the Format menu. In the Character dialog box, pull down the color list and choose the color you want to use: Black, Blue, Cyan, Green, Magenta, Red, Yellow, or White. When you choose the Apply or OK button, Word will change the color of the text you've selected.

Character Formatting Shortcuts

In addition to the Font and Format menus and Character dialog box, Word gives you a number of keyboard shortcuts for formatting characters. To use these shortcuts, you press the Shift and ⌘ keys as you type a character key.

For example, to increase or decrease the size of your text, press Shift-⌘-> or Shift-⌘-<. The effects of the Shift-⌘-> and Shift-⌘-< key combinations will depend on the current type size you are using. If you are currently using 10-point type and you press Shift-⌘->, you'll get 12-point type. If you are currently using 18-point type and you press Shift-⌘->, you'll get 24-point type. Figure 5-59 on page 162 shows the series of point sizes that Word will use in response to your Shift-⌘-> and Shift-⌘-< keystrokes. If you are currently between sizes, Word will increase or decrease the point size to the next nearest size. That is, if you are using 16-point type and you press Shift-⌘->, you'll get 18-point type. (By the way, if you use the Shift-⌘-+ or Shift-⌘- - key combinations to invoke superscripting or subscripting, Word will also decrease the point size of the text according to the series of sizes shown in Figure 5-59.)

Table 5-5 contains a summary of the Shift-⌘-key shortcuts that you can use to format characters in Word.

As with the Format and Font menu commands, if you have highlighted text when you use one of these Shift-⌘-key combinations, Word will assign that format to the selected text. Alternatively, if you want to begin typing in a new format, you can place your insertion point marker at the desired location and use one of the key sequences to specify your new format. When you begin typing, Word will apply that format to all subsequent text until you click on another location in your document or change formats again.

You can toggle many of these formatting options on or off by repeating the same keystrokes. For example, suppose you have selected a block of text and pressed Shift-⌘-] to assign the Word Underline format to it. Then, you decide (too late to use the Undo command) that you did not want to underline that text after all. Just reselect the text block, if necessary, and press Shift-⌘-] a second time to remove the underline formatting from the selected block.

TABLE 5-5

Format	Shift-⌘- Key	Toggle	Full Menus Only
All Caps	k	•	
Bold	b	•	
Change Font	e (plus font name)		•
Decrease Size	<		
Dotted Underline	\	•	•
Double Underline	[	•	•
Hidden	x	•	•
Increase Size	>		
Italic	i	•	
Outline	d	•	
Plain	Spacebar		
Shadow	w	•	
Small Caps	h	•	•
Strikethru	/	•	•
Subscript 2 point	-		
Superscript 3 points	+		
Underline	u	•	
Word Underline	]	•	•

You can press Shift and ⌘ in combination with other keys to invoke character formatting.

Similarly, if you are in the process of typing a sentence and you need to underline the next several words, you can press Shift-⌘-u to begin underlining with the next character, then press Shift-⌘-u again when you have finished typing the text you want to underline. The next characters that you type will appear in Plain Text format (or whatever format you were using before you invoked underlining).

Although some of the formatting options shown in Table 5-5 cannot be toggled on and off, you can still activate and deactivate them as you are typing by pressing Shift-⌘-Spacebar. For example, if you need to apply the Superscript option as you are typing, you can press Shift-⌘-+, type the characters you want to appear in superscript, then press Shift-⌘-Spacebar to revert to the Plain For Style format. Of course, pressing Shift-⌘-Spacebar will also remove any other special character formats, like boldfacing or italics, unless these are part of the style definition.

The change font shortcut is a bit different than the other Shift-⌘ shortcuts because you must type a font name after pressing Shift-⌘-e. For example, suppose you are currently using the New York font and decide that you want to switch to Geneva. You can select the text you want to reformat, or click in the spot where you want to begin using the Geneva type, and press Shift-⌘-e to signal a font change.

Word will display the prompt *Font* in the status box at the lower-left corner of your screen, as shown in Figure 5-68. Just type the name of the font you want to use (the characters that you type will appear in the status box) and press Return or Enter.

FIGURE 5-68

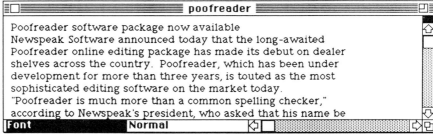

When you press Shift-⌘-e to signal a font change, Word will prompt you for a font name.

If you decide not to change fonts, press the ⌘ and period keys (⌘-.) to cancel the change, or click anywhere in the document window. Also, you can generally abbreviate the font name that you type in response to Word's *Font* prompt. As long as you type enough characters to uniquely identify the font you want to use, the shortcut will work. For example, since we have only one font installed on our System file that begins with the letter *g*, typing *g* will suffice to invoke the Geneva font. To distinguish between the Chicago and Courier fonts, however, you must type at least two characters—*ch* or *co*.

FORMATTING WITH SPECIAL CHARACTERS

So far, we have shown you how to use formatting techniques to control the appearance of characters in your document. Word also offers a number of special characters that can be helpful as you're formatting a document. These include "smart" quotes, nonbreaking spaces, nonbreaking hyphens, and optional hyphens. We'll wrap up our formatting chapter with a look at these characters.

"Smart" Quotes

With Word and a LaserWriter, it's easy to create documents of near-typeset quality. One way to enhance the appearance of your documents even further is to use curved quotation marks and apostrophes (" " ' ') rather than the straight marks that can be produced on a typewriter. Of course, you can create these marks from the Macintosh keyboard, but the process is somewhat awkward, requiring a combination of the Option, Shift, [, and] keys. Word 4 offers a feature that will automatically convert straight quotation marks and apostrophes (" and ') into curved marks as you enter text. To use "smart" quotes, as they're called, just choose the

Preferences… command on the Edit menu and select the "Smart" Quotes option. When you do this, Word will not change any straight quotes that you have already entered in a document. However, each time you type a " or ', Word will enter a ", ", ', or ' in your document.

Spaces

A nonbreaking space is a space that Word treats like a character. If you place a nonbreaking space (or several nonbreaking spaces) between two words, Word will not split those words at the end of a line. As far as Word can tell, the two words and the nonbreaking space are a single unit.

To create a nonbreaking space, just type Option-Spacebar or ⌘-Spacebar. If Show ¶ is in effect, each nonbreaking space will appear as a ⌐ on your screen. Of course, these special markers will not appear in your printed document; instead, Word will print a blank space.

Nonbreaking spaces can be useful when you want to keep two or more words together on the same line. For example, when you enter a date like *February 23, 1989*, in a document, it is a good idea to enter nonbreaking spaces between *February* and *23* and before the year *1989*. You also might use nonbreaking spaces between the different portions of a multipart number, such as a social security number, between a person's first name and middle initial, and between the words that comprise a single proper noun, such as New York.

One important characteristic of a nonbreaking space is that it always has a specific width. You may have noticed that the width of a regular space may vary in a justified paragraph as Word increases or decreases the space between words to keep the left and right margins aligned. A nonbreaking space, on the other hand, is always about the width of a lowercase *n*. (Word adjusts the width of nonbreaking spaces according to the point size you have selected for your text and any character formatting you may have assigned. For instance, a nonbreaking space that appears in the middle of a line of bold text will be slightly larger than a nonbreaking space that falls in the middle of plain text.)

Hyphens

In addition to a regular hyphen, Word 4 offers an optional hyphen and a nonbreaking hyphen. For the most part, Word treats a regular hyphen, which you enter by pressing the - key, like any other character in your document. If the word that is hyphenated happens to fall at the end of a line, however, Word may split that word between two lines. All the characters to the left of the hyphen and the hyphen itself will appear on the first line, and the characters to the right of the hyphen will wrap to the beginning of the next line.

However, there may be occasions when you don't want to split a hyphenated word between two lines. Similarly, words you wouldn't normally hyphenate may need to be split in order to balance lines of text. Word offers two special characters to help you handle these situations: optional hyphens and nonbreaking hyphens.

Optional hyphens

As the name implies, an optional hyphen appears only when the hyphenated word is broken at the end of a line. When you use Word's Hyphenate... command to insert hyphens automatically, Word will insert only optional hyphens. (The Hyphenate... command is discussed in detail in Chapter 6.) If you want to create an optional hyphen manually, press the ⌘ key as you type the hyphen. An optional hyphen appears on the screen as ⁻ when the Show ¶ feature is activated. When you choose Hide ¶, an optional hyphen will not appear at all, unless it occurs at a line break. If an optional hyphen occurs at a line break, it will look like a regular hyphen and will appear on the screen regardless of whether the Show ¶ feature is activated.

We recommend that you use an optional hyphen whenever you hyphenate a word to break it at the end of a line. That way, if you later revise your document so that the word does *not* fall at the end of a line, Word will not hyphenate the word in the middle of a line.

Nonbreaking hyphens

The second kind of special hyphen in Word is the nonbreaking hyphen. A nonbreaking hyphen is similar to a nonbreaking space. If you hyphenate a word, such as *great-grandfather*, and that word occurs at the end of a line, Word may break the word at the hyphen. If you don't want a word to break at the hyphen, then you should use a nonbreaking hyphen. To create a nonbreaking hyphen, press the ⌘ key as you type a ~. You don't need to press the Shift key as you type ⌘ and ~.

For example, suppose you are writing about the software program Lotus 1-2-3. To prevent Word from breaking *1-2-3* at the end of a line, you should always use nonbreaking hyphens between the *1* and *2* and between the *2* and *3*. Nonbreaking hyphens are always visible on your screen, though they are marked by the ⁼ symbol when Show ¶ is activated and look like regular hyphens when you choose Hide ¶. When Word prints a nonbreaking hyphen, it looks like a regular hyphen.

Other hyphens

You can use the hyphen key to create dashes as well as hyphens. A dash (or "long hyphen") is often used to introduce a pause in a sentence or to set apart an explanatory phrase. Word offers both a long dash and a short dash. If you want to create a long dash (—), type Shift-Option-Hyphen. If you want to create a short dash (–), type Option-Hyphen. Word will treat the — and – characters just as it does a normal hyphen.

Other Characters

Most of the text we have shown in our sample documents so far has been created by standard keyboard characters that you enter into your document by typing a letter or number, or by pressing the Shift key and typing a letter or number. Some additional characters are also available through the ⌘ and Option keys. These characters vary according to the font you're using at any given time. For example, if you are working with the Geneva font, the Shift-Option-~ key combination will yield a ✦ character. In the Times font, however, the same key combination would result in a Ÿ character. You can use the Key Caps desk accessory, described on page 12, to see the various characters available in each font.

Another important character is the ellipsis (…), which you can enter into your document by pressing the Option key as you type a semicolon (Option-;). Although the ellipsis looks like three period characters, Word treats it as a single character. Therefore, Word will not change the spacing between the periods when you justify text, and will always keep the three periods on the same line.

The Symbol font

Word's Symbol font is full of special characters and symbols that you'll find convenient for entering scientific and mathematical text. To make it easier to use the Symbol font, Microsoft has provided a handy Shift-⌘-key shortcut to let you enter single symbol characters into your text as you are typing. Rather than stopping to issue the Character… command or choosing Symbol from the Font menu, just press Shift-⌘-q, then type the Symbol font character that you want to use. (Of course, the Symbol font must be installed in your System file in order to use this technique.)

**Using
ASCII Codes**

ASCII, which stands for American Standard Code for Information Interchange, is the language that Word and other programs use to define the characters you enter into your document. Every letter, number, punctuation mark, and other symbol is defined by an ASCII code. Even special instructions, like carriage returns, paragraph breaks, page breaks, and tabs, are defined in an ASCII code table.

Word allows you to create characters by typing their ASCII codes. Word also can tell you the ASCII code for any character you select in a document. To enter a character by typing its ASCII code, first make sure that either no text is selected in your document or that your selection is larger than a single character. Then, just type Option-⌘-q. The prompt *Code* will replace the page number in the status box at the lower-left corner of your screen, as shown in Figure 5-69 on the following page. You can then type any ASCII code, using numbers at the top of the keyboard or NumLock and the numeric keypad, and press Return. Word will insert into your document the character represented by that code. (If you enter an invalid code, Word will beep and take no action until you correct the error.)

After you've pressed Option-⌘-q once during a Word session, you can simply click on the page number in the status box to invoke the *Code* prompt. Naturally, you won't use this technique to create characters that you can type from the keyboard. However, Word's ability to interpret ASCII codes can be very helpful when you need to create certain special symbols or foreign alphabet characters. Appendix 3 contains a table listing the ASCII codes you can use in your Word documents and the character associated with each.

As we mentioned, Word can tell you the ASCII code for any character that you select. This can be helpful if you need to search for strange characters that show up in a file that's been imported from another program. (These characters may be represented as boxes on your screen.) To find a character's ASCII code, just select that character and press Option-⌘-q. The code for the selected character will appear in the status box, replacing the page number. After pressing Option-⌘-q once, you can simply click on the page number in the status box to see the ASCII code for a selected character.

FIGURE 5-69

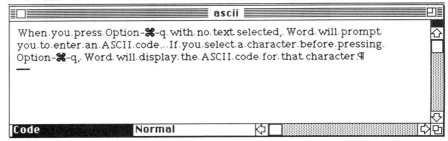

When you press Option-⌘-q with no text selected, or when your selection is larger than a single character, Word prompts you for an ASCII code.

Other Techniques

In addition to the many special characters available directly from the keyboard, Word allows you to create sophisticated special effects by entering character formulas into your document. We'll talk more about this topic in Chapter 13.

EDITING 6

You have a number of tools at your disposal for editing text in Word. In Chapter 4, we covered Word's most basic editing functions: inserting, deleting, and overwriting text. In this chapter, we'll introduce you to Word's "scissor and glue" functions—the Cut, Copy, and Paste commands—and to Word 4's new Clear command.

Next, we'll explore some of Word's more sophisticated editing features, like finding and changing, spell-checking, and automatic hyphenating. We'll also show you how the Clipboard and Scrapbook facilities are designed to aid your editing tasks.

As with formatting, generally, your first task in editing a document is to select the text you want to work with. We suggest that you refer to the selection and navigation techniques presented in Chapter 4 as you practice the editing concepts presented here. By learning to select text blocks quickly and accurately, you will speed your editing time significantly.

COPYING AND MOVING TEXT

Word's Cut, Copy, and Paste commands are the scissors and glue that make editing your text much faster than working with hard copy documents. With just a few keystrokes or mouse clicks, you can easily reorganize your document or repeat a block of text—and simultaneously reflow the entire document to adjust for your changes. You can also copy items from one Word document to another or even from one Macintosh program to another. We'll cover copying and moving text within Word in this chapter. In Chapter 15, we'll show you how to share information with other Macintosh programs.

Moving and copying text in Word is a two-step process: First, you select the text you want to copy or move, then you select the spot where you want to paste that text. Word also offers a few keyboard shortcuts that let you copy character or paragraph formats only and select text to paste at the current insertion point. Let's start with the more straightforward Copy, Cut, and Paste commands, then look at these handy keyboard shortcuts.

Copying Text

Rather than typing the same block of text over and over, you can use Word's Copy and Paste commands to copy a selected block and repeat it in one or more locations throughout your document. As you might expect, the Copy command can be a great time-saver when you need to duplicate a word, a paragraph, or even an entire document in another location.

To copy a block of text, begin by highlighting the characters you want to copy, then select the Copy command from the Edit menu. Now, point to the location where you want the copy block to appear, then click. When you select Paste from the Edit menu, a copy of the text you selected will appear to the left of the insertion point. The insertion point marker will appear at the end of the pasted block. If you are pasting a large block of text, Word will automatically scroll the end of the pasted block into view for you. The original block of text will remain unchanged.

For example, suppose you want to insert the word *revitalization* to the left of the word *efforts* in the twelfth line of the sample document in Figure 6-1. Rather than retyping the word, you could double-click on the word *revitalization* in the sixth line of the document (to select the word and the trailing blank space), issue the Copy command, click to the left of the word *efforts* in the twelfth line, and issue the Paste command. As you can see in Figure 6-2, a duplicate of the copied word will appear to the left of the word *efforts*.

By the way, you can save yourself a few mouse clicks by pressing ⌘-c to copy the selected block of text, then—after you have selected a new insertion point— pressing ⌘-v to paste it into another location. If you have an expanded SE or Mac II keyboard, you can press [F3] to copy and [F4] to paste.

Replacing as you paste

If you want to paste your copy block over an existing block of text, select the text you want to overwrite before issuing the Paste command. Returning to the sample document shown in Figure 6-2, suppose you want to change the word *revitalization* that you pasted into line 12 to read *preservation* instead. Simply double-click on the word *preservation* from the second line and press ⌘-c or [F3]. Then, double-click on the word *revitalization* in the twelfth line and press ⌘-v or [F4]. As you can see in Figure 6-3 on page 178, Word overwrites the selected text with the pasted text.

FIGURE 6-1

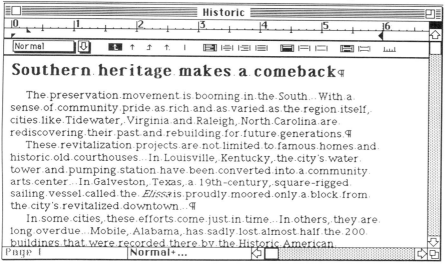

We need to insert the word revitalization *in the twelfth line of this sample document.*

FIGURE 6-2

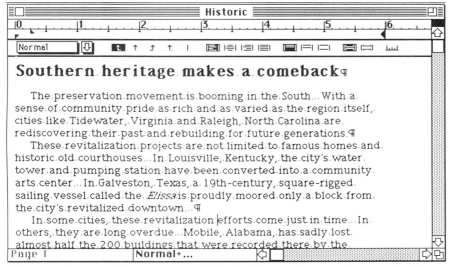

When you issue the Paste command, Word will insert the copy block to the left of the insertion point.

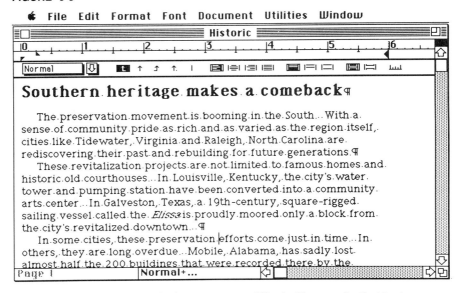

FIGURE 6-3

If you select a block of text before you paste, Word will overwrite that text.

Moving Text

Moving text in Word is much like copying, except that the original selection is removed from its current location and pasted to another location. To move a block of text, begin by selecting the characters you want to move, then select Cut from the Edit menu. Now, place the insertion point marker at the spot where you want the text to appear, and select Paste from the Edit menu.

To illustrate, let's move the sentence that begins *In Louisville* in Figure 6-3 to follow the sentence that begins *In Galveston*. Begin by pressing the ⌘ key and clicking on the sentence that begins *In Louisville*. Select the Cut command from the Edit menu, then click just to the right of the sentence that begins *In Galveston* and issue the Paste command. You'll need to press the Spacebar twice to insert the proper number of blank spaces between the two sentences. Figure 6-4 shows the results.

Again, when you paste a block of text, Word will insert the text to the left of the insertion point, then move the insertion point marker to the end of the pasted block. As you would expect, Word reflows the area from which you cut the text as well as the area in which you pasted the text. You can speed up the move process by pressing ⌘-x or [F2] to cut a selection and ⌘-v or [F4] to paste it into another location.

FIGURE 6-4

Use the Cut and Paste commands to move a block of text.

As with the Copy and Paste procedure, if you make a selection before you issue the Paste command, Word will delete the selected block and paste the cut selection in its place.

Replacing as you paste

For instance, suppose you want to move the sentence *The preservation movement is booming in the South.* in the second line of Figure 6-4 to the first line in the document. Since you want this sentence to serve as your headline, you will need to replace the existing headline with the selected phrase as you paste.

Begin by pressing the ⌘ key and clicking on the first sentence in the second paragraph, then press ⌘-x or [F2]. Next, highlight the phrase that begins *Southern heritage* in the first line and press ⌘-v or [F4]. Figure 6-5 on the following page shows the result.

As you can see, Word replaced the headline with the selected sentence and retained the sentence's original character formatting. This brings us to our next topic: copying and moving formats.

When you copy or cut a block of text and paste it in another location, Word will generally retain the original character formats you assigned to that text as it pastes the characters in the new location. When you copy or move an entire paragraph, Word will also retain the paragraph formats of the copied selection when you paste. If you copy or move only a portion of a paragraph, however—that is, if the ¶ marker is not included in your selection—Word will use the paragraph formats you have assigned to the surrounding text in the paste area.

Copying and moving formats

FIGURE 6-5

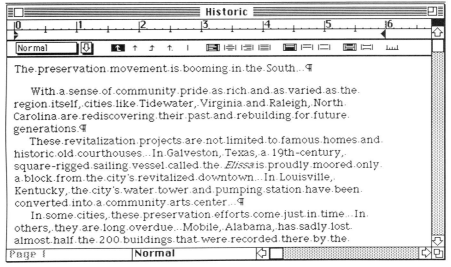

You can also use the Paste command to overwrite a block of text.

You may need to revise the character and paragraph formats of the pasted text to match the formats of the surrounding text. Often, you can use Word's Format From and Format To shortcuts to speed up this process. We'll show you those techniques in a few pages.

The effects of your Paste command may vary slightly if you are using Word's style sheet facility to format your document. In Chapter 8, we'll talk about the effects of editing text that is formatted with style sheets.

Pasting to other Word documents

There may be occasions when you want to use the same block of text in two or more Word documents. Rather than retyping this text, you can copy the original block to your other documents. For example, Figure 6-6 shows two document windows open on the Word DeskTop. Suppose you want to repeat the paragraph that is displayed in the top document window (sales report1) in the second document (sales report2).

First, click in the sales report1 document window to activate it if it isn't already active, then double-click in the invisible selection bar next to the paragraph you want to copy. Now, issue the Copy command and click in the sales report2 window to activate it. Point to the spot where you want to paste the paragraph (or make a selection if you want to overwrite some existing text in the second window) and issue the Paste command. We decided to insert the copied paragraph in front of the paragraph that begins *As for our*, so we clicked in front of the word *As* before issuing the Paste command. As you can see in Figure 6-7, a copy of the paragraph from sales report1 now appears in the sales report2 window.

FIGURE 6-6

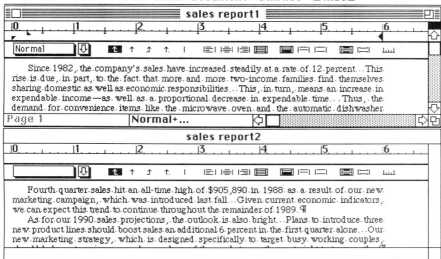

We want to copy the paragraph in the top document window into the bottom document window.

FIGURE 6-7

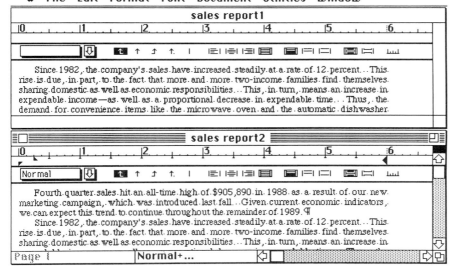

A copy of the paragraph now appears in the bottom document window as well.

By the way, you can use Word's File and Window menu commands to open new documents, retrieve existing files, or activate an open document window before you paste. Word will remember your copy block until you issue another Copy or Cut command, or until you quit from the program.

The Clipboard

When you issue the Cut or Copy command, Word places the text you have selected on the Clipboard. The Clipboard is a temporary holding area where Word stores your cut and copy blocks until they are needed.

Although the Clipboard can accommodate any size text block—ranging from one character to an entire document (memory permitting)—it is very important to understand that the Clipboard can hold only one selection at a time. If you issue the Cut or Copy command, then issue another Cut or Copy command before you paste the first selection back into your document, that selection will no longer be on the Clipboard. Of course, if you are only copying the text, you have lost nothing but time. You must go back and reselect the block and issue a new Copy command. However, if you have issued the Cut command, then cut or copied another block of text before pasting the first block, that first block will be lost.

You can paste a cut or copied selection as many times as you like, as long as you don't overwrite the contents of the Clipboard by issuing another Copy or Cut command. Word will remember the current contents of your Clipboard even if you issue other commands or edit your document before you paste. You can even open and edit new documents without losing the contents of your Clipboard.

If you are ever in doubt about the last selection you have cut or copied, you can select the Show Clipboard command from the Window menu to see the contents of the Clipboard. Figure 6-8 shows the contents of the Clipboard after we copied the paragraph in Figure 6-6.

FIGURE 6-8

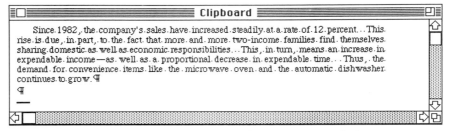

The Clipboard window reflects the last selection you cut or copied.

The Clear command

Word 4 offers a new feature on the Edit menu called the Clear command. This command clears highlighted text without placing it on the Clipboard. If you are storing some text on the Clipboard for pasting to various parts of your document, the Clear command will not disturb that text. You can also use the Backspace key to delete text without disturbing the Clipboard. The Undo command on the Edit menu also undoes the actions of the Clear command.

While the Clipboard saves only one piece of data at a time, the Scrapbook can hold as many items as you can accommodate on your startup disk. In fact, the Scrapbook is a great place to store commonly used text, graphics, and other data. As you'll learn in Chapter 15, you can even use the Scrapbook to transfer information from one application to another. (You can also save commonly used data in a glossary file, as explained in Chapter 13, but you won't be able to transfer that data to other programs.)

The Scrapbook

If you have issued a Cut or Copy command and want to save that piece of text for later use, you can place it in your Scrapbook. Then, you can freely cut and copy other blocks of text without fear of losing the first block. To place a selection in the Scrapbook, select the text you want to cut or copy, then select Scrapbook from the menu.

If you have copied a selection to the Scrapbook before, the last selection you pasted will appear in the Scrapbook window. Otherwise, you'll see the phrase *Empty Scrapbook* in this window, as shown in Figure 6-9. If you select Paste to enter our sample paragraph into the Scrapbook, your window will look like the one in Figure 6-10 on the following page.

FIGURE 6-9

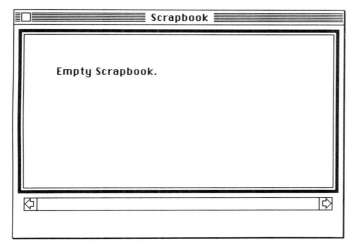

The Scrapbook window appears when you select Scrapbook from the menu.

FIGURE 6-10

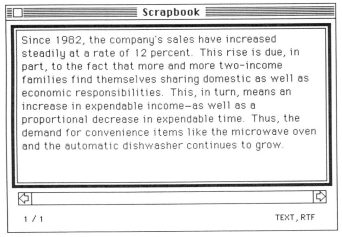

Your pasted block will appear in the Scrapbook window.

Notice that a set of status messages now appears at the bottom of the Scrapbook window. The notation on the left indicates that the entry you are viewing is 1 of 1 item in the Scrapbook. When you add another item, that item will be labeled *1 of 2*, and the previous item will become *2 of 2*. You can enter as many items into the Scrapbook as you can accommodate on your startup disk. Your most recent selections will always appear at the beginning of the list. As soon as you add a second item to the Scrapbook, Word will activate the scroll bar in the lower portion of the window so that you can move from one item to another.

In the lower-right portion of the Scrapbook window, you'll see the notation *TEXT,RTF*, indicating that the selection you pasted was a text block. As you'll see in Chapter 10, you can also use the Scrapbook to store graphics.

To close the Scrapbook window and resume working on the Word DeskTop, just click on the close box at the upper-left corner of the Scrapbook window. If you like, you can leave the Scrapbook window open and click in one of your document windows to begin working again in Word. The Scrapbook will remain open and accessible until you quit from Word.

To retrieve a selection from the Scrapbook, select Scrapbook from the ⌘ menu again (or click on the Scrapbook window if it is already open), then scroll to the selection you want to use. Now, issue another Copy or Cut command to place the selection on the Clipboard. If you issue the Cut command, the selection will be permanently removed from the Scrapbook, and the remaining selections will be renumbered to reflect this change. If you use the Copy command, however, your selection will remain in the Scrapbook, available for reuse later.

Don't worry if you can't see your entire selection in the Scrapbook window. Although there is room to display only about 11 lines of text in this window, you'll be able to retrieve the entire selection by issuing the Copy or Cut command. If you have assigned special formats to the selection you pasted in the Scrapbook, those formats will be retained, even though they are not reflected in the Scrapbook window. The contents of the Scrapbook window will always appear in 12-point Geneva Plain font, even though Word's default font is 12-point New York Plain.

Creating multiple Scrapbooks

The contents of your Scrapbook remain on disk even after you quit from Word and reboot your Mac. In fact, you can even copy your Scrapbook from one startup disk to another and rename the file so you can keep multiple Scrapbooks. To copy your Scrapbook to another disk, just open the System folder on your startup disk and drag the Scrapbook icon to the System folder of the second disk. If the second disk already contains a Scrapbook file, you'll see the message *Replace items with the same name?* If you want to overwrite the existing Scrapbook file on the target disk, click OK. Otherwise, rename the Scrapbook file on the target disk before you begin the Copy procedure.

When you select the Scrapbook command from the menu, Word will always open the file with the name Scrapbook. However, if no file called Scrapbook is present on your startup disk, Word will present a new empty Scrapbook window.

To maintain multiple Scrapbooks, you must rename each Scrapbook file at the Finder level. For example, you might use names like Graphics Scrap, Sales Scrap, and so forth, to identify your various Scrapbook files. When you need to reuse a Scrapbook, just assign the name *Scrapbook* to that document at the Finder level before you load the Word program.

Keyboard Shortcuts

In addition to the ⌘-c, ⌘-x, ⌘-v, [F3], [F2], and [F4] shortcuts you can use to copy, cut, and paste text in Word, you have three other keyboard shortcuts at your disposal. These Option-⌘-key shortcuts let you quickly copy and move text and copy formats from one location to another. You can use these shortcuts only when the Full Menus setting is in effect.

Copy From and Copy To

Rather than using separate Copy and Paste commands to duplicate a block of text, you can use Word's Option-⌘-c or Shift-[F3] shortcut to reduce this process to one step. The effect of the shortcut depends on whether you have selected any text before you issue the command. If you have selected a block of text, that highlighted text will become your copy block. Word will ask you where you want to paste the selection. If you haven't selected any text before pressing Option-⌘-c or Shift-[F3], Word assumes that you want to paste text at the current insertion point location and asks you to select a copy block.

For example, suppose you are typing the sample document shown in Figure 6-11 and you want to include the company name *Consolidated Industrial Manufacturing Company* at the insertion point. (Your insertion point marker is at the end of the document right now, just to the left of the last ¶ symbol.) Rather than typing this long name, you can copy it from the paragraph above.

FIGURE 6-11

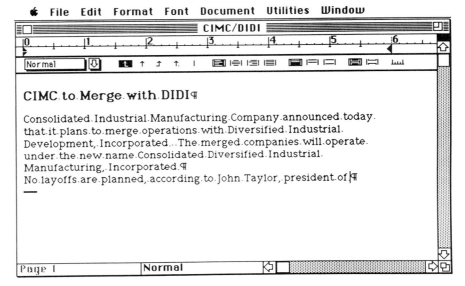

You want to repeat the phrase Consolidated Industrial Manufacturing Company *at the current insertion point.*

To use the Copy From technique, begin by pressing Option-⌘-c or Shift-[F3]. You will see the prompt *Copy from* in the status box at the lower-left corner of your screen. Just drag through the phrase *Consolidated Industrial Manufacturing Company* in the second paragraph—Word will display a dotted line beneath the selected copy block, as shown in Figure 6-12. When you press the Return or Enter key to lock in your copy selection, the copy phrase will appear where your insertion point marker was. Notice that your insertion point marker automatically jumps to the end of the pasted block so that you can resume typing without interruption. (After you type a period to end the sentence, your document will look like the one in Figure 6-13.)

Suppose you discover that John Taylor is actually president of Diversified Industrial Development, Incorporated, not Consolidated Industrial Manufacturing Company. You decide to go back and copy the name *Diversified Industrial Development, Incorporated* from the second paragraph. You can use a similar Option-⌘-c or Shift-[F3] technique to copy and paste that block in one step.

FIGURE 6-12

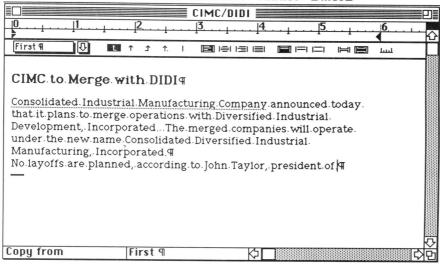

Word will display the prompt Copy from *in the status box and underline your copy selection.*

FIGURE 6-13

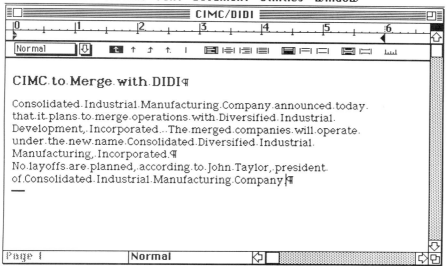

When you press Return or Enter, Word will copy the selected block at the insertion point.

Begin by highlighting the phrase *Diversified Industrial Development, Incorporated*, then press Option-⌘-c or Shift-[F3]. You'll see the prompt *Copy to* in the status box at the lower-left corner of your screen. Now, select the spot where you want to place a copy of the selected text. If you simply click on a new insertion point, Word will display a vertical gray bar at the paste location. If you drag through some text in your document, Word will display a dotted line under your selection to indicate that those characters will be overwritten when you press Return or Enter to lock in your paste selection. Since we want to overwrite the words *Consolidated Industrial Manufacturing Company* in the third paragraph, we'll drag through that company name, as shown in Figure 6-14. When we press Return or Enter, our document will look like the one in Figure 6-15.

FIGURE 6-14

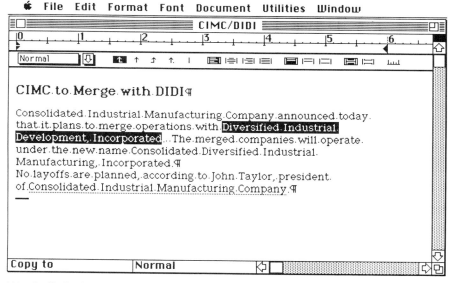

Word will display the prompt Copy to *in the status box and indicate your paste selection with a dotted underline.*

Incidentally, you can use this shortcut to copy text from one document to another as well as within an active document window. You can click on an open document window to activate it, then drag and resize any open window, if needed, to bring another window into view. When you activate another window, the *Copy to* or *Copy from* message will appear in that window's status box.

However, you cannot use the File or Window menus to open or activate another file. Both the source and destination files must be open before you can use the Option-⌘-c or Shift-[F3] shortcut. If you try to use the File or Window menus, Word will cancel the Copy procedure. You may also cancel it by pressing the ⌘ and period keys (⌘-.) or by pressing Esc.

FIGURE 6-15

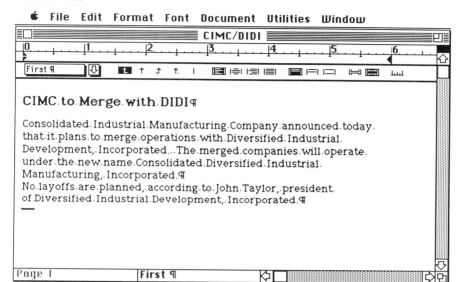

When you press Return or Enter, the copy block will overwrite the underlined text.

Move From and Move To

You can use a similar keyboard shortcut—Option-⌘-x or Shift-[F2]—to move text in your document quickly from one location to another. This keyboard shortcut works just like the Copy From shortcut: If you have selected a block of text when you press Option-⌘-x or Shift-[F2], you'll see the message *Move to* in the status box. Just click on a new insertion point to specify a paste location for the selected text. When you press Return or Enter, Word will delete the selected text from its current location and place it in the new location you have specified. If you drag through a block of text rather than clicking an insertion point when you are choosing your paste location, Word will display a dotted line under that text and overwrite it when you press Return or Enter.

If you do not select any text before pressing Option-⌘-x or Shift-[F2], Word assumes that you want to move a block of text to the current insertion point and will display the message *Move from*. Just drag through the text you want to move and press Return or Enter.

For example, suppose you want to move the sentence that begins *The merged companies will operate* in the second paragraph of the sample document in Figure 6-15 to the end of the third paragraph. Assuming that your insertion point is already at the end of the third paragraph, press Option-⌘-x or Shift-[F2]. When you see the message *Move from*, press the ⌘ key and click anywhere on the sentence that begins *The merged companies will operate* to select that entire sentence. Figure 6-16 on the next page shows the document window at this point. When you press Return or Enter, your document window will look like the one in Figure 6-17.

FIGURE 6-16

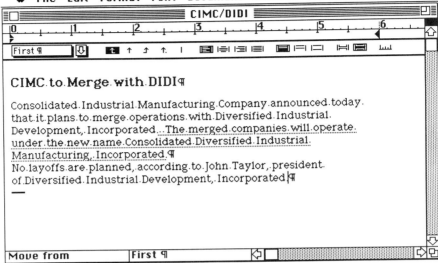

To move a block of text to the current insertion point, press Option-⌘-x or
Shift-[F2], then mark the text you want to move.

FIGURE 6-17

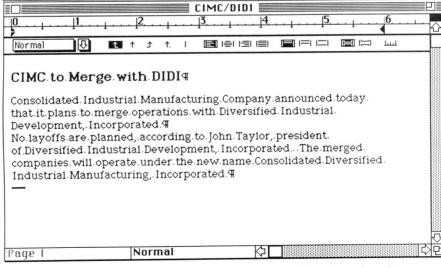

When you press Return or Enter, Word will move the selected text from its
current location to the insertion point.

As with the Copy procedure, you can drag, resize, or activate document windows while you're performing a Move From or Move To operation. If you try to use the File or Window menu commands to access another window, Word will cancel the Move procedure. You may cancel the procedure at any time by pressing the ⌘ and period keys (⌘-.) or by pressing Esc.

When you use Option-⌘-key techniques or the Shift and function keys to copy and move text, Word does not place a copy of your text on the Clipboard. This is not necessary because the original selection remains highlighted and is not removed from your document. If you have previously issued a Cut or Copy command to place a block of text on your Clipboard, that text will remain undisturbed while you carry out the Option-⌘-key maneuver.

Option-⌘-key shortcuts and the Clipboard

Thus, Option-⌘-key or Shift-function key shortcuts not only streamline the Copy and Move procedures, they let you perform intermediate moves and copies without losing your last Clipboard selection. This capability is quite handy when you need to rearrange some data before pasting a selection in your document.

Word 4 also allows you to copy the paragraph and character formats from one block of text to another by pressing Option-⌘-v or Shift-[F4]. Again, the effects of this shortcut depend on whether you have selected any text before pressing these key combinations. If you have selected a block of text, Word assumes that you want to copy the formats of the current selection to another part of your document; if you have not selected any text, Word assumes that you want to copy the formats of another text block to your current insertion point. (As we explained in Chapter 5, if you select new character formats while no text is selected, your new formats will apply to the next characters you type.)

Format From and Format To

Suppose you want to format the heading in the third paragraph of the sample document in Figure 6-18 on the next page to appear in the same format as the heading at the top of the screen. Rather than reformatting the text manually, select one or more characters from the first headline, which is already formatted, and press Option-⌘-v or Shift-[F4]. Word will display the prompt *Format to* in the status box. Now, drag through the characters you want to format. As you can see in Figure 6-19 on the next page, Word displays a dotted line under your *Format to* selection. When you press Return or Enter to confirm your selection, your document will look like the one in Figure 6-20 on page 193. As you can see, Word has changed the character formats of the original selection without changing its content.

FIGURE 6-18

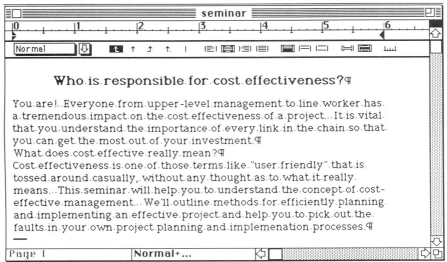

We want to copy the character formats from line 1 to line 6.

FIGURE 6-19

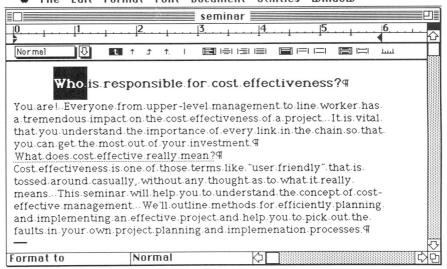

When you press Option-⌘-v or Shift-[F4], Word will prompt you to select the text block to which you want to copy your formats and then will display a dotted line under the Format to *selection.*

FIGURE 6-20

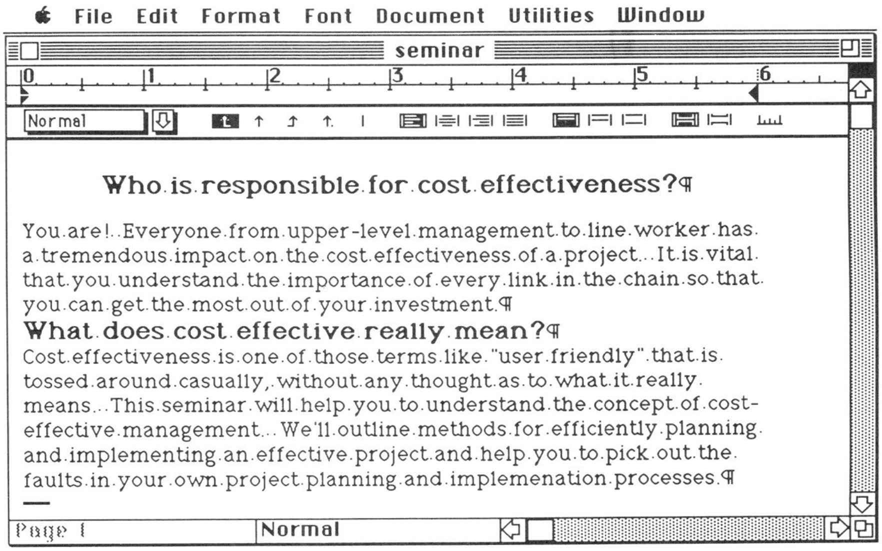

The second heading now carries the same character formats as the first.

Notice that Word has copied the character formats from line 1 to line 6, but not the paragraph formats. Line 1 has centered alignment with spacing above and below the paragraph, while line 6 displays flush-left alignment and no paragraph spacing above and below. If you want to copy paragraph formats, you need to double-click in the selection bar to select your entire source paragraph, then press Option-⌘-v or Shift-[F4] and double-click in the selection bar to select your target paragraph. When you use this technique, Word will transfer paragraph formats only—not character formats.

Of course, if you want to copy both character and paragraph formats, you can always perform the Option-⌘-v or Shift-[F4] operation twice—once with the desired characters selected and once with entire paragraphs selected. For example, to copy the paragraph formats from the first paragraph in Figure 6-20 to the third paragraph, you would double-click in the selection bar next to the first paragraph in line 1, then press Option-⌘-v or Shift-[F4]. Then, you would double-click next to the third paragraph, as shown in Figure 6-21, and press Return or Enter. As you can see in Figure 6-22, our paragraph formats have now been transferred as well.

FIGURE 6-21

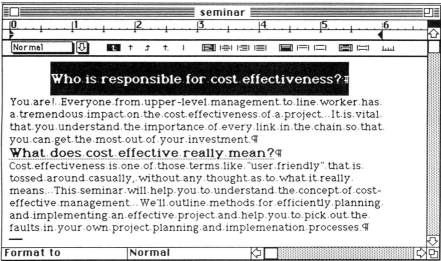

To copy paragraph formats, perform the Option-⌘-v or Shift-[F4] procedure with an entire paragraph selected.

FIGURE 6-22

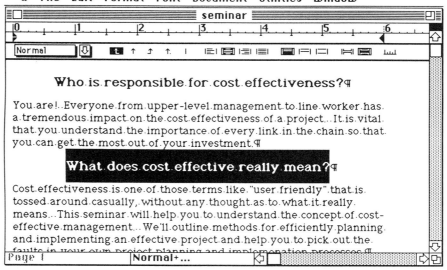

The target paragraph now carries the same character and paragraph formats as the source paragraph.

If you want to change character formats as you type, just press Option-⌘-v or Shift-[F4] without making a selection. Word will display the prompt *Format from* in the status box. Now, click on or drag through a character or block of text in your document that carries the character formats you want to use, and press Return or Enter. Any new text that you type at the current insertion point will appear in the selected format.

As with the Copy and Move shortcuts, you can drag, resize, or activate document windows while you're formatting. If you try to use the File or Window menu commands to access another document window, Word will cancel the Format From or Format To procedure. You may also cancel this procedure at any time by pressing the ⌘ and period keys (⌘-.) or by pressing Esc.

Another way to copy a paragraph format is to copy the paragraph marker (¶) from the end of one paragraph and paste it over the paragraph marker at the end of another paragraph. When you do this, Word will transfer all the paragraph formats from the first paragraph to the second. If the first paragraph has been assigned a named style, that style will be applied to the second paragraph. You can select a paragraph marker by double-clicking on it, just as you would double-click on a word to select it.

Copying a paragraph marker

Like the search-and-replace procedures in many word processing programs, Word 4 allows you to search through a document to find occurrences of a particular word or character sequence. In other words, you can instruct Word to find every occurrence of a given character sequence and replace it with a different sequence of characters. When we use the term "character sequence," we are talking about any string of characters. It can be as small as a single letter or as long as several sentences. However, the sequence you are searching for cannot exceed 255 characters. Typically, your character sequence will be only one or a few words.

Finding and changing can be two of the most useful capabilities in any word processing program. Word 4 takes these capabilities further than most other word processors, letting you change formats as well as characters. In this section, we'll explain how to use the Find... and Change... commands on Word's Utilities menu. We'll also show you a few special ways to apply these features and warn you about certain traps that can arise when you use the Find... and Change... commands.

THE FIND... AND CHANGE... COMMANDS

To find a character sequence, just choose the Find... command on the Utilities menu. Word will display the dialog box shown in Figure 6-23. When this dialog box first appears, you'll see a blinking insertion point marker in the Find What edit bar. Type the characters you want to search for—this is called your find text—then click the Start Search button.

Finding Text

FIGURE 6-23

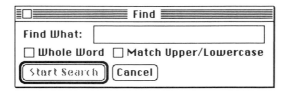

To search for a character sequence, enter your find text in the Find dialog box.

Although there is room in the Find What edit bar to display only about 25 characters, your find string can be as long as 255 characters. The characters on the left side of the edit bar will scroll out of view as you type, but you can view and change any hidden characters by dragging to the left or right to scroll the hidden portion of the find text into view.

In performing a search, Word begins at the insertion point marker's current location in your document and scans forward to the end of the document. When it finds the first occurrence of your find text, Word highlights that occurrence and temporarily halts the Find procedure. To continue the search, just click the Find Next button in the dialog box. (The Find Next button replaces the Start Search button once the Find procedure is underway.) Figure 6-24 shows how your screen might appear when Word finds an occurrence of the word *silver*.

FIGURE 6-24

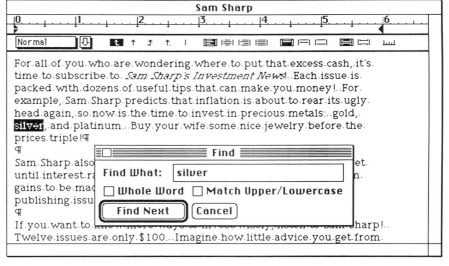

When Word locates an occurrence of the find text, it will highlight that occurrence in your document.

As Word scans through your document looking for your find text, it will scroll the document on your screen as necessary to bring the next occurrence of the find text into view.

When you want to stop searching, click the Cancel button or click the close box in the Find dialog box. Word will save the find text in the dialog box. In fact, this text will remain in the Find dialog box until you replace it, remove it, or quit from Word. You can even open another file or activate another document window to search for the same text string in two or more documents. However, the next time you issue the Find... command, you will notice that the contents of the Find What edit bar are highlighted; therefore, any characters you type will replace the current contents of the Find What edit bar.

Once you have closed the Find dialog box, you can use a shortcut to locate the next occurrence of the find text. Just choose the Find Again command from the Utilities menu or press Option-⌘-a instead of choosing the Find... command. As we'll discuss in a few pages, this shortcut is particularly helpful when you want to edit your document as you search for the find text.

When Word has searched through the end of the document, you'll see the Continue Search alert box shown in Figure 6-25. This does not necessarily mean that the search is complete; it just tells you that Word has reached the end of your document. If you want Word to continue the search by cycling back to the beginning of the document, click Yes in the Continue Search alert box. Word will then go to the beginning of your document and continue scanning for your find text. If you want to halt the Find procedure, click No in the Continue Search alert box. Because the Find dialog box will remain open, you can type a new find text string or click Cancel to stop the Find procedure altogether.

FIGURE 6-25

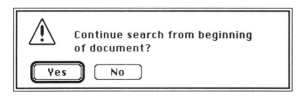

To search from the top of your document, click Yes in the Continue Search alert box.

If you click Yes in the Continue Search alert box, Word will find each occurrence of your find text, starting at the beginning of your document. When Word reaches the end of the document for the second time, however, you'll see an alert box with the message *End of document reached.* When you click OK in this alert box, the Find dialog box will remain open, so you can enter new find text or halt the Find procedure by clicking the Cancel button. If your insertion point marker is positioned at the beginning of your document when you issue the Find... command, Word will display the *End of document reached* message after one complete pass through the document. You won't see the Continue Search alert box at all.

If Word displays the *End of document reached* message without highlighting any occurrences of the find text, this tells you that no occurrences of the find text could be located. If you're puzzled by this, you might try retyping the find text. Keep in mind that Word looks for exact matches to your find text. (Case does not matter unless you click the Match Upper/Lowercase option, which we'll talk about in a few pages.) Therefore, if you've entered extra blank spaces or typed a single character incorrectly in the Find What edit bar, Word won't be able to locate the find text in your document.

Navigating with the Find... command

The Find... command offers a quick way to jump from one part of your document to another as you make revisions. For example, suppose you want to edit a section of your document that appears under the heading named *Part II*. To move quickly to this section of your document without scrolling, you can issue the Find... command and type *Part II* as your find text. When you click Start Search, Word will scroll your document on the screen to bring the *Part II* heading into view. You can then close the Find dialog box and perform any needed revisions.

You may even want to insert hidden "bookmarks" into your text to help you find key sections quickly. Use short, easy-to-remember symbols or codes to mark selected areas. For example, if there is a paragraph in your document that you want to remember to verify later, you might enter the characters **check** just in front of that paragraph, then highlight those characters and use the Character... command to assign the Hidden format to them. (This command does not suppress the display of hidden text on your screen. The Show Hidden Text option in the Preferences dialog box does that.) When you are ready to return to that paragraph, just issue the Find... command and type **check** as your find text.

As long as you display the hidden text on your screen, Word will be able to locate that text when you issue the Find... command. If you use the Preferences... command to suppress the display of hidden text, however, Word will not be able to locate your bookmark. (As you'll see in Chapter 7, you can instruct Word to omit this hidden text when the document is printed.)

Find options

The Find dialog box offers two options, Whole Word and Match Upper/Lowercase. The Whole Word option is used primarily when your find text is a short word, such as *the* or *for*. If you do not select the Whole Word option, Word will search for any character sequence that matches your find text, even if it occurs in the middle of another word. For example, if you type *for* in the Find What edit bar, Word will highlight occurrences in such words as *forecast* and *platform*. To avoid this, just click the Whole Word option before you click the Start Search button.

The Whole Word option also can be useful in cases where you want to find only the singular or present tense of a word. For instance, suppose you enter the word *book* as your find text. By selecting the Whole Word option before you begin searching, you will avoid finding the plural form of the word, *books,* or the past tense, *booked*. Although there will be times when you want to find different forms of a word, in general, we recommend that you select the Whole Word option before you start your search. You can always activate this option in the middle of a search by clicking the Whole Word check box before you click the Find Next button.

The Match Upper/Lowercase option works exactly as you might expect. If you do not activate this option, Word will ignore case as it searches for occurrences of your find text. For example, if you enter *Microsoft* as your find text and do not click the Match Upper/Lowercase option, Word will highlight such occurrences as *microsoft*, *MicroSoft*, and *MICROSOFT*. If you select the Match Upper/Lowercase option, Word will find only those occurrences where the capitalization exactly matches the capitalization of your find text. All other occurrences will be ignored.

The Match Upper/Lowercase option can be helpful when you need to search for a proper noun that has the same spelling as a common noun. For example, suppose you want to search a document for all references to the software program *Word*. However, you do not want to find other occurrences of the word *word*. Enter *Word* as your find text, then click the Match Upper/Lowercase option before you start the search. (You may also want to activate the Whole Word option.) Of course, there's one possible disadvantage to using the Match Upper/Lowercase option. If you have accidentally used the improper case in some instances—for example, if you've entered the name of the software program as *word* instead of *Word*—your Find procedure will not highlight those occurrences. Keep in mind that you may, at times, want to perform a search without the Match Upper/Lowercase option activated so you can check for the correct case of a certain word.

Using wildcards

One very helpful feature of Word's Find... command is its ability to use the question mark character (?) as a wildcard. You can use a ? in place of any single character in your find text. For example, if you enter *ba?e* as your find text, Word will highlight occurrences of *bale*, *base*, *bane*, *bake*, and any other words that begin with *ba* followed by a single character and an *e*.

Wildcards come in handy for a variety of situations. For example, suppose you are working on a document in which you have not been consistent in spelling the name *Anderson*. In some cases, you have entered *Anderson* with an *o*, and in other cases, you've entered *Andersen* with an *e*. You can find all occurrences of the name by using the Find... command and entering *Anders?n* as your find text. Of course, you will probably want to change some of the occurrences so that the spelling will be consistent throughout the document. We'll show you how to do that when we discuss the Change... command.

Since Word considers a question mark in your find text to be a wildcard, you may be wondering how you can search for a literal question mark in a document. Fortunately, there is a way to do this. Just enter ^? (a caret followed by a question mark) as your find text. This tells Word that, instead of using the ? as a wildcard, you want to find all occurrences of a literal question mark. Of course, you can combine ^? with other characters as you are entering the find text. For example, suppose you want to find all occurrences of the question *Is this correct?* in your document. You can do this by entering *Is this correct^?* or perhaps just *correct^?* as your find text.

Finding hidden text

When you assign the Hidden format to text in your document, keep in mind that Word will not be able to locate occurrences of your find text if it is hidden from view. If you want Word to locate occurrences of your find text within a hidden text block, you must activate the Show Hidden Text option in the Preferences dialog box before you begin your search.

Finding formats

Word also lets you find character and paragraph formats. First, select the character sequence or paragraph that has the formatting you want to find. (To select a paragraph, double-click in the invisible selection bar at the left edge of that paragraph.) Then, press Option-⌘-r. Word will find and highlight the next character or paragraph whose formatting is the same as your selection.

You cannot use the Option-⌘-r technique to search for *both* a paragraph format and a character format. If the text you select before pressing Option-⌘-r includes a ¶ symbol marking the end of a paragraph, Word will assume that you want to find the next block of text with the same paragraph formats as your selected text. If your selection does not include a ¶ symbol, Word will assume that you're looking for text with the same character formats.

One terrific application for this feature is moving quickly between subheadings in a large document. For example, suppose you have formatted the second-level subheadings in a document in 12-point Helvetica bold type. You can select one subheading, then press Option-⌘-r to move directly to the next subheading that has 12-point Helvetica bold formatting.

This technique can find only one format at a time. For example, suppose you have a heading that includes some 12-point bold text and some 12-point, bold, italic text. If you select the entire heading and press Option-⌘-r, Word will find the next character in your document that has either 12-point bold formatting or 12-point, bold, italic formatting. Word decides which format to search for by looking at the format of the last character in the text you selected and using that as its guide. So, for example, if the last character in the heading has 12-point, bold, italic formatting, Word will search for the next character in the document with that same formatting.

Finding special characters

Another useful feature of Word's Find... command is its ability to search for special markup characters in a document, such as end-of-line markers, nonbreaking spaces, and optional hyphens. To find a special character, you must insert a caret symbol (^) in your find text. Table 6-1 summarizes the markers that you can search for, and the character combination for each.

TABLE 6-1

Find Text	Finds all occurrences of
^ p	Paragraph marker (¶)
^ t	Tab marker (➡)
^ n	End-of-line marker (↵)
^ s	Nonbreaking space (˜)
^ -	Optional hyphen (-)
^ d	Section-break marker (:::::::) or page break
^ w	White space
^ 5	Footnote reference marker
^ 1	Graphics

You can use these codes to locate special markers.

Word can find markup characters in your text even when they are not visible on the screen. For example, if you've chosen the Hide ¶ command from the Edit menu, the ¶ symbols at the end of every paragraph will not be visible on your screen (nor will other special markers, such as the dots that mark blank spaces and the arrows that mark tab spaces). However, if you use a code like ^p in your find text, Word will highlight the space following each paragraph instead of the ¶ marker. Similarly, Word can find tab markers, optional hyphens, and end-of-line markers even when they are not displayed on the screen.

The seventh item in the table, ^w, needs a little explaining. When you specify ^w as your find text, Word will find the blank space that appears between any two characters in your document. This will include the single spaces that occur between words as well as whole line spaces. The amount of white space that Word highlights on the screen will vary, depending on the situation. For example, suppose you have two blank lines between two paragraphs in your document, and the second paragraph begins with a $1/2$-inch tab. As you can see in Figure 6-26 on the following page, when you search for white space in this document, Word will highlight the ¶ at the end of the first paragraph, as well as the two blank lines between paragraphs and the space created by the tab.

As you might guess, your find text can include any combination of these special markup characters and other text. For example, to find every instance of a paragraph that begins with the word *For,* you can choose the Find... command and enter *^pFor* as your find text. Word will highlight the paragraph symbol at the end of the previous paragraph as well as the word *For* at the beginning of the next paragraph.

In addition to the special markers listed in Table 6-1, you can search for any character by entering a caret followed by the three-digit ASCII code for that character as your find text. For example, if you enter *^097* as your find text, Word will find every occurrence of the letter *a.* Interestingly, even though 097 is the ASCII code for a lowercase *a* and 065 is the ASCII code for an uppercase *A,* Word will find every *a,* regardless of case, unless you activate the Match Upper/ Lowercase option.

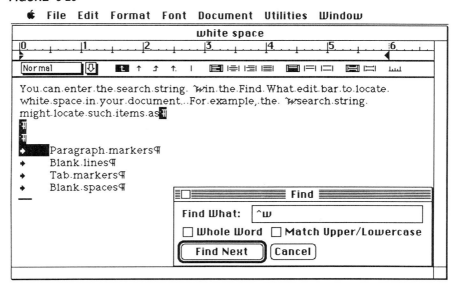

You can use the find text ^w to locate white space in your document.

Editing as you find

Word will not let you edit text while the Find dialog box is active. However, if you want to make changes to your document during a Find procedure, you can switch between your document window and the Find dialog box. After Word locates an occurrence of your find text, just click anywhere on the document window to activate it. The Find dialog box will then move behind your document window, although it will still be open on your DeskTop. While the document window is active, you can access all of Word's menu commands and type any characters from the keyboard.

After you've made your editing changes, you'll probably want to locate the next occurrence of your find text and make additional changes. To locate the next occurrence of the find text, reactivate the Find dialog box and click the Find Next option. There are a couple of ways to reactivate the dialog box. First, you can resize your document window so that it no longer overlays the dialog box, then click anywhere on the dialog box. Second, you can type ⌘-f, which will cause the active dialog box to overlay your document window again. If you plan to do a lot of finding and editing, you may want to resize your document window, then drag the Find dialog box so that at least part of the dialog box will be visible when your document window is active, as shown in Figure 6-27. This way, you can quickly switch between the dialog box and your document by clicking on one or the other.

FIGURE 6-27

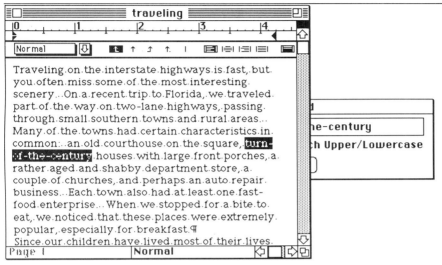

You can create nonoverlapping windows to view the Find dialog box and your document window simultaneously.

Shortcuts

Instead of reactivating the Find dialog box and clicking Find Next, you can locate the next occurrence of your find text simply by typing Option-⌘-a or choosing Find Again from the Utilities menu. You can use Option-⌘-a even when the Find dialog box is not open. Recall that when you close the Find dialog box, Word does not discard the contents of the Find What edit bar. So, when you type Option-⌘-a, Word will be able to locate the next occurrence of the find text even if the Find dialog box is closed.

There's another shortcut you can take advantage of when you are editing as you find text. After you make a change to one occurrence of your find text, you can make the same editing change to the next occurrence by choosing the Again command from the Edit menu or simply by typing ⌘-a. For example, suppose you want to boldface your company name everywhere it appears in a document. You could begin by selecting the Find... command from the Utilities menu and entering the company name in the Find What edit bar. Then, click Start Search in the Find dialog box. When Word highlights the first occurrence of the company name, click anywhere on your document window, then choose Bold from the Format menu. (Since Word will have selected the company name in the text, there's no need to drag through the name before you choose the Bold command.) After boldfacing the first occurrence, press Option-⌘-a to go to the next occurrence of the company name. Then, press ⌘-a to boldface this occurrence as well. You can continue this procedure until you have boldfaced every occurrence of your company name in the document.

If you do not want to boldface every occurrence, you can skip some of the occurrences without losing the shortcut advantage. Just press Option-⌘-a to skip from one occurrence to another, and press ⌘-a only when you reach an occurrence that you want to change. Keep in mind that Word remembers and repeats only your most recent editing change. So use this ⌘-a technique only when you haven't made any other intermediate editing changes to your document.

With certain kinds of changes, you must also be careful that you do not erase an occurrence of your find text when using the ⌘-a technique to edit that text. For example, suppose you want to change the word *system* from its singular form to the plural form *systems*. You begin by finding the first occurrence of the word *system*, then you click to the left of the space at the end of the word and type an *s*. Next, press Option-⌘-a to find the next occurrence. When you find this occurrence, be sure that you click to the left of the space at the end of the word before you press ⌘-a to repeat the editing change. Otherwise, Word will erase the highlighted occurrence of the word *system* and replace it with a single *s*.

Because of the limitations you encounter when using the ⌘-a shortcut, you will probably want to use the Change... command when you need to make a significant number of editing changes to your document. Let's look at the Change... command in detail.

Changing Text

The Change... command on Word's Utilities menu is closely related to the Find... command. Instead of just finding every occurrence of a character sequence, however, the Change... command lets you find and replace each occurrence with a different character sequence. If you've used other word processors, you may know this feature as search and replace.

When you choose the Change... command from the Utilities menu, you will see the dialog box shown in Figure 6-28. Notice that this dialog box is very similar to the Find dialog box shown in Figure 6-23.

FIGURE 6-28

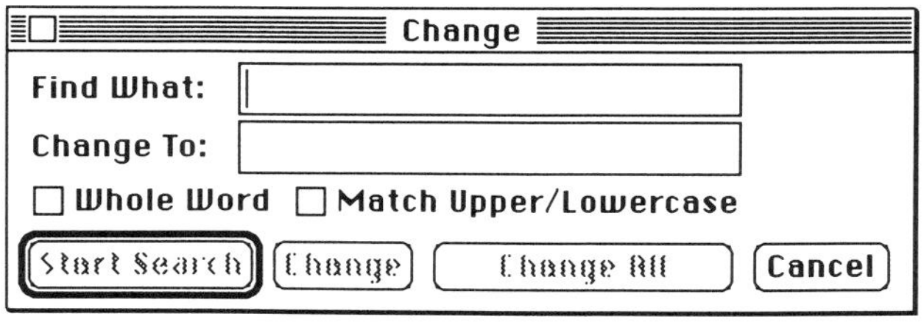

The Change dialog box is similar to the Find dialog box.

Enter the text you want to find and change in the Find What edit bar. (As in the Find dialog box, you will see a blinking insertion point marker in the Find What edit bar when you first open the Change dialog box. If you have used the Find... or

Change… command in a previous Find or Change procedure, the Find What edit bar will reflect the last find text you entered.) After entering your find text, press the Tab key to move the pointer to the Change To edit bar (or click anywhere on that edit bar) and enter your replacement text. Your replacement text can contain from zero to 255 characters, though only about 25 characters will be visible in the edit bar.

If you want to change every occurrence of the find text in your document, click the Change All button. Beginning at the current insertion point and moving to the end of the document, Word will automatically replace every occurrence of your find text with the replacement text you specified. As the replacement text is pasted into your document, it will assume the same format as the find text that it replaces. (If you leave the Change To edit bar blank, Word will delete every occurrence of the find text when you click the Change All button.)

For example, suppose you want to replace every occurrence of the word *year* with the word *period* in the sample document shown in Figure 6-29. Your insertion point marker is currently at the beginning of the third paragraph. Begin by issuing the Change… command, then enter *year* as your find text and *period* as your replacement text. When you click Change All in the Change dialog box, your document will look like the one in Figure 6-30 on the next page.

FIGURE 6-29

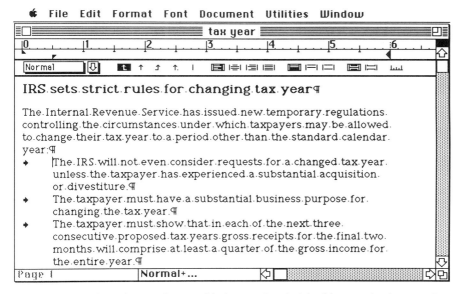

We want to replace the word year *with the word* period *in this sample document.*

FIGURE 6-30

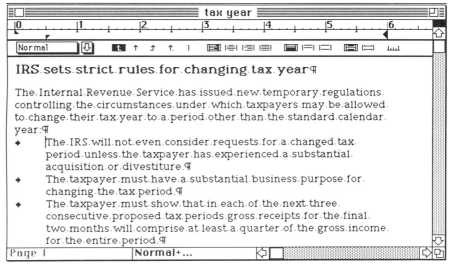

Word replaced text from the current insertion point to the end of the document.

Notice that all occurrences of the word *year* in the last three paragraphs have been changed. However, Word has not changed the text in the first two paragraphs. When you start a Change procedure from the middle of your document, clicking the Change All button will cause Word to replace every occurrence of the find text from the insertion point location to the end of your document. Then, it will show you the alert box depicted in Figure 6-25. (This dialog box will not appear if the insertion point marker was at the very first character space in the document when you issued the Change… command.) If you want the Change procedure to continue from the beginning of the document, click Yes. If you want to halt the Change procedure at this point, click No. If you click No, Word will display in the status box the number of changes made and reactivate the Change dialog box. At this point, you can click the close box or the Cancel button to close the Change dialog box, or you can enter new find text or new replacement text to perform another Change operation.

If you choose to continue the Change procedure from the beginning of your document, Word will change all occurrences of the find text from the beginning of the document to the original insertion point location. When Word has completed all the changes, you'll see a message in the status box telling you how many changes were made.

In many cases, you will not want to replace every occurrence of one character sequence with another character sequence indiscriminately. Word allows you to perform selective changes in two ways. First, you can examine each occurrence of the find text as you go, then decide whether you want to change it. Second, you can change every occurrence of the find text in only a selected portion of your document.

If you want to examine each occurrence of your find text as you go and decide whether to change it, click the Start Search button in the Change dialog box. Beginning with the current insertion point location, Word will highlight the next occurrence of your find text on the screen. If you want to change this occurrence, click the Change button. If you want to skip this occurrence and examine the next occurrence of the find text, click the No Change option. (No Change replaces the Start Search button once the Change procedure is underway.)

In either case, Word will follow your instructions, then highlight the next occurrence of the find text on your screen. Again, you can choose either Change or No Change. Word will scroll your document on the screen to bring new occurrences of the find text into view. Occasionally, you may need to drag the Change dialog box out of the way so that you can see the highlighted find text.

One advantage of examining each occurrence of the find text as you go is that you can alter the contents of the Change To edit bar. This is useful when you want to use a different tense or form in the replacement text. Suppose you are changing the word *walk* to *run*. As you're going through the document, you run across a past tense occurrence of the find text, *walked*. If Word were performing the Change procedure automatically, this occurrence would become *runed*. However, when you come across an occurrence like this, you can alter the contents of the Change To edit bar to *ran* before you click the Change button. (Another way to solve this type of problem is to click the Whole Word option, which we'll discuss in a minute.)

Instead of altering the replacement text in the Change dialog box, you may want to make changes directly to the document. Just click anywhere on your document to activate it, then you can type characters from the keyboard or access any of Word's menu commands. As in a Find procedure, if you click on your document window during a Change procedure, Word does not close the Change dialog box. Instead, it moves the dialog box behind your document window on the DeskTop. To reactivate the Change dialog box, you can either resize your document window and click anywhere on the dialog box, or you can type ⌘-h, which will bring the dialog box back on top of your document window and activate it. You also can press Option-⌘-a or choose Find Again from the Utilities menu to go to the next occurrence of your find text.

After you've located and changed your find text, Word will display the *Continue search from beginning of document?* message shown in Figure 6-25 when it reaches the end of your document. You can stop the Change procedure at this point

Selective changing

Examining each occurrence of the find text

or continue your selective changing, starting at the beginning of the document. If you continue to see this alert box, Word is trying to tell you that it cannot find additional occurrences of the find text in your document. Then, you'll see the message *End of document reached.*

Changing all occurrences of the find text in a selected area

If you select a portion of your document before you choose the Change... command, Word lets you change all occurrences of the find text within that selection only. Continuing with the sample document in Figure 6-29, suppose you want to change the word *year* to *period* within the second paragraph of your document only. Begin by selecting that paragraph, then issue the Change... command. When the Change dialog box appears, you'll see that the Change All button now reads Change Selection.

To perform the Change procedure, just enter your find text (*year*) and your replacement text (*period*), then click the Change Selection button. Word will automatically change every occurrence of the find text within the paragraph you selected. Again, the number of changes will be reflected in the status box.

When you want to change a character sequence within a selected portion of your document, do not click the Start Search button when you begin the Change procedure. If you do, the text you selected before issuing the Change... command will no longer be selected. Instead, only the first occurrence of the find text will be selected. When you click Change Selection, Word will change only the currently highlighted occurrence of the find text, instead of every occurrence in the selected portion of the document.

Change options

You've probably noticed that the Change dialog box offers the same two options that appear in the Find dialog box: Whole Word and Match Upper/Lowercase. The Whole Word option works exactly like the one in the Find dialog box. When you activate this option, Word will change only whole-word matches to your find text. Again, this option is likely to be important when your find text is a single short word. For example, suppose you want to replace every occurrence of the word *top* with the word *bottom*. If you do not activate the Whole Word option, Word will replace the characters *top* in such words as *topic* and *stop*. Your document may end up with some nonsensical "words," such as *bottomic* and *sbottom*.

The Whole Word option can also come in handy when the word you are changing appears in more than one tense or form throughout your document. For example, suppose you want to change every occurrence of the word *boy* to *child*. If your document happens to contain the plural form of *boy*—*boys*—and you do not select the Whole Word option, Word will change *boys* to *childs*. To avoid this kind of problem, you can use the Whole Word option to perform separate Change procedures for each form of the word.

The Match Upper/Lowercase option works a little differently in a Change procedure than it does in a Find procedure. You may recall that when you activate this option in the Find dialog box, Word will search only for those occurrences where capitalization exactly matches that of the find text in the Find dialog box. This rule still applies when you issue the Change... command. However, the Match Upper/Lowercase option also affects your replacement text. If you do not activate this option during a Change procedure, and you enter your Change To text in lowercase letters, Word will use the existing capitalization of each occurrence of the find text to determine the capitalization of the replacement text.

For example, suppose you want to replace the word *May* with the word *April* throughout the sample document shown in Figure 6-31. If you enter your find and replacement text in all lowercase letters and do not activate the Match Upper/Lowercase option, Word will find all occurrences of *may*, ignoring case, and replace them with the word *april*, as shown in Figure 6-32 on the following page.

FIGURE 6-31

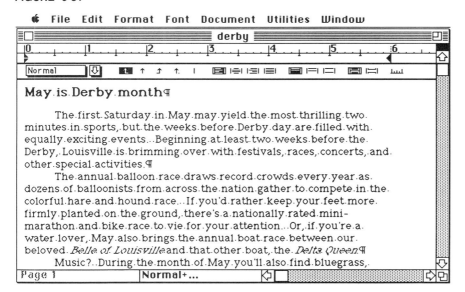

We want to change the word May *to* April *in this sample document.*

Notice that in every instance where the word *may* appeared capitalized, Word also capitalized the replacement text, *april*. However, if you capitalize the first letter of the Change To text, *April*, Word will capitalize all instances of the replacement text when it executes the Change... command, as you can see in Figure 6-33 on the next page.

Notice that the second occurrence of the word *may* in the second line of our document was changed to *april* in Figure 6-32, even though we intended to change only the month names with our search-and-replace procedure. We could get around this problem by using the Match Upper/Lowercase option.

FIGURE 6-32

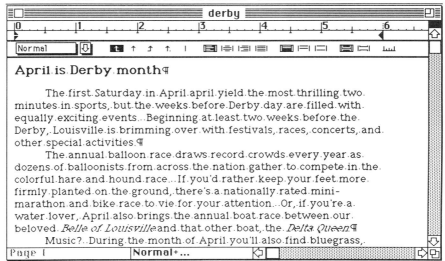

If you enter your find and replacement text in all lowercase letters and do not activate the Match Upper/Lowercase option, Word will use the existing capitalization to change all occurrences of the find text.

FIGURE 6-33

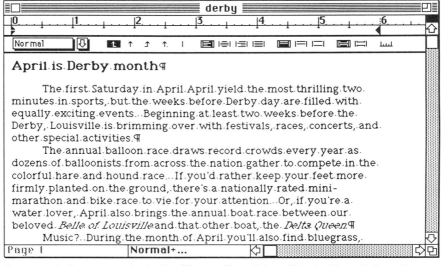

If you capitalize your entry in the Change To edit bar, Word will capitalize all instances of the replacement text.

If you activate the Match Upper/Lowercase option, Word will find only those occurrences of the find text whose capitalization exactly matches that of the find text in the Change dialog box. Word will always paste your replacement text exactly as you have entered it in the Change To edit bar, rather than adapting the replacement text to fit the style of each occurrence of the find text. Figure 6-34 shows the effect of the Change... command on our sample document when we used the Match Upper/Lowercase option to change *May* to *April*. Notice that the second occurrence of the word *may* in the second paragraph remains unchanged in this example.

FIGURE 6-34

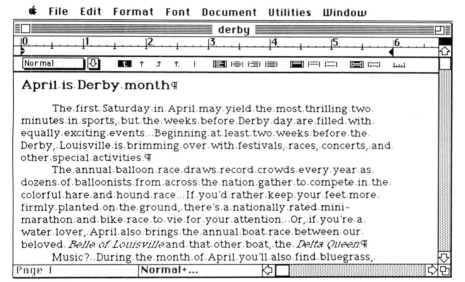

When you use the Match Upper/Lowercase option, Word will change only those words that exactly match the capitalization of the find text.

Using wildcards

The ? wildcard is available in a Change procedure just as it is in a Find procedure. However, you can use a wildcard only in your find text. If you include a ? as part of your replacement text, Word will interpret it as a literal question mark. Sometimes, the ? wildcard can enable you to perform only one Change procedure where you otherwise might need two. For example, suppose you want to replace every occurrence of *software* and *hardware* with the words *computer supplies*. After you choose the Change... command, enter *????ware* as your find text, then enter *computer supplies* as your replacement text. Word will look for all words that begin with any four characters followed by *ware* and replace those words with *computer supplies*.

Changing hidden text

The Change… command will affect hidden text only if you have chosen to display that text on your screen. If you use the Preferences… command to suppress the display of any text that carries the Hidden format, Word will ignore that text when it performs the Change procedure. Thus, if you want to change hidden text, we recommend that you activate the Show Hidden Text option before you begin a Change procedure.

Changing text and formats

When you enter replacement text in the Change dialog box, there is no way to format that text. Word formats your replacement text to match the format of each occurrence of the find text that it replaces. This is exactly what you want in most cases. For example, suppose you are replacing a word that appears both in the body of your document and in several headings and subheadings. You probably want the replacement text to assume the same format as the surrounding text. Fortunately, Word handles all of this automatically.

Suppose, however, you want your replacement text to be pasted into your document in a special format. Word allows you to change formats as well as text by storing your replacement text on the Clipboard. First, type and format the text that you want to use as your replacement text (either in your current document or in another document that is open on your DeskTop). Then, select that text and use either the Cut or Copy command from the Edit menu to place it on the Clipboard. Next, issue the Change… command and type your find text in the dialog box. Instead of entering your replacement text in the Change To edit bar, enter ^c. The ^c code instructs Word to use the contents of the Clipboard as replacement text during the Change procedure. Now, you can choose either Change All (or Change Selection), or you can click the Start Search button to examine each occurrence of the find text.

There are two primary reasons you might want to enter replacement text from the Clipboard. First, when you store your replacement text on the Clipboard, you are not bound by the 255-character limitation that applies in the dialog box. Second, when your replacement text is on the Clipboard, it will come into your document in the same format that appears on the Clipboard. Therefore, you can include special style characteristics (different fonts, point sizes, character formats, and so forth) in your replacement text.

Let's use the ^c technique to replace every occurrence of the word *Excellence* with the full title *Excellence: The Microsoft Excel User's Journal* in the sample document shown in Figure 6-35. You want this title to appear in bold, italic type as well.

Begin by highlighting the full title in lines 1 and 2, then issuing the Copy command to place a copy of the formatted replacement text on the Clipboard. Then, issue the Change… command, type *Excellence* in the Find What edit bar and ^c in the Change To edit bar. When you click Change All, the sample document will look like the one in Figure 6-36.

FIGURE 6-35

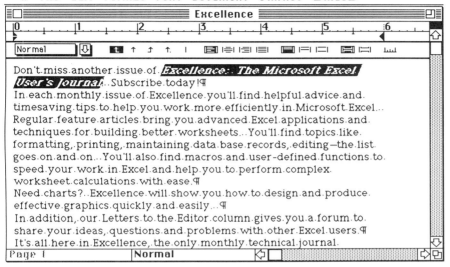

We want to change Excellence *to* Excellence: The Microsoft Excel User's Journal, *then we want to format the replacement text to appear in bold, italic type.*

FIGURE 6-36

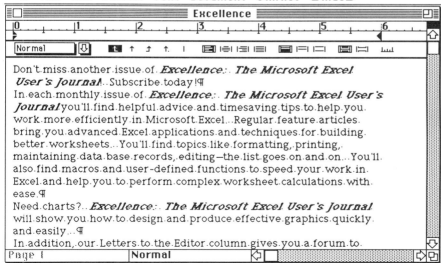

If we copy the replacement text to the Clipboard, Word will apply our character formats when we issue the Change… command.

Although Word allows you to use special formatting in your replacement text, and allows you to search for a particular format using the Option-⌘-r technique, there's no way to search for one format and replace it with another. For example, suppose you have formatted certain words throughout your document using 12-point, bold, italic type. You would like to find every word that has this formatting and change it to 14-point italic with no boldfacing. If you select any character sequence that has 12-point, bold, italic formatting, you can find another occurrence of a character with that same formatting by pressing Option-⌘-r. However, if you change the formatting of the first occurrence from 12-point, bold, italic to 14-point italic, then you cannot use Option-⌘-r to find the next occurrence of 12-point, bold, italic text. In other words, once you have changed from the old format to the new format, the old format will no longer appear on your screen, so you cannot select it and use Option-⌘-r to find the next occurrence.

Using special markers in replacement text

On page 200, we explain how you can search for special markers in a document. For example, if you want to search for every paragraph marker (¶), you can enter ^p as your find text. Table 6-1 summarizes the codes you must use when you want to search for special markers throughout a document. Each code, with the exceptions of ^w, ^l, and ^5, can also be included in your replacement text. For example, suppose you want to replace every normal hyphen in your document with an optional hyphen. (As we explain in Chapter 5, a normal hyphen always appears in your document, whereas an optional hyphen appears only when that hyphen occurs at the end of a line.) Choose the Change... command from the Utilities menu and type a single hyphen as your find text. Then, enter ^- as your replacement text. As with any other change, you can choose the Change All option or click Start Search to search for and replace each occurrence individually.

Your change text also can consist of a ^ followed by the three-digit decimal ASCII code for a character. For example, if you enter ^065 as your change text, Word will paste an uppercase *A* in your document as the replacement text. If you enter ^097, Word will paste a lowercase *a* in your document if the selected occurrence of the find text is lowercase, or an uppercase *A* if the selected occurrence is uppercase.

"Cleaning up" an imported file

When you import a file from another program into Word, some of the characters represented by upper-level ASCII codes and by ASCII codes 0-31 will be displayed on your screen as a retangular box (▯). If the document you've imported contains a lot of these boxes, you could spend a long time getting rid of them using manual editing techniques. Unfortunately, you cannot use the Change... command and specify this box as your find text. However, if you know the ASCII code for a character that's represented as a box, you can enter that ASCII code as your find text.

The first step in eliminating extraneous characters is to find out what ASCII code they represent. You can do this by highlighting a box and pressing

Option-⌘-q. The page number in the status box will change to a three-digit number in reverse video. This is the ASCII code for the character the box represents. (Once you've pressed Option-⌘-q, click in the page number in the status box to make Word display the ASCII code for subsequent characters.) You now can issue the Change... command and enter that code, preceded by a caret, as your find text, then enter nothing in the Change To edit bar as shown in Figure 6-37. If you select the Change All button, you will strip your document of extraneous characters.

FIGURE 6-37

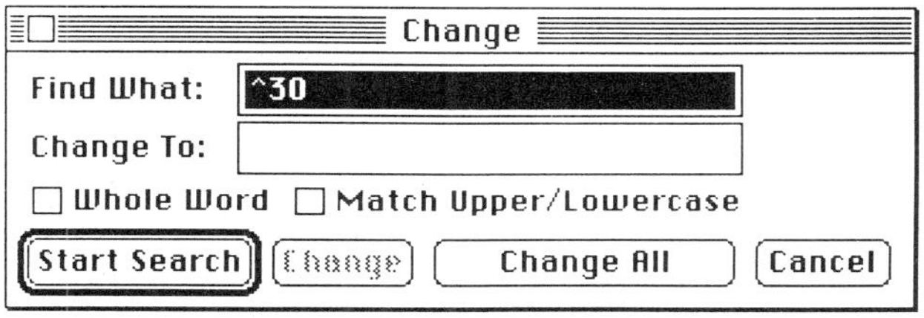

To delete a character, enter its ASCII code, preceded by a caret, in the Find What edit bar, and leave the Change To edit bar blank.

If your document has different extraneous characters, you will have to issue a separate Change... command for each character. After you've deleted one group of extra characters (or boxes), you'll need to highlight another extraneous character and click in the page number box or press Option-⌘-q to discover what ASCII code that character represents. Then, you can use the Change... command to delete all occurrences of that character. Repeat this process until your document is free of all extraneous characters.

CHECKING SPELLING

Your Word 4 package includes an MS Dictionary file of more than 80,000 words. Word uses this dictionary to identify misspelled words in a document. In addition to the MS Dictionary, you also can develop your own custom dictionaries to check for and correct misspelled words. Typically, a user-created dictionary will contain proper nouns, technical terms, and other words that are not found in the MS Dictionary. Before you use any dictionary to spell-check a document, there are a few minor housekeeping details you need to take care of, so we'll address these first.

Diskette Considerations

In order to avoid disk-switching when you're spell-checking a document, you will probably need to copy the MS Dictionary file from your utilities disk onto another disk. Since the MS Dictionary file occupies about 180K of disk space, you may need to reorganize your files in order to copy the dictionary onto another disk. If you're using a Macintosh with a hard drive, copy the MS Dictionary and any user dictionaries onto your hard disk. If you don't have a hard drive, then you should, if possible, copy the MS Dictionary and any user dictionaries onto the disk that contains the document file you want to spell-check.

Spell-checking with the MS Dictionary

Before we get into the subject of custom dictionaries, let's examine the process of spell-checking a document using the MS Dictionary. To check the spelling in a document, choose the Spelling... command from the Utilities menu or press ⌘-l. Word will go to disk and open the MS Dictionary file. If Word cannot find the MS Dictionary file on one of the currently active disks, it will ask you to locate the file. Use the Eject button to replace one of your active disks with the utilities disk or another disk that contains the MS Dictionary file. Click on the name MS Dictionary, as shown in Figure 6-38, and click the Open button. As soon as Word opens the MS Dictionary file, you will see the dialog box shown in Figure 6-39.

FIGURE 6-38

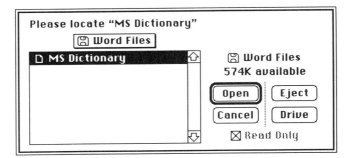

Word will ask
you to locate the
MS Dictionary
file if it is not
available on your
startup disk.

FIGURE 6-39

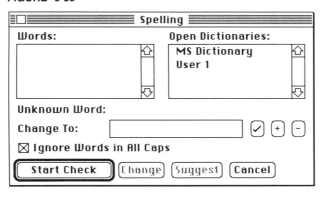

The Spelling dia-
log box appears
once Word has
loaded your MS
Dictionary file.

We will explore the various elements in the Spelling dialog box as we go along, but for now, let's get a quick overview of each item. At the upper-right corner of the dialog box is the Open Dictionaries list box. This box will always show the MS Dictionary plus any user dictionaries you have opened. Word always opens the User 1 dictionary automatically and displays its name in this list box when you first issue the Spelling... command.

Next to the Open Dictionaries list box is the Words list box, which displays Word's suggested correction text and entries from your user dictionaries. Below the two list boxes is the Unknown Word line. During a spelling check, Word displays unrecognized words in this area of the dialog box.

You'll use the Change To edit bar to correct misspelled words and to add new words to user dictionaries. Next to the Change To edit bar are three buttons—a check, a plus, and a minus. You can use the check to see if a word you type in the Change To edit bar is in one of the open dictionaries. As you'll see in a few pages, you'll use the plus and minus buttons to add words to and delete words from your user dictionaries.

The next item in the dialog box is the Ignore Words in All Caps option. This option does exactly what you might expect. When you select it, Word will not check the spelling of any word that appears in all uppercase letters. This option is handy when you are spell-checking a document that contains a number of special codes or acronyms.

Finally, the Spelling dialog box includes four buttons: Start Check (which also appears as No Change and Continue Check), Change, Suggest, and Cancel. As you're spell-checking a document, the purpose of each of these is clear.

A quick tour of the Spelling dialog box

After you've issued the Spelling... command, the first thing Word checks is the spelling of the word on which the insertion point marker is positioned (or the word immediately to the left of the insertion point marker). Assuming that this word is spelled correctly, you can start scanning forward through the rest of the document by clicking the Start Check button. At first, it may appear as if nothing is happening. However, when Word finds a word that it does not recognize—that is, a word that is not in the MS Dictionary—it will highlight that word in your document, then display it in the dialog box, as shown in Figure 6-40 on the following page.

When Word finds an unknown word and displays it in the dialog box, you have several options. If you want to leave the word as it is, click the No Change button. (Notice that No Change replaces Start Check in the dialog box.) Word will then continue scanning the document until it finds another word it does not recognize.

By the way, after you've clicked No Change once for an unknown word, Word will not display subsequent occurrences of that term in the Unknown Word line of the dialog box. However, Word will continue to highlight any additional occurrences of that term in your document window as it scans the text. In fact, Word will remember the term for the duration of the Word session. If you issue the Spelling... command again (even in another document), Word will not pause and display the term in the Unknown Word line.

Finding and correcting misspelled words

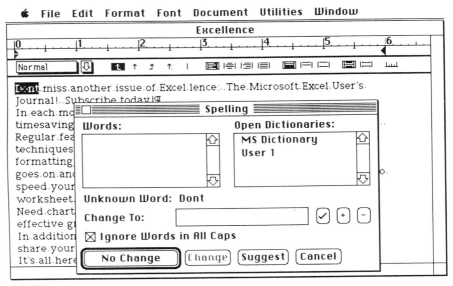

FIGURE 6-40

When Word finds a term it does not recognize, it highlights that word in your document and displays it on the unknown word line in the Spelling dialog box.

If, when you reissue the Spelling… command, you do want Word to pause again at every term it doesn't recognize, then hold down the Shift key as you issue the Spelling… command. Holding down the Shift key will erase the list of words and replacements you have compiled since you began your Word session. (You can use the Shift key to erase the Spelling… command only if you choose Spelling… from the Utilities menu. It won't work if you've used the ⌘-l keyboard shortcut to choose the Spelling… command. You'll notice that as you hold down the Shift key, Word changes the name of the Spelling… command to Reset Spelling….)

Making manual corrections

If you want to change an unknown word, there are several approaches you can take. First, you can simply type a new word in the Change To edit bar and then click the Change button. Word will replace the misspelled word in your document with the word you type in the Change To edit bar and automatically continue checking for more unrecognized words. Instead of typing a new word from scratch, you can click on the unknown word that's highlighted in the dialog box to display it in the Change To edit bar. Once it is in the edit bar, you can edit the unknown word, then click Change to correct the error and continue with the spelling check.

Sometimes, the typographical error in your document may be the result of an unintentional blank space or other error that cannot be corrected directly in the Change To edit bar. If that is the case, you can click on the document window and type your change manually. The Spelling dialog box will remain open, but will move behind the document window. Once you have made your change, issue the Spelling... command again to continue your spelling check.

For example, in Figure 6-41, the Spelling dialog box displays the unknown character string *lence*. If you look at the document window, you will see that the correct word is really *Excellence*, but because there is a blank space in the middle of the word, Word treats it as two words. In order to correct this spelling error, you will need to click on the document window and erase the blank space manually.

FIGURE 6-41

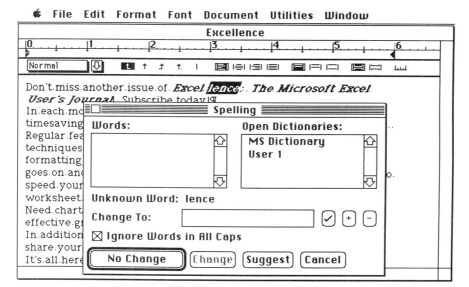

You may have to correct some spelling errors manually.

Another way to change a misspelled word is to click the Suggest button. Word will display a list of similar words in the Words list box. For example, after Word finds the misspelled word *tihs*, if you click the Suggest button, you'll see the list of words shown in Figure 6-42 on the next page.

Using the Suggest button

Notice that the first word in the list of suggested words also appears in the Change To edit bar. If you want to substitute this word for the misspelled word in your document, just click the Change button. Word will make the substitution and continue checking your document. If you want to use a different word in the list as your replacement, just click on that word before you click Change.

For example, suppose in Figure 6-42 you realize you want to use the word *this* instead of the suggestion in the edit bar, *ties*. You can simply click *this* in the Words list box to display that word in the Change To edit bar. If you then click the Change button, Word will substitute the word *this* in the Change To edit bar for the unrecognized word in your document and then continue scanning for other possible misspellings.

FIGURE 6-42

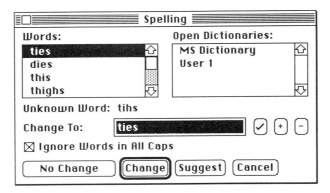

You can use the Suggest button to see a list of suggested alternatives for a misspelled word.

By the way, if the unknown word in your document begins with an uppercase letter, then the suggested list of alternatives in the Words list box will also appear in this form. For example, suppose your document contains a reference to a book called *Business Statistics*, and you have misspelled the word *Business*. When Word flags this misspelling and you click the Suggest button, you'll see a list of alternatives that all begin with a capital *B*. Similarly, if a misspelled word appears in your document in all uppercase letters, then the suggested alternatives will also appear in all uppercase letters. (Keep in mind that unless you deactivate the Ignore Words in All Caps option, Word will skip any misspelled words that appear in all uppercase letters.)

Occasionally, Word will be totally perplexed by the unknown word and will not be able to make an intelligent guess about alternatives. In that case, you'll see an alert box that says *Unable to suggest alternative*. In this case, you must type the correct word in the Change To edit bar. Another problem with the Suggest feature is that it occasionally gives you a list of alternatives that are not even close to the correct answer. This is most likely to happen when the first letter of a word is incorrect. For example, when we misspelled the word *during* as *suring*, Word suggested alternatives that all began with the letter *s* or *c*, such as *surfing*, *curing*, and *surging*.

Using the Change To edit bar

As we mentioned earlier, you can use the Change To edit bar to enter an alternative for a misspelled word or to correct a misspelled word. By using the Change To edit bar creatively, you can make even more significant changes to a document without having to activate your document window and halt the spelling check. Returning to the example in Figure 6-42, suppose you've misspelled the word *this* as *tihs* in your document. After Word catches the misspelling and suggests *this* as a possible alternative, you realize that, instead of the word *this*, you want to use the word *these*. All you have to do is edit *this* in the Change To edit bar to *these*, and click the Change button. Word will then substitute *these* for the misspelled word in your document and continue scanning for more unrecognized words. To help you see the context of an unknown word, you can move the Spelling dialog box on your screen by dragging its title bar.

When you're editing the contents of the Change To edit bar, you are not limited to typing a single word. Although the edit bar can display only about 19 characters, you can type many more characters than this. You can even type a sentence or more, if you want.

Normally, Word will not alert you if the text you type in the Change To edit bar is misspelled. Once you've entered a correction in the Change To edit bar, however, you can check the spelling of your correction text against the entries in all open dictionaries. To do this, click the check symbol next to the edit bar before you click the Change button. Word will look for that term in the open dictionaries. If the term you typed cannot be found in an open dictionary, Word will place a copy of that term in the Unknown Word line in the dialog box. If Word does find the term you typed in a dictionary, the Unknown Word line will be blank. You can assume that the word is spelled correctly and click the Change button to correct your document. Unfortunately, you can check only single-word entries in the edit bar. If you've typed more than one word, Word will automatically see the contents of the edit bar as "unknown."

Repeated misspellings

If you have made the same spelling error more than once in your document, Word will remember the last editing change you made and suggest that solution the next time it runs into the error.

For example, suppose you commonly transpose the letters *a* and *h* in the word *that*. The first time Word highlights the character sequence *taht*, you click on the word in the Unknown Word line of the Spelling dialog box, change the typographical error to *that* in the Change To edit bar, and click the Change button. The next time Word highlights the character sequence *taht*, it will automatically enter the word *that* in the Change To edit bar. You can simply click the Change button to accept Word's suggestion.

Notes

It's interesting to note that, in addition to misspelled words, the Spelling... command will find words that appear to have unusual patterns of uppercase and lowercase letters. For example, Word will flag such occurrences as BOok, boOk, and BooK. These occurrences will be flagged even if the Ignore Words in All Caps option is activated.

If your document contains a hyphenated word, such as well-dressed, then Word will check each part of that word separately. For example, if you've entered *well-dressd*, then Word will flag only the *dressd* portion as an unknown word. Word can recognize any combination of hyphenated words as long as all the component words are in the MS Dictionary and are spelled correctly within your document.

Word also can recognize most words that are created by adding common prefixes and suffixes. However, the program is not completely foolproof in this regard; it's possible that an illogical combination of a word and a prefix or suffix will not be flagged during a spelling check.

If you have assigned the Hidden character format to text in your document, Word will check the spelling of that text as long as it is displayed in the document window. If you use the Preferences... command to suppress the display of your hidden text, however, Word will not check the spelling of any hidden words.

Halting the spelling check

When Word has checked every word from the insertion point to the end of your document, you'll see an alert box that asks, *Continue checking from beginning?* If you click OK, Word will go back to the beginning of the document and continue checking for misspelled words. When Word reaches the end a second time, you'll see the *End of document reached* message. If you click Cancel, Word will halt the spelling check and remove the Spelling dialog box from your screen.

You also can cancel the spelling check at any other time. If you press the ⌘ and period keys (⌘-.) while Word is scanning your document, Word will stop scanning, but the Spelling dialog box will remain open. If Word is not scanning your document, you can cancel the spelling check by clicking the Cancel button, by clicking in the close box to close the Spelling dialog box, or by typing ⌘-period.

If you click anywhere on your document window while the Spelling dialog box is open, Word will activate the document window but will not close the Spelling dialog box. To reactivate the Spelling dialog box, just click anywhere on that box, choose Spelling... from the Document menu, or type ⌘-l.

Spell-checking a selected portion of the document

Word makes it easy for you to check for spelling errors in only a selected portion of a document. Simply drag through the part of the document you want to check, then issue the Spelling... command. When you choose Spelling... from the Utilities menu, Word will pause until you click the Start Check button. After you click this button, Word will proceed to scan only the text you have selected and flag any unrecognized words. After scanning the entire selection, you'll see the alert box shown in Figure 6-43. When you click OK to close this box, Word will also close the Spelling dialog box.

Spell-checking a single word

To check the spelling of a single word, just select that word and issue the Spelling... command. Instead of selecting just the word you want to check, you can select that word and any following text. It's important, however, that the word you want to check be the very first item in your selection. After you make your selection and issue the Spelling... command, Word will check the word against the entries in all open dictionaries. If Word cannot recognize the word you have selected, that word will appear in the Unknown Word line of the Spelling dialog box. You can then correct the word using the methods we described earlier, or you can click the No Change button to leave the word intact. After you've corrected the word or clicked No Change, Word will display the alert box shown in Figure 6-43. (If you've selected more than one word, you won't see this alert box until Word has checked your entire selection.) When you click OK in the alert box, Word will close the Spelling dialog box and terminate the spelling check.

FIGURE 6-43

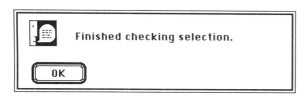

After checking the selected text, Word presents this alert message.

Instead of selecting the word whose spelling you want to check, you can click anywhere on that word (including just before or just after that word), then issue the Spelling... command. Again, if Word does not recognize the word on which you've positioned the insertion point marker, that word will appear in the Unknown Word line of the Spelling dialog box. You can then correct the word, or click the No Change button. In either case, Word will proceed to scan forward through your document for other unrecognized words. If you don't want Word to scan any further, close the Spelling dialog box and change the word manually, if it needs to be corrected. If the word already is correct, just close the dialog box without clicking No Change.

You can also use the Spelling... command to check the spelling of text in your header, footer, and footnote windows. We'll talk about headers and footers in Chapter 7 and footnotes in Chapter 11.

In order to use Word's Spelling... command efficiently, you will almost certainly want to create at least one user dictionary or custom dictionary that you can use in conjunction with the MS Dictionary. Chances are, your documents will contain one or more frequently used words that are not in the MS Dictionary file. It can be annoying and time consuming for the program to flag these words as "unknown" when they are perfectly legitimate terms. You can get around this problem by adding these terms to a user dictionary, then opening that dictionary file each time you perform a spelling check. Since Word automatically checks your document against all open dictionaries, it will be able to recognize any specialized

User
Dictionaries

terms that you have stored in a user dictionary. Of course, if your document contains a specialized term that is misspelled, Word will flag it during a spelling check. You will then be able to consult your user-created dictionary to obtain the correct spelling for that term.

There are a couple of ways to add new terms to a custom dictionary. First, you can add them during a spell-checking procedure—whenever Word finds a legitimate word that is not in its MS Dictionary, you can simply add it to a user dictionary. Second, you can type terms directly into the Spelling dialog box. We will discuss both methods as we explain how to create a custom dictionary.

In addition to adding words to a user dictionary, you can revise and delete earlier entries. You also can copy terms from one user dictionary to another. Of course, any changes like this must be saved to disk if they are to be permanent.

Although Word offers a great deal of flexibility with user dictionaries, it does not allow you to make changes to the MS Dictionary. That file is protected so you can neither add nor delete terms, nor can you revise an existing word in the MS Dictionary.

Creating a custom dictionary

Creating a custom dictionary involves three steps: opening an empty user dictionary, adding terms to that dictionary, and saving it to disk. When you issue the Spelling... command for the first time during a Word session, Word automatically opens a dictionary called User 1 (in addition to opening the MS Dictionary). Unless you've added terms to this dictionary and saved them to disk, the User 1 dictionary will be empty. You also can open other empty user dictionaries and add terms to them.

Opening a new user dictionary file

To start a new user dictionary, just choose New from the File menu while the Spelling dialog box is open. Word will automatically open another user dictionary called User x, where x is a sequential number. For example, the first time you choose New from the File menu, Word will open a dictionary called User 2 (since User 1 is already open). The second time you choose New, Word will open the User 3 dictionary, and so forth. Of course, each of these dictionaries is initially blank, much like a new Word document file.

You can have up to four user dictionaries open at once, RAM permitting. As you are adding new terms to your dictionaries, you may want to have two or more open at once so that you can place different kinds of terms in different dictionaries.

Adding new terms during a spelling check

As you are spell-checking a document, Word may occasionally flag a word it does not recognize, which, in fact, is a legitimate word. The most likely candidates are proper nouns, such as company names, technical jargon, and other specialized terms. When Word displays an unrecognized word in the Spelling dialog box, you can add it to a user dictionary by clicking on the unknown word to display it in the Change To edit bar, then clicking the plus button in the dialog box. Unless you have selected another dictionary name from the Open Dictionaries list box, Word will add the term to the first user dictionary in the list of open dictionaries (probably User 1). If, during the course of the current spell-checking procedure, you've added a word to another user dictionary, Word will "remember" that dictionary and use it when you click the plus button (unless, of course, you select another dictionary name before clicking the plus button).

Now that you have "legitimized" the term, Word will remove it from the Unknown Word line of the dialog box and display it in the Words list box. If this term is the first one to be added to the dictionary, it will be the only entry in the Words list box. For example, Figure 6-44 shows the Spelling dialog box after we have added the word *Helvetica* to the User 1 dictionary.

FIGURE 6-44

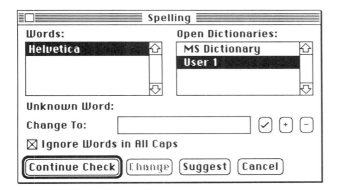

You can add new terms to the User 1 dictionary.

If you want to add the term to a dictionary other than the first user dictionary on the list, just click on the name of that dictionary in the Open Dictionaries list box before you click the plus button. If more than one user dictionary is open when you add a word to a dictionary, that word will remain displayed in the Change To edit bar until you click the Continue Check button or close the dialog box. If you want to add the term to another dictionary, just click on the name of the dictionary in which you want to place the term, then click the plus button again.

You do not have to wait until Word flags an unrecognized word before you add that word to a user dictionary. Another way to add a term is to open the Spelling dialog box, type that term in the Change To edit bar, click the name of the dictionary in which you want to place the term, then click the plus button. For example, suppose you are about to spell-check a legal document that contains numerous references to a person named Schaeffer. You can add this name to the User 1 dictionary before you begin checking your document. Simply choose Spelling... from the Utilities menu, type *Schaeffer* in the Change To edit bar, and click the plus button. Word will automatically add this word to the User 1 dictionary (or whatever user dictionary is first in the list of open dictionaries).

Adding new terms by typing

Capitalization

When you add a new term to a user dictionary, you need to keep in mind how Word deals with capitalization during a spelling check. If the term you add to a dictionary is in all lowercase letters, Word will be able to recognize any occurrence of that word in a document, no matter what case is used. If you use one or more uppercase letters in the term you add to a dictionary, Word will recognize only occurrences that have the same letters in uppercase. For example, suppose you add the name MacArthur to a user dictionary. In performing a spelling check, Word will flag any occurrence of this name where either the *M* or the *A* is not capitalized. Thus, Macarthur, macarthur, and macArthur would all be unrecognized words.

Because of the way Word handles capitalization, you should add any nonproper words in all lowercase letters. For example, the word *repaginate* is not in the MS Dictionary. If you add this word to a user dictionary, be sure that you enter it in all lowercase letters. If you don't—for example, if you enter it with an uppercase *r*— Word will flag all occurrences of that word where the *r* is not capitalized.

Capitalization also affects the way Word displays dictionary terms in the Words list box. At the top of a list of user dictionary terms, you'll see all the words that begin with an uppercase letter, arranged alphabetically. Following these, you'll see a list of all other words, also arranged alphabetically.

Editing a user dictionary

Fortunately, Word's user dictionaries are very flexible. Not only can you add new terms to a dictionary, you also can revise existing terms, delete terms, and even copy terms from one user dictionary to another. If there's a dictionary that you use during most of your spelling checks, you will probably need to make frequent changes to that file in order to adapt it to different situations.

Revising a dictionary term

To revise a term in a user dictionary, open the Spelling dialog box, then open the dictionary file that contains the term you want to revise. When you click on the name of that dictionary file in the Open Dictionaries list box, its contents will appear in the Words list box. Click on the word you want to revise to display it in the Change To edit bar. You can then edit the term in any way you want. Once you have completed your revisions, click the plus button to add the edited term to your dictionary. When Word places the edited term in the user dictionary, it will not automatically delete the original term on which the edited term is based. If you want to remove the original term from the dictionary, you must use the minus button to delete it.

Deleting a dictionary term

To delete a term, click on the name of the dictionary that contains the term you want to delete. Then, click on the term you want to delete in the Words list box. When that word appears in the Change To edit bar, click the minus button. This will remove the word from the dictionary, but the word will still appear in the Change To edit bar. If you want, you can edit the term and add the edited version to the dictionary that contained the original term. Alternatively, you can select another dictionary and add the term to that dictionary.

If you have two or more user dictionaries open, you can easily move a term from one to another. Simply click on the name of the dictionary that contains the term you want to move, then select that term in the Words list box. Word will then place the term you selected in the Change To edit bar. Next, click on the name of the dictionary to which you want to copy that word, and click the plus button. The word will now be in both the original dictionary and the dictionary to which you copied it. If you want, you can now delete the term from the original dictionary.

Moving a term from one dictionary to another

As we mentioned earlier, once you have added terms to a user dictionary, you will need to save that dictionary to disk in order to use those terms again. After a dictionary has been saved, it can be recalled for use with any document. The dictionary on disk is an independent file; it is not in any way "attached" to the particular document that was open when the dictionary was created. However, Word will remember the names of user dictionaries that were open when you ended the last Word session. Thus, you may not need to reopen your user dictionaries each time you issue the Spelling... command.

Managing dictionary files

Interestingly, Word will automatically open no more than three user dictionaries when you issue the Spelling... command in a new Word session. If you had four user dictionaries open during the last Word session, Word will open the first three only. Of course, you can open the fourth one by using the Open... command.

When Word opens the user dictionaries that were open during the last session, it will not open a new, blank user dictionary named User 1. Thus, if you would like to create a new dictionary, you will need to choose the New command on the File menu while the Spelling dialog box is open. Word will then add a User 1 dictionary name to the Open Dictionaries list. You can add terms to this new dictionary and then save it to disk.

You can close user dictionary files when you no longer need them by clicking on the name of the dictionary in the Open Dictionaries list box and selecting Close from the File menu.

Word does not allow you to have more than four user dictionaries open at one time, so you may need to close one dictionary in order to open another. Moreover, you may be able to speed up a spell-checking procedure by closing any extraneous dictionary files. In fact, we recommend that you create one general user dictionary file that contains frequently used terms, and open only this file whenever you spell-check a document.

In addition, you can create a handful of specialty dictionaries, each of which contains terms that are used in a particular kind of document. You would then open one of these specialty dictionaries only when you need to spell-check the kind of document for which it was created.

As you might expect, Word won't let you close the MS Dictionary file. Once that file has been opened, it will remain open until you quit from Word.

Saving a user dictionary

Saving a user dictionary is similar to saving any type of file. To save a user dictionary for the first time, click on that dictionary name in the Spelling dialog box, then—while the dialog box is still open—choose Save or Save As... from the File menu. Word suggests the name User *x* in the Save Current Dictionary As edit bar. Word also displays in dim video the names of other files on the current disk (if any) in the list box.

You can either save the dictionary under the suggested User *x* name or you can type a new name in the edit bar. Once you decide on a name for the dictionary, just click the Save button to save the dictionary to the current disk. Of course, you can use the Drive and/or Eject buttons if you want to save the file on a different disk. After a file has been saved once, you can save it again under the same name by simply opening the Spelling dialog box, clicking on the name of the dictionary you want to save, and then choosing Save from the File menu.

In general, we recommend that you type a new name when you save a dictionary file rather than using the suggested User *x* name. Here's why: Suppose you save a dictionary under the name *User 2*, then quit from Word. The next time you load Word, you decide to create another user dictionary. When you choose New from the File menu, Word will automatically add the name *User 2* to the list of Open Dictionaries in the Spelling dialog box. However, this User 2 dictionary is not the same as the User 2 dictionary that you saved to disk in the earlier Word session. Like all new dictionaries, it will be blank. Suppose you then decide to open the User 2 dictionary that's stored on disk. When you do this, your Open Dictionaries list box will display *two* User 2 dictionaries! Obviously, this could lead to some confusion.

Another reason for saving user dictionaries under a name other than User *x* is to help you remember which dictionaries in the Open Dictionaries list box have been saved to disk and which have not. When you save a dictionary under a different name, Word replaces the original User *x* name in the Open Dictionaries list box with the name of the file on disk.

By the way, if you make changes to a user dictionary and do not save those changes to disk, Word will alert you to this fact when you choose Quit from the File menu. You'll see an alert box with a message like *Save changes to dictionary User 2?* If you click Yes, Word will save the terms in that dictionary under whatever name is highlighted in the Open Dictionaries list box. If you click No, Word will quit to the Finder level without saving the dictionary, and if you click Cancel, Word will return to your document and not quit to the Finder level.

If there are two or more dictionaries with unsaved changes when you issue the Quit command, Word will display this alert box for each dictionary. In each case, you can click Yes, No, or Cancel.

After a user dictionary has been saved to disk, you can open it by choosing Open... from the File menu after you issue the Spelling... command. Word will then search the current disk for dictionary files and display a list of those files (along with other files) in the Open dialog box.

Select the file you want to open by double-clicking on its name in the list box. Of course, you can use the Drive or Eject buttons to access a dictionary file on a different disk. As soon as you open a dictionary file, its name will appear in the Open Dictionaries list box in the Spelling dialog box.

To close a dictionary, just click on its name in the list of Open Dictionaries, then choose Close from the File menu. Word will then delete the name from the list of Open Dictionaries in the Spelling dialog box. If you have made changes to the dictionary that have not been saved to disk, Word will alert you with a dialog box that asks, *Save changes to Dictionary?* If you want to save those changes before you close the dictionary file, click Yes. If you click No, Word will close the dictionary without saving the changes. There's also a Cancel option, which allows you to back out of the Close procedure altogether.

By the way, Word will not allow you to close the MS Dictionary file. As we mentioned earlier, once you issue the Spelling... command and open the MS Dictionary, it will remain open until you quit from Word.

You can delete a dictionary file from within Word just as you would delete any file. When you choose Delete... from the File menu, Word will display a list of all the files on the current disk, including dictionary files. Just click on the name of the dictionary file you want to delete, then click the Delete button (or double-click the file name). Next, click Yes in the Delete dialog box to complete the deletion.

By the way, as with document files, Word will not allow you to delete a dictionary that is currently open. Before you can delete a dictionary that you have opened during a spell-check session, you must click on the dictionary name in the Spelling dialog box and choose Close from the File menu.

In most instances, using a dictionary that you've created is no different from using the MS Dictionary. Once a dictionary file is open, Word will automatically refer to the terms in that dictionary as it spell-checks a document. However, you cannot use the Suggest feature with a user dictionary. Whenever you click the Suggest button, Word looks only in the MS Dictionary for alternatives to an unknown word.

Of course, you can still access an alternative word from a user dictionary. To do this, click on the name of that dictionary in the Open Dictionaries list box. Word will then display the entries in that dictionary in the Words list box, as shown in Figure 6-45.

FIGURE 6-45

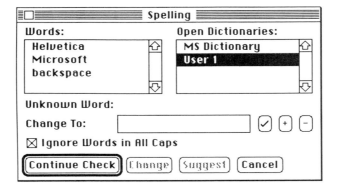

To see the entries in a user dictionary, click on the dictionary name in the Open Dictionaries list box.

If the dictionary contains more words than can be displayed in the Words list box, you can click the scroll arrows to bring additional words into view. When you find the word you want to use as a replacement for the misspelled word, just click on it to place it in the Change To edit bar. You can then click the Change button to make the replacement in your document.

One interesting thing you can do with user dictionaries is create temporary entries—that is, entries you use for only one Word session. All you have to do is add the terms to a user dictionary without saving that dictionary. The words will remain in the user dictionary until you close the dictionary file or quit from Word. For example, suppose you're writing a letter that describes your hometown of Plano, Texas. You can add the word *Plano* to the User 1 dictionary (or to any user dictionary), then spell-check the letter. If you don't think you'll need to use the Plano entry again, quit without saving the dictionary. Of course, you can also save the dictionary and delete the word later, when you're sure you won't need it.

A Final Note

As a final note, we must remind you that Word's ability to find misspelled words does not necessarily mean that you'll discover every wrong word in a document. The program has no way of recognizing incorrect tense or form or improper usage of a word. Always supplement your spelling checks with a thorough reading.

HYPHENATION

Like many other word processing programs, Word 4 offers a hyphenation feature. Word will not automatically hyphenate words as you enter text. However, you can use the Hyphenate... command on the Utilities menu to hyphenate text you've already created. Of course, the benefit of using hyphenation is that it allows you to create better-looking documents. Hyphenation is particularly helpful when you are using justified paragraphs and/or narrow columns of text. By hyphenating selected words, you can avoid the unsightly extra spaces that Word occasionally inserts to achieve a justified right margin. If you are using left-aligned paragraphs instead of justified paragraphs, hyphenation can help you create more uniform lines of text.

Word's Hyphenate… command allows you to hyphenate an entire document or only a selected portion of a document. You also can check each potential hyphenation point as you go or have Word perform all the hyphenation automatically. We'll talk about the different hyphenation options as we explain how to use the Hyphenate… command.

One major advantage of Word's hyphenation feature is that it inserts optional hyphens instead of "regular" hyphens. An optional hyphen appears in your printed document only if the word you have hyphenated occurs at a line break. If you edit or reformat your text so that the hyphenated word gets shifted to the middle of a line, then Word will not print the optional hyphen.

The optional hyphen is one of two special hyphens offered by Word 4. Word also offers a nonbreaking hyphen, which can be created by typing ⌘-~. This will appear on your screen as ≂. By the way, you can create an optional hyphen manually by typing the ⌘ key followed by a hyphen (⌘- -). When Show ¶ is activated, each optional hyphen will appear on your screen as ¬. In Chapter 5, we discussed special hyphens in more detail. For now, however, you just need to be aware of how an optional hyphen differs from a regular hyphen.

Before we discuss how to use Word's Hyphenate… command, we need to go over a few details related to managing your disks during a Hyphenation procedure. As you might expect, the issue of how to arrange disk files is more critical for those using floppy disk drives than for those using a hard drive.

Diskette Considerations

Word's Hyphenate… command calls up a special algorithm that is stored in the Word Hyphenation file, which is on the utilities disk in your Word 4 package. When you first issue the Hyphenate… command during a Word session, the program will look for this file on one of the current disks. If the file cannot be found, Word will display the dialog box shown in Figure 6-46 on the following page. When you see this dialog box, eject one of your current disks and insert the utilities disk or another disk that contains a copy of the Word Hyphenation file. Then, click on the file name *Word Hyphenation* and click the Open button.

To make the Hyphenate procedure simpler when you use floppy disk drives, you can copy the 24K, Word Hyphenation file to your program disk. Be sure to delete the Word 4 ReadMe file from your program disk before you copy the Word Hyphenation file. There is very little space on your program disk, so you need to conserve as much of that space as possible.

FIGURE 6-46

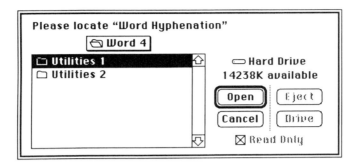

Word will ask
you to locate the
Word Hyphena-
tion file if it is
not on your
startup or
program disk.

Using the Hyphenate... Command

To hyphenate a document, choose Hyphenate... from the Utilities menu or press Shift-[F15]. After Word reads the hyphenation instructions from disk, you'll see the Hyphenate dialog box shown in Figure 6-47.

FIGURE 6-47

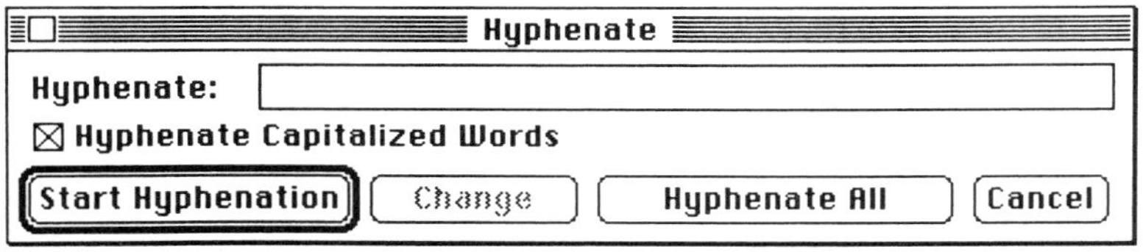

The Hyphenate dialog box appears once the Word Hyphenation file has been loaded.

At this point, you have two choices. First, you can use automatic hyphenation by clicking the Hyphenate All button, which will cause Word to scan through the entire document and automatically hyphenate words at line breaks, where possible. Instead of clicking Hyphenate All, you can click Start Hyphenation. Word will then pause each time it finds a word to hyphenate and display that word in the Hyphenate edit bar. Word will highlight the place where it plans to hyphenate the word. You will then have the choice of accepting the suggested word break. The Word reference manual refers to this pause-and-check procedure as "confirming hyphenation."

Whether you use automatic or confirming hyphenation, you have the choice of ignoring or hyphenating capitalized words. As you can see in Figure 6-47, the Hyphenate Capitalized Words option is selected when you first open the Hyphenate dialog box. If you do not want to hyphenate words that begin with an uppercase letter, click this option to deselect it.

If you click the Hyphenate All button, Word will automatically decide which words to break between lines and how to break each word. This automatic hyphenation occurs very rapidly and affects all the text between the insertion point and the end of the document. When Word reaches the end of the document, you will see the alert box shown in Figure 6-48. If you click OK, Word will cycle back to the beginning of the document and automatically hyphenate words at line breaks until it reaches the end of the document. Word will then display the message *End of document reached.* If you click Cancel in the Continue Hyphenation alert box, Word will stop the Hyphenation procedure and automatically close the Hyphenate dialog box.

Automatic hyphenation

FIGURE 6-48

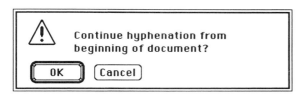

You'll see this alert box when Word has hyphenated from the insertion point to the end of your document.

You can cancel the automatic Hyphenation procedure by pressing the ⌘ key as you type a period (⌘-.). You also can undo hyphenation after the procedure is completed. At the end of this chapter, we will explain a couple of methods for undoing hyphenation.

In general, we recommend that you avoid automatic hyphenation since it can lead to some problems. First, Word may hyphenate words at the end of two or more consecutive lines in your document. This is not good form since it makes the document more difficult to read. Second, Word may hyphenate words that already are hyphenated. For example, if your document contains the word *long-suffering*, Word may hyphenate the *suffering* portion at the end of a line. A final reason for avoiding automatic hyphenation is that Word's syllable breaks are not always correct. For example, in one of our documents, Word hyphenated the word *dictionary* between *dictio* and *nary*, rather than between *diction* and *ary*. If you use confirming hyphenation instead of automatic hyphenation, you can avoid these kinds of problems during the Hyphenation procedure.

Problems with automatic hyphenation

Instead of clicking the Hyphenate All button, you can click Start Hyphenation in the Hyphenate dialog box. Starting at the insertion point, Word will look through your document for the first possible word to hyphenate and display that word in the Hyphenate edit bar. Word also will highlight in your document the letter that will appear after the suggested word break. For example, Figure 6-49 shows how the Hyphenate dialog box will look when Word has found a word to hyphenate.

Confirming hyphenation

FIGURE 6-49

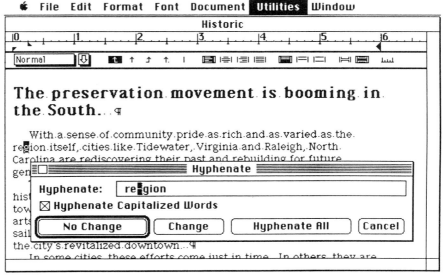

Word will suggest a word break when it locates a "candidate" for hyphenation.

With very few exceptions, when a word contains two or more syllables, Word will display all the syllable breaks in the Hyphenate edit bar. Word will highlight in the edit bar the place where it plans to hyphenate the word. Of course, this corresponds to the word break that's highlighted in the document. If you want to accept Word's suggested hyphenation, just click the Change button in the dialog box. If you do not want to break this word, click the No Change button. (No Change replaces the Start Hyphenation button.) Word will then look for the next word to hyphenate and display it in the edit bar.

If you want to hyphenate the word in the edit bar, but you want the word break to occur at a location other than that suggested by Word, you can simply click on the place where you want the hyphen to occur. For example, in Figure 6-50, Word suggests that the word *generations* be broken between *gen* and *erations*. (Notice that the *e* is highlighted in the document text.) Suppose you want to break the word between the *gener* and *ations*. Just click at the spot where you want to insert your hyphen. Word will highlight that syllable break in the edit bar, as shown in Figure 6-50. Click the Change button to implement the syllable break.

By the way, you can hyphenate a word between any two letters—you do not have to break it between syllables. If you click somewhere other than on a syllable break in the edit bar, Word will display a vertical bar at that place rather than highlighting the break. This flexibility in placing word breaks is very helpful in those few situations where the syllable breaks that Word displays in the edit bar are incorrect.

FIGURE 6-50

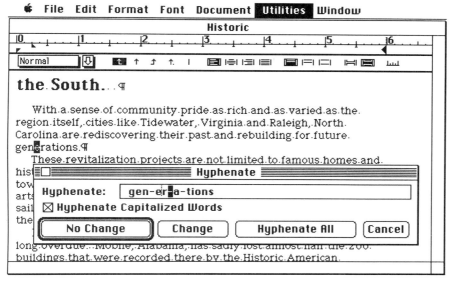

You can highlight the syllable break where you want Word to insert a hyphen.

You might notice a dotted vertical line appearing on a word in the edit bar. This is a guideline for the approximate number of characters in the word that will fit on the current line. In general, if you try to hyphenate the word to the right of the dotted line, there will not be enough room on the previous line to accommodate the first part of the hyphenated word. Word will still insert the optional hyphen in your document, however, without breaking the word. For instance, in the dialog box shown in Figure 6-50, if you clicked between *genera* and *tions*, Word probably would not be able to break the word. However, it still would place an optional hyphen in your document at the location you specified.

After Word has scanned to the end of your document looking for possible word breaks, you'll see the alert box shown in Figure 6-48. If you want to cycle back to the beginning of the document and look for more word breaks, click OK. If you want to stop the Hyphenation procedure, click Cancel in the dialog box. Word will then close the Hyphenate dialog box.

One last note about confirming hyphenation: Although you have considerable flexibility in hyphenating words, you cannot edit your document while the Hyphenate dialog box is open. You may recall that as you are performing some dialog box procedures, such as finding and changing, Word allows you to click on your document window and edit text without closing the dialog box. With the Hyphenate... command, however, you must close the dialog box before you can access your document text.

Hyphenating a selected part of a document

If you select a portion of your document before you issue the Hyphenate… command, Word will perform the Hyphenation procedure only on that selection. Your selection can be as small as a single word, though you probably will want to select at least a paragraph or more. Again, you will have the choice of using either automatic or confirming hyphenation. If you select a block of text in your document, then issue the Hyphenate… command, you'll see a Hyphenate Selection button in the Hyphenate dialog box instead of the Hyphenate All button. If you click Hyphenate Selection, Word will automatically break words at the ends of lines and insert hyphens, as necessary, throughout the selected text. When Word has completed hyphenating the selection, you'll see the alert box in Figure 6-51. When you click OK, Word will close the Hyphenate dialog box.

FIGURE 6-51

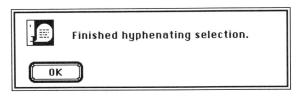

Finished hyphenating selection.

OK

You'll see this alert box after Word has hyphen- ated a selection of text.

If you click Start Hyphenation instead of Hyphenate Selection, Word will pause and display each suggested word break, just as it does when you are performing a confirming hyphenation on an entire document. Again, you have the option of choosing No Change or breaking a word at a place other than the location that Word suggests. When Word has scanned the entire selection, you'll see the alert box shown in Figure 6-51. Just click OK to close the Hyphenate dialog box and stop the procedure.

Editing after You Hyphenate

If you make substantial changes to a document after you've used the Hyphenate… command, you will probably change the location of a number of hyphenated words. Instead of occurring at the ends of lines, some hyphenated words will end up in the middle of lines. Moreover, a number of words that need to be hyphenated will not be. You can solve the second problem by simply issuing the Hyphenate… command again. Before you reissue the Hyphenate… command, however, you may want to get rid of the hyphens that are now in the middle of lines of text. We explain in the next section how you can use the Change… command to search for and delete unnecessary hyphens. Keep in mind that, if you don't eliminate these hyphens, they will not affect the appearance of your printed document since Word does not print optional hyphens unless they appear at line breaks.

In general, we recommend that you delete any unnecessary optional hyphens before you rehyphenate your document. That way, you can reduce the clutter on your screen, which can make your document more difficult to read. For example, the document shown in Figure 6-52 has been through several Hyphenation procedures. Although none of the midline hyphens will appear in your printed text, they make it difficult to read and edit text on the screen.

FIGURE 6-52

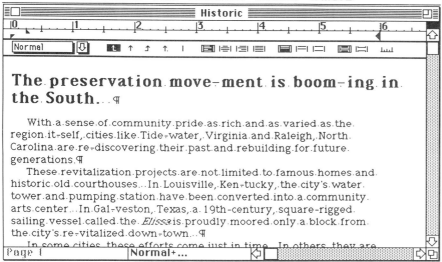

To eliminate clutter, you'll probably want to delete unnecessary optional hyphens from your document.

Undoing Hyphenation

After you have hyphenated a document or a selected portion of a document, you have the option of using an Undo command to delete all the hyphens. As with other Undo commands, you must select Undo Hyphenation from the Edit menu immediately after you complete the Hyphenation procedure. If you perform another action first—typing a few characters, changing formats, etc.—the Undo Hyphenation command will no longer be available.

Fortunately, another way to undo hyphenation is by using the Change... command to delete all the hyphens that were added during a Hyphenation procedure. Just choose Change... from the Utilities menu and enter a caret followed by a hyphen (^-) in the Find What edit bar. Leave the Change To edit bar blank. Then, click Change All if you want to delete every optional hyphen in your document. If you want to delete only some of the hyphens, click Start Search instead of Change All. Word will then pause at each optional hyphen and give you the choice of deleting or leaving it. For more information on using the Change... command, see pages 204-215.

PRINTING 7

After creating, formatting, and editing a document, you're ready to print. Of course, if you're like most Word users, you'll probably print at least one draft of your document long before you complete all your editing and formatting changes. Fortunately, Word's default Print and Page Setup settings are generally adequate for printing quick drafts and simple documents. After you have installed and selected a printer, you simply choose the Print... command from the File menu and click OK in the Print dialog box.

Of course, with a program as powerful as Word, it's no surprise that printing can also be very complex . Word lets you specify a number of settings that apply directly to printing, such as the number of copies you want to create, which pages of a document you want to print, and the method of feeding the paper into the printer. In addition, you can add certain elements to a document that enhance the printed pages, such as page numbers and headers and footers.

In this chapter, we'll explore the various settings that can affect printing and show you how to number your pages and create headers and footers. Then, we'll show you how to use the print preview screen and Word's page view to see how the printed document will look—without actually printing. Let's begin, however, with a look at the procedures you follow to install and select a printer.

INSTALLING A PRINTER

In order to use a printer, you must first install the appropriate driver or printer resource file on your startup disk—this is simply a matter of copying the driver file into your System folder. Then, after you start up your Macintosh, you must use the Chooser command to select that printer driver.

If you use an ImageWriter, ImageWriter LQ, a LaserWriter, or a LaserWriter SC, you will find the driver files for these printers stored on your Macintosh Printing Tools disk. To obtain a new driver, contact your Apple dealer for a Systems Software Update. If you use a daisy wheel printer, you'll find a card in the Word 4 package that you can send to Microsoft (along with a minimal fee) to obtain the Mac DaisyLink serial printer drivers. The printer drivers you receive will work only with Word. However, the package you receive will include an order form for obtaining the full DaisyLink set, which will contain printer drivers for other Macintosh applications.

To install a driver on your startup disk, just place the disk containing the driver in one of your disk drives and place your startup disk in another drive. (Of course, if you're using a hard disk, you only need to insert the disk containing your printer drivers.) Next, double-click on the icon for the disk containing the printer drivers so you can view its contents. Now, click on the icon that represents the printer you want to use, and drag that driver file to the System folder on your startup disk. You must be sure that the driver is in your System folder; otherwise, the Chooser won't recognize it.

If you plan to use more than one printer, be sure to copy all the appropriate driver files. If you are using a LaserWriter, you will need to copy two files to your startup disk: the LaserWriter printer driver file and the file labeled Laser Prep. Finally, if you plan to use background printing with MultiFinder, be sure that you have a copy of the PrintMonitor file in your System folder.

Making Room on Your Startup Disk

If you are using a floppy disk as your startup disk, you may see the alert message *There isn't enough room on the disk to duplicate or copy the selected items* when you try to install a new printer driver. To solve this problem, click on the icon for the printer driver you want to use, and select Get Info from the File menu. You'll then see a window that displays, among other things, the amount of disk space required for the driver file. For example, if you open the Info window for the LaserWriter driver, you'll see that it consumes quite a bit of disk space—from 37K to 64K, depending on which version of the printer driver you have. (By the way, later versions of the LaserWriter driver, which require significantly more disk space, can be used with any Apple LaserWriter PostScript printer. However, earlier versions of the LaserWriter driver cannot be used with newer printers. If you want to obtain the most recent version of the LaserWriter driver file, contact your Apple dealer.)

As we've mentioned, in order to use a LaserWriter printer, you need not only the LaserWriter driver file on your startup disk, but also the Laser Prep file, which consumes an additional 28K of disk space. As its name suggests, the Laser Prep file prepares your document for printing on the LaserWriter.

Once you've determined how much disk space you need, take a look at the files on your startup disk and decide which ones you can do without. For example, your startup disk may contain a driver file for the ImageWriter printer. If you don't plan to use this printer, drag the icon for this printer driver into the Trash and select the

Empty Trash command from the Special menu to free up another 31K to 38K (depending on the version) on your startup disk. (You should first make sure that you have a copy of the ImageWriter driver on another disk in case you ever need it.)

After discarding any unnecessary files from your startup disk, if you still don't have enough space to install the desired printer driver, you can use the Font/DA Mover to delete some fonts and desk accessories. (Your *Macintosh Utilities User's Guide* explains this process in detail.) You must keep the Chooser and Control Panel desk accessories on your startup disk. Also, we recommend that you keep the Key Caps desk accessory, since it's a useful adjunct to any word processing program.

If you commonly use more than one printer and you can't make enough room on your startup disk for all the printer drivers you need, we recommend that you make two or more copies of your startup disk, installing a different printer driver on each disk. Then, load the Word program with the startup disk that contains the printer driver you plan to use during that session.

Before you use any printer, you need to use the Chooser desk accessory on the ⌘ menu to select that printer. You can issue the Chooser command from the Finder level, or you can issue it anytime after you load the Word program. Before you select Chooser, however, your Macintosh should be connected to the printer you plan to use.

When you select Chooser, you'll see a dialog box like the one in Figure 7-1. The contents of the dialog box will vary, depending on the number and type of printer drivers you have installed. The dialog box in Figure 7-1 shows that drivers for both the LaserWriter and the ImageWriter are installed on the startup disk. The design of the icons may also vary, depending on which version of a printer driver you're using.

SELECTING A PRINTER

FIGURE 7-1

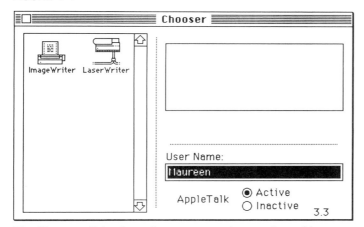

The Chooser dialog box allows you to select a printer driver.

Selecting an Imagewriter

If you plan to use an ImageWriter printer, begin by clicking on the ImageWriter icon on the left side of the Chooser dialog box. You'll then see an alert box with the message *Be sure to choose Page Setup and confirm the settings so that the application can format documents correctly for the ImageWriter.* When you click the Continue button in this box or press Return, you'll see an additional set of icons on the right side of the Chooser dialog box, as shown in Figure 7-2. These icons represent your printer port (the printer icon) and your communications or modem port (the telephone icon).

FIGURE 7-2

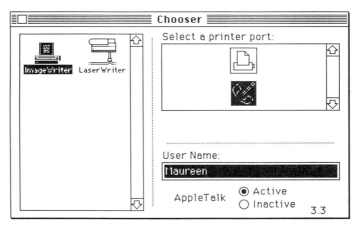

When you choose the ImageWriter printer icon, Word will ask which port you plan to use.

Click on the icon that represents the port you want to use. Generally, you'll attach an ImageWriter to the printer port. Do *not* select the communications port if you've attached a hard disk to that port or your hard disk might be erased!

If you choose the printer port while the AppleTalk setting is active, you'll see another alert box with the message *ImageWriter cannot be used on the Printer port while AppleTalk is active. Do you want to make AppleTalk inactive? Access to current network services will have to be reestablished.* If you click OK in this alert box, you'll see the message *Please make sure that the AppleTalk Personal Network is disconnected.* When you click Continue in this alert box (or press Return), Word will automatically change the AppleTalk setting to Inactive. If you choose Cancel when you see the alert message, Word will leave the AppleTalk setting at Active and will not select the printer port, leaving the modem port selected.

Selecting a Laserwriter

If you plan to use a LaserWriter, first click the Active option in the lower-right portion of the dialog box to indicate that you are hooked into the AppleTalk network.

When you do this, you'll see the message *Please make sure that you are connected to an AppleTalk network.* Choose Continue in this alert box, then click on the LaserWriter icon. If you click on the LaserWriter icon while the Inactive AppleTalk option is selected, you'll see the alert message *LaserWriter requires AppleTalk. Please make sure that you are connected to an AppleTalk network.* When you click OK in response to this alert message, Word will select the Active option.

After you click on the LaserWriter icon in the Chooser dialog box, you'll see the message *Be sure to choose Page Setup and confirm the settings so that the application can format documents correctly for the LaserWriter.* When you click Continue in this alert box, one or more printer names will appear on the right side of the dialog box. You'll also see the On/Off options for Background Printing, as shown in Figure 7-3. If the PrintMonitor file is not in your System folder, the Background Printing options will appear dimmed. (We'll talk about background printing a little later in this chapter.)

FIGURE 7-3

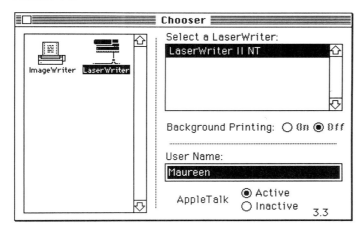

When you choose the LaserWriter printer icon, you'll see a list
of available printers.

Only the names of those printers that are connected to your Macintosh will appear. (If you don't see any names, check your printer cable to make sure there is a secure connection.) Just click on the name of the printer you want to use. Then, type your name or initials in the User Name edit bar. This edit bar appears primarily for users who are sharing a printer on an AppleTalk network. When more than one Macintosh is connected to the same printer, the Mac presents a status box that identifies the user who is currently printing. (By the way, you'll need to type your name only once; the Mac will remember the text you type in the User Name edit bar. You can, however, change the name in this edit bar at any time.)

After completing these steps, close the Chooser dialog box to lock in your selections. If you use only one printer, you probably won't have to issue the Chooser command again. If you want to switch to another printer, however, you'll need to reissue the Chooser command and select the printer and AppleTalk settings you want to use. As long as the appropriate printer driver file is located on the startup disk you used to load Word, you can change printers at any time during a session—either from the Finder level or from within Word.

Other Printers

It is not within the scope of this book to discuss all the possible hardware configurations for printing from the Macintosh. Your *Macintosh System Software User's Guide* and your printer owner's manual will give you more information on using other printers. If you have trouble with any of the steps outlined above, refer to those manuals or contact your local hardware dealer. Also, if you use a printer other than the ImageWriter or LaserWriter, see your owner's manual for special instructions on installing that printer on your startup disk.

THE PRINT... COMMAND

Once you have installed and selected your printer, you can use the Print... command on the File menu to produce a hard copy of your document. This command will print only the document that is currently active on your DeskTop. Any other documents that happen to be open on the DeskTop will not be printed unless you activate those document windows individually and issue a separate Print... command for each.

When you issue the Print... command, Word will present a dialog box containing several options. The contents of this Print dialog box will vary depending on the type of printer you selected with the Chooser. Figures 7-4 and 7-5 show the Print dialog box for the ImageWriter and the LaserWriter.

FIGURE 7-4

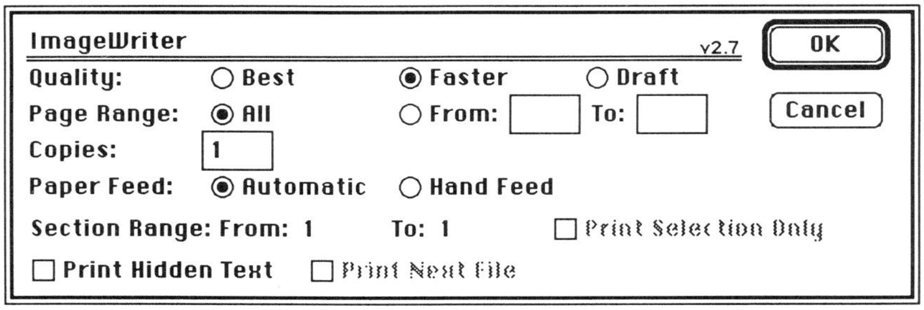

ImageWriter			v2.7	**OK**
Quality:	○ Best	● Faster	○ Draft	
Page Range:	● All	○ From: [ ] To: [ ]		Cancel
Copies:	[1]			
Paper Feed:	● Automatic	○ Hand Feed		
Section Range: From: 1	To: 1		☐ Print Selection Only	
☐ Print Hidden Text	☐ Print Next File			

This is the Print dialog box for an ImageWriter printer.

FIGURE 7-5

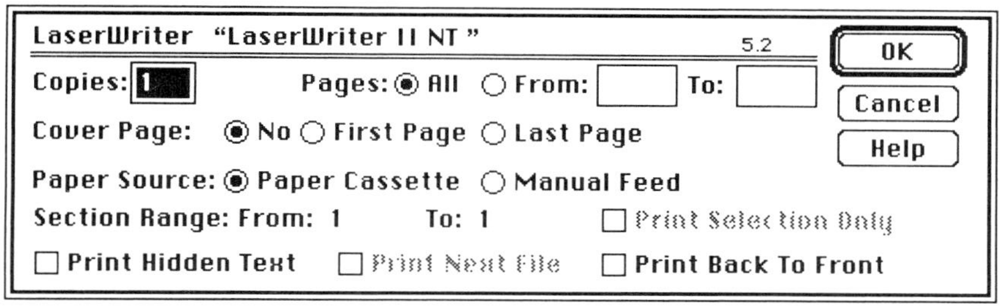

```
┌─────────────────────────────────────────────────────────────┐
│ LaserWriter  "LaserWriter II NT "            5.2    ╭──────╮  │
│ Copies: █         Pages: ◉ All  ○ From:        To:  │  OK  │  │
│                                                     ╰──────╯  │
│ Cover Page:   ◉ No ○ First Page  ○ Last Page        │Cancel│  │
│ Paper Source: ◉ Paper Cassette  ○ Manual Feed       └──────┘  │
│ Section Range: From: 1     To: 1    ☐ Print Selection Only│Help│
│ ☐ Print Hidden Text  ☐ Print Next File  ☐ Print Back To Front│
└─────────────────────────────────────────────────────────────┘
```

This is the Print dialog box for a LaserWriter printer.

After you have made your selections in the Print dialog box, you can click the OK button to begin printing. As each page of your document is processed for printing, you'll see the page number in the status box at the lower-left corner of your screen. You can cancel the Print procedure by pressing ⌘-period.

Let's back up a step and take a closer look at the options in the Print dialog boxes. When you make selections in these dialog boxes, Word will remember your settings for these options: Print Hidden Text, Print Next File, Print Back to Front (LaserWriter only), and Quality (ImageWriter only). In other words, your selections for these options will remain in effect from one Print... command to the next, and, in some cases, even from one Word session to the next. (In Chapter 14, we will explain which Print settings are document-specific and which settings will be carried over from one Word session to the next.)

Your selections for the following options will not be saved: Copies, Pages (or Page Range in the ImageWriter Print dialog box), Section Range, Cover Page (LaserWriter only), Paper Source (or Paper Feed in the ImageWriter box), and Print Selection Only. The Copies setting will always revert to 1, the Pages or Page Range setting will revert to All, and the Section Range settings will revert to From: 1 and To: 1 (for a one-section document) or will be blank (for a multiple-section document). The Cover Page option in the LaserWriter dialog box will revert to No. The Paper Feed option in the ImageWriter dialog box will return to Automatic, and the Paper Source option in the LaserWriter dialog box will return to Paper Cassette. Let's look first at the dialog box options that are common to both printers, then we'll discuss the printer-specific options.

When you issue the Print... command, Word's default settings will print your entire document. If you want to print less than a full document, Word allows you to specify what part of the document you want to print: a selection of text, a range

**The Print
Dialog Boxes**

*Specifying a
print range*

of pages, or specified sections of a document. By combining a section range with a page range, you can even print specific pages from different sections. In this chapter, we'll look at only two of the techniques for printing part of a document: printing a text selection and printing a range of pages. In Chapter 10, we'll explain the Section Range settings as part of our discussion of multisection documents.

Printing a text selection

If you select some text—even as little as a single character—before you issue the Print... command, Word will make the Print Selection Only option available in the Print dialog box. Activating this option tells Word to print only the text you've highlighted on the screen. The Print Selection Only option provides an easy way to print just a few lines or paragraphs of text, although you can use it to print a selection of any size.

If your selection encompasses more than one page, you can use the Pages settings (or the Page Range settings in the ImageWriter dialog box) to print only certain pages of the selected text. Similarly, if the selection includes text in different sections, you can use the Section Range settings to print only part of the selection.

When you print a selection, Word will begin printing at the top-left corner of the page, even if the text you have selected would normally appear in the middle of a page. If you have added any page numbers, headers, or footers to your document (we'll talk more about these items in a few pages), they will not appear when you print text using the Print Selection Only option.

Specifying a range of pages

To print a specified range of pages, just enter the starting page number in the From edit bar and the ending page number in the To edit bar. You must use Arabic numerals to specify your From and To settings—even if you have used letters or Roman numerals to number the pages of your document. Of course, you can specify a range of pages for printing even if you have not numbered your document pages.

As soon as you make an entry in the From or To edit bar, Word will activate the radio button next to the From setting and deactivate the radio button next to the All setting. For example, suppose you want to print pages 5 through 11 of a 25-page document. After you issue the Print... command, just click on the From edit bar and type the value 5. Then, press the Tab key or click on the To edit bar and enter the value 11.

If you make an entry in the To edit bar but leave the From edit bar blank, Word assumes that you want to begin printing with the first page of the document and print to the end of the specified To page. Similarly, if you make an entry in the From edit bar but leave the To edit bar blank, Word assumes that you want to start printing at the beginning of the specified From page and print to the end of the document.

For example, to print pages 1 through 10 of a 25-page document, you can leave the From edit bar blank and simply type the value 10 in the To edit bar. To print from page 10 through the end of the document, you can leave the To edit bar blank and type the value 10 in the From edit bar.

To print only one page of a document, enter the same number in the From and To edit bars. For example if you want to print the third page of a document, enter 3 in both the From and To edit bars.

If you have numbered your document pages beginning with a number other than 1, you must be sure that the page numbers you enter in the From and To edit bars correspond to the page numbers that will appear in your document. For example, suppose the starting page number in your document is 3. You would like to print pages 4 and 5—or the second and third pages—of the document. All you need to do is enter 4 in the From edit bar and 5 in the To edit bar. If you were to enter 2 and 3 in these edit bars (since pages 4 and 5 are the second and third pages of the document), Word would print only the first page of the document, or the page on which the number 3 appears. As far as Word can tell, page 2 doesn't exist in this document. Taking this a step further, if you were to enter 1 and 2 in the From and To edit bars, Word would not print any pages, since, according to your page numbers, the document does not contain pages 1 or 2.

Specifying a page range for printing can get a little complicated if your document contains multiple sections with different page numbering schemes in each. Fortunately, Word 4 has From and To settings for sections as well as pages. We'll look at these settings in Chapter 10 and show how you can use them in conjunction with your From and To page settings to print part of a document.

Copies

If you want to print more than one copy of your document at a time, just type the number of copies you want in the Copies edit bar. If the document is longer than one page, Word will begin by printing all the copies of page 1, followed by all the copies of page 2, then all the copies of page 3, and so on, until you have the number of copies you specified. When you're using a LaserWriter, this method of printing multiple copies is faster than printing complete document sets. That's because a certain amount of time is required to convert each page into a format that the LaserWriter can use and to send this data to the printer. By printing all the copies of each page at once, this process does not need to be repeated for each copy. However, there is one drawback to doing it this way: When your pages come out of the printer, you must collate them.

*Printing
hidden text*

If you have assigned the Hidden format to text in your document, you can opt to print this text along with the rest of your document or hide it in the printed version. The appearance of hidden text in your printed document is completely independent of the appearance of hidden text on your screen. In other words, if you activate the Print Hidden Text option, Word will print any text that has been assigned the Hidden format, even if it is not currently visible on your screen. On the other hand, if you use the Show Hidden Text option in the Preferences dialog box to display your hidden text on the screen, Word will not print that text unless you select the Print Hidden Text option in the Print dialog box.

For example, we assigned the Hidden format to the third paragraph of the sample document shown in Figure 7-6. If we select the Print Hidden Text option, Word will print this paragraph as usual. If, on the other hand, we deselect the Print Hidden Text option in the Print dialog box, Word will omit the third paragraph from our printed document, as shown in Figure 7-7. Notice that Word prints the second and fourth paragraphs sequentially, with no blank space between, as if the hidden text did not exist.

FIGURE 7-6

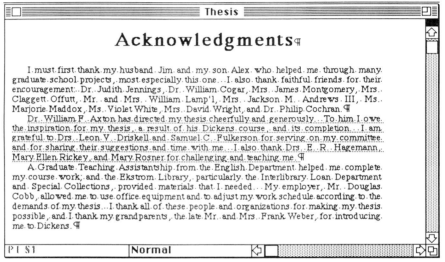

We have assigned the Hidden format to the third paragraph in this sample document.

By the way, when you deselect the Print Hidden Text option, Word will still show that hidden text in the page view and in the Print Preview window, provided you've selected the Show Hidden Text option in the Preferences dialog box.

Hiding markup characters

When you use the Hidden format in a document, you must hide any special markup characters surrounding that text, such as paragraph and tab markers. Otherwise, your printed document will contain extra blank lines or spaces.

For example, if you assign the Hidden format to an entire paragraph, make sure you assign the Hidden format to the paragraph marker (¶) at the end of that paragraph as well. (The gray line that indicates hidden text extends only halfway into the ¶ marker if you apply the Hidden format to it.) If you want to hide an entire sentence, make sure you hide the blank space that separates that sentence from the next. Finally, if you want to hide a word, make sure you hide the blank space or other demarcation character that appears after that word.

FIGURE 7-7

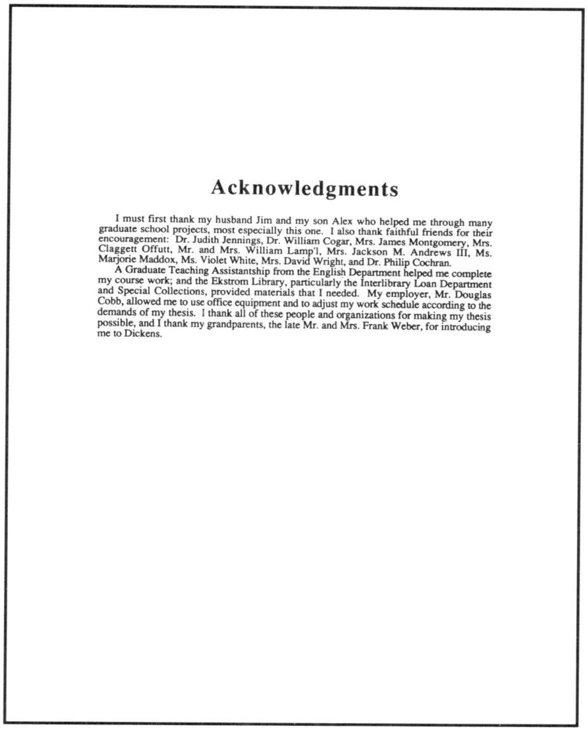

If we deselect the Print Hidden Text option, Word will not include the hidden text in our printed document.

Suppose we assign the Hidden format to all the text in the third paragraph of Figure 7-6, but not to the ¶ marker at the end of that paragraph. If we choose to omit this hidden text when we print this sample page, our document will look like the one in Figure 7-8 on the following page. Notice that a blank line appears between the second and third paragraphs.

On occasion, you may want to string together two or more document files to print consecutively. In order to do this, you must click the Next File... button in the Document dialog box and then select the document you want to print immediately after the current document. Then, you can print the documents consecutively by activating the Print Next File option in the Print dialog box. We'll talk more about linking files in this manner in Chapter 10, when we discuss techniques for working with long documents.

The Print Next File option

FIGURE 7-8

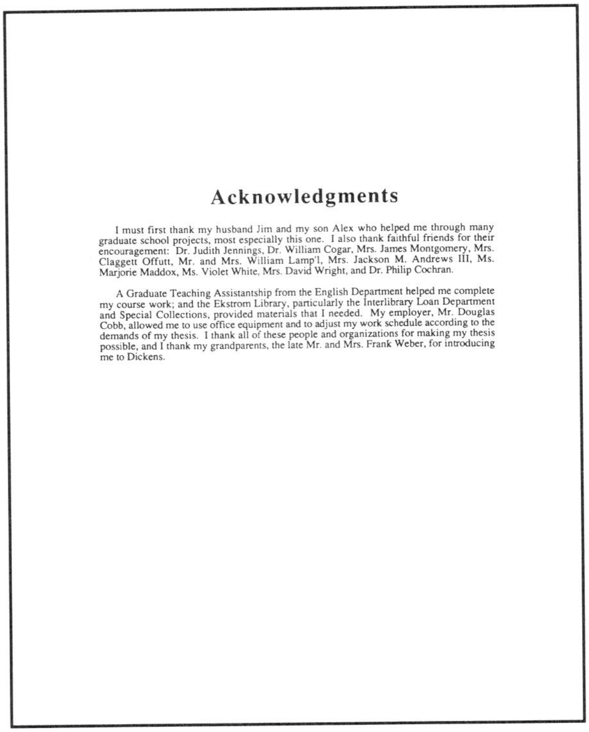

Acknowledgments

I must first thank my husband Jim and my son Alex who helped me through many graduate school projects, most especially this one. I also thank faithful friends for their encouragement: Dr. Judith Jennings, Dr. William Cogar, Mrs. James Montgomery, Mrs. Claggett Offutt, Mr. and Mrs. William Lamp'l, Mrs. Jackson M. Andrews III, Ms. Marjorie Maddox, Ms. Violet White, Mrs. David Wright, and Dr. Philip Cochran.

A Graduate Teaching Assistantship from the English Department helped me complete my course work; and the Ekstrom Library, particularly the Interlibrary Loan Department and Special Collections, provided materials that I needed. My employer, Mr. Douglas Cobb, allowed me to use office equipment and to adjust my work schedule according to the demands of my thesis. I thank all of these people and organizations for making my thesis possible, and I thank my grandparents, the late Mr. and Mrs. Frank Weber, for introducing me to Dickens.

If you see an extra blank line in your printed document, check to see if the ¶ marker was assigned the Hidden format.

LaserWriter options

In addition to the options discussed above, the Print dialog box for the LaserWriter offers several other printing options: two Paper Source options (Paper Cassette and Manual Feed), three Cover Page options (No, First Page, and Last Page) and the Print Back to Front option. Let's look at how you might use each option.

Choosing a paper source

In most situations, you'll want your LaserWriter to feed paper into the printer automatically from a paper tray. In these cases, you won't need to change your Paper Source setting from Word's default, Paper Cassette. On occasion, however, you may want to print on a few sheets of special paper or on envelopes that you feed into the printer by hand. To do this, you must select the Manual Feed Paper Source option. When the Manual Feed option is active, your LaserWriter won't attempt to print a page until you insert a sheet of paper. After printing one page, the red Paper Out light on your printer will flash, indicating that the printer is ready for another sheet. If you don't feed paper into the printer within about a minute, the print job will be cancelled.

The Cover Page options are handy when you need to document the date and time that you printed a document or when several users share the same printer. When you select either the First Page or Last Page option, Word prints a sheet like the one shown in Figure 7-9 to identify your document.

Printing a cover page

FIGURE 7-9

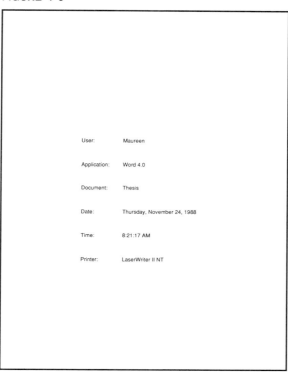

User:	Maureen
Application:	Word 4.0
Document:	Thesis
Date:	Thursday, November 24, 1988
Time:	8:21:17 AM
Printer:	LaserWriter II NT

When you choose to print a cover page, Word produces a sheet like this one.

As you can see, the cover page sheet lists the user's name (the name or initials you type in the User Name edit bar of the Chooser dialog box), the application from which the document was printed, the document name, the date and time at which the document was printed, and the name of the printer.

The Print Back To Front option tells Word to print the pages of your document in reverse order. Whether you use this option will depend on the type of LaserWriter you are using. Some versions of the LaserWriter will release pages with the printed side facing up. In such a case, the pages will be stacked in the reverse order from which they were printed. For example, if you print a ten-page document on a regular LaserWriter or a LaserWriter Plus without activating the Print Back To Front option, Word will print the pages in order from 1 to 10, as you might expect.

Printing back to front

However, when you retrieve the printed document from the paper tray, you'll have to reverse the order of the pages since page 10 will be on top of page 9, page 9 will be on top of page 8, and so forth.

To get around this problem, choose the Print Back To Front option. Word will then print the pages in reverse order—from 10 to 1—so that they will be in the correct order when you retrieve the printed document from the paper tray. The Print Back to Front option is particularly convenient when you are printing long documents or when you are printing multiple copies of a document.

If you are using a LaserWriter II NT or a similar printer, you won't need to activate the Print Back to Front option since these printers stack printed pages face down as they are released from the printer. As a result, when you retrieve your printed document, the pages will appear in the order in which they were printed. Of course, if you ever want to retrieve the pages in reverse order, you can activate the Print Back to Front option.

ImageWriter options

If you use the ImageWriter, you'll find three Quality options in the Print dialog box in addition to the options we have already discussed. These Quality settings are Best, Faster, and Draft. For proofreading and for informal use, we recommend that you use the Faster or Draft option.

The Best option produces darker and denser characters, but it requires more time to print. When you use the Draft option, Word will print your document very quickly, but it will ignore virtually all of your character formatting. In the middle quality range is the Faster option. The Faster option recognizes all your fonts and character formats, but the text is not as dark and dense as that produced with the Best option. However, the Faster option, as the name implies, allows your documents to be printed considerably faster than the Best option.

Figures 7-10, 7-11, and 7-12 show the differences between the Best, Faster, and Draft Quality options. All three text samples are formatted in 12-point Geneva, with the first line Plain, the second line bold, and the third line italic. As you can see, Word ignores our font and character formatting (except for boldfacing) when we use the Draft option.

PRINTING FROM THE FINDER LEVEL

As you already know, when you issue the Print… command from within Word, only the active document will be printed. If you need to print several documents, you may be able to save some time by printing them from the Finder level. Here, you can select several documents to print at the same time by dragging across all the files you want to work with or by pressing the Shift key and clicking on each document icon in turn. Once you have highlighted all the files you want to print, select the Print command from the File menu.

The Print dialog box will appear only once when you use this Finder-level printing technique. Word will print all of the documents, using the same Print dialog box settings for each. The documents will be printed in the order in which they appear on the DeskTop—from left to right and top to bottom.

FIGURE 7-10

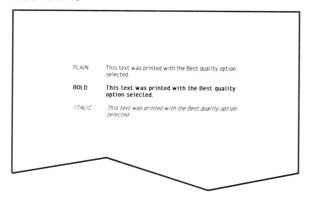

The Best option produces high-quality results but causes slower printing.

FIGURE 7-11

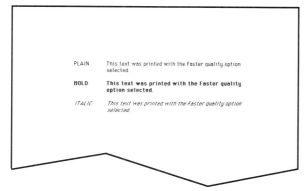

The Faster option retains all your character formats and allows you to print fairly quickly.

FIGURE 7-12

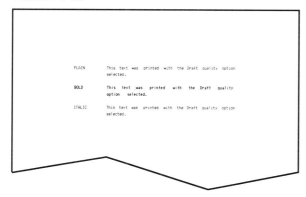

Use the Draft option when you want to print quickly and do not need special formatting.

BACKGROUND PRINTING WITH MULTIFINDER

If you share a LaserWriter on a network with several other users, you may want to take advantage of MultiFinder's ability to print documents "in the background" while you work in Word. As we mentioned earlier, in order to take advantage of background printing with MultiFinder, you must ensure that the file named PrintMonitor is in the System folder on your startup disk. You can find a copy of PrintMonitor on your Macintosh Printing Tools disk.

To use MultiFinder, you must choose the Set Startup... command from the Special menu while you're at the Finder level. Then, in the Set Startup dialog box, choose the MultiFinder option and click OK. Now, restart your computer. When you do this, MultiFinder will be active, as indicated by the 🗐 icon that appears at the far right edge of the menu bar. When you open your Word document, this icon will change to a small version of the 🔶 icon that represents the Word program at the Finder level.

After starting your computer with MultiFinder, open the Chooser dialog box to make sure that the On option for Background Printing is selected. When you're ready to print, just issue the Print... command and specify your Print dialog box settings as you normally would. When you click OK, the PrintMonitor program will take over and spool your file to your startup disk, then it will send the file to the printer. While the file is being printed, you can continue to work in Word, although you'll notice that the program is considerably slower while background printing is on.

Memory Considerations

Because Word 4 requires a considerable amount of memory, you may encounter some problems when you try to print using PrintMonitor, particularly if your Mac is installed with 1 megabyte of RAM or less. For example, you may see a message telling you that there is not enough memory to load the PrintMonitor program. When this happens, you'll have the option of telling PrintMonitor to reconfigure itself to consume less memory. Once you've done this, however, you still may not have enough memory to print, especially if you're working with a relatively long document. When you issue the Print... command, you'll see the message *There is insufficient memory to print at this time. PrintMonitor will attempt to print again when there is more memory available. Quitting one or more applications is a way of making memory available.* At this point, you need to open the Chooser dialog box and turn off the Background Printing option. Then, reissue the Print... command and print as you normally would.

Other PrintMonitor Features

Besides background printing, the PrintMonitor program lets you queue up two or more files for printing and specify a time at which you want to print each. The PrintMonitor program spools the files to disk and prints them in order or at the specified time. Again, your ability to use this feature will be limited by the amount of RAM installed in your Macintosh. We recommend that you save all open files before you attempt to queue up two or more files for printing. For more information on using PrintMonitor, see your *Macintosh System Software User's Guide.*

While the Print dialog box contains options that you are likely to change from one printing session to the next—like page ranges and number of copies—the Page Setup... command lets you define settings that control the overall appearance of a document. In fact, we introduced the Page Setup... command in Chapter 5, where we explained how your choice of paper and print orientation affect the layout of your individual document pages. Since the Page Setup settings fundamentally affect the appearance of a document, once you have specified the settings you want to use, you probably won't change those settings for the current document unless you decide to make a significant alteration to your document design.

To open the Page Setup dialog box, choose Page Setup... from the File menu or press Shift-[F8]. Like the Print dialog box, the Page Setup dialog box will look different, depending on the printer you have selected with the Chooser. Figures 7-13 and 7-14 show the Page Setup dialog box for the ImageWriter and the LaserWriter printers, respectively.

THE PAGE SETUP... COMMAND

FIGURE 7-13

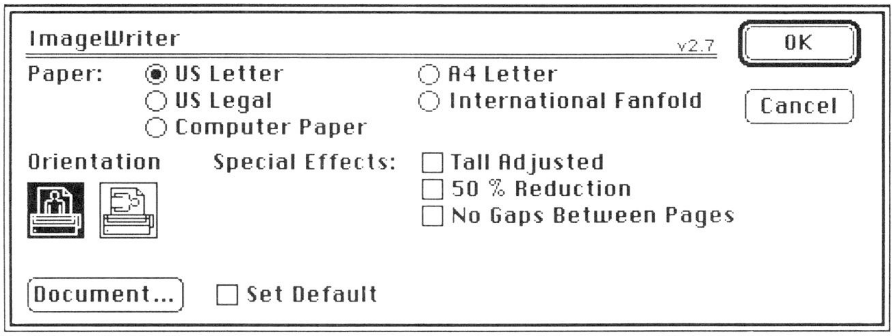

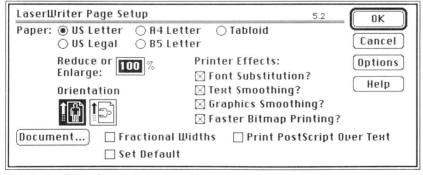

This is the Page Setup dialog box for the ImageWriter printer.

FIGURE 7-14

This is the Page Setup dialog box for the LaserWriter printer.

The Page Setup options you select are saved to disk with your document. In addition, any changes you make in the Page Setup dialog box—except your selections for the LaserWriter's Fractional Widths and Print PostScript Over Text options—will apply to the currently active document and to any new documents you open during the current Word session. For example, suppose you select the US Legal Paper option for one document, then, without quitting from Word, you open a new document. When you open the Page Setup dialog box in this new document, you'll see that the US Legal Paper option is already selected. However, if you open an existing document stored on disk, the Paper setting you originally selected for that document will be unchanged.

As we explained in Chapter 5, the Paper and Orientation options in the Page Setup dialog box are critical in determining a document's page layout. For that reason, we chose to discuss these settings along with other basic formatting issues. If you need to review these settings, see the section entitled "Basic Page Layout" that begins on page 98. The remaining settings in the Page Setup dialog box are different for the LaserWriter and the ImageWriter, so we'll consider each printer's Page Setup dialog box separately. Both versions of this dialog box, however, have a button labeled Document…. Clicking this button allows you to open the Document dialog box, where you can change such settings as your margins, page gutter width, and so forth.

ImageWriter Page Setup Options

The Page Setup dialog box for the ImageWriter contains three options under the heading Special Effects—Tall Adjusted, 50% Reduction, and No Gaps Between Pages. We'll look at these options in this section. First, however, we need to consider a feature that is available only with an ImageWriter printer: the ability to specify a custom paper size.

Choosing a paper size

If you used Word 3, you may recall that it allowed you to specify any paper height and width instead of simply choosing a standard paper size. Unfortunately, Word 4 offers this flexibility only if you are using an ImageWriter printer. To specify a custom paper size for an ImageWriter, you must choose the Preferences… command on the Edit menu. In the Preferences dialog box, which is shown in Figure 7-15, you'll see Width and Height edit bars for specifying the dimensions of your custom paper. If your chosen printer is a LaserWriter, these edit bars will be dimmed.

After you enter the dimensions of your custom paper in the Preferences dialog box, Word will add a Paper option to the Page Setup dialog box to reflect the new paper size. For example, suppose you specify a custom paper size in the Preferences dialog box of $7^1/_2$ inches wide by $9^1/_4$ inches high, as we've done in Figure 7-15. When you open the Page Setup dialog box, you'll see this option added to the standard Paper options, as shown in Figure 7-16.

FIGURE 7-15

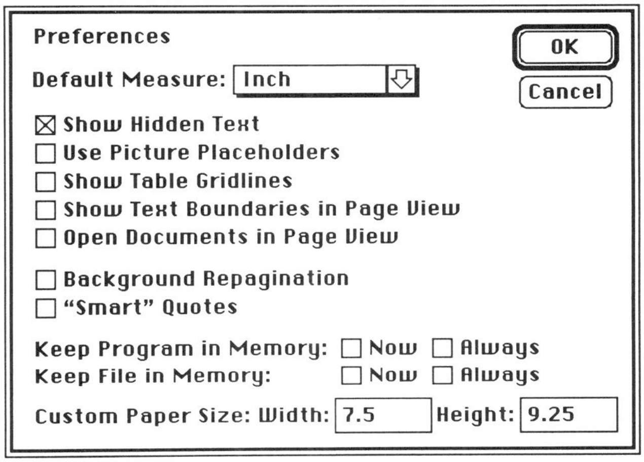

```
┌─────────────────────────────────────────────────────┐
│  Preferences                          ┌────────────┐ │
│                                       │     OK     │ │
│  Default Measure: │ Inch        │⬇️│  └────────────┘ │
│                                       ┌────────────┐ │
│  ⊠ Show Hidden Text                   │   Cancel   │ │
│  ☐ Use Picture Placeholders          └────────────┘ │
│  ☐ Show Table Gridlines                              │
│  ☐ Show Text Boundaries in Page View                 │
│  ☐ Open Documents in Page View                       │
│                                                      │
│  ☐ Background Repagination                           │
│  ☐ "Smart" Quotes                                    │
│                                                      │
│  Keep Program in Memory: ☐ Now  ☐ Always             │
│  Keep File in Memory:    ☐ Now  ☐ Always             │
│                                                      │
│  Custom Paper Size: Width: │ 7.5 │  Height: │ 9.25 │ │
└─────────────────────────────────────────────────────┘
```

To specify a custom paper size, you must open the Preferences dialog box.

FIGURE 7-16

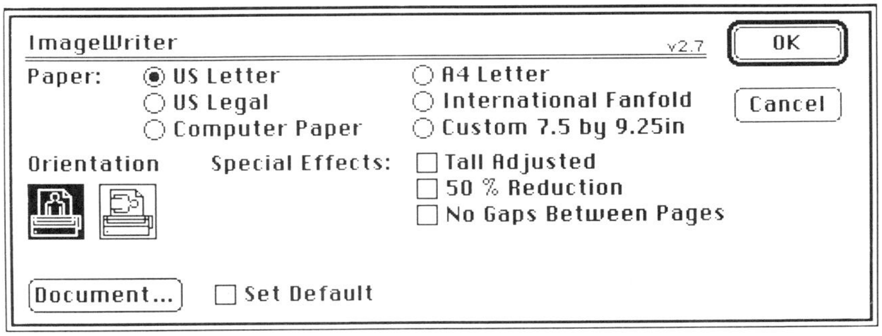

```
┌────────────────────────────────────────────────────┐
│  ImageWriter                        v2.7 ┌─────────┐│
│                                          │   OK    ││
│  Paper:  ⦿ US Letter      ○ A4 Letter    └─────────┘│
│          ○ US Legal       ○ International Fanfold   │
│          ○ Computer Paper ○ Custom 7.5 by 9.25in  ┌────────┐│
│                                                   │ Cancel ││
│  Orientation   Special Effects: ☐ Tall Adjusted  └────────┘│
│   ▨  ▨                          ☐ 50 % Reduction   │
│                                 ☐ No Gaps Between Pages │
│                                                    │
│  ┌──────────┐  ☐ Set Default                       │
│  │ Document...│                                     │
│  └──────────┘                                       │
└────────────────────────────────────────────────────┘
```

After you've specified a custom paper size in the Preferences dialog box, Word will add that option to the ImageWriter Page Setup dialog box.

In some cases, your custom paper option will displace one of the standard Paper options. If you want to use the displaced standard option, you'll need to reopen the Preferences dialog box and delete your custom paper settings. Then, when you reopen the Page Setup dialog box, all the standard Paper options will appear.

Specifying a custom paper size can be helpful when you are printing a document on standard-size paper, but plan to reproduce on paper of a different size. For example, suppose you are setting up a form that you plan to have reproduced on a 3- by 5-inch index card. You may not be able to use a paper stock of this size since it is too small to feed through the printer's rollers properly. However, you can still enter the values 5 and 3 in the Width and Height edit bars of the Preferences dialog box to define the size of your finished document. By entering your finished document size rather than the actual size of the paper stock you plan to print on, you can eliminate some of the guesswork from defining your document layout.

The Tall Adjusted option

You use the Tall Adjusted option primarily to enhance the appearance of graphics that you've imported into a Word document. When you select this option, however, the characters in your printed text will appear a little wider. This will change the number of characters that can fit on each line and, as a result, alter the way your lines of text wrap. You won't be able to see this change in your text on the screen, however, since the adjustment is made by the printer.

The 50% Reduction option

The 50% Reduction option does exactly what its name implies—it reduces your text to half its original size. When you activate this option, Word can fit more characters on each line. For example, Figure 7-17 shows a sample page printed on the ImageWriter in normal size, while Figure 7-18 shows this same page printed with the 50% Reduction option in effect. Notice that the 12-point type in the first figure is virtually unreadable when it's reduced to half size.

FIGURE 7-17

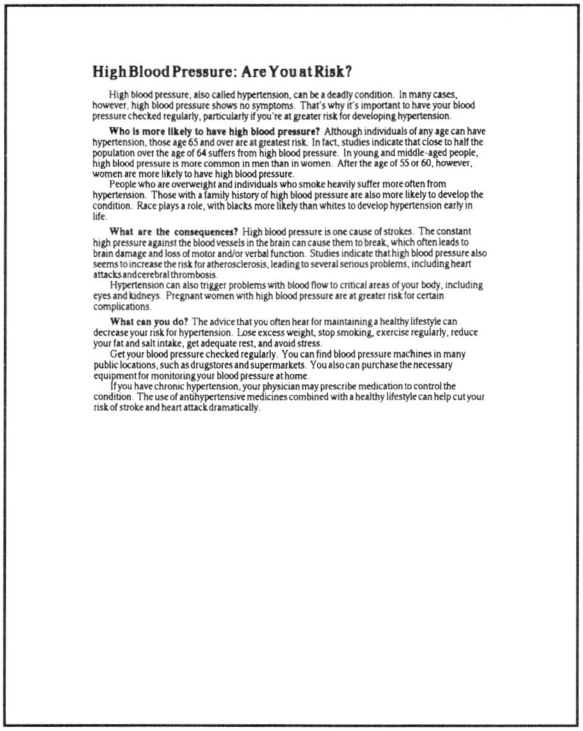

High Blood Pressure: Are You at Risk?

High blood pressure, also called hypertension, can be a deadly condition. In many cases, however, high blood pressure shows no symptoms. That's why it's important to have your blood pressure checked regularly, particularly if you're at greater risk for developing hypertension.

Who is more likely to have high blood pressure? Although individuals of any age can have hypertension, those age 65 and over are at greatest risk. In fact, studies indicate that close to half the population over the age of 64 suffers from high blood pressure. In young and middle-aged people, high blood pressure is more common in men than in women. After the age of 55 or 60, however, women are more likely to have high blood pressure.

People who are overweight and individuals who smoke heavily suffer more often from hypertension. Those with a family history of high blood pressure are also more likely to develop the condition. Race plays a role, with blacks more likely than whites to develop hypertension early in life.

What are the consequences? High blood pressure is one cause of strokes. The constant high pressure against the blood vessels in the brain can cause them to break, which often leads to brain damage and loss of motor and/or verbal function. Studies indicate that high blood pressure also seems to increase the risk for atherosclerosis, leading to several serious problems, including heart attacks and cerebral thrombosis.

Hypertension can also trigger problems with blood flow to critical areas of your body, including eyes and kidneys. Pregnant women with high blood pressure are at greater risk for certain complications.

What can you do? The advice that you often hear for maintaining a healthy lifestyle can decrease your risk for hypertension. Lose excess weight, stop smoking, exercise regularly, reduce your fat and salt intake, get adequate rest, and avoid stress.

Get your blood pressure checked regularly. You can find blood pressure machines in many public locations, such as drugstores and supermarkets. You also can purchase the necessary equipment for monitoring your blood pressure at home.

If you have chronic hypertension, your physician may prescribe medication to control the condition. The use of antihypertensive medicines combined with a healthy lifestyle can help cut your risk of stroke and heart attack dramatically.

This page was printed with normal size text.

FIGURE 7-18

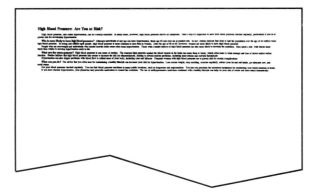

We activated the 50% Reduction option before printing this page.

Of course, by reducing the size of the characters, Word is able to print more information on each page. To illustrate this on your screen, Word will move the right indent marker on your ruler as well as the dotted vertical line that marks the right edge of your text. For example, if you are using Word's default Left and Right margin settings, the US Letter Paper option, and Tall orientation, Word will move the right edge of your text area from the 6-inch mark on the ruler to the $14^1/_2$-inch mark. This does not actually mean your printed text area will be $8^1/_2$ inches wider. It simply shows how much text you will be able to fit on each line when you print.

Word's No Gaps Between Pages option works hand-in-hand with the Top and Bottom margin settings to print your document as a continuous stream of text. When you choose the option and set your Top and Bottom margins at 0, Word will treat the paper that's being fed into your printer as though it were one single, long sheet. You might use this option when you need to print a long table or graphic that won't fit on a single page, or when you simply want to squeeze as much information as possible onto each page.

The No Gaps Between Pages option

As you might expect, there are quite a few more Page Setup options for the LaserWriter than for the ImageWriter. In fact, the number of options you see in the Page Setup dialog box will depend on which version of the LaserWriter printer driver you're using. Our discussion is based on Version 5.2.

LaserWriter Page Setup Options

Word allows you to reduce and enlarge the page image when you print documents on the LaserWriter. Just type the reduction or enlargement percentage you want to use in the Reduce or Enlarge edit bar. You can specify any reduction or enlargement setting between 25% and 400%—that is, from one quarter to four times the original image size—but you must type a whole number as your Reduce or Enlarge setting.

Reducing and enlarging the page image

If you used the reduce and enlarge feature in Word 3, you may recall that Word would not actually attempt to fit more or less data on a page. It would simply decrease or increase the entire page image. In Word 4, this feature works differently. When you type a number less than 100—that is, when you reduce the size of your text—Word will fit more characters on a line and more lines on a page. As a result, you'll be able to print your document on fewer pages.

Entering a Reduce or Enlarge setting that's greater than 100 has exactly the opposite effect. With larger characters, Word will be able to fit fewer characters on each line and fewer lines on each page. Figures 7-19, 7-20, and 7-21 show part of a document printed in normal size, reduced to 50%, and increased to 150%.

FIGURE 7-19

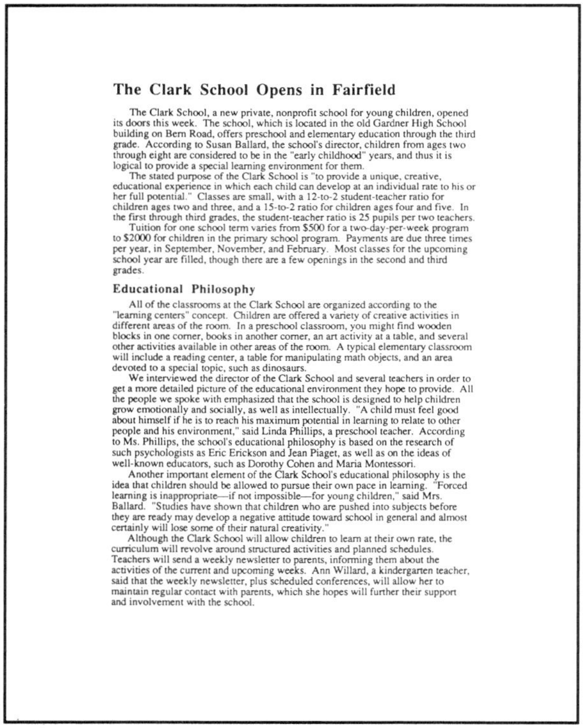

The Clark School Opens in Fairfield

The Clark School, a new private, nonprofit school for young children, opened its doors this week. The school, which is located in the old Gardner High School building on Bern Road, offers preschool and elementary education through the third grade. According to Susan Ballard, the school's director, children from ages two through eight are considered to be in the "early childhood" years, and thus it is logical to provide a special learning environment for them.

The stated purpose of the Clark School is "to provide a unique, creative, educational experience in which each child can develop at an individual rate to his or her full potential." Classes are small, with a 12-to-2 student-teacher ratio for children ages two and three, and a 15-to-2 ratio for children ages four and five. In the first through third grades, the student-teacher ratio is 25 pupils per two teachers.

Tuition for one school term varies from $500 for a two-day-per-week program to $2000 for children in the primary school program. Payments are due three times per year, in September, November, and February. Most classes for the upcoming school year are filled, though there are a few openings in the second and third grades.

Educational Philosophy

All of the classrooms at the Clark School are organized according to the "learning centers" concept. Children are offered a variety of creative activities in different areas of the room. In a preschool classroom, you might find wooden blocks in one corner, books in another corner, an art activity at a table, and several other activities available in other areas of the room. A typical elementary classroom will include a reading center, a table for manipulating math objects, and an area devoted to a special topic, such as dinosaurs.

We interviewed the director of the Clark School and several teachers in order to get a more detailed picture of the educational environment they hope to provide. All the people we spoke with emphasized that the school is designed to help children grow emotionally and socially, as well as intellectually. "A child must feel good about himself if he is to reach his maximum potential in learning to relate to other people and his environment," said Linda Phillips, a preschool teacher. According to Ms. Phillips, the school's educational philosophy is based on the research of such psychologists as Eric Erickson and Jean Piaget, as well as on the ideas of well-known educators, such as Dorothy Cohen and Maria Montessori.

Another important element of the Clark School's educational philosophy is the idea that children should be allowed to pursue their own pace in learning. "Forced learning is inappropriate—if not impossible—for young children," said Mrs. Ballard. "Studies have shown that children who are pushed into subjects before they are ready may develop a negative attitude toward school in general and almost certainly will lose some of their natural creativity."

Although the Clark School will allow children to learn at their own rate, the curriculum will revolve around structured activities and planned schedules. Teachers will send a weekly newsletter to parents, informing them about the activities of the current and upcoming weeks. Ann Willard, a kindergarten teacher, said that the weekly newsletter, plus scheduled conferences, will allow her to maintain regular contact with parents, which she hopes will further their support and involvement with the school.

This page was printed with no reduction or enlargement.

As you can see in Figures 7-20 and 7-21, Word changes the width of all your margins when you reduce or enlarge text. For example, the left margin in the document shown in Figure 7-19 is $1^1/_2$ inches wide. When we reduce the text to 50% of its original size, Word reduces the margin width to $^3/_4$ inch. By the same token, when we enlarge the text to 150% of its original size, Word increases the width of the left margin to $2^1/_4$ inches. Of course, if your document includes graphics, they also will be reduced or enlarged by the percentage you specify.

FIGURE 7-20

The Clark School Opens In Fairfield

Educational Philosophy

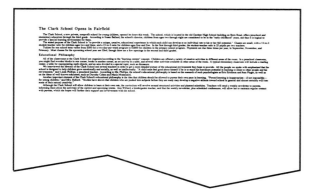

The text on this page has been reduced to 50% of its original size.

FIGURE 7-21

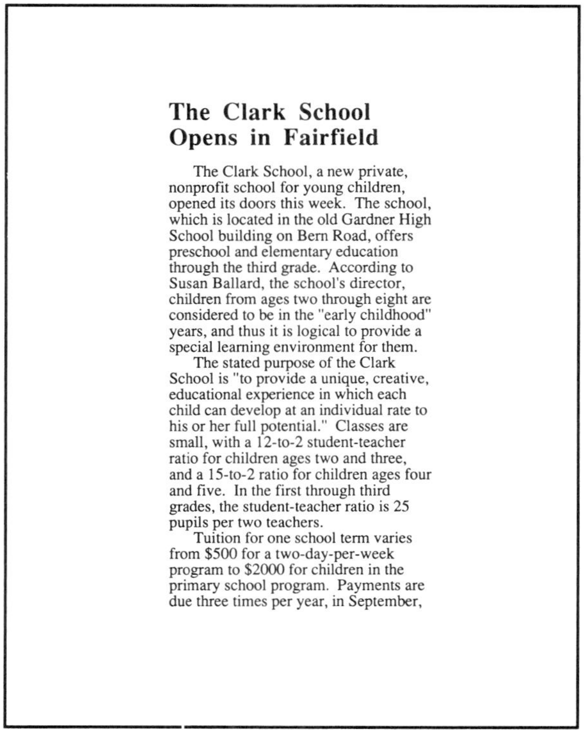

The Clark School Opens in Fairfield

The Clark School, a new private, nonprofit school for young children, opened its doors this week. The school, which is located in the old Gardner High School building on Bern Road, offers preschool and elementary education through the third grade. According to Susan Ballard, the school's director, children from ages two through eight are considered to be in the "early childhood" years, and thus it is logical to provide a special learning environment for them.

The stated purpose of the Clark School is "to provide a unique, creative, educational experience in which each child can develop at an individual rate to his or her full potential." Classes are small, with a 12-to-2 student-teacher ratio for children ages two and three, and a 15-to-2 ratio for children ages four and five. In the first through third grades, the student-teacher ratio is 25 pupils per two teachers.

Tuition for one school term varies from $500 for a two-day-per-week program to $2000 for children in the primary school program. Payments are due three times per year, in September,

We enlarged the text on this page to 150% of its original size.

Font substitution

As you may know, certain fonts, including Helvetica, Times, Symbol, and Courier, are designed specifically for the LaserWriter printers, while other fonts, including New York, Monaco, and Geneva are designed for the ImageWriter. If you have installed any new fonts on your startup disk, you should also know whether they are designed for an ImageWriter or a LaserWriter printer. Some fonts, such as Chicago, are designed for the Macintosh screen display, and do not have a corresponding printer font.

Although you can print documents using any of the fonts that are installed on your startup disk, regardless of the printer you have selected, ImageWriter fonts, such as Geneva and New York, do not give the finished appearance that Helvetica and Times do when you print them with a LaserWriter.

The Font Substitution option in the LaserWriter Page Setup dialog box tells your LaserWriter to convert certain ImageWriter fonts you have used in your document to an appropriate LaserWriter font. For example, if you have used Word's default New York type to format your document text, and you activate the Font Substitution option when you print that document on a LaserWriter, your printed text will be converted to the Times font. The substitution will not appear on your screen—even if you turn on page view. You must print your document in order to see the font substitution.

Table 7-1 describes some examples of font substitutions that will take place when the Font Substitution option is selected.

TABLE 7-1

If your document contains...	The LaserWriter will print...
Boston	Boston
Dover PS	Dover PS
Dover	Dover
Chicago	Chicago
Geneva	Helvetica
Monaco	Courier
New York	Times
Venice	Venice

The LaserWriter will make these font substitutions when you have activated the Font Substitution option.

As you can see, the LaserWriter offers no substitutes for the Boston, Chicago, Dover PS, Dover, or Venice fonts. If you use these fonts in your document, the LaserWriter will create a bitmap of the font characters in order to print them.

You'll find that printing with Font Substitution can take significantly longer than usual. In addition, Font Substitution may produce unsightly gaps between letters and words in your printed document. Although this decrease in quality may be acceptable if you are preparing a mockup or "proof copy" of a document that will be typeset or reprinted later, you generally won't find Font Substitution acceptable for a finished document.

If you turn the Font Substitution option off, the LaserWriter will print the fonts you have selected for your document without converting them. Again, the LaserWriter will need to produce a bitmap of the font characters in order to print them. Although the LaserWriter can use this procedure to create any font shown on your screen, you probably will find that the quality of the non-LaserWriter fonts is not acceptable. (You may be able to improve the quality somewhat by turning on the Text Smoothing option.) In addition, you'll find that it takes much longer to print text that is formatted with ImageWriter fonts.

Overall, your best bet is to use fonts that are designed for your printer. If the available fonts do not suit your needs, ask your software dealer about the many fonts packages that are available for the Macintosh. If you purchase a fonts package, however, make sure that it is designed specifically for your printer.

By the way, you can use fonts designed for the LaserWriter when you are printing on the ImageWriter. Generally, the Times, Helvetica, and Courier fonts can be reproduced quite effectively on the ImageWriter.

Text and graphics smoothing

The Text Smoothing option helps smooth out the rough edges when you print ImageWriter fonts or Macintosh screen fonts on the LaserWriter. For example, suppose you have used the Venice font—which does not have a corresponding LaserWriter font—to format some characters in your Word document. Figures 7-22 and 7-23 show the difference in print quality when you use the Text Smoothing option to print this font on the LaserWriter.

FIGURE 7-22

These characters were printed without Text Smoothing.

FIGURE 7-23

These characters were printed with Text Smoothing.

The Graphics Smoothing option is similar to the Text Smoothing option, except that it helps improve the appearance of graphic images in your document by smoothing jagged edges. Text Smoothing can be especially helpful if your graphic contains a number of rounded or diagonal lines. We'll talk more about graphics in Chapter 15.

Faster bitmap printing

As we've mentioned, the LaserWriter can produce nonstandard font characters by creating a bitmap. When your document contains graphics, these also are printed from a bitmap. By activating the Faster Bitmap Printing option, you often can speed up the printing of documents that contain bitmapped characters and graphics. For example, we printed a document that contained two graphic images and two bitmapped fonts. Without activating Faster Bitmap Printing, 50 seconds elapsed from the time we clicked OK in the Print dialog box until the LaserWriter began printing the first page. After we selected Faster Bitmap Printing, however, the waiting time was reduced to 35 seconds.

Fractional widths

Selecting the Fractional Widths option allows the LaserWriter to achieve more accurate character and word placement by activating its ability to work with fractional pixel widths. You'll find that the Fractional Widths option will improve the appearance of most fonts in a printed document. When you choose Fractional Widths, you'll also notice a difference in the placement of characters, words, and line breaks on your screen. In some cases, the character placement will appear rather distorted on your screen. This problem does not occur, in the printed document. In other cases, however, you may encounter alignment problems with Fractional Widths that appear only in your printed document. If this happens, you will probably need to deselect the option.

By the way, Fractional Widths is incompatible with Font Substitution. If you activate Fractional Widths, your printer will print only the fonts that appear on your screen and will not attempt to substitute a LaserWriter font.

Printing Post-Script over text

If you have inserted a PostScript code into your document to create graphics or special effects, you may want your PostScript images to be printed "on top of" your normal Word text or any graphics you have inserted into your document. By printing PostScript images over your Word text, you can do such things as place a shaded block over some text or add arrows and other special symbols to a graphic illustration. As the option name implies, when you select Print PostScript Over Text, the LaserWriter will print your text and any inserted graphic images first, then print any PostScript images on top of this. For more on the PostScript language, see Appendix 4.

The Page Setup dialog box for a LaserWriter also includes a button labeled Options. When you click this button, Word will make six additional options available, as shown in Figure 7-24. In most instances, each time you click an option, the canine image on the left side of the dialog box will be redrawn to show you how that option will affect your printed document.

Other options

FIGURE 7-24

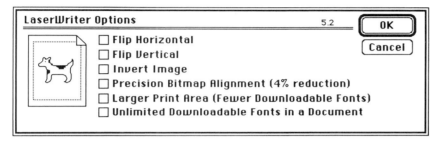

When you click the Options button in the Page Setup dialog box, you'll access these additional printing options.

The Flip Horizontal option tells your LaserWriter to print a "mirror image" of your document pages. When you choose this option, the lines of text in your document will run from right to left across the page, instead of left to right, and each letter will be printed backwards. For example, Figure 7-25 on the following page shows some normal text, while Figure 7-26 shows this same text printed with the Flip Horizontal option activated. If you were to hold the text in Figure 7-26 up to a mirror, its reflected image would look like normal text.

Flip Horizontal

The Flip Vertical option causes the LaserWriter to print an upside-down mirror image of your document pages. For example, Figure 7-27 on the next page shows the text from Figure 7-25 printed with the Flip Vertical option active. (We turned off the Flip Horizontal option before printing.)

Flip Vertical

Selecting Invert Image causes your LaserWriter to print white text on a black background instead of the normal black text on a white background. For example, Figure 7-28 on the next page shows the text from Figure 7-25 printed with the Invert Image option activated. Notice that the black background does not extend all the way to the edge of the page since this is the LaserWriter's "no print" zone.

Invert Image

FIGURE 7-25

This text was printed with no special printing options.

FIGURE 7-26

We activated the Flip Horizontal option to create this sample text.

FIGURE 7-27

This text was printed with the Flip Vertical option activated.

FIGURE 7-28

The Invert Image option creates white text on a black background.

The Precision Bitmap Alignment option will reduce your text and graphics by 4% and, in some cases, give a slightly cleaner appearance. It also can speed up the printing of graphics and bitmapped fonts. You'll find that activating Precision Bitmap Alignment does not always result in a noticeable improvement in your printed text and graphics. However, if you want to enhance the appearance of printed graphics and bitmapped fonts, you should try this option and see if it helps.

Precision Bitmap Alignment

As you may know, the LaserWriter normally cannot print any closer than about $^3/_8$ inch from the edge of the paper. If you have text or graphics that extend into this "no print" zone, they simply will not appear in the printed document. When you activate the Larger Print Area (Fewer Downloadable Fonts) option, the unprintable area is reduced to approximately $^1/_4$ inch. This gives you a larger area on the page in which to print. Increasing the size of the print area consumes some of the LaserWriter's memory, allowing for fewer downloadable fonts. Because different fonts require different amounts of memory, it's impossible to specify exactly how many fonts can be downloaded with this option activated.

Larger Print Area

As the name implies, the Unlimited Downloadable Fonts in a Document option allows you to use any number of downloadable fonts in a document. The LaserWriter will download one set of fonts, create a partial page image, clear its memory, then download another set of fonts and repeat the procedure. As you might guess, this process of switching downloadable fonts in and out of memory can make for much slower printing.

Unlimited Downloadable Fonts in a Document

Unless you specifically instruct it to do so, Word will not automatically add page numbers to each page of your printed document. There are two ways to add page numbers: with the Auto Page Number option in the Section dialog box or with headers and footers. Let's talk first about Word's Page Number settings, then we'll look at headers and footers.

ADDING PAGE NUMBERS TO YOUR PRINTED DOCUMENT

To add page numbers to your printed document, just choose the Section... command on the Format menu and select the Auto check box in the Page Number portion of the dialog box. Figure 7-29 on the following page shows the Section dialog box with this option selected.

When you select the Auto option, the From Top and From Right edit bars will become active. Word's initial default values for these settings is .5, meaning that the page numbers will be printed $^1/_2$ inch from the top and right edges of the page—or in the upper-right corner, as shown in Figure 7-30 on the next page. You can change the From Top and From Right settings to anything you want. For example, if you want your page numbers to appear $^1/_2$ inch from the bottom of the page (assuming you are using $8^1/_2$- by 11-inch paper), you might change your From Top setting to 10.5; if you want your page numbers to appear in the center of the page, you might enter a From Right setting of 4.25.

FIGURE 7-29

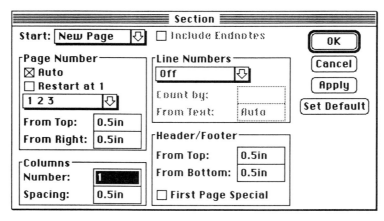

To add page numbers to your printed document, you can select the Auto check box in the Section dialog box.

FIGURE 7-30

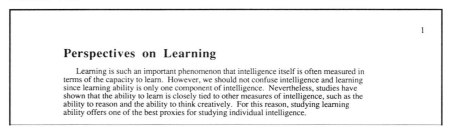

Word's default placement for automatic page numbers is $^1/_2$ inch from the upper-right corner of the page.

If you have activated the Even/Odd Headers option in the Document dialog box, Word will automatically adjust the position of your page numbers on odd and even pages. For more on this topic, see the discussion of right and left pages in Chapter 10.

Keep in mind that your Page Number settings will apply only to the current section. If you have created more than one document section, you'll probably want to apply the Auto Page Number option to each section. As we'll explain in Chapter 10, you can use different numbering schemes for each section or change the position of page numbers from one section to another.

Word uses a style named *page number* to determine the format of page numbers you create with the Auto check box. Since this style is based on your document's *Normal* style, your page numbers will appear in that style. Thus, if you have not changed the definition of the *Normal* style, your page numbers will appear in the New York 12-point Plain format. To change the character format of your page numbers, you must change the definition of the *page number* style. Chapter 8 explains how to do this.

If you have created your page numbers in a header or footer window, Word uses the *header* or *footer* style to determine their formats. Thus, to alter the character format of the page numbers in a header or footer, you can change the definition of the *header* or *footer* style. You also can open the header or footer window, select the page number, and manually change its format.

Formatting Page Numbers

You can choose one of five numbering schemes for your page numbers: Arabic numerals, uppercase Roman numerals, lowercase Roman numerals, uppercase letters, and lowercase letters. Word's default numbering scheme is Arabic numerals. To choose a different numbering scheme, just select an option from the dropdown list box that appears with the other Page Number settings. Figure 7-31 shows the options on this list.

Numbering Schemes

FIGURE 7-31

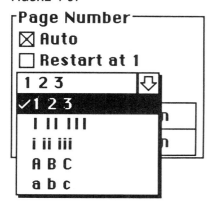

You can choose from five numbering schemes for your page numbers.

If you use one of the alphabetic numbering schemes and you need to number more than 26 pages, Word will use the characters AA, BB, CC, and so forth, for pages 27 through 52. Pages 53 through 78 will be numbered AAA, BBB, CCC, and so forth.

By the way, you do not need to select the Auto check box option in order to access the list of page numbering schemes. If you've already added page numbers in a header or footer, you can open the Section dialog box and choose a numbering scheme for those page numbers from the dropdown list.

Specifying a Starting Page Number

If you have created several documents that you want to link with consecutive page numbering, you must ensure that each document's starting page number is correct. To use a starting page number other than 1 (or A or I, if you're numbering with letters or Roman numerals), choose the Document... command from the Format menu and, in the Document dialog box, enter a starting page number in the Number Pages From edit bar. In Chapter 10, we'll show you how to link two or more documents for printing. When you do this, you can enter 0 in the Number Pages From edit bar, telling Word to set each document's starting page number automatically.

Eliminating Page Numbers on the First Page

When you number the pages of a document, you may want to leave the page number off the first page, particularly if that page is a title page. You can do this by selecting the First Page Special option in the Header/Footer portion of the Section dialog box. When you select First Page Special, Word will remove the page number from the first page and begin with page number 2 on the second page of the document. (Of course, if you've specified a starting page number other than 1 in the Document dialog box, Word will adjust the page number on the second page accordingly.)

HEADERS AND FOOTERS

You see headers and footers in just about every book, magazine, and other publication you read. Generally, headers and footers serve as guideposts for the reader, carrying such information as page numbers and the name of the publication. Longer publications sometimes have variable headers and footers that reflect the names of sections and chapters as well. On dated materials, like periodicals or technical materials that are subject to frequent updates, information such as the date of publication and volume and issue numbers often appear in the header or footer.

Word offers the most flexible system we've seen for creating, formatting, and editing headers and footers. In Word, headers and footers can carry any character and paragraph formats you choose and can be as short as a single character or as long as several paragraphs. You can also vary the appearance and content of headers and footers for odd and even pages and even control the appearance of headers and footers on the first page of a document or section.

In this section, we'll show you how to create, format, position, and edit headers and footers in your document. In the next section of this chapter, you'll also see how you can use the Print Preview window to quickly reposition headers and footers.

As the names imply, headers generally appear at the top of each page in your document while footers appear at the bottom. However, Word allows you to control the positioning of headers and footers so that you can place them anywhere on the printed page.

While you're using the galley view, the headers and footers you create will not appear in your document window. Instead, they will be tucked out of sight in separate windows that are stored along with your document when you save it to disk. To see how the header or footer will appear on each document page, you must switch to the page view or use the Print Preview window.

Let's get started by creating a sample header, then we'll look at some of the handy tools that Word offers for tailoring headers and footers to fit your publication needs. The steps you follow to create, format, and position footers are almost identical to those you follow to create, format, and position headers. If you know how to work with headers, you will be able to work with footers as well. Therefore, in this section, we will illustrate Word's header and footer techniques with examples that focus mainly on headers. However, we'll address any minor differences relating to footers as they arise.

To add a header or footer to a document, begin by selecting the Open Header... or Open Footer... command from the Document menu. A small window will appear at the bottom of your screen. If you're using the Short Menus setting, your header window will look like the one in Figure 7-32. If you are using Full Menus, your header window will look like the one in Figure 7-33. Notice that Word adds a Same As Previous button to the header window when you're using the Full Menus setting. This button is used only when you create headers or footers in a document with two or more sections (a topic we'll address in Chapter 10). Since you cannot create multisection documents using Short Menus, Word eliminates the Same As Previous button.

A Brief Tour

FIGURE 7-32

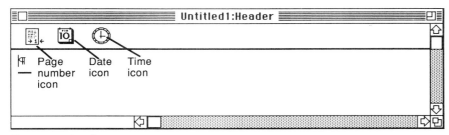

If you're using Short Menus, your header window will look like this.

FIGURE 7-33

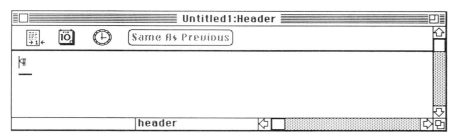

If you're using Full Menus, Word will add a Same As Previous button to your header window.

Also, notice that your insertion point marker initially appears at the first character space in this empty window, much as it does in a new document window. The horizontal bar that currently appears just below the insertion point serves as an end mark—just like the one you see in your document window.

In most ways, this header window functions just like a standard document window. It has a title bar, a close box, a zoom box, scroll bars, and a size box. You use the Show ¶ and Show Ruler commands in this window just as you would in a standard document window. A status box even appears at the bottom of the window. Although you won't see page numbers in the status box, you can use this area to make glossary entries, apply styles, and perform other actions from the keyboard. The status box contains a style name, just as it does in a normal document window. In a header window, you will initially see the style name *header* in this status box.

The title bar in the header window displays the name of the document to which the header is attached, as well as the word *Header*, to help you identify the contents of the window. (Obviously, in a footer window, you'll see the word *Footer*.) As we'll demonstrate a little later, Word allows you to create a separate header and/or footer on the first page of a document. When you open the header or footer window for this page, you'll see *First Header* or *First Footer* at the top of the window. If your document is divided into sections, you'll also see notations like *(S1)* and *(S2)* that tell you which section's header you're working with. If you're using different headers or footers on right and left pages, Word will display *Even Header*, *Odd Header*, *Even Footer*, or *Odd Footer* at the top of the window to tell you what type of header or footer you are working with. See Chapter 10 for a complete discussion of multisection documents and even/odd—or right and left—page layouts.

At the top of the header window, you'll also find three new icons. As we'll show in a few moments, you can use the page number, date, and time icons to add dynamic page numbers, dates, and times to your headers and footers.

A new footer window looks exactly like the header windows we've shown, except for two minor details. As we've mentioned, the word *Footer* appears in the window's title bar. In addition, you'll see the style name *footer* in the status box in the lower-left portion of the window. As we will explain in Chapter 8, Word automatically creates the styles named *header* and *footer*, which you can use to format your header and footer text.

Creating a Header

First, let's type some text into our empty header window and see how we go about formatting that information. Let's suppose you are creating a project proposal called *Managing Computer Documentation Projects*, and you want the name of the report to appear at the top of each page. Begin by typing the phrase in the empty header window, as shown in Figure 7-34.

FIGURE 7-34

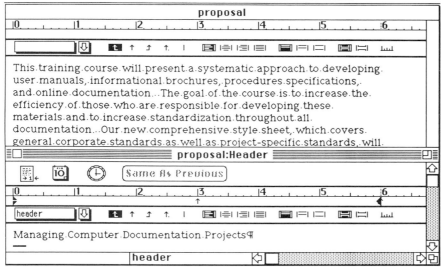

To create a header, just type the text you want to use in the header window.

Notice that the text of the header initially appears in Word's default style: 12-point New York Plain. If you use the Show Ruler command to turn on the ruler display in the header window, as we have done in Figure 7-34, you'll also see that the header's paragraph formats are initially flush left, with a centered tab at 3 inches and a right-aligned tab at 6 inches. At this point, our right indent marker falls at the 6-inch mark since we are using Word's default Document and Page Setup dialog box settings. Of course, your ruler settings in the header window will vary according to the Document and Page Setup options you specify, just as they do in your document window. See Chapter 5 for more on the relationship between margin settings and the ruler.

All the character and paragraph formats we have described are defined in a style named *header*. Because the *header* style is based on the *Normal* style, the text in a header window will have the same character formatting that's defined in the *Normal* style. You can modify the format of a header by changing the definition of the *header* style. We'll show you how to do this in Chapter 8. As you'll see in a moment, you also can change a header's format simply by selecting the text and issuing various formatting commands.

Although we'll certainly want to do some more work on this sample header, let's pause for a moment to see what happens when we print the document. To lock in your new header text, all you need to do is click the close box in the header window title bar. Word will remove the header window from the screen and reactivate the document window.

As you can see in Figure 7-35, when we print the sample document, our header appears $1/2$ inch from the top of the page. The body of our document begins $1/2$ inch below the header, 1 inch from the top of the page. Notice also that the header begins $1^1/4$ inches from the left side of the page, in alignment with our body text.

FIGURE 7-35

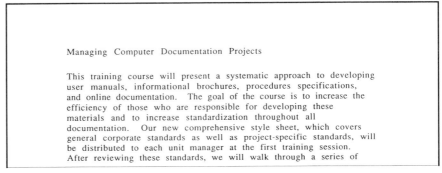

The header initially appears $1/2$ inch from the top of the page, left-aligned with the body text.

Formatting and Positioning the Header Text

Now, suppose you want to reformat the header text to appear in 12-point Helvetica bold type, centered on the page. Simply select the text and format it, just as you would in a document window. Begin by clicking in the invisible selection bar on the left side of the header window to select the entire line, then issue the Character... command and select the Helvetica and Bold settings from the Character dialog box. Next, click on the Centered alignment icon on the header window ruler. Figure 7-36 shows the results.

FIGURE 7-36

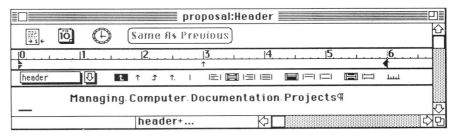

We have now formatted the header text to appear in 12-point Helvetica bold type with centered alignment.

As you can see in Figure 7-37, when we print our sample document with this header in place, Word will center our formatted header text between the left and right margins.

FIGURE 7-37

Managing Computer Documentation Projects

This training course will present a systematic approach to developing user manuals, informational brochures, procedures specifications, and online documentation. The goal of the course is to increase the efficiency of those who are responsible for developing these materials and to increase standardization throughout all documentation. Our new comprehensive style sheet, which covers general corporate standards as well as project-specific standards, will be distributed to each unit manager at the first training session. After reviewing these standards, we will walk through a series of

Our formatted header text is centered between our left and right margins.

If you want to right align your header text, just click on the Right alignment icon. If you're creating a multiline header, you may want to use the Justified alignment icon to align the left and right margins of your header text. You also might use borders to jazz up your headers and help separate them from your body text.

Placing headers in the left and right margins

There may be occasions when you want your header text to appear in your document margins rather than aligned with your main document text. For example, in the sample page shown in Figure 7-38, we've placed our header—consisting of the document title and current date—in the left margin of the page. (We'll show you how to add a date to a header in a few pages.) To create this header, we used a left indent of negative $1^1/_4$ inches, as shown in the header window in Figure 7-39 on the following page.

FIGURE 7-38

6/12/89
Update

This update replaces all previous procedures, policies, and instructions for operation of the CSHS Automated Security Control System. Please remove pages 1-23 through 1-36 from your CSHS user manual and replace them with these updated pages. You will note on page 1-25 of the update that a new password procedure will be in effect beginning 6-30-89. Because of this change in procedure, some users will be issued new passwords. Please see your unit manager for more details.

We placed our two-line header in the left margin.

FIGURE 7-39

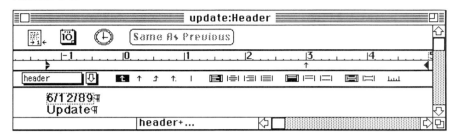

We used a negative left indent to format this header.

To create the negative indent, you must first display the ruler in the header window. Then, press the Shift key and drag the first-line and left indent markers to the left of the zero point on the ruler. If you want to place your header in the right margin of the printed page, just drag the right indent marker to the right, then move the first-line and left indent markers past the dotted line that marks your right margin. (For more on changing a paragraph's left and right indents, see Chapter 5.)

Multiline headers

Notice that the sample header in Figure 7-38 is two lines long. As we mentioned earlier, your header (or footer) can contain as many lines of text as you like. For example, you might want to create your company's letterhead in the header window, as shown in Figure 7-40. Figure 7-41 shows the resulting printed header.

FIGURE 7-40

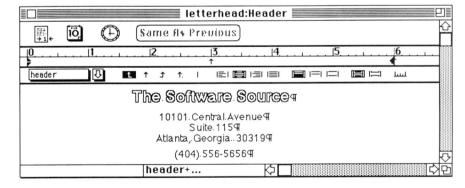

Your header can contain more than one line of text.

FIGURE 7-41

```
                    The  Software  Source
                     10101 Central Avenue
                          Suite 115
                     Atlanta, Georgia  30319

                        (404) 556-5656

      Ms. Laura S. Hartley
      President
      Software Design Corporation
      2707 Redmond Road
      Palo Alto, California   94301
```

Word expands the top margin to make room for a multiline header.

Word will automatically expand the top margin of a document to make room for a multiline header. For example, in Figure 7-41, the first line of text in our document, which normally starts 1 inch from the top of the page, now appears about $1^3/_4$ inches from the top of the page. If we look at our Document dialog box, however, we'll see that Word has not changed our default Top margin setting of 1 inch. It simply overrode this margin setting to avoid overlapping the header text and the main body of the document.

You'll see a similar situation when you create a multiline footer. Word will automatically expand the bottom margin of your document to accommodate the footer text. However, your Bottom margin setting in the Document dialog box will not change.

Notice that Word does not add any extra white space between the header and the first line of text. If you want to insert extra space between the header and the first line of text in your document, you'll need to manually change your Top margin setting in the Document dialog box or use the Before and After settings in the Paragraph dialog box. This brings us to the next topic: controlling the vertical positioning of headers and footers.

Vertical positioning

As you've seen, you can use the ruler in the header window to alter the horizontal positioning and alignment of a header. However, we haven't yet shown how you can move the header vertically on the page. As you already know, the distance between the top of the page and the first line of regular text on the page is controlled by the Top margin setting in the Document dialog box. However, the distance between the top of the page and the first line of a header is controlled by the From Top setting in the Header/Footer portion of the Section dialog box shown in Figure 7-29 on page 268.

Similarly, the distance between the bottom of the page and the last line of regular text on the page is controlled by the Bottom margin setting in the Document dialog box, while the distance between the bottom of the page and the last line of your footer is controlled by the From Bottom setting in the Section dialog box.

The default From Top setting in the Section dialog box is .5 or $\frac{1}{2}$ inch, while the default Top margin setting in the Document dialog box is 1 inch. This leaves $\frac{1}{2}$ inch between the header and the first line of text in your document. However, as you saw in Figure 7-41, if your header takes up more than $\frac{1}{2}$ inch of space (because of the number of lines in the header and/or because of the font size you've chosen), Word will expand the top margin to make room for the header.

Suppose we decide to add extra space between the top of the page and the first line of our header in the sample page shown in Figure 7-41. We would simply issue the Section... command and type a new value—1.5, for instance—in the From Top edit bar. Figure 7-42 shows the results.

FIGURE 7-42

```
                        The  Software  Source
                        10101 Central Avenue
                              Suite 115
                        Atlanta, Georgia  30319
                          (404) 556-5656
        Ms. Laura S. Hartley
        President
        Software Design Corporation
        2707 Redmond Road
        Palo Alto, California   94301
```

You can use the From Top setting in the Section dialog box to add extra white space above a header.

As you can see, Word adds an extra inch between the top of the page and the first line of the header. Word also pushes the first line of text in our sample document down an inch to make room for our expanded header space.

Now, suppose we want to add extra white space between the last line of the header and the first line of text on our sample page. We would issue the Document... command and enter a new value in the Top edit bar. Since our header occupies a total of about $1\frac{3}{4}$ inches (including the space between the top line of the header and the top edge of the page), we might set our top margin to $2\frac{3}{4}$ inches (by typing 2.75 in the Top edit bar) to add an additional inch between the bottom of the header and the top of the text area.

Using the Before and After settings

In addition to changing the From Top and From Bottom settings in the Section dialog box, you can alter the distance between your header and footer text and the top and bottom of the page by using the Before and After settings in the Paragraph dialog box. For example, to open up more space between a header and the top of the page, select the first paragraph of header text, then choose Paragraph... from the Format menu. In the Paragraph dialog box, enter a number—such as 12—in the Before edit bar, then click OK. Word will then automatically allow 12 points of space above your header text—in addition to the amount of space specified in the From Top edit bar of the Section dialog box. As usual, Word will also expand the top margin to make room for the additional space that you've inserted in the header.

Similarly, you can add more space between a header or footer and the body text of a document by using the Before and After settings. For example, suppose you want to insert another $1/_4$ inch of space between a footer and the last line of document text on each page. Begin by selecting the first paragraph of your footer text, then open the Paragraph dialog box. Type 18 in the Before edit bar, then click OK. Word will add 18 points of space ($1/_4$ inch) above the footer text and expand the bottom margin to accommodate the extra space. (For more on the Before and After settings in the Paragraph dialog box, see Chapter 5.)

Although it is convenient that Word automatically adjusts your top margin to make room for long headers, you may occasionally want to override this automatic adjustment to enter your header below the top margin of the page. In other words, you may want to place your header in your text area. For example, consider the sample header shown in Figure 7-38 on page 275. We assigned a negative $1^1/_4$-inch left indent to this header so that we could print it in the left margin of the page.

Placing headers in the text area

Now, suppose you want to print this header in the left margin and align it with the top line of your body text. You want both the header and the first line of text to begin 1 inch from the top of the page. As you learned in the previous examples, if you simply add extra space above the header, Word will move down your first line of text to accommodate the larger header area. To override Word's automatic top margin adjustment, you can enter a negative number as your Top margin setting. Just choose the Document... command from the Format menu. In the Document dialog box, specify a Top margin setting of -1 inch. By typing -1 in the Top edit bar of the Document dialog box, you're not telling Word that you want to create a negative margin—the minus sign simply indicates that you want to make your 1-inch margin setting absolute. This absolute margin setting prevents Word from adjusting the top margin to accommodate the header.

Next, choose the Section... command from the Format menu and type 1 in the From Top edit bar to place the header 1 inch from the top of the page. Figure 7-43 shows the resulting printed page. Notice that the header and body text are now evenly aligned 1 inch from the top of the page.

FIGURE 7-43

6/12/89 **Update**	This update replaces all previous procedures, policies, and instructions for operation of the CSHS Automated Security Control System. Please remove pages 1-23 through 1-36 from your CSHS user manual and replace them with these updated pages. You will note on page 1-25 of the update that a new password procedure will be in effect beginning 6-30-89. Because of this change in procedure, some users will be issued new passwords. Please see your unit manager for more details.

Both the header and the main body text now appear 1 inch from the top of the page.

Another way to place a header in the margin of a page is to use the Position... command. As we'll explain in Chapter 10, with the Position... command, you can place selected text in a fixed position on the page and let Word flow the rest of the text around it. For example, to position a header in the left margin, as shown in Figure 7-43, you could select the text in the header window, then choose Position... from the Format menu. In the Position dialog box, enter .45 in the Horizontal edit bar and click on the Relative to Page option. Then, enter 1 in the Vertical edit bar and click the Relative to Page option there as well. In the Paragraph Width edit bar, type 1. For more about the Position... command, see Chapter 10.

Formatting headers and footers with the style sheet

As we have shown, it's very easy to select and format text in a header window; the process is no different from selecting and formatting text in your main document window. However, as you'll learn in Chapter 8, you also can format your header text by altering the definition of the style named *header* on your style sheet. (Word automatically adds this style to the style sheet whenever you create a header.) Similarly, you can format the text in a footer window by using either manual formatting techniques or by altering the *footer* style on the style sheet. If you've used different headers and footers for different sections of a document (we'll show you how to do this in a few pages), the *header* and *footer* styles will apply to all sections. In other words, Word does not create a separate style to format the header and footer of each new section. In some cases, you can use this to your advantage. When your document contains variable headers and/or footers, you can format all of them consistently by changing the *header* or *footer* style instructions. In situations where you want to use a different format for the headers and footers of each section, however, you can either use manual formatting techniques or define some new styles (such as *header2*, *header3*, and so forth) on your style sheet.

Adding Dates, Times, and Page Numbers

As you've probably guessed by now, the icons at the top of the header window let you insert the current page number, date, and time into your header text. (These icons are also available in the footer window.) These three elements are dynamic; that is, Word updates the date and time whenever you open the header window or print your document so that they remain current. (By the way, to adjust the date and time settings, use the Alarm Clock desk accessory.) The page number that appears in the header window reflects the number of the page that is currently being displayed in your document window. Of course, when you print the document, the page number entry will change for each page in the document.

To insert a dynamic date, time, or page number entry into the header text, place the insertion point at the spot where you want that information to appear, then click on the appropriate icon at the top of the header window. For example, Figure 7-44 shows a sample header in which we've entered the time, date, and page number.

FIGURE 7-44

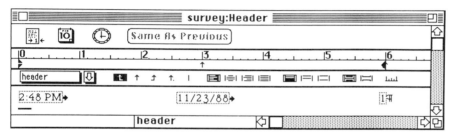

You can enter dynamic times, dates, and page numbers into your header.

When the Show ¶ setting is in effect, as in Figure 7-44, Word displays a dotted border around the time, date, and page number to indicate that they are dynamic entries. Of course, these borders do not appear when you print the document, nor will they appear if you choose Hide ¶.

Word treats each dynamic time, date, and page number entry as a single character. As a result, any character formats you assign to these entries will apply to the entire entry. For example, you cannot assign a character style, such as bold, to just the month portion of a date. To select the time, date, or page number, just double-click anywhere on that item.

Although you can assign any character formats to your date, time, and page number entries, you cannot change the content of those entries—the date will always appear in the form M/D/YY, and the time will always appear in the form H:M AM/PM. However, as we'll explain next, you can use the Section... command to change the form of your page number entries.

If you want to insert a static date or time in a header or footer (a date or time that will not change), you can simply type the date or time or you can insert one of the date or time entries in the glossary. Chapter 13 covers the glossary in detail.

When you add a dynamic page number entry to your header text, Word uses the numbering scheme you selected in the Section dialog box to format those numbers. Figure 7-31 on page 269 shows the available numbering schemes. For example,

Working with page numbers

the page number in the sample header shown in Figure 7-44 appears in Word's default Arabic format. If you want these page numbers to appear in uppercase Roman numerals, open the Section dialog box and select the **I II III** option from the dropdown list in the Page Number portion of the dialog box.

Again, keep in mind that the numbering scheme you select will apply to the current section only. If your document contains more than one section, you can apply the same numbering scheme to all sections. Simply select some text in each section, open the Section dialog box, and choose the numbering scheme you want to use.

By the way, we explained earlier in this chapter how you can use the Auto option in the Section dialog box to add page numbers to your printed document. When you add a dynamic page number entry to your document's header or footer, you probably will want to deselect the Auto option and place the page number in the header or footer only. Otherwise, you'll end up with two page numbers on each page. (If you used Word 3, you may recall that it would automatically turn off automatic page numbering in the Section dialog box whenever you inserted a page number in a header or footer. Word 4 does not attempt to eliminate duplicate page numbers in this manner.)

**Creating
a Different
First-Page
Header**

Often, you'll want the first page of a document to display a different header or footer than the rest of the document. In fact, you may want the first page of a document to display no header or footer at all. To change the header or footer on the first page, just choose the Section... command from the Format menu, and in the Header/Footer portion of the Section dialog box, click the First Page Special option. (If your document contains more than one section, you can activate this option for any or all of the sections. If you want a special header or footer for just the first page of the document, make sure that the insertion point is in the first section of the document before you open the Section dialog box and click the First Page Special option.)

After you close the Section dialog box, you'll see two new commands on the Document menu: Open First Header... and Open First Footer.... When you choose one of these commands, Word will open a new header or footer window with the words *First Header* or *First Footer* in the title bar. For example, Figure 7-45 shows a first-page header window.

The first-page header and footer windows will initially be blank. If you want to eliminate the header or footer on the first page of a document, you only need to activate the First Page Special option. If you want to create a new header or footer on the first page, just enter the text in the header or footer window.

FIGURE 7-45

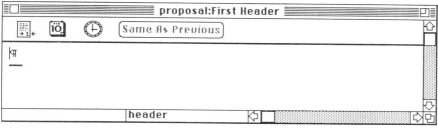

When you select the First Page Special option in the Section dialog box, Word will create new header and footer windows for the first page.

Editing Headers and Footers

In general, you edit headers and footers as you edit any other text in your document. All the techniques for selecting, inserting, deleting, and overwriting text that we discussed in Chapters 4 and 6 apply here as well. You can use the Cut, Copy, and Paste commands in the header and footer windows, just as you do in a document window. You also can copy and move text between your header, footer, and document windows. In fact, you can even use Word's Find..., Change..., Spelling..., and Hyphenate... commands in your header and footer windows.

When you edit a header or footer window for one section of your document, keep in mind that your changes may also affect any subsequent "linked" headers or footers. As we explain in Chapter 10, the effects of your editing changes depend on which header or footer window you edit and whether you have broken the link between that header or footer and subsequent headers and footers.

Copying and moving text in header and footer windows

When you are copying or moving text, you treat your header and footer windows just as you would treat any other document window. For example, suppose you have included the heading *Policies and Procedures* in your document, and you decide to use this title in your document header. Rather than retyping the text, just highlight the heading in your document, and issue the Copy command. Next, select Open Header... from the Document menu, click at the spot where you want to add the heading, and issue the Paste command. After you've finished editing and formatting your header, just click the close box in the header window title bar to lock in your changes and close the window.

If you need to copy several items between your document and header or footer windows, keep in mind that the header and footer windows will remain open on your screen if you simply click on another window, rather than use the close box to remove the header or footer window from the DeskTop. You may want to temporarily resize and reposition the windows on your DeskTop to make it easier to access your header, footer, and document windows.

Unfortunately, you can open only one header or footer window at a time. For example, if you are using odd and even headers (these are discussed in Chapter 10), and you want to copy an item from the even header window to the odd header window, you must first open the even header window, select the text you want, and issue the Copy command. Then, you must open the odd header window, and issue the Paste command. Similarly, if you have created a multisection document and you want to copy a selection from one section header to another, you must issue separate Open Header... commands to access the header windows for each section.

For example, to copy an entry from your *Header (S1)* window to the *Header (S3)* window, you must click in the first section, open the header window, select the item you want to copy, and issue the Copy command. Then, you must click in section three and issue a new Open Header... command before you can issue the Paste command.

Other editing techniques for headers and footers

When you use Word's Find... and Change... commands to locate text or to replace one series of characters with another, Word finds and changes only the occurrences in the active window. This means that Word won't typically locate occurrences of your find text in a header or footer window, even if that window is open on the DeskTop when you issue the Find... or Change... command.

If you want to perform a search or replace operation in a header or footer window, however, just activate that window before you issue the Find... or Change... command. If the window is already open on your DeskTop, click on the window to activate it. If the header or footer window you want to work with is not currently open, select one of the Open Header... or Open Footer... commands from the Document menu. Then, while the header or footer window is active, perform the find-and-change procedure as you normally would in the document window. If you are using different odd, even, or first-page headers and footers, you'll have to open each header or footer window in turn and perform separate find-and-change procedures. In a multisection document, you'll have to click in the appropriate section of your document, then open the header or footer window for that section.

Similarly, when you use the Hyphenate... command in your document, Word will not automatically check your header and footer after it checks the main document. You must activate each of your header and footer windows before you can use the Hyphenate... command in those windows. Once you activate the header or footer window you want to check, you can proceed with your editing just as you would in a standard document window. (See Chapter 6 for more on the Find..., Change..., and Hyphenate... commands.)

Interestingly, when you use the Spelling... command, Word will automatically check for misspelled (or unrecognized) words in your headers and footers. When Word locates a misspelled word, it will display it in the Spelling dialog box as usual, but it will also display a notation indicating in which header or footer the unrecognized word was found. For example, if your header contains the misspelled word *Compayn*, Word will display *Compayn - from Header* in the Spelling dialog box when it locates this word. If your document contains different headers for different sections, odd and even pages, and so forth, the notation in the Spelling dialog box will identify which header or footer contains the error. For example, if the misspelled word appears in the header for the second section of a document, you'll see *Compayn - from Header (S2)* in the Spelling dialog box.

When you issue the Spelling... command in a document that contains headers or footers, Word will begin looking for misspelled words at the insertion point location and search through the end of the main document. After checking all of the main document, Word will check each header and footer window, starting at the beginning of the document. For example, in a two-section document, Word will check the header(s) in the first section, then check the footer(s) in the first section. After that, it will check the header(s) and footer(s) in the second section. If you have created a separate first-page header in a section, it will be checked before other headers in that section. Chapter 6 explains the Spelling... command in detail.

To delete a header or footer, open the header or footer window, select all the text, then press the Backspace key. (You also can choose Cut from the Edit menu to delete the text.) After you've deleted the text, just close the header or footer window.

Deleting Headers and Footers

We've talked about a number of commands and settings that let you control the appearance of your printed document. However, it can sometimes be a bit confusing to figure out how all of these elements work together. Fortunately, Word offers two commands, Page View and Print Preview..., that let you preview your document before you print.

The Print Preview... command, which is located on the File menu, gives you a "bird's-eye view" of your document, allowing you to see entire page layouts on the screen. The Page View command, on the other hand, shows you a full-size preview of your printed document with headers, footers, and other special elements in place. However, because the text is shown in full size, only a portion of the page can be seen on the screen. Page View is a toggle command on the Document menu that also can be accessed by pressing ⌘-b or by clicking the Page View button in the Print Preview window. Both the Print Preview... and the Page View commands can help you avoid time-consuming (and possibly costly) bad print runs. We'll look first at the Print Preview... command, then we'll talk about using Word's page view.

PREVIEWING YOUR PRINTED DOCUMENT

When you choose the Print Preview... command from the File menu (or press ⌘-i), Word displays a window like the one in Figure 7-46. The icons on the left side of the Print Preview window let you add page numbers to your document; change the position of various elements on the document page; display single or facing pages; and print your document.

The Print Preview... Command

FIGURE 7-46

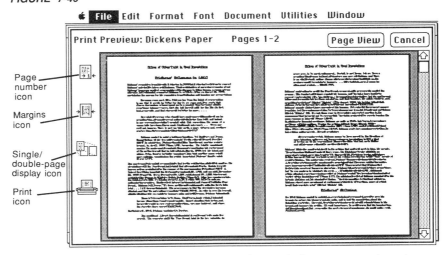

Page number icon

Margins icon

Single/ double-page display icon

Print icon

The Print Preview... command lets you preview and alter your page layout.

The first time you use the Print Preview... command, Word will display two document pages on your screen. To see only a single page, click on the single/ double page display icon (above the printer icon) on the left side of the screen. When you click on this icon, Word will display only the first page of the two-page spread, as shown in Figure 7-47. To bring the two-page display back, just click on the single/ double page display icon once more.

To close the Print Preview window, just click the Cancel or Page View button at the upper-right corner of the screen. You also can close the Print Preview window by pressing ⌘-w (or ⌘-.). As you might guess, choosing the Page View button will display your document in the page view. Choosing the Cancel button or pressing ⌘-w (or ⌘-.) will display your document in whatever view was active (galley, page, or outline) at the time you issued the Print Preview... command.

Navigating in the Print Preview window

When you issue the Print Preview... command, Word will automatically repaginate your document through the page that is currently visible on your screen and display a preview of that page and the following page. The number of the page or pages that are currently being previewed will appear in the top center of the screen. For example, in Figure 7-46, the notation *Pages 1-2* appears at the top of the window.

If you want to see a different page while the preview screen is open, you can use the vertical scroll bar on the right side of the preview window or the direction keys to bring other pages into view. Click on the scroll arrows or in the gray area of the scroll bar to move through the document a page at a time. Or, press ↓ or 2 on the numeric keypad to move forward one page, or press ↑ or 8 on the numeric keypad to move back one page.

FIGURE 7-47

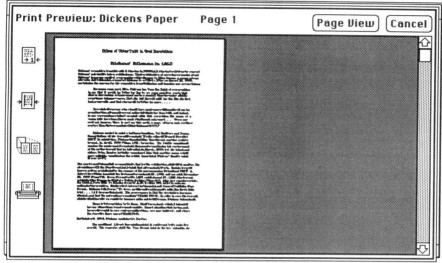

To preview a single page, click the single/double page display icon.

Generally, if you are using a two-page display, moving forward by one page will cause the page on the right side of your preview screen to move to the left, while a new page is brought into view on the right side. When you move back by one page, the effect is the opposite: The page on the left side shifts to the right side, and a new page is brought into view on the left. For example, if you are viewing pages 4 and 5 on the preview screen and you press ↑, Word will display pages 3 and 4.

If you have activated either Mirror Even/Odd Margins or Even/Odd Headers, or if you've specified a Gutter setting in the Document dialog box, navigating from page to page is a bit different. When you're viewing the beginning of a document, a blank page will appear on the left side of your screen, and page 1 will appear on the right. As you move forward or backward through the document, Word will shift both of the display pages in order to maintain this even-odd layout. For example, if you are viewing pages 4 and 5 on the screen and you press ↑, Word will bring pages 2 and 3 into view.

To move through several pages on the preview screen, just drag the scroll box. As you do this, you'll see the page numbers flash by at the top of the screen. Just release the scroll box when you see the number for the page you want to preview.

Word will not let you edit your document or change its character and paragraph formatting while you are viewing it through the Print Preview window. However, if you notice an error or an item you want to change while you are viewing a page on the preview screen, you can quickly go to that spot in your document to make your change. When you close the Print Preview window, Word will display the text that is currently visible on the preview screen in your document window. If, after making your editing or formatting change, you want to preview the results of your efforts, just issue the Print Preview… command again. As long as the text you want to view is visible in your document window, Word will display the page on which that text is located when you choose the Print Preview… command.

Page size

All the sample page preview screens we've see thus far have been standard letter-size pages with Word's default Tall (🖵) Orientation setting. If you use other page sizes or a different Orientation setting, Word will adjust the size and proportion of your preview pages to reflect your Page Setup dialog box specifications.

For example, the sample preview page in Figure 7-48 shows a letter-size page that we set up to be printed with Wide (🖵) Orientation. The sample preview page shown in Figure 7-49 was set up to be printed on 3- by 5-inch index card stock. To create this layout, we opened the Preferences dialog box and specified a custom paper size with a Width setting of 5 inches and a Height setting of 3 inches. Then, we selected this Paper option in the Page Setup dialog box. (As we've mentioned, custom paper sizes are available only for the ImageWriter in Word 4.) In the Document dialog box, we specified Top, Bottom, Left, and Right margin settings of .5 inch. Notice that Word has adjusted the size of the preview page image to display as much detail as possible.

FIGURE 7-48

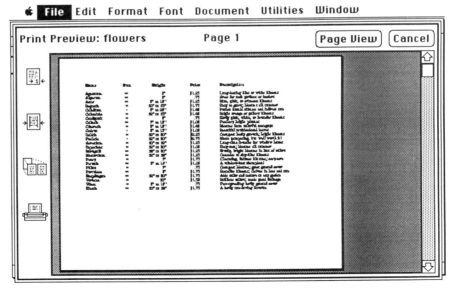

Word will rotate your preview page images to display pages in the orientation you have selected.

FIGURE 7-49

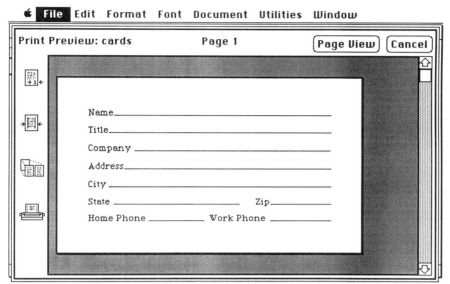

This document is set up to be printed on 3- by 5-inch index cards.

As we mentioned earlier, you can change many of your page layout specifications while the Print Preview window is open on your DeskTop. For example, you can add and reposition page numbers, move your document margins, change your document's page breaks, and reposition your headers and footers. We suspect that many users will find it easier to format their documents "visually" on the preview screen, rather than using the Document, Page Setup, and Section dialog boxes. While you're viewing the Print Preview window, Word also lets you move items that have been positioned with the Position... command. We'll talk more about this when we explain the Position... command in Chapter 10. For now, let's look at how you can change page numbers, margins, page breaks, and headers and footers.

Formatting in the preview window

You can use the page number icon on the preview screen to add page numbers to your document and to reposition existing page numbers. Using this icon has the same effects as clicking on the Auto option in the Page Number portion of the Section dialog box and typing your page number positions in the From Top and From Right edit bars. As with the Page Number options, if you're working in a multisection document, your changes to the page number positions on the preview screen will apply to the current section only.

Adding and positioning page numbers

When you click on the page number icon (the top icon on the left side of the Print Preview window), your pointer will take on the shape of the number 1. Just click at the spot where you want your page numbers to appear. To fine-tune your page number position, you can drag the mouse as you're pointing to the page number. Word will display a pair of coordinates at the top of the screen to let you know exactly where the page number will appear. These coordinates correspond to the From Right and From Top entries that you would make in the Section dialog box. For example, if you see the coordinates *(1.00, 4.50)* at the top of your screen, this tells you that the page number is positioned 1 inch from the right edge of the page and $4^1/_2$ inches from the top of the page.

If you have not yet added any page numbers to your document, you can double-click on the page number icon to automatically position your page number at the default position—$^1/_2$ inch from the top-right corner of the page. After adding a page number, you can reposition it by clicking on the margins icon, then clicking on the number and dragging it to the desired position on the preview page. As you drag, Word will flash new position coordinates at the top of the preview window. You also can reposition the page numbers at any time by clicking again on the page number icon and then clicking at a new spot on the preview page. Word will remove the page number from its current position and place it at the new position.

If you are using the Even/Odd Headers option in the Document dialog box, Word will reverse the position of your page numbers on even pages. For example, if you place the page number 1 inch from the right edge of an odd page, that number will appear 1 inch from the left edge of your even pages.

Changing margins

In Chapter 5, we showed how you can set margins by entering Top, Bottom, Left, and Right margin settings in the Document dialog box. You also can set—or change—your margins in the Print Preview window. Begin by clicking on the margins icon, the second icon on the left side of the preview screen. Then, if you are viewing two pages, click on the page you want to work with. When you click on the margins icon, Word will display dotted lines that represent your current margin positions, as well as your header and footer positions and page breaks, as shown in Figure 7-50. If you have used the Position... command to place an object on the page you're previewing, the boundaries of that object will also be marked with a dotted line when you click on the margins icon.

Notice the black squares or handles that appear at the edge of the top, bottom, left, and right margin markers in Figure 7-50. To change a margin setting, just click on one of these handles and drag it to the desired position. When you move the pointer to a handle, it will assume a crosshair shape. Then, when you click on the handle, Word will display the margin setting at the top of your screen. This setting will change as you drag the margin marker. The value that's displayed when you release the mouse button to lock in your change will be transferred to the appropriate margin edit bar in the Document dialog box.

FIGURE 7-50

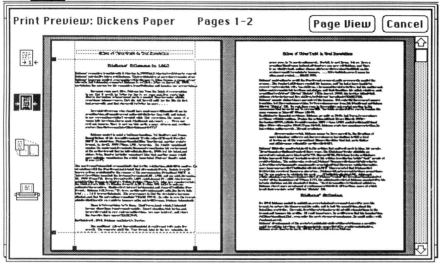

When you click the margins icon, Word will display dotted lines that represent the current page layout settings.

For example, suppose you want to increase the Left and Right margin settings for the sample document shown in Figure 7-50 to $1^3/_4$ inches each. Begin by clicking on the margins icon, then click on the handle at the bottom of the left margin line and drag it to the right. Release the mouse button when you see the value *1.75* at the top of the preview screen. To adjust the right margin, click on the handle at the bottom of the right margin line and drag it to the left. Again, release the mouse button when you see the value *1.75*.

Once you've positioned your margins, click on the margins icon or click anywhere outside the page display portion of the screen to see the effects of your changes. Word will repaginate your document and redraw the pages on your screen to reflect the new margins. Keep in mind that your margin settings apply to your entire document, not just to the page or section you are previewing.

You can also insert manual page breaks into your document from the preview screen by dragging the page-break line that appears below the last line of text on the preview page. This line appears between the lines marking your left and right margins; it does not extend all the way to the edge of the page as do your top and bottom margin markers. In addition, a page-break line does not have a handle—you simply point to any part of the line to drag it. When you release the mouse button,

**Changing
page breaks**

Word will immediately repaginate the document. If you move the page-break line up, any text that appears below that line will move to the top of the next page. If you drag the page-break line down, Word will pull text from the top of the next page down to the bottom of the current page. Of course, if the Widow Control option in the Document dialog box is active, Word will not leave the first line of a paragraph "stranded" at the bottom of a page or move the last line of a paragraph to the top of the next page.

For example, suppose you want to move the last three lines at the bottom of page 1 in Figure 7-50 to the top of page 2. All you need to do is drag the page-break marker up three lines, as shown in Figure 7-51. As you can see, Word will reflow the document and reposition the lines. When you return to your document window, you'll also see that Word has inserted a manual page-break marker at this spot in your document.

FIGURE 7-51

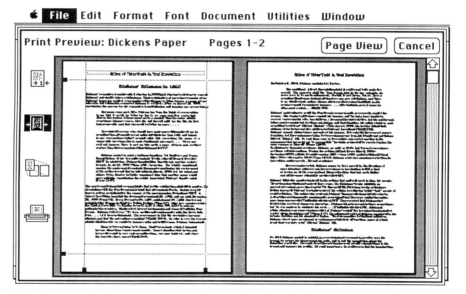

Word automatically inserts a manual page break and reflows your text when you drag the page-break line.

By the way, the page-break line will often appear just above the line marking the bottom margin. This can make it difficult for you to distinguish the page-break line from the margin marker. However, you can move the page-break line without affecting your bottom margin marker. In order to drag the page-break line, you must click between the left and right margins on the preview screen. Since the bottom margin marker must be dragged by its handle—which appears on the left edge of the page—you'll be able to move the page-break line independently of the margin marker. Word will not let you use the page-break line to flow text past the bottom margin marker. However, if you have inserted a manual page break in your document and you decide to remove it, you can drag the page-break line past the bottom margin marker on the preview screen. Word will reflow your document to fill the current page.

Repositioning headers and footers

When you click on the margins icon in the Print Preview window, Word displays a dotted border around your headers and footers. To reposition a header or footer, just click anywhere within this border and drag the header or footer up or down to the desired position. This action is equivalent to changing the value in the From Top or From Bottom edit bar in the Section dialog box. As you drag the header or footer, Word will display the distance between the header or footer and the edge of the page at the top of the preview screen.

After you drag the header or footer, click on the margins icon or click in the gray area of the preview screen. Word will then redraw the screen to show the header or footer in its new position.

If your headers and footers require more space than is currently available in the top and bottom margin areas, you'll want to reposition your top and bottom margin markers before you move the headers and footers. Word will not allow you to drag a header or footer past your top or bottom margin marker.

For example, suppose you want the header shown in Figure 7-51 to appear 1 inch from the top of the page. Because the current Top margin setting is 1 inch, you'll need to drag the top margin marker down before you can move the header. First click on the handle on the right side of the top margin marker and drag it until you see *1.75* at the top-center of the preview screen. Then, click on the header and drag it to the 1-inch position. You should also remove the manual page break that was inserted earlier by dragging it off the page. Figure 7-52 on the next page shows the results.

If you want to drag a header or footer past the current top or bottom margin so that it will print in the text area, just press the Shift key as you drag the header or footer on the preview screen. This is equivalent to using a minus sign to type an absolute Top or Bottom margin setting in the Document dialog box. (See page 279 for more on placing headers and footers in the text area.)

If you're working in a multisection document, your changes to the header and footer positions will apply to the current section only. If you want to change the header and footer positions in more than one section, you may find it easier to highlight some text in two or more sections in your document window and then use the Section... command to make your adjustments. (Chapter 10 explains this process in more detail.)

FIGURE 7-52

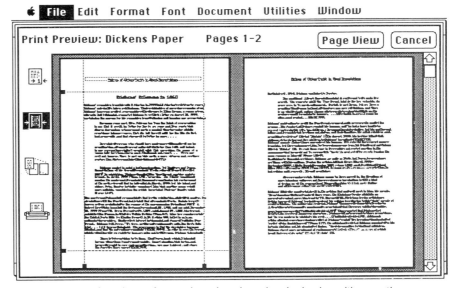

To reposition a header or footer, just drag it to the desired position on the page.

Printing from the Print Preview window

The last icon in the Print Preview window looks like a printer. When you click on this icon, Word will open the Print dialog box. You can change some of the Print settings, or just click OK to print the document with the existing settings. The Print Preview window will remain open after the page has been printed.

Using Page View

A new feature of Word 4 is the page view. Like the preview screen that you see when you choose the Print Preview… command, the page view shows you a preview of your printed document pages with headers, page numbers, footnotes, and other special elements in place. However, unlike the preview screen, the page view displays your page and text in their full size. In fact, the page view feature has replaced the magnifier icon that appeared on the preview screen in Word 3. If you used Word 3, you may recall that you could use the magnifier icon to "zoom in" on part of a preview page. However, once you were viewing the preview page in full size, you could not make any editing or formatting changes to the text. Now, with page view, you not only see a full-size preview of your printed document pages, but you also can make changes as you're viewing those pages.

Although the page view is quite helpful for seeing how your printed pages will be laid out, you'll find that Word runs significantly more slowly when the page view is active. Therefore, you probably will not want to use it for the majority of your text creation, editing, and formatting. We recommend that you stay with the galley view most of the time and use the page view only to check the layout of your document in the final stages.

There are four ways to access the page view. First, you can simply select the Page View command on the Document menu. When you do this, Word will refresh your screen, changing from the view you were using (galley or outline) to the page view. Page View is a toggle command—when you want to turn off page view and switch to the galley view, just choose the command once more. You also can go from page view to outline view by choosing the Outlining command on the Document menu. While page view is active, a check mark will appear next to the command name on the menu. Word will remove the check mark when another view is active. Instead of selecting the Page View command on the Document menu, you can toggle between page view and the galley view (or outline view) by pressing ⌘-b or [F13].

Accessing page view

Another way to access the page view is to click the Page View button at the top of the Print Preview window. This allows you to move from the "bird's-eye view" of the preview screen to the close-up view of the page view screen. Finally, you can set up Word to open all your documents in page view instead of the galley view. To do this, choose the Preferences... command from the Edit menu and, in the Preferences dialog box, activate the Open Documents in Page View option. When this option is active, Word will open both new and existing documents in the page view. Of course, you can switch to the galley view at any time by selecting the Page View command on the Document menu.

When you choose the Page View command from the Document menu, Word will first repaginate your document from the first page through the page on which the insertion point is located. If your document is quite long, you may have to wait several seconds or longer before the page view screen appears. While you're in page view, if you move forward to another page in the document, Word will repaginate through that point as well.

As you're editing and formatting in page view, Word will not automatically repaginate your document unless you've turned on Background Repagination in the Preferences dialog box. The one exception to this is when you make an editing or formatting change that causes text to flow from one page to the next. For example, if you insert a paragraph on a page, causing several lines to be pushed to the next page, Word will automatically repaginate in order to ensure that the page you're viewing reflects your current document layout. Similarly, changing your document margins will also cause Word to repaginate. Of course, you can always select the Repaginate Now command from the Document menu. In page view, however, this command will repaginate only through the current page.

Let's use the page view to take another look at the sample document shown in Figures 7-50 through 7-52. When we issue the Page View command, Word will display the page view screen shown in Figure 7-53.

A brief tour

FIGURE 7-53

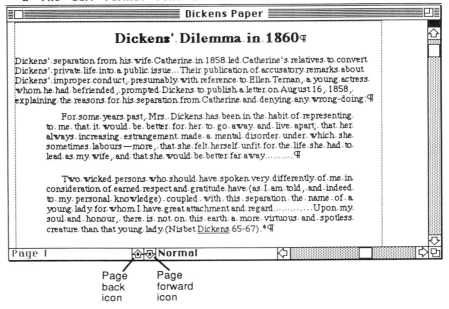

Page
back
icon

Page
forward
icon

When you switch to the page view, Word will display the main text area of the
current page at the top of the screen.

When you first switch to page view, Word will display the main text area of the
current page at the top of the screen. For example, if your document has a 1-inch
top margin with a header, that margin and header will be just out of view, with the
first line of your document's main body text appearing at the top of the window. To
bring other parts of the page into view, just click on the vertical or horizontal scroll
bar. To see a different page, you can drag the scroll boxes or click on the page back
and page forward icons (the up and down arrows) at the bottom of the page view
screen. (More on this in a moment.)

When you scroll in page view, Word will show you edges of your page instead
of marking page breaks with a horizontal line. For example, Figure 7-54 shows the
page from Figure 7-53 after we scrolled the upper-right corner into view. Notice that
Word uses a shaded background to help distinguish the page area. Notice also that
you now can see the header at the top of the page. If we were to continue scrolling
up this document, Word would bring the bottom of the previous page into view.

FIGURE 7-54

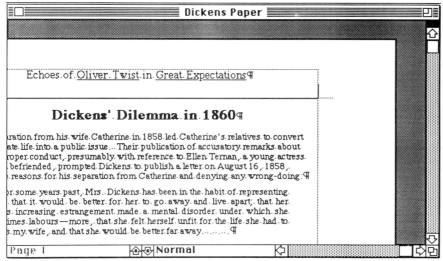

You can scroll the edges of a page into view on the page view screen.

Text areas

In page view, different elements of your page layout are considered to be separate text areas. In a simple page layout, you would have only one text area—the single column of text that's bounded by your left, right, top, and bottom margins. In a multicolumn layout, each column is a separate text area. Each header and footer is also considered to be a text area, as are positioned objects, tables, and individual cells of a table. In Chapter 10, we'll explain how to create multicolumn layouts and tables, and show you how the Position… command works.

The concept of text areas becomes significant as you move around and select text in page view. As you'll see in a moment, Word offers several keyboard shortcuts for moving from one text area to another. In addition, each text area in page view has its own selection bar. Before we talk about these topics, however, let's look at one way you can identify the separate text areas on a page.

Boundary lines

To help you keep your bearings as you scroll around in page view and to distinguish individual text areas on a page, Word displays boundaries, or dotted lines, around the different text areas in a document. These boundary lines are similar to the margin, header, and page-break lines you can see in the Print Preview window, although you cannot drag the boundary lines in page view.

Whenever Show ¶ is active, Word will display boundary lines in page view. Thus, turning boundary lines off and on is as easy as choosing Show ¶ or Hide ¶ from the Edit menu. Figure 7-55 shows the page from Figure 7-54 after we turned off the display of boundaries.

FIGURE 7-55

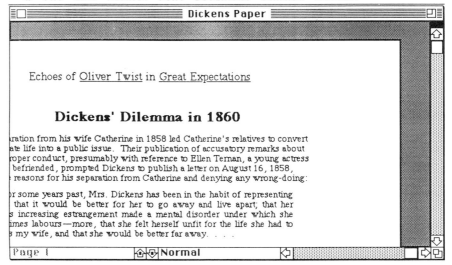

You can turn off the display of boundary lines by choosing Hide ¶ from the Edit menu.

To see boundary lines even after you've selected Hide ¶, just open the Preferences dialog box and select the Show Text Boundaries in Page View option. That way, Word will always display boundary lines.

Going back to Figure 7-54, you can see two types of boundary lines. The vertical and horizontal lines that intersect in the upper-right corner of the page are the margin boundaries. If you were to scroll to any corner of the page, you would see these intersecting lines. Above the line that marks the top margin, you'll see the header boundary. This line appears $1/2$ inch from the top edge of the page—or the distance we've specified as the From Top setting in the Section dialog box. If a page contains a footer, the bottom boundary of the footer would be marked by a similar line.

If your page is laid out in two or more snaking columns, each column will also be surrounded by its own boundary line. Any object to which you have assigned a special position using the Position... command will also appear within its own boundary. Boundary lines will also appear around tables that you have created with the Insert Table... command and around each cell in the table.

We've mentioned briefly that you can use the vertical and horizontal scroll-bars to move around while you're in the page view mode. We've also mentioned the page back and page forward icons that appear at the bottom of your window when you're using page view. When you click the page back icon (🏠), Word brings the top of the previous page into view. Clicking the page forward icon (🔽) will bring the top of the next page onto your screen. In both cases, Word moves the insertion point to the beginning of the new page.

To move quickly through a large portion of your document, just drag the scroll boxes or issue the Go To... command and specify the page number you want to see.

Word also offers a number of keyboard shortcuts for moving around in page view. These keyboard techniques allow you to move quickly from one text area to another on a single page. Table 7-2 summarizes these keyboard shortcuts, which involve using the Option key, the ⌘ key, and the keys on the numeric keypad. As you use these shortcuts, Word will scroll the page on your screen to bring the insertion point into view.

Navigating in page view

TABLE 7-2

This key combination...	Moves the insertion point to...	Example
Option-⌘-8	Text area immediately above	Move from main text area to header
Option-⌘-2	Text area immediately below	Move from main text area to footer
Option-⌘-4	Text area immediately to the left	Move from right column to left column in a two-column layout
Option-⌘-6	Text area immediately to the right	Move from left column to right column in a two-column layout
Option-⌘-3	Next text area on page	Move from first column to top of second column
Option-⌘-9	Preceding text area on page	Move from second column to top of first column

With the numeric keypad, you can use these keyboard techniques to move from one text area to another on a page.

Selecting text in page view

We mentioned earlier that each text area in the page view has its own selection bar. You can see evidence of this as you move the pointer around on the screen. Each time the pointer moves over the selection bar for a text area, it will change from the I-beam shape into a right-pointing arrow. For example, suppose you are working with a two-column layout in page view. Your document window will have a selection bar on the far left as it normally does. However, this selection bar is for the left column only. There will also be another selection bar just to the left of the right column. So, if you want to select a paragraph of text in the right column, move the pointer into the selection bar just to the left of that paragraph and double-click.

If you want to select all the text in a document, just move the pointer to any selection bar—except the selection bar for a header or footer—and press the ⌘ key as you click the mouse button. Other selection techniques that are described in Chapter 4 work the same in page view as in galley view. You can even select text on two or more pages by dragging your selection beyond the top or bottom border of the window. However, you'll find that making a selection like this is much slower in page view than in galley view. Once again, we recommend that you use the galley view for major editing and formatting changes.

Editing and formatting in page view

Although you'll probably want to use the galley view for most of your editing and formatting, you'll often need to make minor changes in the page view as well. For example, if you spot a misspelled word in your header, you can simply click on the misspelling and correct it. There's no need to return to the galley view and open a header window. As you're viewing your document, you also might discover that your margins aren't as wide as you would prefer. To correct this, just open the Document dialog box and enter new settings. You can open the Document dialog box quickly in page view by double-clicking in the corner of a page, between intersections of the lines that mark your side and top or bottom margins. Of course, you also can change your margins by choosing the Print Preview... command, clicking on the margins icon, and dragging your margin markers.

In short, any editing and formatting changes that you can make in the galley view can also be made in the page view. This includes altering your Document, Section, Paragraph, and Character dialog box settings; changing style definitions; cutting; copying; pasting; and finding and changing. You also can insert page breaks and section breaks and use any of Word's special features, including the Spelling..., Hyphenate..., and Sort commands.

Working with headers and footers in page view

As Figures 7-54 and 7-55 illustrate, the page view shows your headers and footers in position on each page. If you want to alter a header or footer, just click on the text and make your change. Word will apply your change to all headers (or footers) in the current section. If your document has multiple sections, changing a header or footer on one page will affect any linked headers or footers in subsequent sections. (Chapter 10 explains sectional headers and footers in detail.)

To add a header or footer in page view, just choose Open Header... or Open Footer... from the Document menu. Word will then move the insertion point to the first character in the header or footer area of the page. You can now enter and format the text for your header or footer. If you have activated Even/Odd Headers in the Document dialog box, Word will use the text that you enter only on like pages. For example, suppose you create a header on page 2. If you scroll to page 3, you'll see that no header appears, since that is an odd page. However, if you scroll to page 4, the header text from page 2 will appear. As long as you're in the page view, only the Open Header... and Open Footer... commands will appear on the Document menu. However, when you switch to the galley view, you'll get the full range of commands for even, odd, and first-page headers and footers.

Although page view is a helpful feature, there are a number of instances when it cannot give you an accurate representation of your printed document. As we said earlier, as long as Show Hidden Text is activated in the Preferences dialog box, any text with the Hidden format will appear in page view—even if you've deselected the Print Hidden Text option in the Print dialog box. If you've chosen to use line numbers in a document, these will not appear in page view, though they will show up in the Print Preview window. Of course, if you've embedded a PostScript code in a document, that code will not be interpreted until you actually print.

Limitations of page view

Finally, many of the options that are available in the Page Setup dialog box will not affect the appearance of your document in page view since these options are implemented by your printer. For example, if you select Font Substitution, the substituted font(s) will appear only when you print. When you view your document in page view, you'll see whatever font(s) you have chosen with the Font menu or the Character dialog box. If you reduce or enlarge your text by specifying a percentage other than the 100% displayed in the Page Setup dialog box, Word will still display the text in normal size in page view, although it will rewrap the text in shorter or longer lines. Again, you must print your document in order to see the new text size. (Interestingly, the Print Preview window does adjust the size of your text when you choose to reduce or enlarge it.) Finally, the various options that appear when you choose Options in the Page Setup dialog box will not affect the appearance of your document in page view or in the Print Preview window. In order to see the results of the Flip Horizontal, Flip Vertical, Invert Image, and other special options, you must print your document.

THE COBB GROUP

The Best

GUARANTEED

Advanced Techniques

Section 3:
Advanced Techniques

In Section 2, you learned all the basics you need to use Microsoft Word. By now, you should have mastered skills like creating, selecting, editing, formatting, and printing text. You should also have a handle on designing a page layout, creating and using document windows, and navigating in Word.

In this section, we'll go beyond these Word basics to look at a number of special features, like style sheets, outlining, the glossary, indexes, multi-column formatting, footnotes, form letters, and character formulas. You'll also learn how to customize your Word menus and control many default settings so that you can tailor the program to fit your needs. We'll show you how to share data with other programs—including SuperPaint and Microsoft Excel—and describe how you can integrate graphics into your Word documents. We'll also introduce you to Word 4's powerful macro capability.

We encourage you to explore these exciting, powerful features and take advantage of them. These are the added attractions that take Word 4 beyond simple word processing into the realm of desktop publishing.

STYLE SHEETS 8

Style sheets are a powerful feature of Word 4. With style sheets, you can define the character and paragraph formats you want to use for various parts of your document and instruct Word to apply those formats automatically. Style sheets can save you a tremendous amount of time and ensure that your document is formatted consistently. As you'll learn in this chapter, you can even copy style sheets from one document to another to maintain consistent formatting characteristics.

Each style sheet contains a collection of named styles. A named style is simply a set of instructions for formatting a paragraph. These instructions control the appearance of a paragraph by specifying both the character format options, such as font and point size, and the paragraph format options, such as indents and line spacing. (By the way, keep in mind that a paragraph in Word may be a block of text or a single line of text, such as a title, as long as it's followed by a paragraph marker.)

WHAT IS A STYLE SHEET?

Typically, the instructions for a named style will control a combination of formatting features that you need to use in many paragraphs throughout a document. By recording these instructions on a style sheet, you won't need to repeat the same formatting process for similar paragraphs. Instead, you can simply apply a named style from the style sheet.

For example, a style named *Figure Caption* might control all the formatting features you need to apply to each figure caption in a document. Every time you create a figure caption, you can format it with one command, instead of issuing two or three commands and clicking on various ruler icons.

Style sheets also make it much easier and faster to modify a document's formatting. Once you have applied a named style in several places throughout a document, you can alter, in only one step, the format of every part of the document that uses this style. All you have to do is change the instructions for that named style on the style sheet. Word will then automatically reformat the appropriate parts of your document, using the new instructions.

Although style sheets are pretty complex, this topic is definitely worth mastering. Using style sheets can greatly cut down on the time and tedium involved in creating and formatting documents, particularly lengthy documents. Once you begin to use style sheets, you'll find that they are one of the most important tools available in Word.

We'll begin our discussion of style sheets by covering a few basic concepts. Then, we will walk through a brief example that illustrates some important style sheet techniques. After presenting this example, we'll examine each style sheet concept and technique in detail.

STYLE SHEET BASICS

Whenever you start a new document, Word automatically creates a default style sheet for that document. Initially, the default style sheet will contain only one style, which is called *Normal*. You can modify the default style sheet to include other styles, if you want. (We will explain how to do this in the section called "Changing Defaults" at the end of this chapter.)

Each document's style sheet is permanently linked to that document. However, you can change a document's style sheet in a number of ways. You can add new styles, modify styles, delete styles, and even borrow styles from other documents. When you save a document, the style sheet—including any changes you've made—will be saved automatically.

It's important to note that every document uses a different style sheet. If you have more than one document open on your DeskTop, then each of those documents will have its own style sheet. Of course, several documents can use an identical collection of named styles. In fact, this is likely to be true if you've taken advantage of Word's ability to copy named styles from one document to another. (We'll explain how to do that later in this chapter.)

If you want to view the style sheet for a document, choose Styles... or Define Styles... from the Format menu. Generally, you'll use the Styles... command to apply styles in your document and the Define Styles... command to edit your style sheet. However, you can apply styles from either dialog box. For example, when you begin a document, and *Normal* is the only style on the style sheet, issuing the Styles... command will summon the dialog box shown in Figure 8-1.

Word 4 provides a new alternative for applying styles to your document. Directly under your ruler, on the left side of the screen, you will see a dropdown list box containing all the styles in your document. You may select from this list box any style you want to use for a paragraph. However, if you want to view the definition of a style, you need to issue the Styles... or Define Styles... command.

As you can see in Figure 8-1, the default *Normal* style specifies 12-point New York type with flush-left paragraph alignment. Text formatted with the *Normal* style will also have single spacing between lines and no indents. (As you may remember from Chapter 5, these are the default paragraph and character formats in Word.) You can change these default specifications for the *Normal* style.

FIGURE 8-1

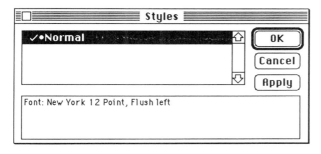

In a new document, Word's default style sheet will contain only the Normal *style.*

The *Normal* style is what Word uses to format the main body text in a document. In fact, you can think of the *Normal* style as the default style for a document—any text that is not specifically assigned a different style will be formatted in the *Normal* style. Figure 8-2 shows how text that is formatted with the default *Normal* style will appear on your screen.

FIGURE 8-2

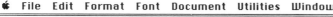

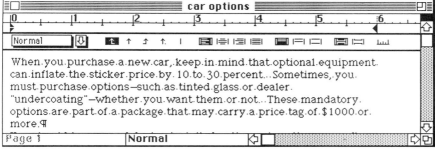

This screen shows how Word's default Normal *style will format text.*

As we mentioned in our introduction, every style sheet is made up of one or more named styles. A style sheet might contain only one named style or as many as 255 styles. Each named style on a style sheet consists of a set of formatting instructions that control the appearance of a paragraph. We've already seen the instructions for the default *Normal* style and the effect of that style on the

Named Styles

appearance of text. Those instructions are fairly simple and straightforward. In many cases, however, a style's instructions will be more complicated than those you see in Figure 8-1. For example, Figure 8-3 displays the instructions for a style named *list*, which we've added to the style sheet.

FIGURE 8-3

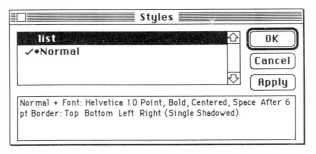

Style instructions can become fairly lengthy and complex.

You can use any named style on the style sheet to format any paragraph in a document, and you can apply a named style to as many paragraphs as you want. However, you cannot use a named style to format any part of a document that is less than a full paragraph. For example, you can use a named style to format several subheadings in a document, but you cannot use that style to format only one word in a subheading. (There are a few exceptions to this "full paragraph" rule. Word uses a named style to format page numbers and line numbers, when you choose to use them, and to format footnote references—the numbers or symbols you use to designate footnotes in the body text of a document.)

Whether you choose to format your document using named styles or format your document text manually, every paragraph in a document will have a named style associated with it. Word displays the style name for the current paragraph in the status box at the bottom of the document window.

In most cases, unless you specifically choose another style, Word will assign the style named *Normal* to each paragraph in a document. This does not necessarily mean that each paragraph will manifest all of the formatting characteristics of the *Normal* style. The appearance of a paragraph can be controlled by both a named style and other formatting changes that you implement using menu commands and ruler icons. In those cases, you may see a plus sign after the style name on your screen—as shown in Figure 8-4—which tells you that the format of the current paragraph is determined by a named style, plus other manual formatting changes you have made.

FIGURE 8-4

The status box tells you which style has been used to format the current paragraph.

Although it's possible to format a paragraph using a combination of a named style and other formatting commands, you probably will use named styles almost exclusively as you become familiar with style sheets. With a named style, you can control all the characteristics listed in Table 8-1 .

TABLE 8-1

Left, Right, and First-line Indents
Tab Placement
Tab Type (Centered, Right Justified, Left Justified, Decimal)
Tab Leader
Paragraph Alignment (Flush Left, Centered, Flush Right, Justified)
Line Spacing within a Paragraph
Spacing Above and Below a Paragraph
Paragraph Border
Other Paragraph Formats (Page Break Before, Keep With Next ¶, etc.)
Vertical Line Placement
Fixed Positioning
Font
Point Size
Character Format (Bold, Italic, Underline, etc.)
Character Spacing (Normal, Condensed, Expanded)
Character Position (Superscript, Subscript, Normal)
Character Color

You can control these formatting features with named styles.

In addition to the characteristics listed in Table 8-1, the instructions for a style can control which named style should be used next in a document. For example, suppose your style sheet includes the style named *heading 2,* which controls the appearance of some of the subheadings in your document. The instructions for this style might also specify that the first paragraph after a *heading 2* subheading should be formatted according to the *Normal* style. Consequently, when you press Return after typing the *heading 2* paragraph, Word will automatically start a new paragraph that is formatted in the *Normal* style. We will explain the Next Style option in the Define Styles dialog box, and other style characteristics, later in this chapter.

If you want to view the instructions for a particular named style, choose either Styles... or Define Styles... from the Format menu and click on the name of the style whose instructions you want to see. (If the style sheet contains more than a few styles, you may need to scroll more names into view in order to click on the name of the style you're interested in.) Word will then display the instructions for the selected style. We've already seen, in Figures 8-1 and 8-3, how the Styles dialog box will display the instructions for a named style. Figure 8-5 shows the Define Styles dialog box, in which we've highlighted the style name *Normal.*

Viewing the instructions of a named style

FIGURE 8-5

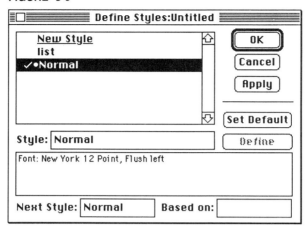

The Define Styles dialog box will display the formatting instructions for the style you select.

Although the instructions in the Define Styles dialog box are identical to the instructions that appear in the Styles dialog box, you might notice that the Define Styles dialog box gives a little more information about the selected style. Specifically, the Define Styles dialog box includes edit bars that list the Next Style and the Based On style.

Sometimes, the formatting instructions for a style will be too long to be displayed in the dialog box. When this happens, you can examine the settings on the ruler and in the Character and Paragraph dialog boxes if you need to see all the characteristics of the selected style.

By the way, if you compare the instructions for the *Normal* style in Figures 8-1 and 8-5 with the list of features in Table 8-1, you'll see that the instructions for the *Normal* style do not spell out every formatting characteristic. For example, the *Normal* style uses no indents, but this is not specifically stated in the instructions. Except for font, point size, and paragraph alignment, a style's instructions will make no mention of those formatting characteristics that are set to Word's defaults. (For additional information about Word's preset defaults, see Chapter 14.)

Notice also in Figures 8-1 and 8-5 that a check mark appears next to the style name *Normal*. This check mark indicates that this is the style that has been applied to the current paragraph in your document (the paragraph on which the insertion point marker is positioned).

Linked styles

Often, the instructions for one named style will be based on the instructions for another style. In this case, the two styles are said to be linked. The "dependent style" is the style whose instructions are based on another style, and the Based On style is the style on which the dependent style is based.

Many different styles can be linked to the same Based On style. One style sheet might contain a dozen or more styles that are based on the style named *Normal*. When you view the instructions for a dependent style, you'll see that those instructions begin with the name of the Based On style. The remainder of the style's instructions will specify those characteristics that are different from the instructions for the Based On style. For example, Figure 8-6 shows the instructions for a style named *Table*, which are *Normal + Centered*. These instructions are a shorthand way of saying, "Use all the style characteristics of the style named *Normal*, except use centered alignment instead of flush-left alignment."

FIGURE 8-6

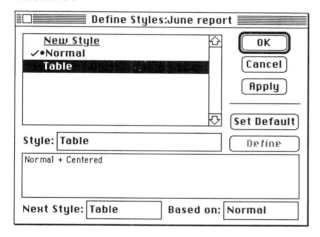

The instructions for a dependent style will specify the name of the Based On style and any characteristics that are different from the Based On style.

As you're setting up a style sheet, it's possible to link more than two styles. For example, you might have a style named *Style2*, which is based on a style named *Style1*. *Style1*, in turn, is based on the style named *Normal*. In this case, *Style2* is indirectly based on *Normal*. Thus, if you change the *Normal* style, *Style2* and *Style1* will change as well.

Throughout our discussion of styles, we will explain more about linked styles—how you can create a linked style, when you should link styles, and how to unlink two styles.

There's a final topic we need to cover in our discussion of style sheet basics: the distinction between automatic and custom styles. Automatic styles are pre-defined styles that are designed to format certain common elements of a document, such as subheadings, footnotes, headers, and footers. In fact, Word comes with a built-in "library" of 33 automatic styles.

Automatic and custom styles

The style named *Normal*, which Word always places on the default style sheet, is one of these 33 automatic styles. The other automatic styles do not appear on the default style sheet initially. However, Word will place them on a document's style sheet automatically as you add different elements to the document. For example, if you add a header to a document, Word will automatically format that header, adding an automatic style called *header* to that document's style sheet.

All the automatic styles are based on the *Normal* style. Therefore, the formatting instructions for each automatic style begin with *Normal +*. As we'll explain in a few pages, Word allows you to modify the instructions for any of its automatic styles.

In addition to automatic or predefined styles, a style sheet can contain custom styles that you create and name. There are a couple of ways to customize a style for a style sheet, as we will explain later in this section. Before we talk about automatic styles, custom styles, and other style sheet concepts, however, let's look at a quick example of creating, applying, and modifying styles.

An Example

Suppose you have begun a document by typing its title, as shown in Figure 8-7. As you can see, this text is formatted with Word's default *Normal* style. You would like to create a new style to format this title in 14-point Geneva bold type, with centered alignment and 12 points of space after the title.

FIGURE 8-7

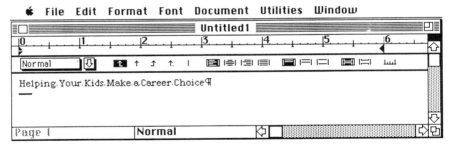

This screen shows the title for a new document.

Begin with the insertion point marker positioned anywhere on this title, and choose Define Styles... from the Format menu. In the Define Styles dialog box, make sure that New Style is selected, and enter the name *Title* in the Style edit bar. Then, without closing the Define Styles dialog box, issue the appropriate commands for formatting the title of the document. Select Geneva and 14 Point from the Font menu, then choose the Bold format option on the Format menu. (The Define Styles dialog box will remain open.) Next, choose Paragraph... to open the

Paragraph dialog box and display the ruler at the top of the screen. In the Paragraph dialog box, enter 12 in the After edit bar. Then, click the Centered alignment icon on the ruler, and click OK in the Paragraph dialog box.

Next, in the Define Styles dialog box, click on the Next Style edit bar and enter the name *Normal*. When you've completed all these steps, the dialog box should look like the one in Figure 8-8.

FIGURE 8-8

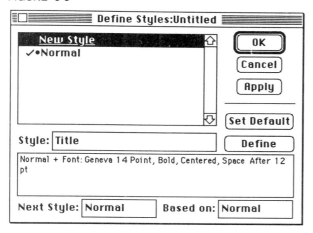

As you're defining a new style, Word will record your format selections in the Define Styles dialog box.

To apply the style to your document title and close the dialog box, click OK. Word will then automatically format the title according to the instructions for the new style you just created.

If you place the insertion point at the end of the title and press Return, Word will start a new paragraph and format it using the *Normal* style. (Recall that we entered *Normal* in the Next Style edit bar of the Define Styles dialog box.) Figure 8-9 on the following page shows how your screen will look after you've formatted the title and entered some body text.

Suppose you decide to change the main body text in this document from 12-point New York to 10-point New York. You also would like to indent the first line of each paragraph by $1/_4$ inch. By changing the definition of the *Normal* style, you can automatically reformat all text that uses this style. Begin by placing the insertion point marker on one of the paragraphs of body text, then open the Define Styles dialog box and click on the style name *Normal* to select it. Next, choose 10 Point from the Font menu, then move the first-line indent marker to the $1/_4$-inch mark on the ruler. To lock in the changes and close the dialog box, click OK. Figure 8-10 shows how your screen will appear at this point.

FIGURE 8-9

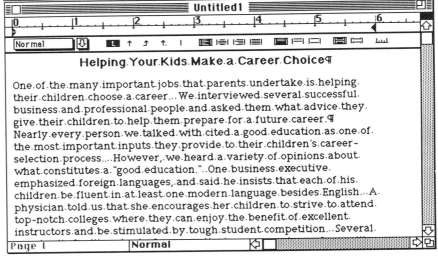

This screen shows the formatted document title and several lines of text formatted in the default Normal *style.*

FIGURE 8-10

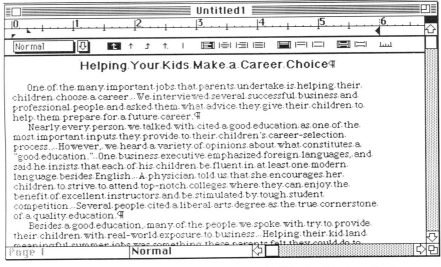

After you alter the instructions for the Normal *style, Word will automatically reformat the body text of the document.*

Notice that you did not need to select any text before you altered the *Normal* style. Word automatically applied the changes to all the text that carried this named style. Of course, in this example, the *Normal* style was used to format only a few paragraphs. You could easily have selected this text and reformatted it manually. If you were working with a longer document, however, you might have *Normal* text scattered among text with different formats—such as figure captions, subtitles, and so forth. When this is the case, changing the *Normal* style on the style sheet saves you the trouble of selecting and reformatting individual sections of body text.

Once you have defined one or more styles on a document's style sheet, you can apply a style to any paragraph in that document. To apply a style, simply place the insertion point marker on the paragraph you want to format, then choose Show Ruler on the Format menu (if the ruler is not currently displayed at the top of the window). Click on the dropdown list box on the left side of the ruler, then select the name of the style you want to apply. Word will then automatically format the current paragraph with that style.

In the example we just described, you probably would not need to apply either of the styles on the style sheet since you've already formatted the title, and Word would continue to use *Normal* to format the remainder of the document. However, many, if not most, of the documents you create in Word will require that you switch from one style to another as you create and format different sections of the document. Later in this chapter, we'll explain in more detail the techniques for applying styles. Before we talk about this and other style sheet techniques, however, let's look at the automatic styles Word creates for you.

AUTOMATIC STYLES

As we explained earlier in this chapter, Word predefines a number of automatic styles. We use the term "automatic" to describe these styles because, in most cases, Word will place a predefined style on the style sheet automatically as it's needed. As you'll see in a minute, you also can add these styles manually.

The *Normal* Style

The *Normal* style is the predominant automatic style in Word. As we've already mentioned, whenever you start a new document in Word, the style sheet for that document will contain only one style—*Normal*. We've also seen in Figures 8-2 and 8-7 how text formatted with the default *Normal* style will appear on your screen. Because the *Normal* style is linked to most, if not all, of the other named styles in a document, it also controls, to some extent, the formatting of other elements in a document.

If you're like most users, the default *Normal* style will be unsuitable for many of your documents. Therefore, you probably will want to modify the *Normal* style each time you start a new document. Of course, it's not imperative that you change the instructions for the *Normal* style on the style sheet. Instead, you can simply issue a few commands to alter the text on your screen in any way you want. However, as we will explain, there are certain advantages to modifying the *Normal* style on the style sheet instead of manually formatting the text in your document.

We've already seen one example of what happens to a document when you modify the *Normal* style after you've entered some text. In many cases, however, you probably will want to modify the *Normal* style before you begin typing any document text. Suppose you want to create a document whose main body text is 10-point Times type, with a $^1/_4$-inch indent on the first line of each paragraph, justified alignment, and double spacing. Before you type any characters in a new blank window, you can modify the *Normal* style to fit these characteristics. To do this, choose Define Styles... from the Format menu and click on the name *Normal* in the Define Styles dialog box. Then, without closing the Define Styles dialog box, choose Times and 10 Point from the Font menu. Next, choose Show Ruler from the Format menu (if the ruler is not already displayed on the screen). Move the first-line indent marker to the $^1/_4$-inch position. Then, click the Justified alignment icon and the double space icon. After you've completed these changes, the Define Styles dialog box will look like the one in Figure 8-11.

FIGURE 8-11

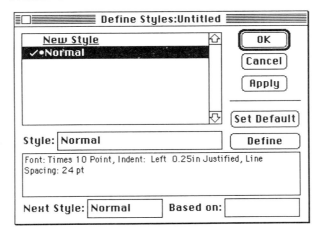

This dialog box shows the modified instructions for the Normal *style.*

Notice that Word has recorded all the changes in the instructions for the *Normal* style. To complete the modification, click Define, OK, or Apply. (After you create or modify style instructions, clicking Define will lock in your changes without closing the dialog box. If you click the Apply button, Word will lock in your changes and apply the style to the current paragraph without closing the dialog box. Clicking OK will lock in the changes, apply the style to the current paragraph, and close the dialog box.)

The procedure we have just described will change the *Normal* style for your current document only. In other words, the main body text of your document will be formatted with all the characteristics you chose after issuing the Define Styles...

command. However, if you start a new document in Word, the *Normal* style in that document will once again have the default style instructions (12-point New York type with single spacing, flush-left alignment, and no indents). Toward the end of this chapter, in the section entitled "Changing Defaults," we will explain how you can modify the default *Normal* style.

Although we recommend that you change the *Normal* style before you type any text in a new document window, you can change the style at any time. As we demonstrated in our earlier example, if you have already typed some text using the default *Normal* style, Word will automatically reformat that text according to any changes you make to the style instructions.

As we have mentioned, Word offers 33 automatic styles that can be used to format certain elements found in many documents. Although these styles don't initially appear on the default style sheet, you can see a list of them by holding down the Shift key and choosing either All Styles... or Define All Styles... from the Format menu. (Word will not be able to display all the automatic styles at one time, but you can scroll through the list of styles by clicking on the scroll bar next to the list box.) You'll notice that a bullet (•) appears next to the name of each automatic style, distinguishing it from the custom styles you have created. Table 8-2 summarizes the name and purpose of each automatic style.

Other Automatic Styles

TABLE 8-2

Style Name	Use to format
footer	Text in a footer window
footnote reference	The number or symbol that designates a footnote in the document
footnote text	Text in a footnote window
header	Text in a header window
heading 1, heading 2,...heading 9	Heading levels that you create in an outline window
index 1, index 2,...index 7	Levels of entries in an index
line number	Line numbers
Normal	All text that has not been assigned another style
page number	Page numbers
PostScript	PostScript commands that are embedded in document text
toc 1, toc 2,...toc 9	Levels in the table-of-contents text

Word's automatic styles are used to format specific elements of a document.

Adding an automatic style to a style sheet

We have mentioned briefly how Word will place automatic styles on a document's style sheet when you add certain elements to that document. For example, if you add one or more footnotes to a document, Word will automatically place two styles on the style sheet. One style, named *footnote reference*, is used to format the number (or other symbol) that you place in the main body of your document to designate a footnote. The other style, called *footnote text*, is used to format the footnote itself.

All of the automatic styles are added to the style sheet in this way, except the *PostScript* style and the styles named *heading 1, heading 2, heading 3,* and so forth. The *PostScript* style must be added to the style sheet manually when you need to format PostScript commands you have embedded in a document. (For more information on PostScript, refer to Appendix 4.) The various *heading* styles, which are designed to format different levels of subheadings in a document, originate in an outline window.

Whenever you use Word's built-in Outline facility to outline the subheadings in a document, Word will format those subheadings according to the automatic styles named *heading 1, heading 2,* and so forth. Word also will add these named styles to the style sheet. If you do not begin your document in an outline window, Word will not automatically use the *heading 1, heading 2,* and so forth, styles to format your subheadings. (Without an outline, Word has no way of distinguishing a subheading from the rest of the document text.) In Chapter 9, we will talk about the link between Word's Outline facility and the automatic styles named *heading 1, heading 2,* and so forth.

If you want to use one of Word's automatic styles to format part of a document, you do not have to wait for Word to add that style name to the style sheet. Instead, you can add the style manually. To do this, hold down the Shift key and choose Define All Styles... from the Format menu. This will cause all of Word's automatic styles to appear in the list in the dialog box. Click on the name of the style you want to add to the style sheet, then click OK or Apply. Apply will add the style to the style sheet and, at the same time, apply the style to the current paragraph. OK will perform both of these actions and close the Define Styles dialog box as well.

If you want to add an automatic style to the style sheet, but you don't want to apply that style to the current paragraph, you should click the Define button after you select the style. In order to make the Define button available (Word will initially display it in dim video), you must click on the Style edit bar where the style name is displayed. Then, after you've defined the style, you can close the Define Styles dialog box by clicking the Cancel button or by clicking the close box.

The Link between *Normal* and Other Automatic Styles

All of Word's automatic styles are based on the *Normal* style. This has two important consequences. First, the format specified by each of the automatic styles will, to some extent, be similar to the *Normal* style. For example, notice the formatting instructions for the automatic style named *header* that are displayed in the Define Styles dialog box shown in Figure 8-12. You can interpret these instructions as "Use all the formatting characteristics of the *Normal* style and add two tab stops: one centered tab at the 3-inch ruler position and one flush-right tab at the 6-inch ruler position." If the *Normal* style specifies 12-point New York type (Word's initial default), then the text in a document's header also will be formatted with 12-point New York type.

Similarly, because the other automatic styles are based on *Normal*, other elements you add to a document, such as a footer, page numbers, subheadings, and so forth, will use the New York font—or whatever font you've specified in the instructions for the *Normal* style.

FIGURE 8-12

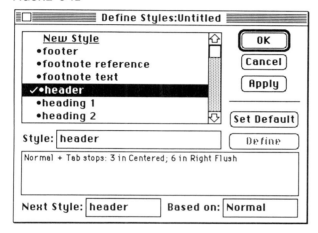

This dialog box shows the default formatting instructions for the automatic style named header.

Another consequence of the link between automatic styles and the *Normal* style is that any change you make to the *Normal* style will affect the other automatic styles. For example, if you change the font for the *Normal* style from New York to Helvetica, then the other automatic styles will use the Helvetica font as well. Of course, the purpose of this is to help you maintain consistency of appearance among the different parts of a document.

We already have explained how you can modify the instructions for the *Normal* style and, in fact, recommended that you do this each time you start a new document. This recommendation is especially important in light of the fact that all of the other automatic styles are based on the *Normal* style. By changing the *Normal* style first, you may be able to save yourself the trouble of changing each of the other automatic styles. On the other hand, if you do not modify the *Normal* style, but manually format the main body text in your document, you probably will need to adjust the formats of other document elements as well.

Suppose you don't modify the instructions for the *Normal* style—you leave them with the default specifications of 12-point New York type with no indents. You then create a document and manually select and format the main body text to appear in 10-point Helvetica type. Suppose you then decide to add a header to the document. Figure 8-13 shows how Word will format the text in the header window.

FIGURE 8-13

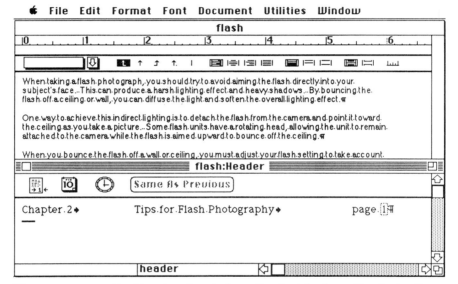

The appearance of text in a header window will reflect the formatting instructions of the Normal *style. Thus, the header won't necessarily match the format of the main body text of your document.*

Notice that the text of the header does not match the main body text of the document. Instead, it is formatted with 12-point New York type since its style is based on the *Normal* style. If you want the format of the header to be consistent with the rest of the document, you must either manually reformat the text in the header window or open the Define Styles dialog box and modify the instructions for the automatic style named *header*. The same thing will happen if you add a footer, page numbers, footnotes, or any other document element that is formatted according to one of Word's automatic styles. Each element will come into your document in a format that is related to the *Normal* style, but inconsistent with the main body text, which has been formatted manually.

To avoid the hassle of reformatting each document element or making extensive changes to the style sheet, one of your first steps in creating a document should be to modify the instructions for the *Normal* style. Then, you won't need to worry about inconsistencies between the main body text and the various elements you add to the document.

Although modifying the *Normal* style offers an excellent starting point for changing Word's other automatic styles, you can, of course, change each of these styles directly. You also can break the link between any automatic style and the *Normal* style. We will talk about the various techniques for modifying styles in a few pages. However, since style modification techniques apply to both custom styles and automatic styles, let's first consider how you can add custom styles to a style sheet.

To add a custom style to a style sheet, you must enter a name for the style and define the formatting instructions for that style. To create (or define) a new custom style, issue the Define Styles... command, type a style name in the Style edit bar, then select menu commands and click on ruler icons to specify the formatting characteristics for that style. As you're choosing commands and manipulating ruler icons, Word records your format selections as instructions for the named style. For purposes of our discussion, we will refer to this method as defining "by selection" since it involves selecting formatting options and ruler icons.

CUSTOM STYLES

Another method for defining a new style is "by example." In other words, you can format a paragraph in your document to have all the characteristics you want to use in a named style, then issue the Define Styles... command and assign a name to that collection of formatting characteristics.

The main difference between these methods is that when you're defining by example, you issue all of the formatting commands before you open the Define Styles dialog box. One major advantage of defining a style by example is that you can see the effects of your formatting specifications before you add them to your style sheet. This is especially helpful when you are designing a new style that may require quite a bit of fine-tuning to achieve just the right appearance.

In addition, formatting by example can come in handy when you've manually formatted a paragraph, then decide that you want to use that format in other locations in your document. Rather than manually reformatting the other text, you can use the first paragraph as your example to define a new style. Then, you can just click on the paragraphs to which you want to apply this style and use the Apply button in the Define Styles dialog box to "copy" the format of your example paragraph to the other text. Let's consider how you might use each of these methods to define a new style.

Suppose you want to create a new style named *Figure Caption*, which specifies 10-point New York bold type with centered alignment. The style instructions will also specify a 12-point line space both above and below the formatted text. To define this style by selection, you would first choose Define Styles... from the Format menu. Word will then display the Define Styles dialog box, as shown in Figure 8-14.

Defining by Selection

FIGURE 8-14

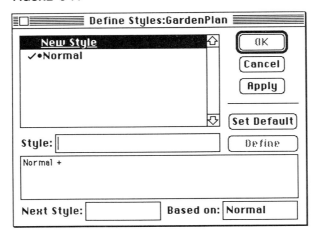

To create a new style, begin by opening the Define Styles dialog box.

There are two things you should notice about this dialog box. First, you can see that Word automatically highlights New Style at the top of the list of styles in the dialog box. Each time you open the Define Styles dialog box, Word assumes you want to add a new style to the style sheet.

Another thing to notice in this dialog box is that Word has begun the instructions for the new style with *Normal +*. Word also displays the style name *Normal* in the Based On edit bar in the lower-right corner of the dialog box. Whenever you define a new style, Word assumes you want that style to be based on the style of the current paragraph (the paragraph where the insertion point marker is located when you issue the Define Styles... command). In our example, the insertion point marker was positioned on a paragraph that was formatted with the *Normal* style when we selected Define Styles.... Therefore, Word assumed that we wanted to create a new style that would be based on the *Normal* style.

In most cases, you will want to base each new style on an existing style, so we won't change this situation in our example. In a few pages, we will discuss the Based On style in more detail and explain how to create a style that's *not* based on an existing style. For now, let's continue the process of defining the new style.

After you've opened the Define Styles dialog box, enter a style name, then select the formatting features you want that style to use. It makes no difference which you do first. In our example, you can begin by entering the style name *Figure Caption* in the Style edit bar. Then, choose 10 Point from the Font menu and Bold from the Format menu. Next, select Paragraph... from the Format menu. In the Paragraph dialog box, type 12 both in the Before and After edit bars. Then, click on the Centered alignment icon on the ruler. Finally, click OK to close the Paragraph dialog box. At this point, the Define Styles dialog box will look like the one in Figure 8-15. Notice that Word has recorded all of our format selections in the style's instructions.

FIGURE 8-15

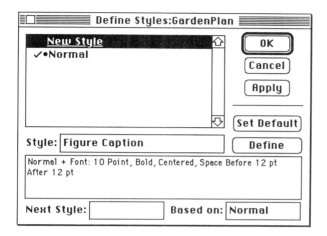

As you're creating a new style, Word will record your format selections in the instructions for that style.

The last step in defining the new style is to add it to the style sheet. You can do this by clicking the Define button. When you click Define, Word will place the style name *Figure Caption* in the list of styles, and the Define Styles dialog box will remain open. If you want to apply the style to the current paragraph at the same time you define it, you should click either Apply or OK. OK will apply the style and automatically close the dialog box, whereas Apply will apply the style without closing the dialog box.

Now, let's consider how you might define this same style by example instead of by selection. Suppose you have entered the text for a figure caption in a document, and you want to format that text. First, you would select the caption paragraph, then issue the appropriate formatting commands. For example, Figure 8-16 on the following page shows an unformatted figure caption that's been selected. To format this as a style example, you would choose 10 Point from the Font menu and Bold from the Format menu. Then, you would select Paragraph… from the Format menu and enter 12 in both the Before and After edit bars. With the caption still selected, you would click on the Centered alignment icon on the ruler. When you click OK to close the Paragraph dialog box, your figure caption will look like the one in Figure 8-17 on the next page.

Of course, in most cases, you won't be able to arrive at an acceptable format for a new style so quickly. Usually, the process of designing a format for a particular part of a document—such as a figure caption—is a matter of trial and error. That's why you might want to experiment with the format on your screen before you define it as a named style.

To save your sample format on the style sheet, choose Define Styles… from the Format menu while the insertion point marker is positioned anywhere on the formatted paragraph. As usual, Word will highlight New Style at the top of the list

Defining by Example

of styles in the dialog box. However, Word also will display the formatting instructions for the current paragraph in the dialog box, as shown in Figure 8-18. Notice that this dialog box looks identical to the one shown in Figure 8-15, except that the style name does not yet appear in the Style edit bar.

FIGURE 8-16

To define a new style by example, begin by entering and selecting the text you want to format.

FIGURE 8-17

This screen shows the formatted text that will serve as the example for a new style.

All you need to do at this point is enter the name *Figure Caption* in the Style edit bar and click either Define, OK, or Apply. Word will then add that style to the style sheet for the current document.

When you're defining a style by example, the instructions for the new style will probably be complete when you open the Define Styles dialog box. However, if you want, you can select additional commands and/or ruler icons after the dialog box is open. If you do this, Word will modify the initial style instructions according to your selections. (You might consider this technique to be a combination of defining by selection and defining by example.)

FIGURE 8-18

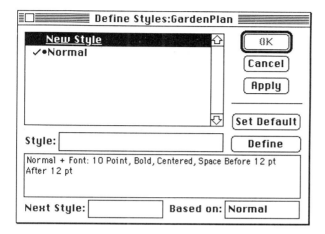

When the insertion point marker is positioned on formatted text, the Define Styles dialog box will display the formatting instructions for that text.

By the way, as you can see in Figure 8-18, the instructions for the new style begin with *Normal* + and the style name *Normal* appears in the Based On edit bar. When you define a new style by example—as when you define a style by selection—Word assumes that you want the new style to be based on the original style of the paragraph you are using as the style example. As you'll see in a moment, you can edit the Based On style to change the links between styles.

The Apply and Define buttons

The Apply button in the Define Styles dialog box also gives you the flexibility to format by trial and error. For example, suppose you want to change the format of a heading in your document, but you are not sure exactly how you want the heading text to look. Begin by placing the insertion point marker anywhere on the paragraph you want to format, and open the Define Styles dialog box. Enter a style name in the Style edit bar and define the instructions for that style. When you've completed the style instructions, click the Apply button. Word will then reformat the paragraph without closing the Define Styles dialog box. If you don't like the results of this new style's formatting, you can issue the appropriate commands to change the style instructions and click Apply again. Each time you click Apply, Word will reformat the text, incorporating any changes to the style instructions.

If the Define Styles dialog box blocks your view of the paragraph you're trying to format, just move the dialog box to the bottom of your screen. When you drag the dialog box by its title bar, Word will allow you to hide almost the entire dialog box from view. About $1/4$ inch of the title bar will remain in view. To display the dialog box again, just drag it back to the middle of the screen.

The Define button lets you define a style without necessarily changing the format of the paragraph in which your insertion point marker is located. When you use the Define button to place a new style name in your style sheet or to change the instructions for an existing style, Word will record your changes and apply them to any paragraphs that carry that style name. If your insertion point marker happens to be on a paragraph that carries another style, however, Word will not change the format of that paragraph unless you click the OK or Apply button. Thus, if you want to change a style definition without changing the format of the current paragraph, just click Define, then click the close box or the Cancel button in the Define Styles dialog box.

Using the ruler to define by example

When you're defining a new style by example, you do not need to open the Define Styles dialog box at all. After you have applied all the formatting to a paragraph that you want to include in a named style, just select it by clicking once on the style name that appears in the style list box on the ruler. Then, type a new style name and press Return. Word will display the message shown in Figure 8-19. When you click Define in this dialog box, Word will define the new style using all the formatting characteristics of the current paragraph.

When you use the technique we just described, you cannot specify a Next Style or Based On style for the new style that you create. You must open the Define Styles dialog box to change the Next Style or Based On style.

FIGURE 8-19

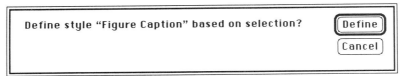

Define style "Figure Caption" based on selection?   [Define]
                                                     [Cancel]

When you type a new style name in the style list box on the ruler and press Return, Word will display a message like this one.

The Based On Style

We have already explained how one style can be based on or linked to another in the style sheet. You might recall that each of Word's automatic styles is based on the style named *Normal*. As we described, this link between *Normal* and the other automatic styles causes each of the automatic styles to reflect, to some degree, the characteristics of the *Normal* style. Moreover, any change you make to the *Normal* style will affect the other automatic styles as well.

As we have just demonstrated, whenever you define a new custom style for a style sheet, Word assumes you want that new style to be based on an existing style. In each of our examples, we created a new style that was based on *Normal*. However, when you create a new style, that style won't necessarily be based on

Normal. In fact, Word always assumes you want each new style to be based on the style of the paragraph in which the insertion point marker is located when you issue the Define Styles... command. This may be the *Normal* style, or it may be another style. In any case, it's a good idea to think about which style you want to use as your Based On style before you begin to define a new style. That way, you may be able to save some time in defining the new style's formatting instructions.

Suppose you want to create a new style named *Style1*, which has all the characteristics of the default *Normal* style except that the first line of each paragraph is indented $1/2$ inch. Since this new style is so similar to *Normal*, it would make sense to use *Normal* as the Based On style. Therefore, before you begin defining *Style1*, you should be sure that the insertion point is positioned on a *Normal* paragraph. Then, when you choose Define Styles..., Word will enter *Normal* in the Based On edit bar and will begin the instructions for the new style with *Normal* +. To complete the definition of *Style1*, you need to drag the first-line indent marker to the $1/2$-inch position on the ruler, then click Define. All the other formatting characteristics of *Style1* will be "borrowed" from *Normal*, the Based On style.

When you're defining a new style, you don't have to use the Based On style that Word suggests. Instead, you can enter a different style name in the Based On edit bar of the Define Styles dialog box. First, drag through or double-click on the style name in the Based On edit bar to select it. Then, type a new style name and click the Define button.

Specifying a different Based On style

There may be times when you want to create a style that is completely independent of other styles in your style sheet. To do this, you can simply erase the contents of the Based On edit bar in the Define Styles dialog box as you are creating the new style.

Creating a new style that is not based on an existing style

For instance, suppose you're defining the *Figure Caption* style that we described on pages 323-325. When you open the Define Styles dialog box, you'll see that the style's instructions begin with *Normal* + and that the word *Normal* appears in the Based On edit bar in the lower-right corner of the dialog box. If you want to make the *Figure Caption* style independent of the *Normal* style, erase the word *Normal* from the Based On edit bar, then click the Define button. After you do this, the Define Styles dialog box will look like Figure 8-20 on the next page.

The instructions are the same as those that appear in Figures 8-15 and 8-18, with a couple of exceptions. First, the instructions no longer begin with *Normal* +. Another difference is that the instructions now specify the New York font. When you eliminate the Based On style, the style that you're defining will retain all the formatting characteristics of the Based On style. However, these characteristics will now be stated explicitly in the style's instructions instead of being implicit in the name of the Based On style.

FIGURE 8-20

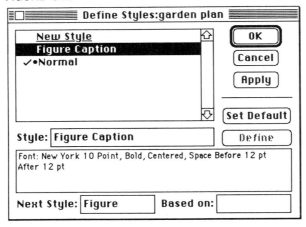

If you break the link to the Based On style, the formatting instructions for the dependent style will specify all the characteristics of the former Based On style.

A word of warning

Although it's possible to create a style independent of any other style, you'll want to avoid this in most cases. We can best illustrate why by using an example.

If you eliminate the link between the *Figure Caption* style and the *Normal* style, the left and right indents for *Figure Caption*—which determine the placement of each line—will no longer be tied to the indents for the *Normal* style. If you do not make any changes to the *Normal* style, this should be of no consequence. Suppose, however, you decide to modify the *Normal* style by dragging the right indent marker to the 5-inch point on the ruler. Word will change the right margin on the main body text in your document by 1 inch. However, since the *Figure Caption* style is no longer linked to *Normal*, any text that was formatted with that style will still be placed as though the right indent marker were at the 6-inch position on the ruler. In other words, all your figure captions will appear off center from the main body text.

Notes on linked styles

One style can be indirectly linked to several styles. However, a style can be directly based on only one other style. For example, you might have a document in which *Style3* is based on *Style2*, which is based on *Style1*, which is based on *Normal*. In this case, *Style3* is indirectly linked to two styles, *Style1* and *Normal*, but it is directly based on only one style, *Style2*.

Word will not allow you to create circular style references. For example, suppose *Style3* is based on *Style2*, which is based on *Style1*. If you then try to make *Style3* the Based On style for *Style1*, Word will beep and display the message *Circular style reference*.

You will also see an alert message if you try to create too many levels of linked styles. Word will allow you to have no more than nine levels of linked styles. For example, you can create a style sheet in which *Style8* is based on *Style7*, which is based on *Style6*, which is based on *Style5*, and so forth, through *Style1*, which is based on *Normal*. However, if you try to create a *Style9* that uses *Style8* as its Based On style, Word will not accept it and will display the message *Too many levels of "Based on:" reference*.

Of course, this does not mean you cannot have more than nine styles that are indirectly linked to one another. For example, Figure 8-21 on the following page shows a diagram that illustrates how you might set up 14 styles in a style sheet that are all directly or indirectly linked to *Style1*, which is directly linked to *Normal*. Notice, however, that this style sheet contains only five levels of linked styles.

Copying and Pasting Style Instructions

When you're creating a new style, Word allows you to copy the instructions for an existing style onto the instructions for the new style. Suppose your document's style sheet contains a style named *Figure Caption*. You would like to create a new style, named *Table Caption*, which has similar or identical formatting characteristics to the *Figure Caption* style. First, open the Define Styles dialog box, and select New Style, enter the style name *Table Caption* and click Define. Next, click on the name of the style whose instructions you want to borrow—*Figure Caption*. With that style selected, choose Copy from the Edit menu. Then, click on the name of the new style that you just created (*Table Caption*), and choose Paste from the Edit menu. Word will then copy the instructions for the *Figure Caption* style into the instructions for the *Table Caption* style. If the style whose instructions you're copying has a Based On style, then the name of that Based On style will also be copied into the Based On edit bar of the dialog box.

After you copy the style instructions, you can use menu commands and ruler icons to make changes and additions to these style instructions. When the instructions are complete, just click Define again to lock them in.

When you copy instructions from one style to another, it's important that you perform the copy-and-paste procedure before you issue commands and click on ruler icons. When you issue the Paste command, Word will overwrite any existing style instructions with the instructions of the style you've copied. As a result, you cannot copy and paste the instructions for more than one style. If you try to do this, the instructions for the second style will completely overwrite the instructions for the first style.

The Next Style

When you open the Define Styles dialog box, you will see a Next Style edit bar in the lower-left corner of the dialog box. You use this edit bar to specify the style you want to apply immediately after a paragraph that's formatted with the style you're currently defining. To enter a style name in the Next Style edit bar, simply click anywhere on the edit bar, and type the name. Then, click Define, Apply, or OK to lock in your Next Style specification.

For example, suppose you are defining a style named *Figure Caption*, which will be used to format the figure captions in your document. You probably will want to follow each caption with a paragraph that is formatted according to the *Normal* style. Therefore, as you are defining the *Figure Caption* style, you should enter *Normal* in the Next Style edit bar.

FIGURE *8-21*

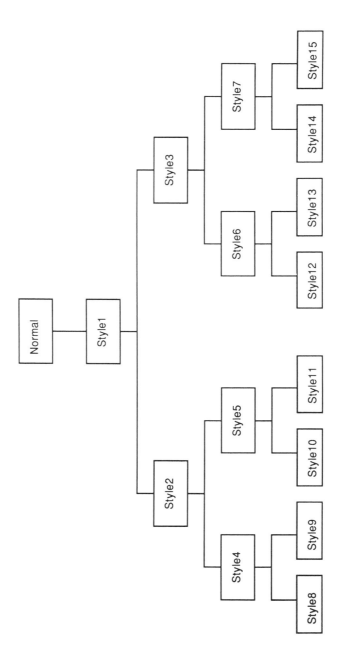

This diagram shows how you might set up links between Style1 and 14 other styles on the style sheet.

The Next Style setting comes into play only when you press Return to end a paragraph. In our example, suppose you apply the style *Figure Caption* to a line of text in your document. When you press Return at the end of that line, Word will begin a new paragraph that is formatted with the *Normal* style. On the other hand, if you were to place the insertion point marker in the middle of the figure caption text and press Return, Word would break that text into two separate paragraphs, but would not apply the Next Style format to the second paragraph. Instead, Word would format the second paragraph with the *Figure Caption* style.

As you're defining a new style, if you do not enter a style name in the Next Style edit bar, Word will use the style you are defining as the Next Style. For example, if you define the style named *Figure Caption*, but you don't specify a Next Style, Word will assume that the paragraph following the figure caption text should also be formatted according to the *Figure Caption* style.

By carefully specifying the Next Style for each style on a style sheet, you can make one style automatically flow into another throughout a document. Each time you press Return to begin a new paragraph, Word will use a different style to format that paragraph. This can be especially helpful when you're creating a document in which you must frequently switch from one style to another. For example, suppose you want to create a list of names and addresses, like that shown in Figure 8-22.

Taking advantage of the Next Style

FIGURE 8-22

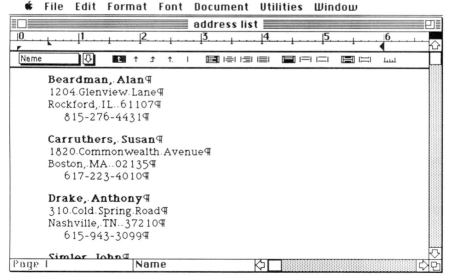

A list of names and addresses might be formatted with several styles.

One way you can greatly speed up the process of creating this list is to set up a style sheet with four styles: *Name*, *Address1*, *Address2*, and *Phone*. As you might guess, the *Name* style will be used to format each person's name; the *Address1* style will be used to format the first line of each person's address; the *Address2* style will be used to format the second line of each address; and the *Phone* style will be used to format each phone number. To help speed up your text entry, you should ensure that the *Name* style uses *Address1* as its Next Style; the *Address1* style uses *Address2* as its Next style; and the *Address2* style uses *Phone* as its Next Style. Finally, to complete the "loop," the style named *Phone* should specify *Name* as its Next Style.

Once you have set up the style sheet as we have described, just start with the *Name* style as you're entering the first name in the list. Each time you press Return, Word will automatically cycle into *Address1*, *Address2*, *Phone*, and back to *Name*.

By the way, there's one minor constraint you need to keep in mind as you are specifying the Next Style. You must enter a valid style name in the Next Style edit bar. This can present a problem if you haven't yet created the style that you want to use as the Next Style. For example, if you are defining the *Name* style but you haven't yet created the style named *Address1*, Word will not allow you to enter *Address1* in the Next Style edit bar. To get around this problem, you may need to modify a style after you've created it, specifying the correct Next Style. (In the next section, we talk about how you can modify an existing style.) Another way to work around this constraint is to define your styles in reverse order. In other words, the first style you define should be the last style you plan to use in your sequence of styles. In our example, you might begin by defining the *Phone* style. Next, you would define *Address2*, then *Address1*, and finally, *Name*. As you're defining *Address2*, *Address1*, and *Name*, the style you want to use as the Next Style will already exist so you shouldn't have any problem entering its name in the Next Style edit bar.

Style Names

As you have seen, entering a style name is an essential step in creating a custom style. However, there are some rules about style names that you need to keep in mind. Word will accept a style name of up to 254 characters but, in general, shorter names are easier to work with. One problem with extremely long names is that you may not be able to see the full style name in the Styles or Define Styles dialog boxes. Word displays only about 25 characters of a style's name in the Style edit bar, and even fewer characters can appear in the Next Style and Based On edit bars.

Each style on a style sheet must have a unique name. If you enter a name of a new style that is identical to the name of an existing style, Word will alert you with the message shown in Figure 8-23. If you click OK when you see this message, Word will replace the existing instructions for the named style with the formatting instructions you have entered for the new style. In other words, Word will alter the style that originally was assigned the name you want to use for the new style.

FIGURE 8-23

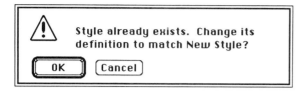

If you enter an existing style name when you're changing the name of a style, you will see this alert box.

Interestingly, Word distinguishes between uppercase and lowercase letters in a style name. For example, a style sheet can include two completely different styles named *Paragraph1* and *paragraph1*.

You can assign two or more names to a style. As you're creating a new style, just enter the different names in the Style edit bar, separating the names with commas. When you assign two names to a style, one name might be relatively long and descriptive to help you remember what the style does, while another name might be extremely short, perhaps only one or two letters. As we will explain later, the shorter style name can speed up the process of applying that style in your document.

When you've assigned more than one name to a style, Word will display both names on the same line in the list of style names in the dialog box. In other words, Word will not treat a style with two different names as though it were two different styles. Suppose you assign the names *Figure Caption* and *FC* to a style. Figure 8-24 shows how Word will display those names in the Styles dialog box. Interestingly, when a style has been assigned two or more names, only the first name will be displayed in the status box at the bottom of a document window.

FIGURE 8-24

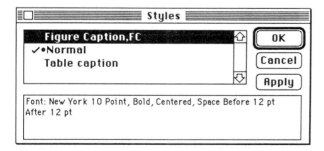

When you assign two or more names to a style, those names will appear on the same line in the style sheet, separated by a comma.

Because Word uses a comma to separate style names, you cannot include a comma as part of a style name. However, you can use any other character in a style name, including the special characters that are created by Option-key combinations (such as ¶ and §).

MODIFYING STYLES

After you have started to work with named styles, you will probably need to make at least a minor change to one or more of them. Earlier in this chapter, we explained briefly how you can modify the *Normal* style. To modify Word's other styles—both automatic and custom—you use virtually the same process.

To modify a style, just choose Define Styles... from the Format menu, then click on the name of the style you want to change. With the style name selected, issue the formatting commands and click on the appropriate ruler icons to alter the style. As you issue commands and click on ruler icons, Word will record all your changes in the instructions for the selected style. When you've completed your changes, you can lock them in by clicking Define.

Suppose you've used the automatic style named *heading 1* to format some of the subheadings in a document, and you decide to change the appearance of those subheadings. The default instructions for the *heading 1* style specify the *Normal* style plus the Helvetica font, with boldfacing, underlining, and a 12-point line space above the subheading. Suppose you want your first-level subheadings to appear in 14-point Helvetica bold type, with centered alignment, a 10-point line space above each subheading, and a 6-point line space below. You also want to remove the underlining that Word adds automatically to each subheading.

To make these changes, first issue the Define Styles... command and click on the name *heading 1* to display those instructions in the dialog box, as shown in Figure 8-25.

FIGURE 8-25

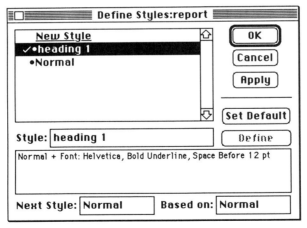

To modify a style, begin by opening the Define Styles dialog box and clicking on the style's name.

To modify this style, open the Character dialog box and choose None from the Underline dropdown list box. Then, type *14* in the Size list box or choose 14 from the dropdown list of sizes. Click OK to close the Character dialog box. To change the line spacing above and below the subheading, open the Paragraph dialog box and replace the *12 pt* in the Before edit bar with *10*. Then, enter *6* in the After edit bar. With the Paragraph dialog box still open, click the Centered alignment icon on the ruler. Finally, click OK to close the Paragraph dialog box. At this point, the Define Styles dialog box will display the altered instructions for the *heading 1* style, as shown in Figure 8-26.

FIGURE 8-26

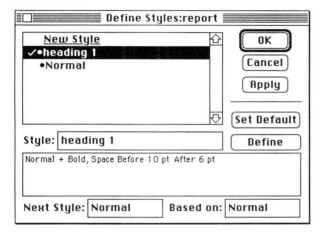

As you issue commands and manipulate ruler icons, Word will alter the style instructions to reflect your changes.

To complete the process of modifying this style, click OK, Apply, or Define. If you click OK, Word will redefine the *heading 1* style in the style sheet, apply it to the current paragraph in your document, and close the dialog box. Word also will reformat any text in your document that has been formatted with the *heading 1* style. The Apply button will have the same effect as OK except that Word will not close the dialog box. If you click Define, Word will redefine the *heading 1* style and apply its new formatting instructions only to text that has been assigned that style. Word will not close the dialog box or apply the *heading 1* style to the current paragraph if that paragraph has not already been assigned the *heading 1* style.

Shortcuts

Word offers a number of keyboard shortcuts that can help you modify a style's instructions. If you want to delete all the instructions for a style except the names of the Based On style and the Next Style, click on the style name in the Define Styles dialog box and press ⌘-Shift-p. For example, suppose you want to delete the instructions for the *heading 1* style that are displayed in Figure 8-25. Figure 8-27 shows how Word will alter the instructions for this style if you press ⌘-Shift-p.

FIGURE 8-27

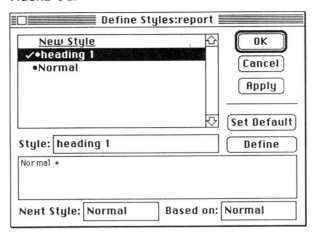

When you press
⌘-Shift-p, Word
will delete all the
instructions for the
selected style ex-
cept the names of
the Next Style and
Based On style.

You can use a similar shortcut to delete only the character formatting instructions for a style. After you open the Define Styles dialog box and click on the name
of the style you want to modify, press ⌘-Shift-Spacebar. Word will then delete such
characteristics as underlining, font, and point size from the style instructions. For
example, Figure 8-28 shows how the Define Styles dialog box from Figure 8-25
would look if we pressed ⌘-Shift-Spacebar.

FIGURE 8-28

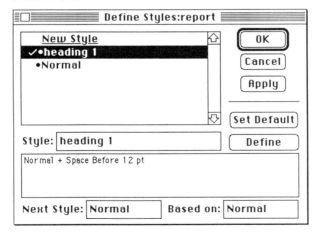

When you press ⌘-
Shift-Spacebar, Word
will delete all the char-
acter formatting in-
structions for a style.

In addition to these two shortcuts, you can use all the character and paragraph formatting shortcuts that are described in Chapter 5. (Appendix 2 includes a summary of these shortcuts.) For example, to specify centered alignment in a style's instructions, you can press ⌘-Shift-c.

Other Modifications

In the example we just presented, we showed how you can modify the formatting instructions for one of Word's automatic styles. To modify the formatting instructions for a custom style, you would follow the same procedure.

In most cases, when you modify a style, you'll change that style's formatting instructions. However, there are other modifications you may want to make as well, such as changing a style's name, specifying a different Based On style, and specifying a different Next Style. Let's look at how you might implement these other style modifications.

Changing a style's name

To change the name of a style, open the Define Styles dialog box and click on the name you want to change. Word will place that name in the Style edit bar. Use the Backspace key to delete the name, then type a new name and click Define. Word will then display an alert box like the one shown in Figure 8-29. If you click OK in this alert box, the new name (in this case, *Line2*) will replace the old name. In addition, all references to the former style name—in the Based On or Next Style edit bars, for example—will be changed so that they refer to the new name.

FIGURE 8-29

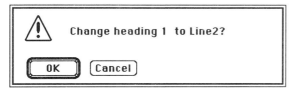

Word will display this alert box when you change the name of a style.

When you enter a new name in the Style edit bar, be sure not to type a name that already exists. If you do this, Word will display a somewhat ambiguous message like *Name matches style. Merge with Style2?*. If you click OK in this alert box, Word will simply eliminate the style whose name you were changing. It will not "merge" that style or any of its characteristics with the style whose name appears in the alert box.

For example, suppose your style sheet contains two styles named *Style1* and *Style2*. The instructions for *Style1* specify the *Normal* style plus boldfacing, while the instructions for *Style2* specify *Style 1* plus 10-point font. Let's assume that you open the Define Styles dialog box and click on the name *Style1* to select it. Then, you change the name of *Style1* to *Style2*. When you click Define, Word will display the *Name matches style...* message. If you click OK in this alert box, Word will eliminate *Style1* from the style sheet. *Style2* will still exist, but its instructions will no longer specify *Style1* as the Based On style.

*Specifying
a different
Based On
style*

To change the Based On style, open the Define Styles dialog box and click on the name of the style whose Based On style you want to change. Drag through the style name in the Based On edit bar to select it, and type the name of the style you want to use as the new Based On style. Then, click Define to lock in the change.

Specifying a new Based On style will in no way change the attributes of the current style. Thus, changing the Based On style does not offer a way to "borrow" some of the attributes from one style and use them in the formatting instructions for another style. For example, suppose you're working with a style sheet that contains three styles: *Normal*, *Style1*, and *Style2*. The *Normal* style specifies 12-point Times type with flush-left alignment and no indents. *Style1* is based on *Normal*, and its instructions read *Normal + Bold Italic, Indent: Left 0.5 in Right 0.5 in, Justified, Space Before 10 pt*. *Style2* is identical to *Style1*, except that it specifies 10-point type. Figure 8-30 shows the formatting instructions for *Style2*.

FIGURE 8-30

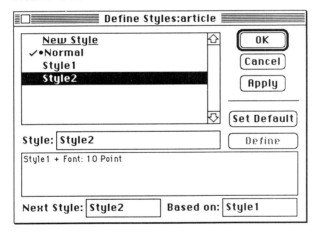

The only difference between Style2 *and its Based On style,* Style1, *is the type size.*

Suppose you want to change the Based On style for *Style2* to *Normal* instead of *Style1*. After opening the Define Styles dialog box, you would click on the style name *Style2*, then select the name *Style1* in the Based On edit bar. Next, type *Normal* as the name of your new Based On style and click the Define button. Figure 8-31 shows the results.

Notice that the new instructions for *Style2* include *Normal* as the Based On style. However, the instructions for *Style2* are now considerably longer than they were before. Since *Style2* is now based on *Normal*, its formatting instructions must spell out all the differences between *Style2* and *Normal*. *Style 2* did not take on any of the formatting characteristics of the *Normal* style.

There is a purpose in specifying a different Based On style. As we've mentioned, any changes that you make to a Based On style may be carried over into the instructions for the dependent style (or styles). Thus, you'll generally specify a new Based On style in order to link two or more styles that are used to format similar elements of a document. Linking styles in this manner helps to ensure that the formatting instructions of these styles are similar.

FIGURE 8-31

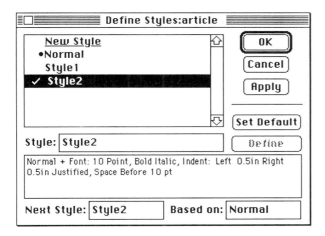

After you change the Based On style, Word will alter the instructions for the dependent style.

Breaking the link to the Based On style

Instead of changing the Based On style, you can delete it altogether. Just select the name in the Based On edit bar, then press Backspace to delete it. Click the Define button to lock in the change. You might recall from our earlier discussion that, in general, it's not a good idea to have a style on your style sheet that is not based on another style. However, if you want to ensure that certain style formats remain unchanged, no matter what style changes you make to other text in your document, Word allows you to do so by eliminating the Based On style.

Specifying a different Next Style

Another modification you may want to make to a style is to specify a different Next Style. Select the name in the Next Style edit bar, type a new style name, then click Define. When you specify a different Next Style, your existing text won't be reformatted. The new Next Style will affect only text that you enter after the change has been made. If you erase the contents of the Next Style edit bar without typing a replacement, Word will beep and display the message *Valid style name is required*.

Using the Ruler to Change a Style

Using the dropdown list of styles on the ruler, you can alter the formatting instructions for a style without opening the Define Styles dialog box. (You cannot alter a style's name, its Based On style, or its Next Style without opening the Define Styles dialog box.) To change the formatting instructions for a style, first click anywhere on a paragraph that's formatted with the style you want to alter. Then, choose the formatting commands and click on ruler icons to format that paragraph with all the attributes you want to include in the style. (This is similar to defining a new style by example.) Now, just choose the style name from the ruler once more. Word will display a dialog box like the one shown in Figure 8-32. Choose the second option (*Redefine the style...*) and click OK or press Return.

FIGURE 8-32

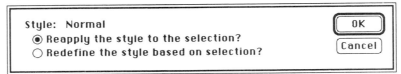

Style: Normal
◉ Reapply the style to the selection?
○ Redefine the style based on selection?

OK

Cancel

When you change the formatting of a paragraph and then reapply the style name to that paragraph, Word will display this dialog box.

The Effects of Modifying a Style

Once you have made changes to a named style, those changes will affect any text in your document that already was formatted with that style. That text does not have to be selected at the time you modify the style in order to be reformatted. For example, suppose your style sheet includes the automatic style named *heading 1*, which you've used to format several subheadings throughout your document. If you change the style instructions for *heading 1*—to specify a different font, for example—Word will automatically reformat all the *heading 1* paragraphs so that they are displayed in the new font. Of course, this automatic reformatting is one of the most important features of Word's style sheets. Since Word applies style sheet changes throughout the entire document, it saves you the time and trouble of reformatting individual sections of the document manually.

When you save a document after you've modified a style, the changes in the instructions for that style will be saved along with the document text. This is true for both automatic and custom styles. Of course, as we've mentioned, if you modify one of Word's automatic styles, your modifications will *not* affect the default instructions for that style. If you create a new document that uses the automatic style, Word will return to its default instructions for that style. However, you can change the default instructions for an automatic style, as we'll explain in the section called "Changing Defaults."

Modifying a Based On Style

If you make changes to a style that serves as the Based On style for other styles, your changes may affect those other styles. For example, earlier in this chapter, we explained how any changes you make to the instructions for the *Normal* style can affect the other styles that are based on *Normal*. Of course, it's possible to make some changes to a Based On style without affecting any dependent styles.

Remember that the instructions for a dependent style spell out the *differences* between that style and its Based On style. If the change you make to a Based On style affects one of these areas of specific difference, then that change will not be reflected in the dependent style's formatting instructions. On the other hand, if the change involves a characteristic that is shared by the Based On style and a dependent style, then the dependent style's instructions will be affected by the change.

DELETING STYLES

To delete a named style from a style sheet, just open the Define Styles dialog box, then click on the name of the style you want to delete. With that name selected, choose Cut from the Edit menu. Word will then display an alert box that asks if you really want to delete the selected style. If you click OK, Word will pause a few seconds, then eliminate that style from the style sheet.

Once you delete a named style, any text that was formatted with that style will lose its special formatting. However, Word will automatically assign the *Normal* style to all the paragraphs that previously were associated with the deleted style.

By the way, Word allows you to delete any style on the style sheet—custom or automatic—except the *Normal* style. Since *Normal* is the style that Word uses whenever a paragraph has not been assigned another style, Word insists on keeping this one style on the style sheet. When you delete one of the other automatic styles—such as the *heading 1* style—from a particular style sheet, you do not, of course, delete that style from Word's library of automatic styles.

If you delete a Based On style, the dependent style will retain all the formatting characteristics of the deleted style. Of course, any formatting characteristics that were derived from the Based On style will now be stated specifically in the style instructions. In addition, Word also will automatically make *Normal* the Based On style in place of the style that was deleted.

If you delete a Next Style, Word will automatically use *Normal* as the Next Style in place of the style you deleted. Of course, Word also will reformat any existing text that was formatted with the deleted style.

USING STYLE SHEETS

Now that we have covered all the ins and outs of creating and modifying named styles, we've come to the heart of our subject: how you can use a style sheet to format a document. In this section, we'll show how you can apply existing styles in a document, make global changes with a style sheet, and copy styles from one document to another.

Applying Named Styles in a Document

Word 4 offers an efficient and easy way to apply a style in a document. Position your insertion point marker anywhere on the paragraph you want to format. Then, turn on your ruler if it is not displayed on your screen. Select from the dropdown list on the ruler the name of the style you want to apply to your paragraph. Immediately, Word will format that paragraph with the style you've selected.

You also can use the Styles or Define Styles dialog box to apply a style. Again, begin by positioning the insertion point marker anywhere on the paragraph you want to format. Then, choose Styles... or Define Styles... from the Format menu. In the Styles or Define Styles dialog box, click on the name of the style you want to apply to the current paragraph, and click Apply or OK. (OK will apply the style and close the dialog box, whereas Apply will apply the style without closing the dialog box.) Instead of clicking the OK button, you can press Return or Enter, which will have the same effect.

Notice that you do not have to select an entire paragraph to apply a style—it's sufficient to place the insertion point marker anywhere on that paragraph before you select a style name from the ruler or choose Styles... or Define Styles... from the Format menu. However, if you want to apply a style to more than one paragraph in a single step, you need to select some text in all of those paragraphs.

Applying styles from the keyboard

If you can remember the name of the style you want to use, there's a shortcut available for applying that style in your document. Instead of opening the Styles... or Define Styles... dialog box, just press ⌘-Shift-s, type the name of the style you want to use, and press Return. When you press ⌘-Shift-s, Word will display the prompt *Style* in the status box, as shown in Figure 8-33. As you type, the style name that you enter will appear in this area, replacing the word *Style*.

FIGURE 8-33

When you press ⌘-Shift-s, Word will display the prompt Style *in the lower-left corner of the current window.*

When you use this shortcut, you do not need to type the full name of the style you want to apply. You can type only enough letters in the style's name to distinguish it from other names on the style sheet. You also don't have to use correct case when you're typing a style name, unless you've created two styles whose names are identical except for capitalization.

If you have assigned more than one name to a style, you can type any of those names when you're applying the style. In our discussion of style names, we suggested that you try to assign relatively short names to styles and, if you assign multiple names to a style, that you make at least one of those names extremely short—perhaps only one or two letters. By sticking to short style names as much as possible, you'll find it easier to apply styles using the keyboard method we've just described.

Word offers another built-in shortcut for applying the *Normal* style. When you choose Short Menus, you'll see, at the far right edge of the ruler, a symbol that looks like an *x* with a vertical bar on either side (I✕I). If you click on this symbol, Word will apply the *Normal* style to the current paragraph in your document (the paragraph on which the insertion point marker is positioned).

There's one minor drawback to accessing this shortcut: You cannot see the I✕I symbol on your screen unless you're using a full-width window. If you've decreased the width of your document window so that the I✕I isn't visible, you can bring the I✕I back into view only by widening the window. You cannot bring it into view by clicking the horizontal scroll bar.

There are two other techniques you can use to apply styles in a document. Both require that you customize Word. First, you can assign a keystroke series to any style name. This allows you to apply a style simply by pressing the assigned keys. Second, you can create a Work menu containing style names. In Chapter 14, we'll explain in detail how to create custom key assignments and custom menus.

In our explanations of how to apply styles, we assumed you had already entered some text you wanted to format. However, you can select a style before you type the text to which you want to apply the style. With the insertion point marker positioned at the beginning of a new paragraph, select a style from the style sheet. Word will apply that style as you begin typing.

As you're formatting a document, you can combine manual format changes with style sheet formatting. In most cases, Word will simply add your manual changes to the formatting features that are specified by the named styles. For example, suppose your document's style sheet includes a style named *Style1* that specifies 12-point Courier bold type. Figure 8-34 shows some text with this style.

Reverting to the Normal *style*

Other methods for applying styles

A note

Manual Formatting vs. Style Sheet Formatting

FIGURE 8-34

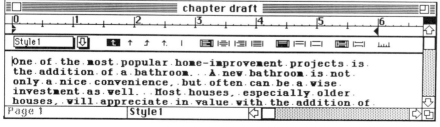

This screen shows some text that has been formatted with Style1.

If you select a paragraph where you've applied this style, then choose Italic from the Format menu, that paragraph will display italic formatting in addition to the boldfacing and other features specified by *Style1*. Furthermore, you can change the indents, margins, and other paragraph formatting features of this paragraph. Figure 8-35 shows a paragraph that has been formatted with both *Style1* and italics. We've changed the first-line indent of this paragraph from the 0 position on the ruler to the $1/_2$-inch position, and we've changed the alignment from flush left to justified.

FIGURE 8-35

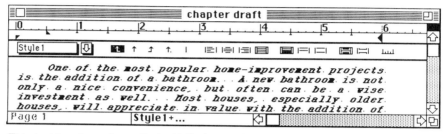

This text has been formatted with Style1 *and italics, which we've added manually.*

When you change the paragraph formatting of some text—for example, the indents or alignment—Word will signify this by adding a plus sign and ellipsis to the style name designation that appears in the status box at the bottom of the window. For example, in Figure 8-35, because we changed the first-line indent and alignment of the paragraph, the style name designation *Style1+...* appears at the lower edge of the window. On the other hand, if you make only character formatting changes (such as assigning a new font, italics, and so forth), Word will not change the style name designation in the status box.

Keep in mind that manual format changes will usually take precedence over style sheet formatting. If you manually assign a formatting characteristic to some text, and that characteristic conflicts with the formatting instructions of the style you've applied to the text, then your manual formatting will override the style instructions. Going back to our example, suppose that after you've applied *Style1* to a paragraph, you select that paragraph and choose New York from the Font menu. Word will then apply the New York font to the text, instead of the Courier font, that was specified by the style instructions.

When you apply a character format that can be toggled on and off (such as italics or boldfacing), your manual format changes may have unexpected results. If you've applied a style to a paragraph and that style's formatting instructions specify italic formatting, for instance, and you later select some text in that paragraph and choose Italic from the Format menu, Word will remove the italics from the selected text.

So far, we've described what will happen when you make manual format changes after applying a style. If you format some text manually before you apply a named style to that text, the rules change a bit. If you manually change the paragraph formatting characteristics of some text (indents, line spacing, alignment, and so forth), then assign a style to that text, the style's formatting instructions will always take precedence over your manual paragraph formatting.

Manual changes to character formats work differently. Word will sometimes combine the formatting characteristics of the named style with the character formats you assigned manually. Other times, however, Word will override your manual formatting. There are reasons why Word preserves your manual format changes or overrides them. If your manual format changes affect a majority of the characters in a paragraph (more than half the characters), Word will override those changes when you apply a style. On the other hand, if your manual formatting is applied to less than half the characters in a paragraph, Word will not override that formatting when you apply a style.

For example, suppose you have created a paragraph, consisting of 200 characters, in Word's default *Normal* style. You then select a word in that paragraph and apply bold formatting. If you later click on the paragraph and reapply the *Normal* style, Word will not remove the bold formatting from that one word. Suppose, however, that instead of applying bold formatting to a single word, you've applied it to the entire paragraph. If you then apply the *Normal* style, Word will remove all the bold formatting.

Because the paragraph consists of 200 characters, you can apply manual character formatting to 100 or fewer characters, and Word will not override that formatting if you later apply the *Normal* style. However, if you applied manual formatting to as many as 101 characters in the paragraph, Word would override that formatting when you reapplied the *Normal* style.

This same "majority" rule will affect how Word toggles formats on and off. As we mentioned earlier, you may get unexpected results when you combine manual character formatting that can be toggled on and off (such as italics or boldfacing) with style-sheet formatting. If your manual formatting affects less than half of the characters in a paragraph, and you later apply a style that specifies that same format, Word will toggle off your manual formatting. However, if you've applied your manual formatting to the majority of the characters in a paragraph, then apply a style whose formatting instructions specify that same format, Word will not toggle off your manual formatting, but will apply the style's formatting to the entire paragraph.

Returning to our example, suppose you've applied bold formatting to one word in a paragraph. Then, you apply a style to that paragraph that specifies bold as part of its formatting instructions. Word will format the entire paragraph in boldface, except for the single word to which you had applied bold formatting manually. Now, suppose you format an entire paragraph to appear in bold. Then, you apply

Applying a named style after making manual format changes

a style to that paragraph that specifies bold as part of its formatting instructions. Word will not toggle off your manual formatting, but will continue to display the entire paragraph in bold.

The Plain Text and Plain For Style options

As we explained in Chapter 5, you can use the Plain Text and Plain For Style options on the Format menu to remove character formatting that you have added to some text. In Word 4, when you select some text and then choose the Plain Text command, Word will remove all character formatting from that selected text except for the font, size, position (superscripting or subscripting), and spacing (condensed or expanded) attributes. Features such as italics, underlining, and color will be stripped away. Word will remove these formatting attributes even if they are part of the style definition for that text.

For example, suppose you have formatted a paragraph with a style named *Style1*. The formatting instructions for *Style1* specify 14-point Times italic type. Now, suppose you select the paragraph that's formatted with the *Style1* style and then choose the Plain Text command. Word will remove the italics from that paragraph so that it appears in 14-point Times Plain type. Word will not alter the definition of *Style1* on the style sheet.

Word 4's new Plain For Style command removes any manual character formatting, but does not affect the formatting that has been applied as a result of a style. Suppose you have formatted a paragraph with the *Style1* style. You then select that paragraph and choose 12 Point from the Font menu and Bold from the Format menu. The paragraph will now appear in 12-point Times bold italic type. Later, you select the paragraph once again and choose the Plain For Style command. Word will remove the bold formatting that you applied manually and return the text to the 14-point size that the *Style1* definition calls for. Word will not remove the italic formatting, however, since it is part of the *Style1* formatting instructions.

Making Global Changes with a Style Sheet

Once you've applied named styles throughout a document, you can make significant format changes to that document merely by changing the instructions of one or more styles. When you change the style sheet, Word will reformat your document text according to those changes. You don't need to select any text before you modify a style's instructions—Word will automatically change any text where that style has been applied. We've already seen examples of what can happen in a document when you modify the instructions for one style. Let's consider an example that shows how you might make even more extensive formatting changes by modifying several styles.

Figure 8-36 shows part of a document in which three styles have been applied. The title has been formatted with a style named *Title* that specifies 14-point New York bold type, flush-left alignment, and a 9-point space after the text. The subheading has been formatted with a style named *Subheading*, which uses *Title* as its Based On style, but specifies 12-point size and a 4-point line space above and a 2-point line space below the subheading. Finally, the body text in this document has been formatted with the *Normal* style, which specifies 12-point New York type, a $^1/_2$-inch first-line indention, and justified alignment.

FIGURE 8-36

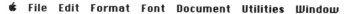

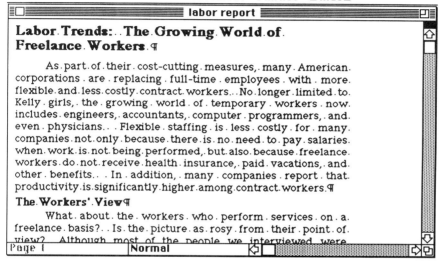

This document has been formatted with three styles: Title, Subheading, *and* Normal.

Suppose you want to change the title and subheading in the document to appear in the Times font with centered alignment. Since the Times font is somewhat smaller than the New York font, you want to change the size of the title text to 18 points and the subheading text to 14 points with centered alignment. You also want to change the main body text to 12-point Helvetica type. In just a few easy steps, you can apply all these formatting changes throughout the entire document.

Begin by opening the Define Styles dialog box and clicking the style name *Normal*. From the Font menu, choose Helvetica from the list of fonts and 12 from the list of sizes. Click OK to close the Character dialog box. Next, click Define in the Define Styles dialog box to lock in these changes to the *Normal* style. Now, select the *Title* style in the Define Styles dialog box, choose Times and 18 Point from the Font menu, then click the Centered alignment icon on the ruler. Again, click Define to lock in these changes. Since the *Subheading* style is based on the *Title* style, the only formatting change you need to make for this style is to choose 14 Point from the Font menu. When you change the font and alignment for the *Title* style, those changes will be carried over into the instructions for the *Subheading* style as well.

After altering all the style instructions, click the close box of the Define Styles dialog box. Figure 8-37 shows how your document will appear at this point.

FIGURE 8-37

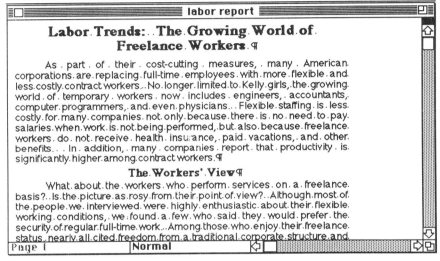

A few simple changes to the style sheet can significantly alter the appearance of a document.

As we've mentioned, one of the nicest advantages offered by style sheets is that you don't need to select any text before you make your formatting changes. When you alter a style's formatting instructions, Word will automatically change any text in your document where that style has been applied. If your insertion point marker is currently on a paragraph that uses another style, you'll want to make sure that you use the Define button to lock in your changes to the style sheet. If you use OK or Apply in the Define Styles dialog box, Word will change the format of the current paragraph to use your altered style instructions as well.

Importing Styles from Another Document

Word allows you to "borrow" styles from other documents and import them into your current document. You can borrow styles one at a time, or import all the styles on another document's style sheet into your current document. Either way, the ability to copy style definitions from document to document can save you the time of redefining styles for each new document, and can provide an efficient way to reformat text.

If you want to copy a style from one document to another, simply copy some text that has been formatted with that style. When you paste the formatted text into a document window, Word will also add the style name and style instructions to that document's style sheet. For example, suppose you're working on a document named Intro in which you've created a style named *First ¶*. You want to use this same style in a document named Summary. Begin by selecting some text that has been formatted with the *First ¶* style in the document named Intro. Then, choose Copy from the Edit menu. Next, open the Summary file and, with that document window active, choose Paste from the Edit menu. Word will copy the text that you selected in Intro—with all of its formatting—into the Summary document window. If you then choose Styles... or Define Styles... from the Format menu, you will see that the style named *First ¶* is now part of the Summary style sheet.

When you use this technique, there are a couple of things you must keep in mind. First, the text you select and copy must include the paragraph marker (¶) at the end of the paragraph. If you copy text without a paragraph marker, Word will not transfer any of the text formatting or the style name to the other document. As soon as you paste the text in the second document, it will be formatted according to that document's *Normal* style.

Second, you need to be aware of how Word handles duplicate style names. Going back to our example, suppose the style sheet for the Summary document already contained a style named *First ¶*. When you paste the *First ¶* text from Intro into Summary, Word will use the existing style instructions for *First ¶* to format that text, rather than import the new style instructions from the Intro file. In other words, in cases of identical style names, the instructions for the style in the destination file will always take precedence over the instructions for the duplicate style name in the source file.

Third, if the style instructions for the paragraph you are copying include a Based On style, Word may need to alter the instructions when you paste the text into the destination file. If the paragraph you copy is based on a style that is not defined in your target document, Word will use *Normal* as the Based On style for the style you are copying. However, Word will retain all the character and paragraph formats you assigned to that paragraph in the source document by creating a more specific set of instructions for that style.

For example, suppose you are working in a document that contains styles named *Sub1* and *Sub2*. The formatting instructions for *Sub1* specify 18-point Helvetica bold type. *Sub2*, which is based on *Sub1*, specifies 14-point Helvetica bold type. Thus, the formatting instructions for *Sub2* read *Sub1 + Font: 14 Point*. Now, suppose you decide to copy a *Sub2* paragraph into a new, blank document window. The only style on the style sheet in this new document is Word's default *Normal* style. After pasting the *Sub2* text into this document, Word will add the *Sub2* style to the style sheet. However, since *Sub2*'s Based On style (*Sub1*) does not appear in this new document, the formatting instructions for *Sub2* will read *Normal + Font: Helvetica 14 Point, Bold*.

If the Based On style name of the paragraph you are copying appears in your destination file's style sheet, Word will continue to use that Based On style. Again, Word will not change the formatting characteristics of the copied style in any way. Suppose you decide to copy some *Sub2* text into a document that already contains a style named *Sub1* (the name of the Based On style for *Sub2* in the original document). However, in the destination document, the formatting instructions for *Sub1* specify 24-point Times italic type. When you copy the *Sub2* text into this file, Word will add the style name *Sub2* to the style sheet. However, its formatting instructions will now read *Sub1 + Font: Helvetica 14 Point, Bold Not Italic*. In other words, *Sub1* is still the Based On style for *Sub2* in the new document. However, in this new document, Word has changed the formatting instructions for *Sub2* so that they spell out all the differences between *Sub2* and *Sub1*.

The best way to avoid wondering about the effect of copying some formatted text from one document to another is to make sure you don't have duplicate style names. Of course, you can't avoid having a *Normal* style in each of your documents. So, one of your first steps in setting up a new document should be to alter the *Normal* style to suit that particular document.

Copying one style at a time can be useful in many instances, but you often will find that it's more efficient to import an entire style sheet, rather than copy individual styles. That is, once you've set up a style sheet in one document, Word makes it easy for you to reuse that style sheet in any other document.

Importing a complete style sheet

To import a style sheet from a file on disk, issue the Define Styles... command. Then, with the Define Styles dialog box open, choose Open... from the File menu. Word will present a list of all the Word document files on the current disk, as shown in Figure 8-38.

If the file containing the style sheet you want to use is not on the current disk, you can click the Drive button to access another disk drive, or you can click Eject and insert a different disk. Once you see the name of the file that contains the style sheet you want to import, click on that name to select it, then click Open (or double-click the file name). Word will automatically add the styles from that file to your current style sheet. (Your style sheet will contain both its original styles and all the styles from the style sheet of the disk file.)

If the style sheet on disk contains one or more styles with the same name as one of the styles in your current document, the style from the disk file will overwrite the existing style. As you might expect, any text in your document that has been formatted with that style will be reformatted according to the instructions of the new style from the disk file.

Every document's style sheet contains the *Normal* style, but the formatting instructions for *Normal* will vary from document to document. Suppose you're working in a document where the *Normal* style specifies 12-point New York type

(Word's default), and you import a style sheet whose *Normal* style specifies 10-point Courier type. Word will replace the instructions for the *Normal* style on your style sheet with the new instructions from the disk file. In addition, the main body text in your current document will be reformatted to display 10-point Courier type.

FIGURE 8-38

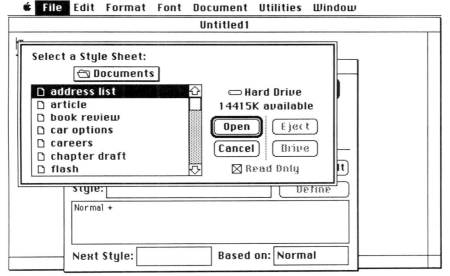

To import a style sheet from another document, choose Open... from the File menu while the Define Styles dialog box is open.

Of course, if the names of all or most of the styles on your current style sheet are identical to the style names that you import from disk, then your document may be radically reformatted. In some cases, this may be exactly what you want. Borrowing another document's style sheet offers an excellent way to reformat an entire document rapidly.

If you plan to use similar formats in several documents, you may want to store those formats in a style sheet template. A style sheet template is a blank document file in which you've defined a number of named styles. Such a template file will typically require only about 2K of disk space, so you can keep a copy of it on each disk where you store your document files or perhaps on your startup disk. Each time you begin a new document, you can set up the style sheet for that document by choosing Define Styles... from the Format menu, then choosing Open... from the File menu and opening the template file. Word will automatically place all the style names from that template file onto your new document's style sheet.

Creating a style sheet template

For example, suppose you must write a report every week that summarizes the activities of your department and lists the goals for the upcoming week. To format this report, you use three styles: *Title* (for the report title), *Normal* (for the main body text), and *List* (for the list of goals). By storing these styles in a style sheet template, you can speed up the process of formatting your report each week.

Let's say that you've just completed one of your reports, which you've saved in a file named Jun10Rpt. To create your style sheet template, begin by opening a new document file. With this new document active, choose Define Styles... from the Format menu. Then, choose Open... from the File menu. In the Open dialog box, double-click the name Jun10Rpt. At this point, Word will load the styles *Title*, *Normal*, and *List*—which are on the Jun10Rpt style sheet—into the style sheet for the new document. Now, all you need to do is save the blank document under a name such as Styles or Template. Then, each week as you begin a new report, your first step should be to load the styles from this file into a new document window where you plan to write your report.

You could load the styles directly from the Jun10Rpt file instead of creating a separate template file. However, as we mentioned before, the template file has the advantage of being small, so you can store copies of it on several disks with your document files. In addition, by keeping a template file, you don't need to worry about discarding your regular document files when you're through with them.

CHANGING DEFAULTS

If there are certain styles that you use repeatedly in different documents, you may want to change the default style sheet so that those styles are automatically available each time you start a new document in Word. In addition, you might want to change the default characteristics of some of Word's automatic styles, particularly the *Normal* style. In this section, we'll explain how to change Word's defaults and how you can recover the original default settings.

Modifying the Default Style Sheet

Initially, the only style on the default style sheet is the *Normal* style. Once you've added other styles—custom or automatic—to a document's style sheet, you can place any of those additional styles on the default style sheet. To add a style to the default style sheet, first open the Define Styles dialog box, then click on the style name that you want to place on the default style sheet. Next, click Set Default. Word will then display the alert box shown in Figure 8-39.

If you click Yes in this box, Word will add the selected style to the default style sheet. Then, each time you open a new Word document, that style will automatically appear on the style sheet for that document.

FIGURE 8-39

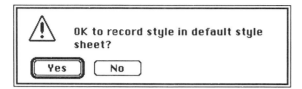

As you are adding a style to the default style sheet, you will see this alert box.

Modifying the Default Characteristics of Automatic Styles

We've already seen an example of how you can change the formatting instructions for an automatic style on a document's style sheet. Suppose, however, you want to make a permanent change to one of Word's automatic styles. That is, you want to modify the instructions for an automatic style so that every time you use that style in any document, the modified instructions will be in effect. You may want to modify the default *Normal* style. Instead of beginning each new document with a *Normal* style of 12-point New York type with flush-left paragraph alignment, you want to use a *Normal* style of 10-point Times type with justified paragraphs and a $^1/_2$-inch indent on the first line of each paragraph. First, you should choose Define Styles... from the Format menu and click on the style name *Normal* to select it. Then, choose Times and 10 Point from the Font menu. Next, click on the ruler icon for justified alignment and drag the first-line indent marker to the $^1/_2$-inch position. After you've made these changes, click the Set Default button in the Define Styles dialog box. Word will then display the alert box shown in Figure 8-39.

If you click Yes in the alert box, Word will alter the *Normal* style both in your current document and in any new documents you create. Any text that you have formatted in your current document using the *Normal* style will be reformatted according to the new formatting instructions. Also, since the other automatic styles are all based on the *Normal* style, any text that carries those styles may also be reformatted. Of course, documents that were formatted in the old default *Normal* style and saved to disk will retain their original formatting.

Returning to the Original Defaults

Word stores the default style sheet and all the instructions for automatic styles in the Word Settings (4) file in your System folder or another configuration file that you specify. If you want to restore the default style sheet and return the automatic styles to their original forms, you can choose the Commands... command on the Edit menu and, in the Commands dialog box, click the Reset button as you press the Shift key. (Chapter 14 explains the Commands... command in detail.)

You also can return to the default style sheet by deleting or renaming the Word Settings (4) file. Word will then automatically recreate the Word Settings (4) file using the original defaults the next time you load Word. *Normal* will be the only style on the default style sheet, and the instructions for each automatic style will return to their defaults.

Of course, if you delete or rename the Word Settings (4) file, or if you press Shift and click Reset in the Commands dialog box, you'll affect more than just style sheets. You also will return all menus, keystroke series, and dialog boxes to their original configurations. (For more on changing defaults and the Word Settings (4) file, see Chapter 14.)

PRINTING A STYLE SHEET

To print a list of all the styles on a style sheet, choose Define Styles… from the Format menu, then choose Print… from the File menu. Word will then print a list like the one shown in Figure 8-40. Notice that it includes the style names in boldface and the formatting instructions for each style. (For more information on printing, see Chapter 7.)

FIGURE 8-40

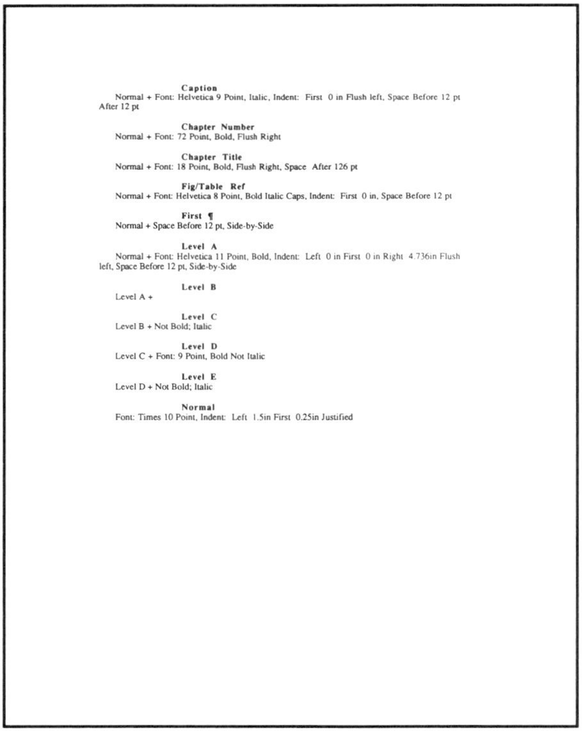

Caption
Normal + Font: Helvetica 9 Point, Italic, Indent: First 0 in Flush left, Space Before 12 pt After 12 pt

Chapter Number
Normal + Font: 72 Point, Bold, Flush Right

Chapter Title
Normal + Font: 18 Point, Bold, Flush Right, Space After 126 pt

Fig/Table Ref
Normal + Font: Helvetica 8 Point, Bold Italic Caps, Indent: First 0 in, Space Before 12 pt

First ¶
Normal + Space Before 12 pt, Side-by-Side

Level A
Normal + Font: Helvetica 11 Point, Bold, Indent: Left 0 in First 0 in Right 4.736in Flush left, Space Before 12 pt, Side-by-Side

Level B
Level A +

Level C
Level B + Not Bold; Italic

Level D
Level C + Font: 9 Point, Bold Not Italic

Level E
Level D + Not Bold; Italic

Normal
Font: Times 10 Point, Indent: Left 1.5in First 0.25in Justified

Word can print a list of all the styles on the current style sheet and their formatting instructions.

OUTLINING **9**

There are times before you create a document, when you know exactly what you want to say and how you want to say it. At other times, however, you just can't seem to get started, or you have so much information that structuring it seems overwhelming. Word 4 comes to your rescue with a powerful Outliner facility that can help you organize your thoughts and build a document from the ground up.

Although Word's Outliner is easy to use, it is highly sophisticated. As you'll see, the Outliner works in conjunction with many of the program's other special features to help you create, edit, and organize your text. The combined power of the Outliner and style sheets lets you format your document quickly and easily. In addition, you can use the Outliner facility to create a table of contents for your document (more on this topic in Chapter 11), to navigate through long documents quickly, and to rearrange blocks of text with just a few keystrokes.

To access the Outliner, make sure that the Full Menus setting is active, then select the Outlining command from the Document menu. In the space that the ruler normally occupies at the top of the document window, you'll see an icon selection bar like the one in Figure 9-1 on the following page. To return to your document window, simply choose Outlining again. You can toggle between the outline and document windows at any time by pressing ⌘-u.

As you assemble your outline, you'll use the Outliner icons to organize, and assign priorities to, information in your document and to expand and collapse your view of the document. We'll look at each of these features as we walk through the process of creating and editing text in the outline window.

FIGURE 9-1

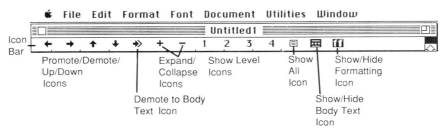

When you issue the Outlining command, this set of icons appears at the top of your screen.

Word's Outliner divides your document text into two categories: headings and body text. Generally, you'll enter your headings in the outline window, then return to the document window to enter your body text. Each heading is assigned a level, labeled *heading 1* through *heading 9*. The remainder of the text is body text.

Heading 1 entries represent your broadest, or most important, categories of ideas, while headings 2 through 9 represent subordinate levels of ideas under your main headings. As you might have guessed, you can use these entries as headings in your finished document, or you can opt to hide them from view once you have completed your document.

Word helps you visualize the relationships between outline topics by indenting the different levels of text that appear in your outline window. Main topics—those labeled heading 1—start at the left margin, while subordinate headings are indented. Heading 2 entries are indented $1/_2$ inch, heading 3 entries are indented 1 inch, and so forth—with each new level indented an additional $1/_2$ inch. Any body text that you enter into an outline window will be indented $1/_4$ inch from where the preceding heading begins. (Actually, the amount of indention that Word uses for the different levels in the outline window corresponds to the default tab stops in your Document dialog box. If you change the Default Tab Stops setting in that dialog box, Word will change the amount of indention for each level of text in the outline window.)

BUILDING AN OUTLINE

The easiest way to learn to use the Outliner is to walk through the creation of a sample document. To illustrate, we'll create an article entitled *Freelancing: A Beginner's Guide*. We'll use the Outliner to organize our ideas, then we'll build on this outline to create a finished document. If you'd like to follow along with our example, begin by opening a new document. Choose Full Menus from the Edit menu, if that setting is not already active, then select the Outlining command from the Document menu.

Figure 9-2 shows a portion of our sample article's outline. To create this outline, start by typing the first heading, *Cutting loose*, then press the Return key to start a new paragraph. Whenever you begin a new outline, Word assumes that your first paragraph will be a heading 1 entry. It also assumes that all subsequent paragraphs will be entered at the same level as the previous entry until you indicate otherwise.

FIGURE 9-2

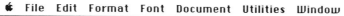
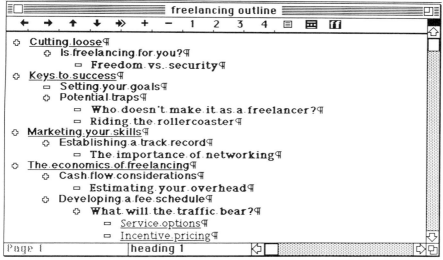

We'll start by entering our ideas in the outline window and assigning priority levels to each idea.

To create the subordinate heading that appears in the second line of the sample outline window, click on the → icon at the top of the window and type the phrase *Is freelancing for you?* You will notice that your second paragraph has been "demoted" to the heading 2 level. Word also indents the paragraph $^1/_2$ inch from the left margin to indicate that this heading is subordinate to the first heading. Press Return again to begin the third paragraph, then click the → icon to indent this entry an additional $^1/_2$ inch to the heading 3 level.

In addition to the various levels of indention, notice that Word has assigned different character formats to the various levels of headings in the outline window. As we'll explain in a few pages, the formats for these headings are controlled by your document's style sheet. If you prefer not to show these various heading formats, you can click on the **ffi** icon, which allows you to hide formatting in the outline window. When you do this, Word displays all the text in the default *Normal* style, as shown in Figure 9-3. You may find that this simplified, unformatted display makes it easier to interpret the structure of your document. To redisplay character formatting, just click on the **ffi** icon again.

FIGURE 9-3

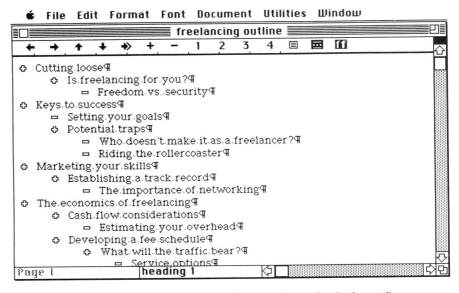

You can click on the ff *icon to suppress character formatting in the outline window.*

After you type the text for the third heading, you're ready to move on to your next major topic: *Keys to success.* Notice that this paragraph is the same level as the first heading in Figure 9-2. When you press the Return key at the end of the third paragraph to enter this heading, however, Word will assume that you want this new paragraph to appear as a heading 3 entry as well. Click the ← icon twice to "promote" the fourth paragraph to a heading 1 entry.

To complete the outline, continue typing the sample text shown in Figure 9-2, clicking the → and ← icons to demote and promote each heading as needed. You can also use the → and ← keys to assign levels to your headings. (Although our sample outline uses only four heading levels, Word allows you to create as many as nine. Generally, the more detailed your outline, the greater the number of heading levels you will use.)

Before you enter your document text, you should familiarize yourself with the outline selection icons you will encounter as you type, promote, and demote text. You'll see these icons to the left of the heading paragraphs in your outline window. An icon's shape indicates whether a paragraph is a heading or body text. The ▫ icon signals a paragraph of body text. The ✛ and ▭ icons signal heading text: the ✛ indicates a heading with subordinate text; the ▭ indicates a heading without subordinate text. (By subordinate text, we mean all the headings and body text between the current heading and the next heading of an equal or higher level.)

As you enter your outline text, keep in mind that the outline window is just another type of window—another view of the document, as far as Word is concerned. Any actions you take in the outline window will also affect the contents of your document window—and vice versa. For example, when you press ⌘-u to return to your document window, after typing the sample outline shown in Figures 9-2 and 9-3, your screen will look like the one in Figure 9-4. As you can see, Word makes it easy to identify the relationship among the headings.

Viewing an Outline in a Document Window

FIGURE 9-4

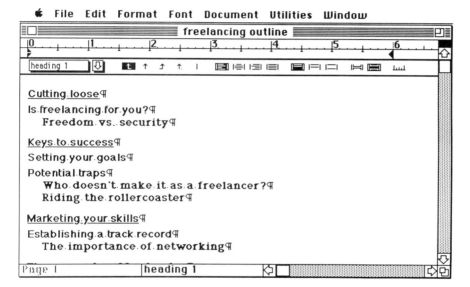

When you toggle back to the document window, the outline text will look like this.

When you return to the document window, you'll see that each heading level carries different character or paragraph formats. If you keep your eye on the status box at the bottom of the screen as you click on the various headings, you'll see that Word has remembered the heading level you assigned to each paragraph.

While you were creating your outline, Word was busy behind the scenes creating a style sheet for your document. For each heading level you entered into the outline window, Word created a corresponding set of style specifications. We'll show you later in this chapter how to use these automatic styles to format your document. First, let's add some substance to our outline and explore some techniques for editing our document through the outline window.

**ADDING THE
BODY TEXT**

After the bare bones of the outline are in place, you can fill in your document by adding your body text. In the document window, begin by clicking at the end of the first paragraph, then press the Return key to begin a new paragraph. As you begin typing the body of the document, part of which is shown in Figure 9-5, Word will automatically format your body text to appear in the default *Normal* style—12-point New York Plain.

FIGURE 9-5

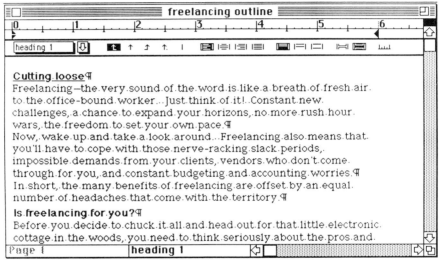

When you click at the end of a heading paragraph and press Return, Word will automatically assign the Normal *style to your body text paragraph.*

Now that we have entered some body text, let's toggle back to the outline window and see what has happened to our outline. As you can see in Figure 9-6, when you return to the outline window, a number of changes will have taken place. First of all, your indentions reappear to give you a clear view of the relationship between each heading in the document. Also, notice that each body text paragraph is indented $1/4$ inch to the right of the heading under which it falls. This half-level indention gives you another visual clue as to the organizational structure of your document.

FIGURE 9-6

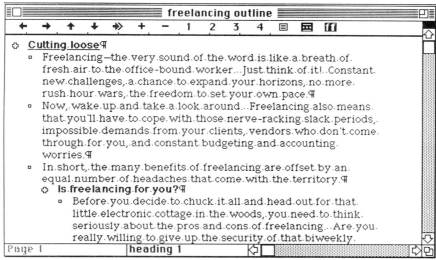

When you return to the outline window, each body text paragraph is indented
1/4 inch to the right of the heading under which it falls.

To help you reduce clutter in the outline window and better view the structure of your document, Word offers a show/hide body text icon, represented by a ☲ symbol. When you click on this icon, Word will condense each paragraph of your body text to only one line, as you can see in Figure 9-7 on the following page, leaving just enough text to remind you of the topic of each paragraph. When you opt to hide the body text in the outline window, ellipses appear at the ends of these lines to indicate that additional text follows. To view the full text of your document again, just click on the ☲ icon a second time.

Simplifying the Document View

Once you have entered your headings and drafted your body text, you'll probably need to make some changes and reorganize information in your document. Word offers a lot of shortcuts for editing your document in the outline window. As in the document window, however, before you can do any editing, you must first select the text you want to work with. Let's look at some of the special selection techniques that Word makes available in the outline window.

When you are working within a single paragraph of an outline, you can use Word's standard selection techniques (described in Chapter 4) to select the text you want to work with. For example, to select an entire word, you can double-click on that word. To select an entire sentence, press the ⌘ key and click on that sentence.

SELECTION TECHNIQUES

FIGURE 9-7

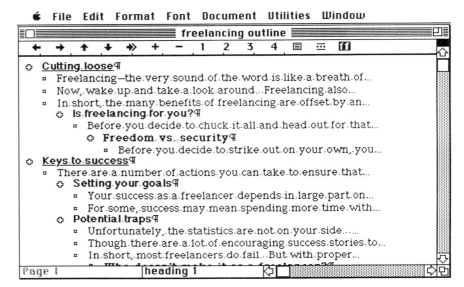

To simplify your view of the document, click on the ⠿ icon to reduce each body text paragraph to one line.

In the document window, when you want to select an entire paragraph, you double-click in the selection bar next to that paragraph. In the outline window, things work a little differently. You need only click once in the selection bar on the left side of the outline window to select an entire heading. (Keep in mind that each heading occupies one paragraph.) You also can select a heading by pressing the Option key and clicking on the selection icon (✛ or ⬚) for that heading.

When you double-click in the selection bar, Word highlights not only the current heading, but all the subordinate text under that heading. Another way to make this type of selection is to click once on the selection icon for a heading.

For example, if you click once in the selection bar to the left of the heading 1 entry *Cutting loose* at the top of the outline window in Figure 9-7, Word will highlight that entire paragraph, including the ¶ marker at the end. If you double-click in the selection bar next to this heading, however, your outline window will look like the one in Figure 9-8. As you can see, Word highlights the paragraph that contains the text *Cutting loose*, as well as its subordinate text. (You can also highlight the entire paragraph by clicking once on the selection icon to the left of the heading 1 entry *Cutting loose*.)

FIGURE 9-8

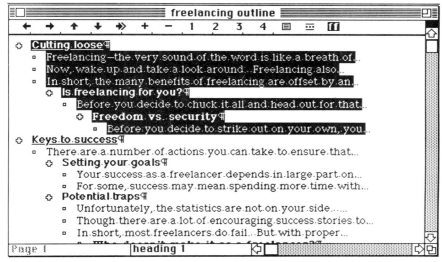

To highlight a heading and all its subordinate text, just double-click in the selection bar next to the heading or click once on the selection icon for that heading.

COLLAPSING AND EXPANDING THE OUTLINE

Even if you have instructed Word to display only the first line of each paragraph of body text in the outline window, your outline can get pretty lengthy once you've created several levels of subheadings and inserted body text under each. If you lose track of all these levels, you can eliminate some of this clutter by collapsing the outline to hide selected headings and body text from view.

For example, suppose you want to see only the heading 1 entries in your outline. To collapse the outline, just click on the **1** at the top of the outline window—this is called the show level 1 icon. As you can see in Figure 9-9 on the following page, all the body text and subheadings under your heading 1 entries will disappear. Word displays a gray line under each heading 1 entry to indicate that additional text is tucked out of sight below those headings.

To expand the outline again, just click on another show level icon. For example, if you click on the show level 3 icon (**3**), Word will expand the outline to display all of your heading 1, heading 2, and heading 3 entries. Your body text will remain hidden from view. To bring all your headings and the body text back into view, click on the show all icon (▤). You can also press the * key on the numeric keypad to redisplay all your outline headings and the first lines of your body text.

FIGURE *9-9*

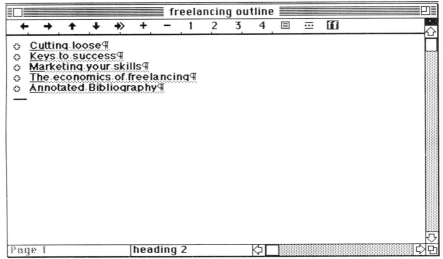

When you click on the show level 1 icon, Word will collapse your outline to show only heading 1 entries.

While the show level icons affect the display of your entire outline, the expand and collapse icons—represented by the **+** and **—** symbols at the top of the outline window—affect only selected portions of your outline display. You can also use the + and - keys on your numeric keypad to expand or collapse portions of your outline.

Suppose you want to collapse the headings and body text that appear under the second level 1 heading in the document shown in Figure 9-8. Simply click on that heading, then click on the collapse icon (**—**), or press the - key on your numeric keypad. As you can see in Figure 9-10, Word will collapse all the body text that originally appeared under that heading. If you click on the collapse icon (**—**) or press the - key again, Word will collapse all the heading 3 levels that appear under that heading, then all the heading 2 levels . To reverse this process, click on the heading again, then click on the expand icon (+) , or press the + key on your numeric keypad.

FIGURE 9-10

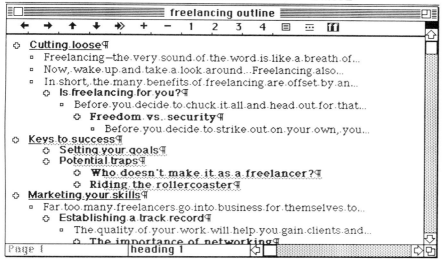

Use the collapse icon or the - key on your numeric keypad to collapse selected portions of the outline.

When you use these expand and collapse techniques, Word will not collapse the other text in your outline; only the text that falls between the current heading and the next heading at an equal or higher level will be affected. In our example, only the text that appears between the second and third heading 1 entries is affected. You also could click on the heading 2 entry *Setting your goals* to collapse all the subtext between that heading and the next heading of equal or higher value, *Potential traps*.

To expand or collapse all the subordinate text under a heading in one step, just double-click the outline selection icon next to that heading. You also can double-click in the selection bar to highlight the entire heading paragraph (including subordinate text), and then click the collapse icon. In addition, you can collapse an entire heading paragraph by selecting the heading and its subordinate text and pressing - on the numeric keypad or by clicking the ▬ icon. You'll need to press + (or click the ✚ icon) repeatedly to regain all the levels of text you collapsed.

For example, to collapse all the subheadings and body text under the heading *Keys to success* in our sample outline, just double-click the selection icon (✚) next to this heading. Word will hide the headings and body text between that heading and the next heading 1 entry, *Marketing your skills*. Figure 9-11 shows the results.

FIGURE *9-11*

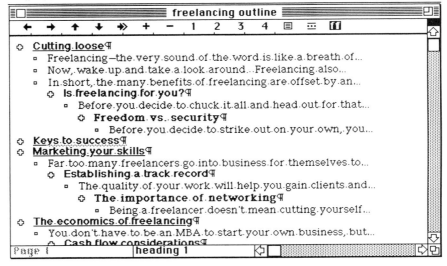

To collapse all the subordinate text under a heading, just double-click the outline selection icon for that heading.

To expand the outline, you can double-click the selection icon once more. You also can reselect the entire paragraph that contains the heading *Keys to success*, and click on the ✚ icon, or press the + key on your numeric keypad to redisplay all the text between that heading and the next heading 1 entry. You can also expand any single heading by highlighting it and pressing ⌘-+ on the numeric keypad. (As you might guess, ⌘- - on the numeric keypad will collapse any selected text.)

A Navigation Tip

When you are working with a long document and want to move to another area, you can use the Outliner to navigate quickly through your document. Just toggle to the outline window, then collapse the outline by clicking one of the show level icons. If the heading 1 entries are too obscure for you to find your place, keep expanding the outline until you locate the spot you want. Next, highlight the heading or body text that represents the section you want to work with. Finally, scroll the highlighted text to the top of your screen. When you press ⌘-u to return to your document window, Word will bring the highlighted text into view.

You can use any of the editing techniques described in Chapters 4 and 6 to edit text in your Word outline. However, when you use the Find... and Change... commands in the outline window, Word will operate only on the text that is visible on the screen.

For example, when you issue the Find... command, Word will not find any occurrences of your find text that are located in a collapsed portion of the outline. If you want to search through all the text in your document, you'll probably find it easier to perform the find operation in the document window. However, if you want to find or change occurrences of a text string only in your document's headings, you may be able to streamline your search-and-replace procedures by working in the outline window.

In addition to these standard document editing techniques, Word offers a number of special editing features to help you edit text in the outline window. Let's look at some of these features.

You can easily change the level of a heading in your outline at any time. Begin by clicking on that heading or by selecting the paragraph that contains the heading, then click on the ← or → icon. You can also use the ← or → keys on your keyboard to promote or demote a heading.

In addition to changing the level number of the selected heading, Word will change the indention of that paragraph to reflect its new level. Word will also adjust the indention of any body text that appears immediately under the selected heading to indicate that it still "belongs to" that heading.

Unless you specifically instruct it to do so, however, Word will not change the levels of other subordinate text in the outline. If you want to promote or demote a heading and all its subordinate text, you must click once on the selection icon for that heading or double-click in the selection bar to select the heading and its subordinate text. Then, click on the ← or → icon.

For example, suppose you want to demote the heading 1 entry *Keys to success* in the sample outline to a heading 2 level. If you simply click on that heading and click the → icon, the outline will look like Figure 9-12 on the following page. As you can see, Word did not demote any of the headings under *Keys to success*.

However, if you click on the selection icon or double-click in the selection bar to select the heading and its subordinate text, then click the → icon, your outline will look like the one in Figure 9-13. As you can see, Word has also demoted all the subordinate headings and body text between the *Keys to success* heading and the next heading 1 entry. In effect, the *Keys to success* heading and its subtext now fall under the first heading 1 entry, *Cutting loose*. Finally, you can demote any selected heading to body text by pressing ⌘-→ or by clicking the ⇒ icon.

EDITING IN THE OUTLINE WINDOW

Changing a Heading Level

FIGURE 9-12

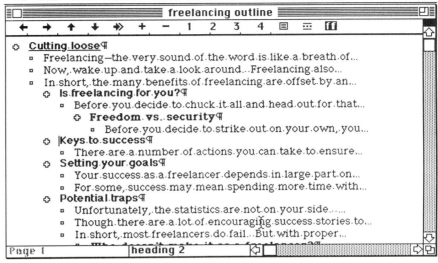

If you click on a heading before you click the ← or → icon, Word adjusts the level of the heading and its body text.

FIGURE 9-13

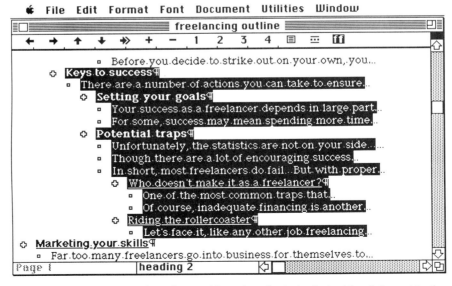

To promote or demote a heading and its subordinate text, double-click next to the heading in the selection bar before you click the ← or → icon.

If you click on a body text paragraph in the outline window, then click the ← icon or press the ← key on your Macintosh keyboard, Word will convert your body text to the same level as its immediate superior heading. For example, if you click on the body text paragraph that begins *Freelancing—the very sound* in the second line of our sample outline in Figure 9-11, and click the ← icon, Word will promote that entire paragraph to a heading 1 level. As you can see in Figure 9-14, when you promote the paragraph to a heading, Word will display the entire contents of that heading, rather than only the first line. (You might use this technique to view or edit the contents of a body text paragraph quickly in the outline window. Then, you can click the demote icon to convert that paragraph back to a body text paragraph when you're through.)

Promoting body text

FIGURE 9-14

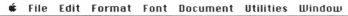

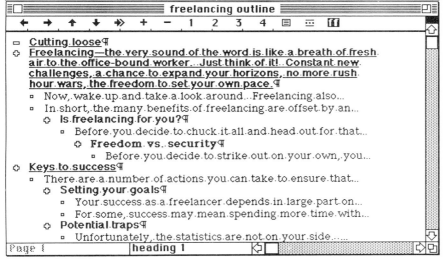

We've used the ← icon to convert the first paragraph of body text to a heading 1 level.

By the same token, if you click on this body text paragraph and click the → icon or press the → key, Word will convert the selected body text to the next subordinate heading level—2. Again, Word will display the entire contents of the body text paragraph. Word also will indent the heading $1/2$ inch to the right of the preceding heading 1 entry.

*Converting a
heading to
body text*

To convert a heading to body text, just click on the heading you want to work with and click the demote to body text icon (➡➤). Alternatively, you can press ⌘-➡ to convert the heading to body text.

When you demote a heading to body text, Word will change the indention of that heading—and any subordinate body text that appears immediately below the heading—to appear $1/4$ inch to the right of the heading immediately preceding it. In short, the heading and its body text become part of the subordinate body text for the preceding heading.

For example, if we select the heading 2 entry *Is freelancing for you?* in our sample outline and click the ➡➤ icon, our outline window will look like the one in Figure 9-15. Notice that the body text that was formerly attached to this heading 2 entry now carries the same indention as the rest of the body text for the heading 1 entry *Cutting loose.* Also, notice that Word now displays the style notation *Normal* in the status box at the bottom of the screen. As you can see, however, Word did not change the heading 3 entry *Freedom vs. security* that appears below the heading 2 entry that we demoted.

FIGURE 9-15

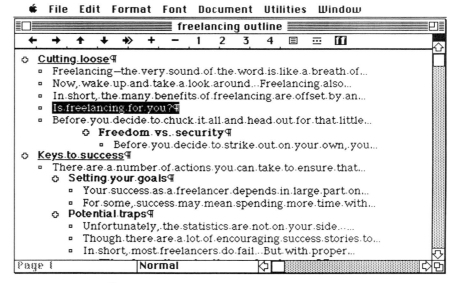

You can use the ➡➤ icon to convert any heading in your outline to standard body text.

Perhaps the simplest way you can promote and demote text is to drag it. If you click on a selection icon but don't release the mouse button, you can drag the entire heading left or right. When you drag left, you promote the heading. When you drag right, you demote it. As you are dragging, you'll notice that Word displays different heading levels in the status box to the left of the horizontal scroll bar. If you drag far enough right, you'll see that your text becomes body text. At that time, the status box will indicate *Normal*.

Dragging text

The easiest way to insert a new heading into your outline is to click in front of the paragraph immediately below the spot where you want your new heading to occur and press ⌘-Option-Return. When you press ⌘-Option-Return, Word will insert a new ¶ marker above the current insertion point. However, your insertion point marker will not jump to the next line but will remain on the same line as the new ¶ marker.

Inserting a New Heading

Initially, your new heading will appear at the same level as the heading you clicked on before pressing ⌘-Option-Return. Of course, you can use the ← and → icons to change the heading level of the paragraph.

Continuing with our sample outline, suppose you want to add a new heading 2 entry—*Success stories*—between the heading 3 entry *Freedom vs. security* and the heading 1 entry *Keys to success*. If you were to click at the end of the heading 3 entry and press Return, your new heading would appear between the *Freedom vs. security* heading and the text paragraph that begins *Before you decide*. If you try clicking at the end of the body text paragraph and pressing the Return key, Word will break that body text paragraph into two paragraphs instead of inserting a new blank heading paragraph after the text paragraph.

To get around these problems, just click in front of the heading 1 entry *Keys to success* and press ⌘-Option-Return. As you can see in Figure 9-16 on the next page, Word will push the heading down a line and insert a new ¶ marker for you. Now, all you need to do is click the → icon to change this paragraph to a heading 2 entry and type your new text. Figure 9-17 shows the results.

If you decide to delete a heading from your outline, be sure to expand the outline before you begin. Otherwise, you may inadvertently delete all the subordinate text for that heading as well. It is important to remember that when you select a heading in a collapsed outline, you also select all the subordinate text for that heading.

Deleting a Heading

For example, if you were to select the heading 1 entry *Cutting loose* in Figure 9-9, then click the show all icon (▤), you would see that Word has highlighted all the subtext between the first and second heading 1 entries in the outline window. In short, any changes you make to a heading while the outline is collapsed will affect all the subtext below that heading.

FIGURE 9-16

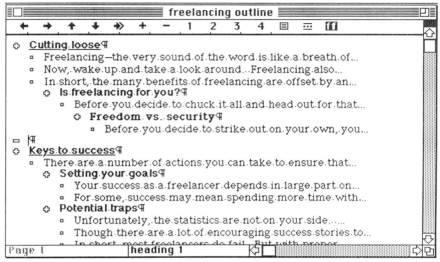

To insert a new heading, click in front of the paragraph immediately below the spot where you want your new heading to occur, and press ⌘-Option-Return.

FIGURE 9-17

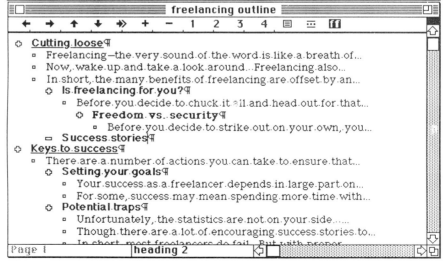

After you create your new blank paragraph, assign the appropriate level and type the new heading text.

Once you have expanded the outline and selected the heading or body text paragraph you want to delete, you can simply press the Backspace key or issue the Cut command to remove that heading from its current location.

There are three ways to move blocks of text in the outline window. The first is the standard cut-and-paste technique—just select the heading and any subordinate text you want to move, issue the Cut command, then click on the spot where you want to place the text and issue the Paste command. You also can use the ↑ and ↓ icons to move text, or click on a selection icon and drag text.

Moving a Heading

As we mentioned in our discussion about deleting text, when you use the Cut command to delete or move text in an outline window, your changes may affect more than the text that is visible on your screen. When you select a heading with collapsed subtext, you are selecting all that subtext as well. If you do not want this subordinate text to be moved along with the selected heading, you'll need to expand your outline before you select the heading and issue the Cut command. However, if you do want the subtext to be included in your selection, you may find it easier to collapse the outline before you begin the cut-and-paste procedure.

Similarly, when you select your paste area, you may want to expand any collapsed text in that area to ensure that you are not inserting text between a heading and its subordinate text.

In addition to the Cut and Paste commands, you can use the ↑ and ↓ icons in the outline window to rearrange blocks of text. For example, suppose you decide to move the heading 2 entry *Setting your goals* and its subtext. You want this text to appear just below the body text paragraph that reads *Before you decide to chuck it all.* If the portion of your outline you want to move is collapsed, simply double-click on the heading to select it and all of its subordinate text. If your outline is not collapsed, you'll need to double-click in the selection bar or click on the selection icon to make your selection.

Now, click the ↑ icon to move the selected text block toward the beginning of the document. (You can also use the ↓ and ↑ keys on your keyboard to move blocks of text up and down through the outline window.) Each time you click the ↑ icon, Word will move the selected block up through the outline window one heading at a time. The program will skip past any body text paragraphs. Just keep clicking the ↑ icon or pressing the ↑ key until the text block is in the desired position. (If you need to move the text block a long distance, you may want to collapse some or all of the outline text before you begin in order to save time.) Figure 9-18 on the next page shows the results.

Just as you can drag text left and right in the Outliner, you can click on a selection icon and drag a heading and its subordinate text up or down to reposition it in your document. By the way, you'll notice that when you move a block of text up in the outline window, you simply change the order of those paragraphs; you do not change your heading levels or the relationship between your headings and body text.

FIGURE 9-18

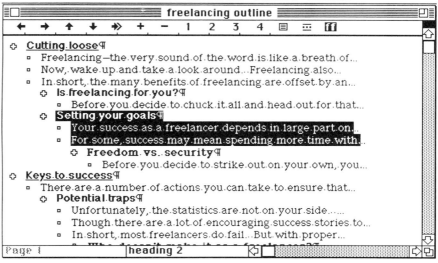

To reposition a selection in the outline window, you can click the ↑ and ↓ icons or press the ↑ and ↓ keys.

**THE OUTLINER
AND STYLE
SHEETS**

As we mentioned at the beginning of this chapter, Word's built-in Outliner is designed to work hand-in-hand with the style sheet facility. When you begin a document in an outline window, Word assumes that you will want to use each topic in the outline as a subheading in your document. As you switch from the outline window to a document window, Word automatically sets up a style sheet, assigning a different style name to each level of the outline.

To illustrate, let's continue with our sample freelancing article. After you switch from the outline window to a normal document window, and place the insertion point on any line, you'll see the level for that text in the status box at the bottom of the screen.

Each level you use in the outline window now has a corresponding style name on the document's style sheet. If you choose Styles… or Define Styles… from the Format menu, you'll see that the style sheet in our sample document includes the style names *heading 1*, *heading 2*, *heading 3*, and *heading 4* . Like other document style sheets, this style sheet will also include the style named *Normal*, as shown in Figure 9-19.

FIGURE 9-19

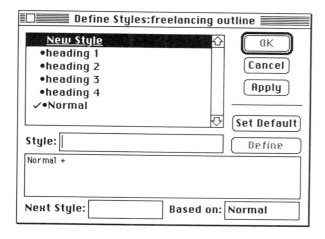

Each level from the outline is now a style name on the style sheet.

Although Word gives you a helpful head start by setting up the styles named *heading 1, heading 2,* and so forth, it does not provide much distinction in the formatting of these *heading* styles. Table 9-1 shows the default formatting instructions for each of these styles.

TABLE 9-1

Style name	Formatting instructions
heading 1	Normal + Font: Helvetica, Bold, Underline, Space Before 12 pt.
heading 2	Normal + Font: Helvetica, Bold, Space Before 6 pt.
heading 3	Normal + Bold, Indent: Left 0.25 in.
heading 4	Normal + Underline, Indent: Left 0.25 in.
heading 5	Normal + Font: 10 Point, Bold, Indent: Left 0.5 in.
heading 6	Normal + Font: 10 Point, Underline, Indent: Left 0.5 in.
heading 7	Normal + Font: 10 Point, Italic, Indent: Left 0.5 in.
heading 8	Normal + Font: 10 Point, Italic, Indent: Left 0.5 in.
heading 9	Normal + Font: 10 Point, Italic, Indent: Left 0.5 in.

These are the default formatting instructions for each of the heading styles.

Suppose you want the main body text in your document to be formatted with Times type, with a $^1/_4$-inch indent on the first line of each paragraph. To alter the *Normal* style to meet these specifications, choose Define Styles… from the Format menu, and click on the name *Normal* to select it. Then, open the Character dialog box and choose Times from the list of fonts. Click OK to close the dialog box. Next, drag the first-line indent marker to the $^1/_4$-inch position on the ruler. Finally, click Define in the Define Styles dialog box to lock in these changes, and click Cancel to close the dialog box. Figure 9-20 shows how the screen from Figure 9-5 will appear after you have modified the *Normal* style as we have described. Notice that the heading 3 text from the outline and all the body text now appear in Times. In addition, each of the headings has been indented $^1/_4$ inch.

FIGURE 9-20

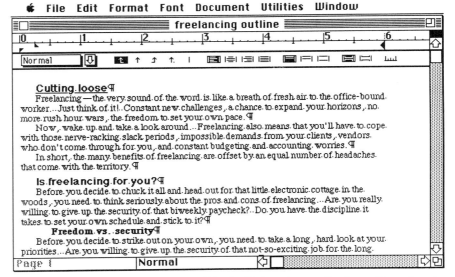

When you modify the Normal *style, Word will also change the formatting of each heading style based on* Normal.

Once you've modified the *Normal* style, you can make additional changes to the instructions for each of the *heading* styles. Continuing with our example, suppose you would like the heading 1 entries to appear in 18-point bold, the heading 2 entries to appear in 14-point bold, and the heading 3 entries to appear in 12-point Helvetica italic with no boldfacing and no indents. You also want to remove the $^1/_4$-inch indent from the heading 1 and heading 2 entries, and display the heading 1 entries without underlining.

To modify each style, you would follow the standard procedure described in Chapter 8. Click on one of the headings that belong to the level you want to format, then choose Define Styles... from the Format menu. In the Define Styles dialog box, click on the name of the style that you want to modify, then select the character and paragraph formats for this heading level. When you click OK, Apply, or Define in the Define Styles dialog box, Word will apply the specified formats to all the headings in your document that carry that level style. Figure 9-21 shows the first few headings in our sample document after we modified the *heading* styles.

FIGURE 9-21

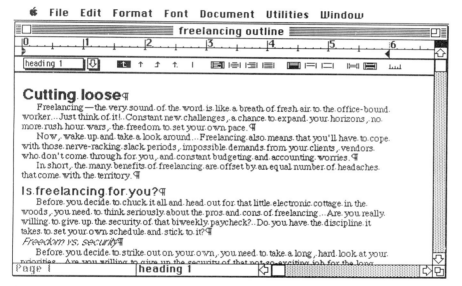

After you modify the instructions for each heading level, Word applies those new formatting instructions to your document.

By the way, if you decide you don't want all of your headings to appear in your finished document, just change the style definition for that heading level to include the Hidden character format. If you turn off Show Hidden Text in the Preferences dialog box, Word will hide all the headings at that level in both your document and your outline windows. However, in the outline window, Word will display an outline selection icon and a ¶ marker at each hidden heading.

As you're changing the formatting instructions for each *heading* style, you may want to change the Based On style as well. Instead of using *Normal* as the Based On style for each of the *heading* styles, you might want to base each *heading* style on the next highest *heading* style. Specifically, the *heading 3* style could be based on *heading 2*, which could be based on *heading 1*, which could be based on *Normal*. That way, when you make format changes to the *heading 1* style—new indention settings, for example—those changes will affect all subheadings.

Also, notice that Word uses the Next Style specification *Normal* for all the *heading* styles. As you saw earlier, when you click at the end of a heading paragraph in your document window and press the Return key to begin a new paragraph, Word assumes you want that text to appear in the *Normal* style. If you want to use a special format for the text below your headings, you can change the Next Style setting.

For example, you might create a style called *First ¶* to format the first paragraph after each heading. Then, you could use the style name *First ¶* in the Next Style edit bar for each *heading* style. Word will treat your *First ¶* paragraphs like standard body text when you return to the outline window. In fact, any text that does not carry the *heading 1* through *heading 9* style names will be treated as body text in the outline window.

As you already know, while you're viewing the document in the outline window, you can change the level of any subheading by placing the insertion point marker on that subheading and clicking the ➡ or ⬅ icon. Word will, of course, change the indention and heading number of the text in the outline window. In addition, when you switch to the document view, you'll see that Word has reformatted that text by applying a different style.

For example, suppose you decide to change the subheading *Freedom vs. security* in Figure 9-18 from a heading 3 entry to a heading 2 entry. In the outline window, you would place your insertion point marker anywhere on this subheading and click the ⬅ icon once. When you switch back to the document window, you will see that this subheading is now formatted with the *heading 2* style instead of the *heading 3* style.

You can also change the level of any heading in the document window with the Define Styles... or Styles... command. When you return to the outline window, your heading will be demoted or promoted to the appropriate level.

PRINTING THE OUTLINE

To print your document outline, just activate the outline window and issue the Print... command as usual. You can print the entire outline or collapse it to print only certain levels. Word will print the outline exactly as it appears in the outline window (as *Normal* text), with one exception: If the first line of any body text paragraphs are visible in your outline window, Word will print those paragraphs in their entirety.

Even though it ignores any character or paragraph formats you may have assigned to the text in your document window, Word does recognize your Document and Section dialog box settings when you print the outline. Any headers, footers, section breaks, or manual page breaks you may have created will also be included in your printed outline.

ADVANCED DOCUMENT DESIGN 10

In Chapter 5, we explained the basics of formatting documents in Word. We showed you how to determine the layout of your document pages, format paragraphs, and apply such character formatting as fonts, type sizes, underlining, and italics. In this chapter, we'll cover Word's more complex formatting features. We'll begin by looking at multisection documents and show you how to use the options in the Section dialog box. Then, we'll show you how to set up different right and left page layouts, or "mirror margins." Next, we'll look at multicolumn layouts and explain how to create snaking or newspaper-style columns.

After this, we'll discuss two important new features in Word 4: tables and the Position... command. The table feature allows you to create sophisticated tabular layouts and side-by-side text. With the new Position... command, you can place a block of text or a graphic anywhere on a page and flow other text around it. Finally, we'll wrap up the chapter with a discussion of Word's special capabilities for creating long documents by linking two or more shorter documents.

MULTISECTION DOCUMENTS

When you create a long or complex document, you may need to break that document into two or more sections. Dividing a document into sections allows you to control certain elements of the document that Word would normally handle automatically. For example, in a multisection document, you can create a separate header and footer for each section instead of using the same header or footer on each page. You also can number the pages of each section independently, which allows you to use a different numbering scheme on each chapter or section of a long document.

Although multiple sections are useful in longer documents, there are times when you'll need to break a shorter document into sections as well. For example, if you want to vary the number of columns from one part of a document to another—or use a varying number of columns on a single page—you'll need to divide the document into different sections. We'll show you exactly how to handle multi-column formatting a little later in this chapter. For now, however, let's consider how to create multiple sections in a document.

Dividing a Document into Sections

Every new document that you begin in Word initially consists of only one section. To create a new section, place the insertion point marker where you want that section to begin and press ⌘-Enter. Word will mark the section break on your screen with a double dotted line, as shown in Figure 10-1. Like page-break markers, section-break markers will not appear in a printed document.

FIGURE 10-1

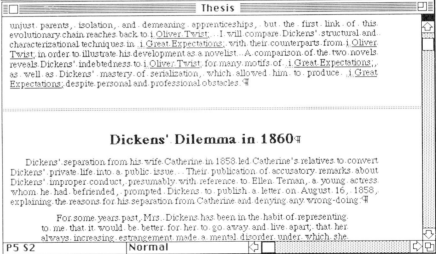

Section breaks are marked on your screen by a double dotted line.

Once you've divided a document into two or more sections, Word will replace the page number in the status box at the lower-left corner of the screen with a page number and a section number. For instance, notice that the status box in Figure 10-1 now displays *P5 S2*. This tells you that the lines displayed at the top of the screen are in the second section of this document and will appear on the fifth page of the printed document.

As we mentioned in Chapter 5, you can format a Word document on four levels: the overall document level, the section level, the paragraph level, and the character level. The various options for section-level formatting are found in the Section dialog box, which is shown in Figure 10-2. To open this dialog box, just choose Section... from the Format menu.

The Section Dialog Box

FIGURE 10-2

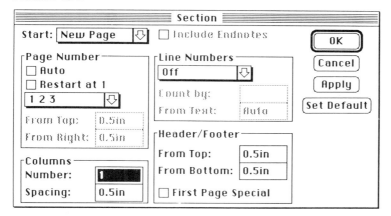

The Section dialog box allows you to vary certain characteristics of your document from one section to another.

Like the Paragraph and Character dialog boxes, the Section dialog box displays the settings for the current section. (The dialog box in Figure 10-2 displays Word's default Section settings.) If you select text in two or more sections before you open the Section dialog box, all of the edit bars will appear blank and the check box options will be grayed.

When you enter settings and choose options in the Section dialog box, your selections will apply to the section in which the insertion point marker is currently located (or to all sections in which you've selected text). If you select a section-break marker before opening the Section dialog box, the settings that you select in the dialog box will apply to all the text preceding the selected section-break marker, up to the next section-break marker or to the beginning of the document if there is no preceding section. If you have not inserted any section breaks in your document, Word will treat the entire document as one section and will apply your Section dialog box settings to the entire file.

As you can see, the Section dialog box is divided into six parts: Start, Page Number, Columns, Include Endnotes, Line Numbers, and Header/Footer. We've already considered some of these settings in Chapter 7. For now, we are interested in the list of Start options, the Page Number settings, and the Header/Footer settings.

Later in this chapter, we'll look at the Columns settings, which you use to create snaking columns in a document. In our discussion of footnotes in Chapter 11, we'll explain the Include Endnotes option and, in Chapter 13, we'll show you how to use the Line Numbers settings to number the lines of a document.

Specifying the Section Start

When you click on the dropdown list of Start options in the Section dialog box, you'll see the options shown in Figure 10-3. These options let you specify where you want a section to begin—that is, whether you want the first paragraph in a section to appear at the top of the next column or page, or whether you want to start the section on an odd or even page.

FIGURE 10-3

Word offers five Start options in the Section dialog box.

As shown in Figure 10-2, Word's default Start choice is New Page. This means that, when you print your document, the first paragraph after the section break will appear at the top of a new page. As a result, part of the previous page may be left blank. When you use the New Page option, Word will not show a page break on the screen in addition to the section-break marker.

If you want to start a new section without beginning a new page, choose the No Break option. As you'll see a little later in this chapter, the No Break option is the key to creating different columnar layouts on the same page.

The New Column option causes a section to begin at the top of a column. Of course, you'll use this option only when your document has a multicolumn layout.

The Even Page and Odd Page options are generally used in conjunction with the Mirror Even/Odd Margins and Gutter settings in the Document dialog box. These Start options will cause a section to begin on the next even-numbered or odd-numbered page, sometimes forcing a blank page to appear in your document. For example, in books, it's common practice to begin each chapter on an odd page. If you are creating a technical publication that contains charts and descriptions, you may want to ensure that all the charts appear on even pages while their corresponding descriptions appear on odd pages. Although you do not have to use Mirror Even/

Odd Margins or a Gutter setting in order to select the Even Page or Odd Page option, you will often find these options useful when the document has different right and left page layouts. (We'll discuss right and left page layouts in more detail later in this chapter.)

Changing Page Numbers from One Section to Another

In Chapter 7, we explained how to number the pages of a document either by inserting a page number in a header or footer or by activating the Auto check box in the Section dialog box. We also introduced the five numbering schemes that are available in Word and explained how you can use the From Top and From Right edit bars to position page numbers. Because the Page Number settings are located in the Section dialog box, you can control page numbering on a section-by-section basis. In other words, you can do such things as number the pages in each section separately or use a different numbering scheme in different sections.

For example, to change the position of page numbers from one section to another, just click on each section in turn, open the Section dialog box, and specify the From Top and From Right settings you want to use for that section.

Like the position of your page numbers, the numbering scheme that you use can change from one section to another. For instance, it's common to use lowercase Roman numerals to number the front matter pages (preface, table of contents, and so forth) of a long publication and Arabic numerals to number the pages of the main body of the document. To change numbering schemes, just click on each section in turn, open the Section dialog box, and select the type of numbering you want to use from the dropdown list.

If you want the pages of each section to be numbered separately, click on each section in turn and then activate the Restart at 1 option. Of course, the first page of each section may not be numbered 1. If you have chosen a numbering scheme other than the default Arabic numerals, Word will begin numbering the pages of each section with *I*, *i*, *A*, or *a*.

When you change numbering schemes in a document section, you'll almost certainly want to apply the Restart at 1 option to that section. For example, suppose you have used the lowercase Roman setting (*i, ii, iii, iv*…) to number the front matter of the document. This section occupies ten pages, which are numbered *i* to *x*. When you reach the first chapter of the document, you start a new section and apply the Arabic numbering option (*1, 2, 3*…). If you don't choose the Restart at 1 option for this new section, your page numbers will start at 11 rather than at 1.

If you activate the Restart at 1 option, Word will change the page numbers in the status box to reflect this. For example, suppose you are working with a ten-page document that you have divided into two sections. The first section occupies pages 1 through 4 and the second section occupies pages 5 through 10. If you use the Restart at 1 option in the second section, Word will number those pages 1 through 6. As you scroll through this part of the document, the status box will display *P1 S2, P2 S2*, and so forth.

Specifying a range for printing

In Chapter 7, we introduced the Print dialog box and explained how you can use the Pages (or Page Range) From and To settings to print a specified range of pages. As we mentioned, specifying a range of pages in a multisection document can get pretty complex. To simplify the task, Word has added Section Range From and To settings to the Print dialog boxes for the LaserWriter and ImageWriter, as shown in Figures 10-4 and 10-5. If your document contains only one section, you won't see edit bars next to the Section Range From and To settings; you will see only the number *1* as both the From and To setting.

FIGURE 10-4

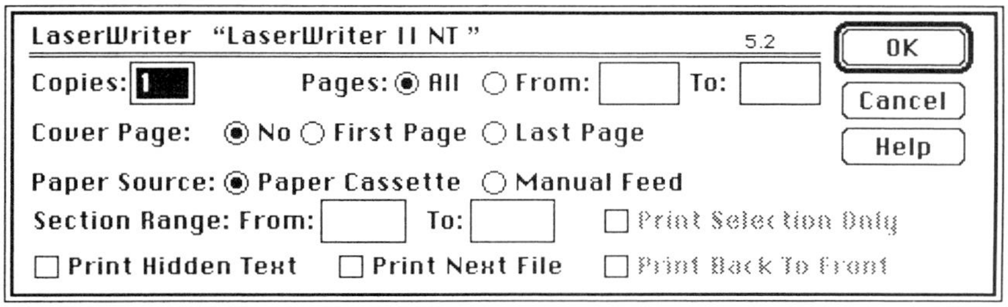

You can print a range of sections by entering section numbers in the Section Range From and To edit bars of the Print dialog box.

FIGURE 10-5

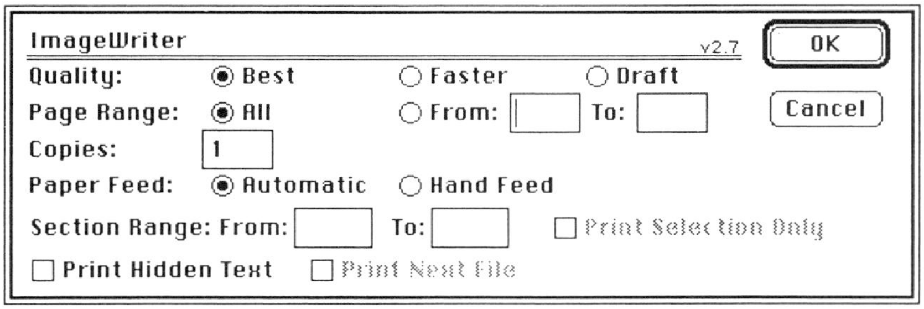

The Print dialog box for the ImageWriter printer also contains Section Range settings.

When you specify Section Range From and To settings without making any entries in the Pages (or Page Range) From and To edit bars, Word will print the sections you specify in their entirety. Suppose you are working in a document that contains five sections. When you issue the Print... command, you leave the Pages (or Page Range) From and To edit bars blank, and you enter 2 in the Section Range From edit bar and 4 in the Section Range To edit bar. When you click OK, Word will print all the pages from sections 2, 3, and 4 of your five-section document.

To print one section in its entirety, just enter the same section number in both the Section Range From and Section Range To edit bars and leave the Pages From and To edit bars blank.

By combining the Section Range From and To settings with the Pages From and To settings, you can print partial sections. Generally, you'll use this kind of combination only when you have numbered the pages of each section separately.

If the pages of a multisection document are numbered sequentially, you can print any part of that document simply by specifying the correct From and To pages; there's no need to specify Section Range settings as well. For example, suppose you have a 20-page document that's divided into two sections, as shown in Table 10-1. You've numbered the pages sequentially, with pages 1 through 12 in the first section and pages 13 through 20 in the second section.

TABLE 10-1

Section Number	Page Numbers
1	1 to 12
2	13 to 20

This table shows the page numbering scheme in a simple two-section document.

If you want to print pages 8 through 15 of this document, enter 8 as your Pages From setting and 15 as your Pages To setting. If you want, you also can enter 1 in the Section Range From edit bar and 2 in the Section Range To edit bar, but this isn't necessary. By the way, if your Section Range settings are not compatible with your Pages (or Page Range) settings, Word may not be able to execute the Print... command. For example, suppose you enter 15 as the Pages From setting and 18 as the Pages To setting. (Both of these pages are in the second section of the document.) If you also enter 1 in both the Section Range From and Section Range To edit bars, Word will not print anything.

When you use separate page numbering for different sections of a document, specifying a print range is not so simple. That's when you may need to use the Pages From and To settings in combination with the Section Range From and To settings.

For example, suppose you have numbered the pages of a two-section document separately, with the pages of section 1 numbered 1 through 12, and the pages of section 2 numbered 1 through 8. To print the last four pages of section 1 and the first two pages of section 2, you would enter 9 in the Pages From edit bar and 2 in the Pages To edit bar. Then, you would enter 1 and 2 in the Section Range From and To edit bars, respectively.

Table 10-2 on the next page describes an even more complex document, consisting of five sections. Table 10-3 shows several combinations of settings you can use to print particular parts of this document.

TABLE 10-2

Section Number	Name	Numbered	Actual Page
1	Introduction	i to iv	1 to 4
2	Chapter 1	1 to 10	5 to 14
3	Chapter 2	11 to 16	25 to 30
4	Chapter 3	17 to 23	47 to 53
5	Appendix	A to H	54 to 61

This table shows a complex numbering scheme for a multisection document.

TABLE 10-3

To print...	Enter these settings...			
	Page Range		Section Range	
	From	To	From	To
Introduction only	blank	blank	1	1
Chapters only	blank	blank	2	4
Appendix only	blank	blank	5	5
Introduction & first five pages of Chapter 1	1	5	1	2
Chapter 2 & first two pages of Chapter 3	11	18	3	4
Last three pages of Chapter 3 & Appendix	21	8	4	5
First page of Introduction	1	1	blank	blank

This table shows some print ranges for the document described in Table 10-2.

The Go To...
command

When you want to go to a specific page in a multisection document, you can select the Go To... command from the Utilities menu and enter a value like *P2S5* in the Page Number edit bar. This will move the insertion point marker to the second page of the fifth document section. If the pages of your multisection document are numbered consecutively, you do not need to specify a section number. For example, suppose you are working in a three-section document in which the pages of the first section are numbered 1 through 12, the pages of the second section are numbered 13 through 20, and the pages of the third section are numbered 21 through 34. If you want to go to page 25, you would simply choose Go To... from the Utilities menu, enter 25 in the Page Number edit bar, and click OK or press Return. There's no need to specify a section number.

When you use the *PnSn* format to specify a page number in the Go To dialog box, you must use Arabic numerals, even if you've numbered the pages of one or more sections in your document with letters or Roman numerals. Word will not accept a value like *Pi S1* or *PA S5* in the Page Number edit bar.

Keep in mind that Word does not automatically repaginate your document when you issue the Go To... command. If you want to be sure that you are going to the correct page, remember to issue the Repaginate Now command before you issue the Go To... command.

Sectional Headers and Footers

In Chapter 7, we introduced headers and footers, showing you how to create them, how to position them on the page, how to format them, and how to create a special header or footer for the first page of a document. As we mentioned, when a document is divided into sections, you can vary the headers and footers from one section to another. In most cases, your section breaks will correspond to major document divisions, like chapters. However, you can change headers and footers at any location in a document by adding a section break.

When you divide a document into sections, each section will initially carry identical headers, footers, and Section dialog box settings. In addition, each header or footer will be linked to the headers and footers in subsequent sections of the document. Any changes you make to the header or footer in one section of a document will apply to all the headers or footers in subsequent sections.

To vary the text or format of a particular section's header or footer, just click anywhere in the section you want to work with, then select Open Header... or Open Footer... from the Document menu. Word will display the section number in the header or footer window title bar to let you know to which section your changes will apply. For example, the header window in Figure 10-6 carries the notation *(S4)*, indicating that it is the header for the fourth section of a document. After opening the header window, you can edit or format the text to suit your purposes.

FIGURE 10-6

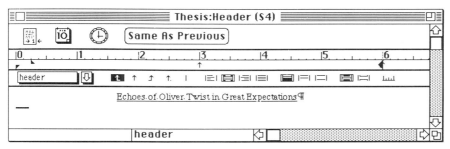

The title bar of a header window displays the section number of that header.

By the same token, to change the position or page numbering scheme for a particular header or footer, just click in the section you want to work with, issue the Section... command, and make your changes in the dialog box.

As we've mentioned, when you reformat or edit the contents of a header or footer window, Word will apply your changes to all successive headers or footers in the document. Any headers or footers that occur before the current section, however, will be unaffected. In addition, once you edit a header or footer, you break the link between it and any previous header or footer windows.

For example, suppose you have created a document that is divided into four sections. You enter the text *Chapter 1* in the header window for the first section. If you then open the header windows for the second, third, and fourth sections of this document, you'll see that they also contain the text *Chapter 1*. Now, suppose you click in the third section of the document, open the header window, and change the header text to read *Chapter 3*. The headers for both the third and fourth sections will now read *Chapter 3*. However, the headers for the first and second sections will still read *Chapter 1*. If you move back to the first section at this point and edit the header text for that section, your change will apply to the first and second sections only. The third and fourth sections will be unaffected by your changes since they are no longer linked to the previous sections' headers.

We mentioned earlier that you can change the Section dialog box settings for two or more sections of a document by highlighting all or part of the sections you want to work with before issuing the Section... command. Unfortunately, this technique does not work for changes that you make to the text or formats of headers and footers. If you select two or more sections of a document and issue an Open Header... or Open Footer... command, the header or footer window will display the header or footer for the first section only. Any changes that you make in this window will apply only to the first section in your selection. If the headers or footers in the sections where you have selected text are still linked, Word will carry your changes through to the other sections in your selection as well. However, if you have created different headers or footers for different sections of a document, you cannot use this technique to make a global change to all the headers and footers. You can, however, make global formatting changes to headers and footers by altering the definition of the *header* and *footer* styles. (See Chapter 8 for more on style sheets.)

Fortunately, if you want to change the From Top and From Bottom settings for the headers and footers in two or more sections, you can simply select text in those sections, open the Section dialog box, and make new entries in the From Top and From Bottom edit bars. Interestingly, if you change the From Top or From Bottom setting in the Section dialog box without selecting any text, your changes will apply only to the headers and footers in the current section, even if the headers and footers in successive sections are linked to the current section. If you want your header and footer positions to be consistent from one section to the next, you may want to select your entire document before you change the From Top and From Bottom settings.

If you want a header or footer to contain the same text and formats as the header or footer in the previous section of a document, you can click on the Same As Previous button that appears at the top of a header or footer window. Word will copy the header or footer text and formats from the previous section into the current window. In addition, Word will re-establish the link between the current header or footer and the previous section's header or footer. Once the link is re-established, you can change the contents of the first header or footer window, and Word will automatically update the second header or footer window to reflect those changes.

The Same As Previous button

If the contents of the header or footer window are already identical to the previous section's header or footer, the Same As Previous button will be dimmed. However, if the current header or footer text differs from the header or footer for the previous section, this button will appear in black.

In Chapter 7, we explained how you can use the First Page Special option in the Section dialog box to create a unique header and/or footer on the first page of a document. You also can use this option to eliminate the header or footer altogether from the first page. Since this option is part of the Section dialog box, you've probably guessed that it can be used to change the header or footer on the first page of each section as well.

The First Page Special option

After activating the First Page Special option, all of the first-page header and footer windows in the document will initially be blank and will be linked. Thus, you can create the same header or footer on the first page of each section by clicking on the first section of the document, choosing Open First Header... or Open First Footer... from the Document menu, and then entering and formatting the header or footer text.

As with regular headers and footers, if you change the text or formatting in one of the first-page header or footer windows, you'll break the link between that header or footer and the first-page headers or footers for previous sections in the document. You can re-establish the link by clicking on the Same As Previous button.

To merge two adjacent document sections, just delete the section-break marker between those sections. You can do this by clicking once in the selection bar to highlight the section-break marker, then pressing the Backspace key. If the two sections have different Section dialog box settings, the new, merged section will display the settings of the second section. (This is similar to what happens when you merge two paragraphs by deleting the ¶ marker at the end of the first one. The merged paragraph will display the paragraph format settings of the second paragraph, whose ¶ marker was not deleted.)

Merging Two Document Sections

RIGHT AND LEFT PAGES

If you are creating a document that you plan to print on both sides of each sheet of paper and bind, you'll probably want to take advantage of Word's ability to create different even and odd (or right and left) page layouts. This type of page layout is sometimes referred to as "facing pages" or "mirror margins," since the left and right margins of facing pages will mirror each other.

There are a couple of ways you can go about creating a document with different formats on right and left pages. First, you can set up "inside" and "outside" margins. In other words, instead of specifying a left and right margin measurement, you specify an inside margin—or the margin that will appear on the binding edge of each sheet of paper—and an outside margin, which is the margin that appears opposite the binding edge. On odd-numbered pages, the left side of the page is considered the binding edge, where the inside margin will appear. On even-numbered pages, the right side of the page is considered the inside margin and the binding edge. Generally, you will make your inside margin larger than your outside margin to allow room for binding.

Another approach to creating right and left page layouts is to use standard right and left margin settings, but add a page gutter to allow room for binding. This gutter will always be added to the binding edge of a page. Again, on odd-numbered pages, the gutter will appear on the left edge, and on even-numbered pages, it will appear on the right edge.

Finally, Word allows you to specify both inside/outside margins and a page gutter. In this situation, the space on the binding edge of each page consists of the inside margin measurement plus the page gutter.

The key to setting up different right and left page layouts is the Document dialog box. After you choose Document… from the Format menu, you'll see three settings in the dialog box that apply specifically to this type of layout: the Mirror Even/Odd Margins check box, the Even/Odd Headers check box, and the Gutter edit bar.

You use the Mirror Even/Odd Margins option when you want to establish inside and outside margins on your document pages. After you select this option, Word will change the labels on the Left and Right margin edit bars to read *Inside* and *Outside*.

For example, suppose you want to create a document with margins that are $1\frac{1}{4}$ inches wide, and you want to allow an additional $\frac{1}{2}$ inch for binding. You could begin by activating the Mirror Even/Odd Margins setting in the Document dialog box. Then, you would specify an Inside setting of 1.75 and an Outside setting of 1.25. Figure 10-7 shows the Document dialog box with these settings.

When you print this document, page 1 will have a left margin that is $1\frac{3}{4}$ inches wide and a right margin that is $1\frac{1}{4}$ inches wide. On page 2, these margins will be reversed: The left margin will be $1\frac{1}{4}$ inches wide, while the right margin will be $1\frac{3}{4}$ inches wide.

FIGURE 10-7

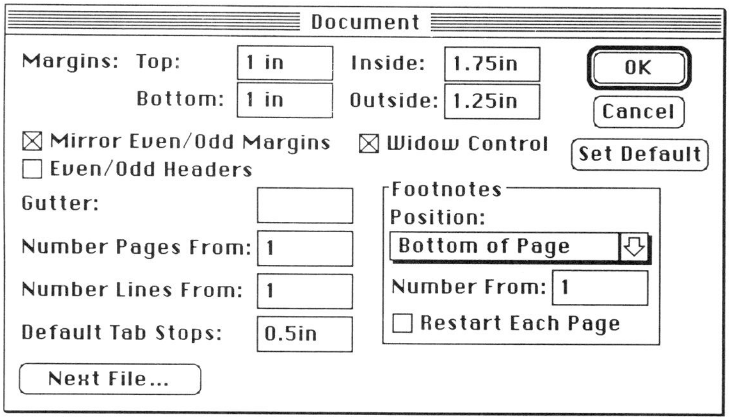

When you activate the Mirror Even/Odd Margins option, the Left
and Right edit bars will be labeled Inside and Outside.

Another way to set up this same page layout is to specify a gutter space in the Gutter edit bar of the Document dialog box. Keep in mind that you do not need to activate Mirror Even/Odd Margins in order to specify a gutter. You could use Word's default Left and Right margin settings of 1.25 and then enter .5 in the Gutter edit bar. When you print this document, Word will add the $1/_2$ inch of gutter space to the left edge of all odd-numbered pages and add it to the right edge of all even-numbered pages.

One advantage of using a Gutter setting is that Word will display the gutter as a shaded area in the Print Preview window. For example, Figure 10-8 on the next page shows the Print Preview window for a document that has the margin and gutter measurements we just described. We've clicked on the margins icon on the preview screen to show the boundaries of the margins. Notice that, unlike the margins, the gutter is not marked by a boundary line. Thus, you cannot adjust the gutter width by dragging it in the Print Preview window as you can the margins.

When you switch to the page view of a document, you won't see the gutter as a shaded area. However, the gutter will increase the amount of white space between your text and the edge of the page as you view a document in page view.

As we've mentioned, you can combine inside and outside margins with a page gutter. In this situation, the binding edge of each page will have white space that is equal to the Inside margin setting plus the Gutter setting. For example, suppose you have activated the Mirror Even/Odd Margins setting in the Document dialog box. You've specified an Inside margin setting of 1.25, an Outside margin setting of 1.5, and a Gutter setting of .75. When you print this document, Word will allow a total of two inches of white space (the Inside margin measurement plus the Gutter measurement) on the binding edge of each page.

FIGURE 10-8

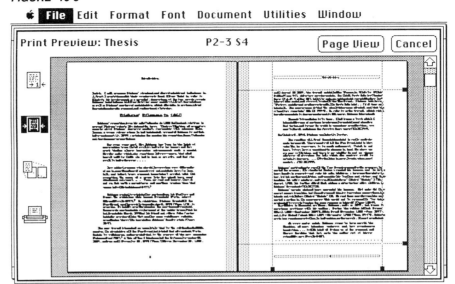

In the Print Preview window, Word displays the page gutter as a shaded area.

**Using the
Ruler with
Right and
Left Pages**

As you might expect, when you use inside and outside margins or a page gutter, Word will adjust the appearance of the ruler on your screen. As we explained in Chapter 5, when you display the ruler in the normal scale, it shows the width of the current text column. In a single-column layout, the width of the text column is the same as the width of the text area on the page. The left edge of a document's text area always begins at the zero point on the ruler, while the right edge of the text area is marked by a dotted vertical line. To compute the width of the text area, Word subtracts the Left and Right margin settings from the width of your paper.

When you use inside and outside margins, Word computes the width of the text area by subtracting the Inside and Outside margin settings from the width of your paper, like this:

Width of paper - Inside margin - Outside margin = Width of text area

If you've specified a page gutter, Word will subtract the Gutter setting as well as your margin settings to obtain the width of the text area, like this:

Width of paper - Left margin - Right margin - Gutter = Width of text area

or:

Width of paper - Inside margin - Outside margin - Gutter = Width of text area

For example, suppose you are using Word's default Left and Right margin settings of 1.25. As you know, this will create a text area that is 6 inches wide (assuming that you're using paper that is $8^1/_2$ inches wide). Now, let's suppose you decide to specify a Gutter setting of .5 inches. This will reduce the width of your text area by $^1/_2$ inch, so the dotted vertical line marking the right edge of your text will move to the $5^1/_2$-inch point on the ruler.

When you turn on the page view and use the page scale on the ruler, Word will account for your Inside and Outside margin settings along with your Gutter setting in determining the placement of the ruler's margin markers. As you scroll from an odd page to an even page, Word will shift the margin markers accordingly. For example, suppose you've specified an Inside margin setting of 1.75 and an Outside margin setting of .75. When you are viewing an odd page on the screen with the ruler displaying the page scale, the margin marker on the left side of the ruler will appear at the $1^3/_4$-inch position. The margin marker on the right side of the ruler will appear at the $7^3/_4$-inch position. When you scroll to an even page, Word will display the margin marker on the left side of the ruler at the $^3/_4$-inch position. The margin marker on the right side of the ruler will move to the $6^3/_4$-inch position. By the way, Word does not adjust the margin markers if you are using the normal galley view (instead of the page view) to look at your document.

Right and Left Headers and Footers

As we've seen, the Document dialog box contains a check box labeled Even/Odd Headers. This setting allows you to vary the content and format of your headers and footers between right and left pages. (Although the option name does not include footers, it allows you to create even/odd footers as well.) As you'll see, this option also allows you to vary the position of automatic page numbers. For example, in many books, you see the book title at the top of even pages and the chapter title at the top of odd pages. Even when the text of a header or footer is the same on both right and left pages, it's common to vary the position of certain elements. For example, in a magazine, you might see page numbers on the outside edge, the name of the publication in the center, and the date on the inside edge of each page.

The Even/Odd Headers option can be activated independently of the Mirror Even/Odd Margins and Gutter settings. This means that you can vary your headers and footers between the right and left pages of your document, even if you are not using inside and outside margins or a page gutter.

Once you activate the Even/Odd Headers option, Word will replace the Open Header... and Open Footer... commands on the Document menu with the commands Open Even Header..., Open Odd Header..., Open Even Footer..., and Open Odd Footer.... As you might expect, you use these four windows to set up the headers and footers on your right and left pages.

For example, Figures 10-9 and 10-10 show a pair of even and odd header windows that we used to create the headers for a book called *Fear and Loathing on the Remodeling Trail.* Notice that we placed a page number on the left side of the even header window and used a right-aligned tab at the 6-inch mark to align the book title with the right margin. In the odd header window, we placed the chapter title, "Dream Kitchen or Nightmare?," on the left and used a right-aligned tab at the 6-inch mark to align the odd page numbers with the right margin. Figure 10-11 shows how these headers will appear when the document is printed.

FIGURE 10-9

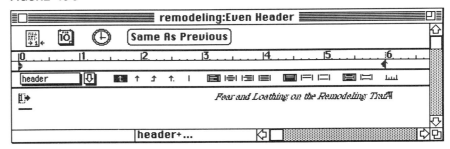

This header is designed for the even pages of a book.

FIGURE 10-10

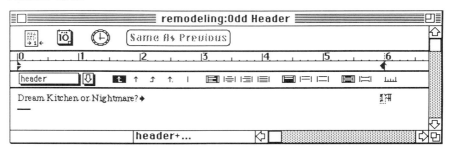

This header is designed for odd pages.

FIGURE 10-11

When we print the document, the page numbers are aligned with the outside edge of each page, while the book and chapter titles are aligned with the inside margins.

In our discussion of multisection documents, we described how the headers and footers for each section are initially linked to the headers and footers of subsequent sections. When you are using Even/Odd Headers with a multisection document, the situation becomes a bit more complex. Basically, the headers and footers for the first section "set the tone" for the corresponding headers and footers in subsequent sections.

For example, let's assume that you are working with a single-section document with no Even/Odd Headers or First Page Special options. You issue the Open Header... command and enter the text *Title* in the header window. Now, suppose you open the Document dialog box and click the Even/Odd Headers option. Word will use the text *Title* in both the odd header window and the even header window. However, if you issue the Section... command and choose the First Page Special option, the header window for the first page will initially be blank.

Now, suppose you decide to split your document into three sections. Initially, the odd and even header windows in the second and third sections will contain the same text that appears in the odd and even header windows for the first section (*Title*). However, the first-page headers in these sections will be blank.

Suppose you now go back to the first section of your document, open the even header window and change the text to read *Chapter 1*. Next, you open the first-page header window and enter the text *First Page*. If you then click in the second section of your document and open the even and first-page header windows, you'll see that they have "inherited" the contents of the corresponding header windows in the first section. The even header window in the second section will contain the text *Chapter 1*, and the first-page header window will contain the text *First Page*. If you click in the third section and open the even and first-page header windows, you'll see that they also have "inherited" the contents of the header windows in the first section.

Now, suppose you change the text in the even header window in the second section of your document to read *Chapter 2*. This will break the link between that header and the even header of the first section. However, the even header of the third section will still be linked to the even header of the second section. Thus, the even header of the third section will now read *Chapter 2*. Any further changes you make to the text of the even header for the second section will carry over to the even header for the third section.

To re-establish the link between the even header for the second section and the even header for the first section, you must click the Same As Previous button in the even header window for the second section. When you do this, Word will change the text in this window to read *Chapter 1* once more. The text in the even header window for the third section will also be changed to *Chapter 1*.

The rules are the same for first-page headers and footers. When you change a first-page header in a document section, that header will no longer be linked to the previous section's first-page header—this is just what you would expect. In addition, Word will automatically change the first-page headers in any subsequent

Linking right and left headers and footers

sections so that they are identical to the header you changed. Going back to our example, suppose you are working in a three-section document. You created the text *First Page* in the first-page header window of the first section, and this text was "inherited" by the first-page header windows of the second and third sections. Now, suppose you open the first-page header window in the second section and change the text to read *Another First Page*. If you then click on the third section of the document and open the first-page header window, you'll see that it also reads *Another First Page*. As you might expect, this header window is still linked to the first-page header window for the second section of the document. Therefore, it displays identical text.

If, at any time, you deselect the Even/Odd Headers option, Word will use the odd header text in each section of your document as the header text for both the even and odd pages in that section. Similarly, if you deselect the First Page Special option, Word will treat the first page of a section just like any other even or odd page. However, if you reselect the First Page Special or Even/Odd Headers options, Word will remember the original text and formats for those headers.

Page Numbers

If you use the Auto Page Number option in the Section dialog box and you've activated Even/Odd Headers, Word will adjust the position of each page number to reflect whether it appears on a right or left page. (You do not need to create a header or footer in order for Word to adjust the positions of the page numbers.) When the page number appears on a right (odd-numbered) page, it will be positioned exactly as you've specified in the From Top and From Right edit bars of the Section dialog box, and the number will be aligned flush left with the From Right position. On left (even-numbered) pages, the position of the page number will be adjusted as though the From Right setting were now a From Left setting. The page number will appear flush right at this position.

For example, suppose you have specified a From Top setting of .75 and a From Right setting of .5. On odd-numbered pages, the page number will be printed flush left at a position that is $1/_2$ inch from the right edge of the paper, and on even-numbered pages, it will be printed flush right with a position that is $1/_2$ inch from the left edge of the paper. By making this kind of adjustment, Word ensures that the page numbers in this document will always appear on the outside edge of the page.

Word will adjust the position of automatic page numbers only if you have activated Even/Odd Headers. If you have not activated this option, but have activated Mirror Even/Odd Margins or used a Gutter setting to create right and left page layouts, Word will not reverse the horizontal position of the page numbers on odd and even pages.

Bar Borders

As you may recall from Chapter 5, one of Word's standard paragraph border options is Outside Bar. When you use Mirror Even/Odd Margins with this type of border, Word will always print the Outside Bar border on the outside edge of the paragraph—that is, on the side opposite the binding edge of the page. On right (odd-numbered) pages, the bar border will appear on the right side of the paragraph and on left (even-numbered) pages, Word will print the bar border on the left side of the paragraph. Figure 10-12 shows two printed pages in which we've used Mirror Even/Odd Margins and an Outside Bar border.

FIGURE 10-12

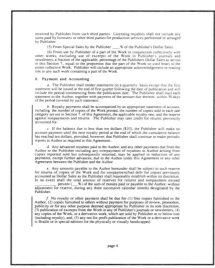 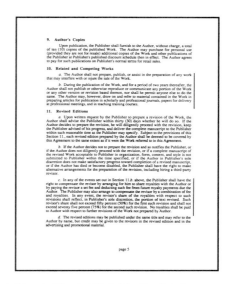

When you use a right and left page layout, Word will print Outside Bar borders on the side opposite the binding edge of the page.

Unfortunately, when you view your document on the screen, the bar border will always appear in the same position (on the left side of the paragraph) unless you're viewing your document in the Print Preview window. Even in the page view mode, Word will not switch the bar position for odd pages.

To create a bar border that always appears on the same side of the paragraph, regardless of whether that paragraph appears on an even or an odd page, select the Custom border type instead of the Outside Bar type in the Paragraph Borders dialog box. Then, in the border diagram, click between the border guides on the side where you want the bar to appear. For example, suppose you want to format several paragraphs with a bar border on the left side of the paragraph. After clicking on or selecting some text in a paragraph you want to format, open the Paragraph Borders dialog box. Select the type of line you want to use, then select the Custom border type. In the border diagram, click between the top and bottom border guides on the left side of the diagram. At this point, the dialog box should look like Figure 10-13.

FIGURE 10-13

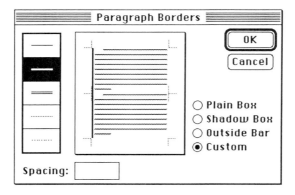

To make sure a bar bor-
der always appears on
the same side of a para-
graph, select the Custom
border type and click in
the border diagram to
indicate where the
border should appear.

Now, when you print this document, the border will always appear on the left side of the paragraph, even if that side is adjacent to the "inside" edge of the page.

MULTICOLUMN FORMATTING

Most of the page designs you've seen in this book have consisted of a single column of text that extends from the left margin to the right margin of the printed page. Of course, there are a lot of publications—newspapers and journals being the most obvious examples—that contain two or more columns of text on each page.

Word offers two types of multicolumn formats: snaking columns and tabular or side-by-side columns. The text in snaking columns, as shown in Figure 10-14, automatically wraps or "snakes" from the bottom of one column to the top of the next. Tabular or side-by-side formatting, on the other hand, can be used to place individual paragraphs side by side on the page. For example, in Figure 10-15 on page 402, we've used Word's table feature to place headings alongside our body text.

By the way, if you used Word 3, you're probably familiar with the side-by-side paragraph formatting feature. In Word 4, the Side-by-Side option is no longer available in the Paragraph dialog box. Instead, you create side-by-side formatting by building a table. If you're more comfortable with the "old" way of setting up side-by-side paragraphs, you can still do so by adding the Side by Side command to your Format menu. We'll show you how to do this when we discuss the table feature later in this chapter.

In this section, we'll show you how to set up snaking columns. Then, we'll discuss the new table feature in Word 4. As you'll see, tables are useful for many kinds of formatting, not just side-by-side paragraphs.

FIGURE 10-14

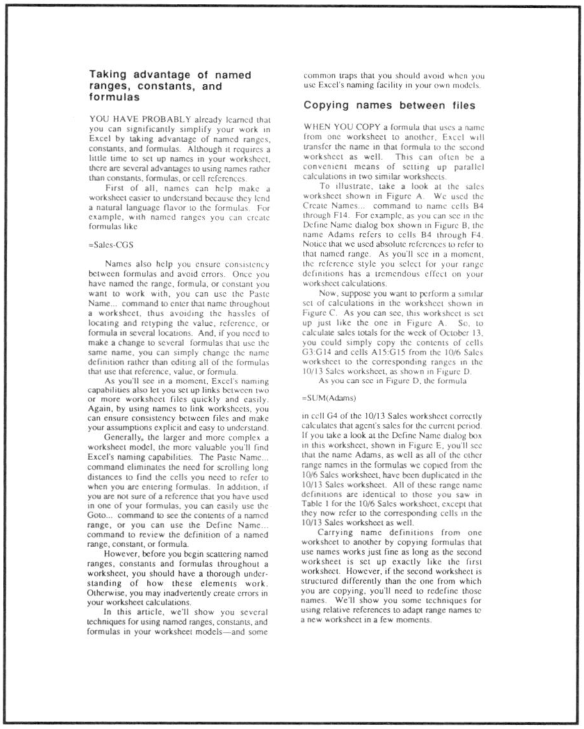

Taking advantage of named ranges, constants, and formulas

YOU HAVE PROBABLY already learned that you can significantly simplify your work in Excel by taking advantage of named ranges, constants, and formulas. Although it requires a little time to set up names in your worksheet, there are several advantages to using names rather than constants, formulas, or cell references.

First of all, names can help make a worksheet easier to understand because they lend a natural language flavor to the formulas. For example, with named ranges you can create formulas like

=Sales-CGS

Names also help you ensure consistency between formulas and avoid errors. Once you have named the range, formula, or constant you want to work with, you can use the Paste Name... command to enter that name throughout a worksheet, thus avoiding the hassles of locating and retyping the value, reference, or formula in several locations. And, if you need to make a change to several formulas that use the same name, you can simply change the name definition rather than editing all of the formulas that use that reference, value, or formula.

As you'll see in a moment, Excel's naming capabilities also let you set up links between two or more worksheet files quickly and easily. Again, by using names to link worksheets, you can ensure consistency between files and make your assumptions explicit and easy to understand.

Generally, the larger and more complex a worksheet model, the more valuable you'll find Excel's naming capabilities. The Paste Name... command eliminates the need for scrolling long distances to find the cells you need to refer to when you are entering formulas. In addition, if you are not sure of a reference that you have used in one of your formulas, you can easily use the Goto... command to see the contents of a named range, or you can use the Define Name... command to review the definition of a named range, constant, or formula.

However, before you begin scattering named ranges, constants and formulas throughout a worksheet, you should have a thorough understanding of how these elements work. Otherwise, you may inadvertently create errors in your worksheet calculations.

In this article, we'll show you several techniques for using named ranges, constants, and formulas in your worksheet models—and some common traps that you should avoid when you use Excel's naming facility in your own models.

Copying names between files

WHEN YOU COPY a formula that uses a name from one worksheet to another, Excel will transfer the name in that formula to the second worksheet as well. This can often be a convenient means of setting up parallel calculations in two similar worksheets.

To illustrate, take a look at the sales worksheet shown in Figure A. We used the Create Names... command to name cells B4 through F14. For example, as you can see in the Define Name dialog box shown in Figure B, the name Adams refers to cells B4 through F4. Notice that we used absolute references to refer to that named range. As you'll see in a moment, the reference style you select for your range definitions has a tremendous effect on your worksheet calculations.

Now, suppose you want to perform a similar set of calculations in the worksheet shown in Figure C. As you can see, this worksheet is set up just like the one in Figure A. So, to calculate sales totals for the week of October 13, you could simply copy the contents of cells G3:G14 and cells A15:G15 from the 10/6 Sales worksheet to the corresponding ranges in the 10/13 Sales worksheet, as shown in Figure D.

As you can see in Figure D, the formula

=SUM(Adams)

in cell G4 of the 10/13 Sales worksheet correctly calculates that agent's sales for the current period. If you take a look at the Define Name dialog box in this worksheet, shown in Figure E, you'll see that the name Adams, as well as all of the other range names in the formulas we copied from the 10/6 Sales worksheet, have been duplicated in the 10/13 Sales worksheet. All of these range name definitions are identical to those you saw in Table 1 for the 10/6 Sales worksheet, except that they now refer to the corresponding cells in the 10/13 Sales worksheet as well.

Carrying name definitions from one worksheet to another by copying formulas that use names works just fine as long as the second worksheet is set up exactly like the first worksheet. However, if the second worksheet is structured differently than the one from which you are copying, you'll need to redefine those names. We'll show you some techniques for using relative references to adapt range names to a new worksheet in a few moments.

The text in snaking columns wraps or "snakes" from the bottom of one column to the top of the next.

Snaking Columns

Creating snaking columns—the kind you commonly see in newspapers and journals—is easy. Begin by choosing the Section... command from the Format menu. In the Columns portion of the Section dialog box, type the number of columns you want in the Number edit bar. In the Spacing edit bar, indicate the amount of gutter space that you want to appear between columns. Word's default Spacing setting is .5 or $^1/_2$ inch.

(The word *gutter* is used to refer to the space between columns of text as well as to the extra binding space that you use when you are printing facing pages. Throughout the remainder of this chapter, we'll use the term *column gutter* to refer to the space between columns and the term *page gutter* to refer to the extra margin space that appears on facing pages.)

When you click OK to close the Section dialog box and return to your document, the text will appear in one narrow column on the screen. You won't see both columns in the document window as they will appear on the printed page, unless you switch to the page view or issue the Print Preview... command.

FIGURE 10-15

Are all mutual company dividends determined by the same method?	No. In most cases your dividends are determined on an annual basis by a complex formula that takes into account the mutual company's investment and claims experience, as well as its cost of doing business. However, methods of determining your dividend shares are likely to vary from one mutual company to the next. Before you decide on a mutual company, you should be familiar with the company's methods for determining dividends.
How does the cash value of my life insurance policy grow from one year to the next?	Your policy's value may increase in two ways: through increased cash value and through dividends. Increases in your accumulated cash value represent your policy's growing equity. Mutual companies also share their profits with their policyholders in the form of dividends. You have the option of receiving these dividend payments directly or applying them to your future policy premium payments.
How can I evaluate my insurance policy's real worth?	Three factors affect the value of your whole life policy: your premium rate, your policy's cash value, and the dividends that you receive. These amounts are interdependent. However, in measuring your policy's value, your actual accumulated cash value is the bottom line. The actual cash value of your policy depends on the guaranteed cash value specified for your policy, as well as those dividends that you use to increase the cash value.
Is a life insurance policy really a worthwhile financial investment?	Only if you really need life insurance coverage. The primary goal of any life insurance policy is to protect the financial security of the policy's beneficiary. However, your life insurance policy does provide an unbeatable combination of protection, savings, and growth. In addition to the steady growth in cash value, with a mutual life insurance policy, you also have the opportunity to participate in the profitability of your insurer through dividends.

By building a table, you can align individual paragraphs in two or more columns.

For example, to create the sample page shown in Figure 10-14, we started with Word's default Document, Page Setup, and Section dialog box settings. Then, we issued the Section… command, specified a Number setting of 2, and used Word's default Spacing setting of .5. Figure 10-16 shows how this document appears on the screen in the galley view. (We also applied justified alignment to the text.)

Notice that the default right edge for our columnar text (indicated by the dotted vertical line on the ruler) now appears at the $2^3/_4$-inch position on the ruler instead of at the 6-inch position. However, if you check the Document dialog box, you'll see that Word has not changed the default Right margin setting of 1.25. If you switch to the page scale on the ruler, you'll see brackets marking not only the left and right margin positions, but also the inside column boundaries. For example, if you were to click on the scale icon of the ruler shown in Figure 10-16, you would see brackets at the $1^1/_4$ and 4-inch positions on the ruler. (These mark the boundaries of the first column.) You also would see brackets at the $4^1/_2$ and $7^1/_4$-inch positions, marking the boundaries of the second text column.

FIGURE 10-16

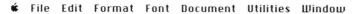

When you're using the galley view, the text in snaking columns appears on your screen as one long column.

When you use the snaking column format, the width of your columns depends on a number of factors, including the width of your document's text area, the number of columns to be placed on a page, and the distance between columns (the column gutter). Let's back up a moment and consider in detail how Word goes about calculating column width.

Calculating column width

To determine the width of each column in a multicolumn layout, begin by calculating the width of your total text area. This tells you how much space you have to work with on the printed page. This space must then be divided among the text columns and the gutter space that appears between columns.

As you may remember from Chapter 5 and earlier in this chapter, to determine the width of a document's text area, you need to take into account the page size and orientation, as well as your Left and Right margin settings (or your Inside and Outside margin settings). If you are using a page gutter, you also need to consider the width of your Gutter setting. Therefore, to calculate the width of a document's text area, you use this formula:

Width of paper - Left margin - Right margin - Page gutter = Width of text area

A document's text area, of course, must accommodate the columns of text as well as the space between columns. For example, in the sample document shown in Figures 10-14 and 10-16, Word divided our 6-inch text area into two columns, allowing 3 inches for each column. Then, to create the $^1/_2$-inch gutter between columns, Word subtracted an equal amount, $^1/_4$ inch, from each column. This resulted in a width of $2^3/_4$ inches for the text in each column.

To determine how wide the columns will be in any document, you can use the formula:

$$\frac{\text{Width of text area - (Column gutter * (Number of columns - 1))}}{\text{Number of columns}} = \text{Column width}$$

Although this formula looks a little complicated, you'll find that it's really quite simple if you walk through it step by step. Let's look first at the formula's numerator. You already know how to compute the *Width of text area* component. The *(Column gutter * (Number of columns -1))* portion of the numerator computes the total amount of space that will be allotted to column gutters. You must subtract this space from the width of your text area before you can determine the amount of space available for the columns of text.

Why do you need to subtract 1 from the number of columns to determine the total amount of gutter space? Because column gutters appear *between* columns—not to the left or right of each column—you'll always have one less gutter than text column. For instance, in a two-column page layout, you'll have one column gutter; in a three-column layout, you'll have two column gutters; and so forth.

After computing the total amount of space available for the columns of text, you must divide that result by the number of columns. The formula's denominator is simply the Number setting you specify in the Section dialog box.

Let's use this formula to compute the column widths for the sample page shown in Figure 10-14:

$$\frac{6 - (.5 * (2\text{-}1))}{2} = \frac{6 - .5}{2} = 2.75$$

As you can see, the formula results in the column width shown in Figure 10-16, $2^3/_4$ inches. If you are creating a three-column layout, you would use a formula like this:

$$\frac{6 - (.5 * (3\text{-}1))}{3} = \frac{6 - 1}{3} = 1.66$$

to determine the total column width. This formula allows room for two $^1/_2$-inch column gutters, rather than one. Thus, you must subtract a total of 1 inch from your text area before you can determine the width of each column.

To test this three-column formula, let's go back to the sample document window shown in Figure 10-16 and issue a new Section... command. If we specify a Number setting of 3 and leave the Spacing setting at .5, our document window (in the galley view) will look like the one in Figure 10-17. Notice that Word has now narrowed our columns to about $1^{11}/_{16}$ inches (or approximately 1.66 inches). Figure 10-18 on the next page shows the resulting printed page.

FIGURE 10-17

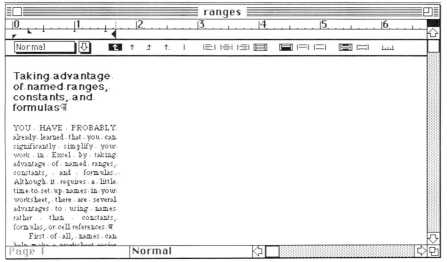

When we use a Number setting of 3 and a Spacing setting of .5, Word narrows our columns to $1^{11}/_{16}$ inches each.

If you find these formulas hard to grasp, you may find it easier to visualize the effects of your column settings by creating a layout sketch of your multicolumn page. For example, Figure 10-19 on page 407 shows a layout sketch of the three-column page that we created in Figure 10-18.

In Chapter 5, we presented several techniques for controlling page breaks in documents. Most of these techniques can be applied in multicolumn documents to control column breaks as well as page breaks. For example, you can use the Widow Control option in the Document dialog box to ensure that no single line from a paragraph will appear alone at the top or bottom of a column. You can also use the Keep Lines Together option in the Paragraph dialog box to prevent Word from splitting a paragraph between two columns. Similarly, the Keep With Next ¶ option in the Paragraph dialog box will ensure that a paragraph appears in the same column as the succeeding paragraph. (When you use these features, Word may need to repaginate your document in order to display the correct column breaks.)

Controlling column breaks

FIGURE 10-18

Taking advantage of named ranges, constants, and formulas

YOU HAVE PROBABLY already learned that you can significantly simplify your work in Excel by taking advantage of named ranges, constants, and formulas. Although it requires a little time to set up names in your worksheet, there are several advantages to using names rather than constants, formulas, or cell references.

First of all, names can help make a worksheet easier to understand because they lend a natural language flavor to the formulas. For example, with named ranges you can create formulas like

=Sales-CGS

Names also help you ensure consistency between formulas and avoid errors. Once you have named the range, formula, or constant you want to work with, you can use the Paste Name... command to enter that name throughout a worksheet, thus avoiding the hassles of locating and retyping the value, reference, or formula in several locations. And, if you need to make a change to several formulas that use the same name, you can simply change the name definition rather than editing all of the formulas that use that reference, value, or formula.

As you'll see in a moment, Excel's naming capabilities also let you set up links between two or more worksheet files quickly and easily. Again, by using names to link worksheets, you can ensure consistency between files and make your assumptions explicit and easy to understand.

Generally, the larger and more complex a worksheet model, the more valuable you'll find Excel's naming capabilities. The Paste Name... command eliminates the need for scrolling long distances to find the cells you need to refer to when you are entering formulas. In addition, if you are not sure of a reference that you have used in one of your formulas, you can easily use the Goto... command to see the contents of a named range, or you can use the Define Name... command to review the definition of a named range, constant, or formula.

However, before you begin scattering named ranges, constants and formulas throughout a worksheet, you should have a thorough understanding of how these elements work. Otherwise, you may inadvertently create errors in your worksheet calculations.

In this article, we'll show you several techniques for using named ranges, constants, and formulas in your worksheet models—and some common traps that you should avoid when you use Excel's naming facility in your own models.

Copying names between files

WHEN YOU COPY a formula that uses a name from one worksheet to another, Excel will transfer the name in that formula to the second worksheet as well. This can often be a convenient means of setting up parallel calculations in two similar worksheets.

To illustrate, take a look at the sales worksheet shown in Figure A. We used the Create Names... command to name cells B4 through F14. For example, as you can see in the Define Name dialog box shown in Figure B, the name Adams refers to cells B4 through F4. Notice that we used absolute references to refer to that named range. As you'll see in a moment, the reference style you select for your range definitions has a tremendous effect on your worksheet calculations.

Now, suppose you want to perform a similar set of calculations in the worksheet shown in Figure C. As you can see, this worksheet is set up just like the one in Figure A. So, to calculate sales totals for the week of October 13, you could simply copy the contents of cells G3:G14 and cells A15:G15 from the 10/6 Sales worksheet to the corresponding ranges in the 10/13 Sales worksheet, as shown in Figure D.

As you can see in Figure D, the formula

=SUM(Adams)

in cell G4 of the 10/13 Sales worksheet correctly calculates that agent's sales for the current period. If you take a look at the Define Name dialog box in this worksheet, shown in Figure E, you'll see that the name Adams, as well as all of the other range names in the formulas we copied from the 10/6 Sales worksheet, have been duplicated in the 10/13 Sales worksheet. All of these range name definitions are identical to those you saw in Table 1 for the 10/6 Sales worksheet, except that they now refer to the corresponding cells in the 10/13 Sales worksheet as well.

Carrying name definitions from one worksheet to another by copying formulas that use names works just fine as long as the second worksheet is set up exactly

This printed page shows the results of our three-column page layout.

When you are working with snaking columns, the only way to tell where the column breaks will occur in your document is to switch to the page view on your screen. When you repaginate a document that contains two or more columns, Word displays only your page breaks—not your column breaks—in the galley view. The page view, on the other hand, shows snaking columns side by side on the screen and displays the column boundaries with dotted lines. For example, Figure 10-20 on page 408 shows the document form Figure 10-17 in the page view. Notice that Word adjusts the location of the zero point on the ruler (in the normal scale) to show the width of the current column. In Figure 10-20, for example, the insertion point marker is on the middle column, causing the zero point on the ruler to be shifted toward the right.

The column boundaries that you see in page view show how much space remains at the bottom of a column that does not quite fill a page. They also show you where Word has created one or more extra blank lines in a column to control a widow, keep two paragraphs together, or keep all the lines of one paragraph in a single column.

FIGURE 10-19

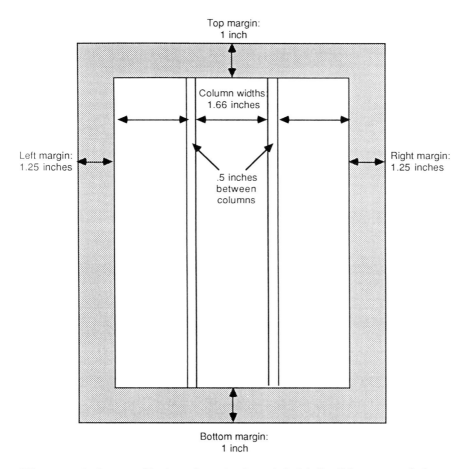

When you design a multicolumn layout, a layout sketch like this one may help you determine your column widths.

By the way, to see the column boundaries, you must choose Show ¶ from the Edit menu. However, if you activate the Show Text Boundaries in Page View option in the Preferences dialog box, Word will display column boundaries even when you've selected Hide ¶.

FIGURE 10-20

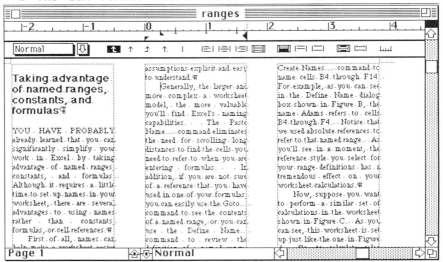

When you switch to the page view, you can see columns of text on the screen as well as dotted lines marking the column boundaries.

FIGURE 10-21

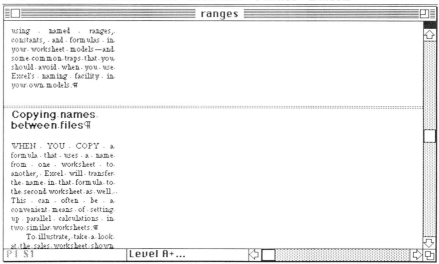

To force a column break in a document, begin by inserting a section-break marker.

Unfortunately, Word does not make it easy for you to insert a column break in a document. If you use the Shift and Enter keys to force a manual page break in a multicolumn document, Word will force all the text after the break to the top of the next page—not to the top of the next column. The only way to force a column break in a document is to create a new section (by pressing ⌘-Enter), then click in the section where you want the new column to start, open the Section dialog box, and choose New Column from the list of Start options.

For example, in the sample document shown in Figure 10-18, suppose we want the headline *Copying names between files* that appears near the bottom of the second column to appear at the top of the third column. In our document window, we would first click in front of the paragraph that contains this heading and press ⌘-Enter to insert a section break, as shown in Figure 10-21. Then, we would click below the section-break marker and issue the Section... command. In the Section dialog box, we would pull down the list of Start options and choose New Column. Figure 10-22 shows the results.

FIGURE 10-22

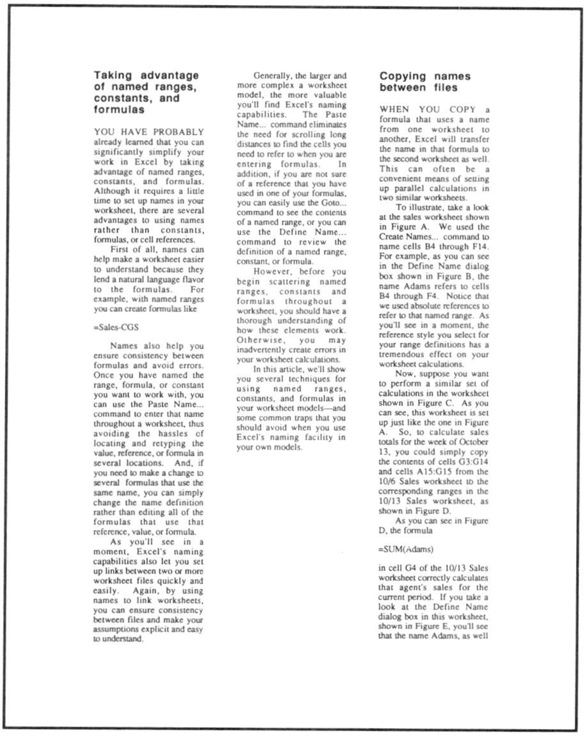

Taking advantage of named ranges, constants, and formulas

YOU HAVE PROBABLY already learned that you can significantly simplify your work in Excel by taking advantage of named ranges, constants, and formulas. Although it requires a little time to set up names in your worksheet, there are several advantages to using names rather than constants, formulas, or cell references.

First of all, names can help make a worksheet easier to understand because they lend a natural language flavor to the formulas. For example, with named ranges you can create formulas like

=Sales-CGS

Names also help you ensure consistency between formulas and avoid errors. Once you have named the range, formula, or constant you want to work with, you can use the Paste Name... command to enter that name throughout a worksheet, thus avoiding the hassles of locating and retyping the value, reference, or formula in several locations. And, if you need to make a change to several formulas that use the same name, you can simply change the name definition rather than editing all of the formulas that use that reference, value, or formula.

As you'll see in a moment, Excel's naming capabilities also let you set up links between two or more worksheet files quickly and easily. Again, by using names to link worksheets, you can ensure consistency between files and make your assumptions explicit and easy to understand.

Generally, the larger and more complex a worksheet model, the more valuable you'll find Excel's naming capabilities. The Paste Name... command eliminates the need for scrolling long distances to find the cells you need to refer to when you are entering formulas. In addition, if you are not sure of a reference that you have used in one of your formulas, you can easily use the Goto... command to see the contents of a named range, or you can use the Define Name... command to review the definition of a named range, constant, or formula.

However, before you begin scattering named ranges, constants and formulas throughout a worksheet, you should have a thorough understanding of how these elements work. Otherwise, you may inadvertently create errors in your worksheet calculations.

In this article, we'll show you several techniques for using named ranges, constants, and formulas in your worksheet models—and some common traps that you should avoid when you use Excel's naming facility in your own models.

Copying names between files

WHEN YOU COPY a formula that uses a name from one worksheet to another, Excel will transfer the name in that formula to the second worksheet as well. This can often be a convenient means of setting up parallel calculations in two similar worksheets.

To illustrate, take a look at the sales worksheet shown in Figure A. We used the Create Names... command to name cells B4 through F14. For example, as you can see in the Define Name dialog box shown in Figure B, the name Adams refers to cells B4 through F4. Notice that we used absolute references to refer to that named range. As you'll see in a moment, the reference style you select for your range definitions has a tremendous effect on your worksheet calculations.

Now, suppose you want to perform a similar set of calculations in the worksheet shown in Figure C. As you can see, this worksheet is set up just like the one in Figure A. So, to calculate sales totals for the week of October 13, you could simply copy the contents of cells G3:G14 and cells A15:G15 from the 10/6 Sales worksheet to the corresponding ranges in the 10/13 Sales worksheet, as shown in Figure D.

As you can see in Figure D, the formula

=SUM(Adams)

in cell G4 of the 10/13 Sales worksheet correctly calculates that agent's sales for the current period. If you take a look at the Define Name dialog box in this worksheet, shown in Figure E, you'll see that the name Adams, as well

By creating a new section and using the New Column Section Start option, we have forced a column break in our sample document.

Combining single and multiple columns

Because snaking columns are controlled by the Section... command, you can change the number of columns that appear in a document on a section-by-section basis. Therefore, to use two or more column formats in the same document, just start a new section and indicate the number of columns you want to use in the Section dialog box. Word also allows you to use two or more column formats on a single page. For example, you might display part of a page in a single-column format and part of it in a two-column format. Each time you want to change column formats, press ⌘-Enter to begin a new section. Then, click in the new section, open the Section dialog box, specify the number of columns you want, and choose No Break as your Start option.

Consider the sample page shown in Figure 10-23. To create this page layout, we used ⌘-Enter to split our document into two separate sections between the introductory paragraph and the list of names, as shown in Figure 10-24. Then, we clicked on the second section (where the list of names appears), issued the Section... command, and entered Number and Spacing settings of 2 and .5, respectively. We also selected No Break from the list of Start options.

FIGURE 10-23

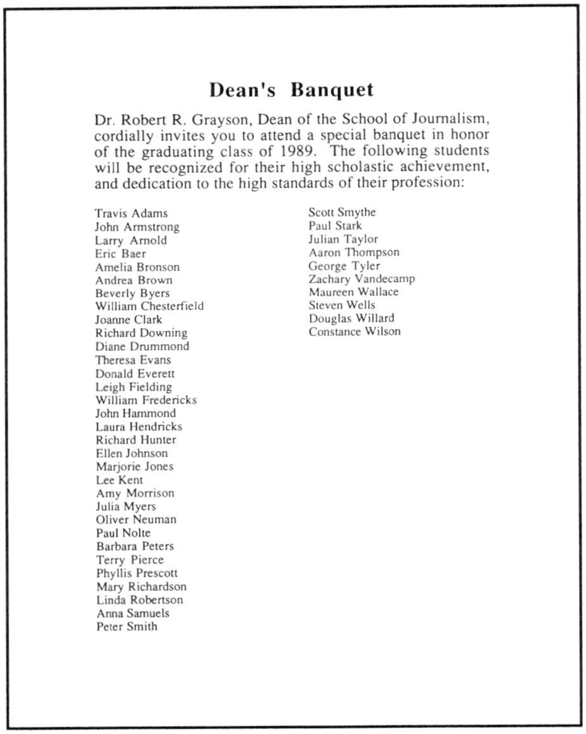

Dean's Banquet

Dr. Robert R. Grayson, Dean of the School of Journalism, cordially invites you to attend a special banquet in honor of the graduating class of 1989. The following students will be recognized for their high scholastic achievement, and dedication to the high standards of their profession:

Travis Adams
John Armstrong
Larry Arnold
Eric Baer
Amelia Bronson
Andrea Brown
Beverly Byers
William Chesterfield
Joanne Clark
Richard Downing
Diane Drummond
Theresa Evans
Donald Everett
Leigh Fielding
William Fredericks
John Hammond
Laura Hendricks
Richard Hunter
Ellen Johnson
Marjorie Jones
Lee Kent
Amy Morrison
Julia Myers
Oliver Neuman
Paul Nolte
Barbara Peters
Terry Pierce
Phyllis Prescott
Mary Richardson
Linda Robertson
Anna Samuels
Peter Smith

Scott Smythe
Paul Stark
Julian Taylor
Aaron Thompson
George Tyler
Zachary Vandecamp
Maureen Wallace
Steven Wells
Douglas Willard
Constance Wilson

Word allows you to combine single-column and multi-column layouts on the same page.

FIGURE 10-24

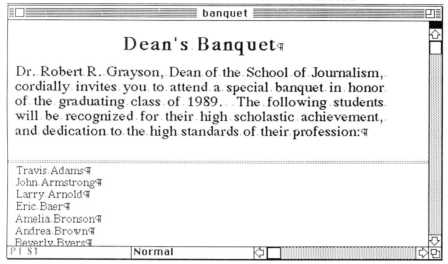

To change columnar layouts, insert a section break and choose No Break as the
Section Start option.

In this document, Word printed the text in the second section, beginning just
below the section break and extending to the bottom margin—this created the first
column. Then, Word wrapped the text in this second section back to the top of the
section—not to the top of the page—creating the second column.

You also can use section breaks and the No Break Section Start option to align
the length of columns. Whenever a document contains one or more sections with
multicolumn formatting, and you choose No Break as the Start option, Word will
break the columns at the section boundaries. As a result, Word will wrap the
columnar text within each section between the section boundaries. In other words,
the No Break Start option in the Section dialog box does not cause the text from one
section to flow into the text of the next section. Instead, it causes Word to place the
text from separate sections on the same page, wrapping the columnar text within
each section separately from the text in other sections. Thus, the location of your
section breaks determines the depth of the columns within each section.

For example, in the document shown in Figure 10-23, the two columns are not
balanced in length. To solve this problem, we might add another section break just
below the last line of text in the two-column section. We again would use the No
Break Section Start option for this third section. Word will then wrap the two-

*Creating columns
of even length*

column text between the section breaks, as shown in Figure 10-25. (We have formatted this last section of the document to have only one column, and we've added some text in this section. However, if our only purpose in adding this third section is to even out the columns in the two-column section, we could have simply entered a section break without typing any text.)

FIGURE 10-25

Dean's Banquet

Dr. Robert R. Grayson, Dean of the School of Journalism, cordially invites you to attend a special banquet in honor of the graduating class of 1989. The following students will be recognized for their high scholastic achievement, and dedication to the high standards of their profession.

Travis Adams
John Armstrong
Larry Arnold
Eric Baer
Amelia Bronson
Andrea Brown
Beverly Byers
William Chesterfield
Joanne Clark
Richard Downing
Diane Drummond
Theresa Evans
Donald Everett
Leigh Fielding
William Fredericks
John Hammond
Laura Hendricks
Richard Hunter
Ellen Johnson
Marjorie Jones
Lee Kent
Amy Morrison
Julia Myers
Oliver Neuman
Paul Nolte
Barbara Peters
Terry Pierce
Phyllis Prescott
Mary Richardson
Linda Robertson
Anna Samuels
Peter Smith
Scott Smythe
Paul Stark
Julian Taylor
Aaron Thompson
George Tyler
Zachary Vandecamp
Maureen Wallace
Steven Wells
Douglas Willard
Constance Wilson

The banquet will begin at 7:30 p.m. on Saturday, June 6 in the Student Union Building Reception Hall. If you plan to attend, please return the enclosed reply card no later than May 31.

We divided our document into three separate sections to create this page layout.

Creating long headings

In a newspaper-style layout, you may want to create headings that stretch across two or more columns. To accomplish this, you might be tempted to simply click on your heading text and drag the right indent marker to the right so that the heading extends across the width of the page. If you use this method, however, the text in your second column will overwrite your heading.

For example, as we pointed out earlier, Word marks the right edge of the text column in the sample document in Figure 10-16 with a dotted vertical line at the $2^3/_4$-inch mark on the ruler. Suppose we decide to alter the heading of this document so that it stretches across both columns. To do this, we might click on the heading and then drag the right indent marker to the 6-inch mark, as shown in Figure 10-26.

FIGURE 10-26

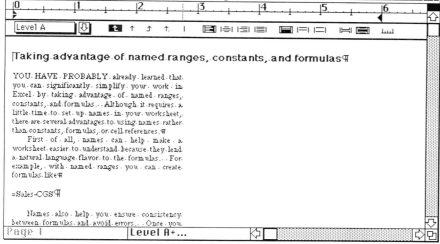

To format the heading for this document, we dragged the right indent marker to the 6-inch mark on the ruler.

Figure 10-27 on the next page shows what happens when we print this document. Although the heading does indeed extend across both columns, the text in the second column wraps to the top of the page and overwrites the wide heading.

To get around this problem, we can place our heading in a separate section. First, we would click on the beginning of the first line after the heading and press ⌘-Enter to insert a section break. Then, we would click anywhere in the first section (which contains the heading text), open the Section dialog box, and change the Number setting in the Columns portion of the dialog box to 1. After closing the dialog box, we would click on the second section, choose the Section... command once more, and select No Break in the list of Start options. Next, we would make sure that the Number setting is 2 and the Spacing setting is .5. As you can see in Figure 10-28, when we print this document, the text in the second column starts on the same line as the text in the first column, rather than wrapping all the way back to the top of the page.

FIGURE 10-27

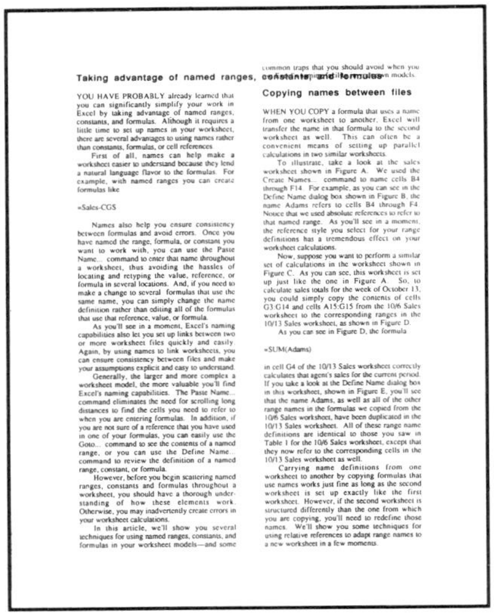
Taking advantage of named ranges, constants, and formulas

Copying names between files

When we print the document, the text in the second column overwrites the heading.

FIGURE 10-28

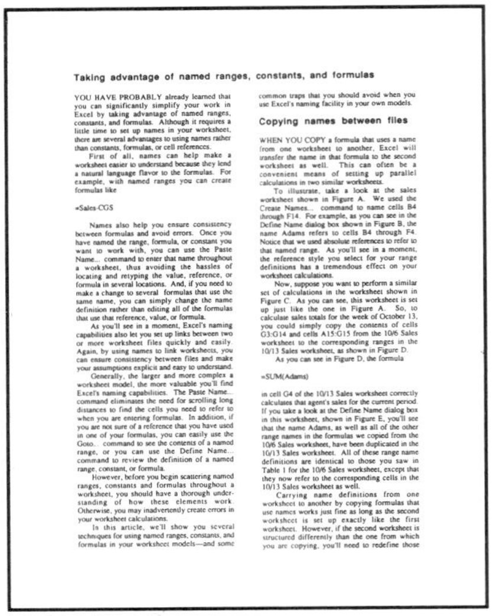
Taking advantage of named ranges, constants, and formulas

Copying names between files

To avoid the overlap problem shown in Figure 10-27, we placed the long heading in a separate, single-column section.

BUILDING TABLES

One of the most useful additions to Word 4 is the new table feature. Tables combine elements of tab formatting, which we explained in Chapter 5, and Word 3's side-by-side formatting. You can use tables to create simple tabular layouts, like a two-column list, or more complex page designs, such as business forms or side-by-side text and graphics. In this section, we'll show you how to create a simple table. Then, we'll demonstrate the various editing and formatting techniques you can use to alter a table to suit your needs.

Creating a Table

There are two ways to create a table in Word. First, you can use the Insert Table... command to create a blank table. Second, you can convert existing text into a table. We'll start our discussion by showing you how to create an empty table and fill in the text. Later in this section, we'll show you how to convert existing text into table format.

Let's begin by creating the two-column table shown in Figure 10-29. Although this is a fairly simple document, notice that the text in the second column wraps from one line to the next. You could create this effect using tabs, but a table makes this type of formatting much easier.

FIGURE 10-29

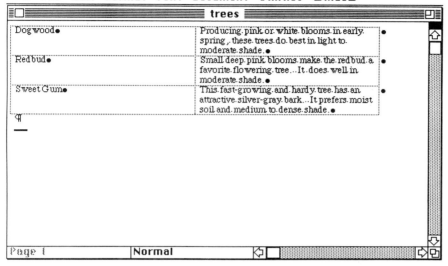

The Insert Table… command makes it easy to create tables like this one.

First, place the insertion point marker at the place you want the table to appear, then choose Insert Table… from the Document menu. Word will present the Insert Table dialog box shown in Figure 10-30. As you can see, Word initially suggests two columns and one row for the table. Since our sample table has two columns, we won't need to change the Number of Columns setting. However, since our table has three rows, we'll need to replace the 1 in the Number of Rows edit bar with 3.

FIGURE 10-30

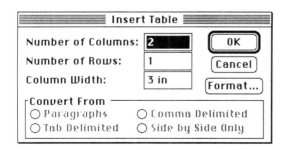

When you choose the Insert Table… command, Word will display this dialog box.

The Insert Table dialog box also contains Word's suggested column width. To determine this setting, Word divides by 2 the width of the text column in which the table is being inserted. As you may recall from Chapter 5, when you use Word's default Page Setup and Document settings, the width of your document's total text area will be 6 inches. In a single-column layout, the text column is, of course, the same width as the text area—6 inches. Thus, Word suggests 3 inches as the width of each column in a two-column table. We'll use this suggested width for now, and later we'll show you how to change column widths.

After specifying the number of columns and rows for the table and a column width, click OK in the Insert Table dialog box. Word will then insert a blank table in your document, as shown in Figure 10-31.

FIGURE 10-31

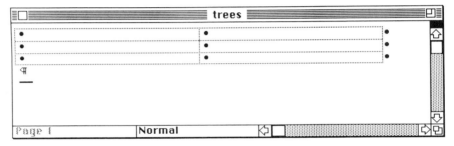

We used the Insert Table... command to create this blank table.

If you insert a table in a document that has a multicolumn format, Word will divide the width of the current text column by the number of columns in the table to obtain the suggested Column Width setting in the Insert Table dialog box. For example, suppose you are working in a two-column document in which each text column is 2 inches wide. If you choose the Insert Table... command, Word will suggest a table with two columns in which each table column is 1 inch wide.

Getting Your Bearings

As you can see in Figure 10-31, our blank table contains gridlines that define the rows and columns of the table. The intersection of each row and column is called a cell. Each cell displays a bold black dot called an end-of-cell marker, which shows how far the text in that cell extends. (Since there is no text in the table yet, the end-of-cell marker appears at the left edge of each cell.) Another black dot, called the end-of-row marker, appears just to the right of each row. This marker comes into play when you want to append a new column onto the right edge of a table.

If you do not see the gridlines and black dots after you create a new table, don't panic. There are a couple of ways to turn on the display of these elements. First, you can choose Show ¶ from the Edit menu. When Show ¶ is active, Word will always display table gridlines and end-of-cell markers. Second, if you select the

Show Table Gridlines option in the Preferences dialog box, Word will display table gridlines (but not the end-of-cell markers), even when you've chosen the Hide ¶ command. In fact, the only way to suppress the display of table gridlines and end-of-cell markers is to deselect Show Table Gridlines in the Preferences dialog box, then choose Hide ¶ from the Edit menu.

You almost undoubtedly will want to keep the display of gridlines turned on while you're working with a table. Without gridlines, it can be virtually impossible to discern many important characteristics of a table, such as the width of columns, the alignment of rows, and the depth of rows.

By the way, if a cell in a table contains no text or only a single paragraph of text, Word will not display a paragraph marker (¶) in that cell. Nevertheless, Word considers the text in separate cells to be in separate paragraphs as well. Thus, the end-of-cell marker also defines the end of the last paragraph of text in a cell.

Of course, Word will not include the table gridlines and end-of-cell markers in a printed document. You can, however, print gridlines in a table by adding borders. We'll show you how to use borders in a table later in this section.

As you work with tables, you'll need to be familiar with the ways in which Word displays the ruler. As we explained in Chapters 2 and 5, Word can show a ruler in three scales: the normal scale, the table scale, and the page scale. Let's begin with the normal scale. Figure 10-32 shows our blank table from Figure 10-31 after we've turned on the ruler display.

Using the ruler with a table

FIGURE 10-32

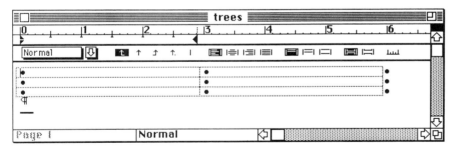

In the normal scale, the ruler shows the width of the text area for the current cell.

You might recall from Chapter 5 that the ruler in the normal scale shows the width of your document's text area. The left edge of the text area begins at the zero point on the ruler, while the right edge of the text area is marked by a dotted vertical line. When you're working in a table, the normal scale on the ruler is somewhat different. Instead of showing the width of the document's total text area, the ruler shows you the width of the current cell's text area. Again, the left edge of the text area begins at the zero point on the ruler and the right edge of the text area is marked by a dotted vertical line.

For example, in Figure 10-32, the insertion point marker is on the first cell of the table. The text area of this cell begins at the zero point on the ruler and extends to the dotted line that appears just beyond the $2^7/_8$-inch point. You may wonder why the dotted line marking the right edge of this cell's text area does not appear at the 3-inch point on the ruler, since each of our columns is three inches wide (according to the Column Width setting in the Insert Table dialog box). The reason for this difference is that Word allows some space between the columns of a table so that the text in adjacent cells won't overlap. We'll talk more about this space in a moment. First, however, let's see what happens when we click on a cell in the second column of the table.

Figure 10-33 shows our table with the insertion point marker in the second column. Notice that the ruler display has shifted so that the zero point is aligned with the left edge of the second column's text area. Similarly, the dotted vertical line at the $2^7/_8$-inch position now marks the right edge of this cell's text area.

FIGURE 10-33

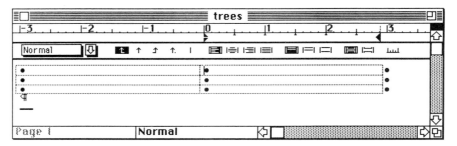

When we move the insertion point marker to the right column, Word shifts the ruler display.

Now, let's click on the scale icon at the far right side of the ruler to switch to the table scale. Figure 10-34 shows our document after making this change.

FIGURE 10-34

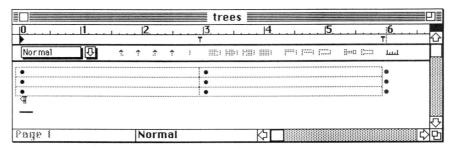

When we switch to the table scale on the ruler, Word will mark the position of our column boundaries.

In the table scale, the zero point on the ruler represents the left edge of your document's text column, while the dotted vertical line (at the 6-inch point in Figure 10-34) marks the right edge of your document's text column. (Note that the right edge of the document's text column extends slightly beyond the right edge of the text area in the last cell on each row—more on this later.)

The position of the left edge of the table is denoted by an indent marker (▶), which we'll refer to as the row indent. Unlike the left and first-line indent markers that appear on the ruler in the normal scale, the row indent marker is a solid arrowhead. In Figure 10-34, the row indent marker is aligned with the zero point on the ruler. As we'll show you later, this won't always be the case.

When you switch to the table scale on the ruler, the right edge of each cell in the current row will be marked by a ▼ symbol just below the ruler line. Notice in Figure 10-34 that each ▼ marker corresponds to a cell boundary, without taking into account the space between cells. You can drag these ▼ markers to change your column widths. We'll show you how to do this in a moment.

Now, let's click on the scale icon once more to see the ruler in the page scale. As you can see in Figure 10-35, positioning the insertion point marker on a table does not affect the appearance of the ruler in the page scale. The ruler looks the same as it would if the insertion point marker were on regular text. The page scale, as we explained in Chapters 2 and 5, shows the width of your page, with brackets marking the left and right margin positions.

FIGURE 10-35

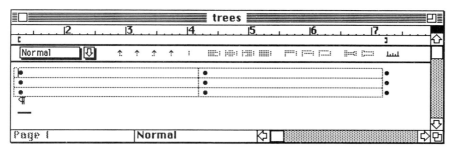

The ruler in the page scale shows the position of our left and right document margins relative to the edges of the page.

Now that we have created a blank table, let's enter some text. Entering text in a table is no different than entering text anywhere else in a document. You simply click on the place where you want the text to appear and begin typing. The text will appear in the *Normal* style for the current document, unless you assign different character and paragraph formats. (In our sample trees table, the *Normal* style definition calls for 12-point Times text.)

Entering Text in a Table

To create the sample table shown in Figure 10-29, we would click on the first cell of the table and type the word *Dogwood*. Then, we would click on the cell at the top of the second column and enter the descriptive text that begins *Producing pink or white blooms....* (We also could press the Tab key to move the insertion point marker from the first cell to the second cell. We'll talk about this and other navigational techniques shortly.)

If the text you enter is longer than the width of the current cell, Word will wrap the text within the cell. For example, Figure 10-36 shows our sample table after entering the descriptive text in the first cell of the second column. Notice that Word also increased the depth of the adjacent cell in the first column, even though it contains only one line of text.

FIGURE 10-36

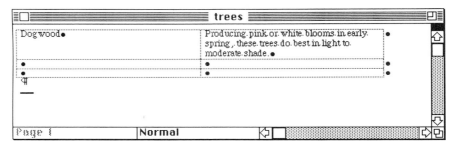

Word can wrap text within each cell of a table.

We can continue filling in the table by clicking on each cell (or pressing the Tab key to move from cell to cell) and then typing the text for that cell. Figure 10-29 shows our sample table after filling in all the text.

Now that we've shown how to create a table and enter text, let's consider some techniques for moving around in a table and selecting text.

Navigating within a Table

Perhaps the easiest way to move around in a table is simply to click on the spot where you want to work, but you also can press the Tab key to move from cell to cell in a table. Each time you press Tab, Word will move the insertion point marker one cell to the right and position it in front of the first character space in that cell. If you press Tab while the insertion point marker is on the last cell of a row, it will jump to the first cell of the next row. (If you're in the last cell of the last row of the table, pressing Tab will append a new row to the end of the table.)

Similarly, pressing Shift-Tab will move the insertion point marker to the cell immediately to the left of the current cell. If you press Shift-Tab while the insertion point marker is on the first cell of a row, Word will move it to the last cell of the row immediately above. (However, if the insertion point marker is on the first cell of the first row of the table, pressing Shift-Tab will have no effect.)

You can also use the arrow keys and the keys on the numeric keypad to navigate in a table. Pressing ↑ or 8 on the numeric keypad will move the insertion point marker to the cell immediately above. Pressing ↓ or 2 on the numeric keypad will move the insertion point marker to the cell immediately below. Pressing ← or 4 on the numeric keypad will move the insertion point marker one cell to the left. Finally, pressing → or 6 on the numeric keypad will move the insertion point marker one cell to the right. The Home key will move the insertion point marker to the first cell of the current table.

In some respects, selecting text in a table is no different from selecting text in any other part of a document: You can use your mouse to drag over text to select it, and you can double-click on a word to select that word. To select a sentence in a table, just press the ⌘ key as you click anywhere on that sentence. You also can use the technique described on page 66 of clicking at the beginning of the text you want to select, moving the insertion point marker to the end of the area you want to select, and pressing Shift as you click once more.

Selecting Text in a Table

Whenever you select text in two or more cells, Word will highlight those cells in their entirety. In other words, Word will not let you select only part of the text in two or more cells. For example, suppose you click in front of the last word in a cell and then drag down. As soon as you cross the cell boundary, Word will select all the text in the original cell and all the text in the cell immediately below.

Although you can click and drag to select different parts of a table, Word also offers several special techniques for selecting text in a table. To use these techniques, you need to be aware that each cell and each column in a table has its own selection bar. If you move the pointer to the left edge of a cell, you'll see that it assumes the shape of a right-pointing arrow, indicating that the pointer is in the cell's selection bar. Similarly, if you move the pointer over the top of a column, you'll notice that it assumes the shape of a downward-pointing arrow, as shown in Figure 10-37. This tells you that the pointer is in the column's selection bar.

FIGURE 10-37

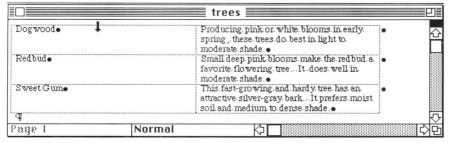

The downward-pointing arrow indicates the pointer is in the column's selection bar.

You can select the contents of a cell by clicking once anywhere in that cell's selection bar. To select an entire row, place the pointer on the selection bar for any cell in that row and double-click. For example, suppose we want to select the second row in our sample table. We could move the pointer to the left edge of either the first or the second column in the table. When the pointer assumes the shape of a right-pointing arrow, we would just double-click. Word would select the entire row, as shown in Figure 10-38.

FIGURE 10-38

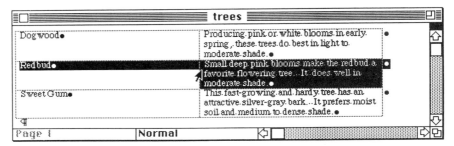

We can select a row in a table by double-clicking in the selection bar for any cell in that row.

To select an entire column of text, you can click in the column's selection bar or press the Option key and click anywhere on that column. To select an entire table, press the Option key and double-click anywhere on the table. (Of course, you also can just drag through the entire table.)

Word will not allow you to use the Option-drag technique described on pages 70 and 71 to select a vertical block of text within a table. If you try to use this technique, Word will select the entire column.

**Changing
the Layout
of a Table**

After you create a table, you may want to change its appearance by altering the width of one or more columns, changing the spacing between columns, or adding and deleting rows and columns. In fact, you may want to use a different number of columns in different parts of the table. You also may want to change the position of the table on the page or the alignment of some of the table's rows. In this section, we'll explain how to make these kinds of changes. We'll look at two new commands: the Cells... command on the Format menu and the Table... command on the Edit menu.

*Adjusting cell and
column widths*

One way to change a table is to alter the width of individual cells or entire columns. Changing the width of a column is simply a matter of changing the widths of all the cells in that column. Let's look first at how you would change the width of an individual cell, then we'll consider how to adjust entire and partial columns.

The easiest way to change the width of a cell is to click anywhere on the row that contains that cell and, on the ruler, drag the ▼ marker that marks the right edge of the cell. If you want to change the width of two or more cells in a column, select those cells before you drag the ▼ marker. If you simply click on one cell and drag a▼ marker, Word will adjust the width of the current cell only without changing any other cells in the column. (Of course, you can use this to your advantage when you need to create a table with different cell widths on different rows.)

As you're dragging a ▼ marker, Word will display the width of the cell that you're adjusting in the status box at the bottom of the window. This measurement will change as the ▼ marker moves, helping you to zero in on the exact width you want. (As you'll see in a moment, you can use the Cells dialog box to achieve maximum precision in specifying a cell width.)

When you drag a ▼ marker on the ruler, Word will simultaneously move all ▼ markers that appear to the right of that marker. This allows you to change the width of one cell without affecting the widths of other cells on the same row.

To change the width of one cell without moving the ▼ markers to the right, just press the Shift key as you drag the ▼ marker. For example, if you press the Shift key as you drag a ▼ marker to the right—making the current cell wider—Word will decrease the width of the cell immediately to the right. Similarly, if you press Shift and drag the ▼ marker to the left to make the current cell narrower, Word will widen the cell immediately to the right by the same amount.

Changing the width of a cell

You also can use the Cells dialog box to adjust the width of a cell or a column. First, click on the cell whose width you want to change (or select all the cells whose widths you want to adjust). Then, choose the Cells... command from the Format menu. Word will then display the dialog box shown in Figure 10-39. (You also can access the Cells dialog box by clicking the Format... button in the Insert Table dialog box.)

Changing the cell width in the Cells dialog box

FIGURE 10-39

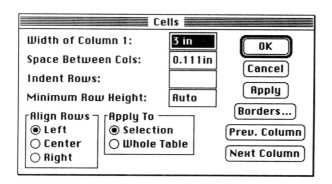

You can use the Cells dialog box to change the features of a table.

Notice that the first edit bar in the dialog box is labeled *Width of Column 1*. As you might guess, the column number in this label will change, depending on where the insertion point marker is positioned or what part of the table is selected. If you have selected cells in two columns, the label will read *Width of Columns 1-2*.

Normally, the Width edit bar will display the width of the current cell(s). However, if you've selected two or more cells of different widths, the edit bar will be blank.

To change the width of the cell(s) you have selected, just enter a measurement in the Width edit bar and click OK or Apply. You can enter your width measurement in inches, centimeters, points, or picas. If you don't specify a unit of measure (such as *in*, *cm*, *pt*, or *pi*), Word will assume inches (or whatever unit you've chosen for the default in the Preferences dialog box).

The Prev. Column and Next Column buttons

In the lower-right portion of the Cells dialog box, you'll see two buttons labeled *Prev. Column* and *Next Column*. When you click on the Prev. Column button, Word will select the cell to the left of the current cell and display its width in the Width edit bar. Similarly, when you click on the Next Column button, Word will select the cell to the right of the current cell and display its width in the Width edit bar. If you click Prev. Column when the first cell on a row is selected, Word will select the last cell in the row. By the same token, if you click the Next Column button when the last cell in a row is selected, Word will highlight the first cell in that row.

If you have selected two or more cells in a row and you click the Next Column button, Word will select the first cell to the right of the highlighted cells. If you have highlighted two or more cells in a row, clicking the Prev. Column button will select the cell to the left of the first cell in your selection. For example, suppose you have selected the second and third cells in a four-cell row. If you click the Prev. Column button, Word will select the first cell on that row.

The Prev. Column and Next Column buttons can be particularly useful when you want to assign different widths to different cells on the same row. You can click on one cell in the row, open the Cells dialog box, and specify a Width setting. Then, instead of clicking the OK button, which will close the dialog box, click Apply to assign the Width setting and keep the dialog box open. Next, click Prev. Column or Next Column to move to a different cell on the row. You can specify a width for this cell, click Apply, then move to another cell by clicking Prev. Column or Next Column. Repeat this procedure until you have adjusted all the cells in the row.

Changing the width of an entire column

As we mentioned, changing the width of a column in a table is really just a matter of changing the widths of all the cells in that column. Fortunately, however, you don't have to change each cell individually.

If you want to use the ruler to change the width of a column, first select that entire column. Then, click the scale icon on the ruler to access the table scale and drag the ⊤ marker for the boundary of the column. As you drag, Word will display the width of the selected column in the status box. (If there are cells of different widths in the column, Word will dim the ruler and display the width of the top cell only. However, the new width you create by dragging the ⊤ marker will apply to all the cells in the selected column.)

Again, Word will automatically move any ⊤ markers to the right of the one that you drag. Because you've selected the entire column, however, Word will shift all the cells in all the columns that appear to the right of the current column.

For example, let's reduce the width of the first column in our sample table. First, we'll select that column by pressing the Option key and clicking on the column. Figure 10-40 shows the column after we selected it.

FIGURE 10-40

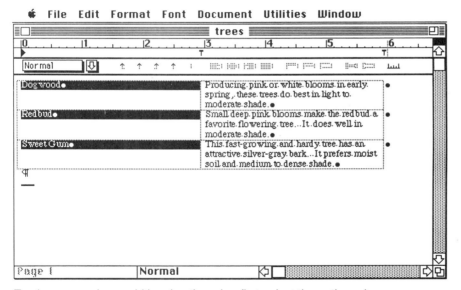

To change a column width using the ruler, first select the entire column.

After selecting the column, we'll click on the ⊤ marker that appears at the 3-inch position on the ruler and drag it to the $1\frac{1}{2}$-inch position. As we do this, the ⊤ marker at the 6-inch position will move to the $4\frac{1}{2}$-inch position. Figure 10-41 shows the results.

FIGURE 10-41

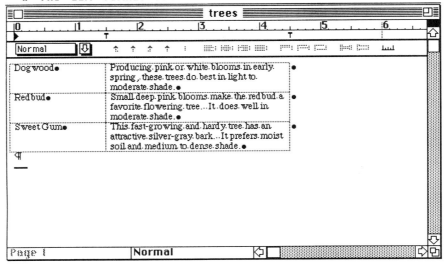

We dragged a ⊤ *marker on the ruler to decrease the width of the first column.*

Changing the column width in the Cells dialog box

Of course, you also can use the Cells dialog box to change the width of an entire column. When you do this, you don't need to select the entire column (although you may). Instead, just click on one of the cells in the column whose width you want to change, then choose Cells... from the Format menu. In the Cells dialog box, enter the column width you want to use in the Width edit bar, then click the Apply To Whole Table option in the lower portion of the dialog box.

To change the width of two or more columns, just select one or more cells in each of those columns before you open the Cells dialog box. Then, specify a Width setting and click the Apply To Whole Table option.

As you're adjusting column widths in the Cells dialog box, you can use the Prev. Column and Next Column buttons we described earlier to move from one column to another. For example, after specifying a new Width setting for one column, you can click the Apply button, then click Prev. Column or Next Column to select a different column and adjust its width as well.

Before we move on, let's take a closer look at the two Apply To options in the Cells dialog box: Selection and Whole Table. If you choose Selection after specifying a new column width, Word will change the width of only the cell on which the insertion point marker is positioned (or only the cells you selected before opening the Cells dialog box) when you click OK or Apply. As we mentioned, however, if you click Whole Table, Word will change the widths of all the cells in the current column. If you've selected cells in two or more columns, Word will change the widths of all the cells in those columns. If you select one or more entire columns before opening the Cells dialog box, Word will dim the Apply To options, although the Whole Table option will be selected.

So far, we've considered how you might change the width of individual cells or entire columns. As you might guess, you also can change the width of any selection of cells in a column. After highlighting the cells whose widths you want to change, drag the T marker on the ruler or specify a Width setting in the Cells dialog box. If you click Prev. Column or Next Column in the Cells dialog box, Word will select the corresponding cells in an adjacent column. For example, suppose you've selected the last two cells in the first column of a table. If you open the Cells dialog box and click Next Column, Word will select the last two cells in the second column of the table.

Partial columns

When you create a table, Word automatically allows some space between the text in each column. This space is not marked on your screen by any gridlines or other indicators. However, as you enter text in a cell, you'll notice that Word allows some space between the left edge of that cell and the first text character. Similarly, Word will not let the text flow all the way to the right edge of a cell; instead, it will wrap the text to a new line, leaving some space between the last character on each line and the right cell border.

Adjusting the space between columns

Word's default spacing between columns is $1/_9$ inch. When you create a new table and open the Cells dialog box, you'll see the value *.111* displayed in the Space Between Cols. edit bar. This Space Between Columns setting can be pretty confusing for several reasons. First, what this setting actually determines is the maximum space between the *text areas* of adjacent columns; it does not change the boundaries of the columns themselves. For example, if you increase the Space Between Columns setting, you won't see any change in the width of your table cells. (However, you will notice that Word shifts the cells to the left and rewraps the text in each cell.)

Another confusing characteristic of the Space Between Columns setting is that you cannot specify a different Space Between Columns setting for different cells on the same row. Unlike the Width setting, the Space Between Columns setting that you specify affects all the cells on the current row(s).

Finally, the way in which Word creates the spacing between columns is a little odd. Word divides the Space Between Columns setting between both ends of each cell on a row. For example, suppose you have specified .5 inch ($1/_2$ inch) as the Space Between Columns setting. Word will allow $1/_4$ inch of space at the right and left edge of each cell. You will not be able to enter text in these areas unless you change the indents for that text (more on this later). Of course, by combining the $1/_4$ inch of space at the right edge of one cell with the $1/_4$ inch of space at the left edge of an adjacent cell, Word achieves the $1/_2$-inch column spacing you've specified.

However—and this is the strange part—Word also inserts the $^1/_4$-inch space at the left edge of the first cell on the row and at the right edge of the last cell on the row. Obviously, this space will not fall "between columns" as the setting name implies.

To get a better handle on the Space Between Columns setting, let's look at the ruler. Figure 10-42 shows a four-column table in which each column is 1 inch wide. Currently, the table is formatted with Word's default Space Between Columns setting of .111.

FIGURE 10-42

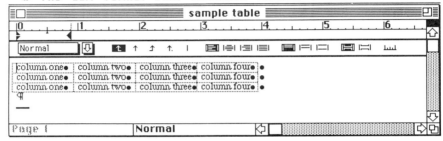

This table displays Word's default Space Between Columns setting of .111 ($^1/_9$) inch.

With the ruler in the normal scale, you can see that the width of the text area in the current cell is slightly less than 1 inch, extending from the zero position on the ruler to the dotted line. This width reflects the width of the cell (1 inch) less the default space between columns ($^1/_9$ inch).

If you look carefully at Figure 10-42, you'll see that the line marking the left boundary of the table falls just to the left of the zero point on the ruler. However, the insertion point marker (and the text in the first column of the table) is aligned with the zero point. The space between the table's left boundary line and the text in each cell is the "space between columns" that Word has allotted to this end of each cell in the first column.

Now, let's see what happens when we increase the Space Between Columns setting to .5 or $^1/_2$ inch. After selecting all the cells in one column, we'll open the Cells dialog box and enter .5 in the Space Between Cols. edit bar. Figure 10-43 shows our table after making this change.

As you can see, the left boundary of the table is no longer visible on the screen. With the increased Space Between Columns setting, Word now allots $^1/_4$ inch of space to each end of each cell. To create this space, Word has simply shifted the left edge of all the column boundaries to the left.

FIGURE 10-43

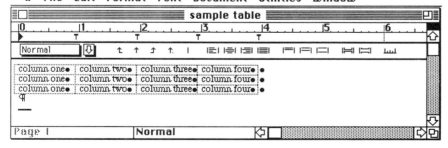

We've now increased the Space Between Columns setting to .5 ($^1/_2$) inch.

In increasing the space between columns, however, Word does not change the relative alignment of the text in the table. To illustrate, notice that the insertion point marker in the first cell is still aligned with the zero position on the ruler. Similarly, the left edge of all the text in all the columns has retained its original alignment.

Notice also that the text area on the ruler is now only $^1/_2$ inch wide. After subtracting the $^1/_2$-inch space between columns from the 1-inch cell width, only $^1/_2$ inch remains for text in each cell. Thus, Word has had to wrap the text in each row to a new line.

Let's see how changing the Space Between Columns setting affects the ruler in the table scale. Figure 10-44 shows our original table from Figure 10-42 with the default .111 Space Between Columns setting. Figure 10-45 on the following page shows the table after increasing the Space Between Columns setting to .5 or $^1/_2$ inch.

FIGURE 10-44

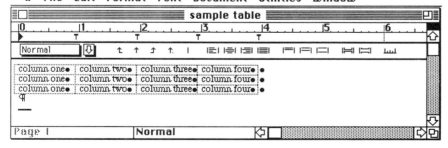

When we switch the ruler to the table scale, T markers will show the location of column boundaries.

FIGURE 10-45

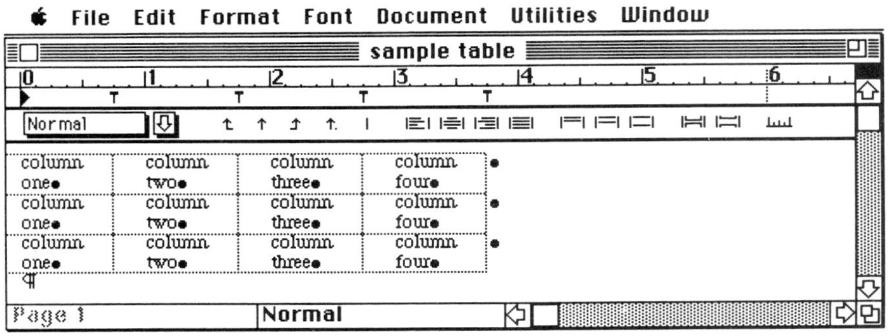

After increasing the Space Between Columns setting, Word will shift the ⊤ markers to reflect the new column boundaries.

As you can see, when you change the Space Between Columns setting, Word shifts the ⊤ markers on the ruler to reflect the change in the column boundaries. Interestingly, Word does not shift the row indent marker at the zero position on the ruler. This marker shows the left edge of the text in the first column, not the left boundary of that column.

Unfortunately, this makes it difficult to figure out how wide each cell is just by looking at the ruler. The positions of the ⊤ markers do not correspond to absolute cell widths. For example, in Figure 10-45, the first ⊤ marker appears at the $3/4$-inch position on the ruler. However, each cell in the first column of the table is actually 1 inch wide. One-fourth inch of each cell's width falls to the left of the zero point on the ruler.

Key points

If you're finding the whole topic of column spacing thoroughly confusing, you're not alone. However, if you keep just a few key points in mind, you should be able to adjust the space between columns to suit your needs. First, remember that Word subtracts your Space Between Columns setting from the cell width, thus decreasing the width of the area available for text in a cell. Second, Word creates space between columns by allotting a blank area at either end of each cell in a row. This blank area appears at the beginning of the first cell on a row as well as at the end of the last cell on a row. Finally, changing the Space Between Columns setting does not affect the horizontal alignment of text on a row. It may, however, change the way Word wraps text and breaks lines within each cell.

As we'll see later in this chapter, you can use paragraph formatting techniques to change the alignment of text within cells (and of individual paragraphs in the same cell). By moving the indent markers on the ruler, you can actually "pull" text into the column spacing area that Word allots at either end of a cell. We'll also show you how to shift the entire table to the right or left.

As you enter text in a table, Word will automatically adjust the height of individual rows to accommodate the text. Both the size of the characters and the number of text lines will affect the height of a row. For example, in the sample table in Figure 10-41, notice how Word has adjusted the height of all the cells in each row to accommodate the wrapping text lines in the second column. If we selected the text in our table and applied a larger font size, Word would increase the row height even further.

Adjusting row height

Word lets you increase the height of rows to allow more white space between the text on each row. For example, going back to the table in Figure 10-41, let's see what happens when we increase the height of the rows in this table. We would begin by clicking anywhere on the table and then opening the Cells dialog box. In the Minimum Row Height edit bar, let's replace the word *Auto* with *.65 in.* Then, we would click the Apply To Whole Table option and click OK. Figure 10-46 shows the result.

FIGURE 10-46

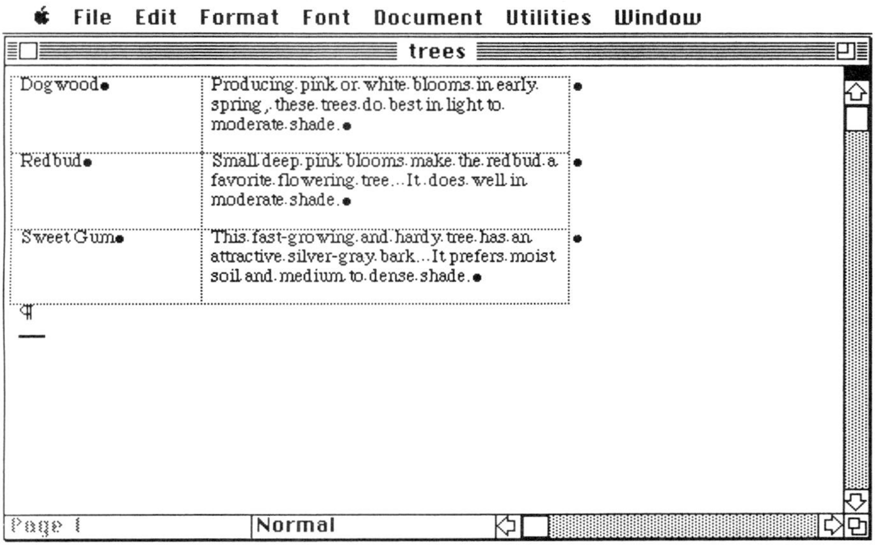

This is how our sample table will look after we increase the row height slightly.

Notice that when Word increases the height of a row, it inserts the additional space below the text. If we want to insert space above the text, we'll need to use the open space icon on the ruler or the Before setting in the Paragraph dialog box. (More on this later.)

Notice also that the Minimum Row Height setting affects all the cells on a row. Word will not allow you to have cells with different heights on the same row.

Moreover, the label for the edit bar—*Minimum Row Height*—should clue you in to how Word interprets your setting. Word will not allow the rows you've formatted to appear smaller than the specified height. However, Word will increase the height of those rows as necessary to accommodate additional text or different formatting.

If you enter a setting that is smaller than the amount of space Word needs to separate the text in adjacent rows, Word will ignore your setting and use automatic spacing so that the rows of your table don't overlap. You can override Word's "overlap protection" by entering a negative number as the Minimum Row Height setting. Word will then use the absolute value of that number and overlap the rows of text. (This is similar to how Word handles a negative Line Spacing setting in the Paragraph dialog box, which is explained in Chapter 5.)

To return a row to the default height, just open the Cells dialog box and enter 0 or Auto in the Minimum Row Height edit bar.

Adding rows

To add a row to the end of a table, just place the insertion point marker anywhere in the last cell of the last row and press the Tab key. A new, blank row will appear at the bottom of the table. This new row will have the same format settings (alignment, indent, and row height) as the last row of the table. For example, to add another tree description to our sample table, we would just click on the last cell of the table (where the description of the Sweet Gum tree appears), and press Tab once. Figure 10-47 shows the result. Using this new row, we can add a new tree description, as shown in Figure 10-48.

FIGURE 10-47

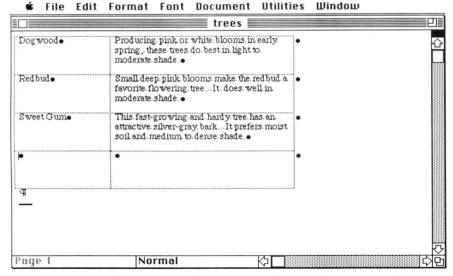

To append a new, blank row onto the end of a table, just click on the last cell of the table and press the Tab key.

FIGURE 10-48

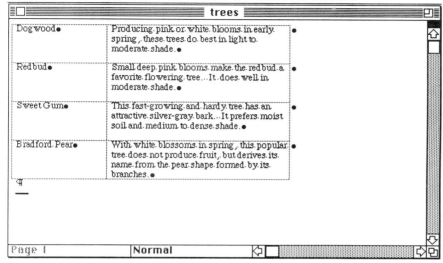

We used the new row to add another tree description to the table.

To add a row to any other part of a table, you must use the Table... command on the Edit menu. This command allows you to insert a row above the current row. Suppose we want to add a row to the top of the sample table. We would begin by clicking on any cell in the top row. Then, we would choose Table... from the Edit menu. Word will display the dialog box shown in Figure 10-49.

FIGURE 10-49

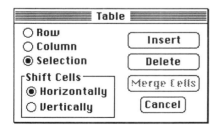

The Table dialog box allows you to insert and delete rows and columns.

In the Table dialog box, Word will suggest the type of insertion we need to make: Row, Column, or Selection. Since we selected less than a full row or full column, Word automatically activated the Selection option. However, we want to add an entire row to the table. Therefore, we'll click the Row option, then click the Insert button. Word will then insert a new, blank row, as shown in Figure 10-50.

This new row will have all the same formats as the row immediately below. As you can see in Figure 10-51, we decreased the row height after entering the title text in each column.

FIGURE 10-50

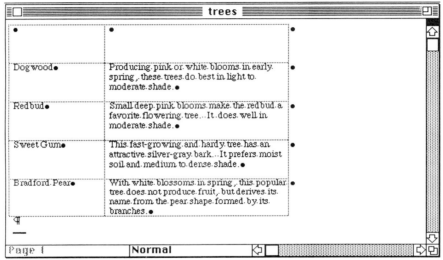

Using the Row option in the Table dialog box, we inserted a new row at the top of our sample table.

Adding
multiple rows

You can add two or more rows to a table in one step. First, select one or more cells in the number of rows you want to insert. For example, if you want to insert three rows in a table, you should select one or more cells in three rows. (Of course, you can select three rows in their entirety, if you want.) Keep in mind that the rows you insert will appear just above the first row in your selection.

After making your selection, choose Table... from the Edit menu. In the Table dialog box, click the Row option and click Insert. Word will add the new rows just above the rows you selected. The new rows will have the same format (row height, alignment, and indent) as the top row in your selection.

Deleting rows

You also use the Table dialog box to delete one or more rows in a table. First, select one or more cells in the row(s) you want to delete. (If you want to delete only one row, just click anywhere on that row.) Then, open the Table dialog box, click the Row option, and click Delete. Word will remove the selected rows and shift up any rows below so that no gap appears in the table.

FIGURE 10-51

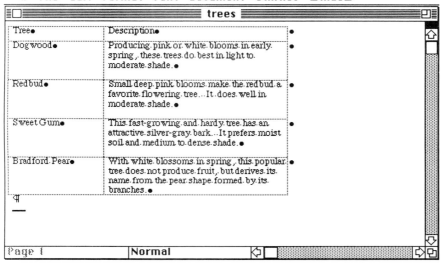

We used the new row in our table to display a title for each column.

If you mistakenly delete rows that you want to keep in your table, you can use the Undo command to recover those rows. However, Word does not place the deleted rows on the Clipboard. Thus, you cannot recover deleted rows by pasting them back into your document.

By the way, if you try to use normal editing commands—Cut or Clear—to delete a row, Word will merely delete the text in the selected row. It will not remove the row from the table.

Adding columns

Word allows you to insert one or more columns in a table in much the same way that you insert rows. Normally, the new column(s) will appear to the left of the current column. You also can insert a new column to the right of the table. We'll show you how to do this in a moment.

Suppose we want to insert a new column in our sample table to display the mature height of each tree. We would begin by clicking anywhere on the second column of the table, then choosing Table... from the Edit menu. In the Table dialog box, we would click the Column option, then click the Insert button. Word will insert a new, blank column, as shown in Figure 10-52 on the next page.

The cells in the new column will have the same width as the first cell in the column immediately to the right (the column you click on before inserting the new column). Of course, you can change the width of the cells in the new column using the techniques we have described. For instance, after inserting the new column in our sample table, we reduced its width to $1\frac{1}{4}$ inches and added text in that column, as shown in Figure 10-53.

FIGURE 10-52

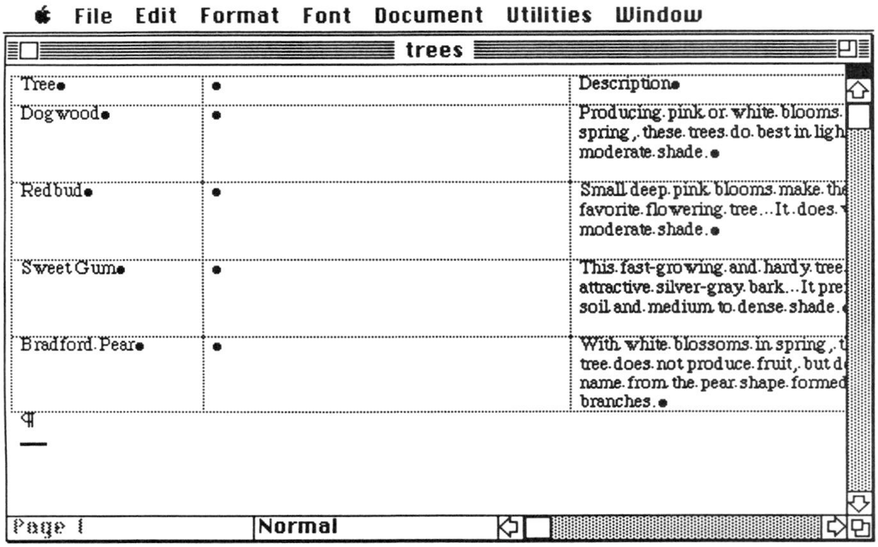

With the Table... command, you can insert a new column in a table.

Adding a column to the right of a table

As we've mentioned, Word also allows you to append a column to the right side of a table. For example, to add a new column to our sample table, we would begin by clicking in the area outside the right edge of the table. Word will position the insertion point marker between the edge of the table and the end-of-row marker (the black dot) just outside the table.

Next, we would open the Table dialog box, click the Column option, and click Insert. Word will insert a new, blank column, as shown in Figure 10-54. As you can see, the new column displays the same width as the column immediately to the left. In fact, in Figure 10-54, we scrolled to the right in our document window in order to display the new column. (Since we won't be needing this extra column, we'll delete it before creating any more examples.)

FIGURE 10-53

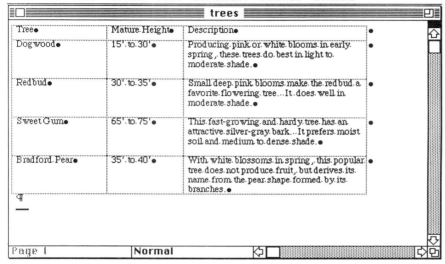

A new column in the middle of the table displays the mature height of each tree.

FIGURE 10-54

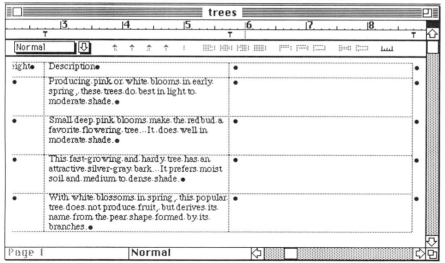

With the Table dialog box, you can add a new, blank column to the right side of a table.

Adding multiple columns

Word lets you add two or more adjacent columns with one Table... command. First, select one or more cells in the number of columns you want to add. For example, if you want to insert two columns in a table, you should select one or more cells in two columns. (Of course, you can select two columns in their entirety.) Keep in mind that the columns you insert will appear just to the left of the first column in your selection.

After making your selection, open the Table dialog box, click the Column option, and click Insert. Word will add the new columns to the left of the columns you selected. The new columns will have the same width as the top cell in the first column of your selection.

Unfortunately, you cannot append two or more columns to the right edge of a table with one Table... command. Each column must be added separately.

Deleting columns

The technique you use for deleting a column is similar to the technique for deleting a row. Begin by selecting one or more cells in the column or columns you want to delete. (If you want to delete only one column, just click anywhere on that column.) Then, open the Table dialog box, click the Column option, and click Delete. Word will remove the selected column(s) and shift the remaining columns so that no gap appears in the table. When it shifts the remaining columns, Word will maintain your row alignment (left, centered, or right).

If you mistakenly delete columns that you want to keep in your table, you can use the Undo command to recover them. However, Word does not place the deleted columns on the Clipboard. Therefore, you cannot recover deleted columns by pasting them back into your document.

Again, if you try to use normal editing commands—Cut or Clear—to delete a column, Word will merely delete the text in the selected column. It will not remove the column from the table.

Adding and deleting cells

You've probably noticed that the Table dialog box includes two Shift Cells options: Horizontally and Vertically. You use these options when you want to insert or delete less than a full column or full row of cells. These options tell Word which way to shift the cells of the table in order to perform the insertion or deletion. Let's consider an example of how you might insert or delete partial rows and columns.

Figure 10-55 shows a simple four-column by six-row table. Notice that we have selected two adjacent cells in the second row. To delete these two cells, we would open the Table dialog box. When we do this, Word will already have selected the Shift Cells Horizontally option. If we click on the Delete button with this option selected, the result would look like Figure 10-56. If we decide that we don't want to delete the cells after all, we can use the Undo command to recover them.

FIGURE 10-55

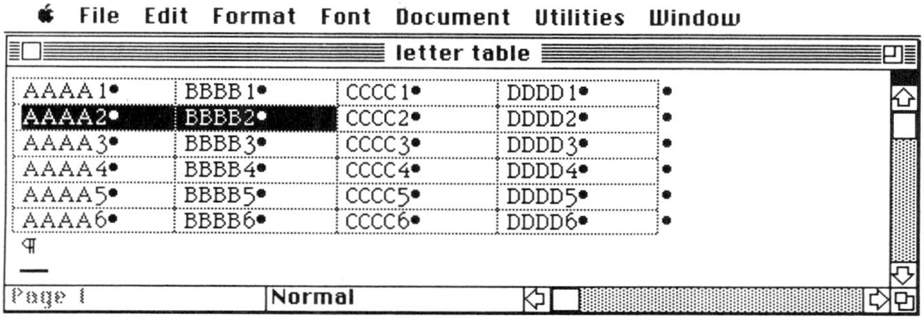

We'll use this simple table to illustrate inserting and deleting cells.

FIGURE 10-56

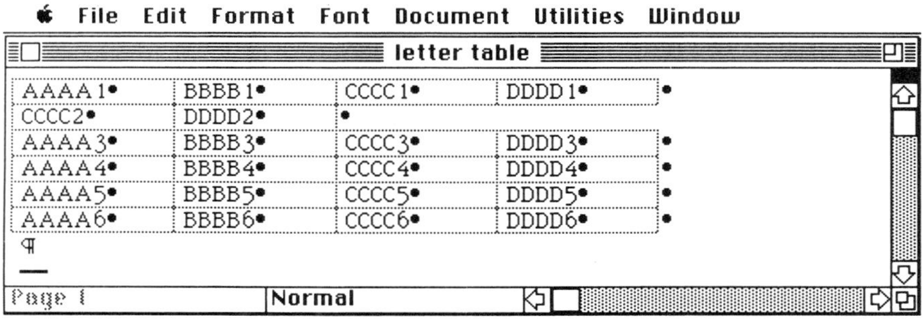

This is the effect of deleting the selected cells and shifting the remaining cells horizontally.

Let's see what happens when we use the Shift Cells Vertically option to delete the selected cells in row two. Figure 10-57 on the following page shows the result. As you can see, Word has moved up by one row all the cells in the first column and the third through sixth rows. Notice that two blank cells now appear in the sixth row of the table.

Word also allows you to merge two or more cells on the same row. (You cannot merge cells in the same column.) To merge cells, just select the cells you want to combine, open the Table dialog box, and click the Merge Cells button. Word will remove the boundaries between the selected cells and create one cell whose width is equal to the combined widths of the merged cells.

Combining and splitting cells

FIGURE 10-57

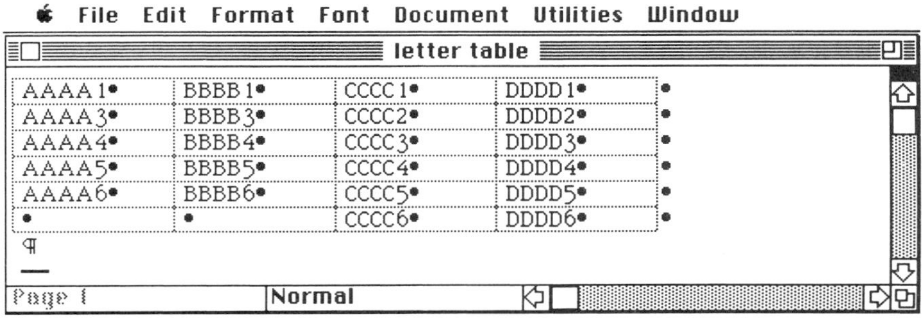

File Edit Format Font Document Utilities Window

letter table				
AAAA1•	BBBB1•	CCCC1•	DDDD1•	•
AAAA3•	BBBB3•	CCCC2•	DDDD2•	•
AAAA4•	BBBB4•	CCCC3•	DDDD3•	•
AAAA5•	BBBB5•	CCCC4•	DDDD4•	•
AAAA6•	BBBB6•	CCCC5•	DDDD5•	•
•	•	CCCC6•	DDDD6•	•

¶
—

Page 1 — Normal

When you delete cells and choose the Shift Cells Vertically option, Word will shift up cells in the rows below.

One excellent use for cell merging is creating a title that stretches across two or more columns in a table. For example, let's add a title row to our sample table shown in Figure 10-53. The first step is to add a new row to the top of the table. After clicking on one of the cells in the top row, we would open the Table dialog box, select the Row option, and click the Insert button. Word would then add a new row, as shown in Figure 10-58.

FIGURE 10-58

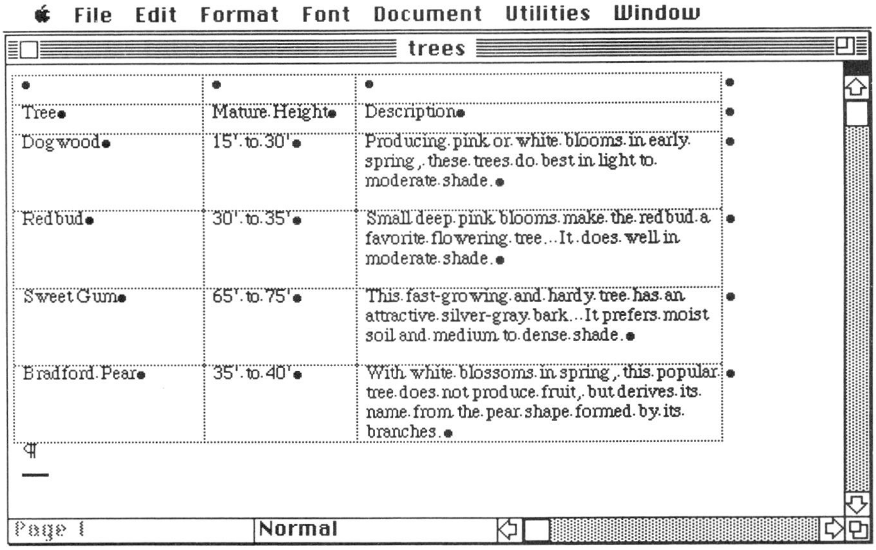

File Edit Format Font Document Utilities Window

trees			
•	•	•	•
Tree•	Mature.Height•	Description•	•
Dogwood•	15'.to.30'•	Producing.pink.or.white.blooms.in.early.spring,.these.trees.do.best.in.light.to.moderate.shade.•	•
Redbud•	30'.to.35'•	Small.deep.pink.blooms.make.the.redbud.a.favorite.flowering.tree...It.does.well.in.moderate.shade.•	•
Sweet Gum•	65'.to.75'•	This.fast-growing.and.hardy.tree.has.an.attractive.silver-gray.bark...It.prefers.moist.soil.and.medium.to.dense.shade.•	•
Bradford.Pear•	35'.to.40'•	With.white.blossoms.in.spring,.this.popular.tree.does.not.produce.fruit,.but.derives.its.name.from.the.pear.shape.formed.by.its.branches.•	•

¶
—

Page 1 — Normal

To create a title for our sample table, we'll begin by adding a new row to the top of the table.

The next step is to merge the cells in this new row into one cell. We would begin by double-clicking on the selection bar for any cell in the row. This will select the entire row. Then, we would open the Table dialog box and click the Merge Cells option. Figure 10-59 shows the result. Notice the two paragraph markers that appear in the merged cell along with the end-of-cell marker. We'll delete these before entering our text.

FIGURE 10-59

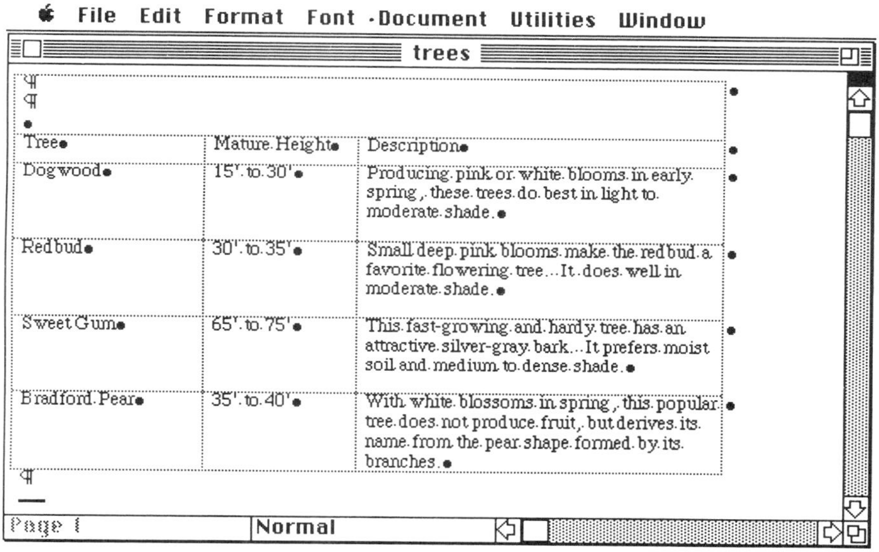

Word has merged the cells in the new row into a single cell.

After entering our title text in the new cell, we'll center that text by clicking the Centered alignment icon on the ruler. Figure 10-60 on the following page shows the table with the title in place.

After merging two or more cells, you can use the Undo command to cancel the merge—provided, of course, that you choose Undo before you perform any other actions. You also can use the Table dialog box to "unmerge" a cell. If you click on a cell that you created by merging two or more cells and then open the Table dialog box, you'll see that the Merge Cells button has been replaced by a Split Cells button. This button appears only after you have used the Merge Cells button to combine cells. In other words, you cannot split any cells other than the ones that were created by merging. When you click the Split Cells button, Word will break the merged cell into its original cell components.

You cannot combine a merged cell with another cell. For example, suppose you have merged the first two cells on a four-cell row. You then decide that you really wanted to merge all the cells on that row. You select the new merged cell and the other cells on that same row and open the Table dialog box. When you do this, you'll see that the Merge Cells button appears dimmed, indicating that it is not available.

FIGURE 10-60

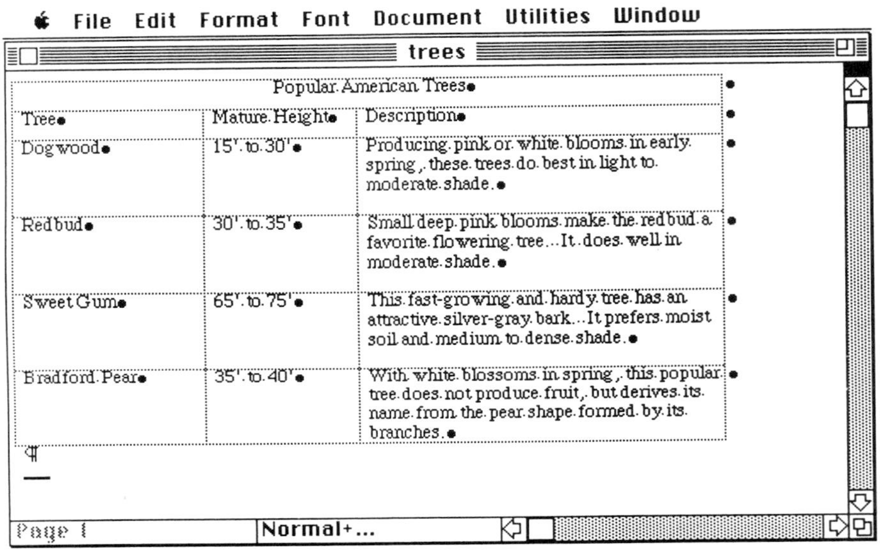

| File | Edit | Format | Font | Document | Utilities | Window |

| | | trees | |

Popular American Trees		
Tree	Mature Height	Description
Dogwood	15' to 30'	Producing pink or white blooms in early spring, these trees do best in light to moderate shade.
Redbud	30' to 35'	Small deep pink blooms make the redbud a favorite flowering tree...It does well in moderate shade.
Sweet Gum	65' to 75'	This fast-growing and hardy tree has an attractive silver-gray bark...It prefers moist soil and medium to dense shade.
Bradford Pear	35' to 40'	With white blossoms in spring, this popular tree does not produce fruit, but derives its name from the pear shape formed by its branches.

Page 1   Normal+...

We entered our title text into the top row and formatted it with centered alignment.

Changing Row and Table Alignment

As we've illustrated, when you first create a table, Word aligns the left edge of the text area in the first column with the left edge of your document's text column. Assuming you're working in a single-column layout and you haven't moved the left or first-line indent markers on the ruler, the position of the left edge of the table text will correspond to the zero position on the ruler. However, the left boundary of the table itself (marked by a dotted line on your screen) will appear just to the left of the zero point.

Using the Cells dialog box (shown in Figure 10-39), you can change the alignment of individual rows in a table or the alignment of an entire table. In other words, you can shift the boundaries of the table horizontally.

The three Align Rows options in the Cells dialog box allow you to change the alignment of a table relative to the current text column. The Left option (the default) will align the left boundary of the table with the left edge of the text column (actually, the table boundary will appear slightly to the left of the edge of the text column due to the Space Between Columns setting). So far, all the tables we have shown in this chapter display left alignment.

With the Center option, you can center the boundaries of a table on your document's text column, and with the Right option you can align the right edge of a table with the right edge of your document's text column. Interestingly, with Right alignment, Word doesn't attempt to compensate for the Space Between Columns setting. Instead, Word aligns the right boundary of the table with the right edge of your document's text column. Because of the Space Between Columns, however, the right edge of the table text will not be aligned with the right edge of your document's text column.

When you choose one of the Align Rows options, you can apply it either to part of the rows in a table or to the entire table. If you select one or more cells in every row of the table, Word will automatically apply to the entire table the Align Rows option you select. If you do not select a cell in every row of the table, you can use the Apply To options—Selection or Whole Table—to specify how you want to apply the Align Rows option.

If you choose Apply To Selection, Word will apply the alignment you choose only to the row on which the insertion point marker is located (or to all the rows in the current selection if you've selected cells in more than one row). If you choose Apply To Whole Table, Word will apply the alignment option to the entire table.

Suppose we want to center our sample table in Figure 10-55. After clicking on a cell, we would open the Cells dialog box, select the Center option, then click the Apply To Whole Table option. Figure 10-61 shows the result.

FIGURE 10-61

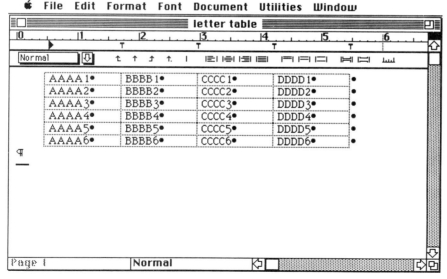

This is how the sample table from Figure 10-55 will look if we choose Center alignment and click the Apply To Whole Table option.

Although in most simple table applications, you'll want all of your rows to display the same alignment, there may be times when you'll need to use different alignment on different rows to create a special effect. For example, if you use a table to design a complex form, you may want to change the alignment of selected rows in the table. In these situations, you can select some cells on just those rows whose alignment you want to change, then choose an alignment option and click the Apply To Selection option. For example, Figure 10-62 shows the sample table from Figure 10-55 after we applied centered alignment to only two rows.

FIGURE 10-62

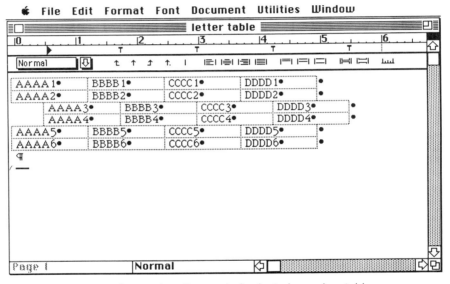

Word allows you to change the alignment of selected rows in a table.

Keep in mind that the alignment of a table (or a row) has nothing to do with the alignment of the text within individual cells of that table. As we'll demonstrate a little later, Word allows you to change the alignment of text in a table without affecting the alignment of the table boundaries. Therefore, you do not need to change the alignment of entire rows in order to achieve different text alignment within a table.

Indenting rows

Besides alignment options, the Cells dialog box also includes an Indent Rows setting that you can use to shift one or more rows—or the entire table—to the right or left. For example, suppose you're using the default Left alignment and you want to shift the entire table $^1/_2$ inch to the right. After opening the Cells dialog box, enter .5 in the Indent Rows edit bar and click the Apply To Whole Table option. When you click OK or Apply, Word will shift all the rows of the table $^1/_2$ inch to the right.

Since Word allows you to place a row in the margin area of your page, you can cause part of a table to "hang" outside the margin by adjusting the indent on one or more rows. For example, suppose you are working on a table that has the default Left alignment. You click on one row, open the Cells dialog box, and enter an Indent Rows setting of -.5. If you use the Apply To Selection option, Word will shift the current row $^1/_2$ inch to the left.

When you use an Indent Rows setting other than the default of 0, that setting will affect the table's alignment. For example, suppose you specify an Indent Rows setting of .5, then you select Center as your Align Rows option and click Whole Table. Instead of centering the table between the right and left edges of the current text column, Word will center the table between the $^1/_2$-inch indent that you've specified and the right edge of the text column.

You also can use the ruler in the table scale to indent one or more rows on a table. As we've pointed out, in the table scale, the ruler displays a row indent marker (▶) at the zero position. By dragging this marker, you can change the indention of selected rows. For example, to indent an entire table by $^1/_2$ inch, select any column in the table. Then, just drag the row indent marker $^1/_2$ inch to the right.

Splitting a Table

To split a table horizontally, you must insert a paragraph marker between two rows in that table. To do this, begin by clicking on the row below where you want the split to occur. Then, press Option-⌘-Spacebar. For example, suppose we want to split the six-row table shown in Figure 10-61 into two three-row tables. First, we would click anywhere on the fourth row of the table, then we would press Option-⌘-Spacebar. Word will insert a paragraph marker (¶) between rows two and three, as shown in Figure 10-63 on the following page. We can enter any text or other data in the blank area between the two smaller tables.

Another way to split a table horizontally is to select one or more rows in the table and then choose the Table to Text… command on the Document menu. (This command replaces the Insert Table… command when you click on or select any part of a table.) In the Table to Text dialog box, select one of the three Convert To options (Paragraphs, Tab Delimited, or Comma Delimited), and click OK. Word will convert your selected rows to normal text. This text will divide the original table into two separate tables. If the rows you selected were blank, Word will simply create one or more blank paragraphs to divide the table. We'll talk more about the Table to Text… command a little later in this chapter.

Word does not offer a method for splitting a table vertically between columns. In other words, you cannot create two tables that appear side by side in a document. However, you can achieve the same effect simply by inserting one or more blank columns in the middle of a table. Just use the Insert button in the Table dialog box as we've described to insert a new, blank column where you want the vertical "split" to occur.

FIGURE 10-63

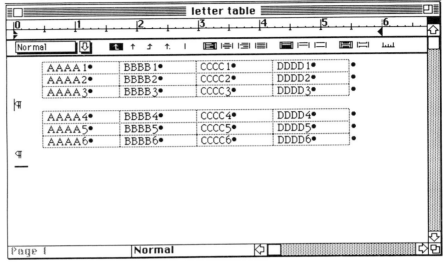

You can split a table by pressing Option-⌘-Spacebar.

Inserting text above a table

Suppose you've inserted a table at the top of a new document and you decide to enter some normal text above that table. To do this, you must insert a blank paragraph above the table. Just click anywhere on the first row of the table, then press Option-⌘-Spacebar. Word will shift the table down slightly and a paragraph marker (¶) will appear above the table.

Altering the Text in a Table

Word allows you to edit and format the text in a table much as you would edit and format any other document text. There are a few differences, however, which we'll point out. We've already shown you how to select text in a table. In this section, we'll begin by discussing how you can edit your table text, then we'll move into the topic of formatting table text.

Editing text in a table

To edit text in a table, you can use many of the same procedures and commands that are used for editing normal document text. For example, you can use all the basic editing techniques we described in Chapter 4 for inserting new text and overwriting or deleting existing text. When you press the Return key, Word will begin a new paragraph in the same cell of the table—it won't move the insertion point marker to the next row on the table.

When you use Word's Cut, Copy, and Paste commands, there are a few rules that you need to keep in mind. First, when you copy and paste or cut and paste, the results of your paste will vary, depending on whether you copied or cut an end-of-cell marker (●). If the selection you copy or cut includes an end-of-cell marker, when you paste that text to another cell in the table, Word will replace the contents of that cell. (By the way, after you've cut or copied an end-of-cell marker, the Paste command on the Edit menu will change to Paste Cells.) For example, Figure 10-64 shows a table in which we've selected the text in a cell and the end-of-cell marker.

FIGURE 10-64

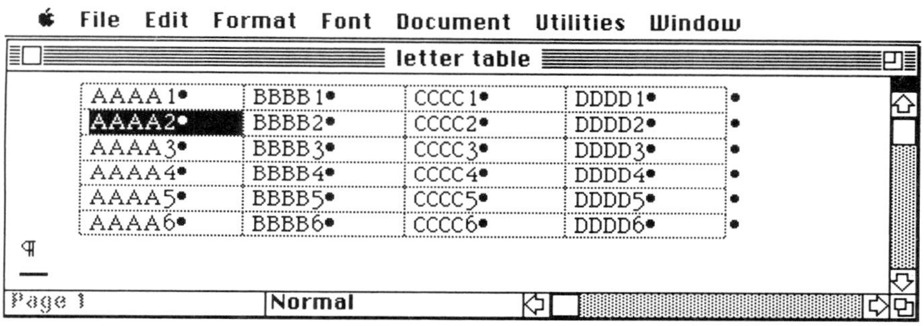

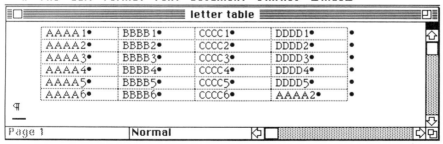

We've selected both the text and the end-of-cell marker in a cell.

Now, suppose we choose the Copy command, then click on the last cell in the fourth column of the table, and choose the Paste Cells command. Figure 10-65 shows the result. As you can see, the text we copied, *AAAA2*, has replaced the text *DDDD6* that formerly appeared in the last cell of the table.

FIGURE 10-65

 File   Edit   Format   Font   Document   Utilities   Window

letter table

AAAA1●	BBBB1●	CCCC1●	DDDD1●	●
AAAA2●	BBBB2●	CCCC2●	DDDD2●	●
AAAA3●	BBBB3●	CCCC3●	DDDD3●	●
AAAA4●	BBBB4●	CCCC4●	DDDD4●	●
AAAA5●	BBBB5●	CCCC5●	DDDD5●	●
AAAA6●	BBBB6●	CCCC6●	AAAA2●	●

¶

Page 1   Normal

Because we copied the end-of-cell marker, Word replaced the contents of the last cell on the last row of the table.

If the selection you copy or cut does not include an end-of-cell marker, Word will simply add that text to the cell where you paste it. For example, suppose the selection in the table shown in Figure 10-64 included only the text *AAAA2* and not the end-of-cell marker. Figure 10-66 shows the result of copying and pasting this text into the last cell of the table. (We also inserted one blank space between the original and copied text.)

FIGURE 10-66

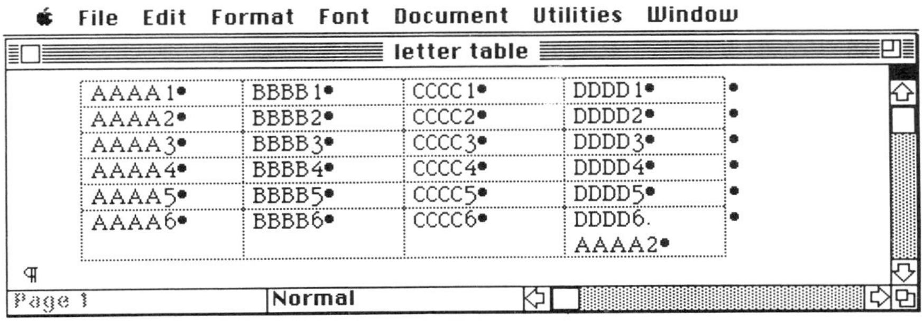

When the text selection does not include an end-of-cell marker, Word adds that text to the text in the cell where you paste.

As we pointed out earlier, there's no way to select text from two or more cells without also selecting the end-of-cell markers. Thus, if you want to copy and paste text from two or more cells into another cell—without deleting the contents of that cell—you must perform separate copy procedures for each cell whose text you want to duplicate. Similarly, if you want to cut text from two or more cells and paste it into another cell without losing the original contents of that cell, you must issue a separate Cut command for each cell whose contents you want to move.

Selecting a paste area within a table

When you move or copy cells within a table, you must select a paste area that corresponds in both size and shape to the area that you cut or copied. For example, suppose we want to copy the first two rows of the table shown in Figure 10-64 and paste them into the last two rows of that table. We would begin by selecting the first two rows and issuing the Copy command. Then, we must select the last two rows in their entirety before choosing the Paste Cells command. If we select anything more or less than two full rows—for example, if we select only the first cell in each of the last two rows—Word will not execute the paste and will display the message *Copy and Paste areas are different shapes*. (By the way, if you're familiar with copying, cutting, and pasting in a spreadsheet, such as Excel, you can see that Word is much pickier about the way in which you must define your paste area in a table.)

As we've shown, the results of moving and copying text within a table will vary depending on whether the text you select to cut or copy includes an end-of-cell marker. The end-of-cell marker also affects what happens when you paste text outside a table. If the text that you select in a table includes an end-of-cell marker and you paste that text outside the table, Word will create a new table. This new table will have the same dimensions and alignment as the cells you copied or cut from the original table. For example, suppose we copied the block of cells shown in Figure 10-67 to an area outside the table. Figure 10-68 on the next page shows the results. Notice that the cells are the same size as the original cells and that Word has applied centered alignment to this new table.

Pasting text outside a table

FIGURE 10-67

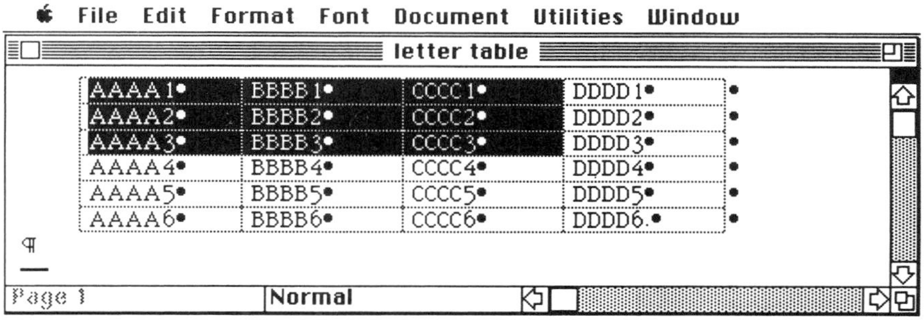

We'll copy this block of cells outside the table.

When we performed the copy procedure shown in Figures 10-67 and 10-68, we left a blank paragraph between the original table and the copied cells. If we had not done this, Word would have appended the cells onto our original table, as shown in Figure 10-69 on the following page.

If you select some text in a table and your selection does not include an end-of-cell marker, Word will paste only the text in your document when you copy or move that text outside the table; it will not create a new table. For example, suppose we select the first cell of the table shown in Figure 10-67, issue the Copy command, click outside the table, then choose Paste. Figure 10-70 on page 451 shows the result. Notice that we did not need to leave a blank paragraph between the table and the copied text.

FIGURE 10-68

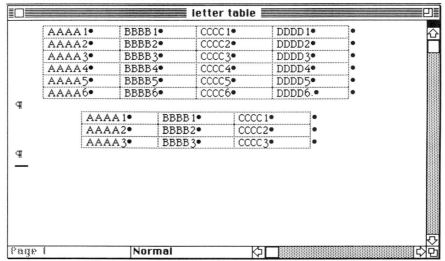

When you paste a block of cells outside the table, Word will create a new table.

FIGURE 10-69

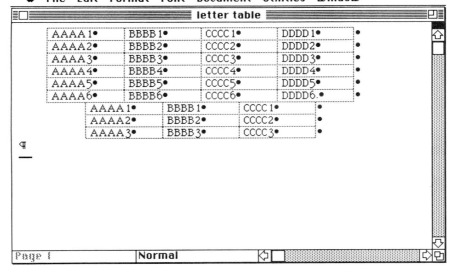

If you don't allow a blank paragraph between the original table and the copied cells, Word will append those cells onto the original table.

FIGURE 10-70

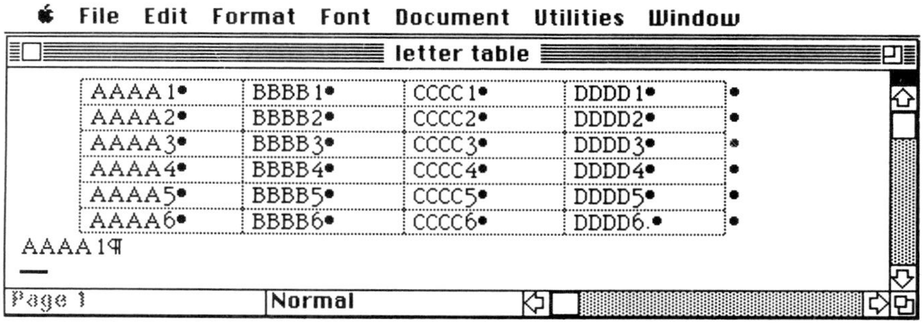

If the text you select does not include an end-of-cell marker, you can paste that text outside the table without creating a new table.

One of the nicest features of tables is the tremendous amount of flexibility you're allowed in formatting the table text. You can apply any combination of character and paragraph formatting to the text of a table. To make formatting faster and easier, you can define and apply styles to your table text.

Each of the paragraphs in a table can be formatted completely independently of other paragraphs. Thus, text that appears in the same row or the same column—or even the same cell—of a table can display different indents, alignment, line spacing, tabs, and so forth. There are only a few restrictions that Word imposes on formatting the text in a table. First, you cannot force table text to flow across a cell boundary. You also cannot create a table within a table, nor can you create a section break in a table. A table must always be contained within a single document section.

To show how to format text in a table, let's apply some paragraph and character formatting to our sample trees table shown in Figure 10-60. We'll begin by formatting the title of the table to appear in 18-point bold type. To do this, we'll select the title text (*Popular American Trees*), then we'll choose Bold from the Format menu and 18 Point from the Font menu. We'll also add 8 points of Before and After spacing to the title. (We've already formatted this title with centered alignment.)

Next, we'll add bold formatting, centered alignment, and Before and After spacing to each of the column headings (*Tree, Mature Height*, and *Description*). We'll also change the size of these headings to 14 point. First, we will select the row on which these titles appear. Then, we'll choose Bold from the Format menu and 14 Point from the Font menu. Next, we'll open the Paragraph dialog box and enter 2 in both the Before and After edit bars. Finally, we'll click the Centered alignment icon on the ruler. (By the way, the ruler must appear in the normal scale in order for the formatting icons to be available.) Figure 10-71 shows the result of our formatting changes.

Formatting text in a table

FIGURE 10-71

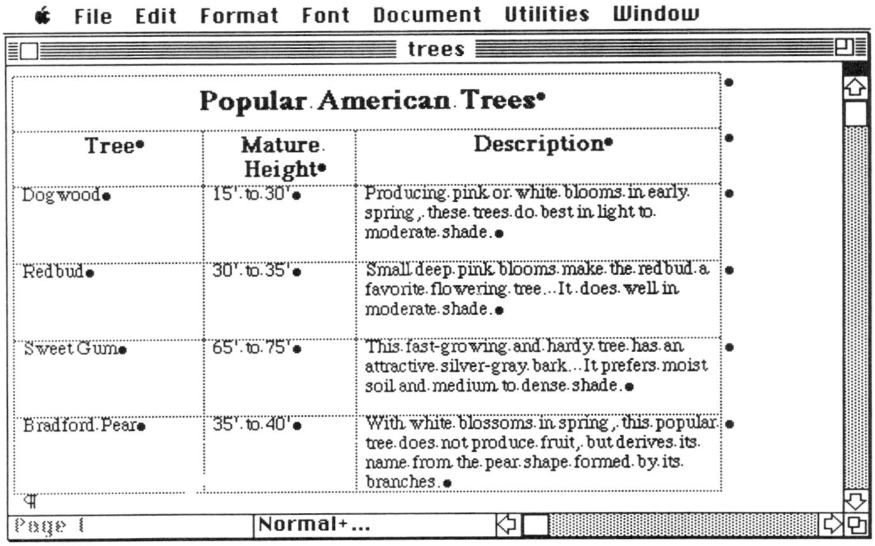

File   Edit   Format   Font   Document   Utilities   Window

trees

Popular American Trees		
Tree	**Mature Height**	**Description**
Dogwood	15' to 30'	Producing pink or white blooms in early spring, these trees do best in light to moderate shade.
Redbud	30' to 35'	Small deep pink blooms make the redbud a favorite flowering tree... It does well in moderate shade.
Sweet Gum	65' to 75'	This fast-growing and hardy tree has an attractive silver-gray bark... It prefers moist soil and medium to dense shade.
Bradford Pear	35' to 40'	With white blossoms in spring, this popular tree does not produce fruit, but derives its name from the pear shape formed by its branches.

Page 1   Normal+...

We've added some formatting to the title and column headings in our sample table.

Using named styles in a table

When you first create a table, Word will assign to every cell in that table the style of the paragraph on which the insertion point marker was positioned at the time you issued the Insert Table... command. If you create a table in a new, blank document, every cell will automatically carry the *Normal* style. You can, of course, apply other named styles to format the text in a table. For example, let's format the tree names in the first column of the table by defining a style named *trees* and applying it. To determine what characteristics we want the *trees* style to have, let's format the first tree name, *Dogwood*, then use its characteristics as the "example" for our new style. After clicking on the cell that contains the name *Dogwood*, we'll click the Centered alignment icon on the ruler. Then, we'll click the open space icon.

Now, to define these characteristics as a new style, we'll click on the style name that appears in the edit bar at the top of the styles list box on the ruler. We will type our new style name, *trees*, and click the arrow next to the edit bar. When Word displays the message *Define style "trees" based on selection?*, we'll click the Define button.

To apply this new style to the other tree names, we will simply select those cells and choose the style name *trees* from the dropdown list on the ruler.

We could follow a similar procedure to define the styles *height* and *description* to format the second and third columns of the table. The *height* style, like the *trees* style, would call for centered alignment and open spacing. The *description* style would call for 6 points of space above each paragraph. Figure 10-72 shows the table after applying our named styles.

FIGURE 10-72

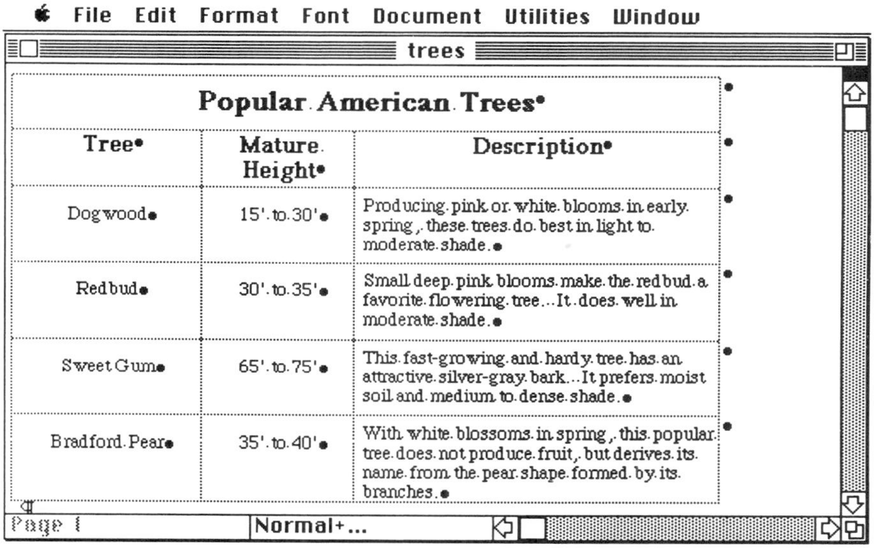

We used named styles to format the columns of our table.

When you use styles in a table, keep in mind that a style will not "carry over" from one cell to the next as you are entering text. Suppose you have applied a style named *cells* to the first cell in a table. After typing some text in this cell, you press the Tab key to move to the adjacent cell. When you begin typing here, Word will use the *Normal* style to format your text (or whatever style has been applied to that cell). If you want to use the *cells* style again, you must apply it to the cell.

Of course, if you press Return to start a new paragraph in the same cell, Word will continue to use whatever style you applied to the previous paragraph—unless that style specifies a different Next Style.

With styles, you also can "preformat" individual cells of a table. After you have created a new, blank table, just apply different style names to the different cells in the table. Then, as you move from cell to cell and enter text, Word will automatically apply the style that's defined for each cell. Of course, instead of "preformatting" the cells of a table as we've described, you can enter all the text in a table and then apply various styles to individual cells and blocks of cells to format the text.

**Indenting
table text**

By moving the indent markers on the ruler, you can change the alignment of text in a table. To change indents, first make sure the ruler is displayed in the normal scale. Then, click on or select the text you want to indent and drag the indent markers on the ruler. If a cell contains two or more paragraphs, you can change the indents for only one of those paragraphs by clicking on it and moving the indent markers on the ruler. The other paragraphs in the cell will not be affected.

You can simultaneously change the indents for the text in two or more adjacent cells in a column. Just select those cells and drag the indent markers on the ruler. (If the paragraphs in your selection have different indent settings, Word will dim the ruler and display the indent markers for the top paragraph in the selection.) You cannot simultaneously change the indent settings for two or more cells in a row. If you select two or more adjacent cells in a row, the ruler will display the indent markers for only the first (leftmost) cell in the selection.

Changing indents can have a similar effect as changing the Space Between Columns setting—it will move your text closer to or farther from the left and right boundaries of the cell. However, you can change indents on a selective basis, whereas the Space Between Columns setting always applies to every cell in a row.

By moving the indent markers on the ruler, you can override the Space Between Columns setting. As you know, Word divides the Space Between Columns between the left and right ends of each cell. If you specify a Space Between Columns setting of .5 ($^1/_2$ inch) for one row of a table, Word inserts $^1/_4$ inch of space at either end of each cell on that row. This can create unwanted space between the left and right boundaries of the table and the table text. To push the text closer to the cell boundaries, select the cells you want to format and move the indent markers on the ruler.

For example, Figure 10-73 shows a table that has two-inch wide columns and a Space Between Columns setting of .5. We've also applied centered alignment to this table. Suppose we want the text in the first column to appear closer to the left table boundary and we want the text in the second column to appear closer to the right table boundary. We would begin by selecting the first column, then, with the ruler in the normal scale, we would drag the left and first-line indent markers $^1/_4$ inch to the left. Next, we would select the second column and drag the right indent marker $^1/_4$ inch to the right. Figure 10-74 shows the result.

**Applying Before and
After spacing to
table text**

The Before and After settings in the Paragraph dialog box (and the open space icon on the ruler) offer a way to create space between the text in a table and the top and bottom boundaries of each cell. When you apply Before and/or After spacing to the text in a cell, Word will adjust the height of that cell (and other cells on the same row) as necessary to accommodate the additional space. In this respect, applying Before and After spacing is similar to changing the Minimum Row Height setting in the Cells dialog box. However, there's one important difference. When you adjust the height of a row in the Cells dialog box, Word does not increase the spacing between the text in that row and the top boundary of that row. With Before and After spacing, however, you can increase the height of a row and control the position of the text in that row relative to the top and bottom cell boundaries.

FIGURE 10-73

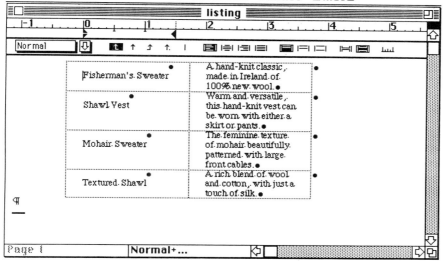

This table has a Space Between Columns setting of .5 inch, which creates extra space between the table boundaries and the table text.

FIGURE 10-74

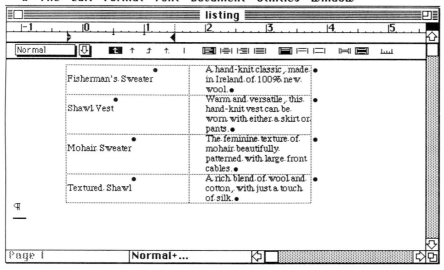

By moving the indent markers on the ruler, we have moved the text closer to the table boundaries.

For example, we used Before spacing to format the paragraphs in our sample trees table shown in Figure 10-72 and to format the text in the first column of the table shown in Figures 10-73 and 10-74. This moved the text away from the top boundary of each cell, making the table more attractive and easier to read.

Using tabs in a table

Word allows you to use tabs to align the text in one or more cells of a table. With tabs, you can split the contents of a cell into two or more "columns" without having to insert a new cell. This can be convenient when only one cell (or a few cells) on a row needs columnar formatting.

Tabs also allow you to create decimal alignment for a column of numbers in a table. In fact, if you format a cell with a decimal tab, Word will automatically align the contents of that cell with the decimal tab. (For more on creating and using tabs, see Chapter 5.)

There's one important difference between tabs that appear in a table and tabs that appear in any other part of a document. To move the insertion point marker to the next tab position in a table, you must press Option-Tab. As we explained earlier, when you press only the Tab key, Word will move the insertion point marker to the next cell in the same row.

Figure 10-75 shows an example of a table that includes tabs. As you can see on the ruler, we used a decimal tab to align the numbers in the second column of the table. We also used a right-aligned tab to align the words *(through Dec. 10)* in the last cell of the first column. Of course, instead of using a tab in this last cell, we could have used the Table... command to insert an extra cell in the fourth row of the table, then adjusted the widths of the cells to align the text properly. As you might guess, however, inserting a single tab stop is a much quicker and easier way to accomplish the same result.

Adding Borders to a Table

As we've mentioned, the gridlines that define the row and column boundaries of a table on your screen do not appear when you print the table. If you want the printed table to include gridlines, you can format the table with borders. When you use borders in a table, you do not need to display lines between every row and every column. You can apply borders selectively to certain rows and columns or even to individual cells. You also can surround an entire table with a border and omit the gridlines within that table.

To add a border(s) to a table, first select the portion of the table on which you want the border to appear. Then, choose Cells... from the Format menu. In the Cells dialog box, click the Borders... button. Word will then display the dialog box shown in Figure 10-76. Notice that this is not the same dialog box that appears when you click the Borders... button in the Paragraph dialog box.

As you can see, the Cell Borders dialog box includes five line style options, just like the Paragraph Borders dialog box: single line, thick line, double line, dotted line, and hairline. The dialog box also includes a border box with a diagram that you can use to "draw" the type of border you want to create. After you select a line style by clicking on it, you can click on different parts of the border diagram to add and remove border lines. For instance, if you want to add a border line to the right side of a selected cell or group of cells, just click on the right side of the diagram to create a line. As with the Paragraph Borders dialog box, double-clicking on the edge of the border diagram will draw a plain box border.

FIGURE 10-75

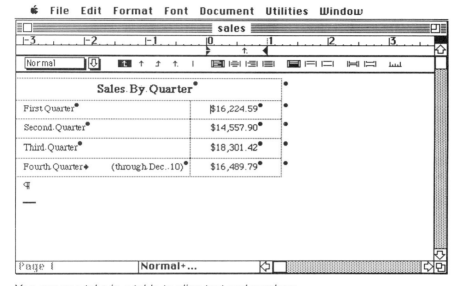

You can use tabs in a table to align text and numbers.

FIGURE 10-76

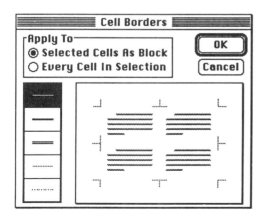

Use the Cell Borders dialog box to create borders in a table.

Notice the two option buttons at the top of the dialog box labeled *Selected Cells As Block* and *Every Cell In Selection*. These are pretty self-explanatory: They allow you to specify whether Word will apply the border you specify around the group of cells you've selected or around every cell individually.

For example, suppose we want to place a plain box border around our sample table shown in Figure 10-72. We would begin by pressing the Option key and double-clicking on the table to select the entire table. Then, we would open the Cell Borders dialog box and click on each of the four sides of the border diagram or double-click the edge of the diagram to "draw" our border outline. Since we want the border to appear around the entire table, we would choose the Selected Cells As Block option. Figure 10-77 shows the dialog box at this point.

FIGURE 10-77

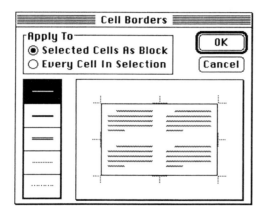

You can use these settings in the Cell Borders dialog box to create a border around an entire table.

Now, to add the border, we would simply click OK in the Cell Borders dialog box and in the Cells dialog box as well. Figure 10-78 shows our table when we print it with the border.

Suppose we now want to add gridlines to our table in addition to the outline border, as shown in Figure 10-79.

FIGURE 10-78

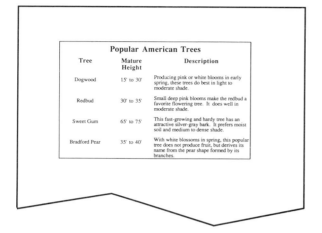

We've now created a
border around our
sample table.

FIGURE 10-79

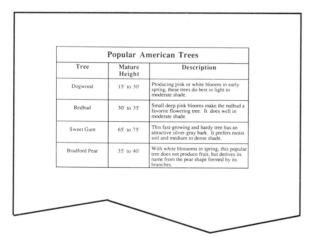

We have added
gridlines to our outline
border.

There are two ways to go about this. First, we could select the entire table, open the Cell Borders dialog box, create a plain box in the border diagram, and click the Every Cell In Selection option. We would not change the lines on our border diagram. However, Word would redraw the diagram to represent a single cell, as shown in Figure 10-80.

FIGURE 10-80

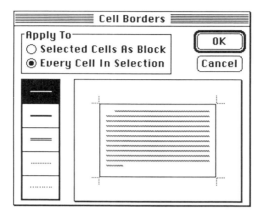

We could use the Every Cell In Selection option to create gridlines in the table.

Another way to add gridlines would be to select the table, open the Cell Borders dialog box, then click in the middle of the diagram to "draw" the lines between cells, as shown in Figure 10-81. After altering the diagram in this manner, we do not need to select the Every Cell In Selection option.

FIGURE 10-81

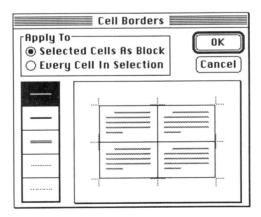

These dialog box settings will also create gridlines in our sample table.

Using different line styles

So far, we've used only the single-line border style. However, you often can enhance the appearance of your borders by using other line styles. For example, the lines in Figure 10-79 look somewhat busy. Let's use a thick line for the outline border and use hairlines for the gridlines between rows and columns. To do this, we would select the table and open the Cell Borders dialog box. In the dialog box, we would click on the thick line style to select it, and then click on each of the outside border sections in the diagram. Next, we would click the hairline border style and click on the border lines that cross in the middle of the diagram. Finally, we would choose the Selected Cells As Block option at the top of the Cell Borders dialog box, then click OK in this dialog box and in the Cells dialog box. Figure 10-82 shows the printed result. (By the way, you can print hairline borders only on a PostScript printer. On the screen, hairlines look like single lines.)

FIGURE 10-82

Popular American Trees		
Tree	Mature Height	Description
Dogwood	15' to 30'	Producing pink or white blooms in early spring, these trees do best in light to moderate shade.
Redbud	30' to 35'	Small deep pink blooms make the redbud a favorite flowering tree. It does well in moderate shade.
Sweet Gum	65' to 75'	This fast-growing and hardy tree has an attractive silver-gray bark. It prefers moist soil and medium to dense shade.
Bradford Pear	35' to 40'	With white blossoms in spring, this popular tree does not produce fruit, but derives its name from the pear shape formed by its branches.

You can use different line styles for a table border.

Word also allows you to use different line styles in each section of an individual cell's border. To do this, select the Every Cell In Selection option in the Cell Borders dialog box. Word will then redraw the border diagram to represent a single cell, as shown in Figure 10-80. You can now click on a line style you want to use and then click on the border section to which you want to apply that style.

Deleting borders

To delete the border(s) in a table, begin by selecting the cells whose borders you want to remove and opening the Cell Borders dialog box. To delete all the borders from the selected cells, just double-click in the edge of the border diagram. To remove only selected parts of the border, click on the individual border sections in the diagram. For example, if you want to delete only the top of the border box on selected cells, you would click the top line in the border diagram. When you click on a border section, make sure that the line style that's selected in the Cell Borders dialog box is the same style that appears in that border section. Otherwise, Word will simply convert the border section to the selected line style.

Sorting in a Table

In Chapter 13, we explain the Sort command on Word's Utilities menu. You can use this command to sort all or part of a table. When you sort a table, Word follows most of the same rules for sorting that we explain in Chapter 13. For example, Word uses ASCII codes to determine how to sort the table. In addition, the default sort order is ascending. To perform a descending sort, you press the Shift key as you issue the Sort command.

Word always sorts a table by rows. In other words, you cannot use the Sort command to rearrange the cells in a row. Furthermore, in determining how to sort a table, Word looks at the first character (or first few characters) in each cell. If a cell contains more than one paragraph, the Sort command will not affect the order of those paragraphs within the cell.

Suppose we want to sort the information in our sample trees table so that it appears in alphabetical order by tree name. To do this, we could begin by selecting just the tree names in the first column. (It's important that we do not select the column heading, *Tree*.) Instead of selecting just the tree names in column one, we could select entire rows of the table. After making our selection, we would choose Sort from the Utilities menu. Figure 10-83 shows the result.

FIGURE 10-83

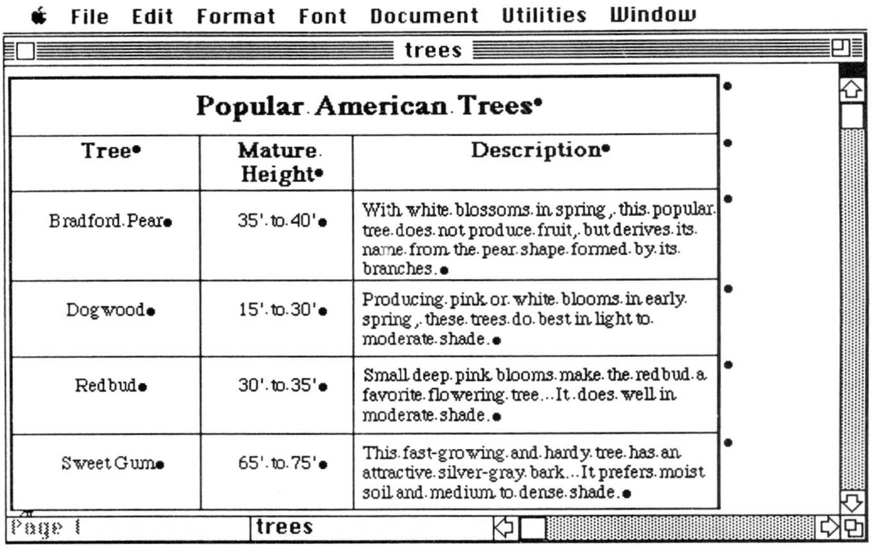

Using the Sort command, we arranged our table in alphabetical order by tree name.

Word sorts the text in *all* the columns of a table—not just the column or columns you select. However, the column you select (or the leftmost column in a selection) serves as the "key" to the sort procedure. For example, to sort the sample trees table by height, we would begin by selecting the second column of the table, as shown in Figure 10-84. (We also could select the second and third columns.) Then, we would choose the Sort command on the Utilities menu. Figure 10-85 shows the result.

FIGURE 10-84

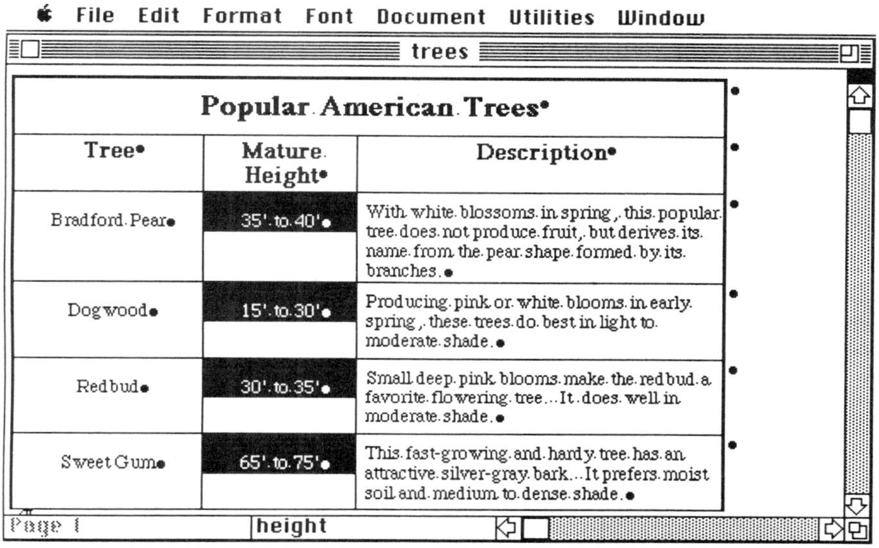

🍎 File Edit Format Font Document Utilities Window

trees

Popular American Trees•		
Tree•	**Mature Height•**	**Description•**
Bradford Pear•	35' to 40'•	With white blossoms in spring, this popular tree does not produce fruit, but derives its name from the pear shape formed by its branches.•
Dogwood•	15' to 30'•	Producing pink or white blooms in early spring, these trees do best in light to moderate shade.•
Redbud•	30' to 35'•	Small deep pink blooms make the redbud a favorite flowering tree...It does well in moderate shade.•
Sweet Gum•	65' to 75'•	This fast-growing and hardy tree has an attractive silver-gray bark...It prefers moist soil and medium to dense shade.•

Page 1 height

The column you select before issuing a Sort command serves as the key for the sort.

FIGURE 10-85

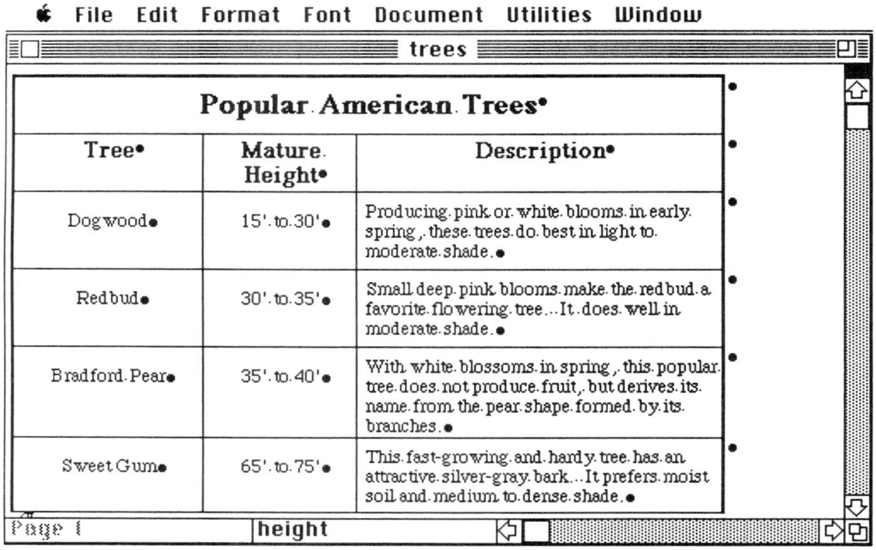

🍎 File Edit Format Font Document Utilities Window

trees

Popular American Trees•		
Tree•	**Mature Height•**	**Description•**
Dogwood•	15' to 30'•	Producing pink or white blooms in early spring, these trees do best in light to moderate shade.•
Redbud•	30' to 35'•	Small deep pink blooms make the redbud a favorite flowering tree...It does well in moderate shade.•
Bradford Pear•	35' to 40'•	With white blossoms in spring, this popular tree does not produce fruit, but derives its name from the pear shape formed by its branches.•
Sweet Gum•	65' to 75'•	This fast-growing and hardy tree has an attractive silver-gray bark...It prefers moist soil and medium to dense shade.•

Page 1 height

Our table is now arranged in ascending order by height.

Deleting a Table

There are several techniques you can use to delete an entire table from your document. First, you can select that table, then choose Table… from the Edit menu and click the Delete button in the Table dialog box. You also can select all the cells in one column of the table, open the Table dialog box, click the Row option, and then click the Delete button. This tells Word to delete all the rows in which you've selected a cell—or the entire table. Finally, you can select an entire row of the table, open the Table dialog box, click the Column option, and then click the Delete button.

If you delete a table by mistake, you can use the Undo command to recover it. Keep in mind that Word does not place the deleted table on the Clipboard. As a result, you cannot recover a table by pasting it back into your document.

Converting Existing Text into a Table

As we mentioned at the beginning of this section, Word allows you to convert existing text into a table. Most often, you'll convert Word 3 side-by-side paragraphs or tab-delimited text into a table. You also can convert comma-delimited text, such as a database that you've imported from another program. Finally, you can create a table by converting plain paragraphs with no tabs, commas, or special formatting.

To convert existing text into a table format, first select that text. Then, issue the Insert Table… command. When the Insert Table dialog box appears, you'll see that the Convert From options in the bottom of the dialog box are activated, as shown in Figure 10-86. (Normally, these options are dimmed.)

FIGURE 10-86

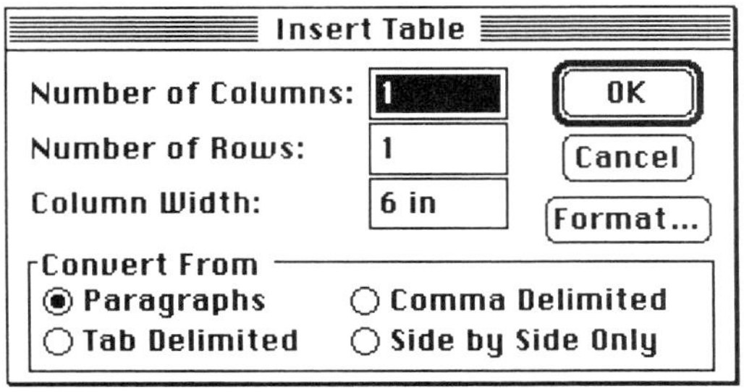

If you select text before issuing the Insert Table… command, the Convert From options in the Insert Table dialog box will be available.

Word will usually select the Convert From option that best describes the type of text you are converting. If your selected text contains a mixture of types—for example, some tab-delimited lines and some comma-delimited lines—Word will be able to convert only one type correctly. For instance, suppose you select one line of text that contains words separated by tabs and another line that contains words separated by commas. Then, you issue the Insert Table… command. Word will automatically select the Tab Delimited option. When you click OK to create the table, Word will place all the text in the comma-delimited line in a single cell. On the other hand, if you select the Comma Delimited option, Word will place all the text in the tab-delimited line in a single cell of the new table.

The Side by Side Only option does exactly what its name implies: It converts any side-by-side paragraphs in your text selection into table format and ignores the rest of the paragraphs in the selection. If you want to convert the other paragraphs into a table format, you must select them, issue the Insert Table... command, and choose the Paragraphs option.

When you convert existing text into a table, Word also will suggest a Number of Columns and a Column Width setting based on your text selection. If you select the Tab Delimited option, Word will use the paragraph with the greatest number of tabs to determine its suggested Number of Columns setting. Similarly, if you select the Comma Delimited option, Word will use the paragraph with the most commas to determine its suggested Number of Columns setting. The width of the current text column will then be divided by the number of columns to determine the Column Width setting.

If you are converting plain paragraphs, Word will always suggest 1 as the Number of Columns setting. When you convert side-by-side paragraphs, Word will suggest neither a Number of Columns setting nor a Column Width setting.

When you select tab-delimited or comma-delimited text, the Number of Rows setting in the Insert Table dialog box will be dimmed. Word automatically sets the number of rows in the new table based on the number of text lines you are converting to table format.

Let's consider a quick example of how you might convert existing text to table format. Figure 10-87 shows a document that lists name and address information.

FIGURE 10-87

FirstName♦	LastName♦	Address♦	City♦	ST♦	Zip¶
David♦	Powell♦	1040.Eastern.Pkwy.♦	Nashville♦	TN♦	37215¶
Sandra♦	Jennings♦	134.Brecker.Blvd.♦	Lansing♦	MI♦	48912¶
Norman♦	Baker♦	2100.Crescent Place♦	Dallas♦	TX♦	75238¶
George♦	Henderson♦	3344.Broadway♦	Baltimore♦	MD♦	21228¶
Julia♦	Fischer♦	1454.East 60th. St.♦	Orlando♦	FL♦	32817¶
Gayle♦	Higgins♦	801.Parkside.Dr.♦	Tulsa♦	OK♦	74127¶
Brad♦	Thomas♦	5987.Norwood.Ave.♦	Liberty♦	IL♦	62347¶
Lisa♦	Schaefer♦	1600.Winchester.Rd.♦	Richmond♦	VA♦	23236¶
Stanley♦	Green♦	709.Market St.♦	Atlanta♦	GA♦	30318¶
Evelyn♦	Peterson♦	111.East Main.St.♦	Louisville♦	KY♦	40205¶
Charles♦	Keller♦	3333.University.Dr.♦	Cincinnati♦	OH♦	45231¶
Michael♦	Ford♦	1217.Maple.St.♦	Greensboro♦	NC♦	27406¶
Gary♦	Fleming♦	8560.Olympic.Blvd.♦	Orange♦	CA♦	92667¶
Nathan♦	Sanders♦	24.Stone.Mill Way♦	Albany♦	NY♦	12205¶
Rachel♦	McLaury♦	176.Quince.St.♦	Natick♦	MA♦	01760¶
Janet♦	Taylor♦	674.Emerald.Dr.♦	Arlington♦	VA♦	22207¶
Robert♦	Haynes♦	1622.Glyndon Ave.♦	Sioux.City♦	IA♦	51104¶
John♦	Lynch♦	12.West 15th.St.♦	New.York♦	NY♦	10011¶
Anna♦	White♦	142.State.St.♦	Hartford♦	CT♦	06117¶
Kim♦	Thayer♦	2413.Briarcliff.Rd.♦	Phoenix♦	AZ♦	85027¶
Daniel♦	Kaufman♦	2004.Jefferson.St.♦	Springfield♦	MO♦	65807¶

You can convert tab-delimited text like this to table format.

You might use a document like the one shown in Figure 10-87 as the data document in a print merge procedure. As you can see, the fields in this document (FirstName, LastName, Address, and so forth) are separated by tab spaces. To convert this text to a table, you would select all the rows of information, then choose Insert Table... on the Document menu. In the Insert Table dialog box, Word will automatically suggest the correct settings for the table, so you can simply click OK to complete the procedure. Figure 10-88 shows the result.

FIGURE 10-88

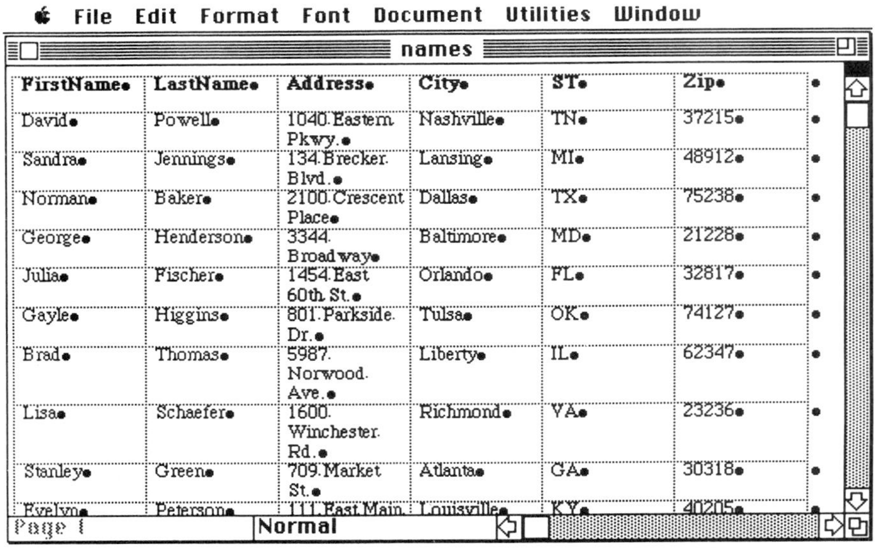

FirstName	LastName	Address	City	ST	Zip	
David	Powell	1040 Eastern Pkwy.	Nashville	TN	37215	
Sandra	Jennings	134 Brecker Blvd.	Lansing	MI	48912	
Norman	Baker	2100 Crescent Place	Dallas	TX	75238	
George	Henderson	3344 Broadway	Baltimore	MD	21228	
Julia	Fischer	1454 East 60th St.	Orlando	FL	32817	
Gayle	Higgins	801 Parkside Dr.	Tulsa	OK	74127	
Brad	Thomas	5987 Norwood Ave.	Liberty	IL	62347	
Lisa	Schaefer	1600 Winchester Rd.	Richmond	VA	23236	
Stanley	Green	709 Market St.	Atlanta	GA	30318	
Evelyn	Peterson	111 East Main	Louisville	KY	40205	

This is the table that Word created from the document shown in Figure 10-87.

In the third column of Figure 10-88, notice that Word has wrapped some of the address information into two lines in order to fit it within the cell boundaries. Of course, you can always widen this column if you want each address to appear on a single line. If the text appears wrapped, however, Word will have no trouble interpreting the information in a print merge procedure.

Converting All or Part of a Table to Text

Word makes it easy for you to convert selected rows of a table—or an entire table—to text. To do this, you must first select the row(s) you want to convert. It's important that you select whole rows; otherwise, Word won't be able to convert the table to text. After making your selection, choose the Table to Text... command on the Document menu. (This command replaces the Insert Table... command when you select text in a table.) Word will then display the dialog box shown in Figure 10-89. Choose one of the Convert To options and click OK.

FIGURE 10-89

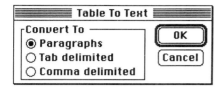

Word will display
this dialog box when
you choose the
Table to Text...
command.

If you select the Convert To Paragraphs option, Word will place the text in each table cell in a separate paragraph. However, if a cell contains two or more paragraphs, those paragraphs will remain separate after the conversion. In addition, any paragraph formatting you may have applied to the table text, such as indents or line spacing, will be preserved.

If you select the Convert To Tab Delimited or Convert To Comma Delimited option, Word will separate the text of each cell on a row with tabs or commas. Each row of the table will be converted into a single paragraph unless one of the cells on a row contains two or more paragraphs. In that case, Word will recognize the additional paragraphs as it converts the text.

A Word about Side-by-Side Paragraphs

As we've mentioned, Word 4's table feature supplants the side-by-side paragraph format that was available in Word 3. However, you can still use the side-by-side format, if you want. In fact, if you open into Word 4 a Word 3 document that contains side-by-side paragraphs, you'll see that these paragraphs retain their side-by-side formatting. Each side-by-side paragraph will be marked by a paragraph properties mark. Because tables can be slow to work with (they slow down both scrolling and screen refreshing), you may, under certain circumstances, opt to use side-by-side paragraphs instead of creating a table.

To apply the side-by-side feature, first click on the paragraph you want to format, then choose the Commands... command on the Edit menu. In the Commands dialog box, you'll see a list box displaying all the commands and features available in Word 4. If you scroll down this list, you'll see the item *Side by Side*. Select this item, then click the Do button.

Instead of opening the Commands dialog box every time you want to apply side-by-side formatting, you can add that option to the Format menu. To do this, open the Commands dialog box and click on the Side by Side option in the list box. Word will then display the menu name *Format* in the Menu edit bar on the right side of the Commands dialog box. Click the Add button immediately below this edit bar and then click the Cancel button. If you now check the Format menu, you'll see that it includes the Side by Side option. You can use this new menu option to toggle the side-by-side format on and off. For more on customizing menus and using the Commands... command, see Chapter 14.

SPECIAL POSITIONING

Another exciting new feature in Word 4 is the Position... command, which allows you to place a paragraph, graphic, or table anywhere on a page, with text flowing around that item. You also can use the Position... command to place one or more rows from a table anywhere on a page. This capability will be an important tool for anyone who plans to use Word for desktop publishing applications.

When you place an item with the Position... command, that item is called a positioned object. For example, Figure 10-91 shows a page of text with a table positioned in the center.

FIGURE 10-91

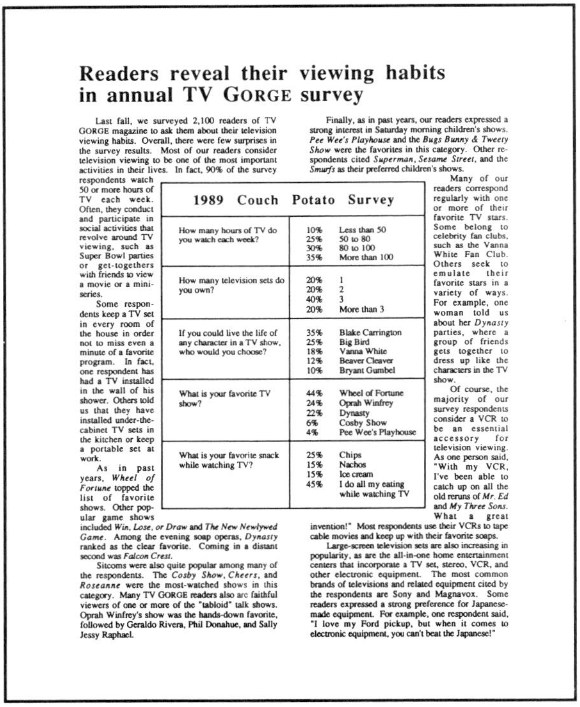

Readers reveal their viewing habits in annual TV GORGE survey

Last fall, we surveyed 2,100 readers of TV GORGE magazine to ask them about their television viewing habits. Overall, there were few surprises in the survey results. Most of our readers consider television viewing to be one of the most important activities in their lives. In fact, 90% of the survey respondents watch 50 or more hours of TV each week. Often, they conduct and participate in social activities that revolve around TV viewing, such as Super Bowl parties or get-togethers with friends to view a movie or a mini-series.

Some respondents keep a TV set in every room of the house in order not to miss even a minute of a favorite program. In fact, one respondent has had a TV installed in the wall of his shower. Others told us that they have installed under-the-cabinet TV sets in the kitchen or keep a portable set at work.

As in past years, *Wheel of Fortune* topped the list of favorite shows. Other popular game shows included *Win, Lose, or Draw* and *The New Newlywed Game*. Among the evening soap operas, *Dynasty* ranked as the clear favorite. Coming in a distant second was *Falcon Crest*.

Sitcoms were also quite popular among many of the respondents. The *Cosby Show*, *Cheers*, and *Roseanne* were the most-watched shows in this category. Many TV GORGE readers also are faithful viewers of one or more of the "tabloid" talk shows. Oprah Winfrey's show was the hands-down favorite, followed by Geraldo Rivera, Phil Donahue, and Sally Jessy Raphael.

Finally, as in past years, our readers expressed a strong interest in Saturday morning children's shows. *Pee Wee's Playhouse* and the *Bugs Bunny & Tweety Show* were the favorites in this category. Other respondents cited *Superman*, *Sesame Street*, and the *Smurfs* as their preferred children's shows.

Many of our readers correspond regularly with one or more of their favorite TV stars. Some belong to celebrity fan clubs, such as the Vanna White Fan Club. Others seek to emulate their favorite stars in a variety of ways. For example, one woman told us about her *Dynasty* parties, where a group of friends gets together to dress up like the characters in the TV show.

Of course, the majority of our survey respondents consider a VCR to be an essential accessory for television viewing. As one person said, "With my VCR, I've been able to catch up on all the old reruns of *Mr. Ed* and *My Three Sons*. What a great invention!" Most respondents use their VCRs to tape cable movies and keep up with their favorite soaps.

Large-screen television sets are also increasing in popularity, as are the all-in-one home entertainment centers that incorporate a TV set, stereo, VCR, and other electronic equipment. The most common brands of televisions and related equipment cited by the respondents are Sony and Magnavox. Some readers expressed a strong preference for Japanese-made equipment. For example, one respondent said, "I love my Ford pickup, but when it comes to electronic equipment, you can't beat the Japanese!"

1989 Couch Potato Survey

How many hours of TV do you watch each week?	10%	Less than 50
	25%	50 to 80
	30%	80 to 100
	35%	More than 100
How many television sets do you own?	20%	1
	20%	2
	40%	3
	20%	More than 3
If you could live the life of any character in a TV show, who would you choose?	35%	Blake Carrington
	25%	Big Bird
	18%	Vanna White
	12%	Beaver Cleaver
	10%	Bryant Gumbel
What is your favorite TV show?	44%	Wheel of Fortune
	24%	Oprah Winfrey
	22%	Dynasty
	6%	Cosby Show
	4%	Pee Wee's Playhouse
What is your favorite snack while watching TV?	25%	Chips
	15%	Nachos
	15%	Ice cream
	45%	I do all my eating while watching TV

You can use the Position... command to place a paragraph, graphic, or table anywhere on a page.

As you can see in Figure 10-91, Word automatically reflows the text around a positioned object on a page. You won't be able to see the reflowed text, however, unless you switch to the page view of your document or issue the Print Preview... command. As long as you're in the galley view, the text will appear in a single column—as it normally would—displaying any formats you have assigned. In addition, the paragraph, graphic, or table to which you've assigned a special position will appear in the same text column as the rest of your document. However, Word will display the paragraph properties mark (■) next to the positioned object to indicate that it has been assigned a special format.

To position a paragraph, graphic, or table row, first click on that object or select it. To position a full table, you must select the entire table; and to position two or more rows in a table, you must select the first cell in each row. Next, choose Position... from the Format menu. Word will then display the dialog box shown in Figure 10-92.

Positioning an Object

FIGURE 10-92

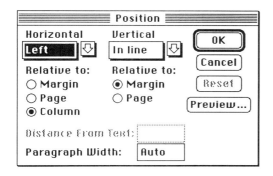

The Position dialog box allows you to specify precisely where you want to place an object on a page.

The settings in this dialog box let you specify the position of the selected object on a page. Notice that there are two dropdown list boxes labeled *Horizontal* and *Vertical*. Below each dropdown list, you'll see the headings *Relative To:* followed by some options. As these items suggest, positioning an object is simply a matter of specifying its horizontal and vertical position relative to a specific part of the page. The horizontal position can be relative to the left and right document margins, the left and right edges of your page, or the boundaries of a text column. (If your document contains only one column of text, the Margin and Column options have the same effect.) The vertical position can be relative to either your top and bottom margins or the top and bottom edges of the page.

Figure 10-93 on the next page shows the options that are available on the Horizontal and Vertical dropdown lists. Instead of choosing one of these standard options, you can type a value in the edit bar at the top of the list. We will show you how to use values for your Horizontal and Vertical settings a little later in this chapter.

Generally, the first step in specifying an object's position is to choose one of the Relative To options. In other words, you need to decide what part of the document page you want to use as your point of reference in positioning the object. Then, you can specify how you want to align the object. For both the horizontal and vertical positions, you can either select an alignment option from the dropdown lists shown in Figure 10-93 (such as Center), or you can type a measurement in the edit bar at the top of the list.

After you've specified a position, you can click OK to apply it and return to your document. Alternatively, you can click the Preview... button to go directly to the Print Preview window and see how Word will place the object on the printed page.

FIGURE 10-93

Horizontal   Vertical

Word offers several standard options for specifying the horizontal and vertical position of an object.

For example, Figure 10-94 shows a graphic that we've positioned two inches from the top margin, aligned with the left edge of the text column. We specified the horizontal position of this object by choosing Left from the Horizontal dropdown list and clicking on the Margin option beneath this list box. Then, to specify the vertical position, we typed *2 in* in the Vertical edit bar and chose the Margin option there as well.

Alignment options

When you first open the Position dialog box, you'll notice that Word's default horizontal alignment is Left Relative To Column. The default vertical alignment is In Line. With these settings, the paragraph, graphic, or table will appear with no special positioning. Let's look at how you can use the other alignment options to change an object's position.

Horizontal options

As you can see in Figure 10-93, the alignment options in the Horizontal dropdown list are Left, Center, Right, Inside, and Outside. Left will align the left edge of the selected object with the left edge of the page, the current column, or the left margin (depending on which Relative To option you select: Margin, Page, or Column). Similarly, the Right option will align the right edge of the selected object with the right edge of the page, the current column, or the right margin. When you choose Center, Word will center the object between the left and right margins, the left and right edges of the page, or between the boundaries of the current text column. Figures 10-95 and 10-96 on page 472 illustrate the Left, Center, and Right Horizontal alignment options.

FIGURE 10-94

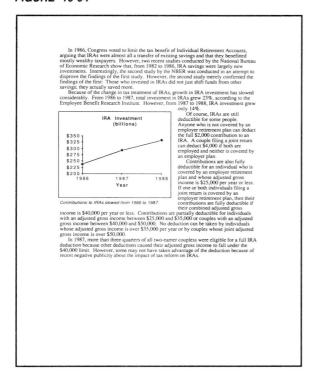

We positioned this graphic two inches from the top margin, aligned with the left edge of the text column.

The Inside and Outside alignment options allow you to specify a position that changes depending on whether the positioned object falls on a right or left (odd or even) document page. You will typically use these options only when you've activated Mirror Even/Odd Margins or specified a Gutter setting in the Document dialog box. However, these options are available even if you have not set up different left and right page layouts.

The Inside option will align the edge of an object with the inside margin, the inside edge of a page, or the inside edge of a column. On odd-numbered or right pages, the left edge of the object will be aligned with the left margin, the left edge of the page, or the left edge of the text column. On even-numbered or left pages, the right edge of the object will be aligned with the right margin, the right edge of the page, or the right edge of the text column.

FIGURE 10-95

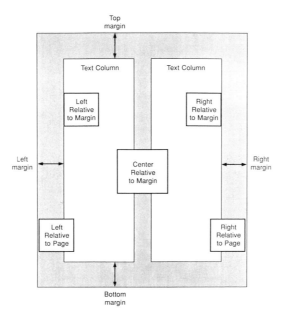

This layout sketch illustrates Horizontal alignment relative to the left and right margins and the left and right edges of the page.

FIGURE 10-96

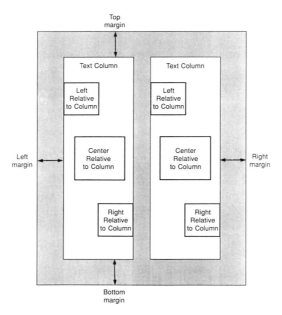

This layout sketch illustrates Horizontal alignment relative to column boundaries.

The Outside option will align the edge of an object with the outside margin, the outside edge of a page, or the outside edge of a column. On odd-numbered or right pages, the right edge of the object will be aligned with the right margin, the right edge of the page, or the right column boundary. On even-numbered or left pages, the left edge of the object will be aligned with the left margin, the left edge of the page, or the left column boundary. Figures 10-97 and 10-98 on the following pages illustrate how the Inside and Outside options will align an object.

The Vertical dropdown list offers the options In Line, Top, Center, and Bottom. The Top, Center, and Bottom options are fairly self-explanatory. Top will align the top edge of the selected object with the top of the page or with the top margin (depending on whether you've selected Margin or Page as the Relative To option). The Bottom option will align the bottom edge of the selected object with the bottom of the page or with the bottom margin. If you select Center, Word will center the positioned object either between the top and bottom margins or between the top and bottom edges of the page.

Vertical options

The In Line option works a little differently. It does not change the normal vertical alignment of an object on a page. When you choose In Line, Word will position the object relative to its surrounding document text. If you insert or delete text above the positioned object, Word will adjust the vertical position of that object accordingly. The Relative To options for vertical positioning have no effect when you choose the In Line option.

Since the In Line option does not change the vertical position of an object, you may be wondering what purpose it serves. By using this option in combination with one of the Horizontal options (or a Horizontal measurement), you can change an object's horizontal position without changing its alignment relative to preceding and subsequent text. This is similar to adjusting the left indent on a paragraph, with one important difference: When you specify a Horizontal position and use In Line Vertical alignment, Word will flow text around the positioned object. In fact, if you choose Left Horizontal alignment Relative To the Margin and In Line Vertical alignment, Word will position the object just as it normally would, but will flow text around that object (assuming that there's room for the text).

For example, Figure 10-99 on page 476 shows some text that we've positioned using In Line as our Vertical position and Left Relative To Margin as our Horizontal position. Notice how the main body of our document flows around the specially positioned text. (To create this effect, we specified a Paragraph Width setting of 3.25 inches. We'll talk more about this setting in a moment. As you can see, we also created a border around the positioned paragraph.)

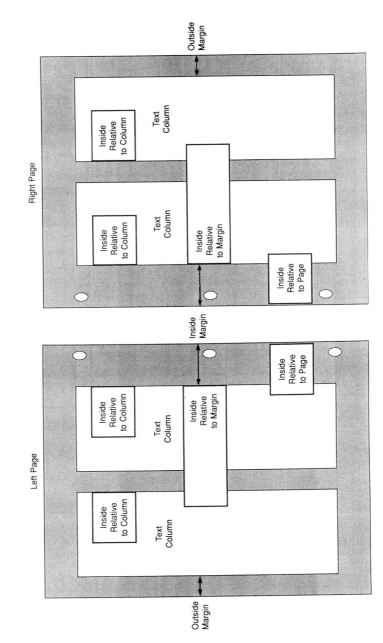

FIGURE 10-97

This layout sketch shows how the Inside alignment option will position objects on left and right pages.

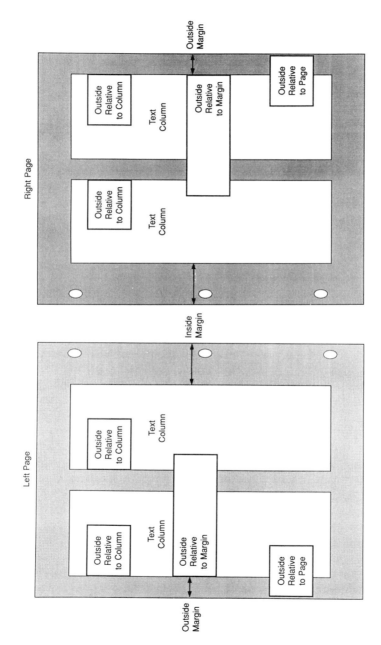

FIGURE 10-98

This layout shows how the Outside alignment option will position objects.

FIGURE 10-99

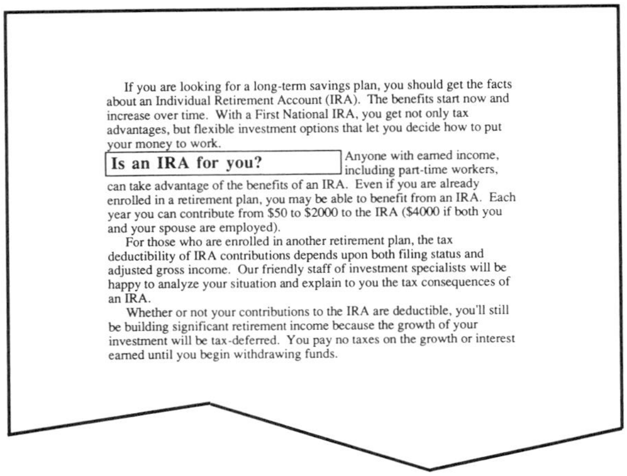

> If you are looking for a long-term savings plan, you should get the facts about an Individual Retirement Account (IRA). The benefits start now and increase over time. With a First National IRA, you get not only tax advantages, but flexible investment options that let you decide how to put your money to work.
>
> **Is an IRA for you?** Anyone with earned income, including part-time workers, can take advantage of the benefits of an IRA. Even if you are already enrolled in a retirement plan, you may be able to benefit from an IRA. Each year you can contribute from $50 to $2000 to the IRA ($4000 if both you and your spouse are employed).
>
> For those who are enrolled in another retirement plan, the tax deductibility of IRA contributions depends upon both filing status and adjusted gross income. Our friendly staff of investment specialists will be happy to analyze your situation and explain to you the tax consequences of an IRA.
>
> Whether or not your contributions to the IRA are deductible, you'll still be building significant retirement income because the growth of your investment will be tax-deferred. You pay no taxes on the growth or interest earned until you begin withdrawing funds.

When you use In Line Vertical alignment, Word will not change the vertical position of an object, but will flow text around it.

Specifying an alignment measurement

Instead of selecting an alignment option from the Horizontal or Vertical dropdown list, you can type a measurement in the Horizontal or Vertical edit bar. The measurement you type must be a positive number, expressed in inches, centimeters, points, or picas. If you do not include a unit (*in*, *cm*, *pt*, or *pi*) in your entry, Word will assume inches (or whatever unit you have chosen as the default in the Preferences dialog box). In addition, Word will convert any entries you make in centimeters, points, or picas to inches (or the default unit of measure).

When you use a measurement to specify an object's horizontal position, Word will align the left edge of that object relative to the left edge of the page, the left margin, or the left column boundary, depending on the Relative To option you select. For example, suppose you enter .5 in the Horizontal edit bar and click the Relative To Page option. Word will position the selected object $\frac{1}{2}$ inch from the left edge of your paper.

Similarly, when you use a measurement to specify an object's vertical position, Word will position the object relative to the top edge of your paper or the top margin. Suppose you enter 3 in the Vertical edit bar and click the Margin option. Word will position the selected object 3 inches from the top margin on the page.

Specifying the Distance From Text

As we've seen, when you position some text or a graphic, Word will flow the remainder of the text on the page around the positioned object. Normally, Word allows $\frac{1}{8}$ inch of white space between the positioned object and the text that flows around it. This space is determined by the Distance From Text setting in the Position dialog box. The default value for this setting is .125 (or $\frac{1}{8}$) inch. As you might guess, you can change the amount of space between a positioned object and its surrounding text by entering a new number in the Distance From Text edit bar.

The Distance From Text setting can be as small as 0 or as large as 22 inches. For example, if you want $1/4$ inch of white space to appear between a positioned object and its surrounding text, enter a Distance From Text setting of .25. A relatively large setting—a few inches or more—will cause the positioned object to appear on a page by itself. When this happens, Word will not "carry over" any of the space that you've specified in the Distance From Text setting to the previous or subsequent pages. In other words, Word will place the positioned object on one page, with the text on the pages before and after the object appearing in the normal text area.

Although Word does a pretty good job in controlling the horizontal distance between a positioned object and its surrounding text, you may find that the space between your text and the top or bottom edge of a positioned object does not exactly match the Distance From Text setting. The reason for this inaccuracy is that Word must consider the leading of the text that flows around the positioned object as well as the Distance From Text setting. Word will not adjust the text leading in order to create the correct amount of space between a positioned object and surrounding text.

Figure 10-100 shows a printed document in which one paragraph has been assigned special positioning. The text flowing around the paragraph measures 12 points. We've specified a Distance From Text setting of .2 for this paragraph. Notice, however, that the distances between the top and bottom edges of the paragraph and the surrounding text are considerably greater than the distances between the left and right paragraph edges and the surrounding text.

FIGURE 10-100

Word may not be able to create the correct amount of space between the top and bottom edges of a positioned object and surrounding text.

As you specify a Distance From Text setting, keep in mind that this value will affect how Word flows text around the positioned object. To flow text beside an object, Word must have at least one inch of space between a positioned object and the boundary of a text column. In determining whether there is one inch of available space, Word considers not only an object's horizontal position, but also the Distance From Text setting. If Word cannot maintain the specified distance between an object and its surrounding text and still have at least one inch of space available for text, it will not flow the text.

For example, suppose you have positioned a graphic one inch from the left margin and you have specified .1 (or $^1/_{10}$ inch) as your Distance From Text setting. Word will not be able to flow text on the left side of that graphic because only $^9/_{10}$ inch remains after allowing for the .1 inch Distance From Text setting. To flow text on the left side of the graphic, you must make sure that the graphic is at least $1^1/_{10}$ inches from the left margin. In other words, you must specify a Horizontal setting of at least 1.1 inches.

If you position an object at the edge of a page, the Distance From Text setting will determine how much space appears between that object and the edge of the page. For example, suppose you have positioned a graphic by choosing Right from the Horizontal list and clicking the Relative To Page option. You've also specified .25 as the Distance From Text setting. Word will not place the right edge of the graphic flush against the right edge of the page. Instead, Word will allow $^1/_4$ inch of space—the Distance From Text setting—between the graphic and the edge of the page. Of course, when you position an object near the edge of a page, keep in mind that the LaserWriter cannot print anything that falls less than about $^3/_8$ inch from the edge of the paper.

Specifying a width

We've just seen how the Distance From Text setting can affect the way Word flows text around a positioned object. Another factor that affects the flow of text is the width of that object. The default width of a positioned graphic is simply the width of the graphic frame. Similarly, the default width of a positioned table is no different from the width of the table without any special positioning. Therefore, when you apply special positioning to a graphic or table, Word will automatically flow text around that object as long as there is sufficient room.

Positioned paragraphs work a little differently. Initially, the width of a positioned paragraph is determined by the width of the text column. For example, if you're using Word's default Page Setup and Document settings, and you have only one column of text, each paragraph—regardless of whether you assign a special position—will be six inches wide. If you are using snaking columns, the width of each paragraph will be equal to the width of a column.

Because Word considers a positioned paragraph to be the same width as the text column, it may not be able to flow text on the right or left side of the paragraph. Even if you move the indent markers on the ruler to make a positioned paragraph narrower or wider, Word will, for positioning purposes, consider that paragraph to be the same width as your text column.

You can see the width of a positioned paragraph by turning on page view and choosing Show ¶ from the Edit menu. When you do this, Word will mark the paragraph's boundaries on your screen with dotted lines. For example, let's go back to the document shown in Figure 10-99. Before we changed the Paragraph Width setting on the positioned paragraph, Word considered that paragraph to have the same width as the document's text area. Figure 10-101 shows this document in page view before we changed the Paragraph Width setting. As you can see, a dotted line marks the boundaries of the positioned paragraph. Notice that, even though the text of this paragraph is quite short, Word extends its boundaries to the full width of the text area and is unable to flow text to the right of the paragraph.

FIGURE 10-101

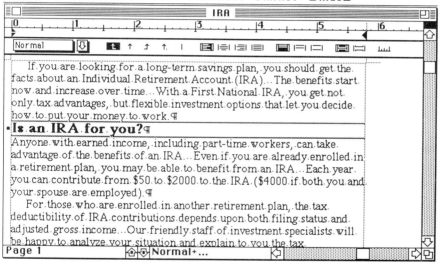

Initially, the width of a positioned paragraph will be the same as the width of a document's text column.

To make the text flow around the positioned paragraph shown in Figure 10-101, you must specify a Paragraph Width setting in the Position dialog box. When you specify a Paragraph Width that is less than the width of the text area, Word will rewrap the paragraph text, if necessary, to fit that setting. In addition, Word will flow text around the paragraph. For example, Figure 10-102 on the following page shows our sample paragraph from Figure 10-101 after we changed its Paragraph Width setting to 3.25 (inches).

You also can specify a Paragraph Width setting that is greater than the width of your text column. When you do this, Word will rewrap the text in the paragraph to align it within the specified width. As a result, the positioned paragraph will hang outside the text column.

Changing the width of a positioned paragraph

FIGURE 10-102

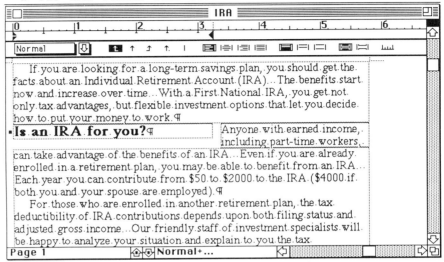

File   Edit   Format   Font   Document   Utilities   Window

After changing the Paragraph Width setting, Word is able to flow text around the positioned paragraph.

Changing the width of a positioned table or graphic

Although you can use the Paragraph Width setting with a positioned table or graphic, you probably will want to leave this setting on Auto. If you specify a setting that is greater than the initial width of the table or graphic, Word will not enlarge the table or graphic; it will simply add some additional white space to the right of the object. However, if you specify a Paragraph Width setting that is less than the initial width of a table or graphic, Word will truncate the positioned object by cropping off part of its right edge.

Formatting a positioned paragraph

You can use the ruler and the Paragraph dialog box to change the alignment and other paragraph formatting characteristics of a positioned paragraph. When you click on a positioned paragraph, the ruler (in the normal scale) will display the width of that paragraph, with the zero position on the ruler representing the left edge of the paragraph and the dotted vertical line representing the paragraph's right boundary (as determined by the Paragraph Width setting). For example, notice in Figure 10-102 that the dotted vertical line appears at the $3^1/_4$-inch mark on the ruler. Initially the left and first-line indent markers for the paragraph will be aligned with the zero position on the ruler, and the right indent marker will be aligned with the dotted vertical line.

If you change the indents or alignment of a positioned paragraph, those changes will be made relative to the paragraph's boundaries. For example, suppose we apply right alignment to the sample paragraph shown in Figure 10-102. As you can see in Figure 10-103, Word will align the paragraph flush with its right boundary. (If we were to move the right indent marker on this paragraph, Word would align it with the indent marker rather than the right boundary.)

Changing alignment and indents

FIGURE 10-103

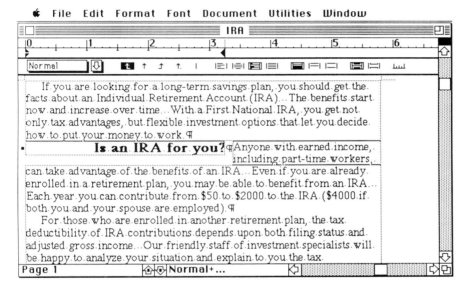

We have applied right alignment to the paragraph shown in Figure 10-102.

Because Word aligns the indent markers relative to a paragraph's boundaries, you should not move these markers until you have specified a Paragraph Width setting. If you move the markers before you change this setting, you may get unexpected results. For example, Figure 10-104 on the next page shows some text that is six inches wide (Word's default text area width). We have moved the right indent marker for the second paragraph two inches to the left, to the 4-inch position on the ruler. We've also assigned a special position to this paragraph: The Horizontal alignment is Center Relative To Column and the Vertical alignment is In Line. We used Word's default Distance From Text setting of .125.

To flow text around the positioned paragraph, we will need to make sure that there are at least $1\frac{1}{8}$ inches of space on either side of the paragraph (1 inch for the text and $\frac{1}{8}$ inch for the Distance From Text setting). To create this space, we need to change the Paragraph Width setting. If we simply move the indent markers on the ruler, Word will wrap the paragraph text in a narrower area, but the paragraph boundaries will remain aligned with the right and left edges of the text column.

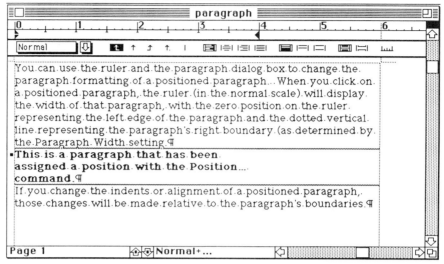

FIGURE 10-104

The right edge of the second paragraph in this document has been indented two inches.

Let's suppose that we open the Position dialog box and specify a Paragraph Width setting of 3. This will create $1^1/_2$ inches of space on either side of the positioned paragraph. (The text column is 6 inches wide. Subtracting 3 from this gives us 3 inches in which to flow text. Word will put half of this space on either side of the positioned paragraph, creating $1^1/_2$ inches of space.)

Figure 10-105 shows the positioned paragraph after changing its Paragraph Width setting. Notice that Word has maintained the 2-inch right indent, so that the text is now wrapped within a 1-inch-wide column.

You can correct the problem shown in Figure 10-105 by moving the right indent marker on the ruler to the dotted vertical line that marks the right boundary of the paragraph. Figure 10-106 shows the document after we made this change.

To avoid the type of problem shown in Figure 10-105, use the Paragraph Width setting—not the indent markers on the ruler—to adjust the width of a positioned paragraph. After setting the Paragraph Width, you may want to move the indent markers on the ruler to fine-tune the appearance of the positioned paragraph.

Word allows you to move the indent markers beyond the left and right boundaries of the positioned paragraph. That is, you can move the left and first-line indent markers to the left of the zero point on the ruler, and you can move the right indent marker to the right of the dotted vertical line. Generally, you'll want to avoid doing this. When the positioned object is pulled into the surrounding text, Word will truncate part of that object.

FIGURE 10-105

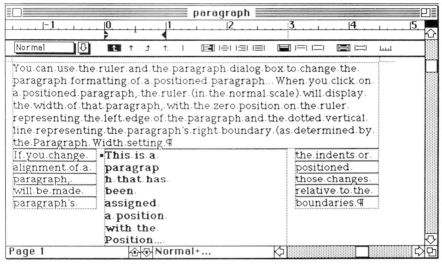

When we change the Paragraph Width setting to 3 inches, Word maintains the 2-inch right indent, wrapping the text in a 1-inch-wide area.

FIGURE 10-106

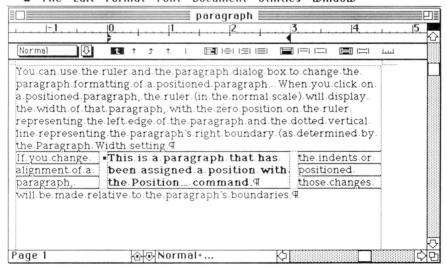

We moved the right indent marker to the 3-inch position on the ruler in order to wrap the positioned paragraph within its 3-inch boundary.

Other paragraph formatting

Another way you can format a positioned paragraph is to change its line spacing. For example, a document might contain a positioned paragraph with double spacing, while the text that flows around that paragraph may have single spacing. You also can create tab stops in a positioned paragraph or add a border.

With the Before and After settings in the Paragraph dialog box or the open space icon on the ruler, you can change the amount of space between the top and/or bottom edges of a positioned paragraph and its surrounding text. In other words, when you insert space before or after a positioned paragraph, Word places that space within the paragraph's boundary.

Viewing the Positioned Object

As we have mentioned, to see special positioning on your screen, you must turn on the page view or use the Print Preview window. When you use the Print Preview window, you can change the position of an object by dragging it. To do this, you must first click on the margins icon to display the boundaries of the object. For example, Figure 10-107 shows the document from Figure 10-91 in the Print Preview window.

FIGURE 10-107

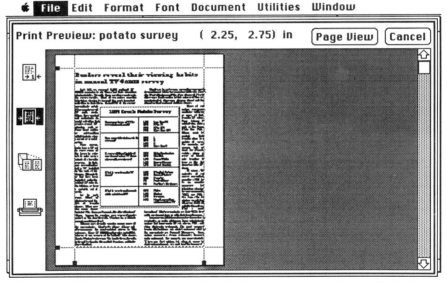

When you click the margins icon in the Print Preview window, Word will display boundary lines around a positioned object.

After clicking the margins icon, you can move the pointer over the positioned object, where it will assume a crosshair shape. When you click on the object, Word will display its horizontal and vertical position coordinates at the top of the preview screen. These coordinates represent the position of the left and top boundaries of the positioned object relative to the left and top edges of the page. For example, the coordinates *(2.25, 2.75)* tell you that the left boundary of the object is $2^1/_4$ inches from the left edge of the page, and the top boundary of the object is $2^3/_4$ inches from the top edge of the page. Word will flash new coordinates as you drag the object to a new position. After you've repositioned the object and clicked in the gray area of the preview screen, Word will move the boundary lines for the positioned object and redraw the screen to show the new flow of text.

Of course, if you want to see a closer view of a positioned object, click on the Page View button at the top of the Print Preview window, or choose Page View from the Document menu. Figure 10-108 shows the document from Figures 10-91 and 10-107 in the page view.

FIGURE 10-108

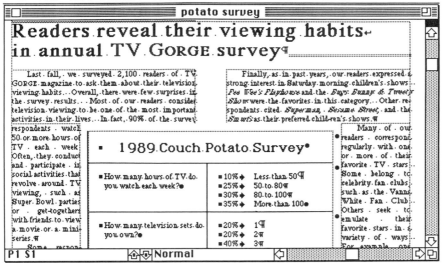

In the page view, Word will display the positioned object in place with text flowing around it.

If you decide that you do not want a paragraph, graphic, or table to have special positioning in your document, you can simply choose the Reset button in the Position dialog box. This will return the object to a normal position. The Horizontal setting will be Left Relative To Column, the Vertical setting will be In Line, and the Paragraph Width setting will become Auto.

Returning to Normal Positioning

In many respects, applying special positioning to a paragraph is no different than applying other, more conventional paragraph formatting. In fact, you can use the settings in the Position dialog box as part of a style definition. For example,

Positioning Tips

suppose you want to place the illustrations throughout a document in one of four standard positions on a page. The easiest way to do this would be to define four named styles whose definitions include your Position settings. To do this, just choose Define Styles... from the Format menu and, in the Define Styles dialog box, select <u>New Style</u> from the list box. Type a name for the style—such as *position 1*— in the Style edit bar, then choose Position... from the Format menu. In the Position dialog box, enter your Position settings, and click OK. Finally, click the Define button in the Define Styles dialog box to complete the style definition. Now, when you want to position one of your illustrations, just click anywhere on the illustration's graphic frame and apply the *position 1* style.

Whenever you want to use the Position... command to place a paragraph, table, or graphic in a particular location on a page, we strongly recommend that you first create and format your entire document without any specially positioned objects. Then, repaginate the document and add the positioned objects, beginning at the top of the document and working your way to the end. After positioning each object, you should repaginate again. We recommend this approach because it's possible for Word to move a positioned object from one page to another as you add and delete text. Keep in mind that the Position... command does not specify on which printed page a positioned object should appear. It merely specifies the location of an object on the current page. Thus, if you edit a document, changing the location of its page breaks, it's likely that an object with fixed positioning will be moved to a different page.

You probably will want to avoid placing a positioned object in the middle of a wide text column—for example, in the middle of a page that contains only one column of text. When you do this, Word will split lines of text at the edge of the positioned object, making it difficult to read the document. In fact, in the sample documents we've shown in this section, whenever we've centered an object on a page, we've always used a two-column text layout (as in Figure 10-91). That way, each text column flows around one side of the positioned object, and the lines of text are not split by the object.

We mentioned at the beginning of this section that you can use the Position... command to position one or more rows of a table—rather than an entire table. To do this, simply apply a position to the first cell(s) of the row(s) you want to position. In order to position the row(s), Word may split the table between different parts of the page.

If you're positioning a graphic and some text that immediately follows the graphic, Word will automatically set the width of the text to be the same as the width of the graphic. This feature is particularly handy when you need to use the Position... command to place an illustration and its caption at a certain spot on the page.

Although the Position... command is a powerful feature, we have found that it often requires some trial and error to create an attractive page layout when positioned objects are involved. We recommend that you have a good working knowledge of Word's Document, Paragraph, and Character formatting features before you attempt to use the Position... command.

Although the Word reference manual states that, given sufficient memory, you can create documents as long as 16 million characters (3,000 pages or more), you'll probably find that files any longer than about 50 pages become slow to work with and difficult to handle. Of course, the practical size limit of any file depends on your Macintosh configuration and the complexity of the document.

If you have created a very long document that is divided into several sections, you may want to consider splitting that document into separate files and then linking the documents through the Document dialog box. Word allows you to print linked documents consecutively and to compile a single index and table of contents for the linked documents. (We'll show you how to do this in Chapter 11.) Linking documents is also helpful when you want the flexibility to mix and match various document files for printing.

For example, suppose you have created a 250-page document that consists of three chapters. Because you want to vary the headers and footers within each chapter and use multicolumn formatting on some pages, you've subdivided each chapter into several sections. As you might imagine, working with this document could get pretty complex. In addition, procedures like finding and changing, hyphenating, spell-checking, repaginating, and saving will slow down considerably when you're working with a document of this length.

The Next File... button in the Document dialog box makes it easy for you to divide a complex document into smaller portions. With this option, you can split a document into smaller individual files and then pull all the sections together when you print.

For example, suppose you've created a series of documents called Chapter 1, Chapter 2, and Chapter 3. Chapter 1 is 85 pages long, Chapter 2 is 97 pages long, and Chapter 3 is 68 pages long. To link these documents, begin by opening the Chapter 1 file and issuing the Document... command. In the Document dialog box, click the Next File... button. Word will then present the Open dialog box, where you should select the name of the file you want to print after Chapter 1 (Chapter 2 in this example) and click Open. If the file you need to access is not on the current disk, you can use the Drive and Eject buttons to access another disk.

After you click the Open button in the Open dialog box, Word will not actually open the Chapter 2 file. However, it will specify that file name in the Document dialog box. The Next File... button will now be labeled *Reset Next File* and the file name *Chapter 2* will appear just to the right of the button.

After choosing Chapter 2 as the Next File for Chapter 1, you should click OK to close the Document dialog box and then save and close the Chapter 1 file. (Word will save your Next File setting to disk, along with your document.) Next, open the

WORKING WITH LONG DOCUMENTS

Chapter 2 file and choose the Document… command on the Format menu. In the Document dialog box, click the Next File… button, select the file name *Chapter 3* in the Open dialog box, and click the Open button. Then, click OK to close the Document dialog box and save Chapter 2. There is no need to enter a Next File setting for the third chapter since it is the last document in the series.

Now, whenever you print the file Chapter 1, Word will automatically print Chapter 2 and Chapter 3 as well. Chapters 2 and 3 do not have to be open when you issue the Print… command. Word will automatically retrieve from disk the information it needs to print those files. In fact, you can even print all three documents from the Finder level without loading the Word program. Just click on the icon for the Chapter 1 file and issue the Print command.

By the way, if you want to print Chapters 2 and 3 only, issue the Print… command from within Chapter 2, rather than Chapter 1. Moreover, if you issue the Print… command while Chapter 2 is active on the Word DeskTop, Word will start printing at the beginning of Chapter 2, even if Chapter 1 is also open on the DeskTop. Also, you may print from the Finder level by clicking the icon for Chapter 2, then issuing the Print command. Your document will begin printing from Chapter 2.

Page Numbering

If you want the pages in your linked documents to be numbered sequentially when you issue the Print… command, you'll need to use the Number Pages From setting in the Document dialog box. Fortunately, in Word 4, you do not need to figure the starting page number for each document in the linked series. Simply type a 0 in the Number Pages From edit bar for each document in the series, except the first one.

When you print the documents, Word will automatically "count" the pages and number each page correctly. It makes no difference whether you've used the Section dialog box or the Header or Footer windows to create your page numbers. In either case, Word will provide sequential page numbering automatically.

Of course, if you decide that you want the page numbers in a particular document of the series to begin at a specified number, then you can enter that number (instead of 0) in the Number Pages From edit bar. For example, suppose you plan to insert five pages of figures or diagrams between the first and second documents in a linked series. We'll assume that the first document in the series contains 20 pages and each of the five inserted pages must display a page number (21 through 25). In this situation, you would enter 26 as the Number Pages From setting for the second document in the linked series. You can use 0 as the Number Pages From setting for the remaining documents.

Line Numbers and Footnotes

If you are using line numbers or footnotes in your linked documents, you'll need to go through a similar process to set the starting values for these items. In the Document dialog box, use the Number Lines From edit bar to specify a starting line number. Similarly, in the Footnotes portion of the Document dialog box, enter a starting footnote number in the Number From edit bar. We'll talk more about these settings when we discuss footnotes in Chapter 11 and line numbers in Chapter 13.

Printing Selected Pages

When you link a series of documents for printing, you can use the Pages From and To options in the Print dialog box to print any series of pages. If you have numbered the pages in each document sequentially, type the From and To values you want in the Print dialog box. For instance, in our previous example, suppose Chapter 1 in your series is 85 pages long and Chapter 2 is 97 pages long. Let's assume that you have numbered the pages in these linked documents sequentially. If you issue the Print… command and enter a From setting of 80 and a To setting of 110, Word will print the last six pages of Chapter 1 and the first 25 pages of Chapter 2. The pages will be numbered 80 through 110, as you might expect.

If you have not used the Number Pages From setting to number the pages of your linked documents sequentially, you may get some unexpected results when you use the From and To settings to print linked documents. If the To setting that you specify is less than the number of pages in the first document in the series, Word will print the selected pages from that document only. However, if your To setting is greater than the number of pages in the first document of the series, Word will begin printing again with the second document. If the second document contains fewer pages than you have specified in the To edit bar, Word will continue printing with the third document, and so forth. Word will keep printing until it finds a document that contains at least as many pages as you have specified in the To edit bar.

Again, suppose Chapters 1 and 2 in your linked series contain 85 and 97 pages, respectively, but you have not used sequential page numbering. When you issue the Print… command and type a From setting of 1 and a To setting of 90, Word will print pages 1 through 85 of Chapter 1 and pages 1 through 90 of Chapter 2.

Other Page Setup and Document Options

When you print linked documents, Word will remember most of the Page Setup and Document dialog box options that you have selected for each file. For example, you can specify different Paper and Margins settings for each document. Word also will remember your Orientation settings for each document. Generally, you'll probably want these settings to be consistent from one document to the next, but the ability to use different formatting options for each document may come in handy on occasion.

By the way, if you are using headers, footers, or page numbers in your linked documents, keep in mind that you must create and format these items separately for each document in your linked series. Word will not automatically apply the headers and footers for your first document to any of the subsequent documents in your series. In addition, you must specify all of your Section dialog box settings for every document in the series—including activating the Auto Page Number option, even if you plan to use the same Section settings for all the documents.

ADDING A TABLE OF CONTENTS, AN INDEX, AND FOOTNOTES

11

One of the most time-consuming and monotonous tasks in creating a document is developing reference aids, such as indexes, footnotes, and tables of contents. Microsoft has taken much of the tedium out of these tasks by adding to Word special index, footnote, and table of contents facilities.

The steps you follow to create indexes and tables of contents are quite similar. You simply enter special hidden identification codes into the body of your document to flag the entries you want to include. Then, you can use the Index... or Table of Contents... command to compile these entries.

Footnotes, on the other hand, are entered in a separate window that is saved to disk with your document (much like a header or footer window). Word will print your footnotes automatically when you print your document.

Since the table of contents is the simplest of the three reference aid features, we'll look at it first. Then, we'll look at Word's indexing and footnoting capabilities.

Word gives you two ways to build entries for a table of contents. First, you can enter special codes into your document to flag the entries you want to include in your table of contents. Second, if you have used the Outline facility (described in Chapter 9) to create your document, you can instruct Word to compile a table of contents directly from the headings you have entered into the outline. We'll take a look at the coding technique first.

CREATING A TABLE OF CONTENTS

Defining Your Table of Contents Entries

A table of contents entry has three parts: a hidden code that identifies the start of the entry, the entry text, and an end-of-entry marker. The three-character code that identifies the start of the entry consists of a period, the letter *c*, and another period (.c.). You must assign the Hidden format to this code; otherwise, Word will not recognize it as a table of contents marker.

The end-of-entry marker may be a paragraph marker (¶), an end-of-line marker (↵), or a semicolon (;). If you decide to use a semicolon, you'll probably want to assign the Hidden format to that character so that it will not appear in your document text. If you want to use the semicolon (or any other special character) as literal text in your table of contents entry, place single quotation marks around the entry text. For instance, if you wanted to create the entry *Division of Parts: Delineation of Roles; Books II and III*, you would surround the entry text with single quotation marks before typing the end-of-entry marker.

For a table of contents entry, you can either type text specifically for the entry or you can use existing text from your document. Generally, you'll want to use existing document headings and subheadings for your entry text, rather than typing new text. However, in order to create a special table of contents entry, you may need to enter new text. If you type some text in your document specifically for a table of contents entry, you'll probably want to assign the Hidden format to that text so that it doesn't appear in your printed document.

We've created three table of contents entries in the document shown in Figure 11-1. The first entry, in the title, takes advantage of an existing heading. Notice that the .c. flag appears with a gray underline, indicating that we have assigned the Hidden format to that code. The ¶ marker at the end of the heading serves as the end-of-entry marker.

The second table of contents entry, *Delineation of roles*, appears just after the first paragraph of body text. This entry, like the first entry, occupies an entire paragraph, but is not part of our document text. For that reason, we have assigned the Hidden format to the entire entry, including the ¶ marker. (As we explained in Chapter 7, if you don't hide markup characters, like blank spaces and ¶ markers, you'll find extra white space in your document when you print.)

The third entry, *Books II and III*, which appears in the last line shown on the screen, also takes advantage of existing body text. Therefore, we assigned the Hidden format only to the .c. and ; portions of the entry to prevent them from appearing in our printed document.

A shortcut: the Insert TOC Entry command

Rather than typing the .c. and end-of-entry marker codes into your document and formatting them to appear as hidden text, you can use the Insert TOC Entry command on the Document menu. This command lets you quickly insert a set of preformatted .c. and end-of-entry codes either for existing or new text.

To designate an existing block of text as a table of contents entry, start by selecting the text you want to appear in the table. Then, simply issue the Insert TOC

Entry command. Word will insert a hidden .c. code in front of the selection, and place a hidden semicolon after the selection. If the selection happens to end with a paragraph marker, Word will not insert the trailing semicolon since it is unnecessary. Once you've inserted a table of contents entry, you can delete it by choosing the Undo Insert TOC Entry command on the Edit menu.

FIGURE 11-1

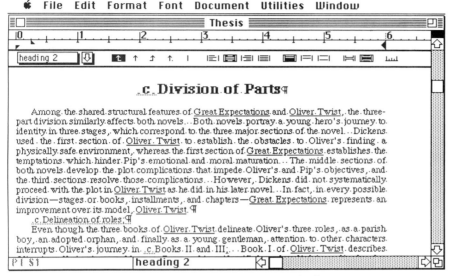

We created three table of contents entries in this sample document.

To insert a set of table of contents markers for new text, just place the insertion point marker at the spot where you want the text to appear, then issue the Insert TOC Entry command. Word will insert the needed .c. and semicolon characters at the current insertion point, then move the insertion point marker between the two codes so that you can type your table of contents text. The .c. and semicolon characters will be assigned the Hidden format, as will the table of contents text you type between the two codes. Although Word assumes that you want the new table of contents text to be hidden, you can select that text and reformat it as needed.

Multilevel table of contents entries

You can create as many as nine levels of entries for your table of contents by including a numeric level argument in your .c. code. As you'll see when you compile a table of contents, Word will indent the entries according to the level you have assigned. To assign a level to an entry, enter a value from 1 to 9 after the *c* character, like this: .c2., .c3., .c4., and so forth. (Be sure to include the period after the level number.) You can enter the first-level table of contents entry codes as .c1., if you like, but the level code is not necessary for first-level entries.

For example, in the screen shown in Figure 11-2, we used a first-level table of contents code to flag the major heading at the top of the screen. We used the .c2. code to mark the text *Delineation of roles* as a second-level entry, and we used a .c3. code to define the inline entry *Books II and III.*

FIGURE 11-2

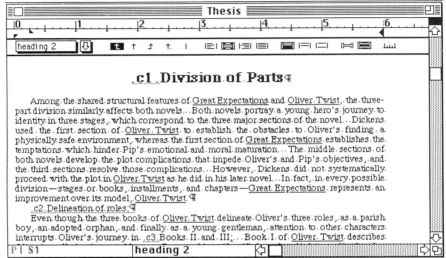

We've created three levels of table of contents entries on this screen.

Combining table of contents entries

There may be times when you want the program to display page numbers only after selected entries. Word allows you to designate subentry levels in a single table of contents entry. When you do this, however, Word will place a page number only after the last entry in the combined entry. For example, you might want to organize your table of contents so that level 1 and 2 entries serve as references to major sections, but do not appear with specific page references. If you then want to include page numbers after your level 3 entries, you can string together a set of table of contents entries like this:

.c.Division of Parts:Delineation of roles:Books II and III;

In this table of contents entry, we used colons to separate the various entry levels. The effects of this entry are identical to those shown in Figure 11-2—Word creates a level 1 entry from the text *Division of Parts*, a level 2 entry from *Delineation of roles*, and a level 3 entry from *Books II and III.* However, Word will place a page number only after the last entry in the series. (Of course, if you've opted not to use page numbers in your table, there is no difference between the two techniques.) One advantage to the latter technique, however, is that it is faster and easier to enter into your document. It also requires less room. Thus, if you don't want the table of contents text to appear in your document anyway, you may want to consolidate your entries with semicolons so you can quickly and easily hide the entire series of entries.

Collecting table of contents entries from an outline

If you use the Outline facility to create a document, you won't have to enter any special codes into that document in order to create a table of contents. As we explained in Chapter 9, when you enter headings into a document through the outline window, Word assigns style names to each level. Major headings are assigned the style *heading 1*; subheadings are formatted with the styles named *heading 2*, *heading 3*, and so forth. (Your document can contain as many as nine levels of styles—the same number of levels available for table of contents entries.)

If you instruct Word to compile the table of contents from your outline, it will search through your document to locate all the paragraphs that carry the style names *heading 1* through *heading 9*. These headings will become the text for the table of contents. As you might guess, the *heading 1* styles will become first-level table of contents entries; the *heading 2* styles will become second-level table of contents entries; and so forth.

Compiling the Table of Contents

Once you have defined the entries you want to use, you can use the Table of Contents... command on the Utilities menu to compile the table of contents. (This command is available only when Full Menus is in effect.) When you issue the Table of Contents... command, you'll see a dialog box like the one in Figure 11-3.

FIGURE 11-3

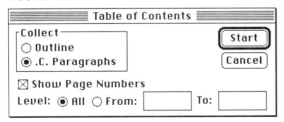

This dialog box appears when you issue the Table of Contents... command.

The option you select in the Collect section of the dialog box tells Word where to look for the table of contents entries. If you want to use the heading levels from your outline, click the Outline option. (The first time you open the Table of Contents dialog box, you'll see that .C. Paragraphs is the default selection under Collect.)

Next, you need to tell Word how many entry levels you want to include in the table of contents. Just click All if you want to include all the entries in the table of contents. Alternatively, you can enter the levels you want to use in the From and

To edit bars. If you want to include page numbers in the table of contents, select the Show Page Numbers option. Finally, click the Start button to begin compiling the table. If you need to halt the compilation for any reason, you can press the ⌘ and period keys (⌘-.) to cancel the procedure.

When you click the Start button in the Table of Contents dialog box, Word repaginates the entire document, overlooks hidden text, searches for the table of contents entries, compiles the table of contents, and inserts the table text in a new section at the beginning of the document.

If you've already compiled a table of contents for your document, Word asks if you want to replace the existing table. Click Yes to replace the old table of contents with a new one. If you click No, Word will place the new table of contents in another new section at the beginning of the document, right in front of the old one. You may want to use this technique to create separate tables for different types of information in your document, such as diagrams, illustrations, and so forth. We'll talk more about creating other types of tables of contents in a moment.

Figure 11-4 shows a sample table of contents compiled in Word. As you can see, each entry contains the table of contents text, followed by a tab marker, dot leaders, the page number (since we have opted to display page numbers), and a paragraph marker (¶) to end the entry. Word also has inserted a section-break marker at the end of the table of contents. Because the table of contents appears in its own section, you can change its page layout and page numbering scheme without affecting the rest of your document.

FIGURE 11-4

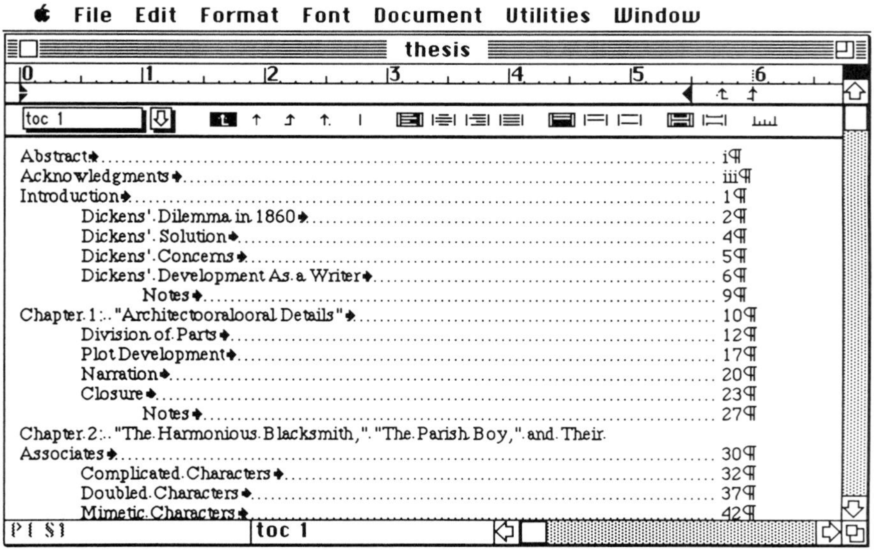

Your compiled table of contents will look like this.

By the way, the best time to compile the table of contents is right before you print the final version of a document. Word automatically repaginates your document when you issue the Table of Contents... command to ensure that the page numbers are accurate. However, if you edit or reorganize the document after compiling the table of contents, the page numbers may change, causing the table of contents entries to be incorrect.

We also recommend that you deselect the Show Hidden Text option in the Preferences dialog box before you compile a table of contents. If you don't plan to include this hidden text in your printed document, you'll need to hide it in the document window so that the document will be repaginated correctly when Word compiles the table.

Formatting the Table of Contents

As we mentioned earlier, the table of contents initially appears in a new section at the very beginning of a document. In addition, the character formatting of the table of contents will match the *Normal* style for that document. For example, if you're using Word's default *Normal* style, your table of contents will appear in 12-point New York Plain. (See Chapter 8 for more on style sheets and defining the *Normal* style.) Although Word does not assign any special character formatting to a table of contents, it does assign certain paragraph formats to each entry in the table. This paragraph formatting determines the amount of indention for each level of entries, as well as the tabs and dot leaders used to position the page numbers in the table.

Of course, once you've created a table of contents, you can change the character and paragraph formats of that text. You also can use the Cut and Paste commands to move the table to another part of your document. The easiest way to reformat your table of contents text is to redefine the style definitions that Word has applied to the table. Let's look at the relationship between the table of contents and Word's style sheet facility.

Using the style sheet

Like the Outline facility we discussed in Chapter 9, Word's table of contents facility is designed to work hand-in-hand with the style sheet facility. For each table of contents entry level you create, Word adds a style name to the document's style sheet. If you choose Styles... or Define Styles... from the Format menu after creating a table of contents, you'll see that your document's style sheet includes the style names *toc 1*, *toc 2*, *toc 3*, and so forth. Like every other document style sheet, this style sheet will also include the style named *Normal*, as shown in Figure 11-5 on the next page. If you have used the Outline facility to build your document, you'll also see the style names *heading 1*, *heading 2*, and so forth.

All the table of contents styles are based on the *Normal* style—that's why the table of contents will display the same character formats as the main body text in your document. All *toc* styles carry a $1/2$-inch right indention—that is, in a standard document with 6-inch text space, the right indent marker will appear at the

$5^1/_2$-inch mark. All *toc* style definitions also contain two tab stops: a left-aligned tab with a dot leader at the $5^3/_4$-inch mark, and a right-aligned tab at the 6-inch mark. (You can see the right indent and tabs on the ruler in Figure 11-4.) In fact, the only difference between the various *toc* styles is that Word assigns different amounts of left indention to each level. In the default style, *toc 1* entries are not indented; they are aligned with the default left margin of your body text. However, each of the remaining *toc* styles is indented an additional $^1/_2$ inch. For example, *toc 2* entries are indented $^1/_2$ inch, *toc 3* entries are indented 1 inch, and so forth.

FIGURE 11-5

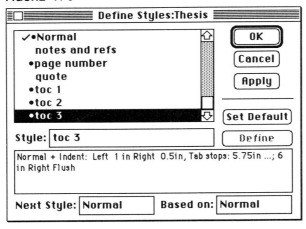

Each level in the table of contents is now a style name on the style sheet.

To modify one of the *toc* styles, just click on one of the table of contents entries that belong to the level you want to format, then choose Define Styles... from the Format menu. In the Define Styles dialog box, click on the name of the style you want to modify (a check mark should appear next to that style name), then select the character and paragraph formats you want to use for this level. When you click OK or Apply in the Define Styles dialog box, Word will apply your new format selections to all table of contents entries in your document that carry that style name.

For example, in the sample document we used to create the table of contents shown in Figure 11-4, the *Normal* style specifies 12-point Times Plain type. As a result, the table of contents also appears in 12-point Times Plain type. If we want the first-level headings in this table of contents to appear in 12-point Times bold type, we can change the format of all the first-level entries by modifying the *toc 1* style on the style sheet. First, we would click anywhere on one of the first-level table of contents entries in the document and select the Define Styles... command from the Format menu. Then, we would click on the name *toc 1* in the list that appears in the dialog box. Next, we would choose Bold from the Format menu. When we click OK to lock in this style change and return to the document window, our table of contents will look like Figure 11-6.

FIGURE 11-6

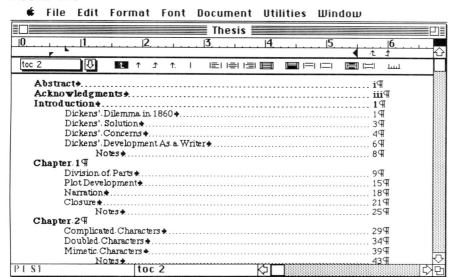

We used the Define Styles... command to apply bold formatting to the first-level
table of contents entries in this document.

As you're changing the formatting instructions for each *toc* style, you may want
to change the Based On style as well. Instead of using *Normal* as the Based On style
for each *toc* style, you might want to base each *toc* style on the next-highest *toc* style.
This can help you maintain formatting consistency among the different levels in a
table of contents. Specifically, *toc 5* could be based on *toc 4*, which could be based
on *toc 3*, which could be based on *toc 2*, which could be based on *toc 1*, which would
be based on *Normal*. That way, when you make a format change to the *toc 1* style,
your change will affect the other *toc* styles as well.

*Numbering the
table of contents
pages*

As you already know, Word creates a new section for each table of contents.
Since the table of contents is generally considered part of a document's front matter,
you'll probably want to create a special numbering scheme for the table of contents
pages (and any other front matter items like the title page, acknowledgments page,
and so forth). Lowercase Roman numerals (i, ii, iii) are useful for this part of
a document.

To number your table of contents pages, click anywhere in that section, issue
the Section... command on the Format menu, and click the Auto option in the Page
Number portion of the dialog box. Select the numbering style you want to use from
the dropdown list box, and specify the position for your page numbers in the From
Top and From Right edit bars.

To use a different page numbering style for the body of your document, click in the first section of the main document and issue another Section... command. Select the numbering scheme you want to use, and click the Restart at 1 option.

If you want the table of contents pages to be numbered sequentially, before your document, you'll need to reserve page numbers for the table before you issue the Table of Contents... command. Otherwise, the page numbers in the table of contents will be inaccurate. To reserve page numbers for the table of contents, just insert a manual page break or section break where the table will appear. You may need to include two or more page breaks if the table will be more than a page long. When you compile the table, Word will include the extra blank pages you have created in its page count as it compiles page numbers for the table of contents.

Creating other tables

You can use the Table of Contents... command to compile other types of tables, such as a list of illustrations or a list of tables. You can accomplish this in two ways. If you've used Word's Outline facility in creating your document, you can compile your main table of contents from the different levels of outline text. Then, you can type .c. codes in your document window to flag the entries for your secondary tables. If you did not use the Outline facility, you can reserve separate .c. entry levels for each table you plan to build.

Let's start with the latter case: If you didn't use the Outliner to create your document, you'll need to reserve different .c. levels for each table you want to create. For example, suppose you have created a document that contains several diagrams and illustrations. For easy reference, you want to create a list of these items that is separate from your main table of contents.

Since you will need to use .c. codes to define both the table of contents entries and the illustration table entries, you need first to decide which level of detail you want to use in the main table of contents. Let's say you want to include four levels of entries in your main table of contents. Use the entry codes .c1. (or simply .c.) through .c4. to define the table of contents entries. Now, use the entry code .c5. to define your illustration table entries.

When you're ready for Word to compile the tables, issue the Table of Contents... command and type the level number *5* in the From edit bar. When you click Start, Word will compile your illustration table entries and place them at the beginning of the document. Now, to compile the main table of contents, issue another Table of Contents... command, and enter the level number *1* in the From edit bar and the level number *4* in the To edit bar. Remember to click No when Word asks if you want to replace the existing table of contents. Word will then compile the second table and insert it in a new section in front of the illustration table. Once you've compiled both tables, you can use the style sheet to format the different levels in each table.

If you created your document using Word's Outliner, the process for setting up multiple tables is even easier. You can compile your main table of contents by issuing the Table of Contents... command and choosing the Outline option. After compiling the main table of contents, you can insert .c. codes in your document window to define the entries for the second table. To compile this table, issue the Table of Contents... command and choose the .C. Paragraphs option. Again, remember to click No when Word asks whether you want to replace the existing table of contents. Word will compile the second table and insert it in front of any existing tables.

When you use this technique, keep in mind that Word will apply the same *toc* level styles to both tables. If you use the style sheet to change one of the *toc* style definitions, Word will apply your changes to any table where an entry is formatted with that style. For example, if you've created two tables, both will have at least first-level entries. Therefore, if you alter the definition of the *toc 1* style, you will affect the format of the first-level entries in both tables. If you want to use different formats for the two tables, you may want to format one of the tables manually or create a new set of style names for the entries in that table.

Although the process is a bit more complex, building an index is much like building a table of contents. Index entries—like table of contents entries—contain three main parts: a hidden code that identifies the start of the entry, the entry text, and an end-of-entry marker. You also can add a number of optional arguments to define subentry levels and to format page number references.

BUILDING AN INDEX

The code that identifies the start of an entry consists of three characters: a period, the letter *i*, and another period (.i.). You must assign the Hidden format to this code, or Word will not recognize your index entry. The end-of-entry marker may be a paragraph marker (¶), an end-of-line marker (↵), or a semicolon (;). If you decide to use a semicolon, you'll probably want to assign the Hidden format to that character so it will not appear in your document text. If you want to use the semicolon (or any other special character) as literal text in an index entry, place single quotation marks around the entry text. For instance, if you wanted to display *Division of Parts: Delineation of Roles; Books II and III,* you would surround the entire text with single quotation marks before typing the end-of-entry marker.

The text you use for an index entry can be either existing text in your document or new text that you enter specifically for the entry. If you decide to type new index text into your document, you'll probably want to assign the Hidden format to that text so that it doesn't appear in your printed document.

For example, we have created three index entries in the sample document shown in Figure 11-7 on the following page. The first entry at the top of the screen, *Division of Parts,* takes advantage of existing text. Notice that the *.i.* flag appears with a gray underline, indicating that we have assigned the Hidden format to that marker. The ¶ marker after the heading serves as the end-of-entry marker.

The second index entry, *Delineation of roles,* occurs just after the first paragraph of body text. Since it is not part of our document text, we assigned the Hidden format to the entire entry, including the ¶ marker. (As we explained in Chapter 7, if you don't hide demarcation characters, like blank spaces and ¶ markers, you'll find extra white spaces in your document when you print.)

The third entry (*Oliver*), appearing in the second paragraph of body text, also takes advantage of existing text. We assigned the Hidden format to the *.i.* and *;* portions of the entry to prevent them from appearing in our printed document.

FIGURE 11-7

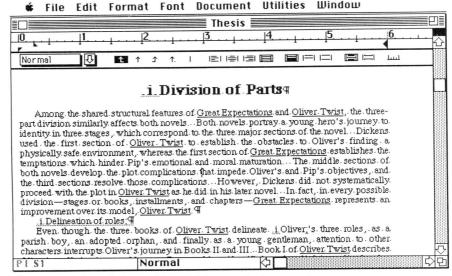

We created three index entries in this sample document.

A shortcut: the Insert Index Entry command

As with the table of contents codes, Word offers a command to help you enter index codes quickly and easily. Rather than typing the .i. and end-of-entry marker codes into your document and formatting them to appear as hidden text, you can use the Insert Index Entry command on the Document menu.

To designate an existing block of text as an index entry, start by selecting the text that you want to appear in the index. Then, simply issue the Insert Index Entry command. Word will insert a hidden .i. code in front of the selection and place a hidden semicolon after the selection. If the selection happens to end with a paragraph marker or other end-of-entry marker, Word will omit the trailing semicolon because it is unnecessary. Once you've inserted an index entry, you can undo it by choosing the Undo Index Entry command on the Edit menu.

To insert a set of index entry markers for new text, just place the insertion point marker at the spot where you want the text to appear, then issue the Insert Index Entry command. Word will insert the needed .i. and semicolon characters at the current insertion point, then move the insertion point marker between the two codes so you can type your index text. The .i. and semicolon characters will be assigned the Hidden format, as will the text you type between the two codes. Although Word assumes you want the new index text to be hidden, you can select that text and reformat it as needed.

You can create as many as seven levels of index entries by adding subentry text to your index entries. Just type the index code, the main index entry, and a colon. Then, add the subentry text and an end-of-entry marker. For example, in the sample document shown in Figure 11-7, you might define the second and third index entries as subentries under the main heading, *Division of Parts,* by typing

.i.Division of Parts:Delineation of roles¶

and

.i.Division of Parts:Delineation of roles:Oliver¶

(Of course, you don't actually type the ¶ marker after each entry; we've included it here simply to indicate that when you press Return after creating each entry, a ¶ marker will appear to serve as the end-of-entry marker.)

Notice that every time you type a subentry, you also must type its main entry. Also, keep in mind that you must use a colon to separate each subentry level. Finally, remember to assign the Hidden format to these entries so that they won't clutter your printed document. Figure 11-8 shows our sample document with the first-, second-, and third-level index entries in place.

Defining Subentries

FIGURE 11-8

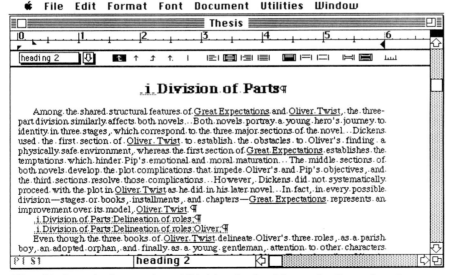

We added a pair of second- and third-level subentries under the main entry, Division of Parts.

The Index...
Command

Once you have defined all your index entries, Word can take over the indexing task. When you issue the Index... command, Word will gather and alphabetize your entries, search for any duplicate entries and merge them, throw out any duplicate page references for an entry, compile the index, insert the correct page numbers, and add the index to the end of your document.

Before you issue the Index... command on the Utilities menu, however, you need to select Preferences... from the Edit menu and make sure that the Show Hidden Text option is deselected. If you skip this step, your document may not be paginated correctly, and you'll end up with inaccurate page number references in the finished index.

After removing the hidden text from your screen, select the Index... command. (This command is available only when the Full Menus setting is in effect.) You will see a dialog box like the one in Figure 11-9.

FIGURE 11-9

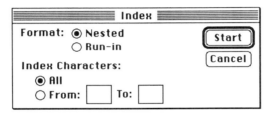

Word presents this dialog box when you issue the Index... command.

If you click the Nested button, Word will indent each subentry on a new line under the main entry, as shown in Figure 11-10. If you click the Run-in button, Word will include each subentry in the same paragraph as its main entry. Each subentry will be separated from the main entry and from other subentries by a semicolon, as shown in Figure 11-11.

Word also allows you to compile a partial index by using the Index Characters option to specify a range of entries to index. For example, you might want to index only those entries that start with the letters *a* through *m*. This option can be handy when you need to compile an index for a long document that contains a lot of index entries. If you find that Word runs out of memory before it can complete the index, you can use this option to compile the index in stages. You can also use this technique to recompile only a portion of an index if you need to make corrections to a specific range of index entries.

To use the Index Characters option, just type the starting letter in the From edit bar and the ending letter in the To edit bar. If you leave these edit bars blank, Word assumes that you want to compile the entire index.

FIGURE 11-10

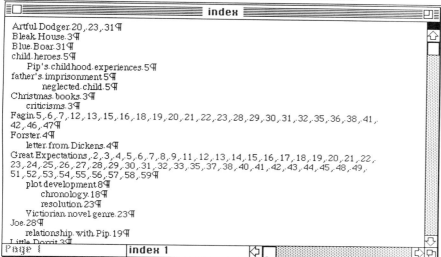

When you click the Nested option, Word will indent each subentry on a new line under the main entry.

FIGURE 11-11

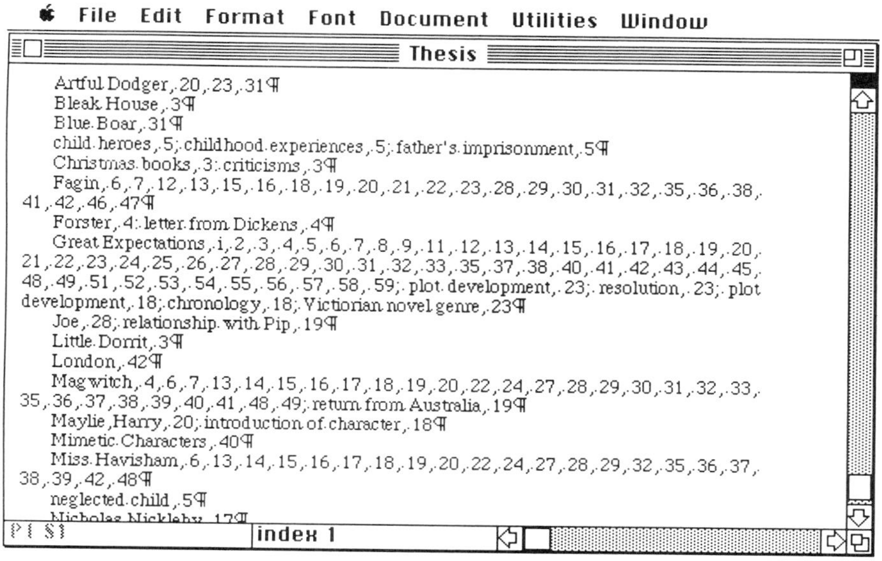

When you click the Run-in option, Word will include your subentries in the same paragraph as the main entry.

When you lock in the Index dialog box settings, Word will create a new section at the end of your document to hold the finished index. (Thus, you'll be able to format it separately from the rest of your document.) If you have already compiled an index for the document, Word will ask whether you want to replace the existing index. If you click No, Word will add the new index in a new section following the existing index. If you click Yes, Word will replace the old index with the new one.

If you're using the Index Characters option to compile an index in stages, you should choose the No button when Word asks whether you want to replace the existing index with the new one. Otherwise, each successive group of index entries will overwrite the previous one. Also, be sure you compile the index in ascending alphabetical order. Otherwise, the index entries will be out of order. For example, if you're compiling the index in three stages, you might use the ranges *a* through *h*, *i* through *p*, and *q* through *z*.

Finally, Word will place a section-break marker between each group of index entries. You'll probably want to erase these extra section breaks once the entire index has been compiled.

Index Arguments

Word offers a number of optional index arguments that let you control the format of the page numbers in index entries, add notes to your entries, and create multipage references. For example, you can format the page numbers to appear in bold type by adding the character *b* to each index code. Just place the formatting code directly after the character *i* but before the period, like this:

.ib.Division of Parts;

In your finished index, this entry will appear like this:

Division of Parts **1**

Similarly, you can add an *i* to your index code to format page numbers in italics. For example, if you enter

.ii.Division of Parts;

your index entry will look like this in the finished index:

Division of Parts *1*

If you add both the *b* and *i* codes to an index entry, Word will format the page number to appear in bold italic type. Thus, the index entry

.iib.Division of Parts;

would result in

Division of Parts *1*

Sometimes it is necessary for an index entry to refer to a range of pages rather than a single page. To let the reader know that a particular topic is discussed on several consecutive pages, add a left parenthesis to the first index entry code and a right parenthesis to the last index entry code. For example, if you type

.i(.Division of Parts;

on page 5 of your document, then move to page 10 and type

.i).Division of Parts;

Word will create an index entry like this:

Division of Parts 5-10

Rather than using a page number reference in an index, you'll sometimes want to refer the reader to another part of the index for further information. For example, rather than create a separate set of entries and page numbers for the topic *Delineation of roles*, you might want to enter a note to refer the reader to the main topic: *Division of Parts*. To replace the page number with text, type a # symbol after the index entry text, then type your cross-reference text. For example, the entry

.i.Delineation of roles#(see Division of Parts);

will appear like this in your finished index:

Delineation of roles (see Division of Parts)

If you like, you can add an i or b code to format the cross-reference portion of the entry to separate it from the main entry text. For example, you might add an italic code like this:

.ii.Delineation of roles#(see Division of Parts);

to create the entry

Delineation of roles *(see Division of Parts)*

Combining Index and Table of Contents Entries

Often, you'll want the same entry to appear in both your table of contents and your index. If you are creating a first-level index entry, you can string together the index and table of contents codes. For example, suppose you want the heading *Division of Parts* in Figure 11-7 to be included in both your index and table of contents. You can set up the entry like this:

.c..i.Division of Parts;

When you want to include a subentry in an index entry, however, you'll need to type a separate entry for the table of contents and for the index. If you don't, Word will include the subentry text in the table of contents, as well as in the index. For example, rather than using the combined entry

.c..i.Division of Parts:Delineation of roles;

you should enter the table of contents and index entries separately, like this:

.c.Division of Parts;
.i.Division of Parts:Delineation of roles;

Remember to assign the Hidden format to the index entry so that it does not appear in your printed document.

Formatting the Index

Initially, the character and paragraph formats of all first-level index entries will match the *Normal* style for your document. Subentries are identical to first-level entries, except that Word indents each subentry $1/_4$ inch.

Of course, once you've created an index, you can assign it any character and paragraph formats. You can also use the Cut and Paste commands to move the index (whole or in part) to another part of your document. The easiest way to reformat your index text is to redefine the style definitions that Word has applied to the index. Let's look at the relationship between the index and Word's style sheet facility.

Like the Outliner and table of contents, Word's index facility is designed to work in conjunction with style sheets. If you use the Nested option to compile an index, Word will create a style name for each index level in your document. These index styles, which are named *index 1*, *index 2*, and so forth, correspond to the various entry levels you have created for your index. Each style is based on the *Normal* style. If you choose the Define Styles… command from the Format menu after creating an index, you'll see a dialog box like the one in Figure 11-12.

Using the style sheet

FIGURE 11-12

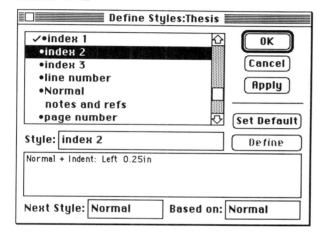

Each level of a nested index has a style name on the style sheet.

If you used the Run-in option to include all the index subentries in the same paragraph as its main entry (as shown in Figure 11-11 on page 505), Word will create only one index style—*index 1*. Since each main entry appears in the same paragraph as all of its subentries, there is no need to create special formatting instructions for different index levels.

You can modify index styles by changing the style instructions on the style sheet. Just click on one of the index entries that belongs to the level you want to format, then choose Define Styles… from the Format menu. In the Define Styles dialog box, click on the name of the style you want to modify, then select the character and paragraph formats for that index level. When you click OK or Apply in the Define Styles dialog box, Word will apply the specified formats to all the index entries in your document that carry that style name. (For a detailed discussion of modifying styles, see Chapter 8.)

For example, in the sample document we used to create the index shown in Figure 11-10, our *Normal* style, which formats the main body text of the document, specifies 12-point Times Plain type. As a result, our index also appears in 12-point Times Plain type. If we want the first-level headings in the index to appear in bold type, we would click on one of the first-level index entries in the document and issue the Define Styles… command. In the Define Styles dialog box, we would click on the style name *index 1*, then choose the Bold option from the Format menu. When we click OK to lock in this change and return to the document window, our index will look like the one in Figure 11-13. Notice that any formatting change you make to an index style affects the entire index entry—both the text and the page number reference.

FIGURE 11-13

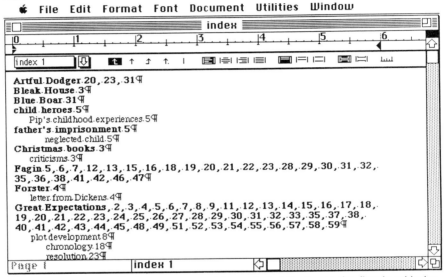

We used the Define Styles… command to apply boldfacing to the first-level index entries in this document.

As you're changing the formatting instructions for an index style, you may want to change the Based On style as well. Instead of using *Normal* as the Based On style for each index style, you might want to base each index style on the next-highest index style. Specifically, *index 5* could be based on *index 4*, which could be based on *index 3*, which could be based on *index 2*, which could be based on *index 1*, which would be based on *Normal*. That way, when you make a format change to the *index 1* style, that change will affect not only the first-level index entries, but also the subsequent levels of index entries.

ADDING FOOTNOTES

The mere mention of footnotes strikes fear in the heart of anyone who has ever struggled through a term paper. But with Word, footnotes don't have to be frightening. Word's footnoting facility allows you to enter footnote text as you create your document (while the information is still fresh in your mind and at your fingertips). Word will automatically number and track the sequence of your footnotes—even if you modify the document by adding and deleting them. Then, when you are ready to print your document, you can tell Word where to place the footnotes and choose how the footnotes will be separated from the rest of the text on a page.

Let's start by showing how you would create a footnote in the sample document shown in Figure 11-14. The first step is to place the insertion point marker where you want the footnote reference marker to appear. In this example, we want to add our sample footnote reference at the end of the first paragraph of body text.

**Creating
Footnotes**

FIGURE 11-14

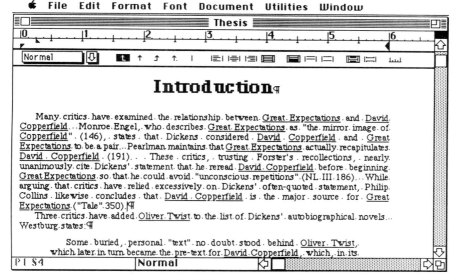

We'll insert a sample footnote reference into this document.

Once you've clicked at the spot where you want to place your footnote reference, choose Footnote... from the Document menu. If you're using Short Menus, you'll see a dialog box like the one in Figure 11-15 on the next page. If you're using Full Menus, you'll see a dialog box like the one in Figure 11-16. We'll take a look at the Separator..., Cont. Separator..., and Cont. Notice... options in a few moments. First, let's examine the Footnote Reference Mark options that appear in both dialog boxes.

FIGURE 11-15

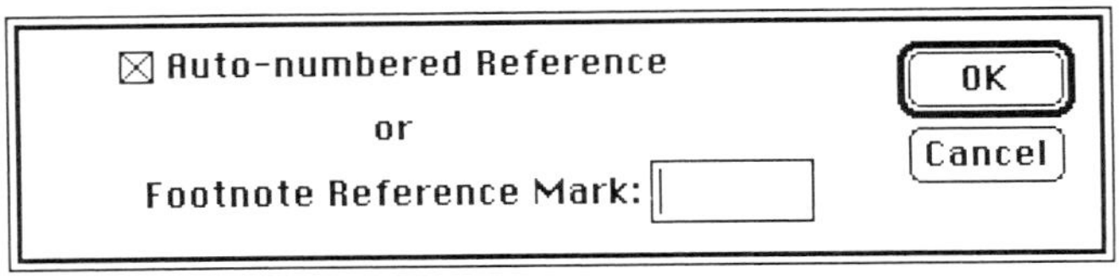

If you use Short Menus, you'll see this dialog box when you issue the Footnote... command.

FIGURE 11-16

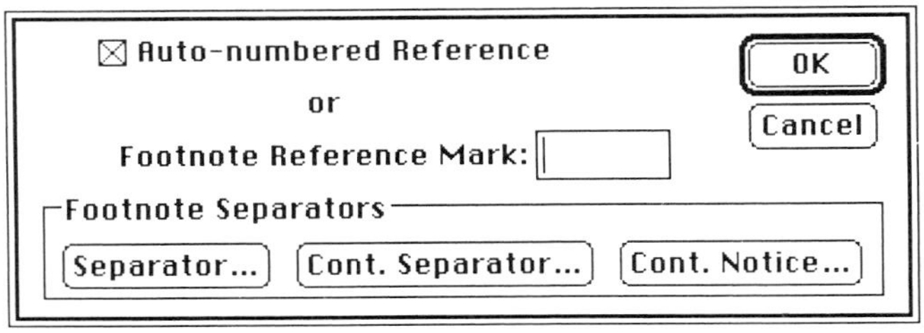

When the Full Menus setting is in effect, you'll see this dialog box when you issue the Footnote... command.

If you want Word to number your footnotes automatically, click the Auto-numbered Reference option in the Footnote dialog box. If you'd rather use your own reference marker, such as an * or † symbol, just type that marker in the Footnote Reference Mark edit bar. You can enter as many as ten characters. Word will automatically deselect the Auto-numbered Reference option when you type an entry in the Footnote Reference Mark edit bar.

When you click OK, Word inserts the correct footnote number or other reference marker just to the right of the current insertion point in your document. Word also splits the document window into two panes, as shown in Figure 11-17, and displays a corresponding reference marker in the bottom window pane.

At this point, all you need to do is type your footnote text after the reference marker in the bottom pane. Figure 11-18 shows the text for our sample footnote. There is no limit to the length or number of paragraphs you can include in a footnote. If your footnote text is too long to view in the bottom portion of the split screen, you can use the vertical scroll bar in the lower pane to bring additional text into view, or you can drag the split bar up to make the bottom pane larger. To drag the split bar, just point to the black rectangle that appears between the two vertical scroll bars on the right side of the window, click, and drag.

FIGURE 11-17

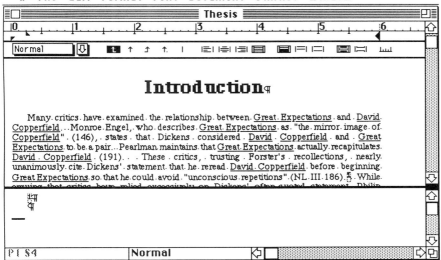

When you click OK in the Footnote dialog box, Word will add a footnote reference marker and split the document window into two panes.

FIGURE 11-18

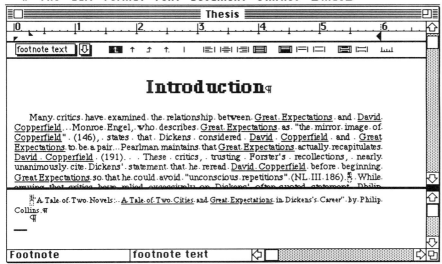

We have entered our footnote text in the bottom window pane.

After entering your footnote text, you can click anywhere in the document window above the split bar to resume working in your document. Word will continue to display the footnote pane at the bottom of the screen.

The document and footnote panes you see in Figure 11-18 resemble the window panes you create by dragging the split bar in a document window. (We explained this technique in Chapter 2.) However, the footnote pane is actually a separate entity. Although footnotes are saved to disk along with a document, Word does not consider footnotes to be a part of the body of the document. (Notice that when the footnote window is active, the word *Footnote* appears in the status box—where the page number normally would appear.)

Microsoft chose to use this split-pane format, rather than create a new window for footnotes as it does for headers and footers, so it could create vertical scroll bars that allow you to move through your document and footnote text with ease. As you scroll through the document window, Word will automatically scroll the contents of the footnote window pane in order to display the footnote text that corresponds to the footnote reference on your screen. By the same token, when you scroll through your footnote entries in the bottom window pane, Word will scroll the corresponding parts of your document text into view in the upper pane.

To expand your view of the document window, you can drag the split bar toward the bottom of the screen. To hide the footnotes altogether, you can drag the split bar past the top or bottom of the document window.

When the Full Menus setting is in effect, you can quickly bring your footnote text back into view by pressing the Shift key as you drag down the split bar. (When a document window is not split into panes, the split bar will appear at the top of the vertical scroll bar.) You also can press ⌘-Option-Shift-s to toggle the footnotes into and out of view.

Shortcuts

To add a new footnote reference to your document, you can access the Footnote dialog box quickly, by pressing ⌘-e instead of selecting the Footnote... command from the Document menu. If you are using the Auto-numbered Reference option (rather than typing your own footnote reference markers), you can bypass the Footnote dialog box altogether by pressing the Return key immediately after you press ⌘-e. Word will insert the appropriate reference number into your document and footnote pane. All you'll need to do is start typing the footnote text.

By the way, after you've finished inserting or editing footnote text in the footnote window, you can return to your previous place in the document window by pressing ⌘-Option-z. If you have a numeric keypad, just press the 0 key to move back to your previous location in the document.

Inserting and Deleting Footnotes

You may have noticed that a dotted border appears around the automatic footnote reference numbers in the sample document shown in Figure 11-18. This border indicates that the footnote references are dynamic—that is, Word will adjust all of your footnote references whenever you insert or delete an automatically numbered footnote. (By the way, the dotted border is visible only when you've chosen Show ¶ from the Edit menu.)

To delete a footnote, just delete the footnote reference marker in the document window. Word will automatically delete the corresponding footnote text as well. Word will also renumber all subsequent footnote references automatically.

To insert a new footnote between existing footnotes, click at the spot in the document window where you want the footnote reference number to appear, select Footnote... (or press ⌘-e), then press Return. Word will insert the correct footnote reference number in the document, move the insertion point marker to the correct location in the footnote pane, and open a new paragraph so you can enter the footnote text. Again, all subsequent footnotes will be renumbered automatically, both in your document and footnote window.

Editing Footnotes

If you have entered your own footnote reference marker (such as a † symbol), and you decide to use a different reference marker, you'll need to edit the marker in both your document and footnote panes. In changing the reference marker in your document, you should not attempt to edit it directly. If you do, Word will delete your footnote reference and text. Instead, select the footnote reference marker in your document, issue the Footnote... command and type a new reference marker in the Footnote Reference Mark edit bar. Word will change the entry in the document window, as well as in the footnote pane.

Once you have created a footnote, use Word's standard editing techniques to edit the footnote text. For example, you can insert, delete, cut, copy, and paste text just as you would in the document window. You can also use the Find..., Change..., Hyphenate..., and Spelling... commands to edit your footnote text. (To search for a Footnote mark in your text, type ^5 in the Find What edit bar after you issue the Find...or Change...command.) Word will automatically check your footnote text when you issue one of these commands from the document window. Unfortunately, if your document is divided into sections with separate footnote numbering in each section, it's impossible to tell which footnote contains a spelling error when more than one footnote uses the same number.

Copying footnotes

Here's a handy shortcut for repeating a footnote entry in two or more locations in your document. If you select a footnote reference marker in your document, issue the Copy command, then paste that reference marker in another part of the document, Word will automatically copy the corresponding text for that footnote as well. The copied footnote text will appear in the appropriate location in the footnote window. When you paste—if you copied an automatically numbered reference marker—Word will also change that number to reflect its new position in the document. Word will then renumber any subsequent reference markers.

Formatting Footnotes

When you insert a footnote into your document, Word automatically adds two new style names to the style sheet: *footnote reference* and *footnote text*. As you can see in Figure 11-19, the *footnote reference* style will format your footnote reference markers to appear in 9-point type, superscripted 3 points. The *footnote text* style will format your footnote text to appear in 10-point Plain type. Both styles appear in the font you have specified for your document's *Normal* style.

FIGURE 11-19

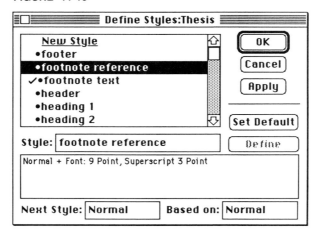

When you create a footnote, Word adds the footnote reference *and* footnote text *styles to the style sheet.*

The easiest way to change the format of your footnote text or reference markers is to change the style definition of *footnote reference* or *footnote text* in the Define Styles dialog box. When you do this, Word will apply the new formatting instructions to all the footnote text or reference markers in your document. (For a discussion of modifying named styles, see Chapter 8.) Because Word allows you to select a reference marker in your document, you can change the formatting of one or more reference markers manually.

Changing Footnote Separators

When you print a document, Word will print your footnotes as well. As you can see in Figure 11-20, Word uses a short horizontal line between your document text and footnote text to separate the two elements on the printed page. When a footnote is too long to fit on one page or when all the footnotes for a page cannot appear at the bottom of that page, Word will automatically place the remaining text on the following page. To indicate that the footnote text on the next page is a continuation, Word uses a horizontal rule that extends from margin to margin.

You can create your own separators by using the Separator… and Cont. Separator… options in the Footnote dialog box. (Remember, these options are available only when you have selected the Full Menus setting.) To access these options, choose Footnote… from the Document menu. Rather than clicking OK to start a new footnote entry, click the Separator… button. Word will close the Footnote dialog box and present a new window, like the one shown in Figure 11-21.

FIGURE 11-20

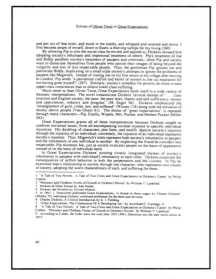

Word uses a short horizontal line to separate your footnotes from your body text and a margin-to-margin line to indicate that the footnotes continue from one page to the next.

FIGURE 11-21

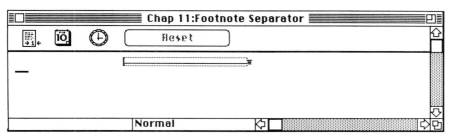

Use this Footnote Separator window to customize the separator line that divides your footnotes from your body text.

Notice that Word displays a horizontal line about $1\frac{1}{2}$ inches long in the Footnote Separator window. Although you cannot change the size or format of this line, you can add characters to the Footnote Separator window, or you can highlight the separator line and overwrite it. (We'll demonstrate this in a moment.) You also can use the icons at the top of the Footnote Separator window to add a dynamic page number, date, and/or time to the separator.

When you click Cont. Separator... in the Footnote dialog box, Word will display the window shown in Figure 11-22. As you can see, this window contains the margin-to-margin line that Word uses as the default separator between document and footnote text when footnotes continue from one page to another. (This window is identical to the Footnote Separator window except for the length of the separator line.) Again, you can insert additional characters or overwrite the separator line if you like.

FIGURE 11-22

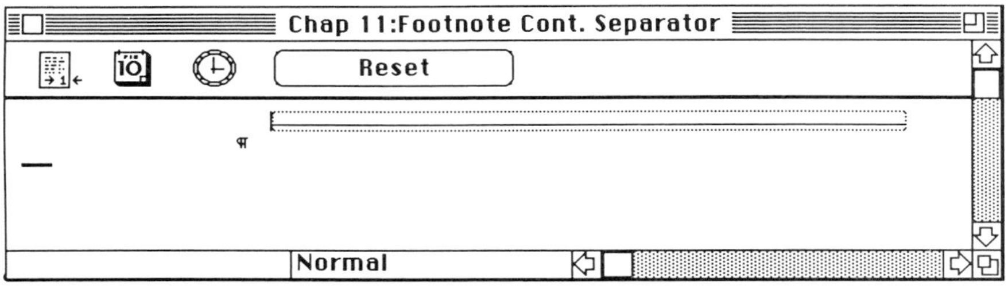

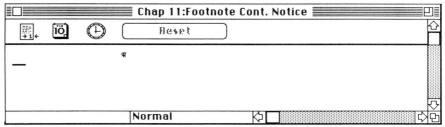

You can enter your own separator characters in the Footnote Cont. Separator window.

In addition to customizing your separators, Word allows you to place a notice at the end of your footnotes on one page to let the reader know that the footnote text continues on the next page. To do this, click Cont. Notice... in the Footnote dialog box. You will then see a blank Footnote Cont. Notice window like the one in Figure 11-23. In this window, you can enter a phrase like *(continued on next page)*. Word will print the contents of the Footnote Cont. Notice window only when footnote text flows from one page to the next.

FIGURE 11-23

You can use this window to notify the reader that a footnote continues on the next page.

To illustrate how you might use the Footnote Separator, Footnote Cont. Separator, and Footnote Cont. Notice windows, let's customize the footnote separators and create a continuation notice for the sample pages in Figure 11-20.

First, make sure that the Full Menus setting is in effect. Then, select the Footnote... command from the Document menu. Next, click on the Separator... button to access the window shown in Figure 11-21. Now, let's suppose you'd like to replace the default line separator with the word *Footnotes*. You want this word to appear in 12-point Helvetica underlined type, and you want to center the separator between your document margins.

Just double-click on the existing separator line to select it, then type the word *Footnotes*. (Word will overwrite the line when you begin typing.) Next, double-click on the word you just typed, issue the Character... command, choose the Helvetica font and 12 Point size, then click the Underline option. Finally, choose Show Ruler from the Format menu and click on the Centered alignment icon. (You also may want to click the Open Space icon to create some extra white space between the last line of body text and your footnote separator.) Figure 11-24 shows the Footnote Separator window at this point.

FIGURE 11-24

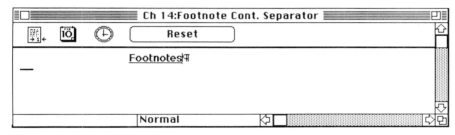

We replaced Word's default line separator with the word Footnotes.

Now, to format the continuation separator, follow the same steps described above, except type the text *Footnotes (Continued)* in the Cont. Separator window. Also, be sure to format the word *(Continued)* in italics. Figure 11-25 shows this window after we typed the new text.

FIGURE 11-25

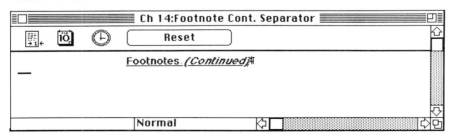

We have modified our continuation separator to display the words Footnotes (Continued).

Finally, to create a continuation notice, open the Footnote Cont. Notice window and enter a message like *(continued on next page)*. Format your continuation notice to appear in 10-point Helvetica Plain type, as shown in Figure 11-26.

FIGURE 11-26

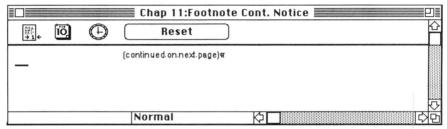

We've added a (continued on next page) *message to the Footnote Cont. Notice window.*

Now, when you print your document, Word will use the new separators and print the continuation notice where necessary, as shown in Figure 11-27.

FIGURE 11-27

These printed pages show our customized separators and continuation notice.

Oddly enough, Word will not allow you to create different separators and continuation notices for different pages in a document. You cannot even change the separators or continuation notice from one section to another. Any changes you make in these windows will affect your entire document. As a result, you may wonder what purpose the Reset button serves in these three windows.

The Reset button that appears in the Footnote Separator, Footnote Cont. Separator, and Footnote Cont. Notice windows is used to return the contents of the current window to the default. For example, if you were to click this button in the window shown in Figure 11-24, Word would remove the *Footnotes* notice and replace it with its default line separator.

The Reset button

Word gives you a number of choices for positioning your footnotes: You can print each footnote on the same page where its footnote reference marker appears; you can group your footnotes at the end of a document section; or you can print all your footnotes at the end of your document. If you want each footnote to appear on the same page as its reference marker, you can tell Word to place the footnotes either at the bottom of the page or directly beneath the last paragraph on the page. (In some cases, the last paragraph on a page may occur somewhere other than at the bottom of the page.) You also can control whether your footnotes will be numbered consecutively throughout a document or separately on each page or in each section.

You control the positioning of your footnotes through the Document dialog box, which offers four options for positioning footnotes: Bottom of Page, Beneath Text, End of Section, and End of Document. This dialog box, shown in Figure 11-28 on the following page, also includes a check box option, Restart Each Page/Section, that determines whether your footnotes will be numbered consecutively throughout a document, or numbered separately on each page or in each section. (If you select End of Section as your Position option, this check box says Restart Each Section.) Finally, the Document dialog box also includes a Number From edit bar, which allows you to begin your footnote numbers at something other than Word's default of 1. We'll talk about this edit bar in the last section of this chapter, "Working with Multiple Documents."

If you choose the Bottom of Page option in the Document dialog box, each footnote will appear at the bottom of the page on which its reference marker occurs, as shown in Figure 11-29 on the following page. If you click Beneath Text, your footnotes will appear on the same page as their reference markers, but Word will print them directly under the last paragraph on the page, as shown in Figure 11-30 on page 523.

When you choose the Bottom of Page or Beneath Text option, you can number your footnotes separately on each page, or you can number them sequentially throughout the document. If the Restart Each Page/Section option is activated in the Document dialog box, Word will use a different set of footnote numbers on each page. If you deselect this option, Word will number your footnotes continuously from page to page.

Positioning and Numbering Footnotes

FIGURE 11-28

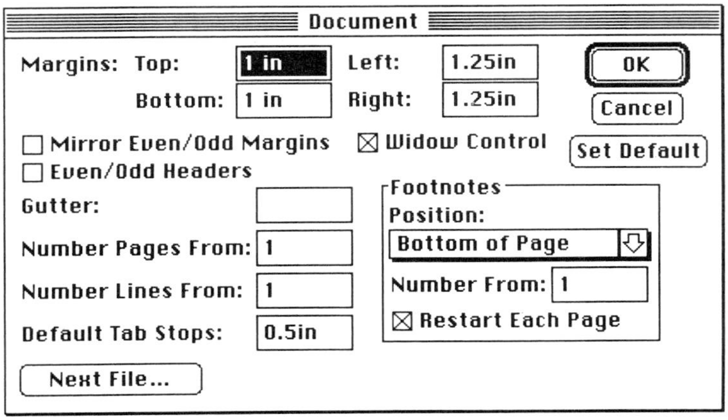

You can position footnotes from the Document dialog box.

FIGURE 11-29

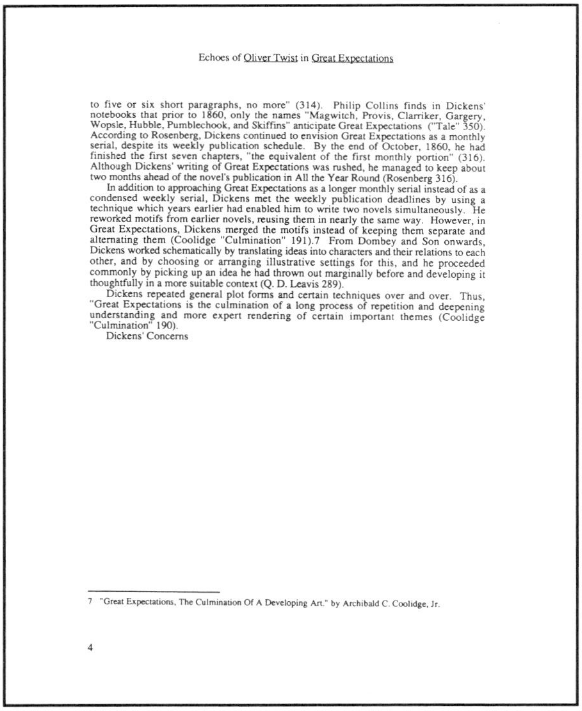

Echoes of Oliver Twist in Great Expectations

to five or six short paragraphs, no more" (314). Philip Collins finds in Dickens' notebooks that prior to 1860, only the names "Magwitch, Provis, Clarriker, Gargery, Wopsle, Hubble, Pumblechook, and Skiffins" anticipate Great Expectations ("Tale" 350). According to Rosenberg, Dickens continued to envision Great Expectations as a monthly serial, despite its weekly publication schedule. By the end of October, 1860, he had finished the first seven chapters, "the equivalent of the first monthly portion" (316). Although Dickens' writing of Great Expectations was rushed, he managed to keep about two months ahead of the novel's publication in All the Year Round (Rosenberg 316).

In addition to approaching Great Expectations as a longer monthly serial instead of as a condensed weekly serial, Dickens met the weekly publication deadlines by using a technique which years earlier had enabled him to write two novels simultaneously. He reworked motifs from earlier novels, reusing them in nearly the same way. However, in Great Expectations, Dickens merged the motifs instead of keeping them separate and alternating them (Coolidge "Culmination" 191).7 From Dombey and Son onwards, Dickens worked schematically by translating ideas into characters and their relations to each other, and by choosing or arranging illustrative settings for this, and he proceeded commonly by picking up an idea he had thrown out marginally before and developing it thoughtfully in a more suitable context (Q. D. Leavis 289).

Dickens repeated general plot forms and certain techniques over and over. Thus, "Great Expectations is the culmination of a long process of repetition and deepening understanding and more expert rendering of certain important themes (Coolidge "Culmination" 190).

Dickens' Concerns

7 "Great Expectations, The Culmination Of A Developing Art." by Archibald C. Coolidge, Jr.

4

If you use the Bottom of Page option, the footnote text will appear at the bottom of the page on which its reference marker appears.

FIGURE 11-30

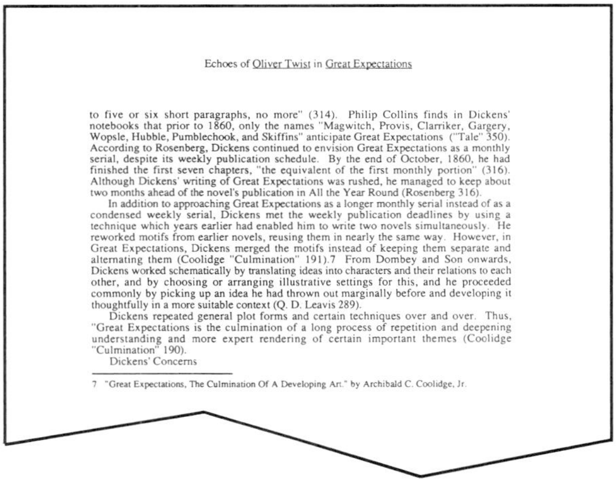

Echoes of Oliver Twist in Great Expectations

to five or six short paragraphs, no more" (314). Philip Collins finds in Dickens' notebooks that prior to 1860, only the names "Magwitch, Provis, Clarriker, Gargery, Wopsle, Hubble, Pumblechook, and Skiffins" anticipate Great Expectations ("Tale" 350). According to Rosenberg, Dickens continued to envision Great Expectations as a monthly serial, despite its weekly publication schedule. By the end of October, 1860, he had finished the first seven chapters, "the equivalent of the first monthly portion" (316). Although Dickens' writing of Great Expectations was rushed, he managed to keep about two months ahead of the novel's publication in All the Year Round (Rosenberg 316).

In addition to approaching Great Expectations as a longer monthly serial instead of as a condensed weekly serial, Dickens met the weekly publication deadlines by using a technique which years earlier had enabled him to write two novels simultaneously. He reworked motifs from earlier novels, reusing them in nearly the same way. However, in Great Expectations, Dickens merged the motifs instead of keeping them separate and alternating them (Coolidge "Culmination" 191).7 From Dombey and Son onwards, Dickens worked schematically by translating ideas into characters and their relations to each other, and by choosing or arranging illustrative settings for this, and he proceeded commonly by picking up an idea he had thrown out marginally before and developing it thoughtfully in a more suitable context (Q. D. Leavis 289).

Dickens repeated general plot forms and certain techniques over and over. Thus, "Great Expectations is the culmination of a long process of repetition and deepening understanding and more expert rendering of certain important themes (Coolidge "Culmination" 190).

Dickens' Concerns

7 "Great Expectations, The Culmination Of A Developing Art." by Archibald C. Coolidge, Jr.

If you use the Beneath Text option, the footnote text will appear directly under the last paragraph on the page.

To group your footnotes at the end of each section in a document, select the End of Section option in the Document dialog box. Of course, if your document contains only one section, this option will place your footnotes at the end of the document (just as if you had chosen the End of Document setting). If your document contains more than one section, you must be sure that the Include Endnotes option is selected in the Section dialog box for each section. (Word's default for Include Endnotes is active if you have selected the End of Section option in the Document dialog box.) This tells Word to include the footnotes for that section at the end of the section. If you turn off the Include Endnotes option for one or more sections, Word will place the footnotes for those sections at the end of the next section for which the Include Endnotes option is active (or at the end of your document if you've deselected Include Endnotes in the remainder of your sections). This can be helpful in situations where you've created separate sections for formatting purposes only.

When you group footnotes at the end of each section, you can choose to number your footnotes sequentially throughout the entire document, or you can number the footnotes separately in each section. Again, the Restart Each Section option in the Document dialog box determines whether you will have continuous footnote numbering. If you activate this option, Word will number the footnotes in each section separately. When this option is deselected, Word will number all the footnotes in the document sequentially. By the way, when you choose the End of Section option in the Document dialog box, Word will always print your footnotes immediately after the last paragraph in a section. Word will not place the footnotes at the bottom of the last page or on a separate page.

If you would like to place all your footnotes at the end of a document that contains multiple sections, you must select the End of Document option in the Document dialog box. Word will save your footnotes until it reaches a section in which you have selected the Include Endnotes setting or until it reaches the end of your document. Word will then print the footnotes just below the last paragraph in the document. When your footnotes appear at the end of a document, Word will always number them sequentially from the beginning of the document.

WORKING WITH MULTIPLE DOCUMENTS

As we explained in Chapter 10, you can use the Next File... option in the Document dialog box to link two or more document files for printing. When you use this technique to consolidate several small documents into one long document, Word can also consolidate your table of contents, index, and footnote entries.

To create a master table of contents or master index, you follow a few simple steps. First, make sure you've entered the correct file name in the Next File... option dialog box for each document you want to link. Also, be sure that you've entered the correct page number in the Number Pages From edit bar of the Document dialog box for each document. (If you don't number the pages of your linked documents sequentially, the page references in your index and table of contents will be incorrect.) Now, just open the first document in the series and issue the Table of Contents... or Index... command. Word will repaginate your current document, then repaginate each of the linked documents on disk. Then, if you're creating a table of contents, Word will place that table of contents in a new section at the beginning of your current document. If you're compiling an index, Word will open the last document in your series of linked documents and place the index in a separate section at the end of that document.

Numbering Footnotes in Multiple Documents

If you want Word to group all your footnotes at the end of the last document in a linked series rather than place them at the bottom of each page or at the end of each section, you'll need to select the End of Document option in the Document dialog box for each document. Then, you must issue the Section... command and deselect the Include Endnotes option for each section of every document—except the last section in the last document.

You'll also need to give Word a starting footnote reference number for each document in the series, except the first. To determine the correct starting footnote number for each document, begin by opening the first document in the series and scrolling to the bottom of your footnotes pane in order to determine the last footnote reference number for that document. Then, open the next document in the series, issue the Document... command, and type the starting reference number for that document in the Number From edit bar. Word will immediately renumber all the footnotes in that document. Now, look at the last footnote in the document to determine the starting footnote reference number for the next document. Follow these steps for each of the remaining linked documents. When you print the linked documents, your footnotes will be numbered sequentially, and Word will print all of the footnotes at the end of the linked series.

MERGING DOCUMENTS 12

If you're like most people, a great deal of the business writing you produce each day is dull and repetitive—sending out billing notices to your clients or churning out dozens of "personal" invitations to the grand opening of your company's new production facility. If you find yourself stuck with these jobs very often, you'll be glad to know that Word's merge facility can take the time and tedium out of these repetitive tasks.

The merge facility is a powerful feature that lets you combine data from two or more files to create customized documents. You provide the standardized text in one document and the variable information in another document. When you issue the Print Merge... command, Word will print multiple versions of the standard text document, automatically customizing each version with a name, address, account balance—or other information—from a second document.

For example, in your grand opening invitations, you might enter the text of your letter in one document and the names and addresses of each guest in another. When you merge the two files, Word will create a personal letter of invitation for each guest. Similarly, when you send out billing notices, you might store the text of the notice in one document and the names, addresses, and amounts due for each client in another document. Then, you can merge the information in these two files to create all of your billing statements with just a few keystrokes.

You commonly hear Word's merge facility referred to as a form-letter facility since it is used so often to customize business letters. However, there are dozens of equally useful applications for the merge facility, such as mailing labels and management reports. For that reason, we prefer the term *merge facility* rather than *form-letter facility*.

USING THE MERGE FACILITY

As we mentioned, you'll need to create at least two files in order to generate a series of merge documents: a main document and a data document. The main document contains your standard text, which will remain constant for each merge document. The data document contains the text that will vary from one merge document to the next. Word combines the information from the data document and the main document to create a series of customized merge documents.

Although only two documents are required to use the merge facility, you can also set up a series of subdocuments and have Word combine the text from those documents into your merge documents as well. We'll show you how to do this in a few pages.

Why Bother?

If you've ever dealt with a cantankerous word processor that makes your form letters look like glued-together bomb threats from an illiterate terrorist, you may feel doubtful about using the merge facility. Perhaps you've even received computer-generated form letters in which half of your name is truncated on the mailing label. You also may have found your name floating in the middle of a gappy line of text because it didn't fill the allotted space. For example, a name like Catherine Hammerschmidt can be rechristened Catherine Hammers (or, even worse, Catheri Hammersc) and Ann Lee can get lost in the middle of a sentence like

```
Just for you, Ann Lee          , we've reserved a…
```

You can now set your doubts to rest. Word has gone a step beyond most other programs to let you develop truly professional merge documents. Because the merge facility includes a number of sophisticated capabilities for extracting and formatting variable information, your form letters don't have to look like conventional form letters. Word adjusts the text in every merge document to accommodate variable-length entries. You can even choose to exclude blocks of text from selected merge documents without leaving gaping holes in your printed document.

There are a number of other advantages to using Word's merge facility to create variable documents. The most obvious advantage is that you can compile and print all your merge documents with a single command—no more typing different names and addresses for each version of a form letter. This not only saves time, but also helps you avoid typographical errors and inconsistencies. You will save even more time—and disk space—by letting Word fill in the blanks for you as it prints, rather than creating and saving each version of your document to disk.

Although your main document and data document may take a little time and planning to develop, once you set them up, you can use those files again and again. In addition, Word lets you mix and match information any way you like. That is, you can use the same data document to "feed" any number of main documents, and you can draw information from any number of data documents into a main document by directing Word to the files you want to use.

Before we can put the merge facility through its paces, we need to create a pair of main and data documents. Let's begin by setting up our data document, then we'll set up the main document and show you how to merge the information from the data document into the main document text.

If you've ever worked with a computerized database program, you should have no trouble mastering data documents in Word. A data document is nothing more than a specially structured collection of entries that are stored in a standard Word file. This file can contain any kind of information—from inventory numbers and prices to names, addresses, and telephone numbers.

Every data document consists of three elements: records, fields, and field headers. Each paragraph in a data document is a record, and each column is a field. When you merge the data and main documents, each record provides the variable data needed to create one new merge document. The field header paragraph, which appears at the top of the data document, identifies the information that is stored in each field. As you'll see in a moment, these field headers are the key link between your data document and main document.

Figure 12-1 shows the sample data document we'll use to create our merge documents. The first line in this document contains our field headers: LastName, FirstName, Address1, Address2, City, ST, ZIP, and Sign. Each line of text after this first one is a separate record, containing information on one person.

SETTING UP THE DATA DOCUMENT

FIGURE 12-1

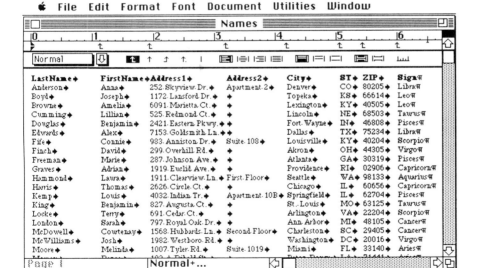

We'll use this data document to create some sample merge documents.

Rules of the Game

Although creating a data document is quite easy, there are a number of rules you must follow as you set up this file. First, the field headers must occupy the very first paragraph of the data document. Otherwise, Word will not be able to locate the correct field entries when you merge the main and data files. Each field name can be as long as 254 characters, the allowable number of characters between a pair of print merge symbols, and each data record can contain as many as 127 fields. For readability and ease of use, we suggest that you use short, easy-to-remember field names.

Although Word allows you to include blank spaces in your field names, we recommend that you avoid them. As you'll see, when you're setting up a main document, you'll have to type the field names exactly as they appear in the data document—including any blank spaces. Therefore, you might be better off avoiding blanks altogether.

We mentioned earlier that each record occupies a single paragraph. Word uses the ¶ marker to signal the end of each record. If your data document contains a lot of fields or if some field entries are very long, then your records may wrap into two or more lines. This is fine—Word will be able to interpret the data in each record as a unit as long as that information appears in a single paragraph and in the same order as the information in the field header paragraph. (As you're entering records, be sure that you do not leave any blank lines in your data document. These will cause error messages when you create your merge documents.)

You must also be sure your field entries are typed exactly as you want them to appear in your merge documents. For example, any extra blank spaces that you include in a field entry will also appear in the merge documents and may cause the text to be misaligned. You should be sure to use the correct case for your field entries—for example, you'll want to capitalize the first letter of each first name, last name, city, and street entry. If you're using standard two-digit postal abbreviations, you'll also want to type the state field entries in uppercase letters—KY, LA, and MO, for example.

Field separators

Notice that the field headers in our sample data document are separated by tab markers. In addition, we've separated the field entries in each record with tabs. If you want, you can use commas instead of tabs to separate the fields in each data record and the names in the field header row. Whether you choose to use commas or tabs, you should use the same delimiters in the field header row and in each data record, for consistency.

We strongly recommend that you use tabs instead of commas to separate the fields in your data document. For one thing, tab-delimited files are much easier to read and, consequently, much easier to edit. Also, with tab spaces, you often can tell at a glance if a particular record is missing a field entry or contains an extra field entry. And, because tabs create clearly defined columns, you will be able to select any field in your data document and sort the document on the contents of that field.

If you have imported your data records from another program, those records may be delimited automatically with commas between the field entries. If this is the case, you can easily use the Change... command, described in Chapter 6, to replace the commas with tab markers. Just enter a comma (,) in the Find What edit bar, and type ^t in the Change To edit bar. Then, click the Change All button to make the switch. We'll talk more about sharing data with other programs in Chapter 15.

Record length

Another important rule to remember is that every data record must contain the same number of fields. Even if you choose to leave some fields blank, you must enter a tab or comma as a placeholder in that field. For example, notice that many of the Address2 fields in the sample database shown in Figure 12-1 are empty. However, we inserted extra tab markers as placeholders for these empty fields. If we do not included these extra separator characters, Word will not be able to complete the merge procedure.

Special characters

Since Word interprets tab markers and commas as field separators, you may be wondering whether you can include commas and tabs in your data records. If you are using tabs to separate the fields and you need to include a tab within a field entry, you must enclose the entire field entry in quotation marks. Similarly, if you are using commas to separate the fields in your data document and you need to include a comma within a field entry, you must enclose that entire field entry in quotation marks. If you do not use quotation marks, Word will not be able to complete the merge procedure and will display the alert message *Data record too long.* Word will not print the quotation marks in your merged documents.

In a tab-delimited data document, you can use a comma in a field entry without enclosing that entry in quotation marks. By the same token, when you use commas to separate the fields of your data document, you can include a tab within a field without enclosing the field entry in quotation marks.

The only characters that are completely off limits for field entries (or field headers) are the guillemet symbols (« and »)—also called international quotation marks. As you'll see in a moment, Word reserves these characters for the merge instructions that you include in the main document.

Tables

Instead of using tabs or commas to separate the fields in a data document, you can format the entire document as a Word table. In order to do this, you must have no more than 31 fields. Each record should occupy a separate row of the table, and each field should occupy a separate column. The first row of the table should contain the data header information (field names), and nothing can appear before the table in the data document. For a detailed discussion of tables, see Chapter 10.

Formatting and Organizing a Data Document

We said earlier that you should type your field entries exactly as you want them to appear in your merge documents, using the correct capitalization, spelling, spacing, and so forth. However, the formats that you assign to the entries in your data document have absolutely no effect on the way that information will appear when you create your merge documents. You'll assign the formatting specifications for the merge documents when you create your main document. (This means that the same field entries can take on different formats in different merge documents. You can even format the same field entry in different ways within the same merge document.) Nevertheless, as you are creating a data document, you may want to use certain Character, Paragraph, Document, and Section formats to make the data records easy to read and edit.

For example, you may have noticed in Figure 12-1 that we entered a series of manual tab stops on the ruler. These ensure that the entries in each column are aligned properly and allow us to make certain that no information is missing. The tabs will also help us edit our field entries and make it easier to extract information from the data document later. However, formatting our fields like this is not required. It makes no difference to Word whether your data document is aesthetically pleasing, as long as all the information is in order.

Organizational tips

Your data document will be much more useful if you organize your information carefully. As you set up your fields, think about how you will use the information when you create your merge documents. Then, try to design the fields so that you can access any piece of information quickly and easily. For example, you may be tempted to type your clients' names in a single field. Instead, consider using three separate fields to hold each person's first name, middle initial, and last name. You may also want to create additional fields for titles like Dr., Mr., and Ms. and for professional designations like C.P.A. and Vice President.

Although it may seem like a lot of trouble to create a separate field for every piece of information in a data document, the importance of this organizational issue will become clearer as you begin sorting data and extracting information from the data document. For example, in the sample data document shown in Figure 12-1, notice that we split our address information into five separate fields: Address1, Address2, City, ST, and ZIP. As we'll demonstrate in a few pages, this technique will allow us to sort and select records on the basis of key information like state and zip code.

Data header documents

If you have imported the text for your data document from another program into Word, your data document may not automatically include a field header paragraph like the one shown in Figure 12-1. To get around this problem, you can either manually edit the imported file to create the field headers, or you can store your header paragraph in a separate header document.

To create a header document, just type your field entries into a Word file. Separate the field names with tabs or commas as usual—just as if you were entering the headers into a standard data document. (A little later, we'll show how you can use the information from a data header document in your merge documents.)

Once you have created a data document, you're ready to build your main document. You create, edit, and format this document exactly as you would any Word file, except that you add placeholders where you want Word to fill in variable information later. Figure 12-2 shows a sample main document that we have created to extract information from the FirstName, LastName, and Sign fields of our sample data document.

FIGURE 12-2

The main document contains special instructions that let you extract information from the data document.

Notice the *«DATA Names»* instruction that appears in the first line of this document. This instruction tells Word the name of the data document that contains the information needed to create the merge documents. This DATA instruction will not appear when we print our merge documents, nor will it affect the line or character spacing for the first line of the document.

The fifth line of our main document contains two field name instructions, *«FirstName»* and *«LastName»*, which tell Word to extract the entries from the FirstName and LastName fields of our data document and place them into the main document. Thus, when Word prints our first merge document, it will insert *Anna* and *Anderson* in the appropriate places. In printing our second merge document, Word will plug in the FirstName entry *Joseph* and the LastName entry *Boyd*. Unless we specify otherwise, Word will create a new merge document for each record in our data document, plugging in the appropriate FirstName and LastName entries for each new version of the merge document.

Our main document includes three more field name instructions in the first paragraph of body text. In the first line of body text, we use the field name instruction *«Sign»* to extract the individual's astrological sign from the data document. Then, in the second line of body text, we use the field name instructions *«FirstName»* and *«LastName»* again. As you might expect, when we create our merge documents, Word will again extract the appropriate information from each record and place it in its proper location in the document.

Before we see how our finished merge documents appear, let's look at some of the rules for entering instructions into the main document file and for formatting the variable text.

Merge Instruction Basics

The sample document in Figure 12-2 uses the two most common types of merge instructions—the DATA instruction and the field name instruction. Later in this chapter, we'll show you some additional merge instructions you can use to vary the contents of your merge documents. Regardless of the type of instructions you are entering, however, the basic rules remain the same.

To separate your instructions from the standard text in your main document, use a pair of guillemet characters (« and »). To enter the opening « character, press Option-\. To enter the closing » character, press Shift-Option-\. If you want, you can enter the guillemet characters directly from the Glossary. Select the Glossary... command on the Edit menu, highlight the term *print merge*, then click the Insert button. Word will place the guillemet characters in your document around the insertion point marker. All you need to do is type the appropriate instruction for your merge documents.

You can also use an end-of-paragraph marker as a delimiter for a merge instruction. As you'll see in a few pages, the ¶ marker can help you avoid awkward line breaks in your merge documents.

The DATA instruction

The first instruction in a main document must be the DATA instruction, which takes the form

«DATA document»

This instruction tells Word where to find the variable information it will use to "fill in the blanks" in your printed merge documents. For example, the DATA instruction *«DATA Names»* tells Word to look in the data file named Names for the variable information.

When you type a DATA instruction, be sure to enter a blank space between the word DATA and the beginning of the data document name. Otherwise, Word will not be able to locate the data document file. If the file name contains blank characters, you should include those blank characters in your argument as well.

Word does not distinguish between uppercase and lowercase letters in a DATA instruction. For example, you can enter the first word of a DATA instruction as *data*, *DATA*, or *Data*. However, we generally find it easier to distinguish our merge instructions from the rest of the text in our main document when we use uppercase letters.

Similarly, the document names you enter into your DATA instructions may appear in either uppercase or lowercase letters. For example, in the sample document shown in Figure 12-2, we could have entered our document name argument as *names* or *NAMES*.

In our discussion of organizing a data document, we explained how, in some cases, you may store your field headers in a separate document. When you have created and saved a data header document, you'll need to add an additional argument to the DATA instruction to direct Word to this header file, like this:

Referring to a data header document

«DATA data header document,data document»

For example, suppose you have stored the headers for a data document called Clients in a file named Client Headers. To let Word know where the header text is stored, you would enter your DATA instruction like this:

«DATA Client Headers,Clients»

Keep in mind that the same header document can apply to any number of data documents. For this reason, you may find it convenient to store a set of headers in a separate file when the information in your data documents must be updated frequently or when you have created several data documents that use the same headers. That way, you can be sure that all your data documents contain correct header information.

As we said earlier, the field names at the top of a data document provide the link between the main document and the information stored in that data document. To plug in text from a specific field in the data document, type the field header, enclosed in guillemet characters. No other arguments are required for this instruction.

The field name instructions

You can refer to the same field as many times as you like in a main document, and you can enter the field name instructions in any order. As long as the field names in your main document exactly match the field headers in the data document, Word will be able to extract the needed information from the appropriate field in each record.

Unlike the DATA instruction, Word does consider case in your field name instructions. For example, we used the field header *FirstName* to identify our first name fields in the sample data document shown in Figure 12-1. If we use a field name instruction like *«firstname»* or *«Firstname»* in our main document, Word will not be able to locate the appropriate field when we merge the documents.

Although Word will accept blank spaces in the field headers of a data document, you must be sure to enter these spaces correctly when you type your field name instructions in the main document. Otherwise, Word will not recognize your instructions.

Rather than trying to remember whether a field name should contain a blank space, we prefer to avoid blank spaces altogether. For example, in our sample data document, we used the field names *FirstName* and *LastName*, rather than *First Name* and *Last Name*. Although this is entirely a matter of preference, you'll run into fewer errors if you develop some rules for consistent field name references.

Formatting Your Merge Text

You may have noticed that the two sets of *«FirstName»* and *«LastName»* field instructions in lines 5 and 7 of Figure 12-2 carry different character formats. In the heading near the top of the document, we used 18-point Times bold text; in the body text, we used 12-point Times Plain. Word will apply these character formats to our variable text when it creates the merge documents. As this illustrates, you can control the character formats of your variable text simply by applying the desired formats to your field name instructions. In fact, Word will use the character formats that you assign to the first character in the field name instruction to format all the text that replaces that instruction in the merge documents.

For example, if you want the individual's astrological sign, which appears in the sixth line of our sample document, to appear in italic type, you can assign the Italic format to the letter *S* in the field name instruction, like this: «*S*ign». (For readability, however, you may prefer to italicize the entire field name instruction, like this: *«Sign».*)

In addition to character formatting, Word will use all the Page Setup, Document, Section, and Paragraph settings that you assign in your main document to format your merge documents. We'll show you some examples of how your Section, Document, and Page Setup dialog box settings affect your merge document formats when we, talk about creating mailing labels in Word.

MERGING THE DOCUMENTS

Once you have created your data and main documents, you're ready to use the Print Merge... command to merge the two files. To create your merge documents, make sure that the main document is active on the Word DeskTop, then select Print Merge... from the File menu.

Your data document does not have to be open on the Word DeskTop when you issue the Print Merge... command. Word can read the data from that file on disk. However, the data document should be located on the same disk—and in the same folder, if you are using folders—as your main document. If Word cannot find your data document, it will present an Open dialog box and ask you to locate the needed file. You'll have to access the disk (or folder) on which the document is located before you can continue with the merge procedure. If your data document is located on another disk, you may have to do quite a bit of disk-swapping as Word builds each of your merge documents.

When you issue the Print Merge… command, Word will display a dialog box like the one in Figure 12-3. If you want to print your documents, just click the Print button or press the Return key.

FIGURE 12-3

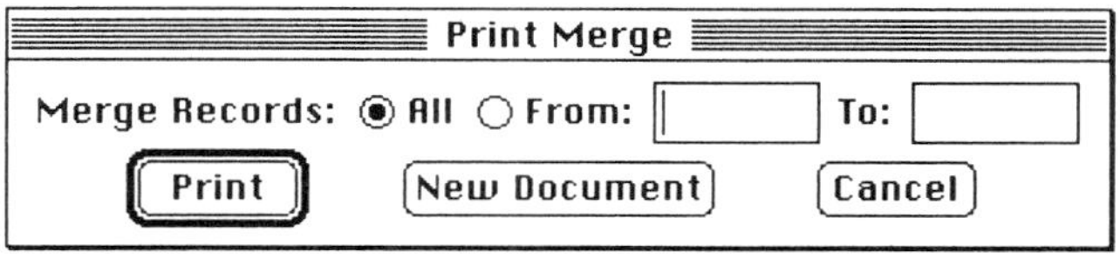

You'll see a dialog box like this one when you issue the Print Merge… command.

The From and To options in the Print Merge dialog box let you control which data records you want to use in your merge documents. If you want to create merge documents for every record in your data document, leave the default All option selected. If you want to print only some of the records, enter the start and end ranges in the From and To edit bars. For example, if you want to merge the data from the fourth, fifth, and sixth data records, you would type the value 4 in the From edit bar and the value 6 in the To edit bar.

When you click on the Print button, Word will present you with a Print dialog box exactly like the one you see when you issue the Print… command to print a standard Word document. (See Chapter 7 for a complete description of the Print dialog box.)

All the options in the Print dialog box work just as they do when you print a standard Word document. Keep in mind, however, that the Pages options in the Print dialog box refer to the number of document pages you want to print, not the number of records—that setting is controlled in the Print Merge dialog box. If you specify a From and To value in the Print dialog box, Word will print the specified range of pages once for each record in your data document. In other words, if you have a four-page document, and you use From and To values of 2 and 3, Word will print pages 2 and 3 of the merge document for every record in your data document. (Of course, if you've instructed Word to merge only a subset of your data records, then the page range will be printed once for each record you've selected.)

Similarly, the Copies option refers to the number of copies of each merge document you want to print, not the total number of documents you want to print. For example, if you use a Copies setting of 3, Word will print three copies of your merge document for each record in the data document. (Again, if you've chosen to merge a range of records from the data document, instead of all the records, Word will print the specified number of copies for each record.)

Figures 12-4 and 12-5 show the first two merge documents that Word will create when we merge the Names data document with the Horoscope main document shown in Figures 12-1 and 12-2. As you can see, Word has printed the text of the Horoscope file, substituting the text from the FirstName, LastName, and Sign fields of the first and second records in our data document for each of the field name instructions in our main document.

FIGURE 12-4

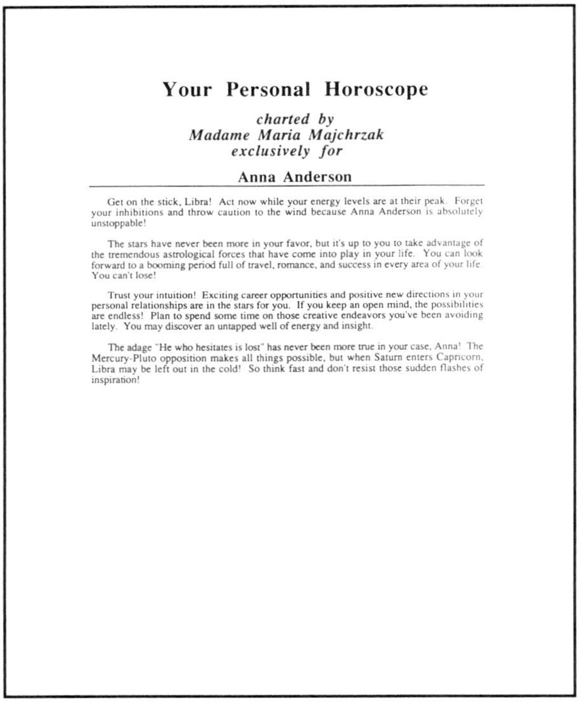

Your Personal Horoscope

charted by
Madame Maria Majchrzak
exclusively for

Anna Anderson

Get on the stick, Libra! Act now while your energy levels are at their peak. Forget your inhibitions and throw caution to the wind because Anna Anderson is absolutely unstoppable!

The stars have never been more in your favor, but it's up to you to take advantage of the tremendous astrological forces that have come into play in your life. You can look forward to a booming period full of travel, romance, and success in every area of your life. You can't lose!

Trust your intuition! Exciting career opportunities and positive new directions in your personal relationships are in the stars for you. If you keep an open mind, the possibilities are endless! Plan to spend some time on those creative endeavors you've been avoiding lately. You may discover an untapped well of energy and insight.

The adage "He who hesitates is lost" has never been more true in your case, Anna! The Mercury-Pluto opposition makes all things possible, but when Saturn enters Capricorn, Libra may be left out in the cold! So think fast and don't resist those sudden flashes of inspiration!

To create this merge document, Word extracted information from the first record in our data document.

After you click OK in the Print dialog box, if Word doesn't recognize one of the field names in your main document, it will display the alert message *Unknown field name*. You will have the option of stopping or continuing the merge procedure. You must remember that if you choose to continue, Word will insert the error message in each of your merge documents.

Creating a Merge File

Rather than routing the merge text directly to a printer, you can use the New Document button in the Print Merge dialog box to "print" your merged text to a Word file. When you use this option, Word will open a new Word document called Form Letters1. Like the Untitled documents that Word creates when you issue the New command, each Form Letters file that you create during a Word session will be numbered sequentially—Form Letters2, Form Letters3, and so forth.

FIGURE 12-5

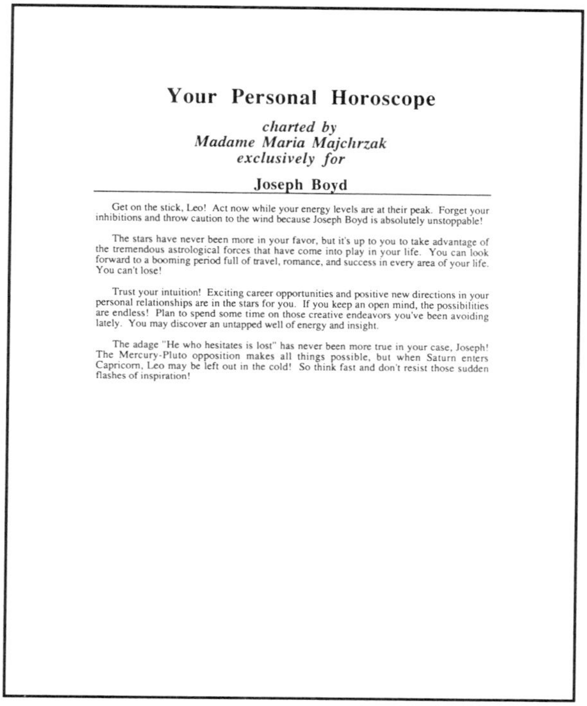

Your Personal Horoscope
charted by
Madame Maria Majchrzak
exclusively for

__Joseph Boyd__

Get on the stick, Leo! Act now while your energy levels are at their peak. Forget your inhibitions and throw caution to the wind because Joseph Boyd is absolutely unstoppable!

The stars have never been more in your favor, but it's up to you to take advantage of the tremendous astrological forces that have come into play in your life. You can look forward to a booming period full of travel, romance, and success in every area of your life. You can't lose!

Trust your intuition! Exciting career opportunities and positive new directions in your personal relationships are in the stars for you. If you keep an open mind, the possibilities are endless! Plan to spend some time on those creative endeavors you've been avoiding lately. You may discover an untapped well of energy and insight.

The adage "He who hesitates is lost" has never been more true in your case, Joseph! The Mercury-Pluto opposition makes all things possible, but when Saturn enters Capricorn, Leo may be left out in the cold! So think fast and don't resist those sudden flashes of inspiration!

To create this merge document, Word extracted information from the second record in our data document.

Instead of creating a new file for each record in your data document, Word places all the merge text into a single Form Letters file. A section break will appear between the text for each record. For instance, if we were to click the New Document button as we merged the files in our example, Word would create the document shown in Figure 12-6 on the following page. As it creates this document, Word creates the merge text for Anna Anderson, then inserts a section-break marker and creates the merge text for Joseph Boyd. (By the way, as you might have guessed, you will not see the Print dialog box when you use the New Document option.)

You can save these Form Letters documents or you can use them as temporary files to see the results of your merge instructions before you print. In order to get a better idea of how the printed merge documents will appear, you may want to use the Print Preview... command, discussed in Chapter 7. If your data document contains many records, you may want to use the From and To options in the Print Merge dialog box to create a merge file from only a few records as a way of previewing your printed merge documents. This spot-checking technique can save you a lot of time, frustration, and paper before you begin printing a series of merge documents.

FIGURE 12-6

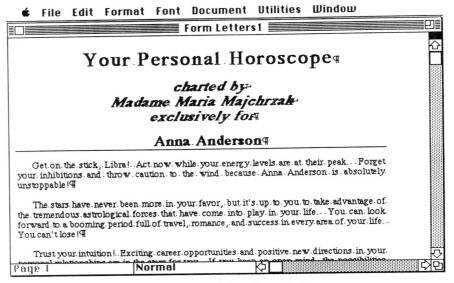

You can save your merge text in a file rather than print it.

If you decide to save your Form Letters document, keep in mind that the file is not dynamic. That is, a Form Letters file is not linked in any way to a main document or data file. If you change the information in either of those files, you'll have to use another Print Merge... command to create a new, updated merge file.

SPECIAL INSTRUCTIONS

In addition to the DATA and field name instructions, Word offers a number of special instructions that let you vary the contents of your merge documents. You can use these instructions to create logical criteria, to update selected information manually each time you issue the Print Merge... command, to combine data from two or more records in the same merge document, and to insert text from other Word files into your merge documents.

The INCLUDE Instruction

The INCLUDE instruction lets you extract text from another Word file and insert it into your merge documents. This instruction takes the same form as the DATA instruction that we discussed earlier:

«INCLUDE document»

To use this instruction, simply type the INCLUDE instruction at the spot where you want the "included" text to appear. If any additional main document text appears after the INCLUDE instruction, Word will print that text immediately after the "included" text. If you want a page or section break to occur before the "included" text, just insert a manual page or section-break marker directly in front of the INCLUDE instruction. Similarly, if you want a page or section break to occur after the "included" text, you can insert a manual break after the INCLUDE instruction.

As with the data document, any files you want to include in your merge document should be located on the same disk and in the same folder as your main document. Otherwise, you'll need to locate the file for Word when you issue the Print Merge... command.

For example, suppose we want to include a "sun sign profile" after the text from our sample Horoscope document. This additional text is located in a file called Profile, shown in Figure 12-7. To include the text from this document in our merge documents, we would type the instruction

«INCLUDE Profile»

at the end of our main document text, as shown in Figure 12-8 on the next page. When we merge the main, data, and include documents, Word will create a series of merge documents like the one shown in Figure 12-9 on the following page.

FIGURE 12-7

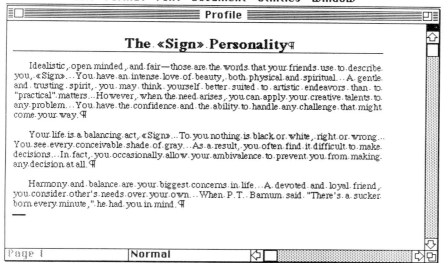

This file contains our sun sign profile text.

FIGURE 12-8

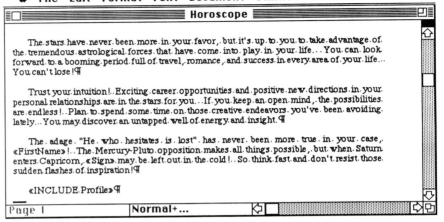

Type the INCLUDE instruction where you want the additional text to appear.

FIGURE 12-9

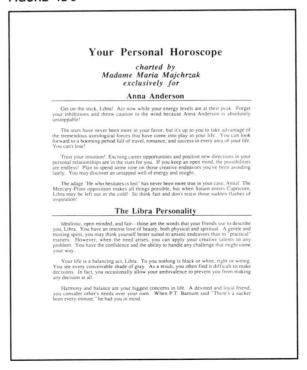

When we issue the Print Merge... command, Word combines the text from all three documents.

Notice in Figure 12-7 that our Profile document also contains field name instructions to fill in the client's sign. An include document can contain any of the special instructions you use in a main document, except for the DATA instruction. Word allows you to use only one DATA instruction at a time, and that DATA instruction must be the first instruction in your main document file.

There are a couple of reasons why you would want to use the INCLUDE instruction to place additional text into your merge documents, rather than simply entering that text into the main document. First of all, you can refer to the same include file in any number of main documents, thus saving yourself the time, effort, and disk space required to enter the "included" text in several files.

In addition, as you'll see in a few pages, you can set up criteria that instruct Word to extract data from different include files, depending on the results of certain conditional instructions.

The SET Instruction

If you need to vary only a few words from one document to the next, you'll probably find it more efficient to use a SET instruction rather than the INCLUDE instruction to create that variable text. The SET instruction lets you manually change the contents of selected fields in your merge documents each time you create a new set of merge documents.

The SET instruction can take three forms:

«SET field name=text»
«SET field name=?»
«SET field name=?message»

Use the *field name* argument to define the name of the field you want to vary each time you create a new set of merge documents. Then, enter that field name into the desired locations in your main document text in order to flag the spots where you want Word to insert your text. In order for Word to recognize each field name in your main document as a special placeholder—and not just another word—the field name must be enclosed in a pair of guillemet characters («»).

The *field name* argument for a SET instruction should be different from the field names that appear in your data document's field header row. Like the field names from your data document, the SET instruction field names will be typed into your main document at each place where you want to vary some text. However, instead of extracting text from the data document, when Word encounters a field name from a SET instruction, it will use text you have provided. If you use a field name in a SET instruction that matches one of the field names in your data document, you'll see the alert message *SET name is also the name of a DATA field.* when you issue the Print Merge... command. This same message will appear in your merge documents at each spot where the duplicate field name appears.

The text option

If you use the first form of the SET instruction, you'll type the text you want to use for the variable field directly into your main document before you issue the Print Merge… command. For example, we mentioned at the beginning of this chapter that you might want to use the merge facility to create a series of personalized invitations to your company's grand opening. Suppose your grand opening party is going to be so big that you must spread it over three days in order to accommodate all your guests.

In order to create three sets of form letters that carry different invitation dates, you could insert into your main document a SET instruction with a *field name* argument called *Date*, like this:

«SET Date=March 1»

Then, to vary the definition of the Date field, you would edit this SET instruction each time you issued the Print Merge… command so that it specifies a different date.

For example, Figure 12-10 shows an invitation letter in which this SET instruction appears immediately after the DATA instruction. After entering the SET instruction to define the Date field, we typed the instruction *«Date»* in the first and third lines of the body text of our letter.

FIGURE 12-10

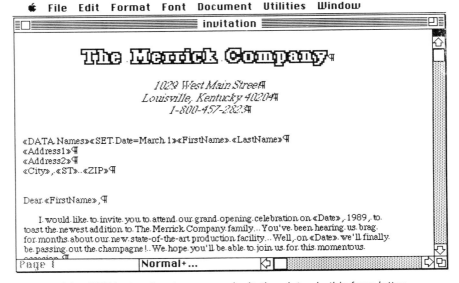

We used the SET instruction to vary our invitation dates in this form letter.

To divide our invitations into three groups (with a different invitation date for each group), we would issue three separate Print Merge... commands. Using the From and To options in the Print Merge dialog box, we would specify a different range of data records for each merge procedure. For example, suppose our data document contains 300 records. We might use From and To arguments of 1 and 100 to print the first batch of invitations, 101 and 200 to print the second batch, and 201 and 300 to print the last batch.

To vary the invitation date from one group of letters to the next, we would simply change the text in the SET instruction before issuing the Print Merge... command. In the second batch, for example, our SET instruction might read:

«SET Date=March 2»

while the SET instruction in the third batch would read *March 3*.

Rather than entering your SET text directly into the main document, you can have Word prompt you for the new date information each time you issue the Print Merge... command. To create a prompt, you use either the second or third form of the SET instruction. If you use the second form of the SET instruction

SET prompts

«SET Date =?»

you'll see a dialog box like the one in Figure 12-11 when you issue the Print Merge... command. Simply type the text you want Word to insert at each *«Date»* instruction in your document and click OK or press Return.

FIGURE 12-11

If you use the question mark form of the SET instruction, Word will prompt you for the text to enter into your SET instruction.

If you have entered more than one SET instruction into your main document, Word's generic *Enter data* message won't be of much help since you may not be able to tell for which field you're supposed to be entering the data. If you would like to see a more descriptive message in this dialog box, you can use the third form of the SET instruction. This form includes a custom message that you create to remind yourself of what kind of data you're supposed to be entering. For example, if you use a SET instruction like

«SET Date =?Enter the invitation date.»

Word will present a dialog box like the one in Figure 12-12.

FIGURE 12-12

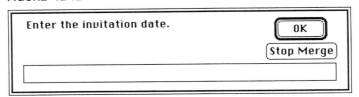

You can also create your own prompts for the SET dialog box.

The ASK Instruction

The ASK instruction is similar to the SET instruction except that it allows you to vary a field entry for each merge document in a set of merge documents. Instead of varying a field for each Print Merge... command, the ASK instruction will vary one or more fields for each merge document you create with a single Print Merge... command. The ASK instruction can take two forms:

«ASK field name=?»
«ASK field name=?message»

As with the SET instruction, the *field name* argument defines a field or placeholder that will appear in the main document. Again, this field name cannot be the same as one of the field names that appear in the data header row of the data document.

The question mark form of the ASK instruction tells Word to present a dialog box like the one in Figure 12-11. This dialog box will appear once for each record in your data document to let you define the field entry you want to use for that record.

To help you remember what type of data you want to enter, Word also lets you specify a prompt message to appear in the ASK dialog box. To create this message, you use the second form of the ASK instruction.

For example, suppose you decide to create a personalized greeting for each guest you plan to invite to your grand opening. You might set up a form letter like the one in Figure 12-13. The ASK instruction in the letter's salutation will cause Word to prompt you for a greeting for each letter.

FIGURE 12-13

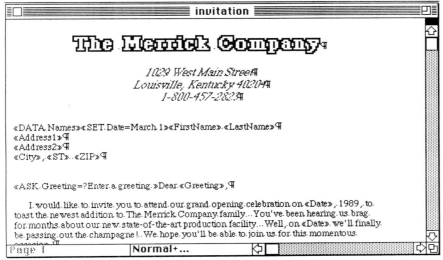

You can use the ASK instruction to vary a field entry for each merge document.

Unfortunately, as you respond to each ASK prompt, you may not be able to tell which record is being processed. As Word creates each letter in the series, the new information for the record that's being processed will appear on the screen behind the ASK dialog box. This will help you see whose letter you are customizing. If you click the New Document button in the Print Merge dialog box, however, you won't see the information for each record as you're responding to the ASK prompts. In addition, depending on how you've set up your main document—how long it is, where you have embedded field names, and so forth—you won't always be able to tell which record is being processed even if you did not click the New Document button.

Here's an easy way to get around that problem: Nest one or more field name instructions in your ASK message to identify the record that is currently being processed. For example, rather than using the instruction

«ASK Greeting=?Enter a greeting.»

in Figure 12-13, you could use an instruction like

«ASK Greeting=?How do you want to greet «FirstName» «LastName»?»

When you issue the Print Merge... command, Word will present a dialog box like the one in Figure 12-14 as it creates the merge text for each record in your data document.

FIGURE 12-14

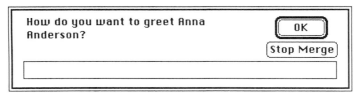

You can embed field name instructions in your ASK messages to keep track of which record is being processed.

The IF and ENDIF Instructions

In many instances, you'll want to create variations in your merge documents that can't be handled with a simple ASK or SET instruction. For example, you may need to insert into your merge documents special text that is dependent on the information in one of the fields in your data document. Word's IF and ENDIF instructions let you handle these situations by setting up conditional tests in the main document file.

The simplest form of the IF instruction is:

«IF field name»text«ENDIF»

This instruction tells Word to check the contents of the specified field in the current record to determine whether that field contains an entry. If there is an entry, then the conditional test is true, and Word will print the text that appears between the IF and ENDIF instructions. If the field is empty (that is, if you have inserted an extra comma or tab to skip past that field in the data document), then the conditional test is false, and Word will omit the text from the current merge document.

The text you enter between the IF and ENDIF instructions can be any length and may even contain page-break markers and section-break markers. You can even include special print merge instructions, such as the SET, ASK, and INCLUDE instructions, within the conditional text. In short, Word considers *anything* between the IF and ENDIF instructions to be conditional on the result of the IF comparison.

Continuing with the sample invitation letter created in Figure 12-10, suppose you want to include a note to your married clients to invite their spouses to the grand opening celebration as well. You have included a field in your data document that contains the name of each client's spouse—if he or she is married. For those who are not married, this field is blank.

FIGURE 12-15

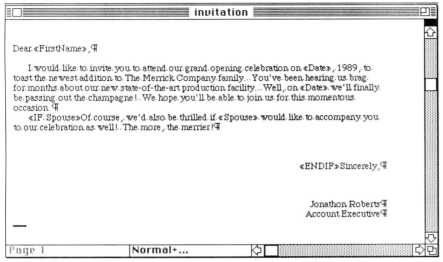

This conditional text will appear only if there is an entry in the Spouse field.

You could set up a conditional instruction like the one shown in Figure 12-15 to test for the presence of an entry in the Spouse field of your data document. If that field contains an entry, Word will print the text *Of course, we'd also be thrilled if «Spouse» would like to accompany you to our celebration as well! The more, the merrier!* (In printing this text, Word will, of course, substitute the name from the Spouse field for the *«Spouse»* field instruction.) If the Spouse field is empty, Word will omit this paragraph.

You may have noticed that we placed the ENDIF instruction after the ¶ marker at the end of our conditional text—just in front of the word *Sincerely* in the closing of our invitation letter. In doing so, we were able to avoid any unwanted blank lines in our merge documents. Remember, when you enter conditional text into your main document, Word considers everything between the IF and ENDIF instructions—including paragraph markers—to be conditional. Thus, by placing the ENDIF instruction at the beginning of the next paragraph—after the ¶ marker—you can ensure that no blank lines will appear in your merge text when the IF condition proves false.

**Comparing text
and numbers**

Rather than simply testing for the presence of an entry in a field, you can use an IF instruction to compare the contents of a field to a string or value that you specify. Word lets you compare text entries as well as numeric values with these two forms of the IF instruction:

«IF field name="comparison text"»text«ENDIF»
«IF field name=comparison value»text«ENDIF»

Notice that the comparison text in the first IF instruction is enclosed in quotation marks. These are required. Be sure you use straight quotation marks (" "), not curved quotation marks (" "). You may need to deselect the "Smart" Quotes option in the Preferences dialog box in order to do this. Generally, you should not include quotation marks around comparison values. If you place quotation marks around numeric values, Word will treat those values as text rather than as numbers. (As we'll explain, there's an exception to this rule.)

Returning to our sample Horoscope document, suppose we want to include a birthday greeting to those persons on the mailing list whose birthdays are approaching. Let's assume that we will be mailing these letters in mid-September, so the Libras are the next group of clients with birthdays on their astral horizons. We could create an IF instruction like the one in Figure 12-16 to include a birthday greeting for clients with the Sign field entry *Libra*.

FIGURE 12-16

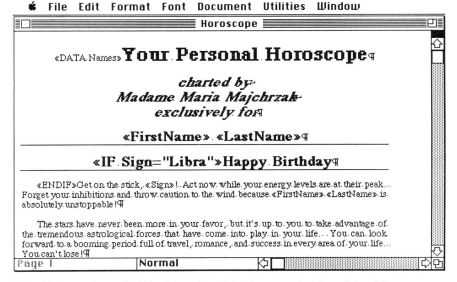

This IF instruction tells Word to print a birthday greeting for all the Libras on our mailing list.

When you're using the IF instruction to compare field entries, you can use a variety of comparison operators. These operators are summarized in Table 12-1. You can use all of these operators with both text and numeric fields. When a field contains text, Word will use the ASCII value of that text to perform the conditional test.

TABLE 12-1

Operator	Meaning
=	Equal to
>	Greater than
<	Less than
>= (or =>)	Greater than or equal to
<= (or =<)	Less than or equal to
<>	Not equal to

You can use these conditional operators to specify an IF condition.

For example, suppose you need to send a series of billing notices to some of your clients. We'll assume that your client data document includes an OD field that lists the number of days that each payment is past due.

Now, suppose you want to issue a particularly strong message to those people whose payments are more than 15 days late. You could use an IF instruction like the one shown in Figure 12-17 on the following page to determine whether the value in the OD field is greater than 15. If the logical test *OD>15* is true, Word will include the sentence *Your bill is seriously past due!* in the billing notice for that client. If payment is 15 days overdue or less, this sentence will not appear in the merge document.

Interestingly, Word recognizes only integer values when you are comparing values. If a field in your data document contains values that are displayed with decimal points, then you must treat those values as labels in the IF instructions by enclosing them in quotation marks, like this:

«IF fieldname="202.33"»text«ENDIF»

Word 4 also allows you to create IF instructions that compare the contents of one field to another within a single record. The form of this instruction is

«IF fieldname1="«fieldname2»"»text«ENDIF»

Again, be sure you use straight quotation marks to surround the *«fieldname2»* portion of the instruction.

FIGURE 12-17

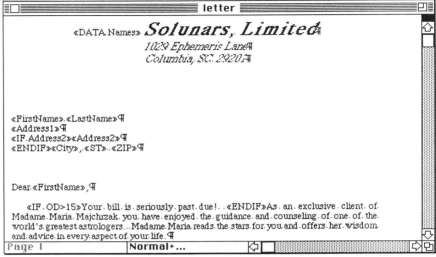

You can use a comparison value in an IF instruction to determine whether each client's payment is more than 15 days overdue.

The ELSE instruction

So far, all our conditional tests have instructed Word to enter a text block into a merge document only if a given condition is true. However, there may be occasions when you want to print alternative text in a merge document when a condition is false. Word's ELSE instruction works hand-in-hand with the IF instruction to let you accomplish this task.

The ELSE instruction, which takes no arguments of its own, is designed to be nested within the IF instruction, like this:

«IF field name»text«ELSE»alternative text«ENDIF»

Continuing with the sample invitation letter shown in Figure 12-15, suppose you want to add an alternative line of text for your unmarried clients (those with no entry in the Spouse field), inviting them to bring a guest. You could accomplish this by changing your IF instruction to look like the one in Figure 12-18.

As you can see, to create the alternative text, you simply add the nested instruction *«ELSE»Please feel free to invite a guest to help us celebrate this momentous occasion!* to your IF instruction.

FIGURE 12-18

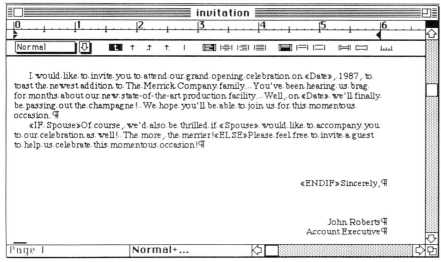

We used the ELSE instruction to add alternative text for unmarried clients.

Using IF to control blank lines

You may have noticed in the sample overdue letter in Figure 12-17 that we used the conditional instruction *«IFAddress2»«Address2»* to create the second line of our address block. We placed the ENDIF instruction just before the *«City»* field instruction in the next line. As you may remember, in the sample data document shown in Figure 12-1, only some of the records contain entries in the Address2 field. The others simply contain extra tab markers as placeholders for this empty field.

To keep from printing a blank line in the address block whenever the Address2 field is empty, we defined the «Address2» field instruction as conditional text. As with the conditional text in Figures 12-15 and 12-18, in Figure 12-17 we chose to place our ENDIF statement after the ¶ marker for the Address2 block to ensure that no extra blank line occurs at this point when the Address2 field is empty.

Nesting IF instructions

You've already seen several examples of nested instructions as we've created sample merge documents throughout this chapter. For instance, we showed how you could nest a field name instruction within an ASK instruction and within an IF instruction. As you might have guessed, you can also nest two or more IF instructions in your main document to test for a number of possible conditions. In fact, by stringing together a group of IF instructions, you can create a fairly sophisticated series of conditional tests.

Depending on the form you use in combining the IF instructions, you can direct Word to print your conditional text only if all of the IF instructions are true or if any one of the IF instructions is true. In other words, like many spreadsheet and database programs, Word allows you to create "logical AND" combinations and "logical OR" combinations. When all of the IF instructions must be true in order for Word to print the conditional text, you might think of your IF instructions as being tied together with logical ANDs. On the other hand, if only one of the IF instructions must be true before Word prints the conditional text, you might think of the IF instructions as being combined with logical ORs.

Logical AND combinations

To combine IF instructions with a logical AND, you would string the instructions together like this:

«IF field name1="comparison text"»«IF field name2="comparison text"»text«ENDIF»«ENDIF»

«IF field name1=comparison value»«IF field name2=comparison value»text«ENDIF»«ENDIF»

Notice that all of the IF instructions appear before the conditional text. Then, following the conditional text, an ENDIF instruction appears for each IF instruction.

Unfortunately, you cannot use an ELSE instruction when you string together two or more IF instructions in a logical AND combination. If you include an ELSE instruction, Word will execute it only when all of the IF conditions are false. If even one of the IF conditions is true, Word will ignore the ELSE instruction.

Logical OR combinations

As we've mentioned, in a logical OR combination, only one IF instruction must be true in order for the conditional text to be printed. When you set up a logical OR combination, you must type the conditional text once for each IF instruction, like this:

«IF field name="comparison text"»text1«ENDIF»«IF field name="comparison text"»text2«ENDIF»

«IF field name=comparison value»text1«ENDIF»«IF field name=comparison value»text2«ENDIF»

Notice that, instead of grouping all of the ENDIF instructions after the conditional text, each ENDIF appears immediately after an IF instruction and conditional text.

As an alternative, you might use the ELSE instruction to create a logical OR combination, like this:

«IF field name="comparison text"»text1«ELSE»«IF field name="comparison text"»text2«ENDIF»«ENDIF»

«IF field name=comparison value»text1«ELSE»«IF field name=comparison value»text2«ENDIF»«ENDIF»

The effect is the same no matter which form of a logical OR combination you choose to use. However, the first form saves you from typing an ELSE instruction between each IF instruction.

As with logical ANDs, you can use either the same field name or different field names in each IF instruction. Unlike a logical AND combination, however, you can vary the conditional text for each IF instruction. For example, in the sample document shown in Figure 12-8, we showed how to create an INCLUDE instruction to extract text from a file named Profile. Suppose we decide to create 12 separate profile documents—one for each astrological sign. We have named these documents Aries, Taurus, Gemini, and so forth. To select the appropriate profile for each client, we could string together a series of 12 IF instructions, like this:

«IF Sign="Aries"»«INCLUDE Aries»«ELSE»«IF Sign="Taurus"» «INCLUDE Taurus»«ELSE»«IF Sign="Gemini"»«INCLUDE Gemini» «ELSE»«IF Sign="Cancer"»«INCLUDE Cancer»«ELSE»«IF Sign="Leo"» «INCLUDE Leo»«ELSE»«IF Sign="Virgo"»«INCLUDE Virgo»«ELSE»«IF Sign="Libra"»«INCLUDE Libra»«ELSE»«IF Sign="Scorpio"»«INCLUDE Scorpio»«ELSE»«IF Sign="Sagittarius"» «INCLUDE Sagittarius»«ELSE»«IF Sign="Capricorn"»«INCLUDE Capricorn»«ELSE»«IF Sign="Aquarius"» «INCLUDE Aquariis«ELSE» «IF Sign="Pisces"»«INCLUDE Pisces»«ENDIF»«ENDIF»«ENDIF» «ENDIF»«ENDIF»«ENDIF»«ENDIF»«ENDIF»«ENDIF»«ENDIF» «ENDIF»«ENDIF»

Notice that the conditional text for each IF instruction is an INCLUDE instruction that directs Word to the appropriate profile document.

The NEXT Instruction

As we have already explained, when you use the Print Merge… command to create a new Form Letters file, Word inserts a section-break marker between the end of the merge text for one record and the beginning of the merge text for the next record. When you print your merge documents, Word again inserts a section break between the merge text for different records and, because the default Section Start setting is New Page, Word automatically starts a new page as it begins printing the text for each new record.

If you would like to omit these page and section breaks, you can insert a series of NEXT instructions in your main document. The NEXT instruction tells Word to extract the information from another record in the data document and continue merging—without starting a new page or inserting a section break. Therefore, after each NEXT instruction, you will also need to enter another copy of the main document text. The NEXT instruction takes no arguments of its own—you insert it in front of other merge instructions to tell Word to extract information from the next record in your data document.

For example, suppose you want to create a list of your clients' names, with ten names printed on a page. If you were to create a main document with the simple field instructions

«FirstName» «LastName»

Word would print only one client name on each page. In order to print ten names on a page, you would set up your main document so that it repeats these field instructions nine times. After the first *«FirstName» «LastName»* sequence, you would include a NEXT instruction in front of each additional field instruction sequence, like this:

«NEXT»«FirstName» «LastName»

Each time Word encounters a NEXT instruction, it will extract the first and last name information from another record in the data document and merge it into the main document where the next *«FirstName» «LastName»* sequence appears.

MAILING LABELS

Our discussion of merging would be incomplete without covering the topic of mailing labels. You might use Word's print merge capabilities to create mailing labels as often as you use it to do any other kind of merging. In this section, we'll cover the basics of creating mailing labels in Word.

In fact, you already know most of what you need to know to create mailing labels. The first step in creating mailing labels is to set up a data document like the one in Figure 12-1 that contains the names and addresses of the people for whom you want to print labels. Next, you must create a main document that defines the form of the mailing labels. Finally, you use the Print Merge… command to print the labels.

Creating Single-Column Labels on an ImageWriter

Let's start with a discussion of creating single-column mailing labels on the ImageWriter printer, then we'll show you how to print multiple-column labels. We'll also look at some formatting problems that might arise as you print mailing labels. Then, we'll discuss some special techniques for creating mailing labels on the LaserWriter printer.

As with any merge document, your first step in creating mailing labels is to set up a data document. Figure 12-19 shows a sample data document that contains the names and addresses of the people for whom you want to print labels. As you can see, this sample data document contains eight fields: FirstName, LastName, MI, Address1, Address2, City, ST, and ZIP.

Creating the data document

FIGURE 12-19

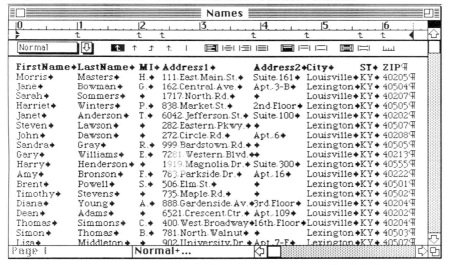

This is the sample data document we'll use to create our mailing labels.

After setting up the data document, you must create a main document that defines the content and format of your mailing labels. Setting up the main document for mailing labels is very similar to setting up the main document for any other print merge application.

Creating the main document

As with most merge applications, there are a number of ways you can approach this problem. However, the sample main document shown in Figure 12-20 illustrates the simplest method we have discovered for creating single-column mailing labels on the ImageWriter printer. Basically, this main document tricks Word into treating each mailing label as an individual page. As we'll explain in a moment, this technique lets you avoid a number of potential alignment problems.

FIGURE 12-20

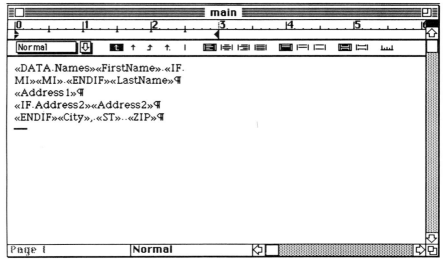

This main document is set up to create single-column mailing labels.

As you can see, the DATA instruction at the beginning of the document refers to the data document called Names, which is shown in Figure 12-19. The main document includes the field instructions *«FirstName»*, *«LastName»*, *«MI»*, *«Address1»*, *«Address2»*, *«City»*, *«ST»*, and *«ZIP»*. Each of these instructions corresponds to one of the fields in the sample data document. We've formatted the field instructions (and thus the resulting merge text) to appear in 12-point New York type. This type size and font allows us to fit as many as five lines of text on each 1-inch high mailing label.

Notice that we've used the logical instruction

«IF MI»«MI» «ENDIF»

to determine whether the MI field in the data document contains an entry. If it does, Word will include that entry in the mailing label, followed by a blank space. If it doesn't, Word will skip the *«MI»* field instruction, omit the blank space so that no unsightly gaps appear between the first and last names, and move on to the *«LastName»* instruction.

Similarly, we've used the logical instruction

«IF Address2»«Address2»¶
«ENDIF»

to determine whether the Address2 field contains an entry. If it does, Word will include that entry in the mailing label. If it doesn't, Word will skip the *«Address2»* field instruction and move on to the *«City»*, *«ST»*, and *«ZIP»* instructions in the next paragraph. The ENDIF instruction appears after the ¶ marker, to ensure that none of the printed labels will contain an extra blank line.

After you've entered the instructions that define your labels, you need to use the Preferences... command to specify a custom paper size. In the Preferences dialog box, first enter the dimensions of your labels in the Custom Paper Size Width and Height edit bars. (These Custom Paper Size settings won't be available unless you've selected the ImageWriter in the Chooser dialog box.) Assuming that you are printing on continuous-feed labels, the Height setting should match the height of your labels (usually 1 or $1^1/_2$ inches). The Width setting should equal the width of your labels. (We'll use a Width setting of 3.5.) As you'll see in a moment, you'll need to use a different Width setting if you are printing multiple-column labels.

After entering your label dimensions as a custom paper size in the Preferences dialog box, you'll need to open the Page Setup dialog box and select the corresponding Paper option. As you'll see, Word will have added the custom paper size to the standard options that normally appear in the Page Setup dialog box. Just click on that option to select it. Also, select the No Gaps Between Pages option.

In order to position the information correctly on the labels, you'll need to change the Left, Right, Top, and Bottom margin settings in the Document dialog box. You'll probably want to enter a value of about .25 or less for the Left and Right settings, since mailing labels typically don't allow much extra room for margins. The Top and Bottom settings should be 0.

As we hinted earlier, by specifying a paper size that matches the size of your labels, you tell Word to treat each label as a page. To ensure that Word will start a new page after it prints each label, make sure that the New Page Start option is selected in the Section dialog box before you issue the Print Merge... command. (New Page is the default Section Start option, so it would be selected automatically if you create a new Word file to hold your main document.)

Printing the labels

Once you've set up your main and data documents, you're ready to use the Print Merge... command to print the labels. As with any merge application, you can opt to route your mailing labels directly to the printer or you can store them in a Word file where they can be reviewed and edited before printing.

Figure 12-21 shows some of the mailing labels that result from the data and main documents shown in Figures 12-19 and 12-20.

FIGURE 12-21

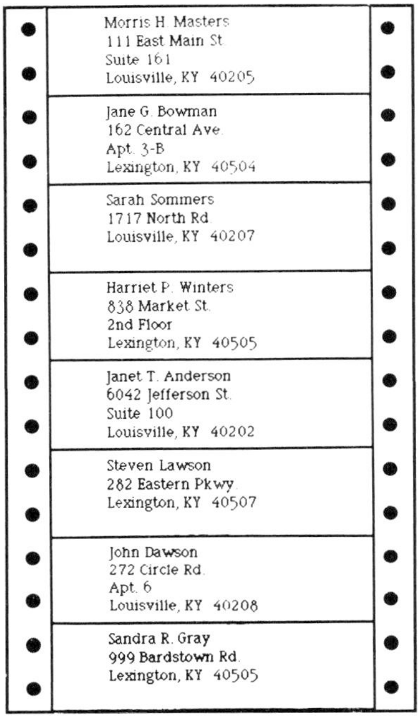

Morris H. Masters
111 East Main St
Suite 161
Louisville, KY 40205

Jane G. Bowman
162 Central Ave
Apt. 3-B
Lexington, KY 40504

Sarah Sommers
1717 North Rd
Louisville, KY 40207

Harriet P. Winters
838 Market St.
2nd Floor
Lexington, KY 40505

Janet T. Anderson
6042 Jefferson St.
Suite 100
Louisville, KY 40202

Steven Lawson
282 Eastern Pkwy
Lexington, KY 40507

John Dawson
272 Circle Rd
Apt. 6
Louisville, KY 40208

Sandra R. Gray
999 Bardstown Rd.
Lexington, KY 40505

A portion of our single-column mailing labels looks like this.

Creating Multicolumn Labels on an ImageWriter

Word also allows you to create multiple-column mailing labels—labels that are printed two, three, or even four across each page. The process of creating multiple-column labels on the ImageWriter is similar to that of creating single-column labels. Rather than tricking Word into treating each label as a separate page, however, you take advantage of Word's columnar formatting capabilities to group two or more labels on each "page."

The first step in generating multiple-column labels is to create one or more additional instruction sets in the main document for each column of labels. Each additional instruction set must begin with a NEXT command. For example, if you're printing labels across three columns, you would have three instruction sets, with a NEXT instruction preceding each of the last two sets. If you're printing labels across two columns, you would have only two instruction sets, with a NEXT instruction preceding the second set.

The NEXT instruction tells Word to pull another record from the data document without inserting a section break. When you set up your main document to include more than one set of instructions, and use the NEXT instruction as we've described, Word will insert a section break—and a page break—after each group of labels. For example, if you're printing labels across three columns, Word will insert a section break after each group of three-across labels.

In addition to adding instruction sets to the main document, you need to use the Section… command to set up columnar formatting in your main document. To do this, enter a Columns Number setting in the Section dialog box that corresponds to the number of labels that you want to fit across the page. If you are printing labels across three columns, you would change the Columns Number setting to 3. For two-column labels, you would enter 2 in the Columns Number edit bar.

You'll also want to enter a Spacing setting to tell Word how much room to allow between columns of labels. Since mailing labels are generally tightly spaced, your Spacing setting should be approximately .25, or perhaps .5, inches.

When you are printing to continuous-form labels, you should also add section breaks between labels and apply the New Page Start option (in the Section dialog box) to the first section, and the New Column Start option to the second and subsequent sections. The first Section Start setting ensures that Word will start a new page—that is, move to the top of the next row of labels—after it prints each set of labels. The New Column setting for the second and subsequent sections ensures that Word will start each new label at the top of a new column—on the same row as the first label.

After setting up the columnar formatting in your main document, you need to open the Preferences dialog box and enter the dimensions of your label forms in the Custom Paper Size Width and Height edit bars. As before, the Height setting should equal the height of a single label. The Width setting that you specify should equal the combined width of the labels. For example, if you're printing labels across two columns and each label is $3^1/_2$ inches wide and 1 inch high, then your Width setting should be 7 and your Height setting 1. If you are printing across three columns, you would triple the Width setting from 3.5 to 10.5. After specifying your Custom Paper Size settings in the Preferences dialog box, open the Page Setup dialog box and select the corresponding Paper option.

You need to make two further adjustments. In the Document dialog box, set the Top and Bottom margins to 0 for maximum depth on your labels. In the Page Setup dialog box, activate the No Gaps Between Pages option.

The section breaks that Word inserts after every group of labels, combined with the columnar formatting that you establish in the Section dialog box, will give you the multiple-column format. When you use columnar formatting, Word will "wrap" your columns separately in each section of a document. This causes each group of labels to be printed across the page instead of in a single column. In other words, each label in a group will appear in its own column on the "page" that you defined in the Preferences and Page Setup dialog boxes.

Figure 12-22 shows a main document that we created to print three-column mailing labels on the ImageWriter. The first instruction set is preceded by a DATA instruction, while the second and third instruction sets are each preceded by a NEXT instruction.

FIGURE 12-22

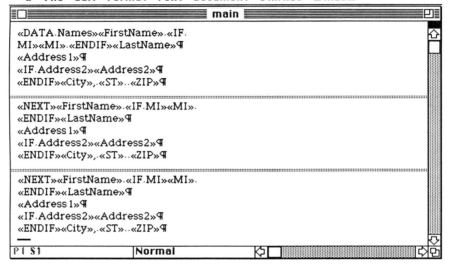

This main document lets us create three-column mailing labels.

Again, to format this main document, we used the 12-point and New York character formats, which allow us to fit five lines of text on each label. We used a Height setting of 1 and a Width setting of 10.5 in the Preferences dialog box to define the size of each "page" or row of labels. In the Section dialog box, we used a Number setting of 3 and a Spacing setting of .25 to define the three-column format.

Figure 12-23 shows the printed mailing labels that result from the main document shown in Figure 12-22.

Using the LaserWriter

If you have access to a LaserWriter, LaserWriter Plus, or LaserWriter Series II printer, you may want to print your labels using that printer. In general, the process of setting up and printing mailing labels using a LaserWriter is similar to that of printing labels on any other printer. However, there is one important difference. Because the LaserWriter cannot accommodate form-feed labels, you're likely to use label sheets to create your mailing labels. For this reason, you will need to set up your main document to contain a full page of three-across labels (or two-across labels if you are using sheets with larger labels.) Word 4's new table feature is the perfect tool for creating this type of layout.

FIGURE 12-23

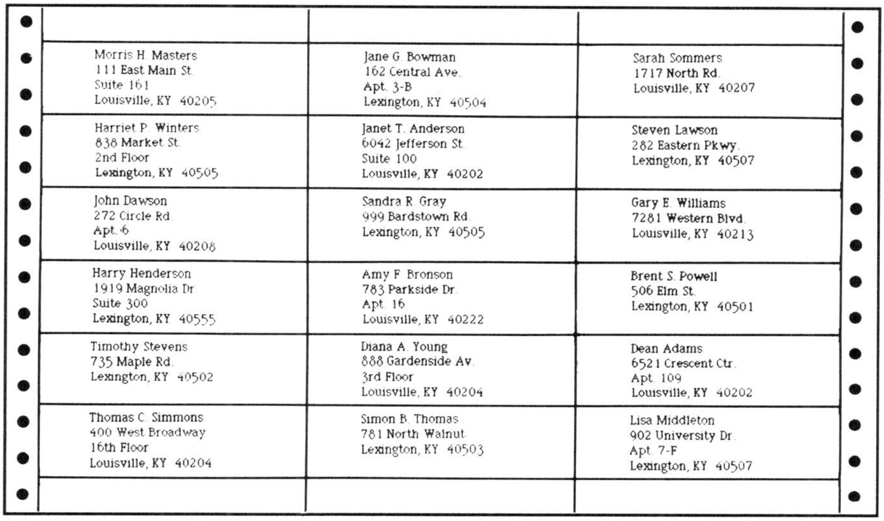

Morris H. Masters 111 East Main St. Suite 161 Louisville, KY 40205	Jane G. Bowman 162 Central Ave. Apt. 3-B Lexington, KY 40504	Sarah Sommers 1717 North Rd. Louisville, KY 40207
Harriet P. Winters 838 Market St. 2nd Floor Lexington, KY 40505	Janet T. Anderson 6042 Jefferson St. Suite 100 Louisville, KY 40202	Steven Lawson 282 Eastern Pkwy. Lexington, KY 40507
John Dawson 272 Circle Rd. Apt. 6 Louisville, KY 40208	Sandra R. Gray 999 Bardstown Rd. Lexington, KY 40505	Gary E. Williams 7281 Western Blvd. Louisville, KY 40213
Harry Henderson 1919 Magnolia Dr. Suite 300 Lexington, KY 40555	Amy F. Bronson 783 Parkside Dr. Apt. 16 Louisville, KY 40222	Brent S. Powell 506 Elm St. Lexington, KY 40501
Timothy Stevens 735 Maple Rd. Lexington, KY 40502	Diana A. Young 888 Gardenside Av. 3rd Floor Louisville, KY 40204	Dean Adams 6521 Crescent Ctr. Apt. 109 Louisville, KY 40202
Thomas C. Simmons 400 West Broadway 16th Floor Louisville, KY 40204	Simon B. Thomas 781 North Walnut Lexington, KY 40503	Lisa Middleton 902 University Dr. Apt. 7-F Lexington, KY 40507

When you merge the main document shown in Figure 12-22 with the data document shown in Figure 12-19, your printed labels will look like this.

To see how the whole process works, let's consider an example. Suppose you want to print sheets of mailing labels like those shown in Figure 12-24 on the following page by extracting the name and address information from the sample data document in Figure 12-25 on page 563.

Before you set up your main document, you need to study the dimensions and layout of your label sheets. In our example, we'll assume that the label sheets are $8^1/_2$ inches wide by 11 inches tall. Each sheet contains 10 rows of three-across labels, and each label is 1 inch high. In addition, an extra row of half labels ($^1/_2$ inch high) appears at the top and bottom of the sheet. If your label sheets do not fit this description, you will probably need to adjust some of the parameters we'll describe for the main document.

FIGURE 12-24

David H. Powell 1040 Eastern Pkwy. Nashville, TN 37215	Sandra M. Jennings 134 Brecker Blvd. Lansing, MI 48912	Norman Baker 2100 Crescent Place Suite 400 Dallas, TX 75238
George B. Henderson 3344 Broadway Baltimore, MD 21228	Julia R. Fischer 1454 East 60th St. Apt. 102 Orlando, FL 32817	Gayle Higgins 801 Parkside Dr. Tulsa, OK 74127
Brad A. Thomas 5987 Norwood Ave. Liberty, IL 62347	Lisa P. Schaefer 1600 Winchester Rd. Richmond, VA 23236	Stanley Green 709 Market St. 12th Floor Atlanta, GA 30318
Evelyn N. Peterson 111 East Main St. Suite 161 Louisville, KY 40205	Charles B. Keller 3333 University Dr. Cincinnati, OH 45231	Michael R. Ford 1217 Maple St. Greensboro, NC 27406
Gary Fleming 8560 Olympic Blvd. Apt. 217 Orange, CA 92667	Nathan F. Sanders 24 Stone Mill Way Albany, NY 12205	Rachel S. McLaury 176 Quince St. Suite 16 Natick, MA 01760
Janet W. Taylor 674 Emerald Dr. Arlington, VA 22207	Robert Haynes 1622 Glyndon Ave. Sioux City, IA 51104	John P. Lynch 12 West 15th St. Apt. 6L New York, NY 10011
Anna White 142 State St. Apt. 13 Hartford, CT 06117	Kim Thayer 2413 Briarcliff Rd. Phoenix, AZ 85027	Daniel C. Kaufman 2004 Jefferson St. Springfield, MO 65807
Martin T. Cates 1150 Park Ave. Apt. 6A New York, NY 10128	Sarah Y. Fleicher 920 Dover Place Suite 56 Austin, TX 78724	Walter Pearson 1325 Garden Dr. Charleston, SC 29406
Frank A. Wagner 8940 Evergreen Rd. Madison, WI 53711	Mary O'Brien 1001 Northfield Dr. Dayton, OH 45419	Jerome P. Butler 2932 Cottage Pl. Apt. H Oakland, CA 94611
Pamela C. Stokes 1400 Willow St. Suite 16 Topeka, KS 66614	Susan B. Sanders 337 Fairmeade Dr. Ashville, NC 28803	Barbara White 8840 Twinbrook Dr. Apt. 3A Harrisburg, PA 17109

With a LaserWriter, you will produce your mailing labels on label sheets.

Creating the main document

The first step in creating the main document is to define the page margins. Since the LaserWriter cannot print any closer than about $^3/_8$ inch from the edge of a sheet of paper, you should specify Left and Right margin settings of .5 inch each. Your Top and Bottom margins will be set to .7 inch each. This allows for the extra half label at the top and bottom of each sheet, plus some space between the edge of the labels on the first and last rows on the sheet and the label text.

Before entering any merge instructions in your main document, choose the Insert Table... command on the Document menu. In the Insert Table dialog box, enter 3 in the Number of Columns edit bar and enter 10 in the Number of Rows edit bar. Then, you can change Word's suggested Column Width setting to 2.5. (You'll need to adjust your column widths slightly after you create the table.) Figure 12-26 shows the Insert Table dialog box at this point. When you click OK, Word will create the blank table grid in the main document, as shown in Figure 12-27 on page 564.

FIGURE 12-25

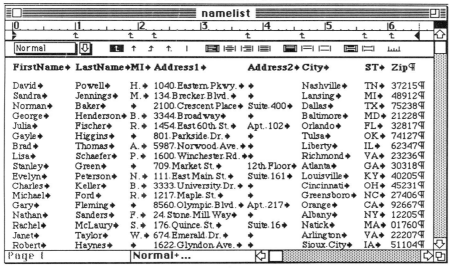

We'll use this data document to produce our mailing labels.

FIGURE 12-26

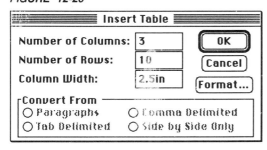

To create a table for your mailing labels, issue the Insert Table... command and specify these settings in the dialog box.

FIGURE 12-27

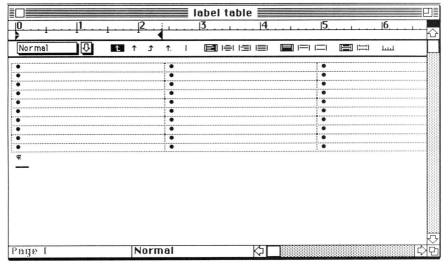

When you click OK in the Insert Table dialog box, Word will produce a blank
table in your main document.

**Adjusting
column widths**

The next step is to adjust your column widths and the spacing between columns.
To do this, click on the first column of the table and choose the Cells... command
on the Format menu. In the Cells dialog box, specify a Space Between Columns
setting of .5, and a column 1 width of 2.625. Also, click on the Apply To Whole
Table option. Figure 12-28 shows the Cells dialog box at this point. Click the Apply
button to lock in these settings.

FIGURE 12-28

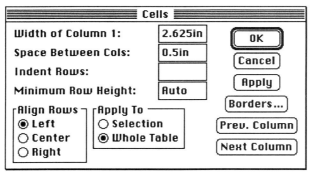

Use these settings in
the Cells dialog box
to format the first
column of the table.

Next, click the Next Column button to format the second column of the table. Leave the Space Between Columns setting at .5 and specify a column 2 width of 2.75. (Again, be sure the Apply To Whole Table option is selected.) Click the Apply button, then click the Next Column button once more to format the third column. Specify a width for this column of 2.625, then click OK to close the Cells dialog box.

Character formatting

After setting the column widths in your table, you need to determine the proper font size for your label text. To do this, first consider the height of your labels. In our example, each label measures 1 inch, or 72 points, in height. Since we need to allow four lines for each label, we can use either 10-point or 12-point type. We used 10-point type to create the labels in Figure 12-24. This allows us to fit any unusually long names or address lines on the labels. (If you decide to use 12-point type, you probably will need to adjust the Top and Bottom margin settings slightly.)

We know that, in most fonts, each line of 10-point type actually occupies 11 points of vertical space—an extra point of leading (white space) appears between the lines. When we multiply 11 by 4, we find that the label text will occupy 44 points of vertical space. Subtracting this from 72 gives us 28 points of space to appear before and after the lines of text—14 points above the first line and 14 points below the last line. (We've discovered from experience that you cannot always use simple math to figure how much space will appear between labels. Sometimes a little trial-and-error is called for.)

By computing the amount of space that must appear above and below the labels, you know that you'll need to insert 28 points after each row of three-across labels, except the last row. We'll show you how to do that in a moment. First, however, let's enter our merge instructions in the table.

The merge instructions

Figure 12-29 on the following page shows our table after entering the merge instructions in the first row. As you can see, the instructions in each cell are identical, except that the first cell contains a DATA instruction, which tells Word the name of the file that contains our data records. The second and third cells each contain a NEXT instruction. These tell Word to pull another record from the data document without inserting a section break.

As we showed in previous examples of mailing labels, each set of instructions includes the logical instruction

«IF MI»«MI» «ENDIF»

This instruction determines whether the MI field in the current record contains an entry. If it does, that entry will be included in the mailing label followed by a blank space. If it doesn't, Word will skip the *«MI»* field instruction and the blank space that follows it.

FIGURE 12-29

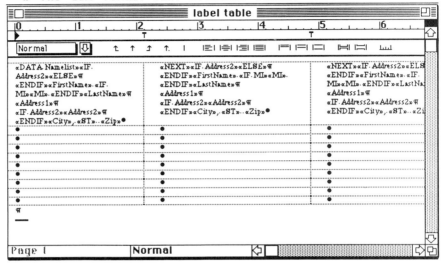

This is how your table will look after entering merge instructions in the first row.

Notice also that each instruction set includes the logical instruction

«IF Address2»«Address2»¶
«ENDIF»

which determines whether the Address2 field contains an entry. If it does, Word will include that entry in the mailing label. If it doesn't, Word will skip the *«Address2»* field instruction and move on to the *«City»*, *«ST»*, and *«Zip»* instructions in the next paragraph. Notice that you must press Return to insert a ¶ marker before the ENDIF instruction. This ensures that no extra blank line will appear in those labels that don't have a second address line.

Because some of the labels will contain four lines of text (those with an entry in the Address2 field), while others will contain only three lines, you need to include a special instruction to ensure that each label begins at the proper position on the label sheet. If you were to print a row of labels in which all three labels contained only three lines of text, the row of labels immediately below that one would begin too high on the label sheet.

To avoid this problem, you need to insert an extra blank line above or below any label that has only three lines of text. To create this extra blank line, you include these instructions just after the NEXT statement in each set of instructions:

«IF Address2»«ELSE»¶
«ENDIF»

Notice the ¶ marker that appears after the ELSE instruction and before the ENDIF. This indicates that Word should add a blank line whenever the IF condition is false. In other words, whenever there is no entry in the Address2 field, Word should "press" Return to insert a blank line before printing the name and address information. When the Address2 field does contain an entry, no extra blank line will be inserted.

Inserting space between rows

As we mentioned, you need to insert 28 points of space after each row of labels, except the tenth row. To do this, you simply click on each line that contains the «City», «ST», and «Zip» instructions, then open the Paragraph dialog box and enter 28 in the After edit bar. (By the way, we found that, when we formatted our labels in 12-point Times type, an After setting of 24 or 25 points worked pretty well.)

If you want, you can specify this After setting for only one of the cells in each row of the table. Since Word forces all cells on the same row of a table to be the same height, inserting 28 points of space after the instructions in one cell will create 28 points of space all the way across the row.

Copying the merge instructions

After creating the merge instructions in the first row of the table, your next step is to copy the contents of this row into the remaining nine rows. Begin by selecting the first row of the table. (Double-click in the selection bar for any cell on that row.) Then, choose Copy from the Edit menu or press ⌘-c. Next, click in front of the end-of-cell marker (●) for the first cell on the second row and choose Paste Cells from the Edit menu.

After making this first copy, you need to edit the instruction set in the first column slightly. When you copied the instructions from the first row to the second row, you copied the DATA statement at the beginning of the first instruction. Since a merge document should contain only one DATA statement, you need to remove this from the copy of the first instruction set that appears in the second row of the table. You also need to add a NEXT statement to this instruction set.

After replacing the DATA instruction on the second row with a NEXT instruction, you can select the second row of the table and copy it into the remaining eight rows. Figure 12-30 shows how your table will look after copying the merge instructions.

FIGURE 12-30

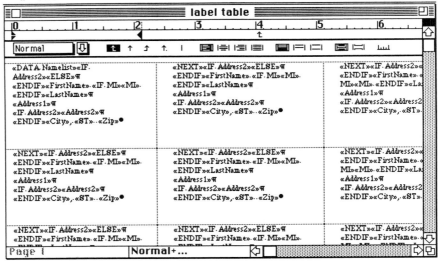

This is how your main document will look after copying the merge instructions into all the rows of the table.

There's one final formatting detail you need to take care of before your main document is complete. You need to remove the 28 points of space after the last line of merge instructions in the last (tenth) row of the table. If you don't do this, Word will not be able to fit this row on the label sheet.

Printing the labels

With your main document complete, you can now print your labels. Just issue the Print Merge… command and click the Print button in the Print Merge dialog box. Figure 12-24 shows the resulting sheet of printed labels.

OTHER SPECIAL FEATURES 13

As you've seen, Word offers a number of special features and capabilities that are designed to make your work easier and faster. In previous chapters, we've looked at the most important special features, including style sheets and the Outliner. In this chapter, we'll show you how to take advantage of several more of Word's special capabilities. We'll begin with a discussion of the glossary. Next, we'll look at line numbering and paragraph numbering, then we'll move into sorting paragraphs and performing calculations in Word. We'll wrap up with a look at Word's ability to create mathematical and scientific formulas and other special symbols with character formulas.

THE GLOSSARY

You've probably seen books that include a glossary, or listing of special terms and their definitions. In Word, the glossary serves a slightly different purpose from what you might expect. Instead of containing definitions for special terms, the Word glossary stores frequently used terms or other text and abbreviations for those terms. Word's glossary feature gives you access to several shortcuts for inserting text into your documents. The entries you store in the glossary might include words that require special formatting or just long terms that are difficult to spell. A glossary item can be as short as a single character or as long as several pages of text. Word even allows you to store graphics in a glossary.

In this section, we'll begin with an overview of how the Word glossary functions. Then, we'll move on to discussions of changing the glossary, creating and updating glossary files, and using the glossary.

**How the
Glossary
Works**

Whenever you load Word, the glossary is activated automatically. You might think of the glossary as a special "memory bin" for storing special terms. When you load Word—either by starting a new document or by opening an existing document file—the glossary initially will contain only the entries that are stored in the Standard Glossary file. You'll find this file on your Utilities 1 disk. It includes some entries that cannot be removed: the various *date* and *time* entries, *page number*, and *print merge*. We will talk more about the Standard Glossary file later in this chapter and in Chapter 14.

**One Glossary,
More Files**

It's important to note that Word has only one glossary, which resides in RAM when Word is loaded. However, you can create many special disk files that store glossary entries. The entries in these files can be loaded into Word's glossary whenever you need them. For purposes of our discussion, we will use the term *glossary* when we refer to the one glossary or "memory bin" that you can access in Word, and we will use the term *glossary file* when we refer to one of the special files on disk that store glossary terms.

*Changing
the glossary*

After you open a document file or start a new document, you can change the contents of the glossary in several ways. You can create your own entries and add them to the glossary; delete entries from the glossary; revise entries in the glossary; and retrieve a glossary file from disk and add its entries to the glossary.

Any changes you make to the glossary—creating and deleting entries or loading entries from another glossary file on disk—will remain in effect until you quit from Word. If you close one document, then open another without quitting from Word, the glossary entries you used with the first document will still be active. Similarly, when you have two or more documents open at one time on your DeskTop, you can access only one glossary, no matter which document you are working in. Therefore, if you need to use different glossary entries for different documents that are open on your DeskTop, make sure that all those entries are loaded into one glossary.

Once you have made changes to the glossary, you may want to save the glossary to disk either in a new glossary file or in an existing glossary file. (If you don't save your changes, they will be lost when you quit from Word.) For example, if you've just opened a new Word document from the Finder level, the only entries in the glossary will be those from the Standard Glossary file, which Word loads automatically. When you create new entries and add them to the glossary, they will join the original entries in the Standard Glossary file. You can save this combination either in a new glossary file or in the Standard Glossary file.

If you save the glossary entries in the file named Standard Glossary, Word will automatically load those entries as it loads the Standard Glossary file each time you open a document. In other words, in each new document, your glossary will contain the combination of the initial Standard Glossary entries and the new entries that you created and saved. In Chapter 14, we'll describe how you can create multiple Standard Glossary files so that you can use a different "automatic" glossary in each Word session.

Note

It's important to remember that no glossary file is "attached" to a particular document file. If you are working in a document, and you make changes to the glossary, you can save both the document and the revised glossary. However, Word will save the document and the glossary entries in separate disk files. The next time you open that document, Word will not automatically load the entries from the glossary file, unless you stored your changes in the file named Standard Glossary. You must open all other glossary files manually.

Now that we've seen an overview of how the glossary functions, let's look at the basics of working with the glossary.

Glossary Basics

To use the glossary in Word, choose Glossary... from the Edit menu. This will summon the dialog box shown in Figure 13-1. In the list box that displays glossary terms, the first entry is always <u>New</u>. You use <u>New</u> only when you want to define a new glossary entry. After <u>New</u>, the list box displays the other glossary terms in alphabetical order. Since there are more terms than can be displayed in the list box, you can click the scroll bar or scroll arrows to view additional glossary terms. As Figure 13-1 shows, the entries in the list box besides <u>New</u> are those that are loaded from the Standard Glossary file: the six *date* choices, the four *time* choices, *page number*, and *print merge*.

FIGURE 13-1

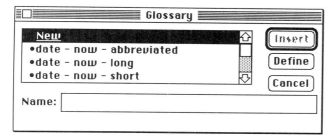

When you choose Glossary... from the Edit menu, Word will display the Glossary dialog box, which lists all the terms that currently are in the glossary.

Earlier, we mentioned that Word's glossary is used to store frequently used terms and their abbreviations. The list box that you see in the Glossary dialog box shows only the abbreviations. In this chapter, we will use the word *glossary term* when we refer to one of the items in this list. The term *glossary text* will refer to the longer text that a glossary abbreviation represents. Finally, we'll use the term *glossary entry* to denote a complete glossary item—both the glossary term and the text it represents.

If you want to see what a particular glossary term stands for, you can open the Glossary dialog box and click on that term in the list box. Word will then display in the lower-left corner of the dialog box, the glossary text that the selected term represents. For example, suppose you want to see what the term *date - now - abbreviated* represents. When you click on this term, the dialog box will look like Figure 13-2.

FIGURE 13-2

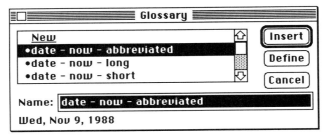

When you click on a term in the Glossary dialog box, Word will display the text for that term in the lower-left corner of the dialog box.

Notice that the term you click—in this case, *date – now – abbreviated*—appears in the Name edit bar. Notice also that the date *Wed, Nov 9, 1988* appears in the lower-left corner of the dialog box. This tells you that the glossary term *date – now – abbreviated* represents the current date in abbreviated format.

Sometimes, the text for a glossary term will be too long to be displayed in the dialog box. In that case, Word will display only as much of the text as will fit in the dialog box, followed by an ellipsis (...). If you want to see all the text, you must click the Insert button to paste it into your document. Then, you can use the Undo or Cut command to remove the text from your document.

Since the entries that are loaded from the Standard Glossary file are not really typical glossary entries, let's create a glossary entry, then we'll show you how to use and save it. Later in this chapter, we will talk more specifically about the *date* and *time* entries.

An Example

Suppose you are creating a document in which you must frequently type the name of your company, International Consolidated Systems, Inc. Since this is a long name that you need to use repeatedly, it makes sense to add it to the glossary. To do this, first type the full company name anywhere in your document. Then, drag through that name to select it. Next, choose Glossary... from the Edit menu to open the Glossary dialog box. With New selected in the list box, type an appropriate abbreviation in the Name edit bar. For example, you might type the abbreviation *ICS*. Then, click the Define button. At this point, the dialog box will look like Figure 13-3. To return to your document, just click the Cancel button, the close box, or anywhere on your document window.

FIGURE 13-3

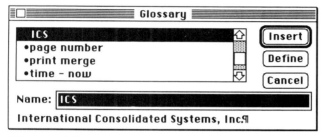

After you define a new glossary entry, Word will display the glossary term both in the Name edit bar and in the list of glossary terms.

The next time you need to use the company name in your document, you can insert it with the Glossary... command instead of typing the full name. Once the Glossary dialog box is open, just click on the term *ICS* in the list box, then click the Insert button. Word will insert the full text for the glossary entry—*International Consolidated Systems, Inc.*—into your document at the current insertion point location and automatically close the Glossary dialog box. By the way, there are a couple of other methods for inserting glossary text in a document, that are even faster than the method we just described. We explain these other methods later in this chapter in the section called "Inserting Glossary Text in Your Document."

After you have added an entry to the glossary, you probably will want to save the glossary with that new entry. Continuing with our example, suppose you want your company name to become a permanent part of the Standard Glossary file so that it will be loaded into the glossary each time you use Word. To save the glossary with this new entry, you must first issue the Glossary... command. Then, with the Glossary dialog box open, choose Save from the File menu. Word will display the dialog box shown in Figure 13-4. As you can see, Word allows you to assign a name to the glossary you are saving. All you have to do is type a name in the Save Glossary As edit bar, then click the Save button to save the current contents of the glossary in that file. (If you want, you can accept the default name *Standard Glossary* that appears in the Save Glossary As edit bar.)

FIGURE 13-4

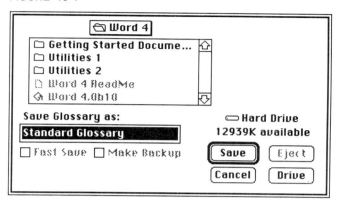

When you save glossary entries in a glossary file, Word will display this dialog box.

The example we just presented describes some of the most basic glossary-related tasks. However, using the glossary can be more complicated than what we have described here. In the remainder of this section, we will talk about the specifics of working with the glossary and glossary files.

Customizing the Glossary

We've just seen a quick example of how you can change the glossary by adding an entry. You can also change the glossary by revising entries, deleting entries, and merging glossary files. In other words, you can customize the glossary to suit any document. Keep in mind that any changes you make to the glossary are only temporary—they remain in effect only until you quit from Word. If you want to make a permanent change—for example, if you want to create a new glossary entry that you can use in later Word sessions—then you must be sure to save the revised glossary in a glossary file. In the section called "Creating and Updating a Glossary File," we explain how to save your glossary changes to disk.

Rules for glossary terms

When you type the glossary term in the Name edit bar, there are a few rules to keep in mind. First of all, Word will not allow you to enter an existing glossary term when you are creating a new glossary entry. If you type a term in the Name edit bar that has already been defined, Word will beep and display the message *That name is already defined*. In determining which terms have already been used, Word does not consider capitalization. For example, a lowercase *g* is considered to be the same as an uppercase *G*. You'll find this makes the glossary easier to use.

You can use any characters you want in a glossary term, including punctuation marks and various special characters produced with Option-key combinations. Interestingly, even though Word does not distinguish capitalization in glossary terms, it does distinguish a character created with an Option-key combination from a regular alphanumeric character. For example, suppose you want to use the symbol © to represent the text for a copyright notice. You can create the glossary term ©

by typing the Option-g combination in the Name edit bar. After you've defined this entry, Word will also let you use the simple letter *g* (or *G*) to define another glossary term. By the way, when you use a special character as a glossary term, Word will place that term at the end of the list of terms in the Glossary dialog box.

A glossary term can consist of two or more words, but cannot exceed 31 characters. However, you'll probably want to keep each glossary term as short as possible so you can type it into the glossary edit bar quickly and remember it easily.

If you do not enter a term in the Name edit bar, but simply click the Define button, Word will supply a name like *Unnamed1*. If you want to use a different name, you can replace the *Unnamed* term with the name you want to use and click Define once more.

Pasting glossary text from the Clipboard

Word allows you to use the contents of the Clipboard as your glossary text. After you have cut or copied some text in your document, Word will store that text on the Clipboard. To use this as the text in a glossary entry, first choose Glossary... from the Edit menu to open the Glossary dialog box. Then, type an abbreviation for the glossary entry in the Name edit bar. Next, choose Paste from the Edit menu and click the Define button in the Glossary dialog box. This tells Word that you want to use the contents of the Clipboard as your glossary text. Word will then display the text (or the first few words of the text) in the lower-left corner of the Glossary dialog box.

Formatted glossary text

When you select text for a new glossary entry, Word stores the formatting for that text in the glossary. Going back to our previous example, suppose you add bold formatting to the *International Consolidated Systems, Inc.* name before you create the glossary entry. Each time you use the glossary term *ICS*, the full name—including bold formatting—will be inserted into your document.

In addition to bold formatting, Word will store different fonts, point sizes, superscripting, italics, and any other character formatting you may have assigned to your glossary text. If your glossary text is a complete paragraph (or several paragraphs), Word will store the paragraph formatting as well—including margins, line spacing, indentions, and so forth.

Although Word stores the formatting for your glossary text, it will not display that formatting when you view the glossary text in the dialog box. As with most other dialog boxes, Word displays all the text in the Glossary dialog box in 12-point Chicago type.

Revising an existing glossary entry

After you have added entries to the glossary, you may need to change one or more of them. Word allows you to change both the glossary term and glossary text, although the procedure is different for each. To change a glossary term (the abbreviation), first choose Glossary... from the Edit menu to open the Glossary dialog box. In the list box, click on the term you want to change. When a term is selected, it will appear in the Name edit bar, as shown in Figure 13-5.

FIGURE 13-5

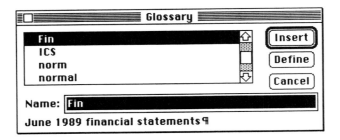

To revise a glossary term, open the Glossary dialog box and click on that term so that it appears in the Name edit bar.

If you begin typing at this point, Word will use the characters you type to replace the existing term in the Name edit bar. After you have typed a new term, click the Define button to lock in your change. Word will then place your new term in the list box and remove the original term. To return to your document, click the Cancel button, the close box, or anywhere on your document window.

Instead of typing a new term, you can edit an existing glossary term using normal editing techniques. For example, suppose you've created a glossary term *Fin*, which stands for the text *June 1989 financial statements*. To make the term a little more understandable, you might change it to *JuneFin*. You can do this by opening the Glossary dialog box and clicking on the term *Fin* in the list box. Then, click at the beginning of this term in the Name edit bar and type *June*. Click Define to lock in the change, then click the close box to return to your document.

Changing the text for a glossary entry is similar to creating a new glossary entry. Word will not allow you simply to edit the existing glossary text; instead, you must replace it with new text. First, type the word or phrase that you want to use as your replacement text in an open document window (if those words do not already exist in your document). Then, select that text and choose Glossary... from the Edit menu. In the Glossary dialog box, click on the term whose text you want to replace. Word will display that term in the Name edit bar and display all or part of the corresponding glossary text in the lower-left corner of the dialog box. To complete the replacement, click the Define button. Word will then display all or part of your new glossary text in the dialog box. You can return to your document by clicking the Cancel button, clicking the close box, or clicking anywhere on your document window.

For example, suppose your glossary includes the term *2EU*, which stands for *2nd Edition Update*. You would like to change the text for this glossary entry to *Current Edition Update*. First, type the words *Current Edition Update* anywhere in your document. Then, select that text and choose Glossary... from the

Edit menu. In the Glossary dialog box, click the term *2EU* to select it, then click Define. Immediately, Word will replace the existing text for that term—*2nd Edition Update*—with the text you've selected in your document—*Current Edition Update*.

To delete a glossary entry, just open the Glossary dialog box and click on the glossary term you want to delete. Then, choose Cut from the Edit menu. Word will display an alert box that asks *Delete glossary entry?* If you click Yes, Word will remove the selected entry from the glossary. The Glossary dialog box will remain open on your screen, so you can insert or delete more entries, if you like.

Word will not allow you to delete the Standard Glossary entries. If you try to delete one of these entries, Word will beep and display an alert box that says *Can't cut a standard glossary entry.* However, there is a quick way to remove all the entries from your glossary except the standard entries. We'll talk about that shortly.

By the way, if the entry you delete is part of a glossary file stored on disk, Word will not delete that entry from the glossary file when you choose Cut from the Edit menu. The next time you open that glossary file, the entry you "deleted" will be loaded into the glossary. If you want to delete an entry from a glossary file, you must open that file and load its contents into the Standard Glossary, delete the entry from the glossary, then save the revised glossary to disk. In a few pages, we'll explain in more detail how to revise a glossary file.

Deleting a glossary entry

Occasionally, you may need to clear all entries from the glossary. For example, before you load the glossary entries from a file on disk, you may want to remove all existing entries from the glossary. With one command, you can delete all entries from the glossary except the standard entries. Just open the Glossary dialog box, then choose New from the File menu. Word will display a dialog box that asks, *Delete all nonstandard glossary entries?* If you click Yes, Word will delete every nonstandard glossary entry. Keep in mind, however, that any changes you have made to your glossary will be lost when you issue the New command, unless you save your changes first.

Deleting all nonstandard glossary entries

So far, we've explained how you can change the glossary by creating new entries, revising existing entries, and deleting entries. There's one more way to make changes to the glossary, and that is by merging entries from two or more glossary files. To do this, however, you must first have created a glossary file by saving glossary entries to disk. Therefore, before we talk about merging glossary files, let's examine how you can save glossary entries to disk.

Working with Glossary Files

Creating and updating a glossary file

After you have made changes to the glossary—particularly when you've created new glossary entries—you may want to save those changes to disk so you can use them in a later Word session. When you save the entries in the current glossary to disk, you can either create a new glossary file, or save the entries in an existing glossary file. At the Finder level, glossary files are represented by a special icon, which is shown in Figure 13-6.

FIGURE 13-6

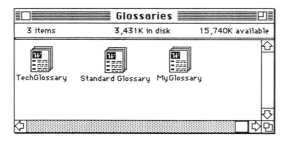

At the Finder level, glossary files are represented by a special icon.

Creating a new glossary file

To save your glossary entries, you must first choose Glossary... from the Edit menu. Then, with the Glossary dialog box open on your screen, choose Save or Save As... from the File menu. Word will then display the dialog box shown in Figure 13-7. If you have not opened a glossary file in the current Word session, the Save Glossary As edit bar will display the file name *Standard Glossary*, as shown in Figure 13-4. If you have opened a glossary file in the current Word session, this edit bar will be blank.

FIGURE 13-7

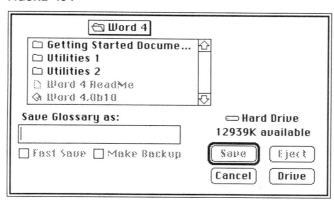

When you save glossary entries to disk, Word will display this dialog box.

If you want to create a completely new glossary file to store the entries in your current glossary, you should type a name for that file in the Save Glossary As edit bar. (If Word is displaying the name *Standard Glossary* in the edit bar when you open the dialog box, you can simply type the file name you want to use, and that name will replace *Standard Glossary*.) After you've entered the name of the file in which you want to store the glossary entries, just click the Save button. (By the way, the Fast Save and Make Backup options are not available when you're saving a glossary file.)

Before you save a glossary to disk, you may want to delete some of the entries in that glossary—particularly if you have loaded entries from several glossary files during the current Word session. Keep in mind, however, that you cannot delete the *page number, print merge*, or the various *date* and *time* entries that are loaded from the Standard Glossary file. Therefore, any new glossary file you create must always contain these entries.

If you make any changes to the glossary, then try to quit from Word without saving the glossary, Word will display the message, *Save changes to glossary?* If you click Yes, Word will open the Glossary dialog box, then open the Save As dialog box shown in Figure 13-7. You can then follow the standard procedure for saving the glossary entries to disk. If you click No in the Save Changes alert box, Word will quit to the Finder level without saving your glossary revisions. By clicking Cancel in the alert box, you can abort the Quit procedure.

If, in addition to glossary changes, you also have made changes to one or more documents and haven't saved those changes, Word's warning procedure will be somewhat different when you choose Quit from the File menu. First, you'll see a message asking whether you want to save changes in the current document. For example, you might see the message, *Save changes to Untitled2?* Whether you click Yes or No, Word will then display the message *Save changes to glossary?* If you click Yes, Word will display the Save As dialog box shown in Figure 13-7, where you can enter the name of the file in which you want to save your glossary entries.

Updating an existing glossary file

Instead of saving the entries in the current glossary in a completely new file, you may want to save those entries in an existing glossary file. To do this, open the Glossary dialog box, choose Save or Save As... from the File menu, then type the name of the existing file in the Save Glossary As edit bar. (Word will display in dim video the names of all files on the current disk in the Save As dialog box.) After you type the name and press Return, you'll see a message asking if you want to replace the existing glossary file on disk. If you click Yes, Word will overwrite that file with the entries in your current glossary. Word will not merge the entries in your current glossary with the entries in the glossary file on disk.

One of the best reasons for saving the glossary into an existing file is to update that file with new entries. For example, suppose you have opened a document and loaded the entries from a file named *MyGlossary* into your active glossary. You then create several new glossary entries so that your glossary contains both the entries from MyGlossary and these new entries. If you want, you can replace the MyGlossary file on disk with the expanded set of entries in your current glossary. First, choose Glossary... from the Edit menu, then choose Save or Save As... from the File menu. Type the name *MyGlossary* in the edit bar. Word will beep and display a dialog box that asks *Replace existing "MyGlossary"?* Click Yes if you want to proceed. Word will then overwrite the contents of MyGlossary on disk with the entries currently in the glossary.

Opening glossary files

To open a glossary file from within Word, just open the Glossary dialog box and choose Open... from the File menu. Word will display the dialog box shown in Figure 13-8, which lists all the glossary files on the current disk.

FIGURE 13-8

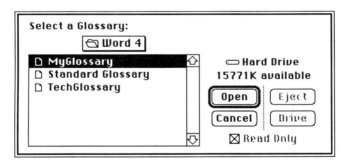

As you open a glossary file, Word will display this dialog box.

To open a glossary file, click on the file name to select it, then click the Open button. (You also can double-click the name of the glossary file you want to open.) As with other File commands in Word, you can access other disks if the glossary file you want to open is not on the current disk. For instance, you would click the Drive button if you wanted to search another disk drive for a glossary file, and you would click the Eject button if you wanted to eject the disk in the current drive and read a different disk.

When you open a glossary file, you won't actually see that file on your screen. However, the glossary terms from the file will appear in the list in the Glossary dialog box as Word adds those terms to the current glossary contents.

To merge two or more glossary files, simply load those files into Word's glossary. Word will expand the glossary to accommodate the entries from all the glossary files that you open (RAM permitting). Suppose you create a glossary file named *Contracts* and you want to merge the entries from this file with the entries in another glossary file named *Legal*. You might begin by opening the Legal file, so that those terms are loaded into the glossary. Then, to merge the entries from the Contracts glossary file, simply open that file, using the procedure we just described.

If any term in the glossary file you are merging is identical to a term that already exists in the glossary, Word will overwrite the existing term with the term from the new file. For example, suppose you have created a glossary entry consisting of the term *mw*, which represents the text *Microsoft Word*. Now, suppose you open a second glossary file that also contains the term *mw*. In this file, however, *mw* represents the text *Michael Williams*. After you open the glossary file, your glossary will contain only one *mw* glossary term, which will stand for *Michael Williams*. The text that was in your glossary before you opened the file—*Microsoft Word*—will no longer be in the glossary.

By the way, Word does not warn you when a glossary entry from a file is about to replace an existing entry. Therefore, before you open a glossary file, it's probably a good idea to save your existing glossary entries to disk so you do not risk losing any of them.

Word allows you to start a new document and open a glossary file in one step. At the Finder level, just double-click on the icon for the glossary file that you want to use. This will load the Word program and open a new, blank document window (just as if you had double-clicked the Word program icon). In addition, however, if you open the Glossary dialog box, you'll see that Word has automatically loaded all the entries from the glossary file you selected at the Finder level. If you want, you can use this technique to load the entries from several glossary files. At the Finder level, press the Shift key, and click on the icon for each glossary file you want to use. Then, choose Open from the File menu. Again, the Word program will be loaded, and you'll see a new, blank document window. When you check the glossary, you'll see that it contains all the entries from the files you selected at the Finder level.

At times, you will want your glossary to contain only the entries from a particular file. In these cases, you must eliminate other entries before you open that file. To delete all the entries in the glossary except the standard entries, which cannot be deleted, just choose Glossary... from the Edit menu, then choose New from the File menu. When you see the alert box shown in Figure 13-9 on the next page, click Yes. After deleting your existing glossary entries, you can choose Open... from the File menu while the Glossary dialog box is still open and select the name of the glossary file you want to open.

If you want to delete a glossary file from within Word, you can do so only if that file has not been opened during the current Word session. To delete the file, just choose Delete... from the File menu. Then, in the Delete dialog box, click on the name of the glossary file you want to remove and click the Delete button. Word will ask you to confirm the deletion before it gets rid of the file.

FIGURE 13-9

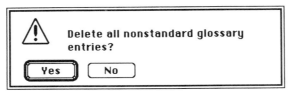

*When you're deleting all entries from the glossary,
Word will display this alert box.*

Once you have opened a glossary file, Word will not let you delete it. In fact, the file name will not even appear in the Delete dialog box. The only glossary file names that will appear in the dialog box are files that have not been opened during the current Word session. Even if you clear the glossary of all the entries that were loaded from a particular glossary file, Word still won't let you delete it. If you want to eliminate a glossary file you've opened during the current Word session, you must quit from Word and delete that file at the Finder level by dragging it into the Trash. (Of course, you can always use the Delete… command to get rid of the file the next time you load the Word program.)

By the way, if you delete the Standard Glossary file by dragging it into the Trash at the Finder level, Word will still load the standard entries into the glossary each time you open a document. However, any other glossary entries you may have stored in the Standard Glossary file will be lost.

Inserting Glossary Text in Your Document

In the example on pages 572-573, we explained one method for inserting glossary text into a document. First, you position the insertion point marker where you want to insert the text. Then, choose Glossary… from the Edit menu and click on the glossary term whose text you want to insert. (Recall that you will see the text for that term in the lower-left corner of the Glossary dialog box—or as much text as will fit in the dialog box.) Finally, click the Insert button to place the glossary text in your document and close the dialog box.

Inserting glossary text from the keyboard

Unless you need to view the text for a glossary entry or you cannot remember a glossary term, opening the Glossary dialog box and clicking the Insert button is not the most efficient way to insert glossary text into a document. Word offers a much easier way to enter glossary text. First, position the insertion point marker where you want to insert the text. Then, press ⌘-Backspace. You'll see a *Name* prompt in the status box, as shown in Figure 13-10. Type the glossary term (the abbreviation) for the text you want to insert in your document and press Return. As soon as you press Return, Word will insert the full glossary text into your document.

FIGURE 13-10

When you press ⌘-Backspace, Word will display a Name *prompt in the status box of the current window.*

Of course, in order to use this technique, you must remember the correct glossary term so that you can type it at the *Name* prompt. Capitalization does not matter when you enter a glossary term. If you cannot remember the correct term or if you decide that you do not want to insert the glossary text in your document, you can cancel this procedure by pressing the ⌘ and period keys (⌘-.) or by clicking anywhere on your screen.

Although using ⌘-Backspace offers a significant shortcut for inserting glossary text, the fastest way to access a glossary entry is to place it on the Work menu. The Work menu is a custom menu you can create in Word to speed up several tasks. The Work menu does not appear on your screen unless you have created at least one custom menu item. Once you've added one or more glossary terms to the Work menu, all you have to do to insert glossary text is select the appropriate term from the Work menu. You don't need to open the Glossary dialog box or type a glossary term. In Chapter 14, we'll discuss the Work menu in detail and explain how to add glossary terms and other items to that menu.

Inserting glossary text from the Work menu

Sometimes, you may need to insert glossary text into your document at several locations. Once you have used the Glossary... command or pressed ⌘-Backspace to enter that term, you can insert it in different locations throughout your document by using the ⌘-a key combination. After inserting your glossary text for the first time, just click at the next spot where you want to insert that text and press ⌘-a. Since, when you press ⌘-a, Word always repeats the last command you issued, you can use this technique only as long as you don't issue another command or make any editing or formatting changes to your document.

Using ⌘-a to repeat a glossary term

After you've inserted some glossary text—using the Glossary... command, the Work menu, the ⌘-Backspace technique, or the ⌘-a method—you can delete that text by choosing Undo Insert Glossary Text from the Edit menu. As with any other Undo procedure, the Undo Insert Glossary Text option will only be available immediately after you insert the glossary text and before you do anything else.

Undoing a glossary insertion

If you're pasting glossary text from the Clipboard, you can remove any text you insert by choosing Undo Paste from the Edit menu. Again, you must choose Undo immediately after you paste. This is no different from using the Undo command to remove any other text you've pasted in a document.

**Working
with Standard
Glossary Entries**

At the beginning of our discussion of the Word glossary, we talked about the *page number, print merge, date* and *time* entries that are stored in the Standard Glossary file. Since Word always loads the entries from the Standard Glossary file into the glossary, and since you cannot remove these entries, any glossary file you create will contain the standard entries.

The *page number* entry inserts a dynamic page number into your document at the current insertion point. This entry provides an alternative to numbering your pages in a header/footer window. The *print merge* entry inserts a pair of guillemet characters («») into the text at the current insertion point. This glossary entry lets you enter merge instructions for your main documents in a print merge procedure.

**The date and
time entries**

Whenever you insert a *date* glossary entry, Word will place the current date into your document in the format indicated by the glossary entry. Similarly, whenever you insert a *time* entry, Word will place the current time in your document in the format indicated by the glossary entry. (Figure 13-12 on page 586 shows the Standard Glossary entries.) These entries are controlled by the Macintosh's internal clock. You can adjust the date and time by using the Alarm Clock desk accessory.

When you use the glossary to place either the date or time in a document, Word will format the date or time in the character format of the surrounding text. For example, if you insert the current date between two words that have bold formatting, the date will also appear in bold.

In the Glossary list box, you'll notice that some date and time entries include the word *now* as part of their name and some include the word *print*. The entries that include the word *now* are static date and time entries. That is, once in your document, the date and time are simply characters, just like those you type from the keyboard. Since they are not dynamic values, you can edit the date and time in your document as you would edit any other characters.

Print designates a dynamic entry, one that updates itself to reflect the current date or time. When you insert a dynamic date or time into your document, Word draws a dotted line around that date or time, as shown in Figure 13-11. This box appears only when Show ¶ is activated.

FIGURE 13-11

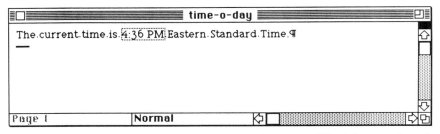

When you insert a dynamic date or time into a document, Word draws a dotted line around it.

Because Word treats these dynamic date and time entries as single characters, you cannot edit them as you can a regular date or time or any other text in a document. You can cut, copy, or paste the entire date or time, but not a portion of it. For instance, you cannot replace the month in a dynamic date. You can also format the dynamic date or time using various fonts or any of Word's formatting commands. As you might expect, you must format the entire date or time, not just a portion of it.

Storing Graphics in the Glossary

Although you'll probably use the glossary mainly to store text, you can also use it to store graphics. Most graphics consist of a picture or chart created in another Macintosh program, then inserted into a Word document. Word considers each graphic a single character, which you can cut, copy, or paste, just as you would regular characters.

To add a graphic to the glossary, you must first paste that graphic into a Word document. (We'll explain how to do this in Chapter 15.) Then, the procedure you use to add the graphic to the glossary is the same procedure you follow to add any other glossary entry. First, click on the graphic to select it. (You'll be able to tell that the graphic is selected by the small black boxes or "handles" that appear on its frame.) With the graphic selected, choose Glossary... from the Edit menu. Then, type a name for the glossary entry in the Name edit bar, and click the Define button. Finally, close the Glossary dialog box to complete the procedure. (By the way, if you change the size of the graphic before you add it to the glossary, Word will store the graphic in its new size.)

Once a graphic is stored in the glossary, you can use all the techniques we have described to paste that graphic into your document. You can open the Glossary dialog box, click on the glossary term for the graphic, then click the Insert button. Or, you can type ⌘-Backspace, enter the graphic name at the *Name* prompt, and press Return. Finally, you can add the glossary term for the graphic to the Work menu or copy it to the Clipboard.

After you have added a graphic to the glossary, you can, of course, save the glossary to disk in a glossary file. This allows you to access the graphic very easily by opening the glossary file in which it is stored. In fact, the easiest way to use a graphic in multiple documents is to store that graphic in a glossary file. That way, you don't have to keep track of the various Scrapbook files that contain graphics.

Printing the Glossary

If you want to get a printout of the contents of the glossary, open the Glossary dialog box and choose Print... from the File menu. Word will print a listing of each glossary term and the corresponding text. Figure 13-12 shows a sample glossary listing.

FIGURE 13-12

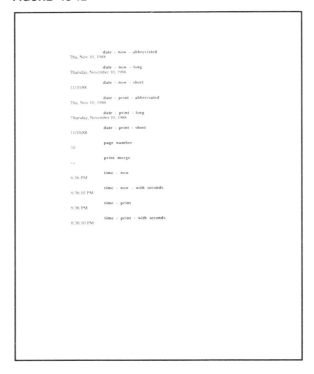

*This figure shows
a sample glossary
listing.*

LINE
NUMBERING

You can create line numbers in your printed documents by activating the Line Numbers option in the Section dialog box. Simply issue the Section... command on the Format menu, then select By Page, By Section, or Continuous from the dropdown list box in the Line Numbers section of the dialog box, as shown in Figure 13-13. When you click OK, Word will number all the lines in the current section of your document according to the setting you specified in the list box. Of course, if your document contains only one section, Word will number all the lines in the entire document.

Line numbers do not appear on the screen unless you use the Print Preview... command to preview your printed document or unless you print the document. (Interestingly, the line numbers will not appear in page view.) However, Word will always include the line numbers in your printed document. For example, Figure 13-14 shows part of a printed document with line numbers.

If your document contains a blank line you created by pressing Return or Enter, Word will number that line. However, if you've formatted a paragraph to have double line spacing or $1^1/_2$ line spacing, Word will not number the blank lines between the lines of text in that paragraph. Similarly, if a paragraph's format specifies a certain amount of space before and/or after the paragraph text, Word will not assign a line number to those spaces.

FIGURE 13-13

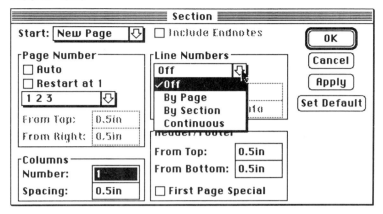

To number the lines in your document, choose the appropriate
Line Numbers option in the Section dialog box.

FIGURE 13-14

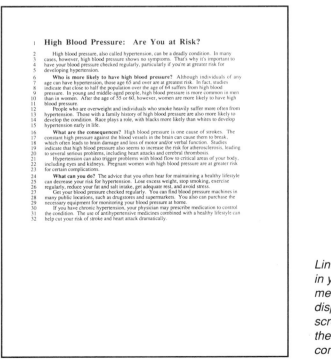

Line numbers appear
in your printed docu-
ment, but are not
displayed on the
screen unless the use
the Print Preview...
command.

Numbering Options

When you activate one of the Line Numbers options, you can control certain features about your line numbers. First, you can specify how often Word should restart its line numbers. You can restart the line numbers at the top of each new page, at the beginning of each new section, or you can choose to number all the lines in a document continuously.

You can also control how frequently Word prints a line number. For example, you can print a number next to every line (this is the default), or you can display line numbers only on every fifth or every fifteenth line. Whatever interval you choose, Word will still include each line in its line count; however, it will print only those line numbers that fall at the interval you specify.

Finally, Word lets you control the placement of line numbers relative to your document text. Default placement is Auto ($^1/_4$ inch from the left edge of each line of text). Let's take a look at each Line Numbers option in detail.

Restarting the line numbers

There are three Line Numbers options to choose among: By Page, By Section, and Continuous. The By Page option tells Word to number the lines on each page separately, beginning with 1. If you prefer to number all the lines in each section continuously without restarting the numbers on each new page, click the By Section option. Actually, this option allows you to restart the line numbers anywhere you want—you simply enter a section break (by pressing ⌘-Enter) whenever you want to restart the line numbering at 1. Of course, if your document contains only one section, the By Section option will cause all the lines in that document to be numbered continuously.

You can use the third option, Continuous, to achieve continuous line numbering in documents with more than one section. When you choose this option, Word will number every line in your document without restarting the line count at section breaks or page breaks. In order for this option to work properly, you must be sure that you've activated line numbering in every section in your document and that you've clicked the Continuous option for each section.

Keep in mind that when you select the By Page, By Section, or Continuous option, your selection will apply only to the current section (the section on which the insertion point marker is positioned when you open the Section dialog box). This allows you more flexibility in numbering lines. For example, suppose your document contains three sections. You would like to number the lines in the first section independently, then number the lines in the last two sections continuously. To achieve this, you would click the By Section option for both the first and second sections. Then, in the third section, click the Continuous option. This tells Word that you want the line numbers in the third section to be continued from the line numbers in the second section, rather than restarting at 1.

As another example, suppose you want your line numbers to restart at the beginning of each new section and at the beginning of each new page. Use the By Page option in those sections that cross from one page to the next and the By Section option in the rest of the sections.

In some cases, you may want to begin line numbering in the first section of a document with a number other than 1. For example, if you're printing a set of linked documents, you may want the line numbers to continue in sequence from one document to the next, rather than starting with 1 at the beginning of each document. You can change the first line number in a document from 1 (Word's default) to any other value by entering a beginning line number in the Number Lines From edit bar of the Document dialog box. For example, suppose you want the first line number in a document to be 463. Choose Document... from the Format menu and enter *463* in the Number Lines From edit bar, as shown in Figure 13-15. (For more on linking documents, see Chapter 10.)

FIGURE 13-15

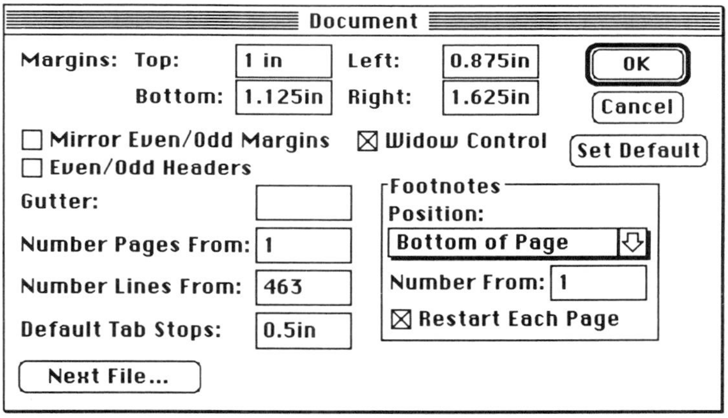

To begin the line numbers in a document at a number other than 1, enter the starting line number in the Document dialog box.

By the way, if you've clicked the By Page or By Section option in the Section dialog box, Word will begin numbering each page or section after the first one with 1, no matter what you've entered in the Number Lines From edit bar.

As we mentioned earlier, you can also control how frequently line numbers are printed in your document. The entry in the Count By edit bar in the Section dialog box determines the frequency of your printed line numbers. Word's default Count By setting is 1; if you do not change this, Word will print a number next to every line in your document, as shown in Figure 13-14. If you want to print line numbers at wider intervals, replace the 1 in the Count By edit bar with a larger number.

Line number frequency

For example, suppose you want line numbers to appear only on every fifth line. In that case, you should enter *5* in the Count By edit bar. Figure 13-16 shows the document from Figure 13-14 after we changed the Count By value. Notice that the first line number that appears in this document is 5.

FIGURE 13-16

High Blood Pressure: Are You at Risk?

High blood pressure, also called hypertension, can be a deadly condition. In many cases, however, high blood pressure shows no symptoms. That's why it's important to have your blood pressure checked regularly, particularly if you're at greater risk for
5 developing hypertension.

Who is more likely to have high blood pressure? Although individuals of any age can have hypertension, those age 65 and over are at greatest risk. In fact, studies indicate that close to half the population over the age of 64 suffers from high blood pressure. In young and middle-aged people, high blood pressure is more common in men
10 than in women. After the age of 55 or 60, however, women are more likely to have high blood pressure.

People who are overweight and individuals who smoke heavily suffer more often from hypertension. Those with a family history of high blood pressure are also more likely to develop the condition. Race plays a role, with blacks more likely than whites to develop
15 hypertension early in life.

What are the consequences? High blood pressure is one cause of strokes. The constant high pressure against the blood vessels in the brain can cause them to break, which often leads to brain damage and loss of motor and/or verbal function. Studies indicate that high blood pressure also seems to increase the risk for atherosclerosis, leading
20 to several serious problems, including heart attacks and cerebral thrombosis.

Hypertension can also trigger problems with blood flow to critical areas of your body, including eyes and kidneys. Pregnant women with high blood pressure are at greater risk for certain complications.

What can you do? The advice that you often hear for maintaining a healthy lifestyle
25 can decrease your risk for hypertension. Lose excess weight, stop smoking, exercise regularly, reduce your fat and salt intake, get adequate rest, and avoid stress.

Get your blood pressure checked regularly. You can find blood pressure machines in many public locations, such as drugstores and supermarkets. You also can purchase the necessary equipment for monitoring your blood pressure at home.
30 If you have chronic hypertension, your physician may prescribe medication to control the condition. The use of antihypertensive medicines combined with a healthy lifestyle can help cut your risk of stroke and heart attack dramatically.

By changing the Count By value to 5, you can print line numbers only on every fifth line.

When you enter a Count By value other than 1, the results can sometimes be confusing because it will be difficult to see where one set of numbers ends and another begins. Suppose your document contains several sections and you've activated the By Section option. If a new section starts in the middle of a page, Word will restart the line numbers at the section break. However, because a printed document does not show every line number, it may be hard to tell where the new section—and the new set of line numbers—starts. For instance, in the document shown in Figure 13-17, a new section begins at the headline in the middle of the page (*Philosophy and Learning*). Notice that, because we've chosen to display line numbers on only every tenth line, there is a significant area of unnumbered lines around the section break. To make matters more difficult, there are two lines numbered 10—one in the first section and one in the second section.

Line number position

As we mentioned before, Word's default position for line numbers is $^1/_4$ inch from the left edge of each line of text. To change this, enter a number in the From Text edit bar of the Section dialog box. For example, to position line numbers $^1/_2$ inch from the left edge of your text, enter .5 in the From Text edit bar.

FIGURE 13-17

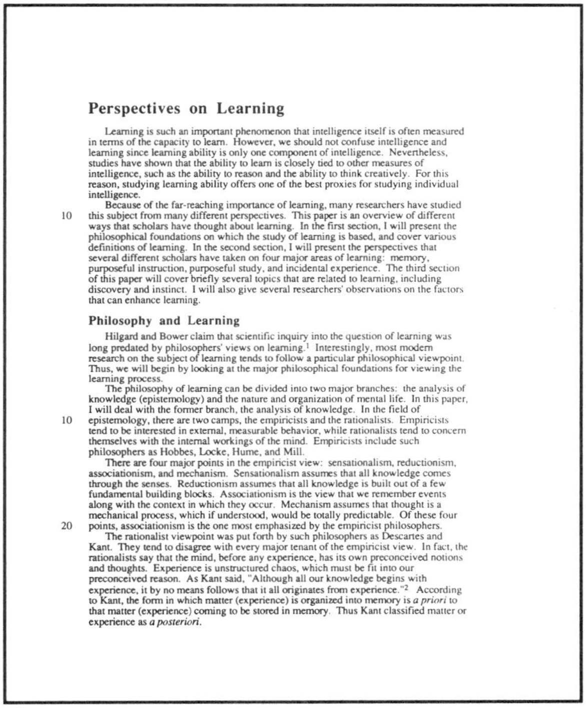

Perspectives on Learning

Learning is such an important phenomenon that intelligence itself is often measured in terms of the capacity to learn. However, we should not confuse intelligence and learning since learning ability is only one component of intelligence. Nevertheless, studies have shown that the ability to learn is closely tied to other measures of intelligence, such as the ability to reason and the ability to think creatively. For this reason, studying learning ability offers one of the best proxies for studying individual intelligence.

Because of the far-reaching importance of learning, many researchers have studied this subject from many different perspectives. This paper is an overview of different ways that scholars have thought about learning. In the first section, I will present the philosophical foundations on which the study of learning is based, and cover various definitions of learning. In the second section, I will present the perspectives that several different scholars have taken on four major areas of learning: memory, purposeful instruction, purposeful study, and incidental experience. The third section of this paper will cover briefly several topics that are related to learning, including discovery and instinct. I will also give several researchers' observations on the factors that can enhance learning.

Philosophy and Learning

Hilgard and Bower claim that scientific inquiry into the question of learning was long predated by philosophers' views on learning.[1] Interestingly, most modern research on the subject of learning tends to follow a particular philosophical viewpoint. Thus, we will begin by looking at the major philosophical foundations for viewing the learning process.

The philosophy of learning can be divided into two major branches: the analysis of knowledge (epistemology) and the nature and organization of mental life. In this paper, I will deal with the former branch, the analysis of knowledge. In the field of epistemology, there are two camps, the empiricists and the rationalists. Empiricists tend to be interested in external, measurable behavior, while rationalists tend to concern themselves with the internal workings of the mind. Empiricists include such philosophers as Hobbes, Locke, Hume, and Mill.

There are four major points in the empiricist view: sensationalism, reductionism, associationism, and mechanism. Sensationalism assumes that all knowledge comes through the senses. Reductionism assumes that all knowledge is built out of a few fundamental building blocks. Associationism is the view that we remember events along with the context in which they occur. Mechanism assumes that thought is a mechanical process, which if understood, would be totally predictable. Of these four points, associationism is the one most emphasized by the empiricist philosophers.

The rationalist viewpoint was put forth by such philosophers as Descartes and Kant. They tend to disagree with every major tenant of the empiricist view. In fact, the rationalists say that the mind, before any experience, has its own preconceived notions and thoughts. Experience is unstructured chaos, which must be fit into our preconceived reason. As Kant said, "Although all our knowledge begins with experience, it by no means follows that it all originates from experience."[2] According to Kant, the form in which matter (experience) is organized into memory is *a priori* to that matter (experience) coming to be stored in memory. Thus Kant classified matter or experience as *a posteriori*.

If you choose not to show all line numbers, you may find it difficult to see when a new set of line numbers begins at a section break.

In positioning line numbers, Word assumes that the left edge of your text is determined by the Left margin setting in the Document dialog box. If, in fact, you've indented your text by moving the indent markers on the ruler, Word won't take this into account in positioning line numbers. For example, suppose that your Left margin setting is 1.25 (Word's default). Suppose also that you've formatted every paragraph in your document by moving the first-line and left indent markers to the 1-inch position on the ruler. This will create a total margin space of $2^1/_4$ inches in your printed document. If you activate line numbering in this document and enter .5 in the From Text edit bar, the line numbers will actually be printed $1^3/_4$ inches from the left edge of the page.

The number that you enter in the From Text edit bar in the Section dialog box must be less than the width of the Left margin setting in the Document dialog box. Otherwise, Word will not be able to fit the line numbers on the printed page.

Word 4 doesn't allow you to enter negative numbers in the From Text edit bar. If you enter 0, Word will automatically convert that setting to Auto and place the line numbers $^1/_4$ inch from the document text. The parameters for the From Text edit bar range from $^1/_8$ to 8.5 inches.

Multicolumn Documents

If you're using a multicolumn page design, and you have selected the Line Numbers option, Word will number the lines in each column. Figure 13-18 shows a two-column document with numbered lines. Notice that the line numbering is continuous from the bottom of the first column to the top of the second column.

FIGURE 13-18

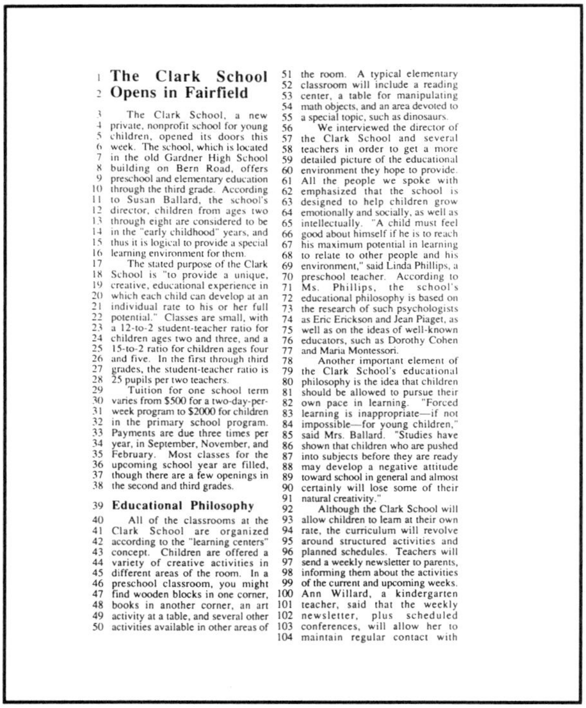

The Clark School Opens in Fairfield

The Clark School, a new private, nonprofit school for young children, opened its doors this week. The school, which is located in the old Gardner High School building on Bern Road, offers preschool and elementary education through the third grade. According to Susan Ballard, the school's director, children from ages two through eight are considered to be in the "early childhood" years, and thus it is logical to provide a special learning environment for them.

The stated purpose of the Clark School is "to provide a unique, creative, educational experience in which each child can develop at an individual rate to his or her full potential." Classes are small, with a 12-to-2 student-teacher ratio for children ages two and three, and a 15-to-2 ratio for children ages four and five. In the first through third grades, the student-teacher ratio is 25 pupils per two teachers.

Tuition for one school term varies from $500 for a two-day-per-week program to $2000 for children in the primary school program. Payments are due three times per year, in September, November, and February. Most classes for the upcoming school year are filled, though there are a few openings in the second and third grades.

Educational Philosophy

All of the classrooms at the Clark School are organized according to the "learning centers" concept. Children are offered a variety of creative activities in different areas of the room. In a preschool classroom, you might find wooden blocks in one corner, books in another corner, an art activity at a table, and several other activities available in other areas of the room. A typical elementary classroom will include a reading center, a table for manipulating math objects, and an area devoted to a special topic, such as dinosaurs.

We interviewed the director of the Clark School and several teachers in order to get a more detailed picture of the educational environment they hope to provide. All the people we spoke with emphasized that the school is designed to help children grow emotionally and socially, as well as intellectually. "A child must feel good about himself if he is to reach his maximum potential in learning to relate to other people and his environment," said Linda Phillips, a preschool teacher. According to Ms. Phillips, the school's educational philosophy is based on the research of such psychologists as Eric Erickson and Jean Piaget, as well as on the ideas of well-known educators, such as Dorothy Cohen and Maria Montessori.

Another important element of the Clark School's educational philosophy is the idea that children should be allowed to pursue their own pace in learning. "Forced learning is inappropriate—if not impossible—for young children," said Mrs. Ballard. "Studies have shown that children who are pushed into subjects before they are ready may develop a negative attitude toward school in general and almost certainly will lose some of their natural creativity."

Although the Clark School will allow children to learn at their own rate, the curriculum will revolve around structured activities and planned schedules. Teachers will send a weekly newsletter to parents, informing them about the activities of the current and upcoming weeks. Ann Willard, a kindergarten teacher, said that the weekly newsletter, plus scheduled conferences, will allow her to maintain regular contact with

When you use columnar formatting in a document, Word will number the lines in every column.

When you number the lines in a multicolumn document, be sure that you allow enough space between columns to display the line numbers. You also should be careful that the From Text setting for your line numbers is less than the Spacing setting for your columns. Otherwise, your line numbers will not fit in the gutter between columns.

Selective Line Numbering

In some cases, you may want to assign line numbers only to certain parts of a document. There are a couple of ways you can number lines selectively. First, if you want to number the lines in only a small part of your document—say, a single paragraph or a few paragraphs—you should place a section break both before and after that part of your document. To insert a section break, just press ⌘-Enter. Word will display a double dotted line on your screen to mark the boundary of the new section. (If you don't want the new section to be printed on a separate page, be sure to choose No Break from the dropdown list of Start options in the Section dialog box.) Figure 13-19 shows a document in which we've inserted a section break before and after a couple of paragraphs.

FIGURE 13-19

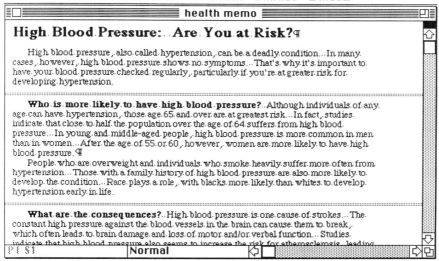

To number the lines in only a small portion of your document, place a section break both before and after that text.

After you've "sectioned off" a part of your document, position the insertion point marker anywhere within the section you want to number, choose Section… from the Format menu, and select By Section from the Line Numbers list box.

Another way you can control line numbering in a document is by turning off the line numbers on selected paragraphs. After you've selected the paragraph(s) whose lines you do not want to number, choose the Paragraph… command from the Format menu to open the Paragraph dialog box. As you can see in Figure 13-20 on the following page, when you first open this dialog box, the Line Numbering check box will be selected. (When you choose a Line Numbers option in the Section dialog box, Word activates the Line Numbering check box in the Paragraph dialog box.) Click this option to turn off line numbering for the selected paragraph(s), then click OK to close the dialog box.

Although you can deselect the Line Numbering option in the Paragraph dialog box for certain paragraphs, you can't apply the Line Numbering option to any paragraph until you have activated that option in the Section dialog box. If you do not select a Line Numbers option in the Section dialog box, the Line Numbering option in the Paragraph dialog box will be dimmed.

FIGURE 13-20

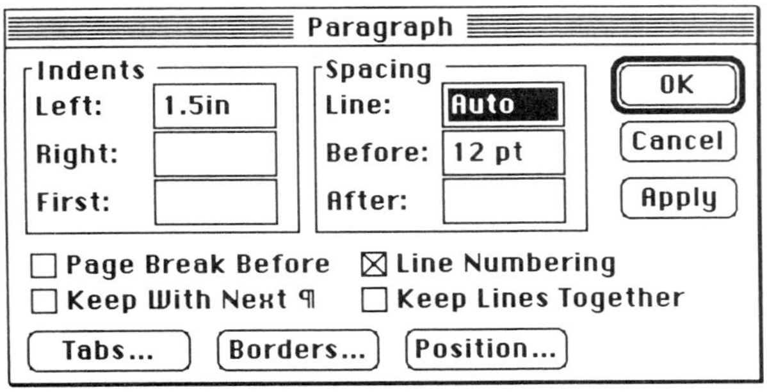

```
╔══════════════ Paragraph ══════════════╗
║  ┌─Indents────┐  ┌─Spacing─────┐  ┌────────┐
║  │ Left:  [1.5in]│  Line:  [Auto]│  ( OK )
║  │ Right: [     ]│  Before:[12 pt]│  (Cancel)
║  │ First: [     ]│  After: [     ]│  (Apply)
║  └────────────┘  └─────────────┘
║  □ Page Break Before   ⊠ Line Numbering
║  □ Keep With Next ¶     □ Keep Lines Together
║  (Tabs...)  (Borders...) (Position...)
╚════════════════════════════════════════╝
```

If you have activated line numbering in a section, Word will activate the Line Numbering check box in the Paragraph dialog box as well.

When you turn off the line numbers for a selected paragraph, Word will not print line numbers next to that text, nor will it include those lines in its line number count. For example, Figure 13-21 shows part of a printed page from a document in which we've numbered all the lines except those in the second paragraph of body text. Notice that the last line before the unnumbered paragraph is numbered 8, while the first line after the unnumbered paragraph picks up the count again with the number 9.

Special Situations

You won't be able to assign line numbers in every situation. For instance, Word does not allow line numbering in headers, footers, footnotes, and Word 3 side-by-side paragraphs. Furthermore, you won't be able to apply numbers to individual rows in a table.

NUMBERING PARAGRAPHS

Word's Renumber... command on the Utilities menu allows you to number paragraphs automatically throughout all or part of a document. When you issue this command without selecting any text, Word will assign a number to every paragraph in the current document. If you select one or more paragraphs before you choose Renumber..., Word will assign numbers only to the selected paragraphs. (By the way, if you select less than a full paragraph of text—say, a word or two—before you choose Renumber..., Word will assume that you want to assign a number only to the paragraph that contains your selection.) In numbering paragraphs, Word doesn't recognize section breaks. The paragraphs before and after a section break will be numbered continuously.

If you decide to add, delete, or rearrange paragraphs, Word's Renumber... command makes it very easy to get your paragraph numbers back in order. You can control several features of your paragraph numbers, including their alignment in relation to your text, the type of numbering scheme used, and the Start At number for a sequence of paragraphs.

FIGURE 13-21

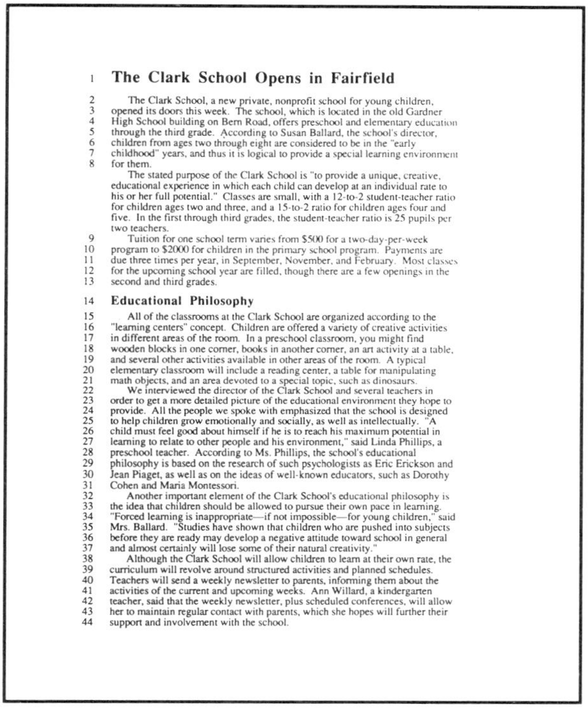

The Clark School Opens in Fairfield

The Clark School, a new private, nonprofit school for young children, opened its doors this week. The school, which is located in the old Gardner High School building on Bern Road, offers preschool and elementary education through the third grade. According to Susan Ballard, the school's director, children from ages two through eight are considered to be in the "early childhood" years, and thus it is logical to provide a special learning environment for them.

The stated purpose of the Clark School is "to provide a unique, creative, educational experience in which each child can develop at an individual rate to his or her full potential." Classes are small, with a 12-to-2 student-teacher ratio for children ages two and three, and a 15-to-2 ratio for children ages four and five. In the first through third grades, the student-teacher ratio is 25 pupils per two teachers.

Tuition for one school term varies from $500 for a two-day-per-week program to $2000 for children in the primary school program. Payments are due three times per year, in September, November, and February. Most classes for the upcoming school year are filled, though there are a few openings in the second and third grades.

Educational Philosophy

All of the classrooms at the Clark School are organized according to the "learning centers" concept. Children are offered a variety of creative activities in different areas of the room. In a preschool classroom, you might find wooden blocks in one corner, books in another corner, an art activity at a table, and several other activities available in other areas of the room. A typical elementary classroom will include a reading center, a table for manipulating math objects, and an area devoted to a special topic, such as dinosaurs.

We interviewed the director of the Clark School and several teachers in order to get a more detailed picture of the educational environment they hope to provide. All the people we spoke with emphasized that the school is designed to help children grow emotionally and socially, as well as intellectually. "A child must feel good about himself if he is to reach his maximum potential in learning to relate to other people and his environment," said Linda Phillips, a preschool teacher. According to Ms. Phillips, the school's educational philosophy is based on the research of such psychologists as Eric Erickson and Jean Piaget, as well as on the ideas of well-known educators, such as Dorothy Cohen and Maria Montessori.

Another important element of the Clark School's educational philosophy is the idea that children should be allowed to pursue their own pace in learning. "Forced learning is inappropriate—if not impossible—for young children," said Mrs. Ballard. "Studies have shown that children who are pushed into subjects before they are ready may develop a negative attitude toward school in general and almost certainly will lose some of their natural creativity."

Although the Clark School will allow children to learn at their own rate, the curriculum will revolve around structured activities and planned schedules. Teachers will send a weekly newsletter to parents, informing them about the activities of the current and upcoming weeks. Ann Willard, a kindergarten teacher, said that the weekly newsletter, plus scheduled conferences, will allow her to maintain regular contact with parents, which she hopes will further their support and involvement with the school.

When you eliminate line numbers from a selected paragraph, Word will not include that paragraph in its line count.

Automatic paragraph numbering is particularly useful in documents with multiple levels of paragraphs—such as legal documents or outlines. In these cases, Word lets you control the numbering scheme of each level. For example, your first-level paragraphs might be numbered *1.*, *2.*, *3.*, and so forth, while your second-level paragraphs are numbered *1-A.*, *1-B.*, and so forth. Before we talk about numbering multiple levels of paragraphs, however, let's examine some of the basics of paragraph numbering. These basic concepts will apply whether your document contains only one or several levels of paragraphs.

Numbering Basics

To number all the paragraphs in a document, just choose Renumber... from the Utilities menu. Word will then display the dialog box shown in Figure 13-22 on the following page.

When you see this dialog box, all you have to do is click OK. Word will then close the dialog box and place an Arabic numeral followed by a period (*1.*, *2.*, *3.*, and so forth) at the beginning of each paragraph. Figure 13-23 shows an example of a document after we've issued the Renumber... command.

FIGURE 13-22

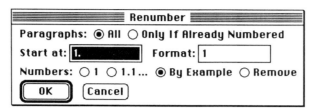

You'll see this dialog box when you choose Renumber... from the Utilities menu.

FIGURE 13-23

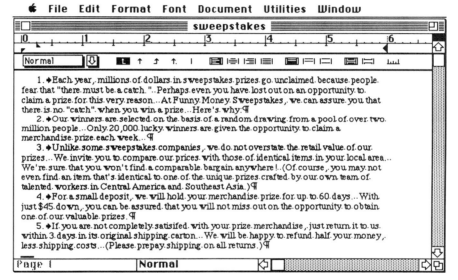

Word's default numbering scheme will place an Arabic number followed by a period at the beginning of each paragraph.

Notice that Word aligns each paragraph number with the first-line indent marker on the ruler. In this example, the first-line indent marker for each paragraph is positioned at the $1/_4$-inch mark on the ruler. Therefore, each paragraph number is indented $1/_4$ inch. Notice also that Word inserts a tab space between the paragraph number and the paragraph text. This causes the first character of text to be positioned at the first tab after the initial indent. Since we have not changed Word's default tab stops, the first character of each paragraph in our example is aligned with the default tab stop that occurs at the $1/_2$-inch position on the ruler. As we'll explain, you can change the alignment of paragraph numbers and text by manipulating your indent markers and tabs.

As we demonstrated in the above example, Word's default numbering scheme for paragraphs uses Arabic numerals. If you prefer to use Roman numerals or alphabetic characters, you can specify your preference in the Renumber dialog box. Just enter the type of character you want to use in the Format edit bar. For example, if you want to use Roman numerals, you can enter *I* in the Format edit bar. To use alphabetic characters in your numbering scheme, you can enter *A*. To specify Arabic numerals, you can type *1* in the edit bar. (Since Arabic numerals are Word's default, you don't need to enter anything in the edit bar unless you are converting existing numbers from another format into Arabic numerals.)

The first time you issue the Renumber... command, you'll notice that the Format edit bar is blank. In fact, this edit bar will always be blank unless the first paragraph in your document (or the first paragraph in your selection) has been numbered. After you've numbered some paragraphs, however, the Format edit bar will display an example of the line numbering scheme for the first paragraph in your document or selection. For instance, if you select some paragraphs that have been numbered with Roman numerals, then choose Renumber..., Word will display an *I.* or *i.* in the Format edit bar.

To use a numbering scheme other than the one that Word suggests, you can just replace the characters in the Format edit bar. For example, suppose you want to change the Arabic numerals in a document to Roman numerals. Issue the Renumber... command, then, in the Format edit bar, drag through the *1.* to select it, and type *I.* or *i.* as a replacement. When you click OK, all your paragraph numbers will be converted to Roman numerals.

As you're specifying a numbering scheme, you don't have to use the first letter of the alphabet, the Roman numeral *I*, or a *1*. You can type any Arabic number to specify an Arabic numbering scheme, and you can enter any letter (except I, V, or X) to indicate that you want to use an alphabetic numbering scheme. Similarly, you can enter almost any Roman numeral to specify a Roman numeral numbering scheme. Interestingly, if you type a high Roman numeral that's only a single character—such as L, C, or M—Word will interpret your entry as an alphabetic character. However, if you enter a high Roman numeral that is made up of two or more characters—such as LIX or CM—Word will correctly interpret your entry as a Roman numeral.

If you choose an alphabetic or Roman numeral numbering scheme, Word will allow you to select either uppercase or lowercase for your paragraph "numbers." The case you use for the entry in the Format edit bar will determine the case of the "numbers" in your document. For example, if you want to use a lowercase alphabetic numbering scheme, you should enter a lowercase letter—such as *c*—in the Format edit bar. Similarly, if you want to use a lowercase Roman numeral numbering scheme (i, ii, iii, and so forth), you should enter a lowercase Roman numeral in the edit bar, as we've done in Figure 13-24.

Choosing a numbering scheme

FIGURE 13-24

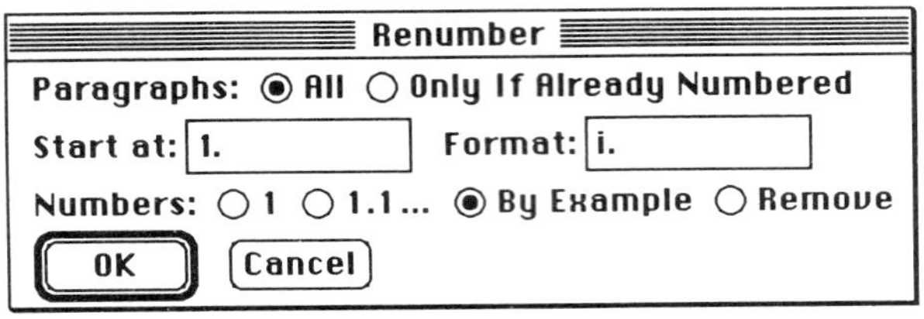

```
┌═══════════════════ Renumber ═══════════════════┐
│ Paragraphs: ● All  ○ Only If Already Numbered   │
│ Start at:│1.        │     Format:│i.        │    │
│ Numbers: ○ 1  ○ 1.1...  ● By Example ○ Remove   │
│ ┌──────────┐  ┌────────┐                         │
│ │   OK     │  │ Cancel │                         │
│ └──────────┘  └────────┘                         │
└─────────────────────────────────────────────────┘
```

The entry in the Format edit bar tells Word what kind of numbering scheme you want to use for your paragraphs.

Choosing the separator characters

As we've already shown, Word's default separator character is a period after each paragraph number. If you want to use a different separator character, you must enter that character—along with a number or letter—in the Format edit bar. For example, suppose you want to use a right parenthesis (with lowercase Roman numerals) as your separator character. In that case, you would enter *i)* in the Format edit bar, as shown in Figure 13-25.

FIGURE 13-25

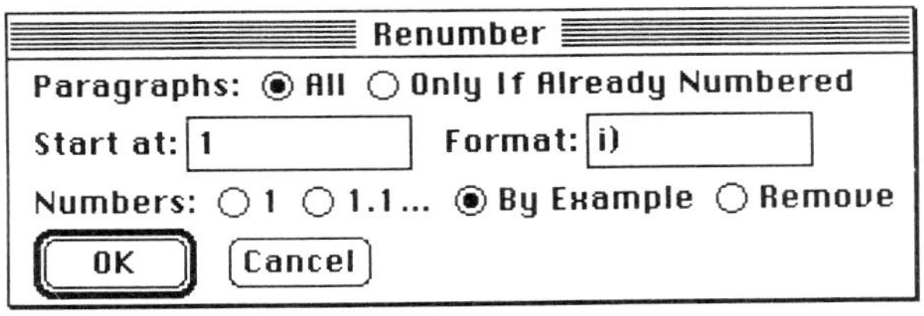

```
┌═══════════════════ Renumber ═══════════════════┐
│ Paragraphs: ● All  ○ Only If Already Numbered   │
│ Start at:│1         │     Format:│i)        │    │
│ Numbers: ○ 1  ○ 1.1...  ● By Example ○ Remove   │
│ ┌──────────┐  ┌────────┐                         │
│ │   OK     │  │ Cancel │                         │
│ └──────────┘  └────────┘                         │
└─────────────────────────────────────────────────┘
```

Your entry in the Format edit bar can also specify a separator character.

Word allows you to use any of the standard nonalphanumeric characters as separators. For example, all the characters produced with the shifted numeric keys are valid separator characters, including #, *, and -. The characters that are produced with the Option-key combinations (such as § and •) are not considered valid separator characters.

You can place a separator character both before and after each paragraph number. If you do this, Word will allow you to use two different characters. For example, you might want to enclose each paragraph number in parentheses, in which case you would enter *(i)* in the Format edit bar.

Interestingly, Word will not allow you to place a separator character before a number without also placing a character after the number. For example, *-1-* and *<i>* are both valid entries for the Format edit bar, but *>1* is not. Word also will not allow any "extra" separator characters. For example, if you type two separator characters before the number in the Format edit bar (such as ***1*), Word will beep and display the message, *Invalid number*. If you place two or more separator characters after the number, such as *1***, Word will simply ignore all separator characters after the first one.

When you're numbering multiple levels of paragraphs, Word will allow you to use a different separator character between each level number. For example, third-level paragraphs might be numbered 2.1-a). We will discuss the format of multiple-level paragraph numbers a little later in this chapter.

When you first issue the Renumber… command for a document or a selection, Word will number each paragraph in sequence, starting with 1, A, or I (depending on the numbering scheme you've chosen). If you want to use a different starting number, you must specify this in the Start At edit bar in the Renumber dialog box. For example, if you want the first paragraph in the document or selection to be numbered 14, you should enter *14* in the Start At edit bar, as shown in Figure 13-26. Word will then number the second paragraph 15, the third paragraph 16, and so forth.

Specifying a start number

FIGURE 13-26

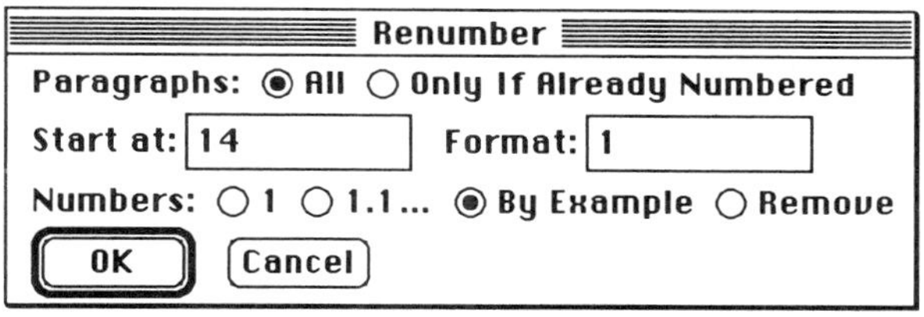

The entry in the Start At edit bar indicates the first paragraph number in your document or selection.

If you select some paragraphs before issuing the Renumber… command, and the first paragraph in your selection has already been assigned a number, then Word will display that number in the Start At edit bar. The same thing will happen when you're renumbering an entire document and the first paragraph of the document has already been assigned a number. Of course, you can still replace Word's suggested Start At number with a different number.

Interestingly, your Start At number does not have to be stated in the same format as your chosen numbering scheme. For example, suppose you want to use an alphabetic numbering scheme and you want to begin "numbering" your paragraphs with the letter *d*. When you open the Renumber dialog box, you would enter *a.* in the Format edit bar to specify an alphabetic numbering scheme, and you could enter either *d.* or *4.* in the Start At edit bar (since *d* is the fourth letter of the alphabet).

As you'll see in a few pages, specifying a Start At number in a document with multiple levels of paragraphs is a little more complicated.

Formatting
paragraph
numbers

Word uses the formatting features of the first character in each paragraph to determine the format of that paragraph's number. In other words, Word will match the character formatting of each paragraph's number—font, size, boldfacing, and so forth—to the format of the first character in the paragraph. This automatic formatting can be especially helpful in documents in which you've used character formatting to distinguish different kinds of topics. For example, Figure 13-27 shows a document with different formatting. Figure 13-28 shows this same document after we've issued the Renumber... command. Notice that some of the numbers appear in New York bold type, while others appear in Helvetica italic.

FIGURE 13-27

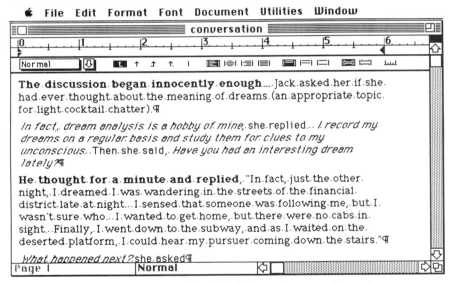

This document contains paragraphs with different character formatting.

After you have numbered your paragraphs, you can change the format of your paragraph numbers. If you reformat the numbers, then change the numbering scheme, Word will not alter your manual format changes. (By the way, if your paragraph numbers are arranged in a column, keep in mind that you can use the Option key to make a block selection and reformat all the numbers at once. Chapter 5 describes this block selection technique in more detail.)

FIGURE 13-28

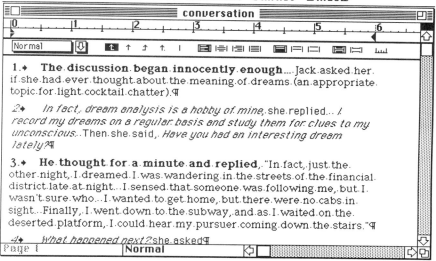

Word uses the formatting characteristics of the first character in each paragraph to determine the format of each paragraph number.

As we explained at the beginning of this section, Word aligns each paragraph number with the first-line indent marker on the ruler. Word also inserts a tab space after each paragraph number so that the first character of paragraph text is aligned with the first tab after the indent. (Of course, the position of the first-line indent marker and the first tab can change from paragraph to paragraph in your document.)

To change the amount of space between a paragraph number and the first character of paragraph text, simply place a tab at the appropriate place on the ruler. For example, Figure 13-29 on the next page shows some numbered paragraphs in which each number is aligned at the left edge of the screen (since the first-line indent marker is at the 0 position on the ruler), while the first character of text in each paragraph is aligned with the $^1/_2$-inch position on the ruler.

Let's say that you want to indent the first character of text by an additional $^1/_4$ inch. First, select these paragraphs, then click on the left-aligned tab icon to select it, and click on the $^3/_4$-inch position on the ruler. The result will look like Figure 13-30.

Aligning numbers and text

FIGURE 13-29

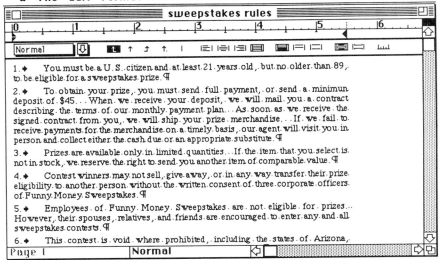

In these paragraphs, the numbers are aligned at the 0 position on the ruler, while the first character of text in each paragraph is aligned at the ¹/₂-inch position.

FIGURE 13-30

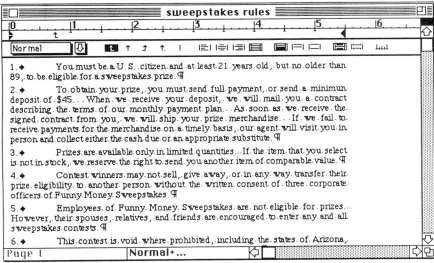

By inserting a tab, you can change the alignment of the first line of paragraph text.

By moving the left indent marker, you can change the alignment of the paragraph text in relation to the paragraph number. For example, you can "hang" paragraph numbers outside the paragraph text. Figure 13-31 shows the paragraphs from Figure 13-30 after we moved the left indent marker to the $^1/_2$-inch position on the ruler.

FIGURE 13-31

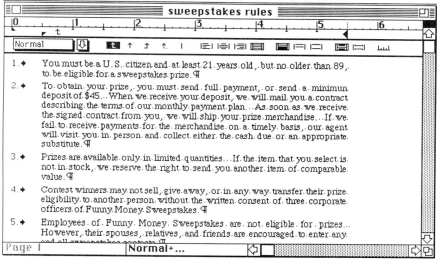

By moving the left indent marker, you can create "hanging" paragraph numbers.

Notice in Figure 13-31 that the first line in each paragraph is no longer aligned with the tab stop at the $^3/_4$-inch position. Instead, it is aligned with the left indent marker at the $^1/_2$-inch position. In deciding where to align the first line of text, Word looks for the first "stopping place" on the ruler after the first-line indent. In many cases, the first stopping place will occur at a tab—either one of Word's default tabs or a tab that you've inserted manually. However, if you move the left indent marker to the right of the first-line indent marker, you may create a "stopping place" before a tab, as we've done in Figure 13-31. In that case, Word will align the first character of text with the left indent marker.

If you were to move the tab to the left of the indent marker, your paragraphs would look like Figure 13-32. Notice that the first line of text in each paragraph is aligned at the tab we've inserted at the $^1/_4$-inch position, while subsequent lines are aligned at the left indent marker, which occurs at the $^1/_2$-inch position. As a result, both the paragraph numbers and the initial text in each paragraph hang outside the left margin.

FIGURE 13-32

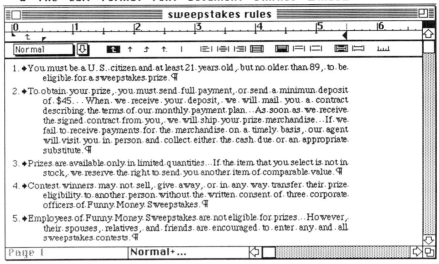

If you move the left indent marker to the right of the first tab, Word will align the first line of text in a paragraph with the tab stop.

Finally, by moving the left indent marker to the left of the first-line indent marker, you can indent the paragraph numbers. In Figure 13-33, we've moved the left indent marker to the -$\frac{1}{2}$-inch position on the ruler.

In the examples we've presented so far, we have changed the alignment of only a few numbered paragraphs. In these cases, you must select those paragraphs before you move the indent markers or insert tab stops. If you want to change the alignment of all the paragraphs in a document, you must select the entire document before you make your ruler changes. A more efficient way to change the alignment of all the paragraphs in your document—or even a few paragraphs—is to alter the style definition (or definitions) for those paragraphs on the style sheet. For information on how to use named styles to format paragraphs, see Chapter 8.

Selective numbering

Chances are, when you number the paragraphs in a document, you will want to exclude certain paragraphs, such as the title, subheadings, figure captions, and so forth. Unfortunately, there's no automatic way to exclude certain paragraphs from the effects of the Renumber... command. However, there are a couple of techniques you can use to achieve selective paragraph numbering.

First, you can number your document a few paragraphs at a time, selecting only the paragraphs to which you want to assign a number. For example, you might begin by selecting all the paragraphs after the main title and before the first subheading, then issue the Renumber... command. After you number these paragraphs, you might select another group of paragraphs between the first and second subheadings, then reissue the Renumber... command. When you number this second group of paragraphs (and all subsequent paragraph groups), be sure to enter the correct number in the Start At edit bar of the Renumber dialog box. Otherwise, your paragraph numbers won't appear in sequence.

FIGURE 13-33

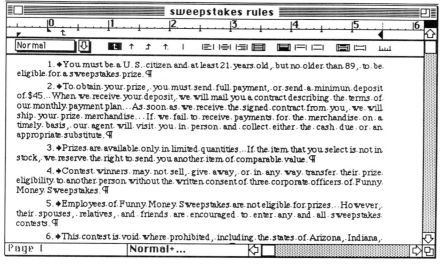

By moving the left indent marker to the left of the first-line indent marker, you can indent your paragraph numbers.

Another technique you can use to achieve selective numbering is to number all the paragraphs in your document, then manually remove each unwanted number. After removing the numbers, you can issue the Renumber... command once more and click the Only If Already Numbered option. Word will then renumber your document, ignoring the paragraphs that don't already have numbers. In other words, the second time you issue the Renumber... command, Word will place all the remaining paragraph numbers in sequence.

Whenever you number the paragraphs in a document, Word skips over blank paragraphs—that is, paragraphs that consist of a ¶ marker with no associated text. However, there may be instances where you want to number these blank paragraphs, perhaps so you can add text to these locations later. To do this, you must manually

Numbering blank paragraphs

enter a number, period, and tab for each of these blank paragraphs. These numbers, which are simply placeholders, do not have to be in proper sequence, nor do they have to use the same numbering scheme as the rest of your paragraph numbers.

After you type a number in front of each blank paragraph, you can use the Renumber... command to make Word replace these placeholder numbers with correct numbers. The Renumber... command will number the blank paragraphs in sequence, using the same numbering scheme (Arabic, Roman, or alphabetic) as the rest of your paragraph numbers.

For example, suppose you want to number each of the blank paragraphs (along with the rest of the document) shown in Figure 13-34. Before you issue the Renumber... command, type a 1 followed by a period and a tab space at the beginning of each blank paragraph. (The period is not absolutely necessary in this case. However, if you use an alphabetic character for your placeholder instead of a numeral—which is perfectly acceptable—you must be sure to type a separator character so that Word can distinguish your "number" from the paragraph text.) Figure 13-35 shows the document with the placeholder numbers.

FIGURE 13-34

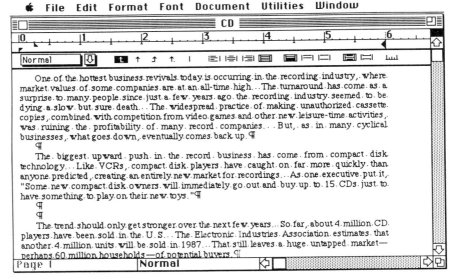

Word normally will not number blank paragraphs like those shown in this document.

The next step is to issue the Renumber... command as you normally would. In this example, let's assume that you enter *A* in the Format edit bar to specify an uppercase alphabetic numbering scheme. When you click OK, your document will look like Figure 13-36. Notice that Word has replaced each placeholder number with the correct letter for that paragraph.

FIGURE 13-35

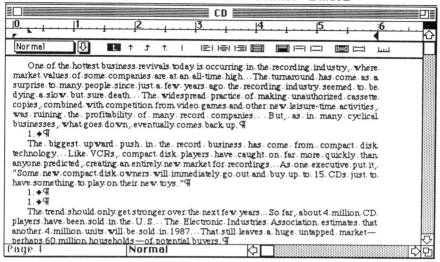

To number blank paragraphs, begin by entering a placeholder number, separator character, and tab before the ¶.

FIGURE 13-36

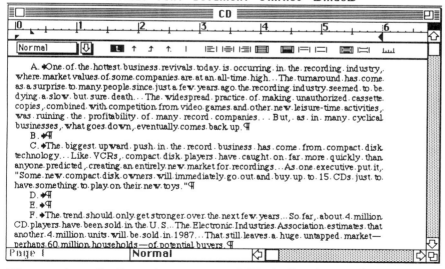

When you issue the Renumber... command, Word will replace each placeholder number with a properly formatted number or letter in the correct sequence.

By the way, you can use this same technique to number blank paragraphs in documents that have multiple levels of paragraphs. When you issue the Renumber... command, just be sure you enter in the Format edit bar the type of numbering scheme you want to use for each paragraph level. Word will then assign the correct number to each blank paragraph, regardless of its level.

Numbering Multiple Levels of Paragraphs

As we mentioned in the introduction to this section, paragraph numbering is perhaps most useful in documents that contain multiple levels of superior and subordinate paragraphs, such as legal documents or teaching materials. When you issue the Renumber... command, Word is able to recognize different levels of paragraphs and assign a different set of numbers to each level. For example, Figure 13-37 shows a document with three levels of numbered paragraphs. Notice that Word uses a different set of numbers for each level.

FIGURE 13-37

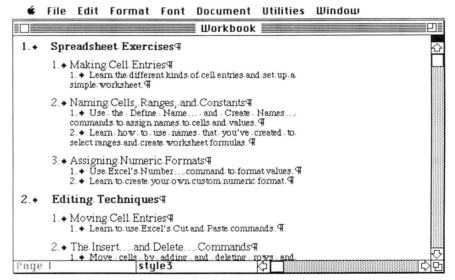

Word is able to assign a different set of numbers to each paragraph level in a document.

Not only is Word able to number each level separately, it can also use a different numbering scheme and different separator characters for each level. For example, Figure 13-38 shows the document from Figure 13-37 in which we've specified two numbering schemes for the three levels of paragraphs. Notice that the first level uses Arabic numerals, while the second level uses uppercase alphabetic characters, and the third level returns to Arabic numerals.

FIGURE 13-38

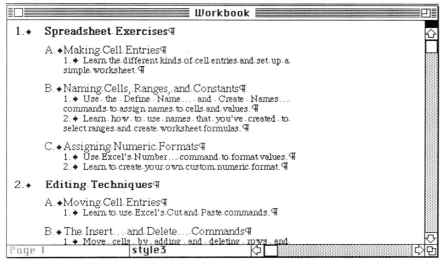

Word can use different numbering schemes to number different paragraph levels.

Word distinguishes the different levels of paragraphs in a document by noting the amount of indention on the first line of each paragraph. The farther right a paragraph is indented, the more subordinate its level. For example, suppose you have a document in which the first line of some of the paragraphs is not indented. In other paragraphs, the first line is indented $1/4$ inch. If you were to issue the Renumber... command, Word would recognize two levels of paragraphs in this document. All the paragraphs with no first-line indention would be considered first-level paragraphs, which Word would number sequentially. The paragraphs with the $1/4$-inch first-line indention would be considered second-level paragraphs. Each consecutive group of these second-level paragraphs would be numbered sequentially. However, when Word reaches a first-level paragraph, that would be its signal to start over when it numbers the next set of second-level paragraphs. In other words, Word assumes that each group of second-level paragraphs "falls under" a particular first-level paragraph.

By the way, a paragraph's indention must be created with the first-line indent marker on the ruler—not by a tab or spaces—in order for Word to differentiate paragraph levels. If you move the first-line indent marker for one or more paragraphs, Word won't automatically change your numbers. However, when you choose Renumber... again, Word will recognize your new indentions and change the paragraph numbering accordingly. Because even a small difference in indention ($1/16$ inch) can signal a new level, we recommend that you use a style sheet to define the formatting of your paragraph levels. That way, you can be sure that every paragraph at the same level will have the same amount of first-line indention.

In addition to indention, Word uses the different parts of an outline created in the Outliner to distinguish various paragraph levels. We'll discuss in detail the relationship between Word's Outline facility and the Renumber... command later in this chapter. First, let's consider the numbering options that are available for multilevel documents.

Specifying a numbering scheme for each level

As we illustrated in Figure 13-38, you can use a different numbering scheme for each level of paragraphs in a document. In other words, you can mix Arabic numerals, Roman numerals, and alphabetic characters among the different levels. You also can use different separator characters for each level.

You don't need to issue a separate Renumber... command for each level of paragraphs in order to specify different numbering schemes. You simply enter in the Format edit bar the type of characters you want to use in numbering each document level. For example, suppose you have a document with three levels of paragraphs in which you want to use a standard outline numbering scheme. Figure 13-39 shows the entry you might make in the Format edit bar of the Renumber dialog box to specify this kind of paragraph numbering. Figure 13-40 shows the results in a document.

FIGURE 13-39

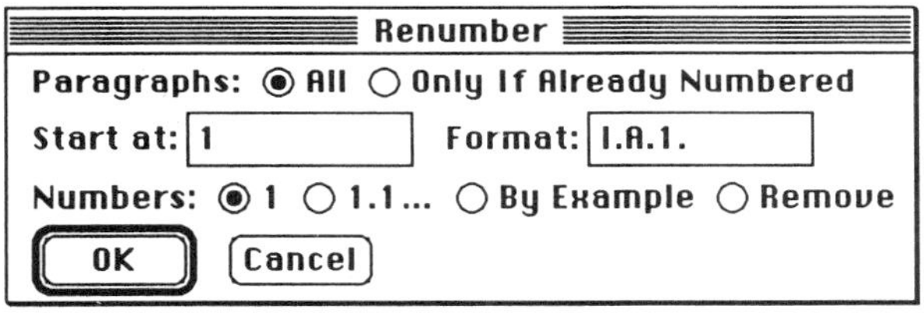

```
╔══════════════ Renumber ══════════════╗
║ Paragraphs: ◉ All  ○ Only If Already Numbered ║
║ Start at: [1]          Format: [I.A.1.]        ║
║ Numbers: ◉ 1  ○ 1.1...  ○ By Example  ○ Remove ║
║ ( OK )   [ Cancel ]                            ║
╚════════════════════════════════════════════════╝
```

In the Format edit bar, enter the type of characters you want to use in numbering each paragraph level in your document.

As with single-level documents, if you do not specify a particular numbering scheme for one or more levels, Word will number the paragraphs at that level with simple Arabic numbers. For example, suppose you're numbering a document with three levels of paragraphs, but you specify only one kind of character in the Format edit bar, a Roman numeral. Word will use Roman numerals to number the first level of paragraphs, but use the default Arabic numerals to number the second- and third-level paragraphs.

FIGURE 13-40

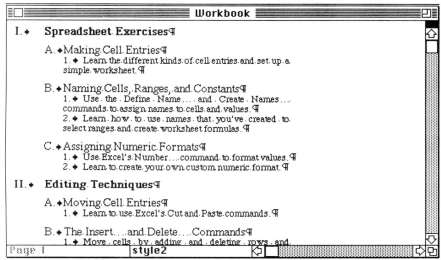

This screen shows the effects of the numbering scheme specified in the dialog box in Figure 13-39.

If you've previously numbered the paragraphs at a subordinate level, you don't have to specify a numbering scheme when you next issue the Renumber... command. The numbering scheme that already appears in your document will override Word's default; that is, if you don't specify a particular numbering scheme in the Format edit bar, Word will not automatically convert the numbers on previously numbered paragraphs to the default Arabic numerals.

Of course, you do not have to specify the format of all your paragraph numbers with one command—though that's usually the easiest approach. If you want to specify the numbering scheme for only one level of paragraphs, select those paragraphs, issue the Renumber... command, and type in the Format edit bar a character representing the kind of numbering you want to use. This technique may require that you issue the Renumber... command several times since all the paragraphs in a single level are not likely to be adjacent in a document.

When you type an entry in the Format edit bar, you must use the same separator character for all paragraph levels. In other words, you must enter something like *1)A)1)a)* or *I-A-1-a-*. If you try to specify different separator characters for different levels—for example, if you enter *I.A.1)a>* —the results will be unpredictable. In most situations, Word will choose one of the separator characters you enter and use

Using different separator characters at each level

it for all paragraph levels, rather than using a different separator character for each level. Word also requires that your separator character appear only after each level's number (not before). For example, if you enter something like *(I)(A)(1)(a)* in the Format edit bar, Word will display the message *Invalid number*.

To use a different separator character for each paragraph level, you must perform a couple of extra steps. For example, suppose you want to number the paragraphs in your document using a standard outline numbering scheme (*I.*, *A.*, *1.*, *a.*). However, instead of displaying a period after each paragraph number, you would like to use a variety of separator characters: a period after the first-level Roman numerals, a right parenthesis after the second-level uppercase alphabetic characters, a period after the third level of Arabic numbers, and another parenthesis after the fourth level of lowercase alphabetic characters.

Begin by issuing the Renumber… command, then enter *I.A.1.a.* in the Format edit bar, click the 1 Numbers option, and click OK. When Word has numbered your paragraphs, as shown in Figure 13-41, select the first "number" at each level and add the appropriate separator character. For example, you would select the first second-level *A.* in line 2 and replace it with *A)*. Then, you would select the first fourth-level *a.* in line 13 and replace it with *a)*. After you've created one "example" paragraph number at each level, your screen will look like Figure 13-42.

FIGURE 13-41

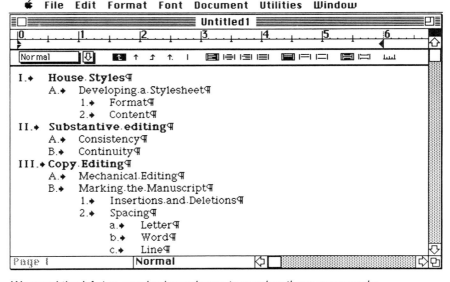

We used the I.A.1.a. numbering scheme to number these paragraphs.

FIGURE 13-42

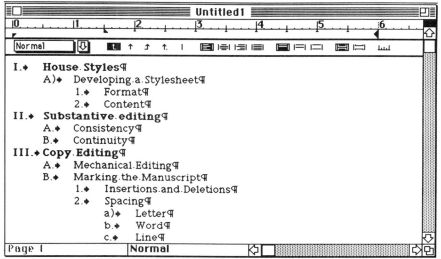

We added our own separator characters to the first "number" at the second and fourth levels.

Now, issue the Renumber… command once more. In the dialog box, erase the contents of the Format edit bar and click the By Example option, then click OK. The results will look like Figure 13-43 on the following page.

Word allows you to include in your paragraph numbers the numbers of all superior levels of paragraphs. To display superior levels, click the 1.1... Numbers option in the Renumber dialog box. For example, going back to Figure 13-40, if you opened the Renumber dialog box and clicked the 1.1... option, the result would look like Figure 13-44 on the next page. Notice that, for each paragraph level, Word displays the number of all superior levels. By the way, when you're displaying superior levels, you can use the method we described earlier to display a variety of separator characters between the number of superior levels—for example, *I.A)1.a)*.

There may be times when you want the numbers for some of your paragraphs to display their superior levels, while the numbers for other paragraphs do not. Using the By Example option in the Renumber dialog box, you can control the display of superior level numbers on a level-by-level basis in your document.

Displaying the number of superior levels

FIGURE 13-43

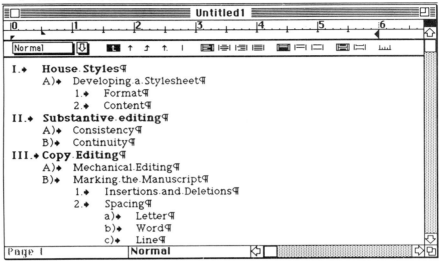

When we reissue the *Renumber...* command and choose the *By Example* option,
Word uses our manual numbering scheme to renumber the paragraphs.

FIGURE 13-44

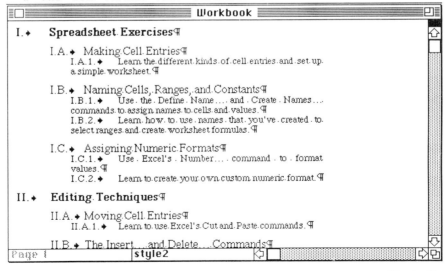

When you click the *1.1...* Numbers option in the Renumber dialog box, Word will
display all superior levels in each paragraph's number.

For instance, suppose you want to display the numbers of superior levels only on the second-level paragraphs in the document shown in Figure 13-44. On the first- and third-level paragraphs, you want to display only the number of the current level. Begin by displaying the numbers of superior levels on all your paragraphs (as we've done in Figure 13-44). Then, for each level on which you do not want to display the numbers of superior levels, edit the number on the first paragraph in that level so that it no longer displays the superior levels. In our example, you must edit the number for the first third-level paragraph (which begins, *Learn the different kinds...*).

After editing the paragraph number, issue the Renumber... command, and in the dialog box, click the By Example option. When you click OK, Word will change the paragraph numbers so that the format of each number at a given level matches the format of the first paragraph number in that level. Figure 13-45 shows our sample document with the numbers of superior levels displayed only on the second-level paragraphs.

FIGURE 13-45

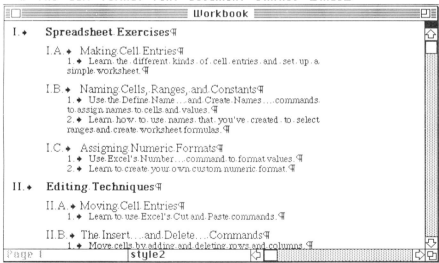

In this document, only the second-level paragraph numbers display the numbers of superior levels.

When you're working with a document that contains multiple levels of paragraphs, specifying a Start At number can be a bit tricky. The number you enter in the Start At edit bar must include the numbers of all superior paragraph levels, but it must not include the numbers of subordinate levels. For example, Figure 13-46 shows a document with three levels of paragraphs that are numbered with a

Specifying a Start At number

standard outline numbering scheme. As you can see, a new second-level topic (*AI Issues*) has been inserted between the second-level paragraphs A (*Software Issues*) and B (*Hardware Issues*). In addition, we've added a couple of third-level topics under the new second-level paragraph.

FIGURE 13-46

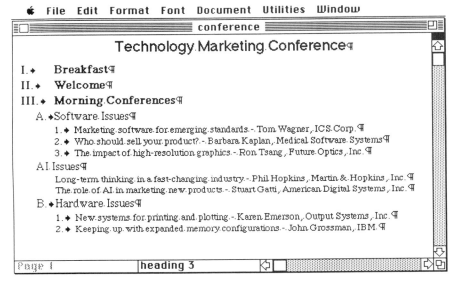

We inserted some new paragraphs in this three-level document.

To renumber this document, you would begin by selecting all the text beginning with the new second-level paragraph. Then, open the Renumber dialog box and enter *I.A.1.* in the Format edit bar. In the Start At edit bar, enter *III.B* or *3.2*, then click the 1 Numbers option. Also, be sure that the All option is activated at the top of the dialog box. Figure 13-47 shows the screen after we selected the text to be numbered and made the appropriate entries in the Renumber dialog box. Figure 13-48 shows the result.

Although we chose to enter our Start At number as *III.B.*, we could just as easily have entered it as *3.2*. Remember, the entry in the Format edit bar tells Word what kind of numbering scheme you want to use at the different paragraph levels (Roman numerals, Arabic numerals, or alphabetic characters). The entry in the Start At edit bar simply indicates where in this numbering scheme you want to start numbering your paragraphs. A Start At number of *3.2*, like *III.B*, indicates that you want to start numbering with the second second-level paragraph after the third first-level paragraph.

FIGURE 13-47

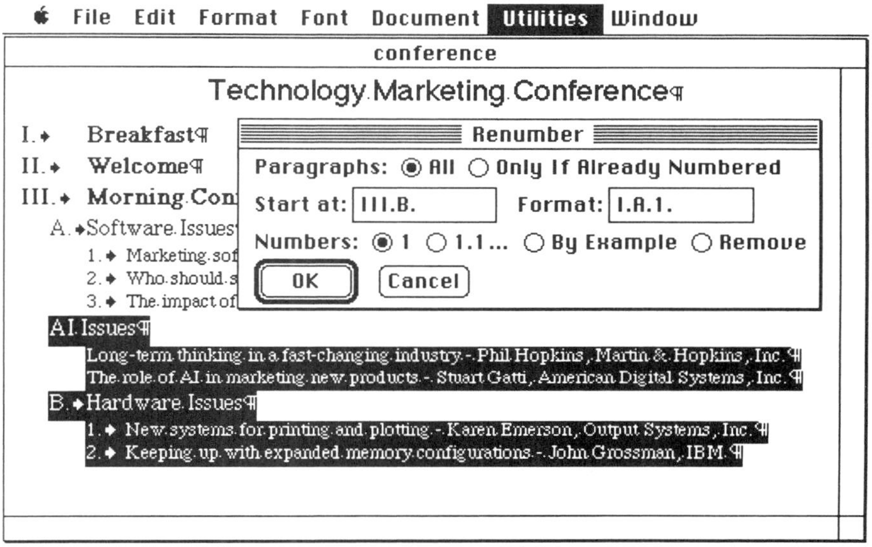

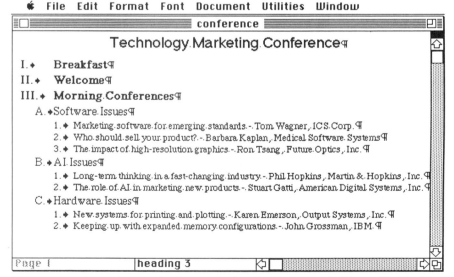

In renumbering paragraphs in a multilevel document, the Start At edit bar should include the number of any superior paragraph levels.

FIGURE 13-48

 File Edit Format Font Document Utilities Window

conference

Technology.Marketing.Conference¶

I.◆ **Breakfast¶**
II.◆ **Welcome¶**
III.◆ **Morning.Conferences¶**

   A.◆Software.Issues¶
     1.◆ Marketing.software.for.emerging.standards.-.Tom.Wagner,.ICS.Corp.¶
     2.◆ Who.should.sell.your.product?.-.Barbara.Kaplan,.Medical.Software.Systems¶
     3.◆ The.impact.of.high-resolution.graphics.-.Ron.Tsang,.Future.Optics,.Inc.¶
   B.◆A.I.Issues¶
     1.◆ Long-term.thinking.in.a.fast-changing.industry.-.Phil.Hopkins,.Martin.&.Hopkins,.Inc.¶
     2.◆ The.role.of.A.I.in.marketing.new.products.-.Stuart.Gatti,.American.Digital.Systems,.Inc.¶
   C.◆Hardware.Issues¶
     1.◆ New.systems.for.printing.and.plotting.-.Karen.Emerson,.Output.Systems,.Inc.¶
     2.◆ Keeping.up.with.expanded.memory.configurations.-.John.Grossman,.IBM.¶

Page 1 | heading 3

This screen shows the result of renumbering the document in Figure 13-46 with the dialog box settings shown in Figure 13-47.

Notice that, even though we want the first paragraph in our selection to be numbered with *B.*, our Start At number includes the *III* of the immediately superior paragraph. Had we entered a *B* as our Start At number, Word would have misinterpreted our intentions. Word considers a *B* in the Start At edit bar to be the same as *2*; both indicate that you want to begin numbering with the second number in the particular numbering scheme you've chosen. In our example, a *B* in the Start At edit bar would have caused the first paragraph in the selection to be numbered with *II* since our entry in the Format edit bar specifies a standard outline numbering scheme in which the second first-level paragraph is always numbered *II*.

Revising Paragraph Numbers

Word's ability to update paragraph numbers is very flexible. Once you've numbered some or all of the paragraphs in a document, you can easily update the numbers to reflect any changes you make, such as adding, deleting, or moving text. If you want to maintain the format of all your numbers as you update them, be sure that the By Example option is selected in the Renumber dialog box and that the first paragraph number at each level is formatted appropriately.

Adding, deleting, and rearranging paragraphs

If you add new paragraphs to your document, delete some paragraphs, or rearrange your existing paragraphs, you can easily update your paragraph numbers by issuing the Renumber... command. Just be sure that no text is selected when you choose Renumber... so that Word will be able to change all the numbers in your document and not just the numbers of selected paragraphs. Of course, there may be times when the changes you make affect only a limited area of your document. In that case, you'll probably find it faster to select just the affected area before you issue the Renumber... command.

When you add or rearrange selected paragraphs, you may need to enter a new Start At number in the Renumber dialog box. If you do this, just keep in mind how Word interprets the entry in the Start At edit bar.

Removing paragraph numbers

Immediately after you issue the Renumber... command and click OK, you can undo your numbering by selecting Undo Renumber from the Edit menu. If you select Undo Renumber after renumbering a document for the first time, Word will delete all the paragraph numbers. If you issued the Renumber... command to reformat or update your paragraph numbers, then Undo Renumber will cancel only your latest change.

You can remove paragraph numbers and the tab space that follows them by clicking the Remove option in the Renumber dialog box. If you don't select any text before you do this, Word will remove all the paragraph numbers in your document. If you want to remove the numbers on only some of the paragraphs in your document, you can select those paragraphs before you choose Renumber... and click the Remove option.

The Renumber... command offers a handy way to number an outline that you've created with Word's Outline facility. Whenever you need to create an outline with numbered points, you'll find that it's much easier to enter your outline text, then use the Renumber... command to number all the outline levels, rather than type the number for each outline point manually. As you might expect, Word is able to recognize the different levels of an outline and number each level appropriately.

Let's consider a simple example of how you might use the Renumber... command in an outline window. As you learned in Chapter 9, the first step in creating an outline is to choose Outlining from the Document menu. This will switch your screen from a normal document view to the outline view. Once you're in an outline window, type the text of your outline and use the → and ← icons at the top of the window to specify the level of each part of the outline. Figure 13-49 shows a completed outline before any numbers were added.

Paragraph Numbers and the Outline Facility

FIGURE 13-49

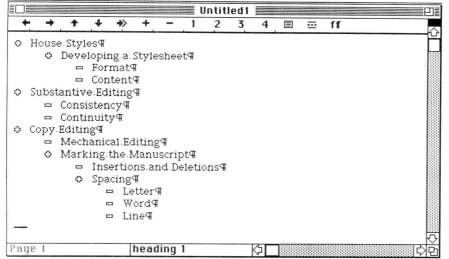

To create a numbered outline, begin by entering your outline text in a blank outline window.

To number the outline, choose Renumber... from the Utilities menu. In the Renumber dialog box, enter the numbering scheme you want to use in the Format edit bar. For standard outline numbering, you would enter *I.A.1.a.i..* (Of course, if your outline contains fewer than five levels, you would not need to enter as many characters in the Format edit bar.) Make sure that the Start At number is 1 and that you have clicked the 1 Numbers option. When you click OK, Word will number each level of the outline so that the result looks like Figure 13-50.

FIGURE 13-50

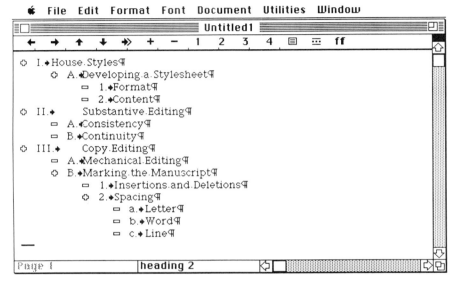

You can use the Renumber... command to number the text in an outline window.

In this example, Word numbered all the outline text since we had not chosen to collapse any part of the outline. If you collapse the outline before you number it, Word will assign numbers only to the visible parts of the outline. For example, going back to the unnumbered outline shown in Figure 13-49, if you clicked on the 2 icon at the top of the screen, Word would collapse the outline so that all text below level 2 is not visible on the screen. If you then issued the Renumber... command, Word would number only the level 1 and level 2 text that is visible on the screen.

By the way, collapsing the outline and choosing Renumber... will not remove existing numbers from the lower levels in the outline. For example, suppose that after you number the entire outline (as shown in Figure 13-50), you decide to click the 2 icon so that all level 3 and level 4 text is collapsed out of view. If you then choose Renumber... again, Word will update the numbers of the visible outline text. However, when you expand the outline to bring the level 3 and level 4 text back into view, you'll see that that text retains the numbers assigned by the first Renumber... command.

Once you've used Word's Outliner to create some outline text, you don't have to number that text in the outline window. If you want, you can switch to the document window before you issue the Renumber... command. Interestingly, even if your outline text does not display different amounts of indention in the document view, Word is still able to recognize the outline levels and number the paragraphs appropriately. For example, suppose you've just created the outline shown in Figure 13-49. If you choose Outlining from the Utilities menu, Word will return to a normal document view like the one in Figure 13-51. As you can see, the level 1 and level 2 topics display the same amount of first-line indention (none), as do the level 3 and level 4 topics ($^1/_4$ inch). However, if you were to issue the Renumber… command, Word would correctly identify the different outline levels and number each level separately.

FIGURE 13-51

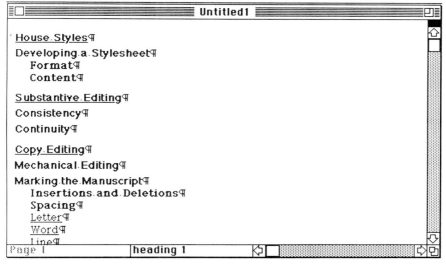

When you switch to the normal document view, your unnumbered outline will look like this.

SORTING

Word's Sort command allows you to rearrange lists, paragraphs, and tables in either ascending or descending order. When you select the Sort command from the Utilities menu, Word will sort paragraphs according to the first character or first few characters in each paragraph. (There are a few cases where Word will ignore the first character in each paragraph. We'll cover those cases later in this section.)

If you don't select any text before you issue the Sort command, Word will sort all the paragraphs in your document. In sorting the paragraphs, Word will ignore section boundaries. If you want to sort only a portion of a document, you can select the text you want to sort before you issue the Sort command. For example, if you want to rearrange five paragraphs, you can select those paragraphs before you choose Sort from the Utilities menu.

One of the most powerful features of Word's Sort command is its ability to sort a table of information based on a single "key column." We'll demonstrate this technique in a few pages. First, however, let's consider a few basic facts about sorting in Word.

Sorting Basics

Word's default sort order is ascending. However, you can sort in descending order by pressing the Shift key as you choose Sort from the Utilities menu. Once you've issued the Sort command, you can undo your sort by choosing Undo Sort from the Edit menu. (Like other Undo commands, this one must be issued immediately after you sort, before you do anything else.)

When sorting, Word uses the ASCII code for a character to determine its sort priority. In an ascending sort, the general priority of characters is: Punctuation marks and other nonalphanumeric characters precede numbers, and numbers precede letters. However, Word will place some nonalphanumeric characters *after* numbers, but before letters. Other punctuation marks will follow letters. (For a listing of characters and their ASCII codes, see Appendix 3.)

If a paragraph begins with an indent, tab, or blank space, Word will ignore the space and sort the paragraph according to the first character after the tab, indent, or space. Similarly, if a paragraph begins with a straight quotation mark ("), Word will sort that paragraph according to the first character after the quotation mark. (This rule does not apply to the single quotation mark (') or to curved quotation marks (" or ').

Completely blank paragraphs—that is, paragraphs that consist of a ¶ with no text—will be ignored in the sort. In other words, when you sort text, Word will not change the location of any blank lines you may have created by pressing the Return key. Another rule of sorting is that uppercase letters precede lowercase letters. For example, a paragraph that begins with *G* will precede one that begins with *g*. Both paragraphs will precede one that begins with an *H*. If two or more paragraphs begin identically, Word will scan the text in each paragraph until it finds differing characters, and sort on that basis.

In addition to these basic rules of sorting, there are some special rules that apply to sorting by numbers. We'll address these next, as we talk about sorting numbered paragraphs and lists of numbers.

Sorting by Number

When Word sorts numbers, it considers each string of digits to be a numeric value; it does not simply look at the first digit in the series. For example, in sorting numbers, Word knows that the number 6 comes before the number 10, even though the first digit in 10, 1, is less than 6. Word is also able to evaluate number-letter combinations correctly. For example, if you're sorting paragraphs that are numbered 1-A, 1-B, 1-C, and so forth, Word will be able to evaluate the numbers properly.

There are a couple of situations you need to avoid when sorting numbered paragraphs. These are likely to occur if you've used the Renumber... command to number paragraphs. First, Word is not able to sort Roman numerals correctly in numbered paragraphs. Word will sort Roman numerals as though they were strings of normal alphabetic characters. Thus, the sorted order of the numbers will be I, II, III, IV, IX, VI, and so forth. Of course, if your paragraph numbers do not go beyond Roman numeral VIII, then you're OK. In general, if you want to sort numbered paragraphs, we recommend that you use Arabic numerals or alphabetic characters.

You also need to be cautious about sorting documents with multiple levels of numbered paragraphs. In some cases, Word cannot keep track of the different levels. Figure 13-52 shows what would happen if you sorted the document from Figure 13-48, which contains three levels of paragraphs in addition to the title. This figure also illustrates a problem you can encounter with Roman numerals.

FIGURE 13-52

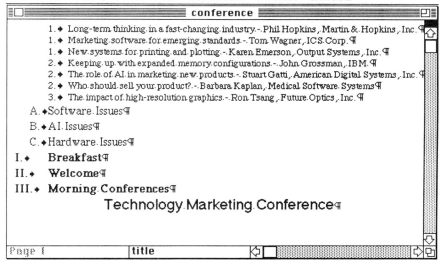

If your document contains multiple levels of numbered paragraphs, the Sort command may not work as you would expect.

To sort a document with multiple levels of paragraphs, you should include the number of all superior levels in each paragraph's number. For example, to sort the document from Figure 13-48 without encountering the kinds of problems shown in Figure 13-52, you would want to number the second-level paragraphs III.A., III.B., and III.C. Then, your third-level paragraphs would be numbered III.A.1, III.A.2,

III.B.3., and so forth. When you display the numbers of superior levels like this, Word will be able to keep the paragraph levels straight when it sorts. (For more on automatic paragraph numbering and displaying superior levels, see the previous section in this chapter entitled "Numbering Paragraphs.")

Using numbered paragraphs to rearrange a document

Word's ability to sort by number offers an easy way to change the order of paragraphs in a document. For instance, suppose you've written a document in which you would like to rearrange several paragraphs. You could cut and paste each paragraph until they're all in the correct order. A faster method, however, is to type a number followed by a period at the beginning of each paragraph, which indicates where you want to place that paragraph relative to the other paragraphs. For example, Figure 13-53 shows a document in which we've typed numbers at the beginning of several paragraphs. You must include at least one blank space between the number and the paragraph text. As you'll see in a moment, this will speed up the process of removing the numbers after you've rearranged the paragraphs.

FIGURE 13-53

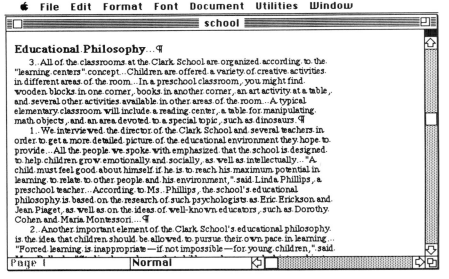

To rearrange paragraphs quickly, begin by placing a number at the beginning of each paragraph to indicate its placement.

Once you've numbered the paragraphs, select them, and choose Sort from the Utilities menu. Word will then automatically rearrange the paragraphs according to their numbers, as shown in Figure 13-54.

FIGURE 13-54

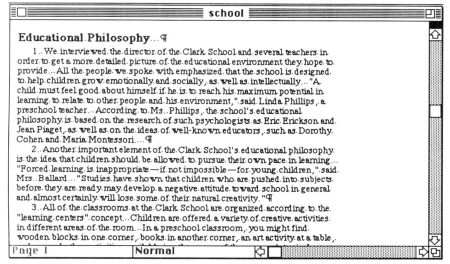

When you issue the Sort command, Word will sort the paragraphs according to their numbers.

You can now remove the numbers, either with manual editing techniques or with Word's Renumber… command. To remove the numbers with the Renumber… command, open the dialog box, click the Remove option, then click OK. This technique will work only if you've included at least one blank space between each number and the first character of paragraph text.

Sorting a Table by Key Column

Word's ability to sort tables of information is similar to that of many simple database programs. Word can sort all the entries in one column (or field) of a table and rearrange the rest of the table according to that sorted column. Word even has a limited ability to use multiple sort keys. Let's consider a simple example that demonstrates Word's table-sorting capability. (In this section, we'll consider how you sort a table that's been created with tabs. In Chapter 10, we explain sorting a table that's been created with Word 4's Insert Table… command.)

Suppose your document contains the table of data shown in Figure 13-55 on the next page. You want to sort this information into ascending order by sales representative. You should begin by selecting the Sales Rep names in the second column of the table. This column is called the *sort key*. To select the column, press the Option key, then click in front of the first name in that column and drag down until you've selected the entire column, as shown in Figure 13-56.

FIGURE 13-55

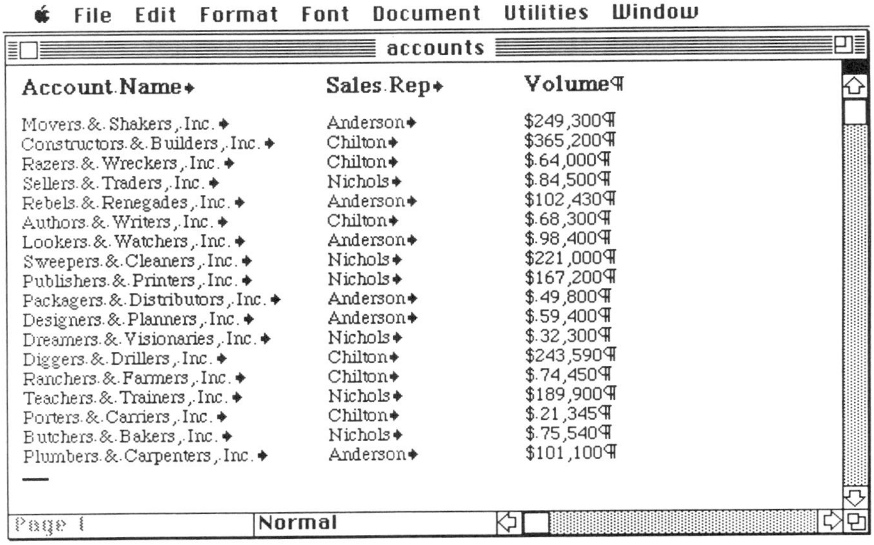

 🍎 File Edit Format Font Document Utilities Window

═□══════════════════ accounts ══════════════════□

Account.Name→	Sales.Rep→	Volume¶
Movers.&.Shakers,.Inc.→	Anderson→	$249,300¶
Constructors.&.Builders,.Inc.→	Chilton→	$365,200¶
Razers.&.Wreckers,.Inc.→	Chilton→	$.64,000¶
Sellers.&.Traders,.Inc.→	Nichols→	$.84,500¶
Rebels.&.Renegades,.Inc.→	Anderson→	$102,430¶
Authors.&.Writers,.Inc.→	Chilton→	$.68,300¶
Lookers.&.Watchers,.Inc.→	Anderson→	$.98,400¶
Sweepers.&.Cleaners,.Inc.→	Nichols→	$221,000¶
Publishers.&.Printers,.Inc.→	Nichols→	$167,200¶
Packagers.&.Distributors,.Inc.→	Anderson→	$.49,800¶
Designers.&.Planners,.Inc.→	Anderson→	$.59,400¶
Dreamers.&.Visionaries,.Inc.→	Nichols→	$.32,300¶
Diggers.&.Drillers,.Inc.→	Chilton→	$243,590¶
Ranchers.&.Farmers,.Inc.→	Chilton→	$.74,450¶
Teachers.&.Trainers,.Inc.→	Nichols→	$189,900¶
Porters.&.Carriers,.Inc.→	Chilton→	$.21,345¶
Butchers.&.Bakers,.Inc.→	Nichols→	$.75,540¶
Plumbers.&.Carpenters,.Inc.→	Anderson→	$101,100¶

| Page 1 | Normal |

You can use Word's Sort command to sort a table like this one.

FIGURE 13-56

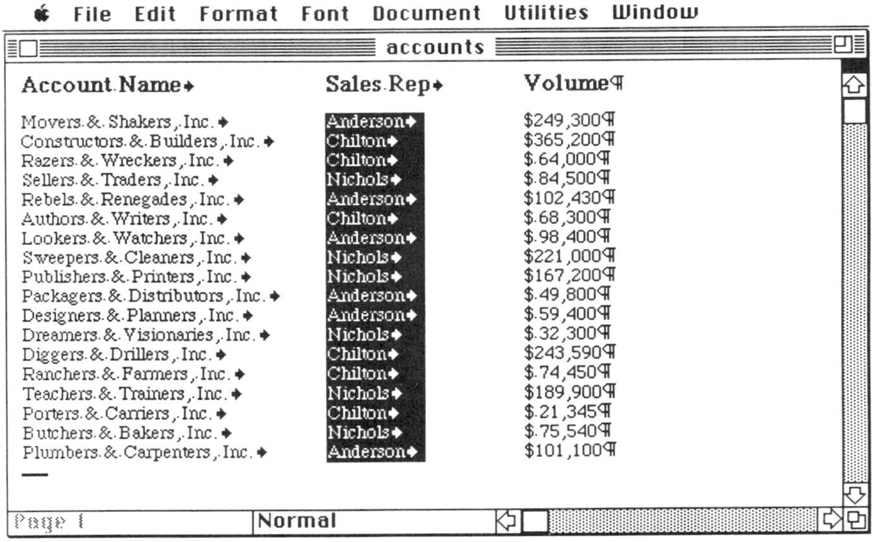

 🍎 File Edit Format Font Document Utilities Window

═□══════════════════ accounts ══════════════════□

Account.Name→	Sales.Rep→	Volume¶
Movers.&.Shakers,.Inc.→	Anderson→	$249,300¶
Constructors.&.Builders,.Inc.→	Chilton→	$365,200¶
Razers.&.Wreckers,.Inc.→	Chilton→	$.64,000¶
Sellers.&.Traders,.Inc.→	Nichols→	$.84,500¶
Rebels.&.Renegades,.Inc.→	Anderson→	$102,430¶
Authors.&.Writers,.Inc.→	Chilton→	$.68,300¶
Lookers.&.Watchers,.Inc.→	Anderson→	$.98,400¶
Sweepers.&.Cleaners,.Inc.→	Nichols→	$221,000¶
Publishers.&.Printers,.Inc.→	Nichols→	$167,200¶
Packagers.&.Distributors,.Inc.→	Anderson→	$.49,800¶
Designers.&.Planners,.Inc.→	Anderson→	$.59,400¶
Dreamers.&.Visionaries,.Inc.→	Nichols→	$.32,300¶
Diggers.&.Drillers,.Inc.→	Chilton→	$243,590¶
Ranchers.&.Farmers,.Inc.→	Chilton→	$.74,450¶
Teachers.&.Trainers,.Inc.→	Nichols→	$189,900¶
Porters.&.Carriers,.Inc.→	Chilton→	$.21,345¶
Butchers.&.Bakers,.Inc.→	Nichols→	$.75,540¶
Plumbers.&.Carpenters,.Inc.→	Anderson→	$101,100¶

| Page 1 | Normal |

The first step in sorting the table is to select the column you want to use as your sort key.

Once you've selected the information on which you want to base your sort, just choose Sort from the Utilities menu. Figure 13-57 shows the result.

FIGURE 13-57

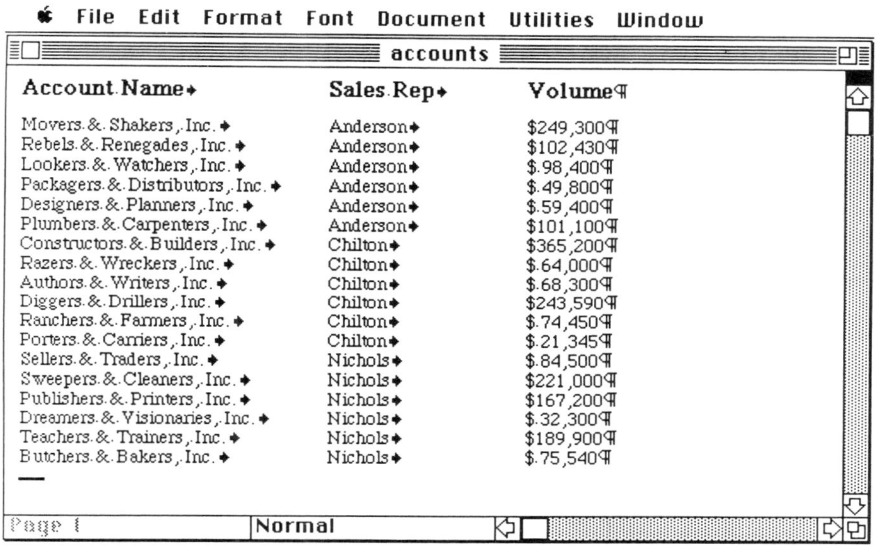

When you choose Sort from the Utilities menu, Word will sort the table according to the column you selected.

As we mentioned, Word's Sort command offers a limited ability to use multiple sort keys—that is, you can sort on more than one column of data. To do this, the sort keys or columns must be adjacent in the table and arranged in order of priority from left to right. For instance, in our example, you could sort the table in Figure 13-55 on the basis of both sales representative and volume. In this case, the Sales Rep column would be your primary sort key since it is in the leftmost column, and the Volume column would be the secondary sort key. To set up this sort, you must select both columns before you issue the Sort command. Figure 13-58 on the following page shows the table with these two columns selected.

When you choose to sort on two columns, Word will first sort the table according to the information in the leftmost column—the primary sort key. Then, Word will sort each group of rows with a common entry in the primary sort column according to the information in the second selected column—the secondary sort key. Of course, you won't see any indication on your screen that Word is performing a "double sort," as we've described. All you'll see is the result. For example, Figure 13-59 shows the table from Figure 13-58 after issuing the Sort command. Notice that the information in this table is grouped not only by the names of the sales representatives, but within each sales representative's grouping, the accounts appear in ascending order by volume.

FIGURE 13-58

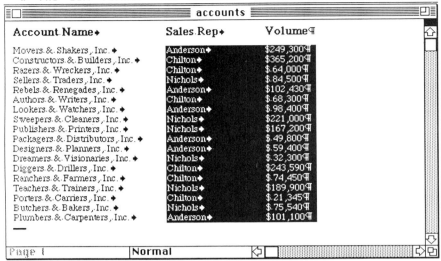

To sort on two columns, select both columns before you choose Sort from the Utilities menu.

FIGURE 13-59

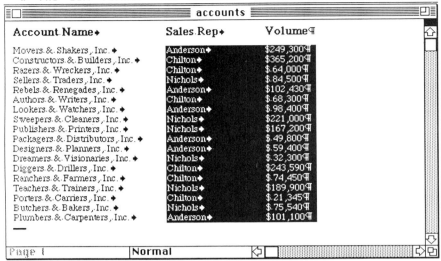

This screen shows the result of sorting both on the sales representatives' names and account volume.

When you use two or more sort keys, Word must apply the same sort order—either ascending or descending—with each of the sort keys. To get around this limitation, you must perform separate Sort procedures. For example, suppose you want to sort the table in Figure 13-55 according to the sales representatives' names and account volume. However, within each sales representative grouping, you would like the accounts to be listed in descending order according to volume.

To accomplish this, sort only by sales representative initially so that your table looks like Figure 13-57. Then, select the volume numbers within each sales representative's grouping and sort into descending order. For example, after you've sorted by sales representative, you would select and sort all the volume information for Anderson. The result is shown in Figure 13-60.

FIGURE 13-60

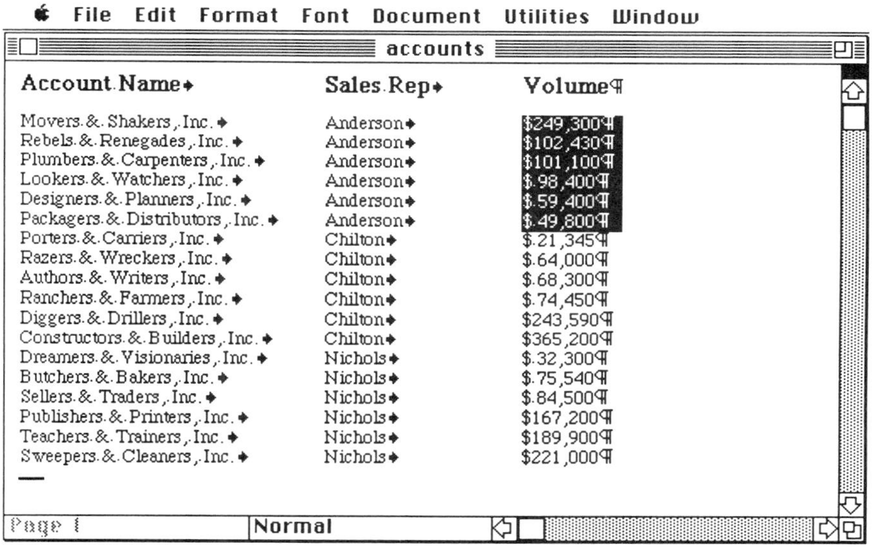

Account Name	Sales Rep	Volume
Movers & Shakers, Inc.	Anderson	$249,300
Rebels & Renegades, Inc.	Anderson	$102,430
Plumbers & Carpenters, Inc.	Anderson	$101,100
Lookers & Watchers, Inc.	Anderson	$ 98,400
Designers & Planners, Inc.	Anderson	$ 59,400
Packagers & Distributors, Inc.	Anderson	$ 49,800
Porters & Carriers, Inc.	Chilton	$ 21,345
Razers & Wreckers, Inc.	Chilton	$ 64,000
Authors & Writers, Inc.	Chilton	$ 68,300
Ranchers & Farmers, Inc.	Chilton	$ 74,450
Diggers & Drillers, Inc.	Chilton	$243,590
Constructors & Builders, Inc.	Chilton	$365,200
Dreamers & Visionaries, Inc.	Nichols	$ 32,300
Butchers & Bakers, Inc.	Nichols	$ 75,540
Sellers & Traders, Inc.	Nichols	$ 84,500
Publishers & Printers, Inc.	Nichols	$167,200
Teachers & Trainers, Inc.	Nichols	$189,900
Sweepers & Cleaners, Inc.	Nichols	$221,000

To sort the accounts into descending order by volume, select the information in the third column for one sales representative, and issue the Sort command as you press the Shift key.

After you've selected the information, hold down the Shift key as you choose Sort from the Utilities menu. When you've repeated this procedure for each of the three sales representative groupings, the table will look like Figure 13-61.

FIGURE 13-61

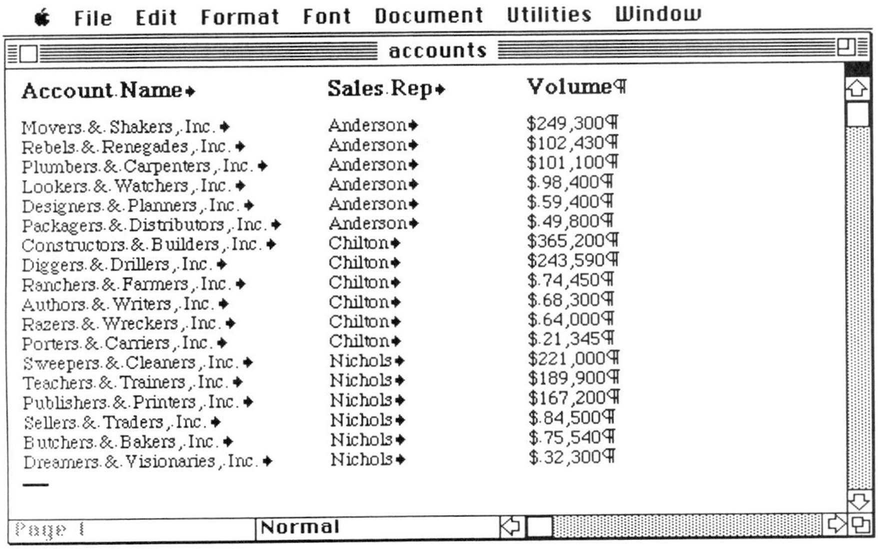

Account Name	Sales Rep	Volume
Movers & Shakers, Inc.	Anderson	$249,300
Rebels & Renegades, Inc.	Anderson	$102,430
Plumbers & Carpenters, Inc.	Anderson	$101,100
Lookers & Watchers, Inc.	Anderson	$ 98,400
Designers & Planners, Inc.	Anderson	$ 59,400
Packagers & Distributors, Inc.	Anderson	$ 49,800
Constructors & Builders, Inc.	Chilton	$365,200
Diggers & Drillers, Inc.	Chilton	$243,590
Ranchers & Farmers, Inc.	Chilton	$ 74,450
Authors & Writers, Inc.	Chilton	$ 68,300
Razers & Wreckers, Inc.	Chilton	$ 64,000
Porters & Carriers, Inc.	Chilton	$ 21,345
Sweepers & Cleaners, Inc.	Nichols	$221,000
Teachers & Trainers, Inc.	Nichols	$189,900
Publishers & Printers, Inc.	Nichols	$167,200
Sellers & Traders, Inc.	Nichols	$ 84,500
Butchers & Bakers, Inc.	Nichols	$ 75,540
Dreamers & Visionaries, Inc.	Nichols	$ 32,300

The information in this table has been sorted into alphabetical order by sales representative, and within each sales representative's grouping, the accounts are arranged in descending order by volume.

Sorting in an Outline Window

The Sort command is available in the outline view, but you should use it with caution. First, Word does not distinguish the levels of an outline when you sort (just as it does not distinguish certain levels of numbered paragraphs). If you're not careful, the Sort command can destroy the structure of superior and subordinate outline levels. For example, Figure 13-62 shows what happened when we sorted the outline from Figure 13-49. (We issued the Sort command before numbering the outline.) Notice that Word has moved some of the subordinate outline sections to the beginning of the outline.

The best way to avoid this kind of problem is to number the outline, using a numbering scheme in which each outline number includes the number of its superior levels. For example, in Figure 13-62, we might undo the Sort command, then number the paragraphs in our sample document *I.*, *I.A.*, *I.A.1.*, and so forth. (For more on numbering an outline and various numbering schemes, see the section in this chapter entitled "Numbering Paragraphs.")

You can use the Sort command in an outline window to rearrange large portions of a document. For example, suppose you created an outline using the Outlining command, then you switched to the document view and filled in the document text. Next, you switched back to the outline view, where Word can display only your document subheadings and the first line of each paragraph of body text, as shown in Figure 13-63.

FIGURE 13-62

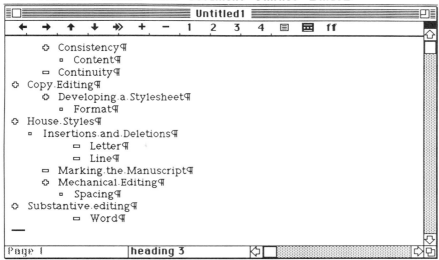

Sorting in an outline window can destroy your outline levels.

FIGURE 13-63

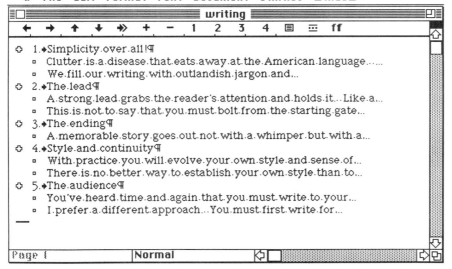

When you switch from a document view to an outline view, Word can display each heading and the first line of each paragraph of body text.

This "bird's-eye" view can be very helpful in checking the organization and flow of your document. Then, if you decide to rearrange your document, you can do so easily in the outline window. For example, in the outline view, you can move one subheading and, in doing so, move all the body text under that subheading as well. The Sort command can be a handy tool for rearranging various parts of a document in an outline window. If you want to use the Sort command, however, you must be sure to collapse out of view any portions of your document you do not want to sort.

For example, suppose you want to reverse the order of sections 2 and 3 in the document shown in Figure 13-63. You can do this by changing the number in front of each section's heading, selecting those headings, and then issuing the Sort command. Before you choose Sort, however, be sure that you collapse the body text out of view. If you do not collapse the body text, the result of the Sort command will look like Figure 13-64.

FIGURE 13-64

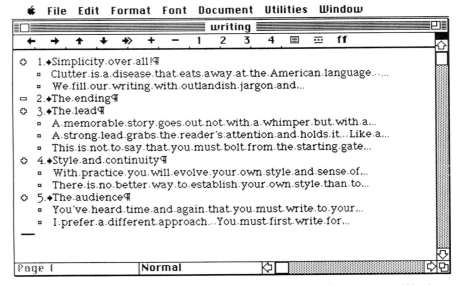

If you do not collapse the body text in an outline window before you sort, Word will sort that text as well as your headings.

Notice that Word has rearranged the outline so that the headings for sections 2 and 3 appear together, with all the body text for both headings underneath. In addition, Word has sorted the body text according to the first word in each paragraph, resulting in a meaningless flow. To correct this problem, you should select Undo Sort immediately.

To avoid this kind of problem, you should click the 1 icon at the top of the outline window so that only the headings you want to sort are visible. Figure 13-65 shows the outline after collapsing the body text.

FIGURE 13-65

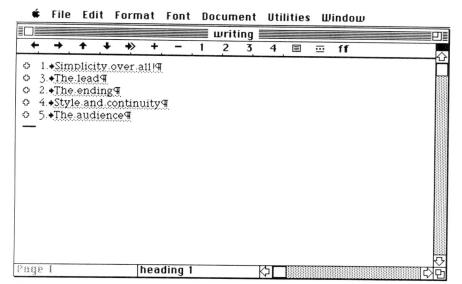

Before using the Sort command to rearrange a document in the outline view, you should collapse the outline so that the body text is no longer visible.

Once you've collapsed the outline, select the headings you want to sort and choose Sort from the Utilities menu. After sorting the headings, you can click the Show All icon (▤) to see what happened in your body text. Figure 13-66 on the following page shows the result. Word not only changed the order of the headings, but also moved the body text so that it falls under the correct heading.

In a simple situation like the one we've just described, you probably would be better off just selecting the text you want to move and using the Cut and Paste commands. However, in a longer document that requires more serious revisions, using the Sort command in the outline window can save time.

Another special feature of Word 4 is its ability to perform basic mathematical calculations. With this capability, you can perform quick calculations, then plug the results of those calculations into your document. Word can calculate percentages and add, subtract, divide, and multiply values.

PERFORMING MATHEMATICAL CALCULATIONS

FIGURE 13-66

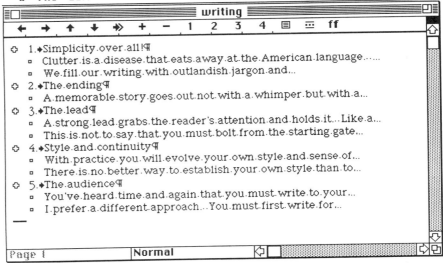

After sorting the selected headings, click the Show All icon to see how the Sort
command affected the body text in your document.

For example, suppose you have created a table of cash receipts like the one in Figure 13-67. You want to compute your total receipts for the week and insert that total value in the table. Begin by highlighting the cells of the table that contain the numbers you want to sum, then press ⌘-= or choose Calculate from the Utilities menu. As you can see in Figure 13-68, Word displays the total value 6025.09 in the status box at the lower-left corner of the screen.

Word also places a copy of this total value on the Clipboard so that you can issue the Paste command (or press ⌘-v) to enter the results of the calculation into your document. For example, if you click to the right of the dollar sign in the Totals line, then select Paste from the Edit menu, Word will paste the value 6025.09 to the right of the insertion point. Figure 13-69 on page 636 shows our table after we pasted the calculated value into the Totals line.

When you add a series of values, as we did in the previous example, Word does not require that you use any mathematical operators. Unless the text you select includes a mathematical operator, Word assumes you want to add the values in that selection.

When you use the ⌘-= technique, Word ignores any alphabetic characters in your selection. It treats the numbers on either side of the alphabetic characters as separate values. For example, if you make an entry like *10x9* in your document, Word will treat this string as two separate values—10 and 9.

FIGURE 13-67

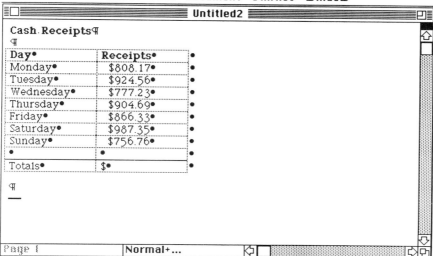

Word can total a column of numbers like the cash receipts shown in this table.

FIGURE 13-68

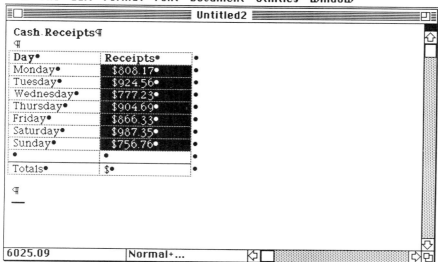

Word displays the result of its calculation in the status box at the lower-left corner of the screen.

FIGURE 13-69

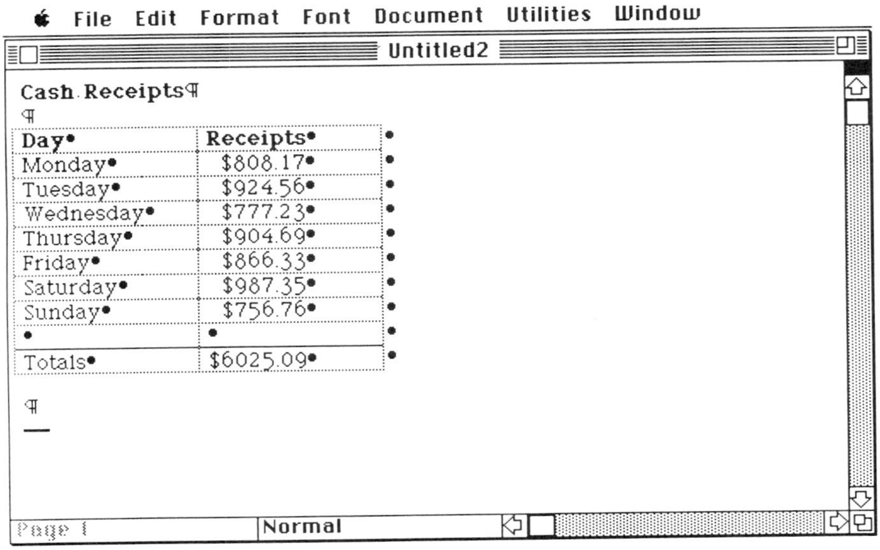

You can paste the result of your calculations into the worksheet.

Since Word ignores alphabetic characters, rather than selecting only the cells that contain the numbers you want to sum, you could select entire rows in the table shown in Figure 13-68 before pressing ⌘-=. Of course, when a table contains more than one column of numbers, you must be sure that you select only the numbers that you want to include in the calculation.

Word also ignores blank spaces and most punctuation and special markup characters like ?, #, @, ¶, and ↵ when you perform a mathematical calculation. There are a few exceptions to this, such as commas, periods, and the +, -, *, /, and % characters. For example, if a value is enclosed in parentheses—(100), for instance—Word treats that value as a negative number.

If you include commas between numbers—as in 100,100—Word will consider those numbers a single value. That's because Word treats commas as separators, dividing hundreds from thousands, thousands from millions, and so on. If a space appears before or after a comma, however, Word will treat the numbers as two separate values.

Similarly, if you include a period between two numbers—as in 100.25—Word will interpret the numbers as a single value since it recognizes the period as a decimal point. Again, if you enter a space before or after the decimal point, Word will ignore the period character and treat the numbers as two separate values. If any of the values you are using in your calculations contain commas and/or decimal points, Word will display commas and/or decimal points in the result as well.

The +, -, *, /, and % characters serve as mathematical operators when you are performing calculations in Word. As you might have guessed, the + character, which is optional, tells Word that you want to add a series of values, while the - sign tells Word that you want to subtract. The * and / signs indicate multiplication and division, respectively. The % operator tells Word that you want to calculate a percentage.

When you want to add numbers in columns or rows, you can do so without typing the + operator. Word assumes that you want to add numbers if you don't specify an operator. (If you want to subtract, but don't want to type a - operator or if you anticipate adding and subtracting in the same calculation, you can type numbers in parentheses. As we said, parentheses signify negative numbers.)

Other Calculations

To perform calculations other than addition, you must enter mathematical operators into your document. For example, to multiply 10 times 2, you would type

    10*2

in your document, select those characters, and press ⌘-=, or choose Calculate from the Utilities menu. Word will display the result, 20, in the status box. As with addition calculations, Word also will place the result on the Clipboard so that you can paste it anywhere in your document by clicking on that spot and selecting Paste from the Edit menu or by typing ⌘-v.

When you use the +, -, *, /, and % operators in your calculations, keep in mind that Word performs its calculations from left to right and from top to bottom. The program does not assign any precedence to the different mathematical operators. If you were to use the ⌘-= technique to calculate the result of an entry like

    10-8*2+15

in your document, you might expect Word to multiply the values 8 and 2 first, thereby reducing the formula to

    10-16+15

to return the value 9. Instead, Word will perform the operations in the order of their appearance and return the value 19. In other words, the program simply takes the calculation arguments in order, like this:

    10 - 8 = 2
    2 * 2 = 4
    4 + 15 = 19

You might be tempted to enclose parts of your formulas in parentheses or brackets to control the order of operations. Unfortunately, Word will ignore any separator characters like these when you use them to isolate portions of your formulas. For example, Word will ignore your parentheses in the formula

10-(8*2)+15

As we mentioned earlier, however, when you place constant numeric values (rather than mathematical formulas) in parentheses, Word will treat the value in parentheses as a negative number. Therefore, Word *will* recognize the parentheses in the formula

10+(8)*2+15

The result of this formula will be identical to the result of the formula

10-8*2+15

To give you a feel for Word's calculation techniques, Table 13-1 shows some sample formulas that you might enter into your Word documents and the result of each.

Notice that you enter the +, -, * and / operators in front of the number you want to add, subtract, multiply or divide by. However, you enter the % sign directly after the number you want it to apply to. Thus, you would use the formula

18%*70

to determine that 18 percent of the value 70 is equal to 12.6. When you place a % sign after a value, Word converts that value to a decimal by dividing by 100. Thus, the formula above is equivalent to

.18*70

Similarly, the formula

20%+5

is equal to

.2+5

TABLE 13-1

Formula	Result
5*4+3	23
4+3*5	35
3+4*5	35
10*(9)	-90
10*9	90
10+(9)	1
10-9	1
10/9	1
10%*6	0.6
10%+6	6.1
10%+10%	.2

This table lists sample formulas you might enter into a Word document and the result of each.

CHARACTER FORMULAS

Another exciting and unique feature of Word is its ability to create special characters using "character formulas." With character formulas, you can create complex scientific and mathematical formulas, such as

$$\int \frac{dx}{x^2 \sqrt{27x^2 + 6 - 1}}$$

that are integrated right into your document. Character formulas can be useful to nearly any writer, not just those with a technical or scientific bent. With a little imagination, you can use character formulas to create a tremendous variety of special symbols and to present ordinary text in an unusual way.

The General Form of Character Formulas

Each character formula begins with a special character, $\backslash$, which tells Word that the next few characters should be interpreted as a formula instead of literal characters. You create the $\backslash$—which looks like a backslash with a period under it—by pressing Option-⌘-$\backslash$. The $\backslash$ is followed by one or more commands, each of which requires one or more arguments. The commands tell Word what action you want to perform, and the command arguments indicate the character or characters to be acted upon. A command's argument(s) must always be enclosed in parentheses.

For example, the Box command is represented by $\backslash$ and the letter *X*. This command draws a box or border around the character(s) that you specify in the command's argument. Figure 13-70 shows an example of the Box command on the screen. In the upper screen of this figure, you see the actual formula, while the lower screen displays the formula result.

FIGURE 13-70

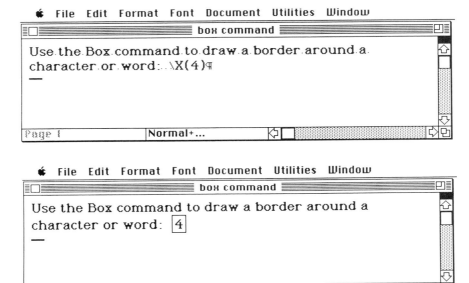

This screen shows an example of a simple character formula. Notice that the command \X draws a border around the argument, 4.

With some commands, you can include options that affect how the command is carried out. When you use an option with a command, that option must be entered after the command name and before the command argument. In addition, you must precede the option with the formula character \ . If you use more than one option, then each option must be preceded with a \ .

For example, when you use the Box command, you can include options that tell Word to draw only the top, bottom, right, or left edge of the box. You also can combine these options so that Word draws just the parts of the box you specify, such as the top and right edges. In a few cases, an option will require its own "argument"—a character that precisely defines how that option should affect the formula. We will describe these "option arguments" where appropriate as we explain each of Word's formula commands.

To summarize, then, the basic form of a character formula is

$\backslash C \backslash On(a1,a2,\ldots an)$

where $\backslash$ is a special formula character; C is the command itself; O is the command option; n is the option's argument; and $a1$, $a2$, and so forth are the command's arguments.

You can enter a character formula anywhere in a document. Begin by typing the special character $\backslash$, then enter the formula's components. You can use either uppercase or lowercase letters for the formula commands and options. When you enter your command arguments, however, be sure that you use the capitalization and formatting you want to appear in the final result. For example, if you want your formula result to display a superscripted character, then you must apply the Superscript format to that character as you're creating the formula.

Word will not display any formula results on your screen until you choose Hide ¶ from the Edit menu. As long as Show ¶ is active, you will see only character formulas, not results. In Figure 13-70, we chose Show ¶ to create the upper screen where the formula is displayed. We used Hide ¶ to display the formula result in the lower screen.

When you print a document that includes formulas, Word will always print formula results. If you enter a formula incorrectly, Word will not be able to evaluate the formula and will not display or print the formula result.

While Show ¶ is active, you can edit and format any of the individual components of a formula. For example, you can select one of the arguments and assign it a different font or size. Of course, any changes like this will affect the appearance of the formula result.

Although you can edit the individual characters in a formula while Show ¶ is active, Word generally considers the formula result to be a single character. Therefore, when you choose Hide ¶, it's usually not possible to cut, copy, or otherwise alter only part of the formula result. In addition, Word requires that a formula's displayed result fit on a single line. (The formula itself can be as long as you want; Word will wrap the formula from one line to another if necessary.) If the displayed result is too long to fit on a single line, then Word will not be able to evaluate the formula. There are a couple of simple ways to get around this length limitation, should you encounter it. First, you may want to enter extremely long formulas as individual paragraphs, rather than integrating them into your text. When you do this, you can change the right indent of any formula paragraphs, as needed. Another solution is to break up a long formula into two or more separate formulas so that each formula's result occupies no more than one line.

Character formula rules

Character Formula Commands

Word offers ten commands you can use to build character formulas. Although you often will use only a single command to achieve a certain result, you can combine different commands in a single formula, and embed one command within the argument of another command. In our examples, we will show you each command in an isolated situation, except in cases where a command is designed specifically to be used with another command.

The Overstrike (\O) command

The Overstrike command, \O, causes two or more characters to appear in the same space. The form of this command is

\O(a1,a2,…an)

where *a1*, *a2*, and so on, represent the characters you want to appear "on top of" one another. Each argument can be as short as one character or as long as several words.

As an example of the Overstrike command, suppose you want to represent the "short" *e* sound, as in the word *pet*. You would like to print a lowercase *e* with a breve symbol (˘) over it. (In some fonts, such as Times and Helvetica, the breve symbol can be created by typing Shift-Option-period. It is not available in all fonts.) Figure 13-71 shows how you can use Word's Overstrike command to achieve the desired result.

FIGURE 13-71

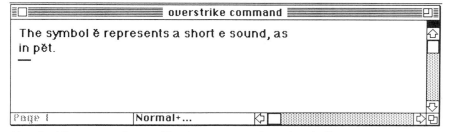

Use the \O command to position two or more characters in the same space.

The Overstrike command offers three options: AR, AL, and AC. These options, which stand for align right, align left, and align center, determine the placement of the character represented by the second argument relative to the character represented by the first argument. If you do not choose one of these options, Word will assume you want centered alignment (AC).

The Box command, \X, draws a border around the argument that you specify. Unlike the Borders options in the Paragraph Borders dialog box, you can apply the Box command to single characters. The Box command has the form

*The Box
(\X) command*

\X(a1)

where *a1* is the character(s) you want to draw the box around.

For example, suppose you want the name of your company, *National Systems Corporation*, to appear in 14-point Helvetica type with a border around it. Figure 13-72 shows a formula that achieves this result.

FIGURE 13-72

You can use the \X command to draw a border around several words.

The Box command can accept only one argument. If you want the argument to include a comma, you must precede that comma with the \ symbol. Otherwise, Word will think you are trying to enter more than one argument and will not be able to evaluate the formula. In cases where your argument must contain a lot of commas, you would be better off embedding the List (\L) command within your argument for the Box command, rather than typing a separate \ for each comma. We'll explain the List command later.

The Box command can accept four options: TO, BO, LE, and RI. These stand for top border, bottom border, left border, and right border, respectively. You use one or more of these options when you want to draw only a partial border around your argument. You can combine these options in any way.

The Fraction
(\F) command

The Fraction command does exactly what you would expect: It creates a fraction using the arguments you specify as the numerator and denominator. The form of the Fraction command is

\F(a1,a2)

where *a1* is the numerator and *a2* is the denominator. The Fraction command does not accept any options. Figure 13-73 shows an example of this command.

FIGURE 13-73

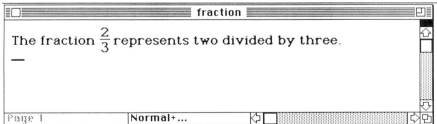

The .\F command creates a fraction using the arguments you specify for the numerator and denominator.

The numerator and denominator arguments do not have to be simple whole numbers, like those used in Figure 13-73. You can use complex formulas, such as $4x^2+12y-23$, or even text as either the numerator or denominator.

The Radical command, \R, draws a radical or "square root" symbol. The form of the command is

\R(a1,a2)

The second argument is optional. If you use only one argument, then that argument will be placed inside the radical to create a square root. If you use two arguments, then Word will place the second argument ($a2$) inside the radical and will place the first argument ($a1$) above the radical to indicate the root being computed. For example, Figure 13-74 shows a formula that displays the square root of 100 and another formula that displays the cube root of 100.

The Radical (\R) command

FIGURE 13-74

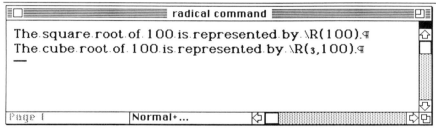

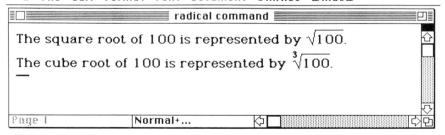

Use the \R command to display the radical symbol in a mathematical formula.

When you use the second argument with the Radical command, you may want to change the point size of the first argument (as we've done in Figure 13-74) so that the exponent outside the radical symbol is smaller than the number inside the radical.

The Array (\A) command

The Array command creates a two-dimensional array using the arguments you specify. The simplest form of the array command is

\A(a1,a2,a3,...an)

The arguments, *a1*, *a2*, and so forth, are the elements of the array you want to create. The simple form of the Array command creates a one-column array with the elements centered on top of one another. Figure 13-75 shows an example of the Array command. Notice that Word stacks the elements, with the first argument, *10*, at the top of the stack.

FIGURE 13-75

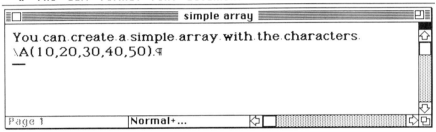

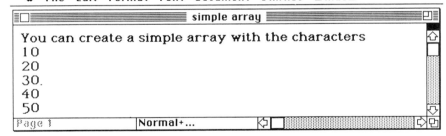

In its simplest form, the \A command will create a one-column array.

There are several options you can use with the Array command to control the number of columns in an array and to control the spacing and alignment of array elements. If you want to create a multicolumn array, you must use the CO*n* option, where *n* is a number that indicates how many columns you want to include in the array.

There also are options you can use with the Array command to control both the horizontal and vertical spacing of the array elements. Normally, Word does not place any space between the columns of an array. In addition, the amount of space between the rows in an array is equal to the leading of normal lines of text. The HS*n* option controls horizontal spacing and the VS*n* option controls vertical spacing. In both cases, *n* is a whole number that indicates the amount of space, in points, that you want to add between the rows or columns of the array. For example, if you use the HS1 option, Word will add one point of space between the rows of the array. This one point is in addition to the normal space that appears between characters. Similarly, if you use the VS1 option, Word will add one point of space between the columns.

There are three more options you can use with the Array command to control the alignment of characters within the columns of the array: AL, AR, and AC which stand for align left, align right, and align center, respectively. If you do not use an alignment option, Word will create an array with left alignment.

The Integral
(\I)command

The Integral command, \I, is used to draw integrals, summations, products, or any other formulas that take a similar form. The simplest form of this command is

\I(a1,a2,a3)

where *a1* is the lower limit, *a2* is the upper limit, and *a3* is the integrand character. Figure 13-76 on the next page shows a simple example of the Integral command. To enhance the appearance of the resulting integral formula (in the lower screen), we assigned a smaller point size to the first two arguments of the command.

The Integral command offers a couple of options that allow you to display a summation symbol, Σ, or a product symbol, π, instead of the integral symbol, $\int$. To create a summation formula, use the SU option in your integral formula. To create a product formula, use the PR option.

You are not limited to the $\int$, Σ, and π symbols when you use the Integral command. By adding the FC or VC option to your formula, you can use any character on the keyboard in place of the default $\int$ symbol. The FC option indicates a character of fixed height: Whatever character you type in the formula is the character Word will use in the resulting formula display. The VC option, on the other hand, indicates a character of variable height. Word will change the size of the character you type to correspond to the size of the third argument in the formula. This option is particularly appropriate in cases where the third argument of the \I command is a fraction. When you use either the FC or VC option, you must type a \ before the option, then type another \ before the character you want to substitute for the $\int$ symbol.

There's one more option you can use with the \I command: IN. This option changes the placement of the first two arguments in the formula result. Instead of the first two arguments appearing above and below the integral symbol (or whatever other symbol you use in the formula), the IN option causes them to appear to the right of the integral symbol in "inline" format.

FIGURE 13-76

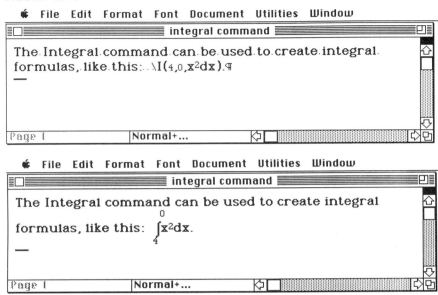

These screens show the \I command in its simplest form.

The Superscript/ Subscript (\S) command

In its simplest form, the Superscript/Subscript (\S) command appears as:

\S(a1)

This command positions the single argument that you specify as a superscript.

For example, Figure 13-77 shows a formula in which we've created a super-scripted 2. In this example, the *10* at the beginning of the formula is not really part of the formula; it merely serves as the "base" for the superscripted 2. (By the way, we lowered the point size of the *2*, in order to enhance the appearance of the formula result.)

When you use the \S command with no options, Word will superscript the argument you specify by three points. If you want to superscript the argument by a different number of points, you can insert an UP*n* option in the formula, where *n* is the number of points by which you want to superscript the argument.

The DO*n* option lets you create a subscript instead of a superscript. Again, *n* is the number of points by which you want to subscript the argument.

Whenever you use either the UP*n* or the DO*n* option, you must specify an *n* value. Otherwise, Word will assume an *n* value of zero and will not superscript or subscript your argument.

FIGURE 13-77

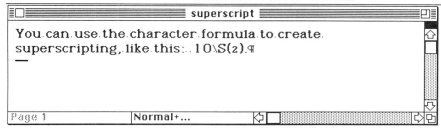

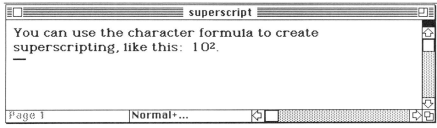

You can use the \S command to create superscripting.

You probably are wondering why anyone would ever use the Superscript/ Subscript command instead of simply choosing Character... from the Format menu and clicking the Superscript or Subscript option. There's really only one difference between using the Superscript/Subscript command and assigning the Superscript or Subscript format from the Character dialog box. The \S command can accept more than one argument, and when you use two or more arguments, Word will superscript the first argument and then "stack" the additional arguments in a column under the first argument. When you use multiple arguments with the \S command, the command will not recognize any UPn and DOn options. There- fore, there's no point in using the UPn and DOn options when your \S command has more than one argument.

The Displace (\D) command allows you to move characters forward or backward by a specified number of points. The Displace command is different from other commands in two important ways. First, it does not accept any arguments. Instead of acting upon an argument, this command always displaces the characters that immediately follow the command. Nevertheless, you must place a pair of parentheses after the Displace command.

The Displace (\D) command

Another important feature of the Displace command is that it requires an option. There are three possible options you can use with this command: FO*n*, BA*n*, and LI. The FO*n* option moves characters forward on the line by *n* points. Similarly, the BA*n* command moves characters backward by *n* points. The LI option draws a line between the character just before the \D command and the character just after the \D command. The LI option must always be used with either the FO*n* or BA*n* option.

The main purpose of the Displace command is to give you precise control over the placement of characters on a line. For example, suppose you want to create exactly $\frac{1}{4}$ inch (or 18 points) of space between two words on a line. Figure 13-78 shows a formula that does this. Notice that we used the FO18 option with this formula to create the 18 points of space.

FIGURE 13-78

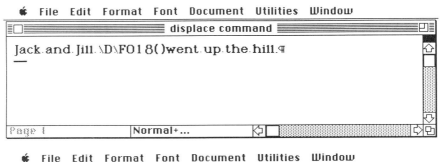

*Use the \D command with the FO*n* option to insert a precise amount of horizontal space on a line.*

The FO*n* option moves all characters that follow the Displace command in the current paragraph forward *n* points. If the *n* value for the FO option is large enough, some characters on the current line will wrap to the next line. This may cause characters on the next line to wrap to another line as well.

The BA*n* option moves all characters that follow the Displace command in the same paragraph backward *n* points. Because the Displace command does not affect the characters that come before the command, the displaced characters will probably overwrite other characters on the same line. If the *n* value that you specify is large enough, the displaced characters will be placed to the left of the beginning of the line. However, the displaced characters won't "wrap up" to the previous line. Instead, they'll be placed in the blank area of your screen beyond the left margin. If you want to view the displaced characters, you must press Shift and click the left arrow in the horizontal scroll bar so that this part of your screen comes into view.

The LI option simply draws a line in the space you create with the Displace command. When you use the LI option with the FO*n* option, Word underlines the space created by the FO*n* option. If you use the LI option with the BA*n* option, Word will draw the line under the characters that have been displaced by the BA*n* option.

The Bracket (\B) command encloses its argument in the bracketing character you specify. In its simplest form, the Bracket command looks like this:

*The Bracket
(\B) command*

\B(a1)

This command places parentheses around the argument, *a1*. For example, the command *\B(ABC)* will enclose the string ABC in parentheses, like this: *(ABC)*.

You probably are wondering why you would use the Bracket command instead of simply typing parentheses. This command is essential when you are building a formula and you want one of your arguments to appear in parentheses in the formula result. If you simply type the parentheses, you could confuse another command in the formula. For example, suppose you want to create the fraction $^3/_4$ surrounded by parentheses. If you type the parentheses as part of the argument for the \F command, you'll create an invalid formula. Figure 13-79 on the following page shows the correct way to create the fraction $^3/_4$ surrounded by parentheses. Notice that in the formula result, Word altered the size of the parentheses to be compatible with the height of the fraction.

The BC option allows you to use bracketing characters other than parentheses. The BC option is always followed by \ and the character that you want to use for bracketing. When you use this option, you need to specify only the opening (or left bracket) character—such as { or [—and Word will supply the closing bracket character.

The LC and RC options allow you to place a bracket character on only the left or right of the argument. The LC option places the bracket character you specify on the left side of the argument. Similarly, the RC option places the bracket character you specify on the right side of the argument. As with the BC option, each of these options must be followed by a \ and the character you want to use.

FIGURE 13-79

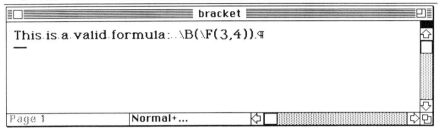

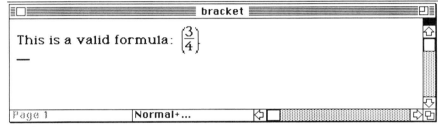

The \B command allows you to display parentheses in a formula result.

The List (\L) command

The List command, like the Bracket command, is designed to be used with other commands. This command simply creates a list, separated by commas, of the arguments you specify. In its simplest form, the List command looks like this:

    \L(a1,a2,...an)

and its result is simply a list of items separated by commas. Since Word normally interprets a comma as an argument separator, the List command comes in handy whenever you want to use a list of items as a single argument. For example, suppose you want to create a list of numbers with a box drawn around the list. Since the Box (\X) command can accept only one argument, the formula \X(10,20,30,40,50) is invalid. As you can see, Figure 13-80 shows how the List command can be used to overcome this limitation.

FIGURE 13-80

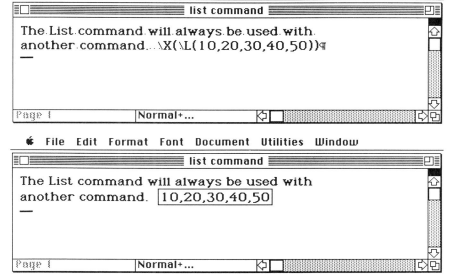

You can use the \L command when your formula result must display items separated by commas.

CUSTOMIZING WORD 14

One of the most useful features of Word 4 is the ability it gives you to customize menus and other program features. You can customize selections on any of Word's menus as well as create a special custom menu called the Work menu. In addition, a new feature in Word 4 is the Commands... command on the Edit menu, which allows you to place any command, feature, or action on any menu and alter the keyboard equivalents of any command.

The main benefit of custom menus and keyboard techniques is that they greatly speed certain tasks that normally require you to open a dialog box. You often can bypass dialog boxes when the option you need to use can be selected from a menu or invoked by pressing a series of keys.

For example, normally the process of superscripting text involves the following steps: First, you select the text you want to appear in superscripted format. Then, you choose Character... from the Format menu. When the Character dialog box is open, you click the Superscript option and enter the number of points for superscripting in the By edit bar (or you can use the default By setting of 3 points). Finally, you click OK to apply the Superscript format and close the dialog box.

Instead of performing all these steps, you can make Superscript an option on your Format menu. (The menu item will specify by how many points you want to superscript, such as *Superscript 3 pt.*) Then, to apply superscripting, all you have to do is select the text you want to format and choose the Superscript option from the Format menu.

Almost all of the check box options, radio button options, or dropdown list box options that appear in Word's dialog boxes can be placed on a menu and/or assigned a series of keystrokes. Generally, you cannot place on a menu, or assign a keystroke series to, the settings that you enter in an edit bar of a dialog box (such as the From Top and From Right settings for automatic page numbers). However, there are some exceptions.

Word also lets you create menu items from the formatting options that are represented by ruler icons and the actions that are invoked by the icons in the outline window. For example, you can create a menu item called Flush Right, which applies right-aligned formatting to a paragraph.

In addition to placing custom options on Word's built-in menus, you can add menu items to a special menu called the Work menu. The Work menu does not appear on your screen until you have placed at least one item on that menu. Typically, the options that you add to the Work menu will not be items that appear in Word's standard dialog boxes. The Work menu will include items that you have created, such as glossary terms, named styles from the style sheet, and file names.

In this chapter, we'll show you how to customize Word's menus and keystroke assignments. We'll also explain the Word Settings (4) file, which stores most of Word's default settings, and we'll describe how you can create other configuration files to store additional sets of defaults. Similarly, we'll show you how to create more than one file for storing standard glossary entries (those glossary entries that Word loads automatically each time you open a document). Finally, this chapter will offer some tips on creating and using document templates.

Before you can take advantage of customizing in Word, you must select Full Menus from the Edit menu. Until you activate the Full Menus setting, you won't be able to add or delete menu items, view any custom menu items you added previously, display the Work menu, or access the Commands... command. Interestingly, if you've removed one of Word's default selections from a menu, that selection will reappear when you select Short Menus from the Edit menu if the selection appeared on Short Menus originally. In other words, Word always displays short menus as they appeared originally.

There are two techniques you can use to customize Word. First, you can use a series of keystrokes to create a new menu option, delete a menu option, or assign a new keystroke series to a command. You also can customize Word with the Commands... command on the Edit menu.

Generally, using the keyboard to customize Word is faster and easier than using the Commands... command. However, the Commands... command gives you more flexibility in designing your own menus and keystroke assignments.

We'll begin our discussion by examining how you can customize menus from the keyboard. We'll include a separate discussion showing you how to create and use the Work menu. Then, we'll show you a keyboard technique for creating your own keystroke assignments. After this, we'll look at Word 4's new Commands... command.

Regardless of which menu you want to customize, the keyboard techniques for adding and deleting items are the same. To add an item, you press the Option and ⌘ keys as you type an equal sign (Option-⌘-=). This will cause the I-beam pointer temporarily to assume the shape of a bold plus sign (✚). Using this special pointer, you perform all the steps that you normally would in executing a certain task. Generally, this will involve opening a dialog box and clicking a selection. Once you've done this, the pointer will resume its normal shape, and you can click OK or Cancel to close the dialog box. If you choose OK, Word will execute the option you've just selected. If you choose Cancel, on the other hand, Word will close the dialog box. However, the option you selected will still appear as a new menu item on the menu to which you assigned it.

By the way, the Word manual instructs you to press the Option, ⌘, and + keys when you want to add an item to a menu. Although + and = occupy the same key on your keyboard, the + requires that you hold down the Shift key. If you press Shift along with Option, ⌘, and =, Word will neither accept your keystrokes nor convert the pointer to the bold plus shape. Therefore, to avoid confusion, we tell you to type Option-⌘-= when you need to add a menu option.

If, after you press Option-⌘-=, you decide that you do not want to add a menu item, press the ⌘ and period keys to cancel (⌘-.) or press the Esc key. The pointer will then return to its normal appearance.

It's possible to add so many items to a menu (particularly the Format menu) that not all of the options will be visible when you click on that menu choice. Word will display a ▼ at the bottom of the visible menu to let you know that more options are available. You can view the options at the bottom of the menu by dragging the pointer beyond the lower edge of the menu. Of course, if a menu gets lengthy, you may want to delete some of its options.

If you want to add two or more similar items to a menu, you don't need to close and reopen a dialog box for each item. After you've added one item, you can press Option-⌘-= while the dialog box is still open. When the pointer assumes the bold plus shape, click on the next item you want to add to a menu. This technique can be especially helpful when you're adding several Character formatting options to the Font and/or Format menus.

Suppose you want to add the options Small Caps and All Caps to your Format menu. You can press Option-⌘-=, issue the Character... command, and click the Small Caps option. Then, without closing the Character dialog box, you can press Option-⌘-= again and click the All Caps option. When you close the dialog box and click on the Format menu, you'll see that it contains both of these options.

Now that we've considered the general technique you use to add items to a menu, let's look more closely at how you go about adding various options to the Format, Font, Document, and Edit menus. After this, we'll consider the Work menu in detail.

CUSTOMIZING MENUS FROM THE KEYBOARD

Adding Character Formatting Options

We've just seen one example of how you can add options in the Character dialog box to the Format menu. You follow a similar procedure to place any of the other Character dialog box options on a menu. Suppose you want to add the Double Underline option to the Format menu. You would press Option-⌘-=, then use the bold plus pointer to open the Character dialog box and choose Double from the dropdown list of underlining options. (Alternatively, you can use the regular arrow pointer to open the Character dialog box and then press Option-⌘-= to switch to the bold plus pointer and select the Double Underline option.)

If you want to add one of the Position options (Superscript and Subscript) or one of the Spacing options (Condensed or Expanded) to the Format menu, you must follow a slightly different procedure. Each of these options requires a numeric setting that tells Word exactly how you want to apply the option. When you create a new menu item from one of these options, that item will include a numeric setting. For example, if you add the Subscript option to the Format menu, the menu item will specify by how many points you want to subscript, such as *Subscript 6 pt*.

To create a Position or Spacing menu item that uses Word's default numeric argument, you can follow the standard procedure for adding that option to the Format menu. For example, suppose you want your Format menu to include an option that will superscript text by 3 points. You would press Option-⌘-=, open the Character dialog box, and click the Superscript option. As soon as you click Superscript, Word will enter *3 pt* in the By edit bar, next to the Superscript option. Also, the pointer will resume its normal shape, which indicates that the option you clicked—and its default numeric argument—have been added to the Format menu. You can complete the procedure by clicking Cancel or OK.

If you want to add to the Format menu a Position or Spacing option that uses a numeric argument other than Word's default, you must follow a slightly different procedure. First, open the Character dialog box. Then, click the option you want to add to the menu. Next, replace Word's default setting in the By edit bar with the number you want to use. Without closing the dialog box, press Option-⌘-=, and use the bold plus pointer to click the option once more. Then, click OK or Cancel to close the dialog box.

For example, suppose you want to create a menu item for superscripting text by 4 points. First, choose Character... from the Format menu. Then, in the Character dialog box, click the Superscript option and type 4 in the By edit bar. Now, press Option-⌘-= and use the bold plus pointer to click the Superscript option once more. The pointer will resume its normal shape, and you can click OK or Cancel to complete the procedure. When you pull down the Format menu, you'll see that it includes the option *Superscript 4 pt*, as shown in Figure 14-1.

FIGURE 14-1

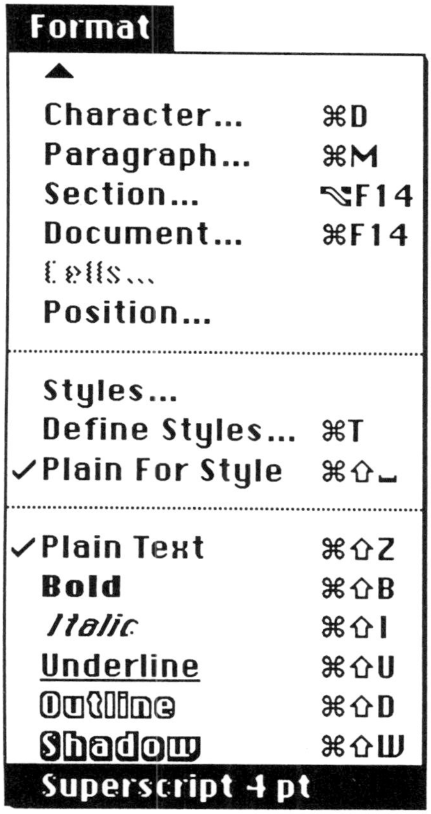

Format

Character...	⌘D
Paragraph...	⌘M
Section...	⌫F14
Document...	⌘F14
Cells...	
Position...	
Styles...	
Define Styles...	⌘T
✓Plain For Style	⌘⇧_
✓Plain Text	⌘⇧Z
Bold	⌘⇧B
Italic	⌘⇧I
Underline	⌘⇧U
Outline	⌘⇧D
Shadow	⌘⇧W
Superscript 4 pt	

This custom Format menu includes an item for superscripting text by 4 points.

When you use the Option-⌘-= technique to select a font name or size in the Character dialog box, Word will add your selection to the Font menu instead of the Format menu. For example, suppose you've installed the Palatino font on your System file and you want to place that font name on the Font menu. Begin by pressing Option-⌘-=. Then, open the Character dialog box and select Palatino from the dropdown list of fonts. The pointer will resume its normal shape, and you can click OK or Cancel to complete the procedure.

You can follow a similar procedure to add a font size to the Font menu. However, in adding font sizes, you are not limited to the standard sizes that appear

Font names and sizes

in the dropdown Size list. To add a nonstandard font size, you open the Character dialog box, type that size in the Size edit bar, then press Option-⌘-= and use the bold plus pointer to click on the new size.

Suppose you want to add the 8 Point font size to the Font menu. First, select Character... from the Format menu. Then, in the Character dialog box, type 8 in the edit bar that appears at the top of the Size list. Now, press Option-⌘-= to tell Word that you want to record a new menu option. Use the bold plus pointer to click on the 8 that you just entered in the Size edit bar. Once you do this, the pointer will change to the arrow shape that you normally see when a dialog box is open. You can then click Cancel or OK to close the Character dialog box. Figure 14-2 shows the Font menu with the 8 Point size added.

FIGURE 14-2

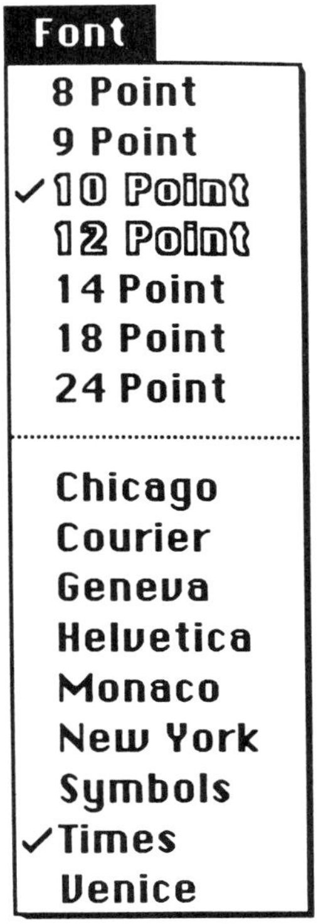

Font

8 Point
9 Point
✓10 Point
12 Point
14 Point
18 Point
24 Point

....

Chicago
Courier
Geneva
Helvetica
Monaco
New York
Symbols
✓Times
Venice

We've added the 8 Point size option to the Font menu.

Adding Paragraph Formatting Options

Adding paragraph formatting options to the Format menu is very similar to adding character formatting options. However, there are some special considerations that you need to keep in mind. First, some paragraph formatting options are controlled by ruler icons rather than by the Paragraph dialog box. You can add most of these options to the Format menu, where they will appear as words, not icons.

Second, Word won't let you create a menu item out of every ruler icon or every option in the Paragraph dialog box. On the ruler, each of the alignment icons, the line-spacing icons, and the open/close paragraph spacing icons can be made into menu options. You also can add the style names that appear in the dropdown style list box to the Work menu. You cannot create a menu item to control tab placement or to control placement of the vertical line.

In the Paragraph dialog box, you can create a menu item from any of the check box options (Page Break Before, Keep With Next ¶, Line Numbering, and Keep Lines Together). However, you cannot create menu items from any of the Indents and Spacing edit bar settings. Table 14-1 summarizes the paragraph formatting features that can be placed on the Format menu.

TABLE 14-1

You can add these Paragraph dialog box options to the Format menu...	
Page Break Before	Keep Lines Together
Keep With Next ¶	Tabs...
Line Numbering	Borders...
You also can create a Format menu option from these ruler icons...	
Left alignment icon	$1^1/_2$ line spacing icon
Centered alignment icon	Double line spacing icon
Right alignment icon	Close paragraph spacing icon
Justified alignment icon	Open paragraph spacing icon
Single line spacing icon	

This table summarizes the paragraph formatting options that you can add to the Format menu.

As you may know, you can access the Tabs dialog box or the Paragraph Borders dialog box by clicking on the Tabs... or Borders... button in the Paragraph dialog box. To speed the process of opening the Tabs and Paragraph Borders dialog boxes, you may want to create a menu item that allows you to open these dialog boxes directly. To do this, just press Option-⌘-=. Then, with the bold plus pointer, choose Paragraph... from the Format menu. In the Paragraph dialog box, click on the Tabs... or Borders... button. Word will add a new item to the Format menu (*Paragraph Borders...* or *Tabs...*) and return the pointer to its normal arrow shape. Word will not, however, open the Tabs or Paragraph Borders dialog box.

Any type of border that you can create in the Paragraph Borders dialog box can be added to the Format menu. However, none of the settings in the Tabs dialog box can be made into menu items. We'll show you how to add borders to the Format menu in a moment. First, however, let's look at an example of how you might add one of the formatting options on the ruler to your Format menu.

Adding ruler options

Suppose you want to be able to apply left alignment to a paragraph by selecting a menu item. Start by pressing Option-⌘-=. Then, if the ruler isn't currently displayed at the top of your window, use the bold plus pointer to choose the Show Ruler or Paragraph... command. Now, just click on the Left alignment icon on the ruler. When you click this icon, Word will add the option *Flush Left* to your Format menu. However, it will not apply left alignment to your current paragraph.

Adding border options

As we've mentioned, Word allows you to add any type of border to the Format menu. To do this, open the Paragraph dialog box, then click on the Borders... button to access the Paragraph Borders dialog box. In the Paragraph Borders dialog box, click on the type of border line you want to use (plain line, thick line, double line, dotted line, or hairline). Then, if you want to create some extra space between the border and the paragraph text, enter a number in the Spacing edit bar. Finally, press Option-⌘-= and use the bold plus pointer to select one of the border type options (Plain Box, Shadow Box, Outside Bar, or Custom). Word will add your border specifications to the Format menu and return the pointer to its normal arrow shape.

If you are creating a custom border, you'll need to click in the border diagram to indicate where you want your border lines to appear. When you click on the border diagram, Word will automatically select the Custom border option (if it's not already selected). Then, to add the custom border to your Format menu, press Option-⌘-= and use the bold plus pointer to click on the Custom option—even though it's already selected. (For a complete discussion of creating paragraph borders, see Chapter 5.)

When you look at the Format menu after adding a border, you'll see a new option like *TLB Thick Paragraph Border*. The capital letters at the beginning of the item indicate where the border lines will appear relative to your text. *T* indicates a line on top of the paragraph(s); *L* indicates a line to the left of the paragraph(s); *R* indicates a line to the right of the paragraph(s); *B* indicates a line below the paragraph(s); and *M* indicates a line between paragraphs.

The next part of the menu option indicates the type of line you have chosen for the border (single, thick, double, dotted, or hairline). If you specified a custom border with two or more line styles, Word will include only one line style in the name of the menu option, but will place a plus sign next to the line style (for example, *TLBR Single* +). If you entered a Spacing setting in the Paragraph Borders dialog box, that setting will not appear as part of the new menu item. However, Word will apply the spacing you specified when you choose that menu item.

Word also allows you to create menu items from most of the options in the Section dialog box. Table 14-2 summarizes the various Section settings that can be added to the Format menu.

TABLE 14-2

You can create a menu item from these Section dialog box settings...	
Start options in dropdown list	Columns Number setting
Page Number options:	Include Endnotes
Auto	Line Numbers options in
Restart At 1	dropdown list
Numbering schemes in	First Page Special
dropdown list	

This table summarizes the Section settings you can place on the Format menu.

Adding most of these options to the Format menu is simply a matter of pressing Option-⌘-= and choosing the option in the Section dialog box. For example, to be able to add page numbers to a document without opening the Section dialog box, you would create a menu item from the Auto Page Number option. Begin by pressing Option-⌘-=, then use the bold plus pointer to open the Section dialog box. In this dialog box, click on the Auto check box, then click OK or Cancel to close the dialog box and complete the procedure. If you now click on your Format menu, you'll see a new menu option, *Auto Page Numbering*. When you select this option, Word will number the pages of the current document using the numbering scheme that's currently selected in the Section dialog box. If you want, you can add the different numbering schemes on the Format menu. This will allow you to turn on automatic page numbering and select the type of page numbers you want to use without opening the Section dialog box.

The procedure for adding a Columns Number setting to the Format menu is similar to the procedure for adding one of the Position or Spacing options in the Character dialog box. First, you enter a Number setting in the edit bar. Then, you press Option-⌘-= and use the bold plus pointer to click on this setting.

As we explained in Chapter 10, when you format text to appear in more than one column, you also must enter a Spacing setting that specifies the amount of space you want to appear between columns. Unfortunately, Word is not able to "store" this setting as part of the menu item for columnar formatting. Therefore, when you've created a menu option for columnar formatting, that option will include the number of columns, but it will not tell you how much space will appear between columns. When you choose the new menu option for columnar formatting, the space between columns will be determined by the current Spacing setting in the Section dialog box.

For example, to create a new menu option specifying a three-column format, begin by choosing Section... from the Format menu. In the Section dialog box, replace the *1* in the Columns Number edit bar with *3*. Next, press Option-⌘-= to convert the pointer to a bold plus sign. Using this special pointer, click on the Number edit bar. Immediately, the pointer will resume its normal shape, and you can click OK or Cancel to complete the procedure. When you check the Format menu, you'll see that it now includes the option Columns 3, as shown in Figure 14-3. When you apply this option, however, the amount of space between the columns will be determined by the current setting in the Spacing edit bar of the Section dialog box. To use a different Spacing setting, you must open the Section dialog box and make the change manually.

FIGURE 14-3

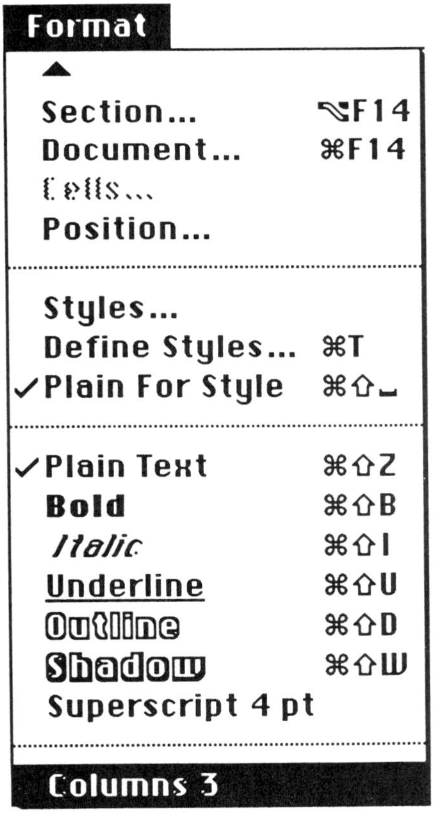

Format	
▲	
Section...	⍁F14
Document...	⌘F14
Cells...	
Position...	
Styles...	
Define Styles...	⌘T
✓ Plain For Style	⌘⇧␣
✓ Plain Text	⌘⇧Z
Bold	⌘⇧B
Italic	⌘⇧I
Underline	⌘⇧U
Outline	⌘⇧D
Shadow	⌘⇧W
Superscript 4 pt	
Columns 3	

This Format menu now includes an option for columnar formatting.

Word allows you to create a new item on the Edit menu from most of the check box options in the Preferences dialog box. To do this, follow the same procedure that we've described for adding other dialog box options to a menu. For example, suppose you want to create a menu item for activating the "Smart" Quotes feature. Begin by pressing Option-⌘-=, then use the bold plus pointer to choose the Preferences... command on the Edit menu. In the Preferences dialog box, just click the "Smart" Quotes option. When the pointer returns to its normal arrow shape, click OK or Cancel to close the dialog box.

Adding Preferences Dialog Box Options

You cannot create a menu option from the units that appear in the Default Measure dropdown list box at the top of the Preferences dialog box. Table 14-3 summarizes the various Preferences options that you can place on the Edit menu.

TABLE 14-3

Show Hidden Text	Open Documents in Page View
Use Picture Placeholders	Background Repagination
Show Table Gridlines	"Smart" Quotes
Show Text Boundaries	Keep Program in Memory Now
in Page View	Keep File in Memory Now

This table summarizes the Preferences dialog box settings that you can add to the Edit menu.

You can create a Document menu option from each icon that appears at the top of an outline window. When you create a menu item from one of these icons, the new item appears on the menu as a word(s) instead of as an icon. To add one of these icons to the Document menu, first choose the Outlining command on the Document menu to switch to the outline view. Then, press Option-⌘-= and use the bold plus pointer to click on an icon. Table 14-4 on the next page shows the menu option that Word will create from each Outliner icon.

Adding Outliner Options

Word also allows you to create options on the Document menu for inserting the current date, time, or page number in a document. To do this, just open a header or footer window. Then, press Option-⌘-= and use the bold plus pointer to click on the date, time, or page number icon that appears at the top of the window. Word will create a new Document menu item called *Insert Date*, *Insert Time*, or *Insert Page Number*.

Adding Date, Time, and Page Number Options

To remove an item from a menu, press the Option, ⌘, and minus keys simultaneously (Option-⌘--). The pointer will then assume the shape of a bold minus sign (▬). Just use this pointer to select the menu option you want to delete.

Deleting a Menu Option

As soon as you've deleted a menu item, the pointer will resume its normal appearance. If you decide that you do not want to delete a menu item after you press Option-⌘--, you can press ⌘-. or Esc to cancel.

TABLE 14-4

When you click this icon...	Word will create this menu option...
←	Promote Heading
→	Demote Heading
↑	Move Heading Up
↓	Move Heading Down
→»	Make Body Text
+	Expand Subtext
—	Collapse Subtext
1	Show Heading 1
2	Show Heading 2
3	Show Heading 3
4	Show Heading 4
▤	Show All Headings
ﬁ	Show/Hide Formatting
▦	Show/Hide Body Text

This table summarizes the menu commands you can create from Outliner icons.

By the way, in customizing your Word menus, you are not limited to deleting only the menu options you have added. You can also delete any of Word's default options. For example, you can remove one of Word's default font sizes, such as 10 Point, from the Font menu. When you remove a menu item, you can, of course, still access that option through a dialog box. For example, if you remove 10 Point from the Font menu, that size will still be available through the less convenient Character dialog box.

If you delete a menu item that is not available in a dialog box—for example, if you delete the Sort command from the Utilities menu—you can use the Commands... command to recover the item and restore it to the menu. You also can use Commands... to execute the deleted menu command. We'll discuss Commands... in detail a little later in this chapter.

Also, if you delete a menu command using the Option-⌘-- technique, you still can issue that command by using its assigned keystroke series. For instance, suppose you remove the Character... command from the Format menu. You'll still be able to open the Character dialog box by pressing ⌘-d.

THE WORK MENU

The Work menu is a special menu you can create to help speed the processes of opening files, inserting glossary text, and applying styles. It may include only one item, such as a glossary term, or it may contain many items, including file names, glossary terms, and style names. (Even though Word 4 lists style names on the ruler, you might want to hide the ruler as you're creating a document and keep the styles you most frequently use on your Work menu.)

Word arranges the items on your Work menu in three separate categories. Word will display file names first, glossary terms next, and style names last. A gray line separates the sections, and within each section, the menu items will be organized alphabetically. For example, Figure 14-4 shows a Work menu that includes two file names, a glossary term, and a style name.

FIGURE 14-4

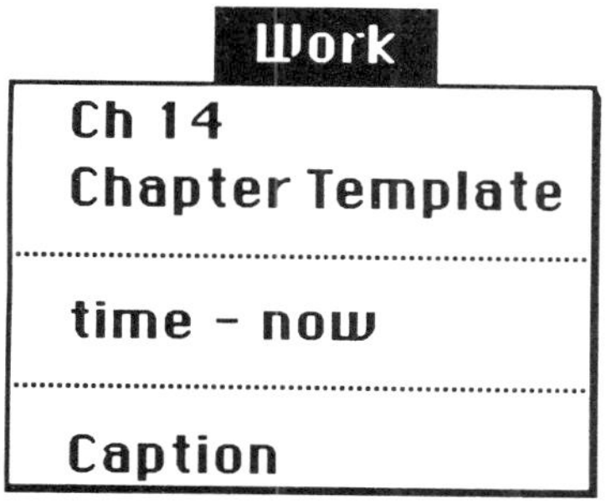

```
          Work
┌──────────────────────┐
│ Ch 14                │
│ Chapter Template     │
│ ....................  │
│ time - now           │
│ ....................  │
│ Caption              │
└──────────────────────┘
```

Word separates the items on the Work menu into three sections, placing file names first, glossary terms next, and style names last.

The procedures for adding file names, glossary terms, and style names to the Work menu are quite similar. To add a file name, begin by pressing Option-⌘-=, then choose Open... from the File menu. Click on the name of the file you want to place on the Work menu, then click the Open button. (You can open and close folders, as needed, to access a particular file name.) When you do, the pointer will resume its normal shape and Word will close the Open dialog box. Word will not open the file you select at this time, but will place its name on your Work menu.

To add a glossary term, press Option-⌘-=, then choose Glossary... from the Edit menu. In the Glossary dialog box, simply click on the term you want to add to the Work menu. Since the Glossary dialog box will remain open, you can press Option-⌘-= again and click on another term. To close the Glossary dialog box, click Cancel or click the close box.

To add a style name, again press Option-⌘-=. Then, use the bold plus pointer to select a style name from the dropdown list on the ruler. Word will add that name to the Work menu, and the pointer will resume its normal shape. Alternatively, you can use the bold plus pointer to open the Styles or Define Styles dialog box and click on a style name. As soon as you click on a style name in one of these dialog boxes, the pointer will resume its normal arrow shape, but the dialog box will remain open. If you want, you can press Option-⌘-= and select another style name to add to the Work menu.

Using the Work Menu

When you select an item from the Work menu, the results will be different, depending on whether you've chosen a file name, glossary term, or style name. If you select a file name, Word will open that file. If Word cannot find the file on one of your current disks, it will display a dialog box like the one in Figure 14-5.

FIGURE 14-5

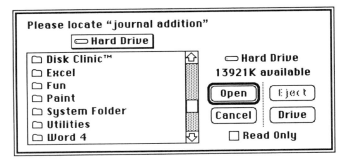

If you choose a file name from the Work menu and that file is not on one of your current disks, Word will display this dialog box.

If you select from the Work menu the name of a document file that's already open, Word will simply create a new window for that document. For example, suppose your Work menu contains a file named *Essay*. If that file is already open and you select Essay from the Work menu, Word will create a new full-screen window named *Essay:2* and rename the original Essay window *Essay:1*.

When you select a glossary term from the Work menu, Word will "type" the text for that term at the current insertion point location. For example, suppose your glossary contains the term *FY89*, which represents the text *Fiscal Year 1989*, and you've added this term to your Work menu. When you select FY89 from the Work menu, Word will insert the text *Fiscal Year 1989* at the current insertion point location, just as if you'd opened the Glossary dialog box, clicked on the term, and clicked the Insert button.

Similarly, when you select a style name from the Work menu, Word will apply that style to the current paragraph, just as if you had opened the Styles or Define Styles dialog box, clicked that style name, and clicked OK, or chosen the style from the dropdown list on the ruler.

Unfortunately, you cannot attach different Work menus to different documents. Unless you open a new configuration file, your Work menu will display the same options, no matter what document is active on the Word DeskTop. (Word stores the Work menu in the Word Settings (4) file or another configuration file. As we'll explain later, you can use the Commands… command to access different configuration files.)

Keep in mind that some of the items on the Work menu may be disabled in certain documents. Specifically, you cannot use a glossary term that appears on the Work menu unless you've opened the glossary file that contains that term. Similarly, you cannot use the Work menu to apply a style unless that style is on your current document's style sheet. If you select an item from the Work menu that Word is unable to use (such as a glossary term that's not in the current glossary), Word will just beep.

Because the Work menu will be the same in all documents, you may want to use identical glossary terms in different documents and identical style names in different document files. That way, you can get more mileage out of fewer menu options since the glossary terms and style names on your Work menu will have different effects, depending on which document you're working in and which glossary file(s) you've opened.

For example, suppose you've added the glossary term *im* to your Work menu. You've also created two different glossary files that contain this term. In one of the glossary files, this term represents the text *international markets*, while in another glossary file, the term stands for *interesting mistake*. When you choose *im* from the Work menu, Word will look at the entries in your current glossary to determine what text to insert in your document. If you've loaded the first glossary file, Word will insert the words *international markets*. If you've loaded the entries from the other glossary file, however, Word will insert the words *interesting mistake*. Of course, if you open both glossary files during the same Word session, the text that's represented by *im* will be the glossary text from the most recently opened glossary file. (See Chapter 13 for more on glossary files.)

Similarly, suppose several documents include a style named *Title*, which you've added to your Work menu. When you choose *Title* from the Work menu, Word will look at the definition of that style on your current style sheet to determine what set of formatting attributes to apply. In several documents, however, the *Title* style can be applied quickly from the Work menu, without opening the Styles or Define Styles dialog box or showing the ruler.

**CREATING
CUSTOM KEY
ASSIGNMENTS**

As you know, Word allows you to issue many commands and assign a number of formatting options simply by pressing a series of keys. For example, you can issue the Print... command by pressing ⌘-p, and you can assign italic formatting to selected text by typing Shift-⌘-i. In Word 4, you can create your own keyboard shortcuts. That is, you can assign a keystroke series to a command that does not have a preset keystroke assignment (such as the Sort command). You also can change the key assignments that have been set by Microsoft and remove any key assignments that you have created or that have been set by Microsoft. In order to remove a keystroke assignment, you must use the Commands... command, which we'll talk about in a moment.

Using just the keyboard, you can assign a keystroke series to any menu command—both Word's default menu commands and any new commands or options that you add to a menu. If you want, you can assign a second or third set of keystrokes to a command that already has a key assignment. However, Word will display only one keystroke series next to the command name on the menu.

To assign a keystroke series using the keyboard, press Option-⌘-+, using the + key on the numeric keypad. (Num. Lock must be turned off.) The pointer will then assume the shape of a bold ⌘ symbol. Using this pointer, select the command to which you want to assign a keystroke series. Word will then ask you to type the key combination that you want to use to invoke that command. As soon as you press the appropriate keys, Word will record the new keystroke assignment.

For example, suppose you frequently create documents that contain tables, requiring you to use the Insert Table... command on the Document menu. Word 4 does not come with a preset keystroke series for this command so you would like to create your own keystroke assignment using the ⌘ and \ keys. Begin by pressing Option-⌘-+ (using the + key on the numeric keypad). Then, click on the Document menu with the bold ⌘ pointer and choose the Insert Table... command. When Word displays the dialog box shown in Figure 14-6, press the ⌘-\ key combination. Word will record the new keystroke series and display it next to the command name on the menu, as shown in Figure 14-7.

FIGURE 14-6

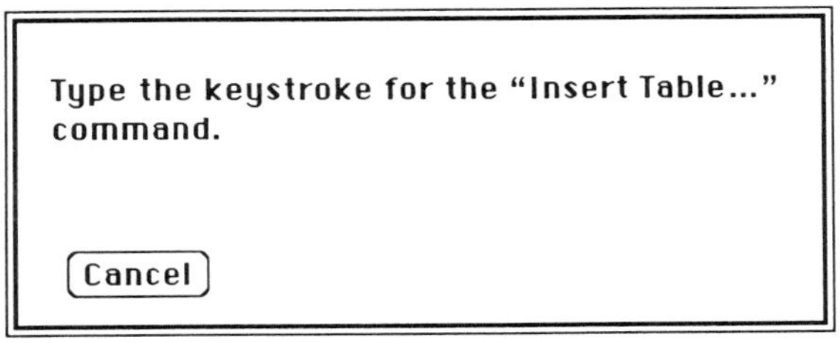

> **Type the keystroke for the "Insert Table..."
> command.**
>
> (Cancel)

*Word presents a
dialog box like this
when you select a
command with the ⌘
pointer.*

FIGURE 14-7

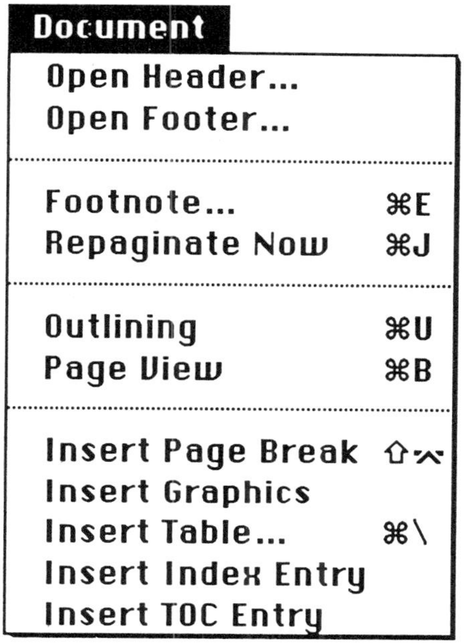

Document

Open Header...	
Open Footer...	
Footnote...	⌘E
Repaginate Now	⌘J
Outlining	⌘U
Page View	⌘B
Insert Page Break	⇧〰
Insert Graphics	
Insert Table...	⌘\
Insert Index Entry	
Insert TOC Entry	

The Document menu shows the new key assignment for the Insert Table... command.

By the way, if you type a keystroke series that already has been assigned, Word will display an alert box like the one shown in Figure 14-8. As you can see, Word gives you the choice of clicking OK, which will remove the keystroke series from the command to which it is currently assigned, or clicking Cancel. If you click Cancel, Word will return to the dialog box shown in Figure 14-6, where you can type a different key combination.

FIGURE 14-8

If you type a keystroke series that has already been assigned to a command, Word will display an alert box like this one.

Valid Key Combinations

As you would expect, Word reserves most of the keys on the Mac keyboard for typing characters. If you want to set up a sequence of keystrokes for invoking a command, you must use certain prescribed combinations. Any key combination that uses the main typing keys on the keyboard must include the ⌘ key. You can combine the ⌘ key with any character key, and you also can create keystroke combinations that use the ⌘ key, a character key, the Shift key, and/or the Option key. If you have a Mac SE or Mac II, you also can use the Control key in a keystroke series. Word won't let you use the Control key in a keystroke series unless you also include the ⌘ key in that series.

Word also lets you use the keys on the numeric keypad to assign a keystroke combination. (Num. Lock must be turned off in order to invoke a command using a key on the numeric keypad.) Your assignment might be a single key, or one of the keypad keys in combination with the Shift, Option, and/or ⌘ keys. Again, if you have a Mac SE or Mac II, you also can use the Control key in combination with one of the keys on the numeric keypad and/or the Shift, Option, and ⌘ keys. (The ⌘ key must be part of any keystroke series that uses the Control key.)

Finally, if you have an expanded keyboard, you can use the function keys ([F1], [F2], and so forth) in your keystroke assignments. Regardless of what key combination you specify, each keystroke assignment must use no more than four keys.

CUSTOMIZING WITH THE COMMANDS... COMMAND

Word 4 offers an accommodating new feature in the Commands... command. The Commands... command allows you to assign new commands to menus or remove commands from menus. It also lets you link any command, feature, or action that Word can perform to any valid key combination. You can even alter the menu selections and key combinations that Microsoft has preset for Word 4.

Commands... also enables you to save various configurations of custom menus, key combinations, and defaults in special configuration files. Through the Commands dialog box, you can access a new configuration file or return to Word's default configuration. We'll consider configuration files in detail a little later in this chapter.

Before you use Commands... , you should decide whether you prefer to use the mouse or the keyboard. If you like to use the mouse, you may want to assign new commands to your menus with the Commands... command. If you prefer to use the keyboard, then you may want to assign your own key combinations to certain commands or dialog box options. Of course, you can place a frequently used option on a menu and assign it a key combination as well.

When you first issue the Commands... command, a complex dialog box will appear on the screen. As you can see in Figure 14-9, a list box dominates the left side of the Commands dialog box. Here, you'll find all the features, commands, and actions that you can assign to menus or custom keystrokes.

FIGURE 14-9

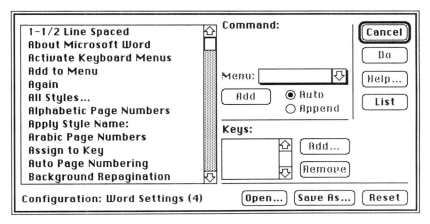

You'll see this dialog box when you issue the Commands... command.

When you highlight an item in the commands list, Word will display the name of that item beneath the word *Command* in the upper-right portion of the Commands dialog box. In addition, a menu name will appear in the edit bar at the top of the Menu list on the right side of the dialog box. If the item you highlighted already appears on one of Word's menus, the menu name will be displayed in dim video and a Remove button will appear below the Menu edit bar. On the other hand, if you highlighted an item that does not currently appear on a menu, the menu name will be undimmed and a button labeled Add will be activated below the Menu edit bar. Also, when you highlight an item in the list box, Word will display any keystroke series that has been assigned to that item in the Keys list box and activate the Add... button next to this list box.

Customizing Menus

Using the Commands dialog box, you can make a number of changes to Word's menus. You can add items, remove items, and move items from one menu to another. We'll begin our discussion by looking at the technique you use to add a command to a menu.

Adding an item to a menu

To add an item to a menu, first click on that item name in the list box on the left side of the Commands dialog box. As we've mentioned, Word will then display a menu name in the edit bar at the top of the Menu list. This is Word's suggested location for the item you selected. If you want to add the item to Word's suggested menu, just click the Add button. If you want to place the item on a different menu, click on the arrow next to the Menu edit bar to pull down the list of menu names. Then, select the menu you want to use.

For example, suppose you want to add the Double Underline option to a menu. When you select Double Underline from the list in the Commands dialog box, Word will display the menu name *Format* in the Menu edit bar, as shown in Figure 14-10. If you want this option to appear on the Format menu, just click the Add button. Suppose, however, you want the Double Underline option to appear on the Document menu. After you select Document from the dropdown list of menu names, as shown in Figure 14-11, click the Add button.

FIGURE 14-10

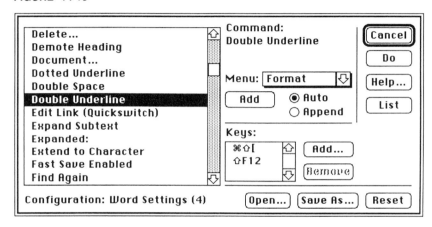

When you select an item from the list box, Word will suggest a menu for that item.

FIGURE 14-11

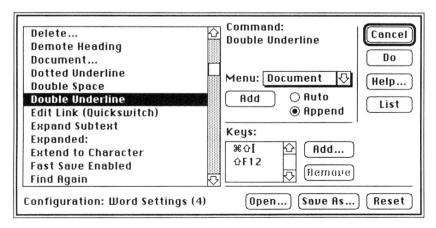

You can select a different menu for the new item.

Two radio buttons that appear below the Menu edit bar—Auto and Append— determine the location of a command on a menu. When you select the Auto option, Word will decide where on a menu a new item should appear. When you select the Append option, Word will add the new menu item to the bottom of the selected menu. If you are adding an item to the menu that Word suggests (the default menu), the Auto option will automatically be selected. You can, however, click on the Append option if you want to place the item at the bottom of the menu.

Whenever you choose a menu other than Word's suggested menu, Word will automatically select the Append option. For example, notice in Figure 14-11 that the Append option is selected. If you click the Auto option, Word will revert to the default menu name in the Menu edit bar. For instance, if we were to click the Auto button in the dialog box shown in Figure 14-11, Word would change the menu name to Format. In other words, whenever you place an item on a menu other than Word's suggested menu, that item will be added to the bottom of the menu.

As you scroll through the list in the Commands dialog box, you'll notice that a colon appears after some items. This colon indicates that you'll need to supply Word with some additional information in order to place that item on a menu. Word will prompt you for this information when you choose one of the items with a colon. For example, notice the *Apply Style Name:* item that appears in Figure 14-9. When you select this item, you must specify the name of the style you want to place on a menu. Figure 14-12 shows what happens when you click on Apply Style Name: in the Commands dialog box.

The Auto and Append options

Items displayed with a colon

FIGURE 14-12

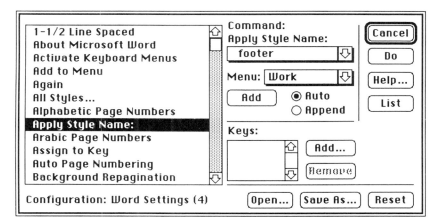

When you select an item that's followed by a colon, Word will prompt you for more information.

Notice in the upper-right portion of the dialog box that Word displays the name of the selected item (*Apply Style Name:*) and, under this, a dropdown list containing the names of all the styles in the current document. If a style already appears on the Work menu, Word will display a ◆ symbol next to its name in the list. You can select a style name from the dropdown list and then click the Add button. Word will place the selected style name on the Work menu. (Of course, you can select a different menu before clicking the Add button, if you want.)

In some cases, when you select an item that's followed by a colon, you will see a combination dropdown list box and edit bar. As you would expect, this allows you to select an item from the list or enter your own setting in the edit bar. For example, if you scroll down the list in the Commands dialog box, you'll see the item *Columns:*. When you select this item, Word will display a combination dropdown list box and edit bar. The list contains four options: Columns 1, Columns 2, Columns 3, and Columns 4. The edit bar simply displays a number—1, 2, 3, or 4. If you want to create a new menu item that specifies a number of columns other than those offered in the list—6, for example—just type that number in the edit bar and click the Add button. Word will then add the item *Columns 6* to the Format menu (or to a different menu, if you so choose).

If you select the Open File Name: item from the list in the Commands dialog box, Word will display a button labeled Open File…. When you click on this button, the Open dialog box will appear. Here, you can select the name of the file that you want to place on the Work menu (or another menu if you'd like). As we've mentioned, when you place a file name on the Work menu, you'll be able to open that file simply by selecting its name from the menu.

Creating a separator line on a menu

Besides adding commands to a menu, Word allows you to append separator lines. Separator lines are the gray lines that divide different categories of menu items. For example, a separator line appears between the Undo command and the Cut command on the Edit menu.

If you scroll to the end of the list of items in the Commands dialog box, you'll see an item called - - -*Separator*- - -. When you select this item, Word won't suggest a menu in the Menu edit bar. You must select the menu on which you want to place a separator line. Once you choose a menu name, you'll notice that Word selects the Append option and dims the Auto option. This indicates that the separator line will be appended to the end of the selected menu. Thus, if you want to create your own menu separators, you must first place them on the appropriate menu(s) and then append additional commands to that menu, below the separator line.

Adding all items to menus

Word offers a special technique for placing all the items listed in the Commands dialog box on the menus. After opening the Commands dialog box, hold down the Option key as you click the Reset button. Word will display the alert message *Are you sure you want to add all the commands to the menus?* If you click OK, Word will load the menus with all the items listed in the Commands dialog box. You can then remove selected items to pare the menus down to a more manageable size. (As we'll explain later, the Reset button serves a couple of other significant functions as well.)

After you have added commands to a menu or performed any other actions in the Commands dialog box, close it by selecting either the Cancel or Do button. When you choose Cancel, Word will close the dialog box. The Cancel button does not revoke any of the changes you have made to menus or key assignments.

When you click the Do button, Word will close the dialog box and carry out the command that's currently selected. For example, suppose you decide to add the command Paragraph Borders… to the Format menu. After selecting this item in the list and clicking the Add button, you can click the Do button to close the Commands dialog box. At the same time, Word will open the Paragraph Borders dialog box.

You can use the Do button to carry out any command in the list that appears in the Commands dialog box. For example, suppose you've opened the Commands dialog box and made several changes to your menus. You now want to return to your document and save it to disk. You can do this in one step by clicking Save in the list in the Commands dialog box and then clicking the Do button.

The Cancel and Do buttons

To remove an item from a menu, you follow a procedure similar to the one we've described for adding menu items. After opening the Commands dialog box, scroll down the list and click on the item you want to remove. As we've mentioned, when you select an item that already appears on a menu, Word will replace the Add button with a Remove button. You simply click this button to delete the menu item.

If you select an item that's followed by a colon, you will need to supply Word with additional information so that it knows exactly which menu option you want to delete. For example, suppose you want to remove the Columns 3 option from the Format menu. To do this, you would first select Columns: in the Commands list. Word will then display the combination dropdown list box and edit bar that contains the various Columns options. Next, select the Columns 3 option from the dropdown list and click the Remove button.

As we've mentioned, once you remove an item from a menu, you can still access that item from the keyboard (if it has a key assignment) or you can open the Commands dialog box to access the item. For example, suppose you remove the Paragraph… command from the Format menu, but you do not alter Word's default key assignments for that command (⌘-m and Shift-[F14]). You can still open the Paragraph dialog box by pressing either key combination. You also can access the Paragraph dialog box by opening the Commands dialog box, selecting Paragraph… in the list of commands, and then clicking the Do button.

Deleting a menu item

Moving a
menu item

To move an option from one menu to another, simply remove that option from its current menu and add it to another. For example, suppose you want to move the Page View command from the Document menu to the File menu. Begin by opening the Commands dialog box and selecting Page View from the list of commands. Word will display the menu name *Document* in the Menu edit bar and display the Remove button below this. Click the Remove button to take the command off the Document menu. Next, click on the arrow next to the Menu edit bar to pull down the list of menus. Select File from this list and then click the Add button. (Since the File menu is not the default menu for the Page View command, Word will append the command to the end of the menu.)

By the way, Word will not allow a command to appear on more than one menu at a time. Thus, you must always remove a command from its current menu before adding it to another.

Customizing Keystrokes

As we've mentioned, the Commands… command lets you assign your own keystroke series to Word's various commands, options, and features. Creating your own keyboard shortcuts is an excellent way to streamline procedures that you use frequently. In fact, you might think of the Commands dialog box as a mini-macro facility for programming your Mac's keyboard. In addition to creating new keystroke assignments, the Commands dialog box allows you to alter and remove the key assignments set by Microsoft.

Any item that can be placed on a menu can also be assigned a keystroke series. However, you don't need to place an option on a menu in order to assign it a keystroke series. For example, Word lets you assign a keystroke series to file names, glossary terms, and style names—items that typically appear on the Work menu. You also can assign a keystroke series to any font name or size and to any window name. None of these items needs to be placed on a menu in order to be assigned a keystroke series.

As you may recall, some items that are listed in the Commands dialog box require that you specify a numeric setting when you place them on a menu. For example, you can create menu options like *Columns 3* or *Superscript 2 pt*. Word also lets you assign keystroke series to this type of item.

Assigning a
keystroke series

To assign a keystroke series to a command or option, first select the item from the list of commands in the Commands dialog box. When you do this, Word will display any keystroke series that currently is assigned to that item in the Keys list box. If the item currently cannot be executed by a keystroke series, the Keys list box will be blank. When you click the Add… button next to the Keys list box, Word will display a message asking you to type the key combination you want to assign to the selected item (like the dialog box shown in Figure 14-6 on page 670). After you press the appropriate keys, Word will display the symbols for those keys in the list box.

As we mentioned briefly, the Commands dialog box allows you to assign a keystroke series to an option that does not appear on a menu. For example, suppose you want to create a keystroke series for invoking the Show Hidden Text option in the Preferences dialog box. You would begin by opening the Commands dialog box and selecting Show Hidden Text from the list box. As you can see in Figure 14-13, the Keys list box will initially be blank when you select this command. When you click the Add... button to the right of the Keys list box, Word will display an alert message similar to the one shown in Figure 14-6. At this point, you type the key combination you want to assign. For our example, we'll assume that you type ⌘-8. When you do this, Word will display that keystroke series in the Keys list box, as shown in Figure 14-14 on the next page.

FIGURE 14-13

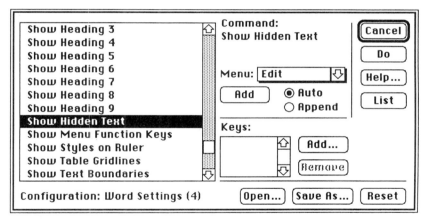

Initially, there are no keystrokes assigned to the Show Hidden Text option.

Word allows you to remove the keystroke assignment from any command. Not only can you remove the custom key assignments that you have created, you also can remove Word's preset keystroke assignments. The technique is simple. Just open the Commands dialog box and click on the item whose keystroke assignment you want to remove. When the keystrokes assigned to that command appear in the Keys list box, just click on the series you want to remove. (In some instances, more than one keystroke series will be displayed in the Keys list box.) Finally, click the Remove button, and Word will delete that keystroke series from the command and from the Keys list box. If you've deleted a preset key assignment for one of Word's menu commands, those keystrokes will no longer be displayed next to the command name on the menu.

Removing a keystroke assignment

FIGURE 14-14

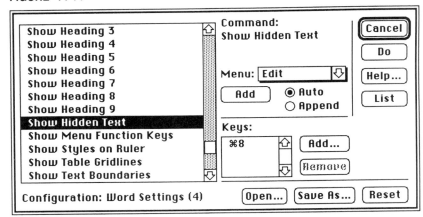

Word will display your new key assignment in the Keys list box.

Altering Word's preset key assignments

You don't have to accept the preset keystroke series that are assigned to Word's commands. You can add a new series of keystrokes to a command's default keystrokes or you can delete the default keystrokes and record an entirely different series.

To add another keystroke series to a command, follow the steps described in the previous section for assigning a keystroke series. Word will display your new keystroke series in the Keys list box below any existing keystroke assignments. It's a good idea to keep the choice of recorded keystrokes to a minimum. Since a keystroke series can be assigned to only one action, you probably will want to conserve the limited number of keystroke combinations so you can make new keystroke assignments later. In addition, when you allow more than one series of keystrokes to activate a command, Word will not list all of them beside the command name on the menu. Only the first keystroke series in the Keys list box will be displayed on the menu.

CREATING A TABLE OF COMMANDS

After customizing Word's menus and keystroke assignments, you may find it difficult to keep up with all the changes you've made. To help you keep track of your menu configurations and keystroke assignments, you may want to create a table of all commands and their associated keystroke assignments. Fortunately, Word automates this process for you. All you need to do is click the List button in the Commands dialog box. When you do this, Word will close the dialog box and create a new document containing a table that lists all the commands and keystroke assignments in the current configuration file. It may take Word several minutes to compile the table. Figure 14-15 shows how this table will look on the screen. Since this list is simply a Word document, you can use the Print... command to create a hard copy of it.

FIGURE 14-15

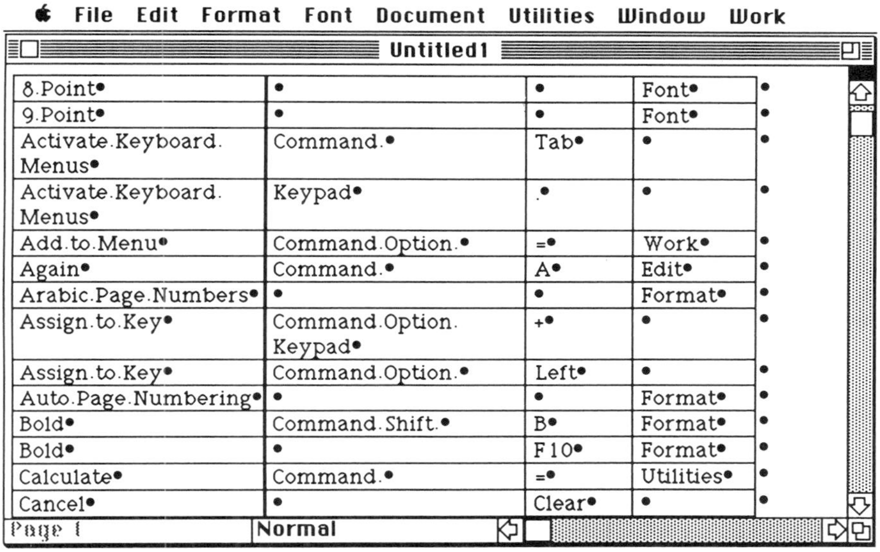

8.Point•	•	•	Font•	•
9.Point•	•	•	Font•	•
Activate.Keyboard. Menus•	Command.•	Tab•	•	•
Activate.Keyboard. Menus•	Keypad•	.•	•	•
Add.to.Menu•	Command.Option.•	=•	Work•	•
Again•	Command.•	A•	Edit•	•
Arabic.Page.Numbers•	•	•	Format•	•
Assign.to.Key•	Command.Option. Keypad•	+•	•	•
Assign.to.Key•	Command.Option.•	Left•	•	•
Auto.Page.Numbering•	•	•	Format•	•
Bold•	Command.Shift.•	B•	Format•	•
Bold•	•	F10•	Format•	•
Calculate•	Command.•	=•	Utilities•	•
Cancel•	•	Clear•	•	•

This table of commands will appear on the screen when you press the List button.

If you press the Shift key as you click the List button, Word will expand the table to include a number of options that do not appear on a menu or that have not been assigned a keystroke series. For example, the expanded list will include style names and glossary terms that do not appear on the Work menu, font names that are installed on the System file but do not appear on the Font menu, and dialog box options that can be placed on a menu or assigned a keystroke series, but currently are not assigned to a menu or key series.

CONFIGURATION FILES

Word automatically saves menus and keystroke assignments in a special file called a configuration file. Word's default configuration file is named Word Settings (4). In addition to menus and keystroke assignments, this file stores other program defaults, including settings in the Page Setup, Preferences, Document, and Section dialog boxes, and the default style sheet.

You'll find the Word Settings (4) file stored in the System folder on your startup disk for Word. The Word Settings (4) file does not exist when you first begin to use

Word. However, Word creates this file automatically the first time you open the program, and loads it automatically every time you start Word. Word also updates the Word Settings (4) file each time you quit to the Finder level. If you discard or rename this file—or even if you remove it from the System folder on your startup disk—Word will create a new Word Settings (4) file with all settings returned to their original defaults.

Fortunately, Word allows you to create additional configuration files to store various groups of default settings. However, only one configuration file can be open at any time. Word displays the name of the current configuration file at the bottom of the Commands dialog box.

The Commands… command is the key to creating and accessing new configuration files. Before creating a new configuration file, however, you must specify the new defaults you want to save in that file. This involves opening the Page Setup, Document, and Section dialog boxes, specifying the settings you want to use, and clicking the Set Default button. To save any custom styles on the default style sheet, open the Define Styles dialog box, click on each of the style names you want to save, and click Set Default. If you want to change the default menus or key assignments, use the techniques we've described to make these alterations. You also may want to change some of the settings in the Preferences dialog box. Many of these settings are automatically saved as Word's new defaults.

Saving Changes in a Configuration File

Once you've made all your alterations to Word's menus, keystroke assignments, and default settings, you can quit to the Finder level and Word will automatically save those changes in the Word Settings (4) file. To save your changes in a different configuration file, issue the Commands… command, and click on the Save As… button at the bottom of the dialog box. Word will then present a dialog box like the one in Figure 14-16, where you can enter a name for the new configuration file. As you can see, Word automatically opens the System folder when saving a configuration file.

You may want to use a distinctive group of names for your configuration files. This will make it easier to identify those files later. For example, as you can see in Figure 14-16, we chose the file name Word Settings (A) to store our new default settings.

After you save your changes in a new configuration file, Word will make that file current. Therefore, any additional changes you make to Word's menus and other default settings will be saved in this new file when you quit to the Finder level. (In a moment, we'll show you how to cancel your changes so that the configuration file on disk is not changed when you quit to the Finder level.)

FIGURE 14-16

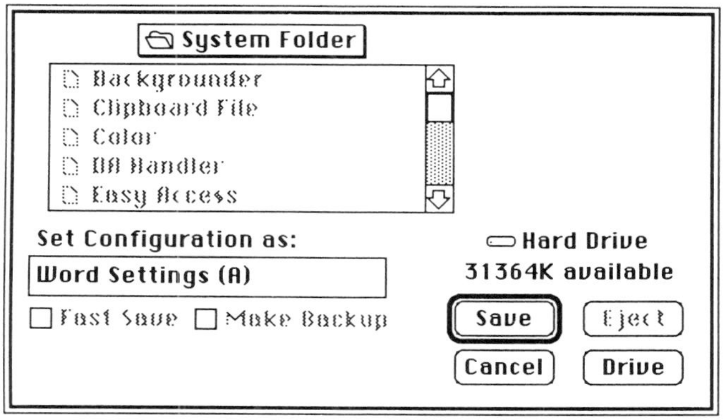

Word will automatically save a configuration file in the System folder.

After saving one or more configuration files to disk, you can use Commands… to access any of those files. After loading Word, open the Commands dialog box and click on the Open… button that appears at the bottom of the dialog box. Word will then present a dialog box much like the standard Open dialog box, except it will display the message *Select a Configuration File.* When you see this dialog box, open the System folder, if necessary, click on the name of the configuration file you want to use, then click the Open button.

When Word opens the new configuration file, all the settings stored in that file, including menus and keystroke assignments, will replace the current settings that are in effect. In addition, Word will display the name of the currently open configuration file at the bottom of the Commands dialog box. Once you've opened a new configuration file, any additional changes you make to Word's menus and other default settings will be saved in this new file when you quit to the Finder level.

As we've mentioned, any changes you make to Word's menus and default settings will automatically be stored in the current configuration file when you quit to the Finder level. If you want to preserve the current configuration file on disk without your changes, there are several techniques you can use. First, you can open the Commands dialog box and click the Reset button before you quit to the Finder level. Clicking the Reset button will cancel any changes you've made since loading the current configuration file.

Opening a Configuration File

Recovering Previous Defaults

You also can save your current settings in a new configuration file or open another configuration file on disk. As you know, when you save your settings in a new configuration file, that file becomes current. In addition, the previous configuration file remains unchanged. Similarly, when you load a configuration file from disk, that file's settings become current, cancelling any changes you may have made since loading the previous configuration file.

By the way, if you don't quit to the Finder level at the end of a Word session—that is, if you simply turn off your computer or if your computer crashes—Word will not record to disk any custom menu changes or other alterations to Word's default settings that you've made since loading the current configuration file (unless, of course, you used the Save As... button in the Commands dialog box to save those changes). When you next load Word, your menus and other settings will be the same as they were at the beginning of the last session.

Returning to Word's preset defaults

To return to Microsoft's original default settings (with Full Menus in effect), just open the Commands dialog box and press the Shift key as you click the Reset button. Word will display an alert message asking if you are sure you want to revert to the default settings. You can click OK to complete the procedure.

If you quit to the Finder level after returning to Word's preset defaults, these original default settings will be stored in the current configuration file. Keep in mind that, if Word Settings (4) is not the current configuration file, then its settings will not be reset to Word's original defaults. To return the Word Settings (4) file to Word's original defaults, load that file before pressing Shift and clicking the Reset button in the Commands dialog box. Alternatively, after you return to the original defaults, you can use the Save As... button in the Commands dialog box to save these settings under the name Word Settings (4).

WORD DEFAULTS

Like other software programs, Word 4 comes with certain preset defaults. These default settings control such items as the page layout, the appearance of the screen, character and paragraph formatting, glossary entries, and print settings. Of course, when you begin a new document, you are not restricted to using Word's default settings. If a particular setting is not suitable for the document you're working on, you can change it. In most cases, your change will not affect Word's default setting. For example, you can change the margins in any document by altering the entries in the Document dialog box. However, when you open a new document, Word will return to its default margin settings.

If you find that you're changing one or more default settings each time you start a new document, then you should consider making a permanent change to that setting. For example, if you are always changing the Left and Right margin settings in the Document dialog box from 1.25 to 1, then you probably should change Word's default settings for the left and right margins. In this section, we'll examine each of Word's default settings and explain how to change them.

Word has a number of default settings that affect various elements of your screen display each time you use the program. These settings include the unit of measure on the ruler and the display of hidden text. Let's look at how you can change these default settings.

Screen Display Defaults

As we explained in Chapter 2, Word's initial default menu configuration is Short Menus. You can change this by selecting Full Menus from the Edit menu. Once you change from Short Menus to Full Menus (or vice versa) and quit from Word, your change becomes the new default. So, after selecting Full Menus, any document you open—even one previously saved to disk—will display Full Menus. Figure 2-3 on page 24 shows the menu selections that are available in Short Menus and Full Menus.

Menus

If you choose to use Full Menus, Word allows you to customize the selections on your menus and create a special menu called the Work menu. In this chapter, we've explained how you can add options to and delete options from the menus and how to create the Work menu. Like the Full/Short Menus setting, your custom menus are stored in the Word Settings (4) file. If you discard or rename the Word Settings (4) file, Word will return automatically to its original default menu configuration. Keep in mind that you can also save and retrieve different menu configurations through the Commands dialog box.

When you begin a new document or open an existing document, you will not see the ruler displayed at the top of the window. You must choose Show Ruler from the Format menu (or press ⌘-r) to bring the ruler into view. The ruler will show up only in the window that's active when you select the Show Ruler command.

Ruler display

Normally, if you close a document with the ruler displayed, then reopen that document, the ruler will no longer appear. However, you can change Word's default hidden ruler so that every window you open automatically displays the ruler. To do this, choose Commands... on the Edit menu. In the list of commands that appears on the left side of the Commands dialog box, select the Open Documents With Ruler command. Then, click the Do button. When Word closes the Commands dialog box, you won't see the ruler at the top of your window unless it already was displayed. However, from now on, when you open a document, Word will automatically display the ruler at the top of the window.

Although, the default unit of measure on Word's ruler is inches, you can change the unit to centimeters, points, or picas. To make a change, just choose Preferences... from the Edit menu. When Word displays the dialog box shown in Figure 14-17, click on the Default Measure dropdown list box, then choose the option you want to use.

Unit of measure

FIGURE 14-17

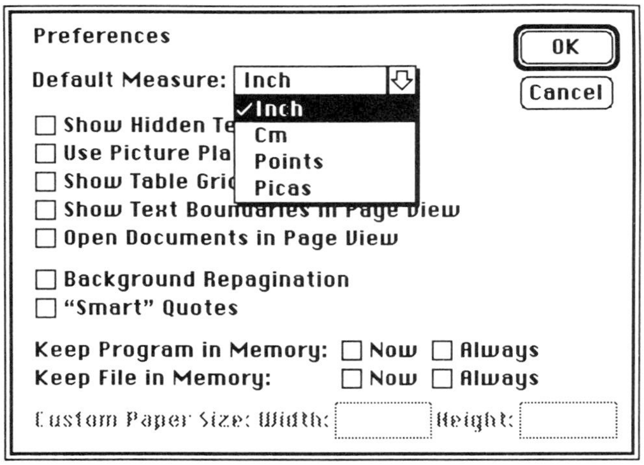

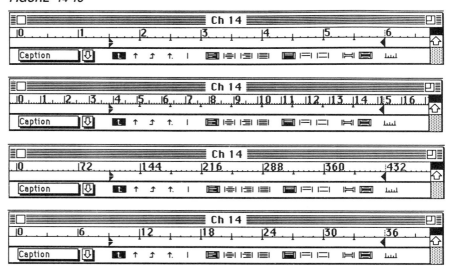

Preferences

Default Measure: [Inch ⬇]
  ✓ Inch
  Cm
  Points
  Picas

☐ Show Hidden Te
☐ Use Picture Pla
☐ Show Table Gri
☐ Show Text Boundaries in Page View
☐ Open Documents in Page View

☐ Background Repagination
☐ "Smart" Quotes

Keep Program in Memory: ☐ Now ☐ Always
Keep File in Memory: ☐ Now ☐ Always

Custom Paper Size: Width: [   ] Height: [   ]

[OK]
[Cancel]

The Preferences dialog box allows you to change the unit of measure in your documents.

Once you select a different unit of measure, Word will change the ruler appearance in all of your documents, even documents that previously were saved to disk with a different ruler measure. The unit of measure that you select is stored in the Word Settings (4) file or another configuration file that you specify. If you discard or rename this file, Word will automatically return to its default unit of measure, inches. Figure 14-18 shows the ruler with four units of measure.

FIGURE 14-18

Word allows you to specify one of four units of measure on the ruler: inches, centimeters, points, or picas.

Word does not change the alignment of text on the screen when you change the ruler measure. All the indents and tabs occur at the same positions. In other words, when you change the Default Measure option in the Preferences dialog box, Word does not merely change the markings on the ruler; it also converts the position of each indent and tab to the new unit of measure.

In addition to changing the appearance of rulers, the Default Measure option will determine the unit of measure in some of the edit bars in your dialog boxes. For example, if you change the unit of measure on the ruler to centimeters, Word will state the Margins settings in the Document dialog box in centimeters. Other dialog boxes that will be affected by a change in the ruler measure are the Paragraph, Section, Cells, and Position dialog boxes.

Besides dialog boxes, the Default Measure option can affect your style definitions. Any named style that specifies one or more indents or tabs will use the new unit of measure in its style definition. Finally, when you change the ruler measure, you'll notice a difference in the Print Preview window. If you click the margins icon (the third icon from the top) and then click on one of the margin "handles" that Word displays, you'll notice that the margin measurement that appears in the lower-left corner of your window will be displayed in the same units you've specified for the ruler. Similarly, Word will display the position of your page numbers, headers, footers, page-break markers, and positioned objects in the same units that you have chosen to display on the ruler.

Display of hidden text

When you apply the Hidden format to some text, Word will not actually hide that text until you print your document. On your screen, the hidden text will appear with a dotted underline. (See Chapter 5 for more on using the Hidden format and Chapter 7 for more on printing hidden text.) If you don't want to display hidden text on the screen, you must change Word's default setting in the Preferences dialog box for displaying hidden text.

The Preferences dialog box includes a Show Hidden Text option, which initially is activated. To suppress the display of hidden text, click on this option to deactivate it.

Once you turn off the Show Hidden Text option, you won't be able to view hidden text in any document, even a document previously saved to disk. That's because the Show Hidden Text option—like other settings in the Preferences dialog box—is stored in the Word Settings (4) file. If you discard or rename this file, or if you open another configuration file in which the Show Hidden Text option is selected, Word will once again display all hidden text on the screen.

Page Layout Defaults

There are a number of settings that control the default layout of any new document you begin in Word. These settings appear in the Page Setup, Document, and Section dialog boxes. We'll consider the default settings in the Page Setup dialog box when we discuss printing defaults. Figures 14-19 and 14-20 show the default settings in the Document and Section dialog boxes.

FIGURE 14-19

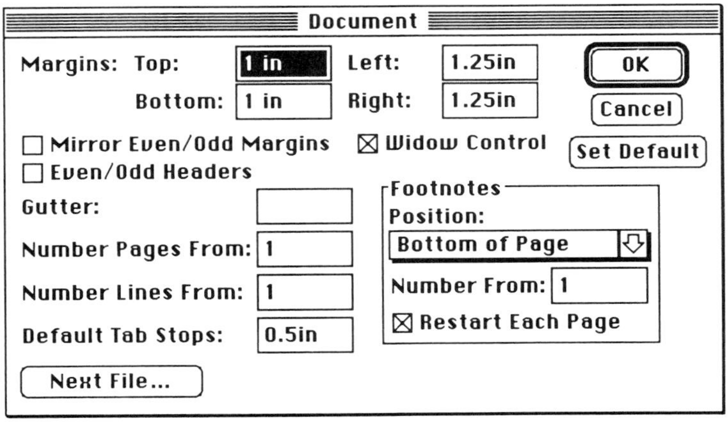

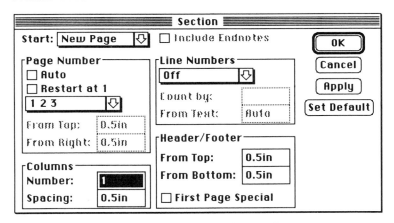

This Document dialog box shows Word's default settings.

FIGURE 14-20

These are Word's default Section dialog box settings.

You can change the default for any of the settings in the Document or Section dialog boxes just by entering a new value for that setting or clicking a new option, then clicking the Set Default button. Keep in mind that when you click Set Default, Word will replace the defaults for all the settings represented in that dialog box with the current settings. For example, to change Word's default margins, you simply enter new margin measurements in the Top, Bottom, Left, and/or Right edit bars of the Document dialog box and click Set Default. Word will save your new default margins in the Word Settings (4) file or another configuration file that you specify.

You can change Word's default Document and Section settings without affecting any documents previously saved to disk and without altering any documents open on your DeskTop. In fact, you can even make a change to one of Word's default page layout settings without affecting your current document. Just click the Cancel button after you click the Set Default button to close the dialog box without changing your current document.

Margins

As we explained in Chapter 5, document margins are controlled in the Document dialog box. Initially, Word's default Margins settings are 1 inch for the Top and Bottom margins and 1.25 inches for the Left and Right margins. If you want to change Word's default margin measurements, just enter the new measurements in the Top, Bottom, Left, and/or Right edit bars of the Document dialog box and click the Set Default button.

Number of columns

Normally, Word assumes that every new document will contain only one column of text. To create a document with two or more columns, you must choose Section… from the Format menu and enter the number of columns in the Number edit bar in the lower-left corner of the dialog box. You also must enter a measurement in the Spacing edit bar to tell Word how much gutter space to allow between columns. (For more on columnar formatting, see Chapter 10.)

To change the default number of columns from one to two (or more), just enter the number of columns in the Section dialog box and the space between columns in the Spacing edit bar, then click the Set Default button. Word will then store both the Number and Spacing settings as its new defaults. (Like many other default settings, the number of columns is stored in the Word Settings (4) file or another configuration file that you specify.) Any time you begin a new document, it will automatically appear in your new default columnar format. Documents saved to disk in the single-column format (or another format that's different from the default) will not be affected by the new default.

Page numbers

Word's initial default settings do not call for automatic page numbering in documents. If you want to change this default, just open the Section dialog box and click the Auto Page Number check box, then click the Set Default button. Word will record the active Page Number setting in your Word Settings (4) file or another configuration file that you specify. Word also will store any special page numbering options that you've selected, such as the numbering scheme you've chosen and the position of page numbers relative to the top and right edges of each page. Once you've changed the default, the Auto Page Number feature will be activated automatically each time you begin a new document. Changing the default will not, however, affect documents previously saved to disk or documents that are open on your DeskTop.

Although you probably will want to start your page numbers with 1, Word allows you to start with any number. To change the starting page number, open the Document dialog box, and enter the new number in the Number Pages From edit bar. If you want this starting number to become your new default, click the Set Default button. As usual, this new default will be stored in the Word Settings (4) file or another configuration file that you specify, and will not affect any documents already saved to disk with a different starting page number. However, any new documents you open will have your new default starting page number in the Number Pages From edit bar.

Line numbers

Line numbering, like page numbering, is controlled in the Section dialog box. To number the lines in a document, open the Section dialog box and choose one of the options in the Line Numbers list: By Page, By Section, or Continuous. (For a complete explanation of numbering lines in a document, see Chapter 13.)

If you want line numbering to be the default in each new document, you should click the Set Default button in the Section dialog box after you choose one of the options in the Line Numbers list. As with page numbering, Word will record not only the activated Line Numbers setting, but also all of the related line numbering options as its new defaults. As you might expect, these new defaults will be recorded in the Word Settings (4) file or another configuration file that you specify.

As with page numbers, Word assumes that your line numbers will begin with 1. To start with a different number, you must enter the starting number in the Number Lines From edit bar of the Document dialog box. To make this new starting line number your default for all new documents, just click the Set Default button in the Document dialog box. Again, Word will store the new default setting in the Word Settings (4) file or another configuration file that you specify.

Headers and footers

Headers and footers are controlled by settings in the Section and Document dialog boxes and by style definitions on the style sheet. Word's initial default settings assume that you want to use the same header and/or footer on every page of your document and position that header/footer $1/2$ inch from the edge of the paper. However, by selecting the First Page Special option in the Header/Footer area of the Section dialog box, you can place a special header/footer on the first page of your document (or on the first page of each section). For more on headers and footers, see Chapters 7 and 10.

As you might guess, you can change Word's default settings so that the First Page Special option will be activated automatically in each new document. Just click on that option in the Section dialog box, then click the Set Default button. When you do this, Word will store the new defaults in the Word Settings (4) file or another configuration file that you specify. Any documents previously saved to disk will not be affected by the new defaults.

To change the position of a header or footer, just enter a new measurement in the From Top or From Bottom edit bar of the Section dialog box. If you want to make the new measurement(s) the default for all new documents, just click on the Set Default button.

You can alter other features of your headers and footers by changing the definitions of the *header* and *footer* styles on the style sheet. To do this, choose Define Styles… from the Format menu, click on the style name *header* or *footer*, and issue the appropriate commands to change the style instructions. (For a complete discussion of modifying styles on the style sheet, see Chapter 8.)

If you want the altered style instructions to become the new default instructions for the style named *header*, click on the Set Default button in the Define Styles dialog box while the *header* style name is selected. When you see the message *OK to record style in default style sheet?*, click Yes. Word will not only change the default instructions for the *header* style, but also will add that style name to the default style sheet. Each time you open a new document, the style named *header*—with your modified instructions—will appear on the style sheet for that document.

Word does not offer any way to define default header or footer text. To create a default header or footer, you'll need to create a document template that includes the standard header or footer, then use that template to build your documents. We'll show you how to create templates in a few pages.

Footnotes

Footnotes, like headers and footers, are controlled by settings in the Section and Document dialog boxes, as well as by style definitions. The dialog box selections determine whether footnotes will appear at the bottom of each page, at the end of each section, or at the end of an entire document. These settings also determine whether the footnotes will be numbered separately on each new page, new section, or continuously through a document. (Chapter 11 explains footnotes in detail.)

Word's default settings in the Document dialog box cause footnote text and footnote numbers to appear at the bottom of each page. Word's default starting number for the footnotes on each page is 1. If you want to change the default footnote settings, select your choices in the Document dialog box, then click the Set Default button. As usual, Word will record your new default settings in the Word Settings (4) file or another configuration file that you choose.

There's only one footnote-related setting in the Section dialog box—Include Endnotes. Include Endnotes comes into play only when a document contains more than one section and you've selected the End of Section option from the Footnotes section of the Document dialog box. Then, Word's default setting for this option is active, and the Include Endnotes setting in the Section dialog box instructs Word to print the footnotes for the current section at the end of that section, instead of printing them at the end of the entire document. If you want all of your footnotes to be printed at the end of the document, you should deactivate the Include Endnotes option. To make the deactivated Include Endnotes option Word's new default, click on Set Default in the Section dialog box.

As we explained in Chapter 11, whenever you use footnotes in a document, Word automatically adds two style names to that document's style sheet: *footnote reference* and *footnote text*. The *footnote reference* style is used to format the number or symbol in your document that calls out the footnote, while the *footnote text* style determines the format of the footnote itself. You can alter either style. After you alter the instructions for one of the footnote-related styles, you can place those altered instructions on Word's default style sheet by clicking on the Set Default button while the style name is selected in the Define Styles dialog box. When you see the message *OK to record style in default style sheet?*, click Yes. Word will not only change the default instructions for the selected style, but also will add that style name to the default style sheet.

Section Start

The options in the Start list in the upper-left corner of the Section dialog box tell Word whether to start a new page or a new column whenever it encounters a section break. Word's default selection for Section Start is New Page. To change this default, select one of the other options in the Start dropdown list box (No Break, New Column, Even Page, or Odd Page), then click the Set Default button. Like other default Section dialog box settings, this one will be stored in the Word Settings (4) file or another configuration file that you choose. Although your new default will not affect previously saved documents, you can expect your default selection to show up in all new documents.

Widow Control

The Widow Control setting in the Document dialog box prevents Word from placing one line of a paragraph on a page by itself. Normally, this setting is active. To change Word's default so that the Widow Control setting is deselected, just open the Document dialog box, click on the check box next to the Widow Control option, then click Set Default. Again, your changes to Word's default Document settings will be stored in the Word Settings (4) file or another configuration file that you specify.

Formatting Defaults

In Chapters 5 and 8, we described Word's default paragraph and character formats. You may recall that the default format for a paragraph specifies flush-left alignment, single spacing, no indents, no tabs other than the defaults, no space before or after the paragraph (other than normal line spacing), no borders, and no special features (such as Keep With Next ¶ or Keep Lines Together). Word's default character formatting calls for 12-point New York Plain type.

As we explained in Chapter 8, Word's default character and paragraph formats are controlled by the definition of the default *Normal* style. In addition, however, a couple of paragraph features—namely, the placement of default tab stops and the treatment of widows—are controlled through settings in the Document dialog box. To change Word's default character and/or paragraph formats, alter the instructions for the *Normal* style and click on the Set Default button in the Define Styles dialog box. Chapter 8 offers a detailed discussion of the *Normal* style, including explanations and examples of how you can alter that style. Like most Word defaults, the definition of the default *Normal* style is stored in the Word Settings (4) file or another configuration file that you specify. If you discard or rename this file after you've altered the default *Normal* style, Word will return to its original defaults for character and paragraph formatting.

Although Word's default style sheet will initially contain only the *Normal* style, there are 32 other automatic styles available. In Chapter 8, we explained how you can modify the default instructions for any of these automatic styles. We also explained how you can add styles—both automatic styles and custom styles—to Word's default style sheet. As usual, the contents of Word's default style sheet will be stored in the Word Settings (4) file. If you discard or rename this file, Word will return to its original default style sheet, which contains only the *Normal* style.

The Default Tab Stops option controls the interval between Word's default tab stops. To change this setting, open the Document dialog box, enter a new measurement in the Default Tab Stops edit bar, and click Set Default.

Default Tab Stops

Most of the settings that affect printing are—quite naturally—found in the Print and Page Setup dialog boxes. Figures 14-21 and 14-22 show Word's default selections in the Print dialog boxes for the LaserWriter and ImageWriter. Figures 14-23 and 14-24 on the next page show the default selections in the Page Setup dialog boxes for the LaserWriter and ImageWriter.

Printing Defaults

FIGURE 14-21

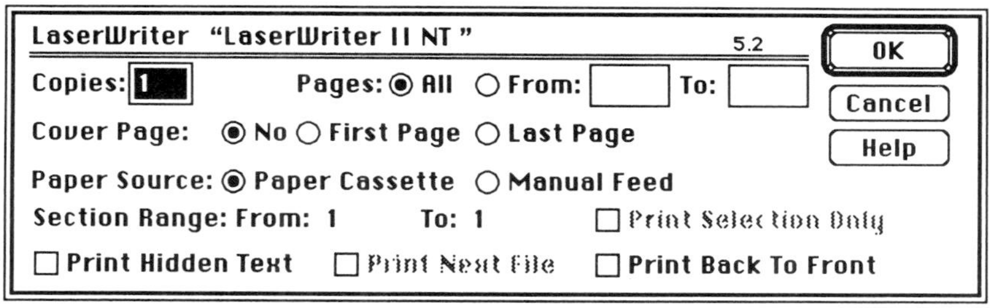

This Print dialog box shows Word's default selections for using the LaserWriter.

FIGURE 14-22

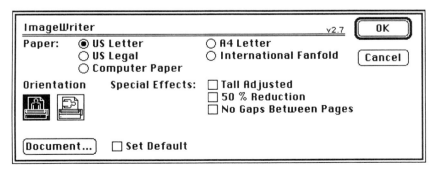

```
┌─────────────────────────────────────────────────────────┐
│ ImageWriter                              v2.7  ┌──────┐  │
│                                                │  OK  │  │
│ Quality:      ○ Best      ● Faster    ○ Draft  └──────┘  │
│ Page Range:   ● All       ○ From: [    ] To: [    ]      │
│                                                ┌────────┐│
│ Copies:       [  1  ]                          │ Cancel ││
│                                                └────────┘│
│ Paper Feed:   ● Automatic  ○ Hand Feed                   │
│ Section Range: From: 1     To: 1      □ Print Selection Only │
│ □ Print Hidden Text    □ Print Next File                 │
└─────────────────────────────────────────────────────────┘
```

This Print dialog box shows Word's default selections for using the ImageWriter.

FIGURE 14-23

```
┌─────────────────────────────────────────────────────────┐
│ LaserWriter Page Setup                    5.2  ┌──────┐  │
│ Paper: ● US Letter  ○ A4 Letter  ○ Tabloid     │  OK  │  │
│        ○ US Legal   ○ B5 Letter                └──────┘  │
│                                                ┌────────┐│
│        Reduce or [100]%   Printer Effects:     │ Cancel ││
│        Enlarge:           ⊠ Font Substitution? └────────┘│
│                           ⊠ Text Smoothing?    ┌────────┐│
│        Orientation        ⊠ Graphics Smoothing?│Options ││
│                           ⊠ Faster Bitmap Printing? └────┘│
│        [↑][↑]                                   ┌──────┐  │
│                                                │ Help │  │
│ [Document...] □ Fractional Widths  □ Print PostScript Over Text │
│               □ Set Default                              │
└─────────────────────────────────────────────────────────┘
```

This Page Setup dialog box shows Word's default selections for the LaserWriter.

FIGURE 14-24

```
┌─────────────────────────────────────────────────────────┐
│ ImageWriter                              v2.7  ┌──────┐  │
│                                                │  OK  │  │
│ Paper:  ● US Letter        ○ A4 Letter         └──────┘  │
│         ○ US Legal         ○ International Fanfold        │
│         ○ Computer Paper                       ┌────────┐│
│                                                │ Cancel ││
│ Orientation  Special Effects: □ Tall Adjusted  └────────┘│
│                               □ 50 % Reduction           │
│ [  ][  ]                      □ No Gaps Between Pages     │
│                                                          │
│ [Document...]  □ Set Default                             │
└─────────────────────────────────────────────────────────┘
```

This Page Setup dialog box shows Word's default selections for the ImageWriter.

Changing Word 4's default print settings is more straightforward than it was in Word 3. While the Print dialog box does not contain a Set Default button, the Page Setup dialog box does. This option allows you to define the defaults for all new documents. Word saves these defaults in the current configuration file when you end your Word session.

LaserWriter Settings

The first six options in the Print dialog box for the LaserWriter are Copies, Pages, Cover Page, Paper Source, Section Range, and Print Selection Only. You cannot change the default settings for any of these options. In fact, if you change any of these settings, your change will affect only the current Print... command.

When you change the Print Hidden Text, Print Next File, and Print Back to Front settings, your changes will become Word's new defaults and carry over from one Word session to another. In fact, any changes to these settings will even affect documents previously saved to disk with a different setting. (The Print Next File setting is available only in those documents for which you've specified a Next File... setting in the Document dialog box. When a document has a Next File... setting, the Print Next File setting will automatically be activated. Also, Word will disable the Print Back to Front option in documents with a Next File... setting.)

Normally, the settings you specify in the LaserWriter Page Setup dialog box will affect the current document only. If you want the settings that you specify to become Word's new default settings, activate the Set Default option. When you do this, your current Page Setup settings will carry over into any new documents you open both during the current Word session and in later Word sessions. However, any documents saved to disk with a different setting will not be affected.

ImageWriter Settings

As in the LaserWriter Print dialog box, Word's default setting for the Page Range option in the ImageWriter Print dialog box is All. Similarly, Word's default Copies setting is 1 and the default setting for the Print Selection Only option is deactivated. If you change one of these settings, your change will affect only the current print session. The next time you print your document, you'll have to respecify the Page Range, Copies, and Print Selection Only settings.

Word does allow you to change the default selections for the Quality, Paper Feed, and Print Hidden Text options. Initially, the Quality selection is Faster, the Paper Feed setting is Automatic, and Print Hidden Text is not active. Any change you make to one of these selections will become your new default. All new documents and any documents previously saved to disk will reflect the new selection.

As in the LaserWriter Print dialog box, the Print Next File setting is available only in those documents for which you've specified a Next File... setting in the Document dialog box. When a document has a Next File... setting, the Print Next File setting will automatically be activated.

Any changes you make to the settings in the ImageWriter Page Setup dialog box will become Word's new defaults when you activate the Set Default option. Your changes will carry over into any new documents you open both during the current Word session and in later sessions. However, the Page Setup settings for documents saved to disk will not be affected.

Selecting
a printer

When you use the Chooser command on the ⬣ menu to select a printer, your choice will become the default until you issue the Chooser command once more and make another selection. The selected printer is a Macintosh setting—it's not controlled by Word. In fact, if you quit from Word, then load another program (such as MacPaint), you'll find that the printer you selected in Word will still be the default printer.

Memory
Management
Defaults

The Preferences dialog box includes two settings, Keep Program in Memory and Keep File in Memory, which allow you to control—to some extent—your computer's RAM utilization. Theoretically, these options can speed processing by loading disk information into RAM. The effects of these options can be temporary, affecting only the current file and Word session (if you click the Now check box), or they can be permanent, affecting each Word session and every document that you open (if you click the Always check box).

If you want to load your current document into RAM, just click the Keep File in Memory Now check box in the Preferences dialog box. Word will then load your document into RAM and close the dialog box. If you want every document you open in Word to be loaded into RAM, click on the Keep File in Memory Always check box. Once you've done this, Word will save the active setting in the Word Settings (4) file or another configuration file that you specify. Then, whenever you open that configuration file, Word will automatically load all open documents (memory permitting) into RAM. Depending on the available memory of your Mac, Word will operate faster because it will not have to go to the disk to read and write data. If your Mac doesn't have enough memory to load an entire document (or documents), it will load as much as it can.

The Keep Program in Memory option can be used to load as much of the Word program into RAM as possible. If you activate the Now check box, the option will be active only for the current Word session. If you click the Always check box, the option will be activated in every Word session. Again, when the Word program is loaded into memory, it will operate faster because it will not have to go to the disk to read and write data. If your Mac doesn't have enough memory to load the entire Word program, it will load as much of Word as possible.

Multiple
Standard
Glossary Files

As we explained in Chapter 13, whenever you open Word, the entries from the Standard Glossary file are loaded automatically into the glossary. Word's default Standard Glossary file contains several *date* and *time* entries as well as a *print merge* entry and a *page number* entry. Word makes it possible for you to store additional entries in the Standard Glossary file. Of course, any new terms that you add to the Standard Glossary file will be loaded into the glossary automatically each time you open a document.

If you want Word to load different sets of terms into the glossary each time you open the program, you can create multiple Standard Glossary files. Once you've done this, you'll be able to access a particular Standard Glossary file by copying that file to the startup disk you use with Word (the disk that contains your System folder).

To create a custom Standard Glossary file, add the desired terms to the glossary as you are working in Word. Before you quit from Word, you can save the contents of the glossary into the file named Standard Glossary. Then, at the Finder level, copy this Standard Glossary file to another disk or folder and then discard that file. Now, to create another Standard Glossary file, load Word again. At this point, the glossary will contain only the default Standard Glossary entries. You can now add to the glossary any terms you want to include in the second Standard Glossary. Then, before you quit from Word, you should save the contents of the glossary into the file named Standard Glossary. You will now have two Standard Glossary files: one on your current startup disk and a second file on another disk (or in another folder).

Before you begin a Word session, you should be sure that the file named Standard Glossary on your startup disk contains the glossary entries you want to use in that session. Of course, if you open Word, then realize that you've used the wrong Standard Glossary file, you can always load the entries from the other file on disk. In Chapter 13, we explained how to open glossary files.

DOCUMENT TEMPLATES

Multiple configuration files and multiple Standard Glossary files can be very useful. However, you probably won't want to create a new set of defaults for every document you create. You will find it more practical to change some settings on a document-by-document basis. However, even this process can be speeded along through the use of document templates—blank document files in which you've preset certain features, such as margins and styles.

To create a document template, first open a new, blank document window. Once the document is open, issue commands to define the margins, styles, and other settings you want to include in the template. If you're creating a template for documents that will use virtually identical text (such as certain kinds of legal documents), you also may want to enter that standard text in the template file. After setting up your formats and entering any text you want to include, you're ready to save the document. To do this, issue the Save or Save As... command and choose a name for the file that identifies the type of template you've created. (You might type the name *Memo* for a template you would use to create memos, *Report* for a report template, and so on.)

Once you've created a template for a specific kind of document, you can use that template whenever you need to create that kind of document. You begin by opening the template file from the Finder level. When Word loads this file, you will see a blank document window (unless, of course, you've entered some standard text). However, all your margins, styles, and other features for this new document will already be defined. You can just type the text of your document in the blank window, then use the Save As… command to save the text under a different name. (Be sure that you don't issue the Save command or press ⌘-s since this will cause Word to overwrite your template with the document you just created.)

By the way, some of Word's settings cannot be controlled with a document template. As we explained earlier, such things as custom menus and the unit of measure on the ruler will show up in all your Word documents unless you open a different configuration file. However, there are many document features you can specify in a template file: Document dialog box settings, the style sheet, Section parameters, headers, footers, and footnotes.

Of course, keeping track of multiple configuration files, Standard Glossary files, and various template files can get to be pretty confusing. We suggest that you don't attempt to use the techniques we've described in this chapter until you're quite comfortable with Word. Then, you might begin by setting up a custom configuration file for your most common applications and, perhaps, create a template or two. As you become more familiar with Word, you'll be able to automate various settings with ease and even create entire turnkey document systems.

SHARING DATA WITH OTHER PROGRAMS 15

If you're like most Word users, you rely on your Mac to do a lot more than word processing. You probably use a spreadsheet program like Microsoft Excel for its number-crunching capabilities or a graphics package like SuperPaint or MacDraw to create illustrations and charts. If you do a great deal of desktop publishing, you may use a page layout application, such as PageMaker, as well.

In this chapter, we'll show you some techniques for combining the power of Word with other applications. We'll cover a wide range of topics, including using MultiFinder to run two or more programs concurrently; integrating graphics into your Word documents; and sharing data with Excel, PageMaker, and other programs.

In many cases, the simplest way to exchange information between Word and other programs is to copy and paste (or cut and paste) that information via the Clipboard or the Scrapbook. (We discussed the Clipboard and Scrapbook in Chapter 6.) Of course, you don't need to load MultiFinder in order to use the Clipboard and Scrapbook. Thus, if your computer doesn't have the memory capacity to use MultiFinder and load two or more applications concurrently, it's still possible to transfer information between Word and other applications.

To transfer information via the Clipboard, first open the file containing the graphic, worksheet data, or other information that you want to copy into Word. Select the information you want to transfer and choose the Copy command. Your selection will be copied to the Clipboard, and will remain there as long as you do not issue another Cut or Copy command or shut down your computer. Now, close

USING THE CLIPBOARD AND THE SCRAPBOOK

the current application and open the Word document in which you want to paste the information you just cut or copied. Click on the location where you want to place the information and choose Paste from the Edit menu. Word will copy the graphic, data, or other information from the Clipboard into your Word document.

As you probably know, the Scrapbook, unlike the Clipboard, stores information on your startup disk, rather than in RAM. Therefore, anything you paste into the Scrapbook will remain there until you remove it. It will not be lost when you copy or cut another selection, or when you shut down your computer.

To transfer a graphic, some worksheet data, or other information to the Scrapbook, just select it, then issue the Copy or Cut command. Next, choose Scrapbook from the menu to open the Scrapbook, and select Paste from the Edit menu to place the selected information in the Scrapbook. Now, you can quit from the current application and load Word. (When you load Word, make sure that you use the startup disk containing the Scrapbook file in which you just pasted the information to be transferred.)

Open a new or existing Word document as you normally would. Once the document is open, choose Scrapbook from the menu. If your Scrapbook contains more than one item (each item being a graphic, worksheet range, text block, and so forth), you may need to click on the scroll bar at the bottom of the Scrapbook window to bring the item you want to use into view. Only one item at a time will be visible in the Scrapbook window.

When the information you want to use is in view, choose Copy from the Edit menu. Then, position the insertion point marker in your Word document where you want the information to appear, and choose Paste from the Edit menu. Word will then copy that information from your Scrapbook into the document window. You can use the techniques we just described to transfer text from Word to other programs. To use only the Clipboard, first select the text that you want to transfer. Then, choose Copy or Cut from the Edit menu. Quit from Word, open the application and file in which you want to paste the text, then issue the Paste command.

USING MULTIFINDER

MultiFinder is a multitasking operating system for the Macintosh. As a result, it lets you operate two or more Macintosh programs concurrently. With just a click of the mouse, you can easily move between a Word document and files created in other programs, such as Microsoft Excel or SuperPaint. By running two or more applications at the same time, you can save a great deal of time in transferring data from one program to another via the Clipboard. MultiFinder also allows you to have constant access to the Finder level, where you can do such things as rename documents, move documents into folders, put files in the Trash, and so forth.

Preparing to Use MultiFinder

To use MultiFinder, your Mac must be installed with System Software, version 5.0 or later, and a minimum of 1 megabyte of RAM. However, in order to run another application simultaneously with Word, you need at least 2 megabytes of RAM. For instance, you won't be able to run Microsoft Excel and Word or load

MacPaint and Word at the same time unless you have 2 megabytes. If, after loading Word, you try to run another application with insufficient RAM, you'll see an alert message telling you that the application could not be loaded. In addition to RAM requirements, you also should have three 800K disk drives or a hard drive for MultiFinder to run effectively.

To use MultiFinder, first make sure your System folder contains the Multi-Finder file. If it isn't there, copy the file from the System folder on the Macintosh System Tools disk. Once you've installed MultiFinder in your System folder, you have to activate it. At the Finder level, choose Set Startup… from the Special menu. Click the MultiFinder option, then click OK. The next time you start your computer, MultiFinder will be turned on. (If you want to activate MultiFinder right away, choose Restart from the Special menu.) You'll know that MultiFinder is loaded when the MultiFinder icon (▣) appears at the far right edge of the menu bar. (If, for some reason, you don't want MultiFinder on when you start your computer, hold down the ⌘ key as you turn on the computer. Continue to press the key until the menu bar appears at the Finder level. MultiFinder will be turned off for that particular session only.)

You load programs into MultiFinder the same way you load them under Finder. The benefit to using MultiFinder, however, is that you don't have to close one program to run another. As we mentioned, the ability to run two or more programs concurrently depends upon the amount of your Mac's memory. Keep in mind that Word requires a great deal of memory—at least 384K.

After you load one application, you can return to the Finder level and open another. To return to the Finder without closing the application, you can choose Finder from the ⌘ menu or click on the application's icon at the far right on the menu bar. Each time a new application is loaded into MultiFinder, the icon at the right side of the menu bar changes. Figure 15-1 shows some of these application icons.

Loading Programs with MultiFinder

FIGURE 15-1

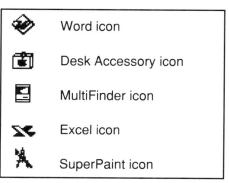

◈	Word icon
▤	Desk Accessory icon
▣	MultiFinder icon
✕	Excel icon
⚘	SuperPaint icon

These are some of the icons you'll see on the menu bar when you use MultiFinder.

Switching among Open Applications with MultiFinder

MultiFinder offers four methods for moving quickly from one open application or desk accessory to another. First, you can click on the icon at the far right side of the menu bar to switch from application to application. Second, you can select an application name from the ⌘ menu, where MultiFinder lists all the open applications. Third, you can double-click on the application's icon in the Finder window. (The icon will be dimmed since the application is already open.) Finally, if you have arranged your DeskTop so that you can see windows for different applications, you can simply click on the window that contains a document in the application you want to access.

Using the Clipboard with MultiFinder

As we've mentioned, once you have loaded two or more programs with MultiFinder, you can quickly copy and paste information between applications. First, select the data you want to copy and choose the Copy command. (Your selection will be copied to the Clipboard.) Then, use one of the methods we just described to switch to the application in which you want to paste the data. In the document, position the insertion point marker in the place you want the copied data to appear, and issue the Paste command.

You can use this same procedure with the Cut and Paste commands to move data from one application to another. After you issue a Copy or Cut command, if the application in which you want to paste the data is not open, you can switch to the Finder level to open it. Then, paste the copied data in the appropriate location.

USING QUICKSWITCH

When you load Word 4 into MultiFinder, you can take advantage of the new QuickSwitch facility to set up dynamic links between your Word documents and files that you have created in Microsoft Excel, SuperPaint, MacDraw, or MacPaint. In other words, the information that you paste into Word from one of these other programs can be automatically updated as you change the source file in which that information was originally created. To use QuickSwitch, your Mac must have enough memory to load MultiFinder, Word, and the application (such as SuperPaint) from which you want to transfer information.

There is really nothing extraordinary about the workings of QuickSwitch. Using it will remind you of using the Clipboard to copy and paste information from one application to another. The only difference, in fact, is that using QuickSwitch automates certain steps, like loading another application and opening a file, and issuing the Copy and Paste Commands.

There are three new commands on Word 4's Edit menu that facilitate dynamic data linking: Paste Link, Update Link, and Edit Link. The Update Link and Edit Link commands are very similar. In fact, the Edit Link command appears only when you press the Shift key and pull down the Edit menu. It then replaces Update Link. Interestingly, you do not need to use these commands with MacPaint or MacDraw files. We'll talk more about transferring and updating MacPaint and MacDraw graphics a little later in this chapter. For now, let's take a closer look at how you use the Paste Link, Update Link, and Edit Link commands.

The Paste Link Command

You use the Paste Link command to paste dynamic data into a Word document from Excel or SuperPaint. After loading both Word and the other application program, simply select the data you want to copy—for example, a range of cells in an Excel worksheet. Then, choose the Copy command. Next, switch to Word, click on the place you want the copied information to appear, and choose Paste Link from the Edit menu. Word will copy the information you selected and insert a special identifier paragraph in front of that information.

The identifier paragraph that appears before the pasted information allows Word to find that data in its source document when you decide to update it. An identifier paragraph consists of the following: an application name followed by an exclamation point, a disk (or drive) name followed by a colon, a file name followed by an exclamation point, and an area name or reference. Word automatically formats the identifier paragraph as hidden text, so it will not appear in your printed document unless you activate the Print Hidden Text option in the Print dialog box. For example, an identifier paragraph for some data that you copy from Microsoft Excel would look like this:

Excel!Hard Drive:Worksheet1!R1C1:R5C2

The identifier paragraph must be, as the name implies, a separate paragraph. As a result, the information that you paste into a Word document will appear at the beginning of a new paragraph.

Creating your own identifier paragraph

If you are using Microsoft Excel 1.03 or another application that doesn't support Paste Link, you can use the regular Paste command to place the copied information into a Word document, then type the hidden identifier paragraph manually. To create an identifier paragraph, place your insertion point marker at the beginning of the pasted text, then type something like *Application!Diskname: Filename!area* where *Application* represents the name of the source program, *Diskname* is the name of the disk on which the file is stored, *Filename* represents the file, and *area* is a named range or a range reference stated in R1C1 format.

The Update Link and Edit Link Commands

The Update Link and Edit Link commands allow you to update information you have added to a Word document with the Paste Link command. You use Update Link after you have edited the information in its original file. For example, suppose you have copied a range of cells from an Excel worksheet to a Word document. After you alter the Excel worksheet, you can switch to Word, select the copied information, and issue the Update Link command. Word will then update that information so that it is current with your changes in Excel.

The Edit Link command, on the other hand, allows you to edit the original file and update Word in one step. First, you select the copied information in Word. Then, you press the Shift key and choose Edit Link from the Edit menu. Word will open the application and the file in which the information was originally created.

You then make any necessary changes and press ⌘-comma. This will return you to Word, where the copied information will be automatically updated. We'll look at some examples of Update Link and Edit Link when we discuss Excel and SuperPaint a little later in this chapter.

GRAPHICS

One of the Mac's greatest selling points is its ability to integrate high-quality graphics images and text. Microsoft has taken advantage of this ability with a number of special tools that let you insert graphics into Word documents. After pasting a graphic into a Word document, you can use the Position... command to place that graphic at any absolute position on a page and flow text around it. Word even lets you size and crop graphics to fit your layout needs. You also can convert text into graphics and insert blank graphics frames into a Word document to serve as placeholders for photographs or illustrations that will be pasted in manually later. Word treats each graphic as a single character, which can be cut, copied, and pasted just like a text element.

Importing Graphics

You can transfer a graphics image from a graphics program, such as SuperPaint or MacDraw, into Word by using either the Clipboard or the Scrapbook, as we described at the beginning of this chapter. If you're using the MultiFinder and your computer has enough memory to run both Word and a graphics program, the fastest way to insert a graphic into a Word document is to copy the graphic to the Clipboard, then switch to Word and paste it into the desired location in your document.

For example, Figure 15-2 shows a SuperPaint screen in which we've drawn the logo for a hypothetical company. Let's suppose we now want to insert this logo into a Word document. To do this, we would use the ⌖ or ⌖ tool to select the graphic, then we would issue the Copy command. Next, we would switch to our Word document, using one of the techniques we described in our earlier discussion of MultiFinder, click at the spot where we want the graphic to appear, and issue the Paste command. At this point, Word will copy the graphic from the Clipboard into the document window, as shown in Figure 15-3.

When you paste a graphic into a Word document, Word will place a dotted line around the graphic, as shown in Figure 15-3. This border, which is not visible when the Hide ¶ setting is in effect, shows the area that the graphic and its surrounding white space occupy in your document. The border will not appear in your printed document.

Using QuickSwitch to import a SuperPaint graphic

If you want a SuperPaint graphic that you paste into a Word document to be dynamic—that is, if you want to be able automatically to update the graphic in your Word document after changing the graphic in its original file—you should use the Paste Link command instead of the Paste command. In order to use QuickSwitch with SuperPaint, use the SuperPaint version that comes with your Word 4 program. Additionally, you won't be able to use the Paste Link command unless you first save the SuperPaint file to disk. That is, QuickSwitch will not allow you to create a dynamic link to an unsaved, untitled SuperPaint file. (Incidentally, you cannot use Paste Link to paste a MacPaint or MacDraw graphic into a Word document. As we'll explain in a moment, Word offers a special technique for automatically updating these graphics.)

FIGURE 15-2

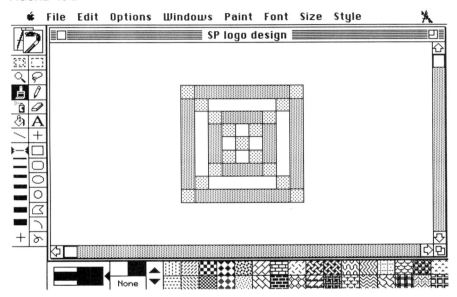

We created this graphic in SuperPaint.

FIGURE 15-3

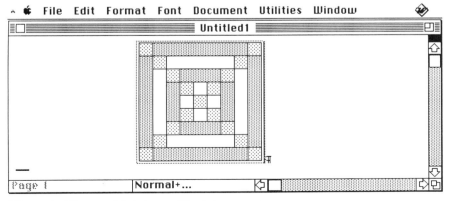

We pasted the graphic into our Word document.

As we explained earlier, when you use the Paste Link command, a hidden identifier paragraph will precede the pasted graphic in your Word document. This identifier paragraph will link the copied information to its source file.

Suppose we want to use the Paste Link command to paste the graphic shown in Figure 15-2 into a Word document. After selecting the graphic in SuperPaint, we would switch to our Word document, click where we want the graphic to appear, then choose Paste Link from the Edit menu. Figure 15-4 shows the result.

FIGURE 15-4

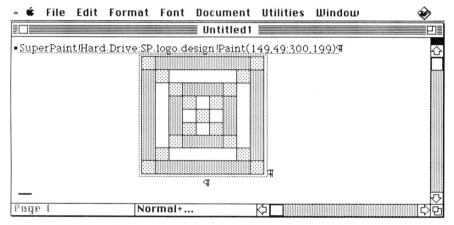

We used the Paste Link command to place this graphic in a Word document.

Notice that an identifier paragraph appears before the graphic. This paragraph contains the application name (SuperPaint), the disk (or drive) and file name (Hard Drive:SP logo design), and the area of the SuperPaint file that contains the pasted graphic (Paint(149,49:300.199)).

Updating a graphic with QuickSwitch

Once you've used the Paste Link command to copy a graphic from SuperPaint into Word, use the Update Link and Edit Link commands to update that graphic. After editing the graphic in SuperPaint, open the Word document that contains the copied graphic. Then, click once in the graphic in your Word document and choose Update Link from the Edit menu. (The graphic must be preceded by an identifier paragraph, as we described earlier.) Word will open the SuperPaint file, copy the updated graphic area, and import it into Word to replace the previous graphic.

Alternatively, you can begin by opening the Word document in which you pasted the SuperPaint graphic. Select that graphic, press the Shift key, and choose Edit Link from the Edit menu. Word will then open SuperPaint and the file that contains the original graphic. You then edit the graphic in SuperPaint, making sure that you do not resize or move the graphic. When QuickSwitch transfers the edited graphic back into Word, it will copy the same area that was originally pasted into Word, so you must make sure that this area contains the correct image.

After making your changes in SuperPaint, press ⌘-comma. QuickSwitch will return to Word and replace the original graphic with the updated graphic. If you want to return to Word without automatically replacing the graphic, just use one of the MultiFinder techniques we described earlier for switching among applications.

You cannot use the Paste Link command to paste a MacPaint or MacDraw graphic into a Word document. Instead, you use the regular Paste command. However, once you've imported a MacPaint or MacDraw graphic into Word, you can use the QuickSwitch facility to update that graphic. Again, you don't use the special commands on the Edit menu—Update Link and Edit Link—to update the graphic. Instead, just start the graphics program (MacPaint or MacDraw) and open a new file. Then, switch to Word and select the pasted graphic. Now, switch back to the graphics program. Word will paste the graphic into the new MacPaint or MacDraw document so you can make any needed changes. After you've made your changes, switch back to your Word document. QuickSwitch will automatically replace the selected graphic in your document with the updated version that incorporates your changes.

Using QuickSwitch with MacPaint and MacDraw graphics

One note of warning: Word will recognize only that portion of the MacPaint or MacDraw window in which you originally pasted the graphic. If you move or resize the graphic, it may not be returned in its entirety to your document window. Thus, if you need to make substantial changes to a MacPaint or MacDraw image, it will probably be easier to start over by pasting an entirely new graphic over the existing graphic in your document window.

When you click on a graphic that you've imported into a Word document, Word will display a frame around that graphic. This frame is similar to the dotted line that appears around a graphic whenever Show ¶ is activated. However, this frame will appear even if you've selected Hide ¶ from the Edit menu. In addition, the frame is a solid-line border and displays three small black squares or "handles." For example, Figure 15-5 on the next page shows the graphic from Figure 15-3 after we clicked on it to display its frame. As you can see, a handle appears on the right side and the bottom side of the frame, as well as in the lower-right corner.

Sizing Graphics

If the frame is larger than the graphic, Word will center the graphic within the frame. To shrink the frame to the smallest size that holds the graphic, just double-click anywhere on the graphic, except on one of the handles of the graphics frame.

You can use the graphics frame to change the size of a graphic. Word lets you resize a graphic in two ways: by cropping or by scaling. To crop a graphic—that is, to resize the frame without changing the scale of the graphic—just drag one of the handles. You can use the bottom handle to change only the height of the graphic, and you can use the right handle to adjust only the width. Dragging the corner handle will alter both the height and width, resizing the graphics frame without altering its original proportions.

FIGURE 15-5

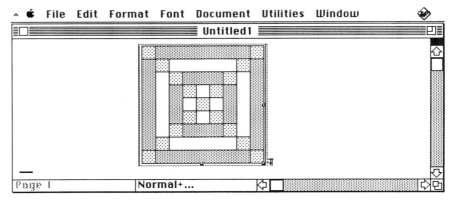

When you click on a graphic, Word will display a graphics frame with handles.

When you crop a graphic, remember that Word will not change the actual size of the image you have pasted into the document. Instead, it will change the amount of space allotted to the graphic. If you increase the size of the graphics frame, Word will insert more white space between the graphics image and its surrounding text. If you decrease the height or width (or both) of the graphics frame, Word will display only as much of the graphic as it can accommodate in the frame. For example, if we click on the graphic shown in Figure 15-5 and drag the corner handle up and to the left, Word will display only part of the original image, shown in Figure 15-6.

FIGURE 15-6

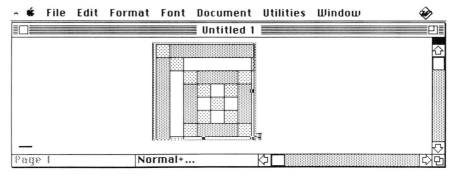

When you crop a graphic frame, Word displays only as much of the graphic as it can accommodate in the frame.

To rescale a graphic—that is, to change the actual size of the image rather than just the frame—you can press the Shift key as you drag a frame handle. As you drag a handle, Word will flash percentages—like *103%*—in the status box. As you might guess, this indicates the new size of the graphic relative to the original size. For example, suppose we press the Shift key as we drag the corner handle of the sample graphic in Figure 15-6, until we see 80% in the status box. Word will reduce the size of the entire graphic image, as shown in Figure 15-7.

FIGURE 15-7

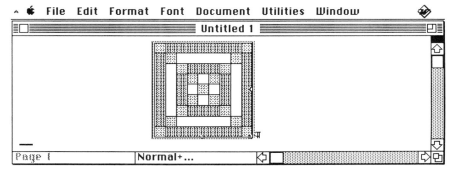

When you scale a graphic, Word will change the size of the graphic image.

Placing a Border around a Graphic

As we've mentioned, the dotted line that appears around a graphic on your screen will not appear in your printed document. If you want to place a border around a graphic, click on that graphic, then choose the Outline option on the Format menu (or from the Character dialog box). This will create a border that is the same size as the graphics frame. To add a drop shadow to the border, choose the Shadow option as well. Choosing the Bold option will increase the thickness of the border line. You also can use the Underline option to place a single line under a graphic.

Another way to frame a graphic is to apply a paragraph border. When you do this, however, Word will create a border that is equal to the width of the current text column—rather than the width of the graphic frame itself. For example, suppose you have pasted a graphic in a document that has a six-inch-wide text column. If you apply a paragraph border to that graphic, the border will be six inches wide also, regardless of the size of the graphic. In addition, the graphic will not automatically be centered within the border. You can make the border narrower or wider by dragging the indent markers on the ruler. You also can change the alignment of a graphic within the paragraph border by clicking one of the alignment icons on the ruler. If a graphic and some text appear in the same paragraph, you can use a paragraph border to enclose both the graphic and text.

**Positioning
a Graphic**

If you press Return to place a ¶ marker after the graphic so that it occupies its own paragraph, you can assign paragraph formats to that graphic. For example, you can use the ruler alignment icons to align a graphic with the left, right, or center of a document's text column, and you can use the Paragraph... command to add space above and below a graphic.

You also can use the Position... command to place a graphic at any absolute position on the page. For a complete discussion of the Position... command, see Chapter 10.

**The Insert
Graphics
Command**

There may be times when you'll want to add an empty graphics frame to a Word document. An empty frame can serve as a placeholder for an illustration that will be pasted in later. You can use the Insert Graphics command on the Document menu to create a blank graphics frame. When you issue this command, Word will place a blank frame at the current insertion point. If Show ¶ is active, you will see a dotted-line border marking the position of the frame. When you click on the graphics frame, you also will see its handles. You can drag these handles to change the size of the empty frame—just as you would resize a frame that contains a graphic. You also can use the techniques we described earlier to create a border in your printed document to mark the location of the graphics frame.

**Converting
Text into
a Graphic**

Some of the text that you create in Word cannot be read by other programs. For example, the character formulas you create using the technique described in Chapter 13 will not translate to other word processors or to desktop publishing programs like PageMaker.

To get around this problem, you can convert text into a graphic. To do this, first highlight the text you want to convert in your Word document, then press Option-⌘-d. When you do this, Word will place a copy of the selection on the Clipboard in graphic form. You can now use the Paste command as usual to paste this text picture onto the Scrapbook or directly back into your document. If you're running MultiFinder and a graphics application program, you can switch to that program and paste the text picture.

**EXCHANGING
DATA WITH
WORD 3**

You can open a Word 3 file in Word 4 without losing any formatting or other characteristics. You open a Word 3 file just as you open any other file: by choosing the Open... command on the File menu.

If you try to open a Word 4 file in Word 3, you'll see the alert message *File does not match file type; will be read as text.* This tells you that Word 3 will open the Word 4 document as a plain ASCII file. When the document appears, it will be pure text with all formatting stripped away (and some strange control characters at the beginning of the file and in other places throughout).

To open a Word 4 file in Word 3 without losing formatting, just save that file in Word 3 format. After choosing Save As... from the File menu, click the File

Format… button. In the ensuing dialog box, select the Microsoft Word 3.0 / Microsoft Write option, then click OK. You may want to specify a new name for the file before you click the Save button to ensure that the Word 3 version does not overwrite the Word 4 version on disk.

If your Word 4 document contains a table, the text in each cell of the table will appear in a separate paragraph in the Word 3 document. However, instead of a paragraph marker (¶) following that text, you will see the □ symbol, indicating a character that Word 3 is unable to translate. You can replace each of these symbols with a ¶ marker. (We'll explain a quick way to do this later in this chapter.)

If you've used the Position… command to assign a fixed position to some text or a graphic, Word 3 will ignore that positioning. However, the text or graphic will appear otherwise unchanged in the Word 3 document.

Word makes it easy for you to share data with a number of other word processing programs. You can use the File Format… option in the Save As dialog box to save a Word document into one of several file formats, which then can be loaded into another program. When you click the File Format… button in the Save As dialog box, you'll see the list of format options shown in Figure 15-8.

EXCHANGING DATA WITH OTHER WORD PROCESSORS

FIGURE 15-8

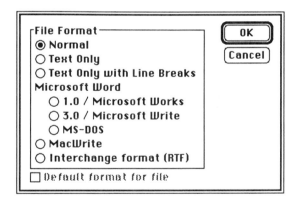

To save a Word document in a different file format, choose Save As… from the File menu, then click the File Format… button to see this list of options.

Notice that you can save a Word document into files that can be read by Word 1.0, Microsoft Works, Word 3.0, Microsoft Write, MS-DOS, and MacWrite. You also can save a Word document into an ASCII text file by selecting the Text Only or Text Only with Line Breaks option. (We'll say more about the ASCII format in a moment.) Finally, you can save a Word document into a RTF (Rich Text Format) file. (We'll talk more about this format later in this chapter.)

After you save a Word document in one of these special formats (with the exception of RTF), you'll be able to load that document directly into another word processing program. In most cases, Word will transfer your character and paragraph formats along with the document text. Of course, special features that are available only in Word 4 will not transfer to the new format.

If the word processor with which you're exchanging files runs on an IBM PC or compatible (or another computer that requires a different disk format), being able to create compatible files may not be enough. You probably also will need to transport the files to a $5^1/_4$-inch disk via modem or special cable before you can load them on your PC. Even if the PC with which you're exchanging data uses a $3^1/_2$-inch disk drive, you still will need to transport the file to another disk, since IBM PCs format disks differently than the Mac does. For example, after you save a Word document in Microsoft Word MS-DOS format, you will need to import that file to a disk that your PC can read. Your computer dealer or consultant can help you with this process.

In addition to saving documents in various file formats, Word can open files created by Word 1.0, MacWrite, Word 3.0, Microsoft Write, or the Microsoft Works word processing program. To open a file created by another word processor, choose the Open... command from the File menu and double-click on the name of the file you want to open. (Sometimes, you'll have to press the Shift key as you choose Open... in order to see the name of the file in the dialog box.) Word performs the translation automatically as it opens the file. As Word is opening the file, you'll see a message like *Converting a MacWrite file. Document will appear in a new untitled window.* in a box on your screen. You can click the Cancel button that you'll see in this message box if you want to stop the file conversion.

When the converted document appears on your screen, it will display all the paragraph and character formatting you assigned to it in the other word processing program. Of course, after you load the document, you can use Word to edit and format it as you would any other text.

Word can also read ASCII text files. Since nearly every word processing program can save documents into ASCII format, you can use this feature to load documents from a number of word processors (and other programs as well) into Word. Let's take a closer look at using the ASCII format to exchange data.

Using the ASCII Format to Exchange Documents

As we've mentioned, most word processing programs, including Word, can save documents to disk in the ASCII file format. In addition, nearly every word processing program and many spreadsheet and database programs can read ASCII files. The ASCII system uses a three-digit code to represent each number, letter, and symbol. For example, your computer knows the character *e* as 101.

You might think of the ASCII file format as the "lowest common denominator" format. When you save a Word file in this format, you create a pure text file without any special character or paragraph formats. Similarly, when you load an ASCII file into Word, you will see plain text on your screen with no special character or paragraph formatting. It's the "plain jane" nature of ASCII files that makes them useful for moving documents from one program to another.

Saving Word documents in ASCII format

If you want to save a Word document into an ASCII file, choose Save As… from the File menu, then click on the File Format… button. Word will present the list of format options shown in Figure 15-8. Click the Text Only or the Text Only with Line Breaks option. Then, click OK in the File Format box to return to the Save As dialog box. Finally, you may want to enter a new file name in the Save Current Document As edit bar. When you've finished, click OK to save the document in ASCII format.

As soon as you execute the Save As… command, Word will replace the document on your screen with the ASCII version of the document. All your character, paragraph, and section formatting will be gone. However, you won't lose your paragraph breaks. If you selected the Text Only with Line Breaks option, you'll see additional paragraph breaks at the end of every line.

Of course, if you had previously saved the document to disk in the normal Word file format (and you didn't overwrite that file with the Save As… command), you'll be able to recover all of your formatting simply by opening that document.

If the purpose in saving your document in ASCII format is to read it into another word processing program, you probably will want to use the Text Only option, not the Text Only with Line Breaks option. This second option is designed primarily for transferring information from Word to spreadsheet and database programs.

Opening an ASCII file in Word

To open an ASCII format file in Word, first press the Shift key, then choose Open… from the File menu. (If you do not press Shift as you select the Open… command, Word may not display the names of the ASCII files in the Open dialog box.) Next, open the ASCII file just as you would open any other file: Double-click on the file name, or click on the file name, then click the Open button. When the file is open, you'll see plain text on your screen. However, you can edit and format this text just as you would any other document. (Sometimes, you may also see some stray coding characters when you import an ASCII file from another program. These can easily be deleted with common editing techniques.) After you've edited and formatted the text to suit your needs, you can save the document in Word format. To do this, just issue the Save or Save As… command as you normally would. (If you don't want to overwrite the plain ASCII file on disk, use the Save As… command, and type a different file name for your new version of the document.)

RTF/DCA Exchanges

The RTF (Rich Text Format) allows you to transfer files between Word and other programs without losing most formatting. When you save a Word document as an RTF file, Word converts every formatting characteristic of the document into an alphanumeric code. If you view an RTF document on your screen, you'll see a rather confusing combination of document text and lots of code text. Microsoft's goal in creating the RTF—also called the Interchange format—was to provide a way to exchange documents between Word and other word processing programs— particularly IBM DisplayWrite—without losing formatting.

Once a Word file is saved in RTF format, you can use the DCA-RFT/MS RTF conversion utility to convert that file into RFT (Revisable-Form Text) format. The RFT file can then be read by word processing programs that use the DCA—or Document Content Architecture—format. You also can use the DCA-RFT/MS RTF conversion utility to transfer DCA/RFT files into the RTF format, which can be read by Word.

The DCA-RFT/MS RTF conversion utility can be found in the Conversions folder on the Word 4 Utilities 2 disk. To use this utility, you must have the Apple File Exchange folder, which is available on your Macintosh Utilities 2 disk. You may want to copy the Apple File Exchange folder onto your hard disk or another disk. Then, you must copy the DCA-RFT/MS RTF conversion utility into this folder.

Converting a Word document into RFT format

To convert a Word document into RFT (Revisable-Form Text) format, you must first save that document in the Interchange or RTF format. To do this, issue the Save As... command, click the File Format... button, select the Interchange format (RTF) option, and click OK. As soon as you click Save in the Save As dialog box, Word will replace the document on your screen with the new Rich Text Format document.

Now, you can quit from Word and use the DCA-RFT/MS RTF conversion utility to transfer this RTF file into RFT format. To do this, just double-click on the icon for the DCA-RFT/MS RTF conversion utility in the Apple File Exchange folder. This will open the Apple File Exchange program, where you'll see a list of all files and folders on the current drive. To access a file on a different drive, just click the Open button at the lower-right corner of the window.

Next, select the name of the RTF file you want to convert and click the Translate button. When the Apple File Exchange program asks what kind of translation you want to make, click the RTF to DCA-RFT... option. The Apple File Exchange program will then convert the file to RFT format.

Once the conversion is complete, you will need to transport the file to a disk that your IBM PC (or compatible) can read. There are several techniques you can use to do this. Your hardware dealer or a consultant can assist you in this process.

When you open the file in the IBM word processing program, you'll see that it retains most of the character and paragraph formatting that you assigned in Word. (You may need to repaginate the document after you open it to see the correct line breaks.) For example, line spacing, tabs, paragraph alignment, bold, and underlining will all be transferred properly. Italic formatting will not be transferred, nor will special formats, such as outline characters, which are not supported by the IBM PC word processing program.

To convert a DCA document into a format that Word can read, you must begin by saving that document into the RFT (Revisable-Form Text) format. Suppose you want to convert a DisplayWrite file. First, you would select the Utilities (6) option on the DisplayWrite main menu. Then, on the Utilities menu, choose the Document Conversion (6) option. In the Document Conversion box, type the name of the document you want to convert and the name you want to assign to the converted file. Then, choose the Document to Revisable-Form Text (1) option.

Converting a DCA document into RTF format

After the file has been converted to RFT format, you will need to transfer that file to a Macintosh-readable disk. There are several ways to do this. Your hardware dealer or a consultant can assist you in this process.

Now, place the diskette with the RFT file in your Mac's disk drive. Open the Apple File Exchange folder and double-click on the icon for the DCA-RFT/MS RTF conversion utility. This will open the Apple File Exchange program, where you'll see a list of all files and folders on the current drive. To access a file on a different drive, just click the Drive button at the lower-right corner of the window.

Next, select the name of the RFT file you want to convert and click the Translate button. When the Apple File Exchange program asks what kind of translation you want to make, click the DCA-RFT to RTF... option. The Apple File Exchange program will then convert the file to RTF format.

Once the file has been converted to the RTF or Interchange format, you can open it directly in Word. After you issue the Open... command and select the document name, Word will display an alert box that asks *Interpret RTF text?* If you click Yes, Word will display the message *Converting an Interchange format (RTF) file. Document will appear in a new untitled window.* You can click Cancel if you want to halt the conversion procedure. When the file appears on your screen, it will display most of the character and all of the paragraph formats that were assigned in the other word processing program. Of course, since Word's formatting capabilities are far superior to those of DCA word processing programs, you probably will want to apply some additional character and paragraph formatting to the document.

If you click No when you see the *Interpret RTF text?* message, Word will load the file directly and display on screen the combination of plain text and RTF format codes.

WordPerfect Exchanges

The Conversions folder on your Word 4 Utilities 2 disk also contains a utility called WordPerfect 4.x/RTF. As you might guess, this utility allows you to convert WordPerfect 4.1 and 4.2 files into RTF format, which you can then open in Word. It also allows you to convert Word RTF files into a format that can be read by

WordPerfect. Like the DCA-RFT/MS RTF utility, the WordPerfect 4.x/RTF conversion utility must be used with the Apple File Exchange program. (You should copy the WordPerfect 4.x/RTF file into your Apple File Exchange folder.)

To convert a WordPerfect document into RTF format, just save that document as you normally would. Then, transfer the file to a Macintosh-readable disk. Next, place that disk in a drive on your Mac and make sure that the Apple File Exchange folder is on another current disk. Open the Apple File Exchange folder and double-click the icon for the WordPerfect 4.x/RTF utility. This will open the Apple File Exchange program, where you'll see a list of all files and folders on the current drive. To access a file on a different drive, just click the Open button at the lower-right corner of the window.

Next, select the name of the WordPerfect file you want to convert and click the Translate button. When the Apple File Exchange program asks what kind of translation you want to make, click the WordPerfect 4.1 to RTF option or the WordPerfect 4.2 to RTF option. The Apple File Exchange program will then convert the file to RTF format. Once the file is in RTF or Interchange format, you can open it directly in Word. All the paragraph and character formatting that you assigned in WordPerfect will be transferred to the Word document.

You follow a similar procedure to convert a Word document into a format that can be read by WordPerfect. First, save the Word document in the RTF (Interchange) format. Then, use the WordPerfect 4.x/RTF utility to convert the file to WordPerfect format. When the Apple File Exchange program asks what kind of conversion you want to make, choose RTF to WordPerfect 4.1 or RTF to WordPerfect 4.2.

After converting the file, transfer it to a disk that can be read by your IBM PC, then load it into WordPerfect just as you would load any other document.

EXCHANGING DATA WITH EXCEL

You can import data from almost any Macintosh spreadsheet program into your Word documents either by copying that data directly into Word via the Clipboard or the Scrapbook, or by saving that data in a text format that Word can read. With QuickSwitch, you also can use the Paste Link command to copy and paste Excel data or an Excel chart into Word and establish a dynamic link between that data and its source file. In addition, you can copy text from a Word document into Excel. If that text appears in a tabular format, it will automatically be divided among cells in an Excel worksheet.

Importing Spreadsheet Data

If you use Excel, you may sometimes want to import data from an Excel spreadsheet or chart into a Word document. In general, all you have to do is copy the information you want to import from the Excel worksheet, then paste that information into your Word document. Of course, the whole process works more smoothly if you use MultiFinder to load both programs simultaneously.

Suppose you have created an Excel sales projections worksheet like the one in Figure 15-9, and you want to import the data from cells A4:F9 into a Word document. Begin by using MultiFinder to load Excel and Word. Once you've loaded the two programs, open the Word document and the Excel spreadsheet.

An example

FIGURE 15-9

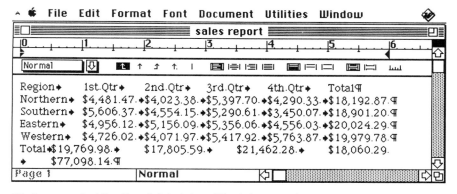

`⌃ ⌘ File Edit Formula Format Data Options Macro Window ✖`

	A	B	C	D	E	F	
			1989 Sales Projections				
1			1989 Sales Projections				
2							
3							
4	Region	1st Qtr	2nd Qtr	3rd Qtr	4th Qtr	Total	
5	Northern	$4,481.47	$4,023.38	$5,397.70	$4,290.33	$18,192.87	
6	Southern	$5,606.37	$4,554.15	$5,290.61	$3,450.07	$18,901.20	
7	Eastern	$4,956.12	$5,156.09	$5,356.06	$4,556.03	$20,024.29	
8	Western	$4,726.02	$4,071.97	$5,417.92	$5,763.87	$19,979.78	
9	Total	$19,769.98	$17,805.59	$21,462.28	$18,060.29	$77,098.14	
10							

We want to copy the data from cells A4:F9 into a Word document.

Next, in the Excel worksheet, highlight the range of cells that contain the information you want to include in your Word document, then issue the Copy command. Now, switch to the Word document, and place the insertion point marker at the spot where you want to insert the Excel data. Then, issue the Paste command to place a copy of the data into your document. Figure 15-10 shows the results.

FIGURE 15-10

`⌃ ⌘ File Edit Format Font Document Utilities Window`

```
Region→    1st.Qtr→   2nd.Qtr→   3rd.Qtr→   4th.Qtr→   Total¶
Northern→ $4,481.47.→$4,023.38.→$5,397.70.→$4,290.33.→$18,192.87.¶
Southern→ $5,606.37.→$4,554.15.→$5,290.61.→$3,450.07.→$18,901.20.¶
Eastern→  $4,956.12.→$5,156.09.→$5,356.06.→$4,556.03.→$20,024.29.¶
Western→  $4,726.02.→$4,071.97.→$5,417.92.→$5,763.87.→$19,979.78.¶
Total→$19,769.98.→   $17,805.59.→   $21,462.28.→   $18,060.29.
→    $77,098.14.¶
```

We have pasted the Excel data into a Word document.

As you can see, when you copy the contents of a worksheet to Word, the data from the worksheet will appear in Word's default *Normal* style. Although any numeric formats you have assigned to your worksheet entries will carry over into Word, any character formats you may have assigned in Excel will be lost. For instance, as you can see in Figure 15-10, the currency format we assigned to the values in Excel are transferred to Word, but the bold formatting is not.

Also, notice that Word places a ¶ marker at the end of each row of data in which tab markers separate the columns of data. We'll talk more about these markers in a few pages when we tell you how to use an Excel database as a Word data document.

Once you've imported information from Excel into Word, you'll probably want to change the tab settings and reformat the data to create a more attractive display, as we've done in Figure 15-11.

FIGURE 15-11

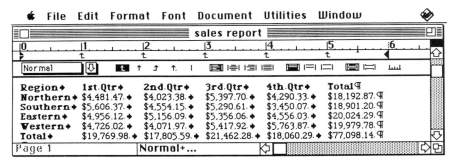

We have formatted the copied worksheet values to create a table in Word.

You also can convert the imported data into a table. Just select the rows of data and choose the Insert Table... command on the Document menu. In the Insert Table dialog box, select the Convert From Tab Delimited option. Word will automatically suggest a number of columns for the table, based on the number of tabs in each line. You can change this setting if you want. When you click OK in the Insert Table dialog box, Word will create the table, placing the data from the Excel worksheet in individual cells, as shown in Figure 15-12. (For more on the Insert Table... command, see Chapter 10.)

Using QuickSwitch

Instead of using the Paste command, you can use the Paste Link command to transfer copied data into a Word document. As we explained earlier in this chapter, when you use the Paste Link command, the data will be preceded by a hidden identifier paragraph, which allows QuickSwitch to maintain the link between the source file and the Word file. (If you are copying data from Excel version 1.3 or 1.4, you'll have to insert the hidden identifier paragraph yourself.)

FIGURE 15-12

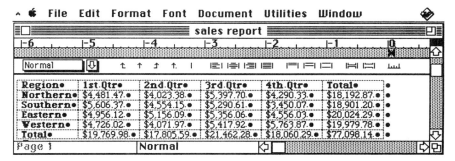

You can use the Insert Table... command to format the imported data as a table.

For example, suppose you used the Paste Link command instead of using the Paste command. Figure 15-13 shows the result.

After importing the Excel data with the Paste Link command (or after typing your own identifier paragraph above the imported data), you can use the Update Link or Edit Link command to update that information. Just follow the procedures we described in our earlier discussion of QuickSwitch.

FIGURE 15-13

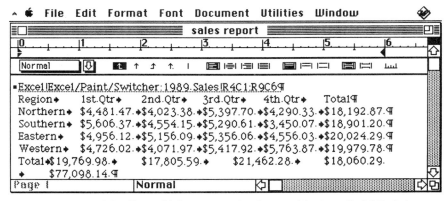

Because we used the Paste Link command to import this data, QuickSwitch automatically placed an identifier paragraph in our Word document.

If you want, you can use Excel database files as data documents for Word merge files. This makes it easy to create mailing labels, form letters, and so forth, from the data in an Excel database.

Using Excel Databases with Word

Since the structure of an Excel database is very similar to that of a Word print merge data document, the chances are good that a database you have set up in Excel is already in a form that can be used as a data document. In fact, to use your Excel database as a merge document, simply save the database worksheet as a text file so that it is readable by Word. To do this, choose the Save As… command on Excel's File menu and choose the Text Only option in the File Format dialog box.

Once you have saved the Excel database as a text file, you can load it into Word as you would any other document. When you load the database text, you'll see that each database record will occupy one paragraph, and that the fields will be separated by tab markers. Your field names will appear above the database text to serve as your field header row. You can reformat the database text by selecting it and moving the tab markers on the ruler. You also can select that text and use the Insert Table… command to convert it into table format.

By the way, if you are using MultiFinder, you can also copy records from your database directly into an open Word file, using the techniques we described earlier for copying standard worksheet entries. If you are copying several records, however, we think you'll find it more convenient simply to save the worksheet as a text file.

Importing Excel Charts

You can also import charts that you've created in Excel into Word. When you issue the Copy Chart… command in the Excel chart environment, Excel will give you the option of copying the chart as it is shown on the screen or as it will appear in print—that is, in the proportions you have specified in Excel's Page Setup dialog box. Simply select the option you want, then switch to your Word document, and choose the Paste Link command to paste the chart into the desired location. This command will establish a dynamic link between the chart in Excel and its replica in Word.

Once you've transferred an Excel chart into a Word document, you can use all the techniques we've described for sizing, formatting, and positioning graphics to change the appearance of that chart.

Exporting Data to Excel

As you might expect, you can also transfer data from Word to Excel, although you probably won't export data to Excel as often as you'll import data from Excel. To export data to Excel, just copy the information from a Word document and then paste that information into your Excel worksheet. Of course, the whole process works more smoothly if you use MultiFinder to load both programs simultaneously.

When you're exporting data to Excel, you will need to use tabs to separate the data that you want to place in different columns of the Excel worksheet. You also can format the text as a Word table. When you export a Word table into Excel, the information in each table cell will appear in a separate cell of the Excel worksheet.

If you do not use tabs or a table to format your Word document, that information will not be divided correctly among the columns of the Excel worksheet. In fact, you cannot use commas to separate the information that you want to place in different columns of a worksheet. With this one exception, however, the format we described in Chapter 12 for print merge data documents is exactly the format you should use to prepare your files for transfer from Word to Excel.

In the preceding section, we showed you how to use the Clipboard and MultiFinder to exchange data between Word and Excel. As we mentioned, you also can use the Scrapbook to transfer data between Excel and Word. You can use the techniques we described for Excel (except the QuickSwitch techniques) to exchange data between Word and other Macintosh spreadsheet and database programs, including Microsoft Multiplan, Microsoft File, and the Microsoft Works spreadsheet and database. Just follow the instructions we gave for exchanging information with Excel.

OTHER SPREADSHEET PROGRAMS

Exchanging data between Word and one of the PC-based spreadsheet or database programs is a little more complicated. The key to this kind of data exchange is the ASCII file format. Before you save a Word document in ASCII format, however, you should check the manual for your PC program to see what special characters that program uses as field delimiters. Unlike the Macintosh programs we've addressed, some PC programs do not recognize tabs as field delimiters. For example, Lotus 1-2-3 requires that you use commas to separate the information in different fields, and that you enclose the contents of each text field in quotation marks. (For a complete discussion of importing ASCII files into 1-2-3, refer to *Douglas Cobb's 1-2-3 Handbook*, published by The Cobb Group, Inc., and Bantam Books.)

PC-based Programs

Once you have set up your Word document with the correct field delimiters, you should save that document in the Text Only or Text Only with Line Breaks format. If you pressed Return to insert a ¶ marker at the end of each line in your document (or if your paragraphs are all quite short), then you can safely use the Text Only option. The ¶ markers will separate your document into discrete lines in the ASCII file, and when you load this file into your PC program, each line will appear in a separate row. On the other hand, if you are transferring a block of text from Word that does not include ¶ markers at the end of each line, you should save the file using the Text Only with Line Breaks option.

After saving your document as an ASCII text file, you will need to transfer that file to a $5^1/_4$-inch IBM PC disk. To do this, you must connect your Mac to the PC using a specially configured cable or a modem, then use communications software to transfer the file.

Since Word can read ASCII files, you also can import data from a PC-based spreadsheet to Word by saving that data in ASCII format. Of course, you will need to transfer the ASCII file onto a Macintosh-readable disk before you can load the file in Word.

Removing Extraneous Characters from an Imported File

If a file that you import from a spreadsheet or database program contains upper-level ASCII characters (ASCII codes 127 and higher), Word may not be able to translate those characters. The same holds true for characters represented by ASCII codes 0 through 31. When Word cannot display a character on the screen, it will display a rectangular box (☐). Although you can use manual editing techniques to delete these, you'll find it much faster to delete them with the Change... command.

To use the Change... command, you must first find out the ASCII code for each rectangular box. (Even if the imported file contains a lot of symbols, they probably represent only one or a few different characters.) To find the ASCII code for one of the ☐ characters, just select it and press Option-⌘-q. Word will display the ASCII code in the status box.

Next, choose the Change... command on the Utilities menu. In the Find What edit bar, type a caret (^) followed by the ASCII code. Suppose you discover that some of the ☐ characters are line feeds, which are represented by ASCII code 10. You would type ^10 in the Find What edit bar of the Change dialog box. To delete these characters, leave the Change To edit bar blank. When you click the Change All button, Word will delete each ☐ that represents ASCII code 10 from your document. You can repeat this procedure to delete other extraneous characters from the file.

EXCHANGING DATA WITH PAGEMAKER

With all its sophisticated page design and formatting capabilities, Word 4 does have a few limitations when it comes to performing full-fledged desktop publishing. If you create a lot of publications, you may want to take advantage of one of the many desktop publishing packages available for the Macintosh. Most of these programs can read Word files directly from disk, with no copying or pasting between applications. To give you an idea of how Word can be used with desktop publishing software, we'll look briefly at the PageMaker program, which is the most sophisticated and popular desktop publishing package on the market.

Working with PageMaker

PageMaker, developed by Aldus Corporation, has the look and feel of an electronic layout board. PageMaker gives you a great deal of control over the layout, placement, and format of your documents. You can use this program to place documents in predefined master page templates that you design with PageMaker's special tools.

Exporting files to PageMaker

Version 3 of PageMaker cannot read Word 4 files directly from disk. To transfer a Word 4 document into PageMaker, first save that document as a Word 3 file, then import it into a PageMaker document. When you import a Word file into a PageMaker document, PageMaker recognizes most of your character and paragraph formatting characteristics. However, it does not carry over your Document or Section dialog box specifications. This is logical, since PageMaker is specifically designed to perform these page layout tasks. Table 15-1 shows the formatting characteristics that PageMaker will carry over when you load a Word file.

TABLE 15-1

Format	Effect in PageMaker
Typefaces	Do carry over into PageMaker as long as that typeface is installed on your PageMaker System file. Otherwise, PageMaker will use its default Times typeface.
Type sizes	PageMaker accepts Word's point sizes.
Character formats	All formats carry over except the Hidden format and the Word, Double, and Dotted Underline formats. PageMaker converts these special underline formats to standard, unbroken underlines. Hidden text will not appear in PageMaker documents.
Carriage returns	All paragraph and line breaks carry over into PageMaker.
Page and section breaks	Manual page breaks and section breaks do not carry over into PageMaker, nor do the Page Break Before, Keep Lines Together, or Keep With Next ¶ Paragraph formats.
Line and Paragraph spacing	Do carry over into PageMaker
Line numbers	Do not carry over into PageMaker
Paragraph numbers	Do carry over into PageMaker
Tabs	All tab formats carry over except the vertical bars you create with the vertical line icon.
Borders	The paragraph borders that you apply do not appear in PageMaker.
Indents	Your First-line, Left, and Right indents do carry over, but PageMaker uses the margins settings you supply for your PageMaker document, rather than the ones you developed in Word. As a result, your line width may vary from Word to PageMaker.
Alignment	Your Left, Right, Centered, and Justified alignment settings carry over.
Multicolumn format	Does not carry over into PageMaker

Format	Effect in PageMaker
Headers, Footers, and Page Numbers	Do not carry over into PageMaker
Indexes, Footnotes, and Tables of Contents	PageMaker will read the text for these elements, but it will strip away the hidden codes you have used to define your index and table of contents entries. Similarly, all footnotes carry over, but PageMaker groups them at the end of your document.
Outlines	Since PageMaker does not recognize your style sheet specifications, it will transfer the text from your outline, but it will not recognize the heading levels you have assigned to that text. However, your style specifications for these elements will remain intact.
Graphics	Any graphics that you have placed in your Word documents will appear in PageMaker, but any text that you have wrapped around the graphic will appear before or after the graphic. In other words, if you have placed a graphic in the middle of a paragraph, PageMaker will insert a paragraph break before and after the graphic. Of course, you can easily position the graphic in PageMaker and flow your text around it.
Tables	Do not carry over into PageMaker. (Table formatting gets stripped out of Word 4 documents in the File Format dialog box when the documents are formatted for Word 3.

Importing files from PageMaker

PageMaker offers an export feature that allows you to write PageMaker files back into a Word format. This tool removes any special PageMaker features that are not supported by Word. It also resets a few features that were removed from the document when it was first imported into PageMaker. For example, if you have used Word's Borders option to draw a box or border around a paragraph, PageMaker will ignore those settings when it imports your Word document. However, when you export that document from PageMaker to Word, your border formats will reappear. The same is true of the Word Underline character format.

There is one important exception to this rule. Since PageMaker strips any hidden characters from your Word files, any codes you have entered for your document index, footnotes, or table of contents will not be re-established when you convert a PageMaker document back into Word format. Of course, the text for the index, table of contents, and so on, will still be a part of the file.

MACROS 16

As you use Word, you'll probably find yourself performing certain tasks repeatedly. For example, you'll frequently transpose letters, boldface words, delete sentences, and so forth. Instead of performing these tasks manually, you can program them into macros. That way, you can perform them simply by pressing a key or a combination of keys.

The Commands... command on Word 4's Edit menu allows you to create simple macros—ones that link a single action to the key or combination of keys that you choose. However, the ability to link a series of two or more actions (keystrokes, mouse movements, commands, etc.,) to a key or key combination is not built into Word. To do this, you must use an external program: AutoMac. A copy of this program comes on Word 4's Utilities 2 disk.

Although AutoMac is packaged with Word, it is not designed exclusively for Word. In fact, you can use it to create macros for any Macintosh application. You can even use it to transfer information between applications. In this chapter, however, we'll concentrate on using AutoMac with Word.

AUTOMAC BASICS

AutoMac is a powerful macro program that can automate tasks that range from simple to complex. The simplest (but perhaps most useful) macros type frequently used words for you. Before we began writing this chapter, for example, we created a macro that typed the word *AutoMac* whenever we pressed the Option-a combination. Complex macros can display custom alert boxes, pause to allow user input, branch to other macros, call subroutines, and more.

You can create AutoMac macros either by recording them or writing them. In most cases, you'll link each macro to a key combination (for example, Option-t).

That way, you can play the macro simply by pressing that combination. When you play a macro, AutoMac performs the actions that are recorded in the macro. For example, it may type characters, move the insertion point, select text, or issue commands—all faster than you could possibly perform those actions yourself.

Installing AutoMac

To use AutoMac, you must drag the AutoMac™ III icon from the AutoMac™ III 2.1 folder on the Microsoft Word Utilities 2 disk into the System folder of the startup disk that you will use with Word. If you want to be able to edit your macros (a good idea), you should drag the MacroEditor and MacroEditor help icons as well. Then, you should restart your Macintosh. Because AutoMac is an INIT file, it will be read each time you start your Macintosh.

The AutoMac Dialog Box

Whenever you start your Macintosh while the AutoMac™ III file is in the System folder, the AutoMac icon (a compressed uppercase *A*) will appear at the upper-left corner of the screen near the menu bar. This icon allows you to access AutoMac. When you click this icon (or press Option-Backspace), AutoMac will display a dialog box like the one shown in Figure 16-1. This is the main AutoMac dialog box.

FIGURE 16-1

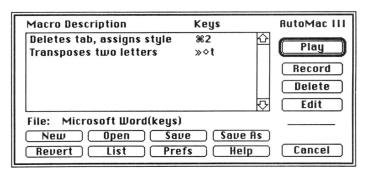

The items in this dialog box—the main AutoMac dialog box—allow you to record, play, and edit macros.

The items in this dialog box allow you to record, play, and edit macros; save and open macro files; and configure, as well as customize, AutoMac. The main portion of this dialog box contains a listing of the active macros. This list is arranged in alphabetical order, on the basis of the descriptions of the macros. The entry to the right of each description specifies the key or key combination (if any) to which that macro is linked. In this list, the symbol ⌘ represents the Command key; the symbol » represents the Shift key; and the symbol ◇ represents the Option key.

If your System folder contained the MacroEditor icon when you started your Macintosh, the fourth button at the right edge of this dialog box will read *Edit*, as it does in Figure 16-1. Clicking this button will access the macro editor. If you did not copy the MacroEditor icon into your System folder, this button will read *Change*. That button allows you to change the description of a macro and/or the keys to which that macro is linked.

RECORDING MACROS

Of the two ways you can create a macro (recording it and writing it), recording is by far the easiest. When AutoMac records a macro, it stores representations of the keys you press and the mouse actions you perform in a portion of your Mac's memory. While AutoMac records these keystrokes and mouse actions, your Macintosh will do whatever those keys and actions normally command it to do.

To record a macro, click the AutoMac icon or press Option-Backspace (Option-Delete on the SE) to reveal the main AutoMac dialog box. Then, click the Record button (or press ⌘-r) to reveal a Record New Macro dialog box like the one shown in Figure 16-2. (You can access this dialog box directly by pressing the Option-= combination.) The principal structures in this dialog box allow you to name the macro that you are about to record, and specify the key combination (or a single key) to which you want to link that macro.

FIGURE 16-2

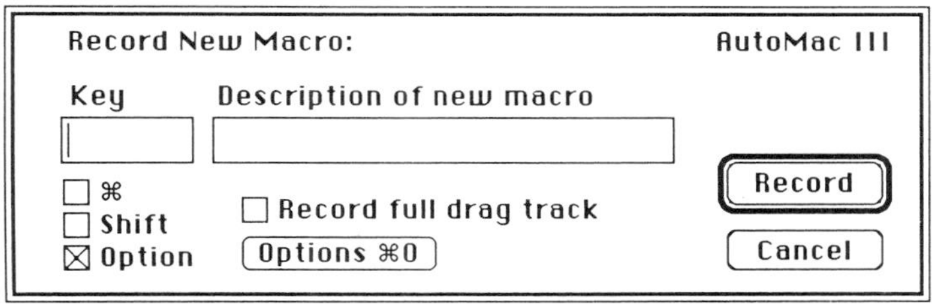

Record New Macro: AutoMac III

Key   Description of new macro

☐ ⌘
☐ Shift   ☐ Record full drag track   Record
☒ Option   Options ⌘O   Cancel

The Record New Macro dialog box lets you name a macro and link it to a key.

Linking the Macro to a Key

In most cases, you'll want to link a macro to a key or key combination. To specify the key(s) to which you want to link the macro, simply type the representation of that key into the Key edit bar, and check the boxes for any modifier keys. For example, to link a macro to the ⌘-Option-b key combination, you would type the letter *b* into the Key edit bar, and then check the boxes for the ⌘ and Option keys.

To enter the representations of most keys into the Key edit bar, you can simply press that key. However, you cannot enter representations of the Backspace, ↑, ↓, ←, →, Enter, or Return keys in this way. To represent these keys, type a series of two or more letters (preferably, a word that describes the key, like *Backspace*, *Up*, *Down*, and so forth) into the Key edit bar. When you later click the Record button, AutoMac will ask you to identify the key that you meant. To do this, press that key.

To link a macro to a key that you must use the Shift key to generate (for example, *A* or *$*), type either the unshifted or shifted version of that key into the Key edit bar, and then click the Shift box. If you type the shifted version of that key into the Key edit bar, but don't click the Shift box, AutoMac will link the macro to the unshifted version of that key—not the shifted version.

Guidelines

In general, you should link a macro to a combination of keys rather than a single key, since single keys are commonly used for other purposes. However, you can link a macro to a single key by entering the representation of that key into the Key edit bar, then deselecting the ⌘, Shift, and Option boxes. If possible, the combination of keys to which you link a macro should not be used for another purpose, either by the Macintosh or by the application in which you'll be working when you invoke the macro. If you assign a macro to a key or a key combination that already has another function, AutoMac will invoke the macro to which that key is linked when you press that key or combination. The original meaning of the key or combination will be obscured. Appendix 2 lists key combinations that are used by Word for specific purposes. As we explained in Chapter 14, however, it's possible to assign the functions of these keys to different keys.

Unnamed macros

If you want, you can create a macro that is not linked to any key or key combination. To do this, leave the Key bar blank. (It doesn't matter whether one or more of the check boxes are selected.) However, linking a macro to a key makes that macro easier to execute. To execute a macro that is not linked to a key, you must use the Play button in the main AutoMac dialog box. We'll explain more about that later in this chapter.

Specifying a startup macro

If you link a macro to the ⌘-Shift-Option-0 (zero) key combination, AutoMac will play it automatically each time you start your Macintosh (or, if you've specified a startup application, as soon as that application is loaded). If you have not specified Word as a startup application, you might want to create a startup macro that opens Word. If you have specified Word as a startup application (using the Set Startup... command on the Special menu at the Finder level), you might want to create a startup macro that loads a "template" document.

Naming the Macro

In addition to specifying the key or key combination to which you want to link a macro, you should type a brief description of the macro into the Description of New Macro edit bar within the Record New Macro dialog box. The description of the macro can be as long as you like; however, the practical limit is 24 characters. The description you specify will appear in the list of macros within the main AutoMac dialog box. If you don't want to provide a description of the macro, you can simply leave the Description of New Macro edit bar blank. In that case, only the representation of the key(s) to which the macro is linked will appear in the main AutoMac dialog box.

Although you don't have to supply either a name or a description, it's a good idea to supply one or the other. Otherwise, the listing for that macro within the main AutoMac dialog box will be blank.

Once you have specified the key(s) to which you want to link the macro and/or typed a description of the macro, you should click the Record button, or press Return or Enter. As soon as you do, AutoMac usually will begin recording your keystrokes and mouse actions. If you specified a key or key combination to which a macro is already assigned (or one that AutoMac reserves for its own purposes), however, AutoMac will beep and display an alert box that tells you so, then allow you to specify a different key or combination. If you decide that you don't want to record a macro after all, you can click the Cancel button (or press ⌘-.) to cancel the recording process.

Once AutoMac has accepted your clicking of the Record button, it will begin recording your keystrokes and mouse actions. While you are recording a macro, you can do most things in Word as you normally do. However, because of the way AutoMac records the effect of clicking and dragging your mouse, you should use keystrokes rather than your mouse to do the following things:

—move the insertion point within a document
—highlight text within a document
—scroll text into and out of view
—select items from list boxes
—adjust settings controlled by the icons on the ruler

When you click or drag your mouse, AutoMac records the position of the mouse pointer relative to the upper-left corner of the screen, one of the four corners of the current window, or the previous position of the mouse pointer. Consequently, unless the screen looks the same when you play a macro as it did when you recorded that macro, the macro will do something other than what you intended it to do. We'll explain this phenomenon in more detail later.

To move the insertion point within a document, you should use the ↑, ↓, ←, and → keys, or any of the key combinations listed in Appendix 2 or discussed in Chapter 4. For example, to move the insertion point two characters to the right, you would press the → key two times; to move the insertion point to the beginning of the current paragraph, you would hold down the ⌘ key and press either the ↑ key or 8 on the numeric keypad; and so forth.

To highlight text within a document, you should use keys (and key combinations) to move the insertion point while holding down the Shift key. For example, to highlight the character to the right of the insertion point, you would hold down the Shift key and press →; to highlight the current word, you would press ⌘-→,

⌘-←, and then ⌘-Shift-→; to highlight the current sentence, you would press ⌘-1 (keypad), ⌘-7 (keypad), and then ⌘-Shift-1 (keypad); to highlight the current paragraph, you would press ⌘-2 (keypad), ⌘-8 (keypad), and then ⌘-Shift-2 (keypad); and so forth.

To scroll text into and out of view while recording a macro, you should use the document-scrolling keys listed in Appendix 2. For example, you should use the ⌘-Option-/ combination or the + key on the numeric keypad to scroll down a line of a document; use the ⌘-Option-p combination, the page up key (on the SE), or 9 on the numeric keypad to scroll up a new screenful of text; and so on.

To select items from list boxes while you are recording a macro, you should use the techniques discussed in Chapter 2. For example, you can use the ↓ and ↑ keys to move the highlight to the next and previous items in a list box, move the highlight to a specific entry by typing its first letter, and so forth. When you click or drag within a dialog box, AutoMac records the action relative to one of the corners of that box. Since the sizes of Word's various dialog boxes do not change, you can safely click check boxes, radio buttons, and regular buttons, and click and drag within text boxes while you are recording a macro.

To adjust the settings that are normally controlled by icons on the ruler, you should use the commands on Word's Format menu. To adjust the position and alignment of tab stops, you should select the Paragraph... command and click the Tabs.... button; to set indents, line spacing, and paragraph spacing, you should use other objects within the Paragraph dialog box; to assign styles, you should use the Styles... command on the Format menu; and to adjust paragraph alignments, you should use the ⌘-Shift-(l, r, j, or c) combinations.

Correcting Mistakes

While you are recording a macro, you may make a mistake, such as typing a character you didn't intend to type, or issuing a command other than the one you wanted to issue. In those cases, you have two choices. First, you can correct the mistake. For example, if you typed the wrong character, you would press the Backspace key and then type the correct one. Of course, AutoMac will record the correction. Consequently, each time you play the macro, AutoMac will make the same mistake you made, then make the correction. If you want, you can edit the macro after you complete the recording, correcting the mistake. We'll show you how to do that later in this chapter.

Second, you can cancel the recording and try again. To cancel the recording of a macro, you should click the AutoMac icon or press Option--, then choose Cancel from the dialog box that AutoMac presents at that point. We'll explain more about the effect of the Cancel button in the next section of this chapter.

Ending the Recording of a Macro

When you have completed the task that you want to record, you should end the recording. To do this, either click the AutoMac icon or press Option--. As soon as you do either of these things, AutoMac will reveal an End of Recording dialog box

like the one shown in Figure 16-3. To end the recording of a macro and save it in
RAM, you should click the Stop button. When you do this, AutoMac will stop
recording, retain what it has recorded, and close the End of Recording dialog box.

FIGURE 16-3

End of Recording: sample macro	AutoMac III
☐ Add a time delay (seconds) [ ]	[**Stop**]
☐ Record full mouse drag track	[Continue]
[Options] [Misc] [Suspend]	[Cancel]

*AutoMac will reveal this dialog box when you click the AutoMac icon
while recording a macro.*

Like the Stop button, the Cancel button ends the recording of a macro. When
you select this button, however, AutoMac discards the macro that it has recorded,
instead of retaining it in RAM. You should click this button if you have made a
major mistake during the recording of a macro.

If, after accessing the End of Recording dialog box, you decide that you want
to continue recording, you should click the Continue button instead of Stop or
Cancel. When you do this, AutoMac will remove the End of Recording dialog box
from the screen and resume recording your actions. None of the actions that you
performed to access or use the End of Recording dialog box will be recorded.

**Suspending
the Recording
of a Macro**

In certain situations, you may want to suspend the recording of a macro. For
example, you may want to test a command to see if it is the one that you want to issue,
without having AutoMac record the process. To suspend the recording of a macro,
simply access the End of Recording dialog box, either by clicking the AutoMac icon
or by pressing Option--. Then, click the Suspend button. When you do this,
AutoMac will stop recording, beep, and display an alert box like the one shown in
Figure 16-4. When you click OK to acknowledge this alert, AutoMac will remove
the box from the screen.

FIGURE 16-4

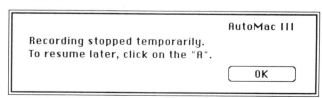

	AutoMac III
Recording stopped temporarily. To resume later, click on the "A".	
	[OK]

*AutoMac will display this alert box when you click the
Suspend button in the End of Recording dialog box.*

To resume the recording of the macro, reaccess the End of Recording dialog box, then click Continue. At that point, AutoMac will resume recording your actions, appending them to the portion of the macro that it recorded before you clicked the Suspend button. If, instead of resuming recording, you want to stop and save the portion that you recorded previously, you should choose Stop instead of Continue. If you want to stop recording and discard what you've already recorded, you should choose Cancel. If you want to continue the suspension of the recording, you should choose Suspend again.

An Example

To demonstrate the process of recording a macro, let's record one that transposes two characters. This macro, which we'll link to the Option-t key combination, will move the character situated to the right of the insertion point to a position immediately to the left of the character situated to the left of the insertion point.

To begin recording this macro, position the insertion point between any two characters that you want to transpose. Next, click on the AutoMac icon or press the Option-Backspace combination to reveal the main AutoMac dialog box. Then, click the Record button to reveal the Record New Macro dialog box. At this point, link the new macro to the Option-t combination by typing *t* in the Key edit bar, clicking the Option box, and deselecting the ⌘ and Shift boxes. Next, type the description *Transposes two characters* into the Description of New Macro edit bar. Finally, click the Record button to begin recording.

To transpose the characters that are situated to the left and right of the insertion point, begin by pressing the ➡ key (or the 6 on the numeric keypad) while holding down the Shift key. This highlights the character to the right of the insertion point— the one you want to move. Then, pull down the Edit menu and select the Cut command. When you do this, Word will cut the misplaced character and place it on the Clipboard. Next, press ⬅ to move the insertion point one character to the left. Finally, pull down the Edit menu and select the Paste command. When you do this, Word will paste the misplaced character into its proper place—immediately to the left of the other character.

Once you have performed these actions, end the recording of the macro by clicking the AutoMac icon or by pressing Option-- to reveal the End of Recording dialog box. Then, click the Stop button. AutoMac will stop recording, close the End of Recording dialog box, and retain the macro in RAM. At that point, you can transpose any two letters simply by moving the insertion point between them and pressing Option-t. We'll explain more about playing macros later in this chapter.

What AutoMac Records

When you press keys and combinations of keys during the recording of a macro, AutoMac records them literally. For example, if you type the word *hello*, AutoMac records the letters *h*, *e*, *l*, *l*, and *o*. Characters that cannot be represented as single characters are represented in a special way, as are combinations of the ⌘, Shift, and Option keys with other keys. When you play a macro, AutoMac "presses" the same keys that you pressed when you recorded the macro.

By default, AutoMac records only two mouse activities: clicking and dragging. If you click the mouse within the active window (which may be a dialog box), AutoMac will record the location of the mouse pointer relative to one of the corners of that window or dialog box (the corner closest to the position of the mouse pointer). If you click outside the active window or dialog box, AutoMac will record the location of the mouse pointer relative to the upper-left corner of the screen.

When you drag the mouse, AutoMac normally records only the position of the mouse pointer when you press the mouse button, and the position of the mouse pointer when you release the button—not the "drag track" (the location of the mouse pointer at various points during the drag). If you begin dragging in the active window or dialog box, both locations are recorded relative to the closest corner of that window or box. If you begin dragging outside the active window or dialog box, both locations are recorded relative to the upper-left corner of the screen.

Importantly, the process of using a mouse to select commands from menus is not recorded in the same way that a drag is. Instead, AutoMac inserts a command into the macro that specifies the name of the command and the name of the menu that contains that command.

If you press a key or combination of keys to which a macro is linked while you are recording a macro, AutoMac will play that macro. However, it will record only the macro-invoking keystroke. This creates a subroutine call. When you play the macro that contains the recording of a key to which a macro is linked, AutoMac will play the subroutine macro. As soon as AutoMac finishes playing that macro, it will resume playing the macro that called the subroutine. We'll explain more about subroutines later when we show you how to play macros.

Recording Options

AutoMac allows you to change many of its recording actions either before you begin recording a macro or at any time during the recording. To alter these settings prior to recording a macro, click the Options ⌘O button in the Record New Macro dialog box. To change these settings once you have begun recording, click the AutoMac icon or press Option-- to reveal the End of Recording dialog box, then click the Options button. In either case, AutoMac will reveal the AutoMac III Recording Options dialog box shown in Figure 16-5 on the next page.

The 14 radio buttons and single check box in the Mouse Relativity section of this dialog box allow you to specify the "point of relativity" for clicks and drags. The radio buttons in the Down column determine the point from which AutoMac will measure mouse clicks and the action of pressing the mouse button at the beginning of a drag. The radio buttons in the Up column determine the point from which AutoMac will measure the action of releasing the mouse button at the end of a drag.

FIGURE 16-5

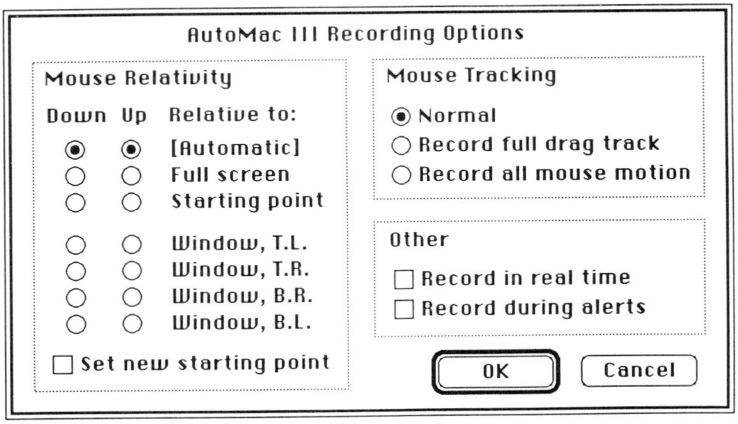

```
┌─────────────────────────────────────────────────────┐
│            AutoMac III Recording Options             │
│ ┌──────────────────────────┐ ┌──────────────────────┐│
│ │ Mouse Relativity         │ │ Mouse Tracking       ││
│ │                          │ │ ◉ Normal             ││
│ │ Down  Up  Relative to:   │ │ ○ Record full drag track││
│ │  ◉    ◉   [Automatic]     │ │ ○ Record all mouse motion││
│ │  ○    ○   Full screen    │ └──────────────────────┘│
│ │  ○    ○   Starting point │ ┌──────────────────────┐│
│ │                          │ │ Other                ││
│ │  ○    ○   Window, T.L.   │ │                      ││
│ │  ○    ○   Window, T.R.   │ │ ☐ Record in real time││
│ │  ○    ○   Window, B.R.   │ │ ☐ Record during alerts││
│ │  ○    ○   Window, B.L.   │ └──────────────────────┘│
│ │ ☐ Set new starting point │  ┌────────┐ ┌────────┐  │
│ └──────────────────────────┘  │   OK   │ │ Cancel │  │
│                               └────────┘ └────────┘  │
└─────────────────────────────────────────────────────┘
```

This dialog box lets you alter AutoMac's recording actions before or during the recording of a macro.

The default setting, [Automatic], causes AutoMac to record these events in the way described above. In almost all cases, this is the setting that you'll use when you record macros for Microsoft Word. However, you can select other buttons, if you want. The Full Screen buttons instruct AutoMac to record the position of mouse events relative to the upper-left corner of the screen; the Starting Point buttons command it to record mouse actions from the current starting point—initially, the position of the mouse pointer (not necessarily the insertion point) when AutoMac began to record the macro. The Set New Starting Point text box allows you to set a new starting point at any point during the execution of the macro. If you click OK while this box is selected, AutoMac will record the position of future mouse events relative to the position of the mouse pointer when you subsequently resume (or begin) recording. The remaining options command AutoMac to record future mouse events relative to the upper-left, upper-right, lower-right, or lower-left corners of the active window.

The three radio buttons in the Mouse Tracking section of the AutoMac III Recording Options dialog box allow you to control what mouse events AutoMac records. The Normal option commands AutoMac to record only clicks and the starting and ending points of drags. This is the option that you'll want to use almost all the time. The second option, Record Full Drag Track, records the position of the mouse pointer every $\frac{1}{60}$ second during a drag. (If you want, you can access this setting through the Record Full Drag Track check box in the Record New Macro and End of Recording dialog boxes.) Consequently, the path of the drag—not just the beginning and ending points—is recorded. This sort of recording is necessary only in programs like MacPaint, where the path of the mouse pointer during a drag is important. The final option, Record All Mouse Motion, records the position of the mouse pointer every $\frac{1}{60}$ second at all times—not just during drags. Consequently, all mouse movements are recorded. Although this sort of recording creates an interesting effect upon playback, it makes for large and complex macros.

The two check boxes in the Other section of the AutoMac III Recording Options dialog box control other recording actions. The first of these boxes, Record in Real Time, determines whether AutoMac records the timing of the events in addition to the events themselves. If this box is deselected (the default condition), AutoMac will record only the events that occur while it is recording. If the box is selected, AutoMac will record the timing of the events as well. For most of your Word macros, you won't want to record the timing of a process.

The second of these check boxes, Record During Alerts, determines whether AutoMac will pause when an AutoMac alert box appears. If this box is deselected (the default condition), AutoMac will pause; if the box is selected, AutoMac will record your response to the alert box. In most cases, you will want to leave this box unchecked.

Once you have changed any settings that you wanted to alter, you should click the OK button. If you have not yet begun to record the macro, AutoMac will return you to the Record New Macro dialog box. To begin recording, simply choose Record from that box. If you have interrupted the recording of a macro to change these settings, AutoMac will return you to the End of Recording dialog box when you click the OK button. In that case, you should click Continue to resume recording at this point. If you don't want the changes that you've made to take effect, you should click Cancel rather than OK from the AutoMac III Recording Options dialog box.

Advanced Recording Techniques

In addition to recording keystrokes and mouse actions, you can add four "special features" to a macro as you record it. First, you can design custom message and alert boxes. Second, you can command AutoMac to beep at any point during the playback of a macro. Third, you can command AutoMac to pause until a certain amount of time has elapsed or until a specific date and/or time or a certain event occurs. Finally, you can command AutoMac to begin executing another macro.

To add any of these features to a macro, you must access the End of Recording dialog box after recording up to the point at which you want that event to occur. To access this dialog box, simply click the AutoMac icon or press the Option-- combination. Once the dialog box appears, click the Misc button. As soon as you do this, AutoMac will reveal the dialog box shown in Figure 16-6—the Misc Recording Options dialog box. The four buttons in this box—Do a Message or Alert Box, Beep Speaker, Stop Playback Until..., and Jump to a Macro—control AutoMac's four special macro features. To add one of these features to a macro, click the corresponding button, do whatever AutoMac asks you to do, and then click OK to return to the End of Recording dialog box. At that point, choose Continue to continue recording, choose Stop to stop recording, or choose Cancel to cancel the recording of the macro.

FIGURE 16-6

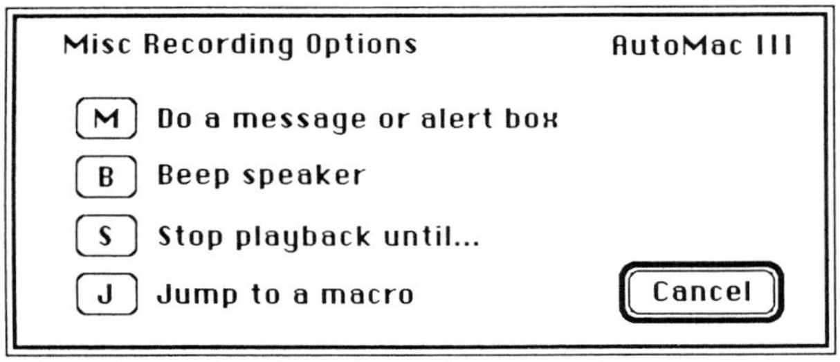

```
┌──────────────────────────────────────────────┐
│  Misc Recording Options          AutoMac III   │
│                                                │
│   [ M ]  Do a message or alert box             │
│   [ B ]  Beep speaker                          │
│   [ S ]  Stop playback until...                │
│   [ J ]  Jump to a macro          [ Cancel ]   │
└──────────────────────────────────────────────┘
```

This dialog box allows you to add special features to your macro.

Creating custom alert boxes

AutoMac allows you to create custom alert boxes that will be displayed on the screen when it executes a macro. These boxes, which can contain text and up to two buttons, allow you to present information to the user and allow the user to determine the course of the macro. A box without any buttons will remain on the screen for the amount of time you specify. A box with one button will remain on the screen until the user chooses that button. At that point, AutoMac will continue with the execution of the macro. A box with two buttons will remain on the screen until the user chooses either of its buttons. If the user chooses the top button, AutoMac will continue the execution of the macro. If the user chooses the bottom button, AutoMac will cancel the execution of the macro.

The buttons in custom alert boxes work just like the buttons in any other alert or dialog box. The single button in a one-button alert box is the default button, as is the upper button in a two-button dialog box. Consequently, you can choose them by pressing Return or Enter. You can select the bottom button in a two-button box by pressing ⌘-period. Of course, you also can select these buttons by clicking them with your mouse.

To design a custom alert box while you are recording a macro, you must choose the Do a Message or Alert Box button in the Misc Recording Options dialog box. When you choose this button, AutoMac will display the dialog box—shown in Figure 16-7. The items in this box—the Do a Message or Alert Box dialog box—allow you to specify the position of the box on the screen, its size, the number of buttons it will have, and the message it will contain.

Once you have accessed this dialog box, you should type into the Text text box the message you want AutoMac to display in the custom alert or message box. This message should be short enough to fit within the confines of the alert box. While you are typing the message, you can use your mouse to highlight text within it, and use the Backspace key to delete all or part of it.

FIGURE 16-7

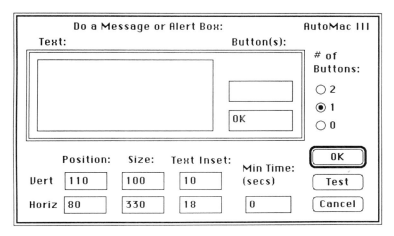

AutoMac will display this dialog box when you choose Do a Message or Alert Box from the Misc Recording Options dialog box.

Next, you should enter the text for the button(s), if any, that you want to appear in the box. Any custom box can contain either zero, one, or two buttons. If you want the box to contain one button, you should type the text for that button into the lower of the two Button(s) edit bars. As you can see, AutoMac provides OK as the default entry in this box. When the user clicks the button in a one-button alert box, AutoMac will continue executing the macro. Therefore, the "text" for the button should be positive, like *OK*, *Continue*, and so forth.

If you want the box to contain two buttons, you should type entries into both of the Button(s) edit bars. The upper bar should contain "positive" text (for example, *Yes*), since AutoMac will continue the execution of the macro when the user clicks the button that corresponds to that text. The lower bar should contain "negative" text (for example, *No*), since AutoMac will cancel the execution of the macro when the user clicks the button that corresponds to that text.

The buttons along the right edge of this dialog box allow you to specify how many buttons the custom message or alert box should contain. If you choose 2, the box will have two buttons. The top button will be the default button, and will contain the text from the upper Button(s) edit bar; the bottom button will contain the text from the lower Button(s) edit bar. If you choose 1, the box will have one button. This button (which will be the default) will contain the text from the lower Button(s) edit bar; AutoMac will ignore any text in the upper Button(s) edit bar. If you choose 0, the box will not have any buttons. In that case, AutoMac will ignore any text in either of the Button(s) edit bars.

The six edit bars at the lower-left corner of the dialog box shown in Figure 16-7 let you specify the position and size of the box you are designing. The value in each of these bars specifies a number of pixels—increments of $1/_{72}$ inch.

The entries in the Position bars determine the position of the upper-left corner of the custom alert box relative to the upper-left corner of the screen. The default values of 110 and 80 position the upper-left corner of the box approximately $1^1/_2$ inches from the top of the screen and 1 inch from the left edge of the screen.

The entries in the Size bars determine the height and width of the custom alert box. The default value in the upper bar, 100, specifies a box that is approximately $1^1/_2$ inches tall. The default value in the lower bar, 330, specifies a box that is approximately $4^1/_2$ inches wide. The sum of the values in the Vert Position and Size bars cannot exceed 341; the sum of the values in the Horiz Position and Size bars cannot exceed 511. If they do, AutoMac will beep and display an alert box when you choose OK to complete the design of the box, or when you choose Test to test it.

The entries in the Text Inset bars determine how far the text within the box will be offset from the top, bottom, left, and right edges of the alert box. The entry in the upper bar controls the offset from the top and bottom borders of the box. The default value in this bar is 10. The entry in the lower bar controls the offset from the left border of any custom alert box, the offset from the right border of a box with no buttons, and the offset from the left edge of the button(s) in a box with one or two buttons. The default value in this bar is 18.

The entry in the Min Time: (Secs) edit bar determines the minimum number of seconds that a custom alert box will remain on the screen. If you are designing an alert box without any buttons, this bar should contain a value greater than 0. Otherwise, the box will disappear as soon as it appears. No matter how long the box remains on the screen, AutoMac will continue executing the macro as soon as it disappears. If you are designing a custom alert box that has buttons (either one or two), the Min Time: (Secs) bar should contain the value 0. Otherwise, the box will remain on the screen for the specified period of time, even if the user clicks a button before that period of time has elapsed.

Once you have designed a custom alert box, you can use the Test button to see what you have created. When you click this button, AutoMac will display the box that is specified by the entries in the Do a Message or Alert Box dialog box. If the box has buttons, it will remain on the screen until you choose one of them. If the box does not have any buttons, it will remain on the screen for the number of seconds specified in the Min Time: (Secs) text box. In either case, AutoMac will return you to the Do a Message or Alert Box dialog box as soon as it clears the custom box from the screen. At that point, you can click OK to "lock in" the definition of the box and return to the End of Recording dialog box, or you can change some of the parameters and test it again. If you choose Cancel, AutoMac will return you to the End of Recording dialog box without adding the custom alert box to the macro.

AutoMac also allows you to make a macro beep at practically any point during its execution. To insert a beep into a macro while you are recording it, access the End of Recording dialog box, either by clicking the AutoMac icon or pressing Option--, choose Misc, and then choose the Beep Speaker button from the Misc Recording Options dialog box. When you do this, your Macintosh will beep once, and AutoMac will add an instruction that will cause it to beep once at that point in its playback. As soon as you choose this button, AutoMac will return you to the End of Recording dialog box. At that point, you can repeat the previous steps to add another beep, or you can continue, stop, or cancel the recording of the macro. You'll often want to use one or more beeps to draw attention to an alert box.

Beeping

The Stop Playback Until... button in the Misc Recording Options dialog box allows you to stop the execution of a macro for a certain span of time or until a certain date and/or time or specified event occurs. When you choose the Stop Playback Until... button, AutoMac will display the dialog box shown in Figure 16-8. As you can see, this box contains six "stop until" options. The option that is selected when you choose OK determines the type of pause that AutoMac will add to the macro. If you choose Cancel instead of OK, AutoMac will return to the End of Recording dialog box without adding a pause to the macro.

Pausing the execution of a macro until a certain event or time occurs

FIGURE 16-8

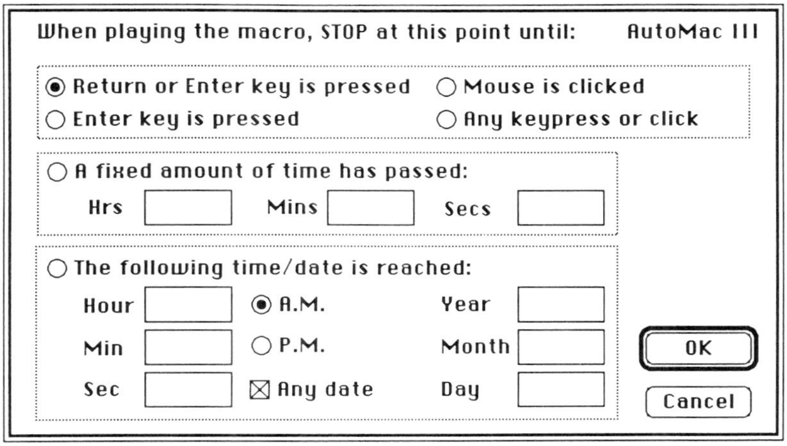

AutoMac will present this dialog box when you click the Stop Playback Until... button in the Misc Recording Options dialog box.

The first four options command AutoMac to pause the execution of a macro until a certain event occurs. If you choose the Return or Enter Key is Pressed option, AutoMac will pause the macro until the user presses the Return or Enter key. If you choose the Enter Key is Pressed option, AutoMac will pause the macro until the user presses the Enter key (not the Return key). If you choose the Mouse is Clicked option, AutoMac will pause until the user clicks his/her mouse. If you choose the Any Keypress or Click option, AutoMac will pause the macro until the user presses any key or clicks the mouse.

The next option, A Fixed Amount of Time Has Passed, pauses the macro for the number of hours, minutes, and seconds that you enter into the three edit bars below that option. For example, if you wanted to pause the execution of the macro for 30 seconds, you would choose this option, enter the value *30* into the Secs edit bar, and either leave the Hrs and Mins bars blank or enter the value 0 into them.

The final option, The Following Time/Date is Reached, pauses the macro until the day and time specified by the entries in the six edit bars below that option. If you want the macro to pause until a particular time on a particular day, you should fill in all six bars and make sure that the Any Date check box is deselected. For example, to make AutoMac pause the execution of a macro until 3:57 AM on November 24, 1989, you would enter the value *3* into the Hour edit bar, enter the value *57* into the Min edit bar, enter the value *0* into the Sec edit bar (or leave it blank), choose the A.M. button, enter the value *1989* into the Year edit bar, enter the value *11* into the Month edit bar, enter the value *24* into the Day edit bar, and make sure that the Any Date check box is deselected.

If you want the macro to pause until the next occurrence of a particular time (that is, if the specific date doesn't matter), you should fill in the Hour, Min, and Sec edit bars, choose either the A.M. or P.M. option, and make sure that the Any Date check box is selected. For example, if you want the macro to pause until 5:30 PM, you would enter the value *5* into the Hour edit bar, enter the value *30* into the Min edit bar, enter the value *0* into the Sec edit bar (or leave it blank), choose the P.M. option, and check the Any Date box. If AutoMac executes the Pause command before 5:30 PM on a particular day, it will pause the macro until 5:30 PM on that day. If AutoMac executes the Pause command after 5:30 PM, however, it will pause the macro until 5:30 PM the next day.

During the pause, any keystrokes or mouse actions that the user performs— including the action that ends the pause—will be passed on to Word. Therefore, Word will do whatever those actions normally command it to do. Consequently, pauses of this sort are intended for situations in which you want the user to supply input during the execution of a macro. In many cases, you'll want to use a beep and/or alert box immediately prior to a pause. The alert box tells the user what to do during the pause; the beep calls attention to the alert box.

After adding a pause to the macro, you'll probably want to suspend recording while you perform the actions that the user will perform during the pause. To do this, simply click the AutoMac icon or press Option-- to access the End of Recording dialog box, click the Suspend button, and then click OK in the alert box that AutoMac presents at that point. For example, if you pause the macro after recording the action of pulling down the File menu and selecting the Save As... command, you'll want to suspend recording while you type a name and click OK. At that point, the document will be in the same condition it would be in after the user performed those actions. Consequently, you would resume recording at that point. To do that, simply click the AutoMac icon or press Option-- to reveal the End of Recording dialog box again, then click the Continue button.

The final button in the Misc Recording Options dialog box—Jump to a Macro—allows you to branch the execution from one macro to the beginning of another macro (or back to the beginning of the same macro). To command AutoMac to branch the execution of a macro to the beginning of another (or the same) macro, click the Jump to a Macro option in the Misc Recording Options dialog box. AutoMac will then present the dialog box shown in Figure 16-9. To identify the macro to which you want to "jump," use the ⌘, Shift, and Option check boxes and the Key Name edit bar to specify the key to which the macro is linked. For example, if you want AutoMac to play the macro that is linked to the ⌘-Option-t combination, you would type *t* into the Key Name edit bar and check the ⌘ and Option boxes. When you click OK, AutoMac will insert the jump instructions into the macro and return you to the End of Recording dialog box. If you click Cancel, AutoMac will return to the End of Recording box without adding the jump instructions to the macro.

Jumping to another macro

FIGURE 16-9

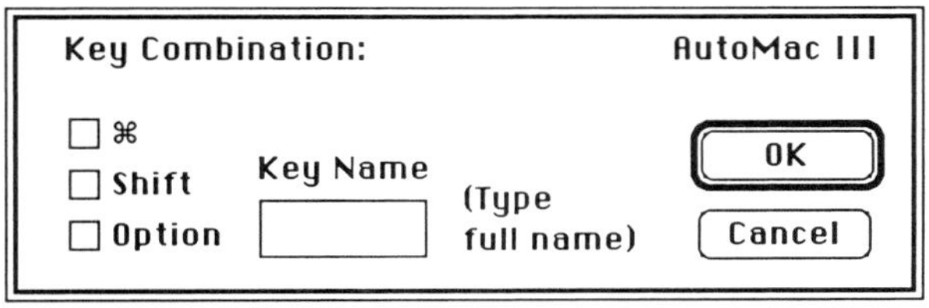

This dialog will appear when you click the Jump to a
Macro button in the Misc Recording Options dialog box.

When AutoMac encounters a jump instruction while playing a macro, it will stop playing that macro and begin playing the macro specified by the jump instruction. Any commands that follow a jump instruction in a macro will never be played. Consequently, you should end the recording of a macro after specifying a jump. To do this, click the Stop button in the End of Recording dialog box.

It's important to differentiate between the effect of recording a jump instruction and simply recording the keystroke to which a macro is linked. A jump instruction creates a one-way rerouting of the execution of the macro. That is, AutoMac will not return to the macro that contains the jump instruction after it completes the macro to which it has jumped. However, recording the key(s) to which a macro is linked causes a two-way rerouting of the macro. As soon as AutoMac finishes playing the "subroutine" macro, it will return to the main macro and resume executing it precisely where it left off.

Delaying the execution of a macro

The Add a Time Delay (Seconds) check box and edit bar in the End of Recording dialog box provide another way to pause the execution of a macro. Unlike the pauses introduced by the Stop Playback Until... button in the Misc Recording Options dialog box, the pauses introduced by this command do not allow user input. Nothing that the user does during the pause will be passed on to Word. This command is most useful for delaying the execution of the next command in a macro until Word has refreshed the screen.

To specify a delay of this sort at a particular point in a macro as you are recording it, simply click the AutoMac icon or press Option-- to reveal the End of Recording dialog box, click the Add a Time Delay (Seconds) check box, type the length of the delay (a number of seconds) into the corresponding edit bar, and then click Continue to resume recording.

An example

As an example of these special techniques, let's record a macro, linked to the Option-b combination, that boldfaces the words you specify. When you play this macro, it should beep and present the alert box shown in Figure 16-10. When you click OK, AutoMac should remove the alert box, pause until you click on the word that you want to boldface, and then boldface that word. Then, the macro should wait for one second, beep, and present the dialog box shown in Figure 16-11. If you click Yes, AutoMac will execute the macro again, allowing you to boldface another word. If you click No, AutoMac will cancel the execution of the macro.

FIGURE 16-10

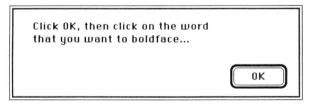

Our boldfacing macro presents this one-button alert box first.

FIGURE 16-11

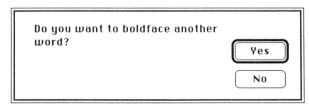

This alert box allows the user to choose between two buttons.

To begin, access the Record New Macro dialog box, either by clicking the AutoMac icon (or pressing Option-Backspace) and then choosing Record, or by pressing Option-=. Then, to specify the key combination for the macro, type *b* into the Key text box, check the Option box, and deselect the ⌘ and Shift boxes. Next, type *Boldfaces specified word* into the Description of New Macro edit bar. At that point, click Record to begin recording the macro.

Before you record any keystrokes, command AutoMac to sound a beep. To do this, click the AutoMac icon or press Option-- to access the End of Recording dialog box, click the Misc button to reveal the Misc Recording Options dialog box, and then click the Beep Speaker button within that box. Next, create the one-button alert box shown in Figure 16-10. To do this, click the Misc button in the End of Recording dialog box, and then click the Do a Message or Alert Box button within the Misc Recording Options dialog box. At this point, type the message *Click OK, then click on the word that you want to boldface...* into the Text edit bar, make sure that the lower Button(s) bar contains the letters OK, and make sure that the 1 option is clicked. At that point, click OK to return to the End of Recording dialog box.

Next, you should command AutoMac to pause until the user clicks the mouse. To do this, again click the Misc button in the End of Recording dialog box. Then, click the Stop Playback Until... button in the Misc Recording Options dialog box. Within the dialog box that AutoMac presents at this point, click the Mouse is Clicked radio button, then click OK.

At this point, you should suspend the execution of the macro while you click on a word you want to boldface. To do this, click the Suspend button in the End of Recording dialog box, then click OK in the alert box that AutoMac presents at that point. After you click on a word that you want to boldface, resume recording by clicking the AutoMac icon or pressing Option-- to reveal the End of Recording dialog box, then clicking Continue.

Next, you should highlight the word in which the insertion point marker is located at the time. To do this, first press ⌘-➡ to move the insertion point marker to the end of the current word. Then, press ⌘-⬅ to move the insertion point marker to the beginning of that word. Finally, press ⌘-Shift-➡ to highlight that word. After highlighting this word, assign it the boldface attribute by pulling down the Format menu and selecting the Bold command.

To give Word time to redraw the screen at this point, you should introduce a one-second delay. To do this, check the Add a Time Delay (Seconds) check box in the End of Recording dialog box, and enter the value *1* into the corresponding edit bar. Then, click Continue to add the delay to the macro.

At this point, you should add another beep to the macro by repeating the steps you used to create the first beep. Next, create the two-button alert box shown in Figure 16-11. To do this, again click the Misc button in the End of Recording dialog box, then click the Do a Message or Alert Box button within the Misc Recording

Options dialog box. Next, type the message *Do you want to boldface another word?* into the Text edit bar, type *Yes* in the upper Button(s) edit bar, type *No* in the lower Button(s) edit bar, click the 2 option, then click OK.

Finally, command AutoMac to replay the macro you are recording. To do this, click the Misc button in the End of Recording dialog box one more time, and then click the Jump to a Macro button in the Misc Recording Options dialog box. At this point, check the Option box in the dialog box shown in Figure 16-9 on page 741, make sure that the ⌘ and Shift boxes are not checked, type *b* in the Key Name edit bar, and then choose OK. Finally, end the recording of the macro by clicking the Stop button in the End of Recording dialog box.

**PLAYING
MACROS**

Once you record a macro, you can play it. If you have linked a macro to a key or a combination of keys, you can play that macro simply by pressing that key or combination. For example, if you linked a macro to the Option-t combination, AutoMac would play that macro whenever you pressed those keys.

Alternatively, you can use the Play button in the main AutoMac dialog box to play a macro. (The Play button provides the only way to play a macro that is not linked to a key.) To do this, click the AutoMac icon or press Option-Backspace to reveal the main AutoMac dialog box. Then, from the list of macros that appears at the left edge of that box, highlight the one you want to play. (This list will contain the descriptions and/or key combinations for all the macros currently in the portion of RAM that is reserved for executable macros.) To select a macro from this list, use the scroll arrows or scroll box to bring that macro into view (the macros will be arranged in alphabetical order by the first characters in their description), then click on it. Finally, click the Play button.

**What Happens
When You Play
a Macro**

When AutoMac plays a macro, it repeats the actions you performed when you recorded that macro. Specifically, it will "press" keys, select commands from menus, and "click and drag" the mouse. Unless the Record All Mouse Motion option was on while you were recording, AutoMac won't actually pull down menus when it issues commands. Instead, it will highlight the name of the menu briefly. Similarly, you won't be able to see the mouse pointer move around the screen unless the Record Full Drag Track or Record All Mouse Motion options were activated when you recorded the macro. AutoMac also will display custom alert boxes, beep, pause for input, and branch to other macros, as instructed by special commands within the macro.

In most cases, AutoMac will execute the keystrokes and mouse movements in a macro one immediately after another, as fast as it can. AutoMac can process commands faster than even the most experienced Word user. If the Record in Real Time option was on when you recorded the macro, however, AutoMac will perform the actions you recorded at the same speed you performed them when you recorded the macro.

If a macro commands AutoMac to press a key that is linked to another macro, AutoMac will stop playing the main macro and begin playing the macro that is linked to that key (the subroutine). As soon as AutoMac reaches the end of the subroutine macro, it will continue playing the main macro, starting with the action that immediately follows the macro-invoking keystroke. If the macro that is linked to the key or key combination no longer exists or is inactive, Word will do whatever that key or combination would normally cause it to do.

An Example

To demonstrate the playing of a macro, let's use the boldfacing macro that we just recorded to boldface the word *Word* on the first line of the document shown in Figure 16-12. Since the macro is linked to the Option-b combination, you should begin by pressing Option-b. AutoMac will beep, then display the one-button alert box shown in Figure 16-10. As soon as you click OK, AutoMac will pause until you click on the word that you want to boldface. In this case, you would click anywhere on the word *Word* on the first line of this document. AutoMac will then continue executing the macro. First, it will press ⌘-➡ to move the insertion point to the left of the first character in the next word (in this case, to the *t* in *to*). Then, it will press ⌘-⬅, which moves the insertion point immediately to the left of the *W* in *Word*. Next, it will press ⌘-Shift-➡, which highlights the word *Word* plus the space that follows it.

FIGURE 16-12

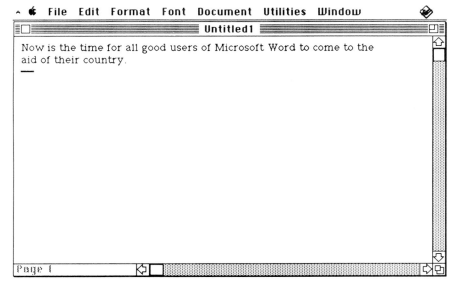

We'll use the boldfacing macro that we recorded earlier to boldface the word Word *on the first line of this document.*

At this point, the macro will select the Bold command from the Format menu. (Since the Record All Mouse Motion option was not activated when we recorded the selection of this command, AutoMac won't actually pull down the Format menu.) Then, AutoMac will pause for one second—enough time for Word to boldface *Word*, as shown in Figure 16-13. At that point, AutoMac will beep again, then display the dialog box shown in Figure 16-11. If you click Yes, AutoMac will repeat the macro. If you click No, AutoMac will cancel the execution of the macro at that point.

FIGURE 16-13

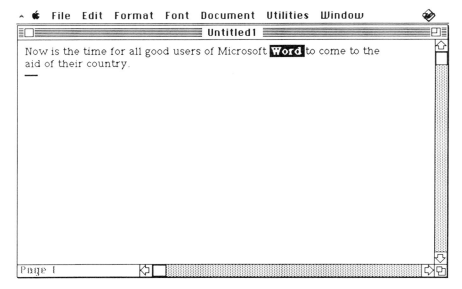

This figure shows the result of using our boldfacing macro to boldface the word Word *in the document shown in Figure 16-12.*

Cancelling the Execution of a Macro

Normally, AutoMac will continue playing a macro until it reaches the end of that macro. However, you can cancel the execution of a macro prematurely by pressing either the Option-. or ⌘-Shift-Option-. key combinations. The Option-. combination will cancel the execution of a macro in all situations except during a "stop until" pause. To cancel the execution of a macro during a "stop until" pause, you must use the ⌘-Shift-Option-. combination.

Deactivating and Reactivating Macros

A macro must be in a special portion of RAM in order to be played. Normally, if the macro that is linked to a key or combination of keys is in that portion of RAM when you press that key or combination, AutoMac will play that macro. However, there will be times when you'll want a key or key combination to have its normal function. To make this happen, you must "deactivate" the macro, either temporarily or permanently.

To deactivate a macro permanently, you must remove it from the portion of RAM in which active macros are stored. We'll show you how to do that in the next section of this chapter. However, you can deactivate macros temporarily without removing them from RAM. To do this, press Option-[. This key combination temporarily breaks the links between all the active macros and their key combinations. Consequently, pressing those key combinations will no longer invoke macros. However, you can still use the Play button in the main AutoMac dialog box to play them. To "relink" the active macros to their keys, simply press Option-].

A Word of Caution

A macro that doesn't do what you intended can have disastrous effects. For example, it can erase a different portion of a document than you intended it to erase, delete files, and, in some cases, cause your Macintosh to "crash." Therefore, we strongly recommend that you back up your work before you invoke any macro that has the potential to do harm—especially untested ones.

SAVING MACROS

When AutoMac records a macro, it stores representations of your actions in the memory of your Macintosh. This is where the macro must be in order to be played. However, unless you save your macros to disk before you turn off your computer, they will be destroyed. Consequently, you'll have to rerecord them before you can use them again.

Fortunately, AutoMac makes it easy to save your macros to disk. To do this, simply click the AutoMac icon or press Option-Backspace to reveal the main AutoMac dialog box. Then, click the Save button in this dialog box. If you have recorded any new macros or changed any of the macros in RAM since you last clicked the Save or Save As buttons, AutoMac will reveal a dialog box like the one shown in Figure 16-14 on the following page. If you have saved the macros previously, AutoMac will list the name of the file in which they are saved within this dialog box. If you have not saved the macros previously, AutoMac will display the name *Untitled*. If you click the Yes button at this point, AutoMac will save the macro currently in RAM to the file specified in the dialog box, overwriting that file. If the macro displays the name *Untitled*, AutoMac will save the macro into a file with the name *application(keys)*, where *application* is the name of the application in which you are working at the time. For example, if you are working in Word 4.0, AutoMac will save your macros into a file named Microsoft Word(keys).

If you want to specify the file into which AutoMac saves your macros, you should click the Save As... button rather then the Yes button within the dialog box shown in Figure 16-14. When you click this button, AutoMac will display the dialog box shown in Figure 16-15. The structures in this box allow you to specify a name, directory, and folder for the file into which AutoMac will save the macros in RAM. If you click Save, AutoMac will save the macros that are currently in RAM into the file you specified, then return you to the main AutoMac dialog box. If you choose Cancel, AutoMac will return you to the dialog box shown in Figure 16-14 without writing anything to disk.

FIGURE 16-14

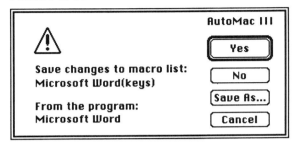

AutoMac will display a dialog box like this one when you click the Save button at the bottom of the main AutoMac dialog box.

FIGURE 16-15

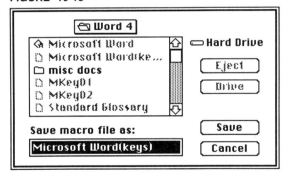

AutoMac will display a dialog box like this one when you click the Save As... button in the dialog box shown in Figure 16-14, or the Save As button at the bottom of the main AutoMac dialog box.

If, after clicking the Save button at the bottom of the main AutoMac dialog box, you decide that you don't want to save to disk the macros that are currently in RAM, you should click Cancel instead of Save. When you do this, AutoMac will return you to the main AutoMac dialog box without writing your macros to disk. However, the current versions of your macros will still be in RAM. If you click No instead, AutoMac won't just fail to write your macros to disk—it will cancel all the changes you have made to the macros in RAM.

If you have not changed any of the macros in RAM since you last clicked the Save or Save As buttons, AutoMac won't do anything when you click the Save button at the bottom of the main AutoMac dialog box. However, the Save As button at the bottom of that box will always work. Whenever you click this button, AutoMac will reveal the dialog box shown in Figure 16-15—the same one it displays when you choose the Save As... button from the dialog box shown in Figure 16-14. The structures in this box allow you to specify a name, directory, and folder for the file into which AutoMac will save the macros in RAM. (By default, AutoMac will supply the name of the file in which those macros are currently stored.) If you click OK, AutoMac will save the macros that are currently in RAM to the file you specified, then return you to the main AutoMac dialog box. If you choose Cancel, AutoMac will return you to the main AutoMac dialog box without writing anything to disk.

When you load an application while AutoMac is active, AutoMac will look for the "default" macro file—the one whose name begins with the name of that application and ends with the characters *(keys)*—and load it into RAM. Therefore, the macros in that file will be available for your use as soon as you enter the new applications. Consequently, it's a good idea to store in the default file the macros that you use most frequently. Macros that you use less frequently should be stored in other files—especially if you have a lot of macros.

MANAGING MACROS

As we stated earlier, a macro must be in RAM in order to be invoked. Specifically, the macros must be in the portion of RAM that AutoMac reserves for executable macros. The macros from only one macro file can be in this portion of RAM at any given time. The name of the file that contains the macros currently in the portion of RAM that is reserved for executable macros always appears to the right of the *File:* prompt near the bottom of the main AutoMac dialog box. This is the active macro file.

Opening Macro Files

To bring the macros from a macro file into the portion of RAM that is reserved for executable macros, you must use the Open button at the bottom of the main AutoMac dialog box. When you click this button, AutoMac will display a dialog box like the one shown in Figure 16-16 on the next page. The items in this box allow you to choose the file that contains the macros you want to activate.

To bring the macros from a particular file into the portion of RAM in which AutoMac stores executable macros, either double-click the name of the file or highlight it and click OK. As soon as you do this, AutoMac will move any macros that are currently in the portion of RAM reserved for executable macros into another portion of RAM. Then, it will bring the macros from the file you specified into the portion of RAM reserved for the executable macros. At this point, the list box within the main AutoMac dialog box will contain only the names of the macros from the file you specified. The name of the file that contains those macros will appear to the right of the *File:* prompt in the main AutoMac dialog box.

FIGURE 16-16

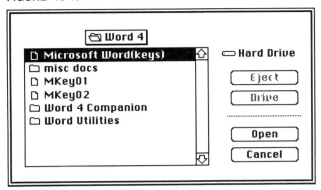

AutoMac displays a dialog box like this one when you click the Open button at the bottom of the main AutoMac dialog box.

If you open a macro file before saving your changes to the macros that are currently in the portion of RAM reserved for executable macros, those macros (complete with changes) will be shifted to another portion of RAM. If you subsequently click the Open button and select the name of the file in which the previous versions of those macros are saved, AutoMac won't read that file. Instead, it will shift the macros from the portion of RAM that they currently occupy into the portion of RAM that is reserved for executable macros.

To save to disk the macros that are in a nonexecutable portion of RAM, simply click the Save button at the bottom of the main AutoMac dialog box. If the macros that are in the nonexecutable portion of RAM contain unsaved changes, AutoMac will present a dialog box like the one shown in Figure 16-14, which allows you to save those changes. (If the macros that are in the executable portion of RAM also contain unsaved changes, AutoMac will present a dialog box that allows you to save those changes as soon as you choose Yes, No, or Cancel from the first box.) To avoid confusion, however, we recommend that you use the Save command to save the changes to the current macro file before you use the Open button to make another macro file current.

In some cases, you won't want to save the changes you've made to the macros in the executable portion of RAM. To undo those changes, you could click the Save button in the main AutoMac dialog box, click No, and then use the Open button to reopen the file that contains those macros. (The Save step is required, since, otherwise, AutoMac will not open the file.) Alternatively, you can simply click the Revert button. When you do this, AutoMac will clear all the macros from the executable portion of RAM and replace them with the macros that are stored in the active macro file.

Moving Macros

AutoMac lets you move and copy macros from one macro file to another. To do this, use the Open command to open the file that contains those macros. Then, in the list of macros in the main AutoMac dialog box, highlight the names of the macros you want to move. (To highlight the name of one macro without unhighlighting another, hold down the Shift key as you click.) Once you have highlighted all of the macros that you want to move, press ⌘-x. When you do this, AutoMac will remove the macros that you selected from the executable portion of RAM and store them on the Clipboard.

If you want to paste the macros into an existing macro file, use the Open button to open that file. If you want to paste those macros into a new file, click the New button instead. Then, in either case, press ⌘-v to copy the macros from the Clipboard into the executable portion of RAM—the portion of RAM that contains the macros (if any) from the file you just opened or created. To save the macros to disk, click the Save button at this point. When you do this, AutoMac will ask if you want to save the changes to the current macro file (the one into which you just pasted the macros). If you choose Yes, AutoMac will add the pasted macros to that file. Then, it will ask if you want to save the changes you made to the file from which you cut the macros. If you choose Yes, AutoMac will remove those macros from the file.

Copying Macros

You can copy macros from one file to another in a similar way. To do this, open the file that contains the macros you want to copy. Then, select the macros you want to copy from the list in the main AutoMac dialog box. Next, press ⌘-c instead of ⌘-x. When you do this, AutoMac will copy (not cut) the highlighted macros to the Clipboard. Consequently, the macros will not be removed from the executable portion of RAM. At this point, use the Open command to activate an existing macro file, or use the New command to create a new one. Then, press ⌘-v to paste the copied macros into the executable portion of RAM. Once you do this, you can use the Save command to save the new macros to that file.

Deleting Macros

In some cases, you'll want to delete one or more macros from a file without adding them to another file. To do this, open the file that contains those macros, highlight them, and click the Delete button at the right edge of the main AutoMac dialog box. When you do this, AutoMac will remove the macros that you highlighted from the executable portion of RAM. However, it will not remove those macros from the file until you click the Save or Save As buttons and click Yes.

Renaming Macros

Once you have recorded a macro, you may want to change its description or the key combination to which it is linked. Both are easy to do. However, the way you do them depends on whether your System folder contained the MacroEditor icon when you last turned on or restarted your Macintosh.

If your System folder does not contain this icon, the fourth button at the right edge of the main AutoMac dialog box will contain the word *Change*. This button allows you to change the key and/or description for a macro. To do either of these things, click the AutoMac icon or press Option-Backspace to reveal the main AutoMac dialog box. Then, in the list at the upper-left corner of that box, highlight the macro whose key or description you want to alter. At this point, click the Change button. When you do this, AutoMac will display a dialog box like the one shown in Figure 16-17.

FIGURE 16-17

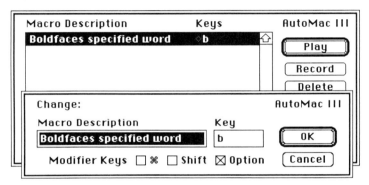

AutoMac will display a dialog box like this one when you click the Change button in the main AutoMac dialog box.

The Macro Description edit bar in this dialog box will contain the current description of the macro. To change the description, simply edit or replace the entry in that bar. The Key edit bar and the three Modifier Keys check boxes will indicate the combination to which the macro is currently linked. To link the macro to a different combination, simply change those settings, and click OK. When you do this, AutoMac will record the changes in RAM and display the altered description and/or key combination in the list within the main AutoMac dialog box. If you click Cancel instead, AutoMac won't make those changes.

If your System folder contained the MacroEditor icon when you last turned on or restarted your Macintosh, then the fourth button at the right edge of the main AutoMac dialog box will contain the word *Edit*. This button allows you to access AutoMac's macro editor. Within this editor, you can change the description of a macro, the keys to which it is linked, and a number of other things. We'll show you how to use the macro editor in the next section of this chapter.

The List Button

The List button in the main AutoMac dialog box allows you to save the listing of macros that appears in that box into a text file. Once you do that, you can print the list from within any word processor. This feature provides a handy way to keep track of which macros are stored in which files. When you click this button, AutoMac will present a dialog box like the one shown in Figure 16-18. To save a copy of the macro list to a file, simply specify the name of the file (as well as a folder and/or directory for that file), then click Save. If, after clicking the List button, you decide you don't want to save a copy of the list, click Cancel instead of Save.

FIGURE 16-18

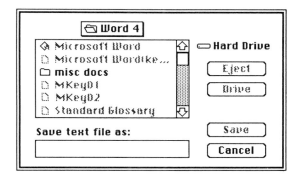

AutoMac will present a dialog box like this one when you click the List button at the bottom of the main AutoMac dialog box.

EDITING MACROS

If, when you play a macro, it doesn't work the way you intended, you can rerecord it. Alternatively, you can correct it within AutoMac's macro editor. To do this, you must drag the MacroEditor icon into your System folder before you start your Macintosh. Once you have done this, the fourth button at the right edge of the main AutoMac dialog box will read *Edit*, not *Change*.

To edit a macro, click the main AutoMac icon or press Option-Backspace to reveal the main AutoMac dialog box, select the macro you want to edit from the list of active macros, then click the Edit button. When you do this, AutoMac will present a dialog box like the one shown in Figure 16-19 on the next page. The main portion of this dialog box contains a listing of the macro that you selected. Within this portion of the dialog box, you can make changes to the macro, such as typing new lines, deleting old lines, and so forth, using standard editing techniques. For example, after clicking an insertion point, you can insert new characters at that point, use the Backspace key to delete the character to the left of that point, and so forth.

The Cut, Copy, and Paste buttons at the bottom of the macro editor dialog box allow you to cut and copy text within a macro or between macros. After dragging your mouse to select a portion of a macro, you can use the Cut or Copy buttons to cut or copy it to the macro editor's Clipboard. Then, after clicking a new insertion point, you can use the Paste button to insert the text from the Clipboard. Alternatively, you can select a portion of the document, then use the Paste command to replace that portion with the text from the Clipboard. To cut or copy a portion of one macro into another macro, use the OK or Cancel buttons in the macro editor dialog box to close the macro from which you cut or copied text. Then, use the Edit button in the main AutoMac dialog box to bring another macro into the macro editor. Finally, click an insertion point within the new macro (or highlight a portion of it) and click the Paste button.

FIGURE *16-19*

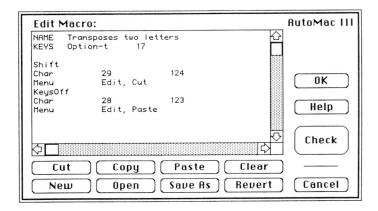

AutoMac will reveal a dialog box like this one when you choose the Edit button from the main AutoMac dialog box.

The Clear and New buttons allow you to remove portions of a macro. To remove a portion of a macro without placing a copy of it on the Clipboard, simply highlight it and then click the Clear button. (Alternatively, you can press the Backspace key.) The New button clears the entire macro from the macro editor dialog box.

The Save As button at the bottom of the macro editor dialog box allows you to save the current macro into a text file. When you issue this command, specify a name, and click OK, AutoMac will save the macro that appears in the macro editor dialog box into the file you specified in text form, exactly as it appears in the macro editor dialog box. Once you have done this, you can open the file into Word and print it. Alternatively, use the Open command to bring it back into the macro editor.

Once you've edited the macro, you should click OK. When you do this, AutoMac will check the macro for syntax errors. If the macro contains errors, AutoMac will beep, insert comments into the macro that pinpoint and explain the errors, and display the alert box shown in Figure 16-20. As soon as you click OK, AutoMac will clear the alert box from the screen, revealing the annotated macro. At that point, you can correct the errors and try again. If the macro does not contain any syntax errors, AutoMac will replace the version of the macro in RAM with the altered version of that macro, clear the macro editor dialog box from the screen, and redisplay the main AutoMac dialog box.

FIGURE 16-20

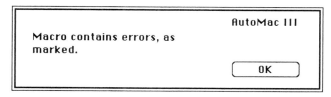

AutoMac will display this alert box if the current macro contains one or more syntax errors when you click the OK or Check buttons.

If you want AutoMac to check for syntax errors before you are ready to exit from the macro editor, click the Check button. When you do this, AutoMac will check the macro for syntax errors. If it finds any, it will annotate them, beep, and display the alert box shown in Figure 16-20. As soon as you click OK, AutoMac will clear the alert box from the screen, revealing the annotated macro.

At any time prior to clicking the OK button, you can "undo" the changes you have made to the macro within the macro editor by clicking the Revert button. As soon as you do this, AutoMac will replace the listing of the macro within the macro editor dialog box with a listing of the original version of that macro. At that point, you can start the editing process again. To cancel any changes and exit from the macro editor, simply click the Cancel button.

Macro Syntax

Although AutoMac does not store macros on disk in an understandable, structured, English-language form, it presents them in that form in the macro editor. Within the macro editor, any macro appears as a series of instructions. For example, Figure 16-21 on the following page shows how the boldfacing macro that we recorded earlier appears in the macro editor. Each instruction commands AutoMac to do something; for example, type a key, click the mouse, select a command from a menu, display a custom alert box, and so forth.

Each action that a macro performs is listed on an individual line of the macro editor. Each of these "command lines" has the form

time delay   command name   parameters

The first entry on each line, *time delay*, is optional. If AutoMac is playing the macro in the real-time mode, this entry tells AutoMac how long to wait before performing the action specified by the command that follows. If AutoMac is not playing in the real-time mode, AutoMac will ignore this parameter, if it exists. In either case, this value specifies a number of ticks (increments of $\frac{1}{60}$ second).

FIGURE 16-21

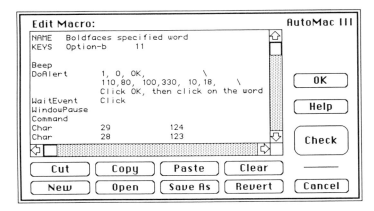

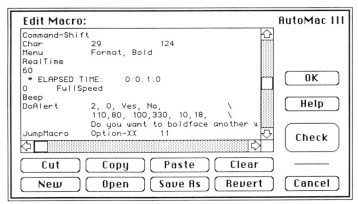

This is how the boldfacing macro that we recorded and played earlier appears in the macro editor.

The second entry on each line, *command name*, identifies the action that AutoMac should perform. (Because the first entry is optional, in many cases, the command name will be the first entry.) This can be as simple as a single letter (which AutoMac will type), or as complex as the DoAlert command, which creates a custom alert box. The case (upper or lower) of the characters in a command's name does not matter. However, we like to type most commands in "proper" form (the first letter of each word capitalized).

Many commands will have required or optional parameters; these parameters supply information to the command. For example, a Click command (which tells AutoMac where to click the mouse) has two parameters—one that specifies a horizontal distance from the origin (usually, the upper-left corner of the current window), and another that specifies a vertical distance from the origin.

If you want to (or have to) break a single macro command onto two or more lines, you must end each line (except the final one) with a backslash. That character tells AutoMac that the command continues on the next line of the macro. When AutoMac records a macro, it always breaks commands that are too long to fit within the width of the macro editor dialog box.

To edit a macro, you must be familiar with the syntax of AutoMac's various macro instructions. In this section, we'll present the instructions that can appear in a macro. If you need help with the syntax of a macro instruction as you are editing a macro, you can click the Help button within the macro editor dialog box. When you do this, a dialog box like the one shown in Figure 16-22 will appear. The text within this box presents the syntax of each macro command.

Macro Commands

FIGURE 16-22

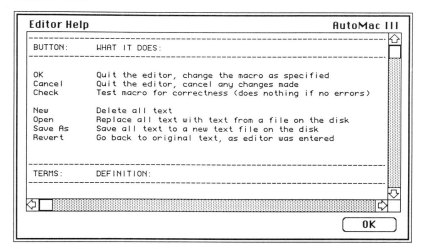

AutoMac will present a dialog box like this one when you click the Help button in the macro editor dialog box.

The NAME and KEYS commands

Two macro commands—NAME and KEYS—will appear at the beginning of almost every AutoMac macro. The NAME command defines the "name" of the macro—the description that will appear in the main AutoMac dialog box, to the right of the key to which the macro is linked. The form of this command is

NAME *description*

where *description* is the description of the macro. For example, a macro named *Boldface current word* would begin with the command

NAME Boldface current word

The NAME command is optional. Without it, however, no name will appear in the main AutoMac dialog box. If a macro contains a NAME command, it must precede all the other commands in the macro, including the KEYS command. (If you reverse the order of the NAME and KEYS commands, AutoMac will switch them into the proper order for you when you finish editing the macro.)

The KEYS command defines the key or key combination (if any) to which the macro is linked. The form of this command is

KEYS *key(s)*   *key code*

where *key(s)* is the representation of the key or key combination to which the macro is linked, and *key code* is the code that identifies that key or combination on the keyboard. If the macro is linked to a combination of keys (as it usually will be), this argument will consist of one or more of the modifier words *Option*, ⌘, or *Shift*, followed by the representation of the main key, all separated by hyphens.

The second argument, *key code*, is optional. If you don't include this argument (which, because this requires the use of a table, you probably won't), AutoKey will ask you to identify the key by pressing it after you choose OK to complete the editing process. At that point, it will add to the KEYS statement the number of the key or combination of keys that you pressed.

If the macro does not contain a KEYS command, you'll have to use the Play button within the main AutoMac dialog box in order to execute the macro. If the macro does contain a KEYS command, it must precede all the other commands in the macro, except the NAME command (if any).

Typing commands

Many of your Word macros will type information into a document or dialog box, or press one or more of the special keys on the keyboard. Consequently, they will contain representations of those keys.

Most keystrokes can be represented within a macro by the character that they produce. Within the macro, each character should appear on its own line; the key number of each character should appear to the right of that character. For example, making a macro type the word *test* would require four lines, as shown below:

t   17
e   14
s   1
t   17

As you can see, commanding a macro to type a series of characters can take a lot of space. If you want, you can use a special command—Type—to make a macro type one or more characters of the kind that can be represented by a single character in a macro. The form of this command is

Type *string*

where *string* is the single character or group of characters you want the macro to type. For example, the command

Type *test*

causes AutoMac to type the characters *test*.

Since the Type command usually provides the most efficient way to represent typing, AutoMac will use it whenever possible. For example, if you type one character per line while editing or writing a macro, and don't include the key numbers to the right of each character, AutoMac will consolidate the characters into a Type command. For example, if you typed *t*, *e*, *s*, and *t* on consecutive lines in the macro editor, AutoMac would replace those characters with the command *Type test* when you chose OK from the macro editor dialog box.

Not all keys can be represented by a single character within a macro. To represent the Tab, Backspace, Return, Enter, Space, and 0 through 9 keys (the ones at the top of the keyboard), you must use the forms shown in Table 16-1 on the next page. Each of these representations must appear on its own line of the macro.

To represent combinations of the ⌘, Option, and/or Shift keys and any other key, you must use three lines. The first line must contain the representation of the modifier key(s): Command, Option, Shift, Command-Option, Command-Shift, Option-Shift, or Command-Option-Shift. The next line should contain the representation of the key that you want pressed in combination with those keys. The third line should contain the command *KeysOff* (unnecessary if the macro ends at that point). For example, you would use the commands

Command-Shift
t   17
KeysOff

to represent the ⌘-Shift-t combination in a macro. (You could replace the second line with the command *Type t*, if you want.)

TABLE 16-1

Key	Represented as:	
Tab	Tab	48
Delete (or Backspace)	Backspace	51
Return	Return	36
Enter	Enter	76
Space	Space	49
0	Digit0	29
1	Digit1	18
2	Digit2	19
3	Digit3	20
4	Digit4	21
5	Digit5	23
6	Digit6	22
7	Digit7	26
8	Digit8	28
9	Digit9	25

The Tab, Backspace, Return, Enter, Space, and 0 through 9 keys must be represented in this way in AutoMac macros.

Although AutoMac usually will sandwich an uppercase character between a Shift command and a KeysOff command, it is not necessary to do so. Instead, you can simply type that character on a line of the macro editor. For example, the simple character *A* represents a shifted *a* as well as the command sequence *Shift-A-KeysOff*.

Many keys cannot be represented in either of the ways demonstrated above. To represent these keys in a macro, you must use the Char command. The form of this command is

Char *ASCII number   key code*

where *ASCII number* is the ASCII number of the character that you want to represent, and *key code* is the code for the key (or combination) that creates that character. In most cases, both arguments are required to define the correct character. Table 16-2 lists the characters that must be represented in special ways.

TABLE 16-2

Key	Represented as:	
↑	Char 30	126
↓	Char 31	125
→	Char 29	124
←	Char 28	123
1 (keypad)	Digit1	83
2 (keypad)	Digit2	84
3 (keypad)	Digit3	85
4 (keypad)	Digit4	86
5 (keypad)	Digit5	87
6 (keypad)	Digit6	88
7 (keypad)	Digit7	89
8 (keypad)	Digit8	91
9 (keypad)	Digit9	92
= (keypad)	=	81
/ (keypad)	/	75
* (keypad)	*	67
- (keypad)	-	78
+ (keypad)	+	69
Enter	Enter	
. (keypad)	.	65
0 (keypad)	Digit0	82
Num Lock	Char 27	71
Help	Char 5	114
Del	WindowPause	117
Home	Char 1	115
End	Char 4	119
Page up	Char 11	116
Page down	Char 12	121
F1	Char 16	122
F2	Char 16	120
F3	Char 16	99
F4	Char 16	118
F5	Char 16	96

Key	Represented as:	
F6	Char 16	97
F7	Char 16	98
F8	Char 16	100
F9	Char 16	101
F10	Char 16	109
F11	Char 16	103
F12	Char 16	111
F13	Char 16	105
F14	Char 16	107
F15	Char 16	113
Esc	Char 27	53

Note: All keys on the numeric keypad will produce actions rather than characters, unless the keyboard is in the Num Lock mode. (To enter the Num Lock mode, you must press the Num Lock key.) Regardless of whether the keyboard is in the Num Lock mode, the keys on the keypad are represented in the same way.

This table shows the keys that must be represented with the Char command in an AutoMac macro.

The Menu command

The Menu command instructs AutoMac to select a command from one of the current application's menus. The form of this command is

Menu *menuname,commandname*

where *menuname* is the name of the menu that contains the command you want AutoMac to select, and *commandname* is the name of that command. For example, the command *Menu Edit,Cut* instructs AutoMac to select the Cut command from Word's Edit menu; the command *Menu File,Save* instructs AutoMac to select the Save command from the File menu; and so forth. If the command reveals a dialog box, the Menu command should be followed by keystroke representations and/or a Type command that selects items from that box. For example, the commands

Menu File,Save As...
backup
Return

would save the current document under the name *backup*.

Since the apple icon cannot be represented in a macro, you should use the menu name *Apple* when you want a macro to select a command from that menu. If the item is a desk accessory, you must preface the name of that accessory with a + sign. For example, to access the control panel, you would use the command *Menu Apple,+Control Panel*.

AutoMac enters special commands into the macro that you are recording when you click the buttons in the Misc Recording Options dialog box. Some of these commands (like Beep) are simple; others (like DoAlert) are complex.

Special commands

The DoAlert command instructs AutoMac to display a custom alert or message box on the screen. The form of this command is

The DoAlert command

DoAlert # *of buttons,duration,button1text,button2text,*
vpos,hpos,vsize,hsize,vinset,hinset,text

where the arguments describe the contents, position, and size of the dialog box. The # *of buttons* argument specifies the number of buttons that the dialog box will contain—zero, one, or two. These buttons will be positioned at the right edge of the box.

The *duration* argument specifies the number of seconds that message boxes will remain on the screen. If the first argument of the DoAlert command is 0 (indicating a box with no buttons), the second argument should be a value greater than 0. Otherwise, the box will disappear as soon as it appears. No matter how long the box remains on the screen, AutoMac will continue executing the macro as soon as the box disappears. If the first argument is 1 or 2 (indicating a box with one or two buttons, respectively), the second argument should be the value 0. Otherwise, the box will remain on the screen for the specified period of time, even if the user has clicked a button before that period of time has elapsed.

The third argument, *button1text*, specifies the text that will appear in the default button for message boxes with one or two buttons. (This argument should be omitted for boxes without buttons.) Since AutoMac will continue executing the macro if the user selects this button, it should contain "positive" text, such as OK, Yes, or Continue. Since this button will be the default button, the user can choose it simply by pressing Return. Of course, the user also can select this button by clicking it.

The fourth argument, *button2text*, specifies the text for the second (non-default) button in two-button message boxes. (This argument must be omitted from DoAlert commands whose first argument is 0; that is, ones intended to create boxes with zero or one buttons.) AutoMac will cancel the execution of a macro when the user chooses this button. Consequently, it should contain negative text, such as Cancel, No, or Stop. To choose the negative button from a custom message box, the user must click on it.

The next six arguments control the dimensions of the custom message box and its position on the screen. All of these arguments specify a number of pixels—increments of $^1/_{72}$ inch. The first two arguments, *vpos* and *hpos*, specify the position of the upper-left corner of the message box relative to the upper-right corner of the screen. The next two arguments, *vsize* and *hsize*, specify the height and width of the message box. For ordinary Macintosh screens, the total of the *vpos* and *vsize* arguments must not exceed 341; the total of the *hpos* and *hsize* arguments must not exceed 511. The next two arguments, *vinset* and *hinset*, specify the distance that the text within the message box will be indented from the top, bottom, left, and right borders of the box. (For boxes with buttons, the *hinset* argument specifies the inset from the button(s) at the right edge of the box.)

The final argument of any DoAlert command, *text*, should be the message that you want to appear in the message box. This message can be as long as you like. However, it should be short enough to fit within the dimensions you specified. If it won't, AutoMac will display only as much text as will fit in the box. To correct this problem, either expand the box or reduce the amount of text.

As an example of the DoAlert command, suppose you want to create a default-sized message box that contains the message *Do you wish to continue?* along with two buttons: one labeled *Yes* (the default button), and another labeled *No*. To do this, you would use the command

DoAlert 2,0,Yes,No,110,80,100,330,10,18,Do you wish to continue?

To create a half-sized one-button dialog box with the message *Click OK to Continue...*, you would use the command

DoAlert 1,0,OK,55,40,50,165,10,18,Click OK to Continue...

Similarly, the command

DoAlert 0,5,72,72,72,144,10,18,This box will disappear in 5 seconds...

would create a message box that is 1 inch tall by 2 inches wide, whose upper-left corner is one inch from both the top and left edges of the screen, that contains the message *This box will disappear in 5 seconds...*, that contains no buttons, and that will remain on the screen for five seconds.

The Beep command

The Beep command causes your Macintosh to sound a single beep. The form of this command is simply Beep—it accepts no arguments. To make your Macintosh beep multiple times, you must enter multiple Beep commands, each on different lines of the macro. AutoMac inserts a Beep command into the macro that it is recording when you choose the Beep Speaker in the Misc Recording Options dialog box.

AutoMac offers four other commands that pause the execution of a macro: WaitPeriod, WaitClock, WaitDate, and WaitEvent. Unlike the Pause command, these commands pass to the Macintosh the actions that you perform during the delay. Consequently, these commands are useful when you want to solicit input from the macro user. AutoMac enters one of these commands into a macro when you choose OK from the dialog box that appears when you choose the Stop Playback Until... button in the Misc Recording Options dialog box.

The WaitPeriod command instructs AutoMac to pause the execution of a macro for a specified amount of time. The form of this command is

WaitPeriod *hours:minutes:seconds:ticks*

where *hours*, *minutes*, *seconds*, and *ticks* specify the duration of the pause. (A tick is $\frac{1}{60}$ second). For example, the command *WaitPeriod 0:0:5:0* would pause the execution of the macro for five seconds. All four arguments are required, even if one or more of them are the value 0.

The WaitClock command instructs AutoMac to pause the execution of a macro until the time you specify. The form of this command is

WaitClock *hour:minute:second am/pm*

where *hour*, *minute*, *second*, and *am/pm* specify the time at which you want AutoMac to resume executing the macro. For example, the command *WaitClock 5:30:0 pm* would pause the execution of the macro until 5:30 PM. All four arguments of this command are required.

The WaitDate command instructs AutoMac to pause the execution of a macro until the date and time you specify. The form of this command is

WaitDate *year:month:day:hour:minute:second am/pm*

where *year*, *month*, *day*, *hour*, *minute*, *second*, and *am/pm* specify the day and time at which you want AutoMac to resume executing the macro. For example, the command *WaitDate 1989:11:23:12:00:0 am* would pause the execution of the macro until midnight on November 23, 1989. All seven arguments of this command are required.

The WaitEvent command instructs AutoMac to pause the execution of a macro until a specified event occurs. The form of this command is

WaitEvent *event1 event2 event3 event4*

where *event1*, *event2*, *event3*, and *event4* are any of the following words: *Return*, *Enter*, *AnyKey*, or *Click*. The word *Return* commands AutoMac to pause until the

The WaitPeriod, WaitClock, WaitDate, and WaitEvent commands

user presses the Return key; the word *Enter* commands AutoMac to pause until the user presses Enter; the word *AnyKey* commands AutoMac to pause until the user presses any key; and the word *Click* commands AutoMac to pause until the user clicks the mouse button.

Only one argument is required for the WaitEvent command; however, up to four can be used. (Since AnyKey is a superset of Return and Enter, however, the use of more than three is redundant.) For example, the command *WaitEvent Return* instructs AutoMac to suspend the execution of the macro until the user presses the Return key; the command *WaitEvent Enter Click* instructs AutoMac to pause until the user presses the Enter key or clicks the mouse button; and so forth.

The first set of buttons in the dialog box that appears when you choose the Stop Playback Until... button in the Misc Recording Options dialog box creates one of the following four WaitEvent commands:

WaitEvent Return Enter
WaitEvent Enter
WaitEvent Click
WaitEvent Return Enter AnyKey Click

To specify any of the other combinations of arguments, you must edit the macro.

The JumpMacro command

The JumpMacro command branches the execution of the current macro to another macro. AutoMac inserts this command into a macro that it is recording when you click the Jump to a Macro button in the Misc Recording Options dialog box. The form of this command is

JumpMacro *key combination key code*

where *key combination* is the representation of the key to which the macro you want to branch is linked, and *key code* is the key code of that combination. Both arguments are required. For example, the command

JumpMacro Option-b   11

instructs AutoMac to stop executing the current macro and begin executing the macro that is linked to the Option-b key combination.

Because the JumpMacro command requires the name of the key to which a macro is linked, it cannot jump to a macro that is not linked to a key. After AutoMac finishes executing the macro that a JumpMacro commanded it to execute, it will not return to the macro that contains the JumpMacro command. Consequently, any commands that follow a JumpMacro command in a macro will not be executed.

Many of AutoMac's macro commands control the movement of the mouse pointer on the screen, as well as specifying the positions of clicks and drags. Since it's not a good idea to use your mouse to move the insertion point and select text when you are recording Word macros, these commands probably won't show up much in your Word macros. However, they will appear if you use your mouse to negotiate dialog boxes.

Mouse-movement commands

The Click command instructs AutoMac to move the mouse pointer to a particular position on the screen and then click the mouse button. The form of this command is

The Click command

Click *y offset,x offset   duration*

where *y offset* and *x offset* specify the position to which AutoMac should move the mouse pointer before clicking, and *duration* specifies how long AutoMac should hold down the mouse button before releasing it. These arguments specify a distance (in pixels) relative to the current origin (not necessarily the current position of the mouse pointer on the screen). The *duration* argument, which is optional, specifies the duration of the click in ticks ($\frac{1}{60}$ second). If you don't supply this argument, AutoMac will supply the value 6 when you choose OK to finish editing the macro.

For example, the command

Click 100,300   10

commands AutoMac to move the mouse pointer to a position 100 pixels below and 300 pixels to the right of the current origin, press the mouse button, hold it down for $\frac{1}{6}$ second, and then release it.

The Down and Up commands instruct AutoMac to drag the mouse; that is, to move the mouse pointer while holding down the mouse button. In Word, as in most programs, this action highlights information in the document. The Down command instructs AutoMac to move the mouse pointer to a particular point on the screen, press the mouse button, and hold it down. The form of this command is

The Down and Up commands

Down *y offset,x offset*

The Up command instructs AutoMac to release the mouse button after moving the mouse pointer. The form of this command is

Up *y offset,x offset*

In both cases, *y offset* and *x offset* specify a position relative to the current origin—not necessarily the current position of the mouse pointer.

For example, the commands

```
Down 72,72
Up 144,144
```

instruct AutoMac to position the mouse pointer one inch below and one inch to the right of the current origin, press the mouse button, hold it down while moving the mouse pointer to a position two inches below and two inches to the right of the current origin, and then release the mouse button.

Setting the origin

As we mentioned earlier, the offsets of the Click, Down, and Up commands specify a position relative to the current origin. The RelScreen, RelTopLeft, RelTopRight, RelBotRight, RelBotLeft, RelStart, and SetStart commands allow you to set the origin. The RelScreen command sets the origin at the upper-left corner of the screen; the RelTopLeft, RelTopRight, RelBotRight, and RelBotLeft commands set the origin at the upper-left, upper-right, lower-right, and lower-left corners of the current window, respectively. The RelStart command sets the origin at the position of the mouse pointer when the macro began. The SetStart command sets the origin at the current position of the mouse pointer.

Any of these origin-setting commands set the origin for any Click, Down, or Up commands that follow, and remain valid until they are changed by another origin-setting command. If an origin-setting command does not appear somewhere above any Click, Down, or Up command, AutoMac will assume that the origin is at the upper-left corner of the screen.

For example, the commands

```
RelTopLeft
MoveTo 100, 200
```

move the mouse pointer to a position 100 pixels below and 200 pixels to the right of the upper-left corner of the current window.

The MoveTo command

The MoveTo command moves the mouse to a particular position on the screen relative to the current origin. The form of this command is

MoveTo *y offset,x offset*

where *y offset* specifies the number of pixels that AutoMac will move the mouse pointer above or below the current origin, and *x offset* specifies the number of pixels it will move to the left or right of the current origin. A positive *y offset* indicates a position below the current origin; a negative *y offset* indicates a position above the current origin; a positive *x offset* indicates a position to the right of the current origin; and a negative *x offset* indicates a position to the left of the current origin. For example, the command

    MoveTo 72,144

commands AutoMac to move the mouse pointer to a position 72 pixels (one inch) below and 144 pixels (two inches) to the right of the current origin. If the current origin were the upper-left corner of the screen, this command would move the pointer to a position one inch below the top border of the screen, and two inches to the right of the left border of the screen.

    The Move command instructs AutoMac to move the mouse pointer relative to its current position on the screen (not relative to the origin, as the MoveTo command does). The form of this command is

    Move *y offset,x offset*

where *y offset* specifies the number of pixels that AutoMac will move the mouse pointer above or below its current position, and *x offset* specifies the number of pixels that AutoMac will move the mouse pointer to the left or right of its current position. A positive *y offset* specifies a movement of the mouse pointer to a position below its current position; a negative *y offset* specifies a movement of the mouse pointer to a position above its current position; a positive *x offset* specifies a movement to a position to the right of the current position; a negative *x offset* specifies a movement to a position to the left of the current position. For example, the command

    Move 72,144

commands AutoMac to move the mouse pointer to a position 72 pixels (1 inch) below and 144 pixels (2 inches) to the right of its current position.

The Move command

    In addition to the macro commands that we've presented so far, AutoMac includes six other commands: RealTime, FullSpeed, Pause, WindowPause, Alert-Start, and AlertEnd. Although these commands probably won't show up in your Word macros very often, we'll discuss them briefly.

Other commands

    AutoMac features several commands that affect the timing of the execution of a macro. The first of these commands, RealTime, instructs AutoMac to pay attention to the time delay values in the subsequent statements in the macro.

The RealTime and FullSpeed commands

Consequently, AutoMac won't begin executing one command as soon as it completes the previous one. Instead, it will wait for the amount of time specified by the time delay value (if any) at the beginning of the next statement.

The FullSpeed command "turns off" the RealTime command. If AutoMac encounters a FullSpeed command in a macro, it will ignore the time delay values (if any) that precede the subsequent statements in the macro. Consequently, it will execute the macro as fast as it can. Full-speed execution is the default; AutoMac will execute all the commands in a macro at full speed, unless the macro contains a RealTime command.

The Pause command

The Pause command allows you to add a delay at almost any point during the execution of a macro. The form of this command is

Pause *hours*:*minutes*:*seconds*:*ticks*

where *hours*, *minutes*, *seconds*, and *ticks* specify the length of the pause. All four arguments are required. For example, to specify a five-second pause, you would use the command *Pause 0:0:5:0*. During the lapse that is caused by a Pause command, none of your actions will be passed on to the Macintosh.

The Pause command should always be used in conjunction with a RealTime command. Unless a Pause command is preceded by a RealTime command, and there is not a FullSpeed command between, AutoMac will remove the Pause command from the macro when you choose OK from the macro editor dialog box. If the Pause command is preceded by a RealTime command (again, without a FullSpeed command between), AutoMac will replace the Pause command with a value that specifies, in ticks, the amount of time specified by the arguments of the Pause command. On the next line, AutoMac will insert a comment in the form ** ELAPSED TIME: a:b:c:d*. For example, AutoMac would replace the command *Pause 0:0:5:0* with the commands

```
300
* ELAPSED TIME:    0:0:5:0
```

The Add a Time Delay (Seconds) check box and text box in the End of Recording dialog box have the same effect as the Pause command. For example, if you entered the value 5 into the Add a Time Delay (Seconds) text box during the recording of a macro, AutoMac would enter the value 300 at the beginning of one line, and the comment ** ELAPSED TIME: 0:0:5:0* onto the next line. If AutoMac is not recording in the real-time mode at the time, it will preface these lines with a RealTime command and follow them with a FullSpeed command.

The WindowPause command instructs AutoMac to delay the execution of the next command in a macro until a few cycles of the current application's event loop have passed. The principal use of this command is to delay the execution of a macro while your application opens a new window. You may see this command in your recorded macros. However, you'll rarely use it when you edit macros or write them from scratch.

Normally, if one of AutoMac's alert boxes (such as the one that asks if you want to save the changes that you've made to the macros in a particular file) appears during the execution of a macro, AutoMac will cancel the execution of the macro. If you want to prevent this from happening, simply enter the command AlertStart into the macro ahead of the command that might cause the alert box to be presented. The AlertEnd command cancels the AlertStart command.

You can include explanatory comments in your macros by preceding the comment with one or more asterisks. AutoMac won't attempt to execute any characters that follow an asterisk. You can place a comment on a line of a macro by itself, or on the same line as a command, to the right of that command. AutoMac automatically inserts comments into macros that have syntax errors when you click OK to exit from the macro editor.

Comment lines

If you want, you can create a macro from scratch by writing it in the macro editor. To do this, begin by clicking the Edit button in the main AutoMac dialog box while none of the macros are selected. When you do this, AutoMac will present a macro editor dialog box like the one shown in Figure 16-23 on the next page. As you can see, this box is blank except for the command NAME, which AutoMac provides for you. At this point, you can complete the command (or erase it). Next, if you want to invoke the macro by pressing a combination of keys, you should enter a KEYS command. Then, you can write your macro.

WRITING MACROS FROM SCRATCH

Once you finish writing the macro, you should click OK. As soon as you do this, AutoMac will check the macro for syntax errors. If it finds any, it will annotate the macro, revealing their positions. If the macro does not contain any syntax errors, AutoMac will store the macro in the active portion of RAM, close the macro editor dialog box, and return you to the main AutoMac dialog box. If you did not include the optional *key code* argument for the KEYS command, AutoMac will ask you to press the key to which you want to assign the macro.

You also can use the New button in the macro editor dialog box to begin writing a macro from scratch. When you click this button, AutoMac will clear the existing macro (if any) from the macro editor dialog box. At that point, you can write the macro from scratch. (Since AutoMac does not provide the beginning of the NAME command in this situation, you'll have to type it yourself if you want to provide a description for the macro.)

FIGURE 16-23

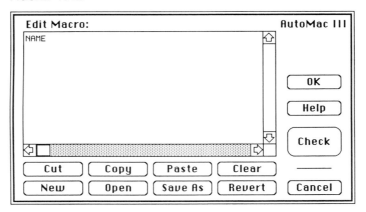

AutoMac will present this dialog box when you click the Edit button in the main AutoMac dialog box when a macro is not selected.

CUSTOMIZING AUTOMAC

If you want, you can change many of AutoMac's default parameters. For example, you can specify which keys reveal each of AutoMac's dialog boxes, alter the amount of memory that AutoMac reserves for macros, and so forth. To do any of these things, begin by clicking the main AutoMac icon or pressing Option-Backspace to reveal the main AutoMac dialog box. Then, click the Prefs button within that box. When you do this, AutoMac will reveal a Preferences dialog box like the one shown in Figure 16-24.

Specifying the Default Modifier Keys

The three check boxes under the heading Default at the upper-left corner of this dialog box allow you to specify the default "modifier" keys. Whichever box(es) (⌘, Shift, or Option) is selected when you click OK will be the one(s) that will be selected by default in the Record New Macro dialog box. For example, if you selected the ⌘ box and deselected the Shift and Option boxes, only the ⌘ box would be active the next time you accessed the Record New Macro dialog box.

Specifying "Illegal" Keys

The None and Next buttons under the heading "Illegal" (Max 16) allow you to specify up to 16 key combinations that AutoMac will not allow to be linked to macros. If you specify one of these illegal combinations in the Record New Macro dialog box, AutoMac will beep and present an alert box as soon as you press OK. By default, the following 14 key combinations are illegal: Option-e, Option-i, Option-n, Option-u, Option-`, Option-Backspace, Option-=, Option--, Option-[, Option-], Option-., ⌘-x, ⌘-c, and ⌘-v. Most of these illegal combinations have a special meaning to AutoMac. For example, the Option-Backspace combination reveals the main AutoMac dialog box, and the Option-= key reveals the Record New Macro dialog box.

FIGURE 16-24

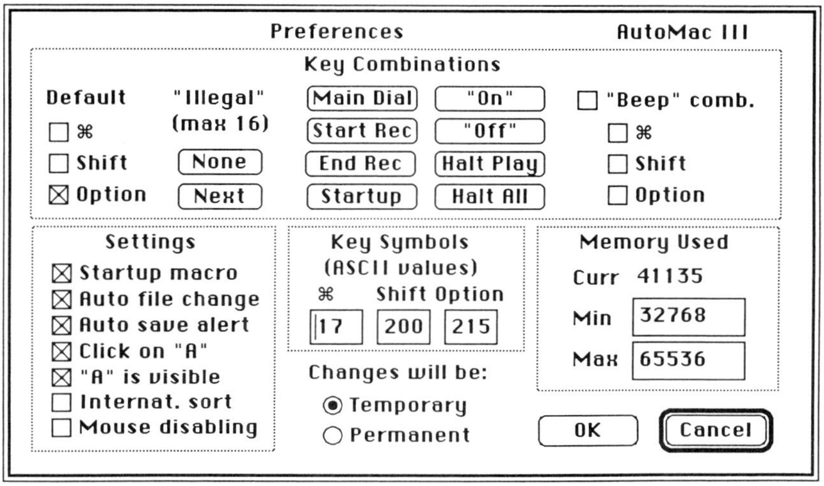

AutoMac will reveal this dialog box when you click the Prefs button in the
main AutoMac dialog box.

To change any of these combinations, begin by clicking the Next button. When
you do this, AutoMac will reveal a dialog box like the one shown in Figure 16-25.
If this box specifies the key combination that you want to replace, use the ⌘, Shift,
Option, and Key Name settings to specify the key that you want to make illegal, then
click OK. If the box does not specify the key you want to replace, click Cancel to
return to the Preferences dialog box, then click Next again. Repeat this process until
the key that you want to replace appears. If you want to specify a new illegal key
without "legalizing" another key, repeat this process until AutoMac reveals a blank
dialog box. To "legalize" all key combinations, click the None key.

FIGURE 16-25

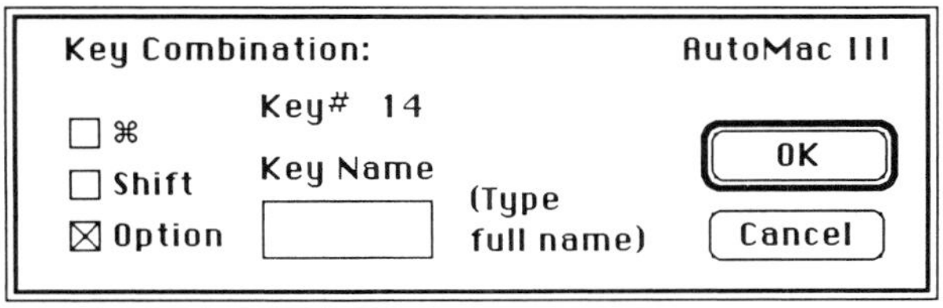

AutoMac will reveal a dialog box like this one when you
choose the Next button in the Preferences dialog box.

Changing AutoMac's Special Keys

The next eight buttons allow you to change the keys that reveal AutoMac's dialog boxes, unlink macros, stop the playing of macros, and so forth. The Main Dial button allows you to specify the key that brings up the main Auto-Mac dialog box (originally, Option-Backspace); the Start Rec button allows you to specify the key that brings up the Record New Macro dialog box (originally, Option-=); the End Rec button allows you to specify the key that brings up the End of Recording dialog box (originally, Option--); the Startup button allows you to specify the key that specifies the startup (auto-executing) macro (originally, ⌘-Shift-Option-0); the "On" button allows you to specify the key that reactivates previously deactivated macros (originally, Option-]); the "Off" button allows you to specify the key that breaks the link between the active macros and their key combinations (originally, Option-[); the Halt Play button allows you to specify the key that cancels the execution of most macros (originally, Option-.); and the Halt All button allows you to specify the key that cancels the execution of any macro (originally, ⌘-Shift-Option-.).

To change the key to which any of these functions are assigned, click the button that corresponds to that function. When you do this, AutoMac will reveal a dialog box like the one shown in Figure 16-25 (the same as the one that AutoMac reveals when you click the Next button). At that point, you can specify the key to which you want to link that function, then click OK.

Reserving Modifier Keys for Macros

The "Beep" Comb. check box and the three check boxes that follow it allow you to disable the ⌘, Shift, or Option keys (or one combination of those keys) except for playing macros. If you press the specified modifier key or combination of modifier keys along with another key, and a macro is not linked to that combination, your Mac will beep instead of doing what that combination would normally instruct it to do. This prevents your Mac from performing an action that you didn't intend it to perform if you accidentally press the wrong key combination when trying to invoke a macro. To specify a "beep" combination, check the "Beep" Comb. box, then check the appropriate modifier box(es).

The Settings Check Boxes

The check boxes in the Settings portion of the Preferences dialog box control other aspects of the way that AutoMac works. The Startup Macro check box allows you to enable and disable the startup (auto-executing) macro feature. If this box is checked, AutoMac will play the startup macro automatically.

The Auto File Change check box allows you to specify whether AutoMac will open the default macro file for an application each time you switch applications. If this box is checked, AutoMac will open the default macro file for each new application. Originally, this box is checked.

The Auto Save Alert check box lets you specify whether AutoMac will ask if you want to save macros to the current macro file each time you change applications. If this box is checked, AutoMac will ask. Originally, this box is checked.

The Click on "A" check box activates and deactivates the AutoMac icon at the left edge of the menu bar. If this box is checked, clicking the *A* will reveal the main AutoMac dialog box. Originally, this box is checked.

The "A" is Visible check box determines whether the AutoMac icon will be visible at the top of the screen. If this box is checked, the *A* will be visible. Originally, this box is checked. This setting does not take effect until the next time you start your Macintosh.

The Internat. Sort check box determines whether AutoMac will use its built-in macro-sorting routine or the Macintosh's sorting routine to sort the macro list that appears in the main AutoMac dialog box. If this box is checked, AutoMac will use the Macintosh's sorting routine. If this box is not checked, AutoMac will use its own sorting routine. Originally, this box is not checked; it should stay that way.

The Mouse Disabling check box controls whether AutoMac will take full control of the mouse during macro playback. Originally, this box is unchecked, and should remain that way.

The Key Symbols Edit Bars

The edit bars in the Key Symbols section of the Preferences dialog box allow you to specify which symbols AutoMac uses to represent the ⌘, Shift, and Option keys in the list of macros within the main AutoMac dialog box. Initially, AutoMac will use the symbol ⌘ to represent the command key, the symbol » to represent the Shift key, and the symbol ◇ to represent the Option key. To change the symbol that AutoMac uses to represent any of these keys, simply type the ASCII number of that symbol into the appropriate edit bar. For example, if you want AutoMac to use the symbol ^ to represent the Shift key, you would type 94 (the ASCII number of that symbol) into the Shift edit bar.

Allocating Memory to AutoMac

The Min and Max edit bars within the Memory Used section of the Preferences dialog box allow you to specify the minimum and maximum amount of memory that will be allocated to AutoMac. Originally, the value in the Min bar is 32768 (bytes); the value in the Max bar is 65536 (bytes). In most cases, these minimum and maximum amounts of RAM are perfectly adequate. If you want to keep a lot of macros in RAM at the same time, you may need to increase these values. To do this, simply type the new value into the appropriate bar. The value in the Min bar must be at least 32768 (32K). The new memory allocations will not take effect until you restart your Macintosh.

Determining Whether the Changes Will Be Temporary or Permanent

The Temporary and Permanent radio buttons at the bottom of the Preferences dialog box determine whether the changes you have made to the settings in the main AutoMac dialog box will remain in effect after you turn off your Macintosh. If you want the changes to be in effect only during the current session (that is, until you turn off your Macintosh), you should click the Temporary button. If you want the changes to apply to future sessions as well, you should click the Permanent button instead.

Of course, none of the changes take effect until you click the OK button within the Preferences dialog box. If you want to return to the main AutoMac dialog box without making any of the changes specified in the Preferences dialog box, you should click Cancel instead.

AUTOMAC KEYBOARD SHORTCUTS

In most cases, you will use your mouse to select items from AutoMac's many dialog boxes. However, you can use various keys and key combinations to select these items. For example, in any dialog box, you can use the Tab key to move between text boxes, use the ⌘-. combination to access the Cancel button, and use the Return or Enter keys to select the default button. Tables 16-3 through 16-11 list the various ⌘-key combinations you can use to select the other items in each of AutoMac's dialog boxes. Table 16-12 on page 779 lists the other key combinations that have special meanings to AutoMac.

TABLE 16-3

To access:	Press:
Record button	⌘-r
Delete button	⌘-d
Change or Edit buttons	⌘-e
New button	⌘-n
Open button	⌘-o
Save button	⌘-s
Save As button	⌘-a
Revert button	⌘-t
List button	⌘-l
Prefs button	⌘-p
Help button	⌘-h

These ⌘-key combinations access the items in the main AutoMac dialog box.

TABLE 16-4

To access:	Press:
Options ⌘O button	⌘-o
⌘ check box	⌘-c
Shift check box	⌘-s
Option check box	⌘-p
Record Full Drag Track text box	⌘-d

These ⌘-key combinations access the items in the Record New Macro dialog box.

TABLE 16-5

To access:	Press:
Continue button	⌘-c
Options button	⌘-o
Misc button	⌘-m
Suspend button	⌘-s
Add a Time Delay (Seconds) check box	⌘-t
Record Full Mouse Drag Track check box	⌘-d

These ⌘-key combinations access the items in the End of Recording dialog box.

TABLE 16-6

To access:	Press:
Down, [Automatic] radio button	⌘-1
Down, Full Screen radio button	⌘-2
Down, Starting Point radio button	⌘-3
Down, Window, T.L. radio button	⌘-4
Down, Window, T.R. radio button	⌘-5
Down, Window, B.R. radio button	⌘-6
Down, Window, B.L. radio button	⌘-7
Up, [Automatic] radio button	⌘-8
Up, Full Screen radio button	⌘-9
Up, Starting Point radio button	⌘-e
Up, Window, T.L. radio button	⌘-r
Up, Window, T.R. radio button	⌘-t
Up, Window, B.R. radio button	⌘-y
Up, Window, B.L. radio button	⌘-u
Normal radio button	⌘-n
Record Full Drag Track radio button	⌘-d
Record All Mouse Motion radio button	⌘-a
Record in Real Time check box	⌘-p
Record During Alerts check box	⌘-i
Set New Starting Point check box	⌘-s

These ⌘-key combinations access the items in the AutoMac III Recording Options dialog box.

TABLE 16-7

To access:	Press:
⌘ check box	⌘-c
Shift check box	⌘-s
Option check box	⌘-p

These ⌘-key combinations access the items in the dialog box shown in Figure 16-17.

TABLE 16-8

To access:	Press:
No button	⌘-n
Save As... button	⌘-s

These ⌘-key combinations access the items in the dialog box shown in Figure 16-14.

TABLE 16-9

To access:	Press:
Do a Message or Alert Box button	⌘-m
Beep Speaker button	⌘-b
Stop Playback Until... button	⌘-s
Jump to a Macro button	⌘-j

These ⌘-key combinations access the items in the Misc Recording Options dialog box.

TABLE 16-10

To access:	Press:
Test button	⌘-t
2 radio button	⌘-2
1 radio button	⌘-1
0 radio button	⌘-0

These ⌘-key combinations access the items in the Do a Message or Alert Box dialog box.

TABLE 16-11

To access:	Press:
Return or Enter Key is Pressed radio button	⌘-1
Mouse is Clicked radio button	⌘-2
Enter Key is Pressed radio button	⌘-3
Any Keypress or Click radio button	⌘-4
A Fixed Amount of Time Has Passed radio button	⌘-5
The Following Time/Date is Reached radio button	⌘-6
A.M. radio button	⌘-a
P.M. radio button	⌘-p
Any Date check box	⌘-d

These ⌘-key combinations access the items in the dialog box shown in Figure 16-8.

TABLE 16-12

To do this:	Press:
Access the main AutoMac dialog box	Option-Backspace
Access the Record New Macro dialog box	Option-=
Access the End of Recording dialog box	Option--
Unlink macros temporarily	Option-[
Relink macros	Option-]
Cancel playback of most macros	Option-.
Cancel playback of all macros	⌘-Shift-Option-.

These are the other key combinations that have special meanings to AutoMac.

Icon	Description		Icon	Description		
⟂	I-beam pointer		⌚	Watch		**Pointer Icons**
⟋	Italic I-beam pointer		✛	Four-pointed outline pointer		
➤	Left arrow pointer		↕	Vertical outline pointer		
➤	Right arrow pointer		↔	Horizontal outline pointer		
⇕	Split-bar pointer		⌘	Assign to Key pointer		
↓	Downward pointing arrow		?	Question mark pointer		
→1←	Page number pointer		+	Plus sign pointer		
+	Crosshair pointer		—	Minus sign pointer		

**Document
Window
Icons**

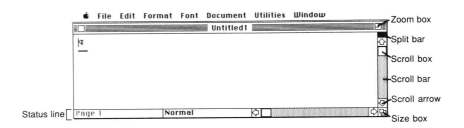

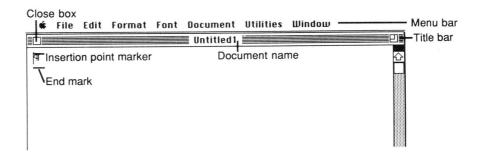

**Dialog
Box Icons**

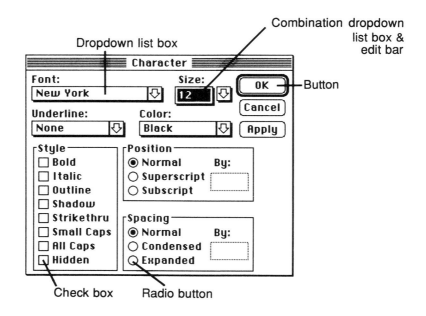

Ruler Icons

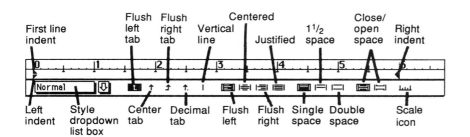

First line indent · Flush left tab · Flush right tab · Vertical line · Centered · Justified · 1½ space · Close/open space · Right indent

Left indent · Style dropdown list box · Center tab · Decimal tab · Flush left · Flush right · Single space · Double space · Scale icon

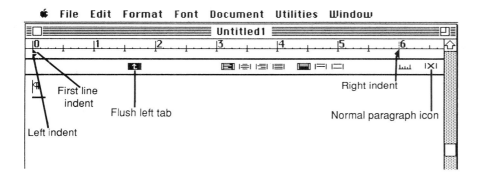

First line indent

Flush left tab

Left indent

Right indent

Normal paragraph icon

Print Preview Window Icons

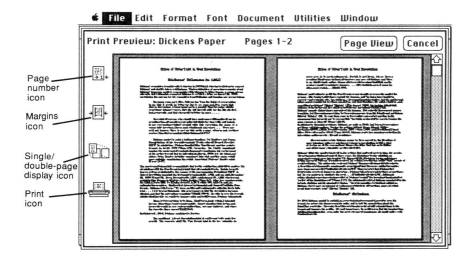

Page number icon

Margins icon

Single/double-page display icon

Print icon

Header, Footer, and Footnote Window Icons

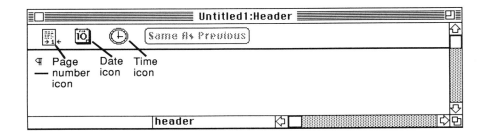

Outline Window Icons

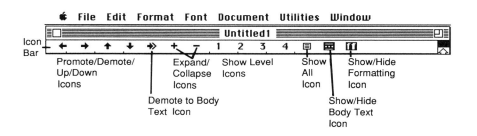

KEYBOARD AND MOUSE TECHNIQUES A2

Select word	Double-click word
Select sentence	Press ⌘ and click on sentence
Select line	Click next to line in selection bar
Select paragraph	Double-click next to paragraph in selection bar
Select column	Press Option key, click next to first character in column, then drag down
Select document	Press ⌘-Option-m or press ⌘ and click in selection bar
Select a graphic	Click inside graphic frame or drag over graphic
Extend selection	Click at beginning of block, then press Shift and click at the end of block
Extend selection to character	Press minus (-) key on keypad, then type character
Move up one line	Press ↑ or 8 on keypad
Move down one line	Press ↓ or 2 on keypad
Move left one character	Press ← or 4 on keypad
Move right one character	Press → or 6 on keypad
Move left one word	Press ⌘-← or ⌘-4 on keypad
Move right one word	Press ⌘-→ or ⌘-6 on keypad
Move to beginning of line	Press 7 on keypad
Move to end of line	Press 1 on keypad
Move to beginning of previous sentence	Press ⌘-7 on keypad
Move to beginning of next sentence	Press ⌘-1 on keypad

Move to beginning of previous paragraph	Press ⌘-↑ or ⌘-8 on keypad
Move to beginning of next paragraph	Press ⌘-↓ or ⌘-2 on keypad
Move to top left of screen	Press ⌘-5 on keypad
Move to beginning of document	Press ⌘-9 on keypad
Move to end of document	Press ⌘-3 on keypad
Move to previous location	Press ⌘-Option-z or 0 on keypad
Move to next text area	Press ⌘-Option-3 on keypad
Move to previous text area	Press ⌘-Option-9 on keypad
Move up one text area	Press ⌘-Option-8 on keypad

Windowing and Scrolling

Activate another window	Press ⌘-Option-w
Make active window full screen size or return to original size	Press ⌘-Option-]
Open/close split window	Press ⌘-Option-s
Scroll up one screen	Press 9 on keypad
Scroll down one screen	Press 3 on keypad
Scroll up one line	Press + on keypad
Scroll down one line	Press * on keypad
Move to bottom of window	Press end
Zoom window	Press ⌘-Option-]
Split window	Press ⌘-Option-s

Editing

Nonbreaking hyphen	Press ⌘-~
Optional hyphen	Press ⌘--
Space	Press Spacebar
Nonbreaking space	Press ⌘-Spacebar
Tab	Press Tab
New line	Press Shift-Return
New paragraph	Press Return or Enter
New paragraph without moving insertion point marker	Press ⌘-Option-Return
New page	Press Shift-Enter
New section	Press ⌘-Enter
Delete character to right	Press ⌘-Option-f
Delete previous word	Press ⌘-Option-Backspace
Delete next word	Press ⌘-Option-g
Delete a selection	Press Backspace
Copy text	Press ⌘-Option-c
Copy formats	Press ⌘-Option-v
Move text	Press ⌘-Option-x
Paste special character	Press ⌘-Option-q
Insert glossary text	Press ⌘-Backspace, then type glossary term and press Return
New ¶ below insertion point	Press ⌘-Option-Return
New ¶ with same style	Press ⌘-Return
Extend To	Press ⌘-Option-h
Insert formula	Press ⌘-Option-\
Find formats	Press ⌘-Option-r

File Commands

New command	[F5]
Open... command	[F6], Shift-[F6]
Save command	[F7]
Save As... command	Shift-[F7]
Print Preview... command	Option-[F13]
Page Setup... command	Shift-[F8]
Print... command	[F8]

Edit Commands

Undo command	[F1]
Cut command	[F2]
Copy command	[F3]
Paste command	[F4]
Paste Link	Option-[F4]
Update Link	Option-[F3]
Edit Link (QuickSwitch)	Option-[F2]
Copy formats	Shift-[F4]
Copy text	Shift-[F3]
Move text	Shift-[F2]

Format Commands

Character... command	[F14]
Paragraph... command	Shift-[F14]
Section... command	Option-[F14]
Document... command	⌘-[F14]
Plain For Style	[F9]
Plain Text	Shift-[F9]
Bold	[F10]
Italic	[F11]
Underline	[F12]
Double Underline	Shift-[F12]
Dotted Underline	Option-[F12]
Outline	Shift-[F11]
Shadow	Option-[F11]
Caps	Shift-[F10]
Small Caps	Option-[F10]
Hidden Text	Option-[F9]

Document Commands

Outlining	Shift-[F13]
Page View	[F13]

Utilities Commands

Spelling... command	[F15]
Hyphenate... command	Shift-[F15]
Word Count... command	Option-[F15]
Renumber... command	⌘-[F15]

Window Commands

New Window	Shift-[F5]

Using the Function Keys

Issuing Commands

Again	Press ⌘-a
Calculate	Press ⌘-=
Change...	Press ⌘-h
Character...	Press ⌘-d
Close	Press ⌘-w
Copy	Press ⌘-c
Cut	Press ⌘-x
Define Styles...	Press ⌘-t
Find...	Press ⌘-f
Repeat Find	Press ⌘-Option-a
Font	Press ⌘-Shift-e, then type font name and press Return
Footnote...	Press ⌘-e
Glossary...	Press ⌘-k
Go Back	Press ⌘-Option-z
Go To...	Press ⌘-g
New	Press ⌘-n
Open...	Press ⌘-o
Outlining	Press ⌘-u
Page View	Press ⌘-b
Paragraph...	Press ⌘-m
Paste	Press ⌘-v
Plain For Style	Press ⌘-Shift-Spacebar
Print...	Press ⌘-p
Print Preview	Press ⌘-i
Quit	Press ⌘-q
Repaginate Now	Press ⌘-j
Save	Press ⌘-s
Show/Hide ¶	Press ⌘-y
Show/Hide Ruler	Press ⌘-r
Spelling...	Press ⌘-l
Undo	Press ⌘-z

Using Dialog Boxes

Move to next group of options	Press →
Move to previous group of options	Press ←
Move to next option	Press ⌘-Tab or decimal point on keypad
Move to previous option	Press ⌘-Shift-Tab
Move to next edit bar	Press Tab
Move to previous edit bar	Press Shift-Tab
Move up in list box	Press ↑
Move down in list box	Press ↓
Choose current item	Press ⌘-Spacebar or 0 on keypad
Choose item directly	Press ⌘-first letter of option
Open folder	Press ⌘-↑
Close folder	Press ⌘-↓

Normal	Press ⌘-Shift-p or click |x| on ruler	**Formatting Paragraphs**
Flush left	Press ⌘-Shift-l	
Flush right	Press ⌘-Shift-r	
Centered	Press ⌘-Shift-c	
Justified	Press ⌘-Shift-j	
Indent first line	Press ⌘-Shift-f	
Nest	Press ⌘-Shift-n	
Unnest	Press ⌘-Shift-m	
Hanging indention	Press ⌘-Shift-t	
Double-space	Press ⌘-Shift-y	
Open Space	Press ⌘-Shift-o	
Apply a style	Press ⌘-Shift-s, then type style name and press Return	
All Caps	Press ⌘-Shift-k	**Formatting Characters**
Bold	Press ⌘-Shift-b	
Dotted underline	Press ⌘-Shift-\	
Double underline	Press ⌘-Shift-[	
Hidden	Press ⌘-Shift-x	
Italic	Press ⌘-Shift-i	
Outline	Press ⌘-Shift-d	
Plain	Press ⌘-Shift-z	
Plain For Style	Press ⌘-Shift-Spacebar	
Shadow	Press ⌘-Shift-w	
Small Caps	Press ⌘-Shift-h	
Strikethrough	Press ⌘-Shift-/	
Superscript	Press ⌘-Shift-+	
Subscript	Press ⌘-Shift--	
Underline	Press ⌘-Shift-u	
Word Underline	Press ⌘-Shift-]	
Font change	Press ⌘-Shift-e, then type font name and press Return	
Larger font size	Press ⌘-Shift->	
Smaller font size	Press ⌘-Shift-<	
Symbol font	Press ⌘-Shift-q	
Promote selection	Press ←	**Using the Outliner**
Demote selection	Press →	
Move selection up	Press ↑	
Move selection down	Press ↓	
Demote heading to body text	Press ⌘-→	
Expand current paragraph	Press + (on keypad)	
Collapse current paragraph and all subtext	Press - (on keypad)	
Expand all hidden text	Press * (on keypad)	

Other Techniques

Repeat last command	Press ⌘-a
Cancel operation in progress	Press ⌘-.
Open a menu	Press decimal point on numeric keypad, then type first letter or number of menu. Press ← or → to move to adjacent menu after a menu has been opened
Select item from open menu	Press ↓ or ↑
Add a command to a menu	Press Option-⌘-=, then issue command
Remove an item from a menu	Press Option-⌘--, then point to menu item
Move left indent marker only	Press Shift and drag bottom marker
Move left or first-line indent marker past zero position	Press Shift and drag marker
Move both left and first-line indent markers past zero	Click on markers, then press Shift and drag
List all files on disk	Press Shift and choose Open…
Repaginate entire document	Press Shift and choose Repaginate Now
Search for formats	Press ⌘-Option-r
Perform descending sort	Press Shift and choose Sort
Move header or footer	Drag into place in Print Preview
Move header or footer into text area	Press Shift and drag into place in Print Preview window
Access Help	Press ⌘-? (pointer changes to a ?)
Ellipsis as one character	Press Option-;
Long hyphen	Press Shift-Option--
Add (delete) fonts	Press ⌘-Option-+ (-)
Add as keyboard command	Press ⌘-Option-←
More keyboard prefix	Press ⌘-Option-'
Outline command prefix	Press ⌘-Option-t
Paste special character	Press ⌘-Option-q

ASCII CODES A3

(The upper-level ASCII codes and characters, those above 217, are accessible in Courier, Helvetica, and Times fonts. You will not be able to reproduce any characters from the ASCII codes above 217 in Chicago, New York, Monaco, or Geneva fonts. For some of the more esoteric fonts, the characters above 217 may change.)

ASCII Code	Character	ASCII Code	Character
6	\	40	(
9	→ (Tab)	41	)
10	(Line feed)	42	*
11	↵ (End-of-line marker)	43	+
12	(Page/Section break)	44	,
13	¶ (Paragraph marker)	45	-
30	– (Nonbreaking hyphen)	46	.
31	⁒ (Optional hyphen)	47	/
32	(Blank space)	48	0
33	!	49	1
34	"	50	2
35	#	51	3
36	$	52	4
37	%	53	5
38	&	54	6
39	'	55	7

ASCII Code	Character	ASCII Code	Character
56	8	96	'
57	9	97	a
58	:	98	b
59	;	99	c
60	<	100	d
61	=	101	e
62	>	102	f
63	?	103	g
64	@	104	h
65	A	105	i
66	B	106	j
67	C	107	k
68	D	108	l
69	E	109	m
70	F	110	n
71	G	111	o
72	H	112	p
73	I	113	q
74	J	114	r
75	K	115	s
76	L	116	t
77	M	117	u
78	N	118	v
79	O	119	w
80	P	120	x
81	Q	121	y
82	R	122	z
83	S	123	{
84	T	124		
85	U	125	}
86	V	126	~
87	W	128	Ä
88	X	129	Å
89	Y	130	Ç
90	Z	131	É
91	[	132	Ñ
92	\	133	Ö
93	]	134	Ü
94	^	135	á
95	_	136	à

ASCII Code	Character	ASCII Code	Character
137	â	177	±
138	ä	178	≤
139	ã	179	≥
140	å	180	¥
141	ç	181	µ
142	é	182	∂
143	è	183	Σ
144	ê	184	Π
145	ë	185	π
146	í	186	∫
147	ì	187	ª
148	î	188	º
149	ï	189	Ω
150	ñ	190	æ
151	ó	191	ø
152	ò	192	¿
153	ô	193	¡
154	ö	194	¬
155	õ	195	√
156	ú	196	ƒ
157	ù	197	≈
158	û	198	Δ
159	ü	199	«
160	†	200	»
161	°	201	…
162	¢	202	(Hard space)
163	£	203	À
164	§	204	Ã
165	•	205	Õ
166	¶	206	Œ
167	ß	207	œ
168	®	208	–
169	©	209	—
170	™	210	"
171	´	211	"
172	¨	212	'
173	≠	213	'
174	Æ	214	÷
175	Ø	215	◊
176	∞	216	ÿ

ASCII	
Code	**Character**
217	Ÿ
218	/
219	¤
220	‹
221	›
222	fi
223	fl
224	‡
225	·
226	‚
227	„
228	‰
229	Â
230	Ê
231	Á
232	Ë
233	È
234	Í
235	Î
236	Ï
237	Ì
238	Ó
239	Ô
240	🍎
241	Ò
242	Ú
243	Û
244	Ù
245	ı
246	^
247	~
248	¯
249	˘
250	·
251	°
252	¸
253	˝
254	˛
255	ˇ

EMBEDDING POSTSCRIPT COMMANDS IN A DOCUMENT A4

PostScript is a powerful, flexible page description language that tells PostScript printers how text, images, and graphics should appear on the printed page. PostScript was first popularized by Apple's LaserWriter printer family, and has since become the computer industry's standard page description language for desktop publishing.

Most applications that run on the Mac, including Microsoft Word, automatically generate the necessary PostScript commands for your printer when you issue the Print... command. These commands tell the printer how to form the characters and symbols that make up your document. If you want, however, you can embed PostScript commands directly in a document. The ability to do this opens up a whole new area of formatting possibilities—ones you might want to explore as you become more familiar with PostScript and its capabilities.

In this appendix, we'll tell you how to embed and format PostScript commands in a Word document, and we'll present a couple of examples that demonstrate this procedure. This discussion does not explain the details of the PostScript programming language—it is aimed at knowledgeable PostScript programmers who want to issue PostScript commands from within Word. For information on the PostScript programming language itself, refer to the following books published by Addison-Wesley Publishing Company:

PostScript Language Tutorial and Cookbook
PostScript Language Program Design
PostScript Language Reference Manual

ENTERING AND FORMATTING COMMANDS

To send PostScript commands to your printer with Word, simply type the commands into a document, then use the Define Styles… command to assign the *PostScript* style to them. Once you've entered and formatted the commands, simply use the Print… command to send the document to the printer. As you'd expect, when your printer receives the document containing the PostScript commands, it will carry out (instead of printing out) the commands.

An Example

By working through a simple example, we'll demonstrate the process of using Word to send PostScript commands to your printer. Suppose you want to send the PostScript commands shown in Figure A4-1, which print an outline of the word *Cobb* at several rotations around a single point. To send these commands to the printer, first select the New command from the File menu to open a new document, then type the commands shown in Figure A4-1. (We've issued the show ¶ command in this document so you can see where the blank spaces appear.)

FIGURE A4-1

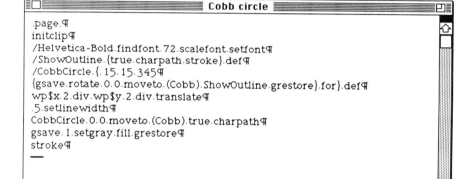

We'll use the commands in this sample document to demonstrate the process of formatting and sending PostScript commands to a PostScript printer.

After you've entered the PostScript commands into your new document, you need to assign the *PostScript* style to the commands. To do this, highlight the entire block of text that contains the commands, hold down the Shift key, then select

Define All Styles... from the Format menu. At this point, a Define Styles dialog box like the one shown in Figure A4-2 will appear. To define the commands you've entered as PostScript commands, click on the PostScript option in the list box. When you do this, the formats for the *PostScript* style will appear below the Style box, as shown in Figure A4-2.

FIGURE A4-2

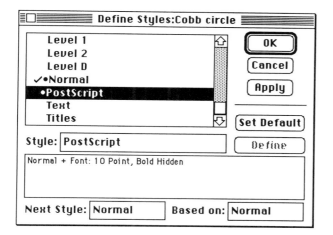

From the Define Styles dialog box, choose the Post-Script *option in the list box and click the Apply button to assign that style to your PostScript commands.*

As you can see, the format for the *PostScript* style is *Normal + Font: 10 Point, Bold Hidden.* You can change the formats for this style, as long as you include the Hidden format in the style definition. If you remove the Hidden format from the *PostScript* style definition, the LaserWriter will print your instructions instead of carrying them out.

After you've specified the *PostScript* style as we've done in Figure A4-2, click on the Apply button to apply that style to the text you've selected. Finally, close the Define Styles dialog box by choosing OK. At this point, your document should look like the one shown in Figure A4-3 on the following page. Notice that the word *PostScript* appears in the status box at the bottom of the screen to indicate that you've assigned the *PostScript* style to the current block of text. Also notice that Word has placed dotted lines beneath this text to remind you that the text will be hidden when printed.

Now, send the document to the printer by selecting the Print... command from the File menu. When the Print dialog box appears, choose the OK option to complete the procedure. Figure A4-4 shows how the sample document will appear when printed on an Apple LaserWriter printer.

FIGURE A4-3

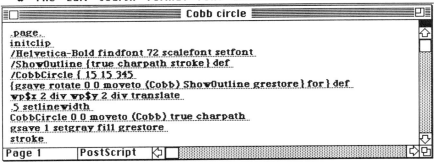

After you've assigned the PostScript *style to the appropriate block of text, moving the cursor into that block causes Word to display the word* PostScript *in the status box at the bottom of the screen.*

FIGURE A4-4

We created this page by sending the document in Figure A4-3 to an Apple LaserWriter printer.

Suppose you want to jazz up the title of a memo you've created in Word. For instance, let's say you want to print the title *Register Now!* in various shades of gray that slightly overlap. To do this, you would enter the PostScript commands shown in Figure A4-5 into your document.

Another Example

FIGURE A4-5

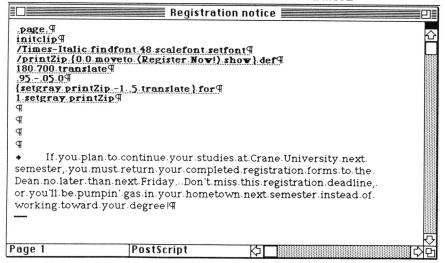

We'll use this sample document to illustrate how PostScript commands can be embedded along with regular text.

As you can see in Figure A4-5, we've entered the PostScript commands at the top of the document, and we've used the Define Styles… command on the Format menu to assign the *PostScript* style to these commands. Since we haven't assigned the *PostScript* style to the document's body text in the lower portion of the screen, the printer will print this text as usual.

When you use the Print… command to send this document to an Apple LaserWriter printer, the resulting document will look like the one in Figure A4-6. As you can see, adding just a few lines of PostScript code can transform a rather boring memo into an eye-catching document.

FIGURE A4-6

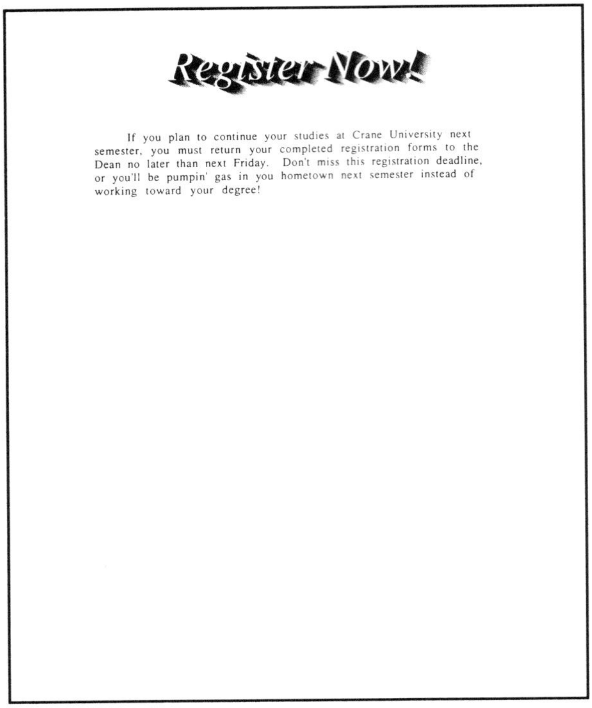

Register Now!

If you plan to continue your studies at Crane University next semester, you must return your completed registration forms to the Dean no later than next Friday. Don't miss this registration deadline, or you'll be pumpin' gas in you hometown next semester instead of working toward your degree!

PostScript commands allow you to turn boring documents into polished, eye-catching reports.

NOTES

If you send a document containing PostScript commands to any printer other than a PostScript laser printer, you'll get unpredictable results. In some cases, the printer will simply ignore the PostScript commands you've entered; in other cases, the printer will produce several pages of gibberish. At present, PostScript is supported on all printers in the Apple LaserWriter family, except the LaserWriter II SC.

Coordinate Systems

Unfortunately, the coordinate system employed by the PostScript language is different from the coordinate system used by Word. As you probably know, PostScript's graphics origin (0,0) initially lies in the lower-left corner of the page, and positive directions are to the right and up. (Word's origin lies in the upper-left corner of the page, and positive directions are to the right and down.) You should always specify coordinates that are consistent with PostScript's coordinate system when entering PostScript commands into a Word document.

All PostScript printers draw within the bounds of an area called the clipping path, or the clipping rectangle. The lower-left corner of the clipping rectangle is called the graphics origin. Although the graphics origin is initially located in the lower-left corner of the page, you can change its position by issuing PostScript's translate command. You can also change the size and shape of the clipping rectangle by issuing PostScript's clip or initclip commands.

The PostScript commands you'll enter into Word are organized into groups. A **Groups** group is made up of sequential paragraphs that are assigned the PostScript style. Each time your PostScript printer encounters a group of PostScript commands, it saves and restores the state of the PostScript printer's virtual memory. For this reason, one group of PostScript commands cannot use the procedures or variables that have been defined by another group.

Each group operates on its own clipping rectangle, and all the commands within a group operate on the same clipping rectangle. There are three types of clipping rectangles available: page, paragraph, and picture. You can specify one of these clipping rectangles by placing one of the commands listed in Table A4-1 in the first paragraph of the appropriate group.

TABLE A4-1

Command	Defines
.page.	Clipping rectangle that extends to the boundaries of the current page.
.para.	Clipping rectangle that is bounded by the next non-PostScript paragraph. If the next non-PostScript paragraph does not fit on the current page, then the clipping rectangle is bounded by the portion that lies on the current page.
.pic.	Clipping rectangle that is bounded by the enclosing frame of the graphic (picture) in the next non-PostScript paragraph. If the next non-PostScript paragraph contains many graphic images, you can enter several .pic. commands, and each command will apply to the corresponding graphic in the following paragraph.

These three groups of commands define the clipping rectangle upon which the current group of commands will operate.

If you do not enter one of the group commands in Table A4-1 at the beginning of a PostScript group, the printer will use the entire page as the clipping rectangle (just as if you'd typed the .page. command). As you might expect, a group command stays in effect until another group command or a non-PostScript paragraph is encountered.

Variables

Word provides several variable names that you can use in your PostScript commands. Variables represent all kinds of important values that describe the current page or paragraph. Table A4-2 lists the variables you can use in all three types of command groups (.page., .para., and .pic.). Table A4-3 lists the variables you can use only in .para. command groups, and Table A4-4 lists the variables you can use only in .page. command groups. As you can see, all three tables list each variable along with the setting it represents. All the values returned by these variables are measured in points (the standard PostScript unit), except the variables that return the current page number, current date string, and current time string.

TABLE A4-2

Variable	Defines
wp$box	Path containing the clipping rectangle
wp$y	Clipping rectangle height
wp$x	Clipping rectangle width
wp$fpage	String representing the current page number in the appropriate format (Arabic, Roman, or alphabetic)
wp$page	Current page number
wp$date	Current date string
wp$time	Current time string

You can use these variables in all three types of PostScript command groups— .page., .para., and .pic..

TABLE A4-3

Variable	Represents
wp$top	Space before the paragraph (same as the Before setting in the Paragraph dialog box)
wp$bottom	Space after the paragraph (same as the After setting in the Paragraph dialog box)
wp$left	Amount of indention from the left margin to the left indent
wp$right	Amount of indention from the right margin to the right indent

You can use these variables only in .para. groups.

TABLE A4-4

Variable	Represents
wp$top	Top margin
wp$bottom	Bottom margin
wp$left	Left margin, including the gutter margin on facing pages
wp$right	Right margin, including the gutter margin on facing pages
wp$col	Number of columns (in the page's first paragraph)
wp$xcol	Width of each column (in the page's first paragraph)
wp$xcolb	Space between columns (in the page's first paragraph)

You can use these variables only in .page. command groups.

Commands to Avoid

Since your PostScript printer will print the text and graphics in your Word document on the same page as the text and graphics generated by the document's PostScript commands, you should not use any of the PostScript commands that reset the printer or that reset the printer's PostScript environment. Table A4-5 lists the commands you should avoid using in all Word documents.

TABLE A4-5

banddevice	initmatrix
copypage	nulldevice
framedevice	renderbands
grestoreall	showpage
initgraphics	

You should not use these PostScript commands in your Word documents.

USING MICROSOFT MAIL IN WORD A5

One of Word 4's most exciting features is its ability to work with the popular electronic mail program Microsoft Mail. If you've installed Microsoft Mail on your Mac along with Word 4, you can compose messages, then send those messages to other people in your network. Similarly, if someone sends you a Mail message he or she has created in Word, you can read, edit, save, or print that message just as you would any other Word document.

In this appendix, we'll cover the mechanics of working with Mail in Word. We'll assume that you've already installed Microsoft Mail on your computer, and that you have a pretty good understanding of how to send and receive messages with this system. If you have not yet installed Microsoft Mail, or if you do not possess basic Mail skills, spend some time with your Microsoft Mail manual before you attempt to learn about Word's mailing facilities. For information on the Microsoft Mail program, call Microsoft's Product Support Department at (206) 882-8089.

USING WORD TO OPEN AND SEND MESSAGES

The commands you'll use to open and send messages in Word are the Open Mail… and Send Mail… commands on the File menu. These commands will work only if your Mac is connected to a Microsoft Mail server on an AppleTalk network, and if you are signed in to your mailbox. For information on installing and signing into the Microsoft Mail system, refer to your Microsoft Mail manual.

Opening Word Messages

To open the Word messages that reside in your mailbox, select the Open Mail… command from the File menu. When you do this, a window like the one shown in Figure A5-1 will appear.

FIGURE A5-1

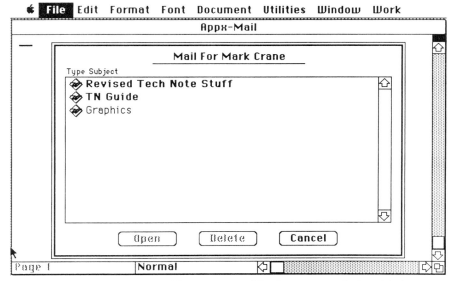

Word's Open Mail... command lets you open Word messages that reside in your Microsoft Mail mailbox.

As you can see, the window in Figure A5-1 indicates that messages entitled *Revised Tech Note Stuff*, *TN Guide*, and *Graphics* currently reside in the mailbox. The titles that appear in boldface (*Revised Tech Note Stuff* and *TN Guide*) are the messages that have not yet been read. To open any message that appears in the window, just double-click on the title of the message you want to read, or click once on the title and then click the Open button. If you want to open more than one message, hold down the Shift key while you click each title, then click the Open button to open all the selected messages at once. As you might expect, Word places each opened message in its own window.

After you open a message in Word, you can edit, save, or print the message like you would any other Word document. The document that you see in Word, however, is a duplicate of the message in your Microsoft Mail mailbox. No matter what you do with the message after you've opened it in Word, the original message will reside in your mailbox until you delete it.

To delete a message from your mailbox, select the Open Mail... command, highlight the title of the message you want to delete, then click the Delete button. If you want to delete multiple messages, hold down the Shift key while you click on each title, then click the Delete button.

The Open Mail... command can open only those messages that are in the form of Word documents. To open messages that are not Word documents, you must use the Microsoft Mail desk accessory on the ⌘ menu. For more information on this, refer to your Microsoft Mail manual.

To send a message you've created in Word to another person's mailbox, first compose the message as you would compose a normal Word document. Afterward, select the Send Mail… command from the File menu. Word will then bring up a window, like the one shown in Figure A5-2, that lists all the people on the Microsoft Mail network. (Fortunately, if you've made any changes to the document you're sending since you last saved it, Word will save the document before it opens the Send Mail window.)

Sending Word Messages

FIGURE A5-2

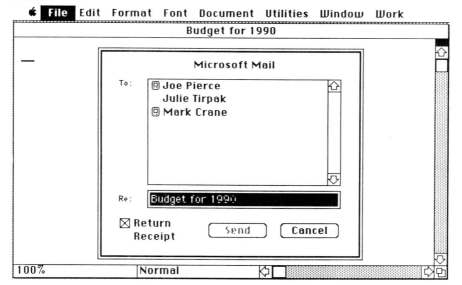

Word's Send Mail… command lets you send a Word document to someone else's mailbox.

In the To box, click on the names of the people to whom you want to send the message. As soon as you click on a name in the list, Word will place a check mark next to that name at the left edge of the To box. If you accidentally click on the wrong name, just click on it again to remove the check mark and to remove the name from the list of recipients. (By the way, the small Macintosh icon that appears at the left of the names *Joe Pierce* and *Mark Crane* indicate the users who are currently signed in on the Microsoft Mail system.)

By default, Word places the title of the document you are sending in the Re box. The text you enter in the Re box will be the message title the recipients will see when they open their mail. As you'd expect, you can accept Word's default message title, or you can select the contents of the Re box and type a different title. (The title you enter will not affect the title of your Word document.)

As you probably know, selecting the Return Receipt check box in the summary window tells Microsoft Mail to notify you when each recipient reads the message. If you do not want to be notified, simply deselect this check box.

Once you are satisfied with all the settings in the Send Mail window, click the Send button to send your Word message to each recipient's mailbox. As soon as you click the Send button, Microsoft Mail will display the message *I'm sending your message to the Microsoft Mail Server....* When the send procedure is completed, the Send Mail window will disappear.

USING MICROSOFT MAIL TO SEND AND READ WORD FILES

If you are using version 1.35 or 1.36 of Microsoft Mail, you can use the Microsoft Mail desk accessory to send and read Word files. (If you are using version 2.0 or later, refer to your Microsoft Mail manual for information on sending and reading Word files.) To bring up the Microsoft Mail desk accessory, select Microsoft Mail from the menu. As soon as you do this, a summary window similar to the one shown in Figure A5-3 will appear.

FIGURE A5-3

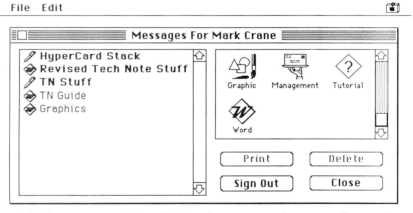

Microsoft Mail's summary window displays the messages in your mailbox on the left, and functions you can use on the right.

Sending Word Messages in Microsoft Mail

If you have used (or another network user has used) Word's Send Mail... command to send a Word file to another person's mailbox, Microsoft Mail will include a Word icon in every network user's summary window, as shown in Figure A5-3. The Word icon allows you to send a Word document as a mail message to another person in the Microsoft Mail network.

When you double-click on the Word icon in the icon list box, Microsoft Mail will present a Send Microsoft Word Message window like the one shown in Figure A5-4. As you can see, this window lets you specify the message's recipient(s) in the To list box, the message's title in the Re box, and comments that accompany the message in the text box at the bottom of the screen. (You'll want to replace the default messages *This message type can be used...* and *See your Word manual...* that appear in the text box at the bottom of the screen with your own comments.) You can also select the Return Receipt... check box, which tells Microsoft Mail to notify you when each recipient reads the message. After selecting the recipient(s), give the message a title, replace the default comments in the text box with your own comments, and click on the File... button. When you do this, Microsoft Mail will present a screen like the one shown in Figure A5-5 on the following page, which lets you specify the file you want to send.

FIGURE A5-4

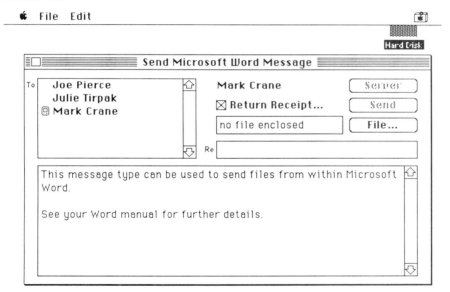

The Send Microsoft Word Message window lets you send a Word document to another person's mailbox.

After you select the file you want to send, the Send Microsoft Word Message window in Figure A5-4 will be reactivated, and the name of the file you've specified will replace the words *no file enclosed* in the text box next to the File... button. When everything in the Send Microsoft Word Message window appears to be in order, click the Send button to send the Word message to the specified recipients. When you do, the message *I'm sending your message to the Microsoft Mail Server...* will appear on the screen. After Microsoft Mail has successfully sent your message, the summary window shown in Figure A5-3 will reappear.

FIGURE A5-5

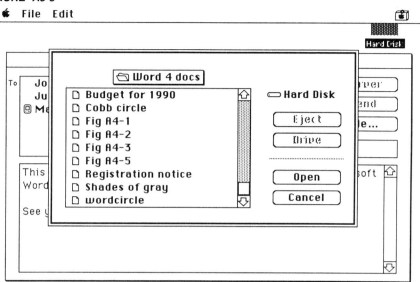

When you click the File... button in the window in Figure A5-4, Microsoft Mail
will present a list of your Word files.

When each recipient opens his or her mailbox with the Microsoft Mail
desk accessory, Microsoft Mail will display in the summary window's message list the title of the Word message you've sent. In addition, Microsoft Mail
will display a Word icon next to the message to indicate that the message is a
Word document.

**Reading Word
Messages in
Microsoft Mail**

The box on the left side of the Microsoft Mail summary window shown in
Figure A5-3 lists the messages that currently reside in your mailbox. As we have
said, Microsoft Mail displays a Word icon next to each message that is in the form
of a Word document.

As we explained earlier in this appendix, when you receive a Word message in
your mailbox, you can open Microsoft Word and use Word's Open Mail...
command to read that message. Alternatively, you can double-click on the
message's title in Microsoft Mail's summary window to bring up the Read
Microsoft Word Message window shown in Figure A5-6.

FIGURE A5-6

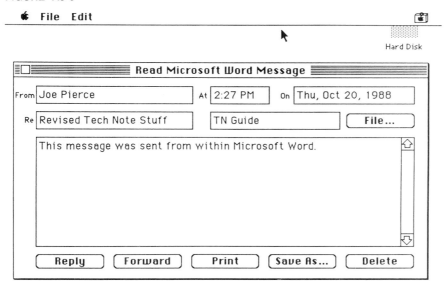

Although you cannot use Microsoft Mail to read a message created in Word, you can use it to manipulate the message in several ways.

The information at the top of this window tells you who sent the message, when the message was sent, and so forth. Although you cannot use Microsoft Mail to read a Word message, the buttons at the bottom of the Read Microsoft Word Message window let you issue a reply to the sender, forward the message to someone else, print the information in the current window, save the accompanying Word message to disk, or delete the Word message from your mailbox. To save the Word message on your own disk drive, click either the Save As... button at the bottom of the window, or the File... button in the upper-right portion of the window, and specify the name under which you want to save the message. After you've saved the message, you can open Word, then open the message as you would any other Word document.

WORD FINDER **A6**

Word Finder® is a desk accessory that allows you to access an online thesaurus. Word Finder can run concurrently with Word—although you can use it without loading Word. With Word Finder, you can quickly locate lists of synonyms for any word. Word Finder also can replace a selected word in your document automatically with a synonym that you choose. As you might guess, Word Finder is a terrific tool for writers and editors.

INSTALLING WORD FINDER

You will find the Word Finder desk accessory and a file called Word Finder® Thesaurus stored in the Word Finder folder on your Word 4 Utilities 2 disk. Because Word Finder is a desk accessory, you must use the Font/DA Mover program to install it on your System file before you can use it. If you don't already have a copy of the Font/DA Mover on your startup disk, you can find it on your Macintosh Utilities Disk 2. To install Word Finder, first make sure that the Font/DA Mover is on one of your current disks and the Word Finder folder is on another current disk. If you have a hard disk, put both items on your hard disk. At the Finder level, open the Word Finder folder, then double-click the Word Finder® DA icon. This will start the Font/DA Mover program and open the Word Finder desk accessory.

When you see the Font/DA Mover dialog box, click the Open… button in the lower-right corner of the dialog box. The Font/DA Mover will then display another dialog box asking you to locate the file you want to open. Since you want to install Word Finder on your System file, you need to locate that file for the Font/DA Mover. After you do this, select the file name *System*, and click the Open button. You will then see a list of all the desk accessories that are currently installed on your System file on the right side of the Font/DA Mover dialog box. On the left side of the dialog box, select the Word Finder file name, as shown in Figure A6-1, then click the » Copy » button. The Font/DA Mover will copy the Word Finder desk accessory to your System file.

FIGURE A6-1

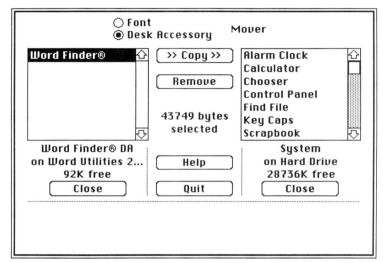

After you open your System file, the dialog box will display all the
desk accessories that are currently installed.

You can now select the Quit button to return to the Finder level. If you check the menu, you will see Word Finder® listed under the other desk accessories. (If you are using MultiFinder, you may need to restart your computer in order to see this new menu option.)

USING WORD
FINDER

To access Word Finder, just select Word Finder® from the menu. When you do this, you will see the message *Please locate the Thesaurus File ...* and a dialog box showing the items in the current disk or folder. After you locate the disk containing the file named Word Finder® Thesaurus, just click on that file name and click the Open button. As soon as the Word Finder® Thesaurus is open, you will see a new menu name—WF— at the far right edge of your menu bar.

If you are using MultiFinder, you will be switched to the Word Finder desk accessory window, where you will see three menu items at the top of the screen: File, Edit, and WF. You'll also see the MultiFinder desk accessory icon ( ) at the far right edge of the menu bar. You will still see your Word document window on the screen, but that window won't be active. Although you can use Word Finder as a stand-alone application, you probably will want to use it to edit your Word document. To do this, just click on the Word document window (or use one of the standard MultiFinder techniques to access Word). When Word is active, the WF menu name will appear on the far right side of the menu bar.

When you click on the WF menu name, you will see the options shown in Figure A6-2. The first item on the menu, Lookup, is the command you use to look up lists of synonyms. We'll explain this command in detail in a moment. The About Word Finder®... command displays a Word Finder copyright screen (for your information). The Change Command Key... command allows you to assign a different keystroke series to the Lookup command. (As you can see, ⌘-1 is the default.) The Window Automatic, Window Above, and Window Below commands allow you to change the placement of the Word Finder dialog box on the screen. As you can see, the default selection is Window Automatic, which means that Word Finder will determine where to position the dialog box. Finally, the Close command, as you might guess, allows you to close the Word Finder desk accessory.

The WF Menu

FIGURE A6-2

WF
Lookup ⌘1
About Word Finder®...
Change Command Key...
✓Window Automatic
Window Above
Window Below
Close

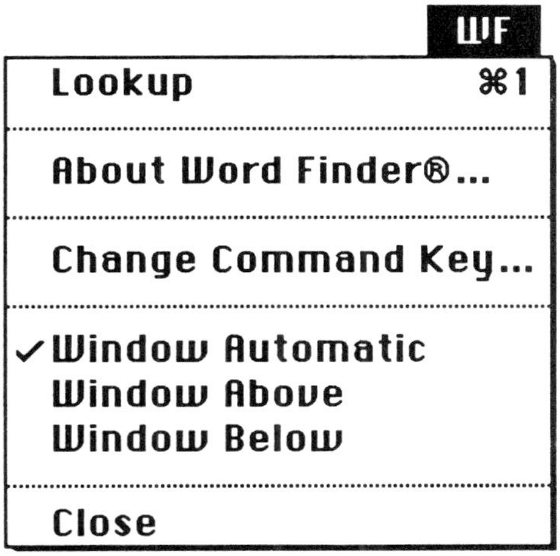

The WF menu offers seven options.

If you want to find a synonym for a word in a document, just select that word, then choose Lookup from the WF menu (or press ⌘-1). Word Finder will display a dialog box on your screen listing various synonyms, as shown in Figure A6-3.

Using Word Finder to Locate Synonyms

FIGURE A6-3

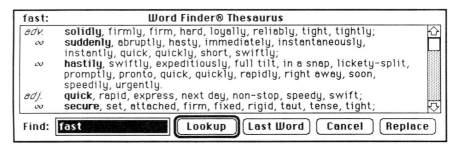

When you select a word and choose the Lookup command, Word Finder will present a dialog box like this one.

In the upper-left corner of the Word Finder dialog box, you will see the word that you selected. That word also will be displayed in the Find edit bar at the lower-left corner of the dialog box. As you can see in Figure A6-3, we selected the word *fast* in our document before choosing the Lookup command.

Notice that Word Finder groups the synonyms for the selected word by parts of speech. For instance, in Figure A6-3, Word Finder displays a collection of adverbs followed by a group of adjectives. If we were to scroll down the list box, we would see more adjectives and some verbs.

Within each part of speech, Word Finder groups words by meaning. For example, as you can see in Figure A6-3, Word Finder arranges the adverbs in three lists. These lists display synonyms for the words *solidly*, *suddenly*, and *hastily*.

Replacing the selected word

If you see a word that you want to substitute for the word you selected, just click on that word, then click the Replace button. Word Finder will automatically overwrite the highlighted word in your document with the word you clicked on, and close the Word Finder window. If you want to undo the replacement, just choose Undo Typing from the Edit menu.

Extending the lookup

You can click on any synonym that's displayed in the Word Finder dialog box and look up more synonyms for that word. For example, suppose we click on the word *rapid* that appears in the list of synonyms for the word *quick*. When we click on that word, it will appear in the Find edit bar. If we then click the Lookup button, Word Finder will present a list of synonyms for *rapid*, as shown in Figure A6-4.

After you have looked up two or more words during a Word Finder session, the Last Word button at the bottom of the Word Finder dialog box will become available. When you click this button, Word Finder will display a list of all the words you have looked up during the current Word Finder session, as shown in Figure A6-5. You can click on one of these words and then click the Lookup button.

(The word you looked up prior to the current—will initially be highlighted.) Word Finder will then redisplay synonyms for that word. For example, if we select the word *fast* in the list shown in Figure A6-5 and then click the Lookup button, Word Finder will again display the words shown in Figure A6-3.

FIGURE A6-4

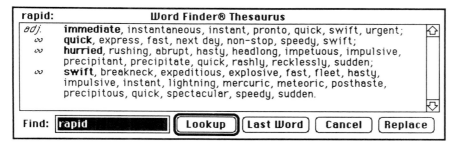

You can look up lists of synonyms for any word that appears in the Word Finder dialog box.

FIGURE A6-5

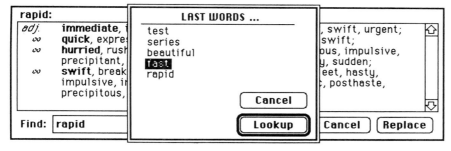

When you click the Last Word button, Word Finder will display a list of all the words you have looked up in the current Word Finder session.

Special situations

You do not need to select a word in your document before you choose the Lookup command on the WF menu. If you select Lookup (or press ⌘-1) but do not select a word, a blank Word Finder dialog box will appear. You can then click the Last Word button to display synonyms for a word that you previously looked up, or you can type a word in the Find edit bar and click the Lookup button.

If you select a misspelled word or if you select more than one word before you choose the Lookup command, Word Finder will display a dialog box like the one shown in Figure A6-6. This dialog box shows words that begin with the same letter(s) as the unrecognized word. For instance, as you can see in Figure A6-6, we misspelled the word *fast* as *fsat*. Since Word Finder could not recognize this word, it presented a list of words beginning with the letters *fr* and *fu*. You can click on one of the words in this list and click the Lookup button, or you can click one of the other buttons in the Word Finder window. You also can correct the spelling in the Find edit bar and click the Lookup button.

FIGURE A6-6

If you select a misspelled word, Word Finder will suggest a list of alternative words.

Closing Word Finder

If you choose the Close command from the WF menu, Word Finder will close the thesaurus file and become inactive. The WF menu will no longer appear on your Word menu bar. If you are using MultiFinder, however, the Word Finder desk accessory will still be active, but you won't be able to look up synonyms without reopening the thesaurus file. You can reopen Word Finder at any time by choosing Word Finder® from the menu, then locating and opening the Word Finder® Thesaurus file. By the way, Word Finder will not automatically become inactive when you quit from Word. However, once you do, you may need to close Word Finder to retrieve enough memory to reload Word.

INDEX

D

Z